Foreword

Global Civil Society 2001 was a landmark publication, launched at the LSE in October 2001. It traced the emergence of a global civil society, the vast contradictory process by which NGOs, social movements, individual activists, and even academic experts became powerful actors on the international stage. With that publication, the editors and authors first put a spotlight on the 'globalisation from below', which is surfacing in conjunction with the 'globalisation from above' essentially led by the political interests of nations, by the activities of corporations, and by other agents connected with them.

The 2001 Yearbook demonstrated how globalisation from below is just as important to our understanding of what globalisation is as globalisation from above. There has been a tremendous acceleration in the number of NGOs working in the world. Big NGOs like Oxfam and Greenpeace are truly global organisations, and, like big corporations, they have a global purchase. On the streets of the world, too, very diverse manifestations and protests are constantly taking place, with wildly different objectives, but with increasingly transnational aspects in their strategies and shared preoccupations. The participants are not just protesting locally, they are protesting globally and they know and use the fact that the image of their protest can be immediately carried around the world.

I am delighted to introduce the first Yearbook's follow-up, *Global Civil Society 2002*. This second Yearbook seeks to deepen and broaden our understanding of global civil society, and begins to explore its relation to the events of September 11. The attacks were a brutal act by any reckoning, but they were not just an act of murder. What happened on September 11 was clearly an act of global communication. It was experienced as an act of global communication; the people who perpetrated it designed it as an act of global communication. An enormous proportion of the world watched the second plane crash into the second tower. It was a global media event, which symbolised something about the kind of commutative interdependence in the world in which we now live.

The authors of *Global Civil Society 2002* explore the relation between global civil society and globalisation, and between global civil society and the September 11 events, from different angles. They discuss the different meanings given to the attacks, and reactions to it, from above, but especially from below. They also show how, on one level, the attacks can be considered as a demonstration of the weakness of global civil society as a cosmopolitan ideal. While criticising the current direction of economic globalisation as dominated by the interests of the West and especially by the interest of the United States, essentially a project for one fifth of the world from which four-fifths of the world are excluded, global civil society, and NGOs in particular, also reproduces those major imbalances of power. Therefore, as different authors make clear, global civil society is not a purely benign force. Civil society produces what Ulrich Beck calls 'ugly citizens'— people who take advantage of democratic rights and procedures—and the growth of civil society produces a diversity of ugly citizens, including, for example, extreme right groups who use the Internet to promote their cause. NGOs are no more elected than the big corporations are, and substituting orthodox democratic politics with a world run by NGOs is therefore problematic. Neither are global media necessarily a civilising and emancipating influence. The new commercialised entertainment media do not necessarily reflect the voice of the poor, and global civil society needs to make a much stronger effort to foster a public interest media that can truly accommodate global public debate.

On the other hand, the different chapters in this Yearbook also continue to provide documentary evidence of the creative, civilising, and empowering character with which global civil society can be credited. Religious doctrines like Gandhian Hinduism, liberal Islam, and liberation theology can be powerful engines for promoting civility and social justice, even though the present secular nature and power realities of global civil society inhibit such influences. Civil society organisations have, sometimes through persuasion, sometimes by applying enormous pressure, changed the way many corporations now think about their responsibilities with respect to human rights, environmental integrity, and social progress. Local mobilisation of people with HIV/AIDS, first in the US but now in countries like Brazil, Thailand, and South Africa, has transformed global health politics. Human rights, legal, peace, and other groups contributed expertise and moral values to the process of establishing an international criminal court, making it a more independent and progressive institution than it would otherwise have been. International NGOs are responding to the challenge of maintaining accountability and internal democracy in an age of globalisation by experimenting with new forms of organisation and governance. Global cities like Hong Kong, Barcelona, New York, and London, while often being sites of great economic inequality, are also 'microsites' of global civil society, which promote new transnational notions of citizenship. An improved and expanded data section of the Yearbook explores the multi-faceted relationship between global civil society, globalisation, and the international rule of law.

As in their first edition, the editors of the *Global Civil Society Yearbook* have made an effort to bring together people from all over the world in order to make the creation of the book itself a global civil society-building exercise. Authors, participants to workshops, research assistants, guest authors of 'boxes', and correspondents were recruited from all over the world in order to contribute to a vibrant debate about the nature of global civil society. In an effort to widen the debate and bring in more voices from the Southern, 'excluded' part of the world, one seminar related to the Yearbook, on HIV/AIDS, was held not at the LSE but in Johannesburg, in partnership with the University of Witwatersrand. This experience was very positive, and more Yearbook-related events are planned in different parts of the world for next year. Even within the LSE however, our own debates are a reflection of a cosmopolitan world, with so many people from so many different countries coming together not just to receive an education but also to listen to and learn from each other.

The editors hope with their Yearbook to stimulate and participate in such debates, because debate, as they say, is the only way to counter the dangers that the world currently faces. It is my pleasure to recommend *Global Civil Society 2002* to you as an important contribution to the debate about the future of the world, about what trajectory of development the world will follow, and what influence we can and should try to have over that trajectory of development.

Anthony Giddens

Director, London School of Economics and Political Science

25 May 2002

Acknowledgements

This Yearbook has been possible only because of the enthusiastic support and the valuable contributions made by many individuals and organisations. We are very grateful to them all; however, the editors hold sole responsibility for the final product.

Editorial Committee

Helmut Anheier, Marlies Glasius (managing editor), Mary Kaldor, Diane Osgood, Frances Pinter, Yahia Said, Sally Stares, Jill Timms (assistant editor).

Consultations

Communicating a New Global Public Sphere? Participation in the Information Age, Expert Seminar, 22 June 2001
Robin Brown, Myria Georgiou, Scott Lash, Chris May, Teri Rantanen, Jayne Rodgers, Hakan Seckinelgin, Roger Silverstone, Glen Tarman, Nuno Themudo, John Tomlinson, Gillian Youngs.

Meaning and Value of the Concept of Civil Society in Different Cultural Contexts, Expert Seminar, 28–29 September 2001
Sola Akinrinade, Leonardo Avritzer, Neera Chandhoke, Bernard Dreano, Chris Hann, Jude Howell, Deborah James, Mustapha Kamel Al-Sayyid, Zdenek Kavan, Smitu Kothari, Ivan Krastev, Kaori Kuroda, David Lewis, Ronnie Lipschutz, Sarah Lister, Ahmad Lutfi, Ference Mislivetz, Mammo Muchi, Bhikhu Parekh, Ali Paya, Jenny Pearce, Pradip Prabhu, Günther Schönleitner, Hakan Seckinelgin, Frank Trentmann, Ivan Vejvoda, Hilary Wainwright.

The Role of Global Civil Society in Dealing with HIV/AIDS and other Infectious Diseases, Expert Seminar, 22–23 February 2002, Johannesburg
Cathi Albertyn, Onanong Bunjumnong, Edwin Cameron, Brendon Christian, Liesl Gerntholtz, Deepika Grover, Mark Heywood, Alec Irwin, Sonam Lamba, Ria Madison, Pedzisani Motlhabane, Jeffrey O'Malley, Richard Pithouse, Marlise Richter, Hakan Seckinelgin, Tumii Thahane, Joseph Tenywa, Sheeren Udin, Jonathan Berger, Anita Kleinsmidt, Jennifer Joni, Diana Pope, Laurie Wen.

Other Input

Special contributions
Bill Burnham (guest box), Meghnad Desai (chapter update), Mark Heywood (guest box), Nadia McLaren (tables), Kerry McNamara (guest box), Leah Margulies (guest box), Dara O'Rourke (guest box), Diane Osgood (chapter update), Mario Pianta (parallel summits data and guest box), Frances Pinter (chapter update), Yahia Said (chapter update and guest box), Sally Stares (tables), Jill Timms (chronology and guest box).

Correspondents: Input on chronology
Mustapha Kamel Al-Sayyid, Leonardo Avritzer, Reine Borja, Joabe Cavalcanti, Hyo Je Cho, Bernard Dreano, Nihad Gohar, Anil Gupta, Svitlana Kuts, Natalia Leshchenko, Alejando Martinez, Nuria Molina, Alejandro Natal, Ebenezer Obadare, Mario Pianta, Jasmin San Juan, Jirina Siklova, Thomas Ruddy, Guy Taylor, Yulia Tykhomyrova, Sebastien Ziegler, Csengeri Zsolt.

Others who provided input or support

Nick Allum, Thomas Buettner, Christine Chinkin, Kim Colaris, Paola Grenier, Fred Halliday, Loek Halman, Fiona Hodgson, Jens Iverson, Jens Johansen, Anthony Judge, Dominic Jukes, Marc Levy, Denise Lievesley, Flavio Lotti, Patrick Lucas, Doug Lynd, Thomas Lyster, Laura Nessling, Eric Neumayer, Mike Oliver, Tammy Parrish, Michael Regnier, Suzanne Shaw, Jay Sheerer, Roger Silverstone, Wojtek Sokolowski, Richard Teahon, Lisa Valeroso, Jan van Deth, Lilian Wanderley, Teresa Woloweic, Nereo Zamaro.

Research and editorial assistance
Lisa Carlson, Rohit Chopra, Isabel Crowhurst, Emily Hauser, Hagai Katz, Anupama Naidu, Amarjit Singh.

Administrative support
Elizabeth Bacon, Barbara Baum, Joanne Hay, Sue Roebuck, Jane Schiemann.

Design and production
Ben Cracknell Studios, Norwich (front cover and inside design and page make-up),
Michael James (copy editor), Mitch Januszki (indexer).
Photographers
Martin Adler, Frank Balthis, Piers Benatar, Annie Bungerath, Joabe Cavalcanti, Rene Clement, Neil Cooper, Tim Dirven, Jeremy Hartley, Crispin Hughes, Denyse Kowalska, Luciano Lanes, Moses Matou, Mark McEvoy, Giacomo Pirozzi, Klaus Reisinger, Karen Robinson, Nick Robinson, Marcus Rose, Irene Slegt, Guy Smallman, Chris Stowes, Chris Tordai, Tayacan, Penny Tweedie, Teun Voeten, Hamish Wilson.

Advisory Board

Paul Anderson, Sergio Andreis, Abdullahi An-Na'im, Andrew Arato, Daniele Archibugi, Anthony Barnett, Peter Baehr, Rosemary Betchler, John Boli, Chris Brown, Jeannette Buiski, Simon Burall, Mark Curtis, Nicholas Deakin, Alex De Waal, Meghnad Desai, Pavlos Eleftheriadis, Mient Jan Faber, Richard Falk, Harriet Fletcher, Ann Florini, Anthony Giddens, Caroline Harper, David Held, Colin Hines, Mark Hoffman, Jason Hunter, Kumari Jayawardene, Anthony Judge, John Keane, Jeremy Kendall, Azfar Khan, Riva Krut, Radha Kumar, Manuela Leonhardt, David Lewis, Ian Linden, Miles Litvinoff, Sarah Lister, Ferenc Miszlivetz, Susannah Morris, Robin Murray, Kumi Naidoo, Ursula Owen, Andrew Passey, Jenny Pearce, Andres Penate, Anne Pettifor, Liz Philipson, Mario Pianta, Margo Picken, Shona Pollock, Babu Rahman, Adam Roberts, Andrew Rogerson, Saskia Sassen, Brita Schmidt, Hakan Seckinelgin, Urmi Shah, Philippe Schmitter, Mukul Sharma, Robin Sharp, Salma Shawa, Hazel Smith, Joseph Tenywa, Nuno Themudo, Fran Van Dijk, Ivan Vejvoda, Hilary Wainwright.

Financial Support

We gratefully acknowledge the financial support of the following organisations:
The Atlantic Philanthropies
BP
Ford Foundation
John D. and Catherine T. MacArthur Foundation
Rockefeller Brothers Fund
Rockefeller Foundation

Contents

Part IV: Records of Global Civil Society

Figures

Maps

Tables

Records
Data Programme

Parallel Summits

Contributors

Professor Abdullahi An-Nai'm is the Charles Howard Candler Professor of Law at Emory University in Atlanta, Georgia, USA. He holds an LLB (Honours) University of Khartoum, Sudan; an LLB (Honours) and Diploma in Criminology, University of Cambridge, England; and a PhD in Law, University of Edinburgh, Scotland. He taught law at the University of Khartoum, Sudan, was visiting professor at several North American and European universities, Scholar in Residence at the Ford Foundation office in Cairo, Egypt, and Executive Director of Human Rights Watch/Africa. He is the director of a Fellowship Program in Islam and Human Rights at Emory Law School. His main research interests are in human rights, Islamic law and politics, and comparative constitutionalism.

Dr Helmut Anheier is Director of the Centre for Civil Society at the London School of Economics and Political Science (LSE) and Professor at the School of Public Policy and Social Research at the University of California, Los Angeles. Prior to this he was a Senior Associate at Johns Hopkins University, Associate Professor of Sociology at Rutgers University, and a Social Affairs Officer at the United Nations. His work has focused on civil society, the non-profit sector, organisational studies and policy analysis, and comparative methodology. He is a founding editor of *Voluntas* and author of over 200 publications in several languages. His present research examines the emergence of new organisational forms in global civil society, the role of foundations, and methodological aspects of social science research on globalisation.

Fackson Banda is Director of the Panos Institute, Southern Africa, and is in charge of the overall running of the Institute in Southern Africa. Formerly Director of Communications and Social Justice at the Christian Council of Zambia and lecturer in Mass Communication at the University of Zambia, he is studying for a doctorate degree in communication with the University of South Africa.

Professor Neera Chandhoke is Professor of Political Science at the University of Delhi. She gained her PhD from the University of Delhi in 1984. Her specialisms include political theory and comparative politics. She was a Fellow at the Centre for Contemporary Studies, Nehru Memorial Museum and Library, Teen Murti House during 1989–92, and Jawaharlal Nehru Fellow during 1997–98. She is author of *State and Civil Society: Explorations in Political Theory* (1995) and *Beyond Secularism: The Rights of Religious Minorities* (1999). A further publication is forthcoming in 2002 titled *The Conceits of Civil Society*. She is also on the editorial board of *Democratization* (University of Warwick) and the *Indian Social Science Review*.

James Deane is Executive Director of Panos London, and one of the founding members of the Panos Institute. He was appointed Director in 1999, having been the Director of Panos' Communications and Social Change Programme. He was earlier Director of the Panos HIV/AIDS Programme when he wrote numerous reports, papers and speeches on HIV/AIDS issues in developing countries. Before that he was in charge of project development and media relations at Panos. He is the author of several publications on new communications technologies and the media, and has advised and been a consultant to many international organisations including the Rockefeller Foundation, UNAIDS, Soul City, the World Bank, the Department for International Development (UK), and USAID. He has a MA (distinction) in International Communication and Development.

Dr Marlies Glasius has been a Research Officer at the Centre for Civil Society, LSE, and managing editor of this Yearbook since 2000. She studied international law as well as English literature at the University of Amsterdam, and holds a PhD with distinction in Human Rights from the University of Utrecht. In 1999 she published *Foreign Policy on Human Rights: Its Influence on Indonesia under Soeharto*. Her research concerns both the theory and the practice of global civil society and its relationship to international law, particularly human rights law. Within this framework, her present interests include the influence of global civil society on the International Criminal Court and the effects of the 11 September 2001 disaster and its aftermath on global civil society.

Professor Mary Kaldor joined the LSE in 1999 as Director of the Programme on Global Civil Society at the Centre for the study of Global Governance. Previously, she taught and conducted research at the University of Sussex for thirty years. She was a founder member of European Nuclear Disarmament (END), founder and Co-Chair of the Helsinki Citizens'

Assembly, and a member of the International Independent Commission to investigate the Kosovo Crisis, established by the Swedish Prime Minister and chaired by Richard Goldstone, which published the Kosovo Report in autumn 2000. Her most recent work, *New and Old Wars: Organised Violence in a Global Era* (1999), has been translated into seven languages. Her book on the idea of global civil society will be published in 2003.

Njonjo Mue is Director of the Panos Institute, Eastern Africa. He is a lawyer by profession and an Advocate of the High Court of Kenya. He received his education at the University of Nairobi and Oxford University, where he was a Rhodes Scholar. He has held various human rights positions including as Legal Adviser to the freedom of expression group, ARTICLE 19. In 2000, he was named Jurist of the Year for his work in defence of human rights, democracy and the rule of law in Kenya. Njonjo enjoys reading, creative writing and the arts.

Melanie Beth Oliviero is a strategist for joint social ventures among civil society, business, and government sectors. Prior to moving into advisory services, she served as a programme officer in the Program for Global Security and Sustainability of the John D. and Catherine T. MacArthur Foundation. She was recently executive director of the Panos Institute, USA, an international information organisation which works with journalists. Her Ph.D. from Georgetown University is in sociolinguistics. She is currently on the faculty of the New School University (formerly the New School for Social Research) in New York, teaching courses over the Internet on civil society, and the media in developing countries.

Professor Saskia Sassen is Centennial Visiting Professor of Geography in the Department of Geography and Environment at LSE and Ralph Lewis Professor of Sociology at the University of Chicago. Her research focuses on globalisation, immigration and cities. She is currently completing her forthcoming book *Denationalization: Territory, Authority and Rights in a Global Digital Age* (2003) based on her five year project on governance and accountability in a global economy. Most recently she has published a new edition of *The Global City* (2001) and edited *Global Networks, Linked Cities (2002)*. Her books have been translated into twelve different languages. She is co-director of the Economy Section of the Global Chicago Project, a Member of the National Academy of Sciences Panel on Urban Data Sets, a Member of the Council of Foreign Relations, and Chair of the newly formed Information Technology, International Cooperation and Global Security Committee of the Social Sciences Research Committee.

Dr Hakan Seckinelgin is a Lecturer in NGO Management at the Centre for Civil Society/ Department of Social Policy, LSE. He holds a master's degree and a PhD in International Relations from LSE. He was an editor of *Millennium: Journal of International Studies*. He co-edited *Ethics and International Relations* (2001) and *Gendering The International* (2002). His research interests focus on 'people's politics' and the relationship between international politics and people's politics that is not underpinned by traditional state-centric conceptions.

Adele Simmons is a former president of the John D. and Catherine T. MacArthur Foundation. The Foundation supports researchers and civil society groups in 61 countries, concentrating on the environment, peace and international security, population and growing inequality addressing corporate responsibility issues. She has served on US presidential commissions on hunger and the environment, and the Commission on Global Governance. Before joining the MacArthur Foundation she was president of Hampshire College in Amherst, Massachusetts. She is now working to mobilise private resources for global equity and serves on the boards of a number of civil society organisations including the Global Fund for Women, the Synergos Institute, the Union of Concerned Scientists, the Rocky Mountain Institute, Environmental Defense and the Field Museum of Natural History in Chicago.

Sally Stares is a research assistant at the Centre for Civil Society at the LSE. She studied social and political sciences at Cambridge University and social science research methods at the LSE. Her research interests are in social science methods and methodologies, in particular the use of multivariate techniques in quantitative data analysis.

Nuno Themudo is Associate Researcher at the Centre for Civil Society, LSE. He teaches on the Masters course 'NGO Management, Policy and Administration' at the same Centre. He is completing his PhD thesis, *Managing the Paradox: NGOs, Resource Dependence and Political Independence*. His interests include NGO and non-profit management, information technology and civil society, and sustainable development.

Part I: Concepts of Global Civil Society

Chapter 1

THE STATE OF GLOBAL CIVIL SOCIETY: BEFORE AND AFTER SEPTEMBER 11

Marlies Glasius and Mary Kaldor

On 10 September 2001, the day before the attacks on New York and Washington, the phenomenon that we call 'global civil society' was flourishing. As we described in *Global Civil Society 2001,* the decade of the 1990s had witnessed the spread of social movements, non-governmental organisations (NGOs), and citizens' networks across national boundaries. Our figures showed a rapid growth in international NGOs during the last decade as well as a dramatic increase in parallel summits, meetings of global civil society actors. Global civil society groups (referred to variously as NGOs and civil society organisations, CSOs: see Box 1.1) had been effective in promoting and influencing a number of important international treaties, for example, on landmines, the International Criminal Court, or global climate change. NGO challenges like that against the pharmaceutical companies' extortionate pricing of medicines, efforts to get former dictators like Pinochet, Soeharto, and Milosevic behind bars, and street demonstrations in Gothenburg, Quebec, and Genoa were becoming part of our daily news. Above all, the period was characterised by the growing importance attached to global norms and values—human rights, the environment, social justice—which were beginning to displace the geo-political discourse of international affairs.

These developments were accelerating during the first nine months of 2001. Indeed, global civil society seemed to be on the verge of a new dialogue with the representatives of global political institutions and global corporations. In the beginning of the year, vice-president of the multinational ABB Björn Edlund, financier and philanthropist George Soros, and two UN officials took up the challenge of taking part in a fierce video-link debate with figureheads of the anti-capitalist movement (Madmundo 2001). After the summer, the IMF and the World Bank responded to an invitation by Global Exchange, Jobs with Justice, 50 Years is Enough, and Essential Action to engage in a public debate, writing that they were prepared to do so in principle provided that it was a non-violent dialogue, conducted with respect for different views (World Bank Group 2001). Around the same time, Guy Verhofstadt, Prime Minister of Belgium and President of the European Union at the time, wrote an open letter to the so-called anti-globalisation movement, published in many major newspapers around the world, and collected the responses in a book (Verhofstadt 2001).

So what was the impact of September 11, the attack on New York and Washington, and of October 7, the day the air strikes against Afghanistan began? On one reading, these two events can be interpreted as an attempt to close down global civil society. If we understand global civil society in a normative sense, as Abdullahi An-Na'im does in Chapter 3, then both Islamic fundamentalism and the use of terror are profoundly inimical to global civil society; indeed, they can be understood as a direct attack on global civil society. At the same time, the global unilateralism of the US administration undermines both the concrete achievements of global civil society and the values and norms promoted by global civil society; it marks a return to geo-politics and the language of national interest and 'realism' in international relations. Above all, the global polarisation, which results both from terror and from the war on terror, squeezes the political space for global civil society.

But there is another reading of September 11 and October 7. These two events could be understood as the moment at which global civil society comes of age. A number of commentators have pointed out that September 11 exposed the vulnerability of all states and demonstrated the reality of global interdependence. September 11, it is argued, represented an opportunity to set the new global agenda and construct a new set of global rules. Some would focus on attempting to humanise and civilise globalisation while others would wish to reverse or transform it; and for yet others the priority is abolition of weapons of mass destruction, real enforcement of human rights, or genuine dialogue between cultures. They would all agree, however, that global civil society is now more needed than ever to express the range of different voices in the world, including weak and excluded ones. Anti-capitalist movements, as well as the peace and human rights movements, have a capacity to reach out across borders to excluded groups in the world, especially among the Islamic community, and so offer an alternative to the appeal of fundamentalist groups.

So which reading is right? Are they, in fact, contradictory? This chapter is about the state of global civil society in 2001, before and after September 11. It is an attempt to develop a way of thinking about the answers to these questions, as indeed are the subsequent chapters of this Yearbook. We start by describing the state of global civil society on September 10. We summarise the results of this year's data collection efforts and then we describe the complex, uneven, and contradictory nature of global civil society through the prism of four global civil society events that took place in the first nine months of 2001: the World Social Forum at Porto Alegre, the NGO presence at the climate change conference in Bonn, the mobilisation around the G8 meeting in Genoa, and the NGO Forum of the World Conference Against Racism in Durban. We then analyse the different ways in which September 11 was experienced and interpreted in different parts of the world and among different strands of opinion, and how these different meanings shaped the responses of governments and international institutions as well as the varied responses of global civil society.

> During the first nine months of 2001, global civil society seemed to be on the verge of a new dialogue with the representatives of global political institutions and global corporations

Global Civil Society on September 10

Continued growth and increasing diversity

The statistics on international non-governmental organisations (INGOs) in *Global Civil Society 2001* showed a dramatic increase both in numbers and in membership after 1990 although, as we show in more detail this year, the increase began earlier. This year's statistics also widen the scope by including 'national organisations with various forms of international activity and concern' as well as more narrowly defined INGOs. The trends we observed last year are confirmed in these new figures; moreover, the growth rate of INGOs shows no sign of slackening

As Helmut Anheier and Nuno Themudo show in Chapter 8, the statistics also reveal that organisations are changing into more varied and fluid forms. They argue that the continued expansion proves that the global environment is still open and welcoming to new organisations, but that an ongoing experimentation to find the most appropriate organisational forms for this complex environment is under way.

Our figures (see Table and Figure R8 in part IV of this yearbook) show that the growth of global civil society and the spread of the rule of law as expressed in the ratification of international treaties are indeed interdependent, as we argued last year, and as is also argued in Chapter 6. However, it seems that the increase in the number of treaties concluded and ratified somewhat preceded the growth of global civil society, reaching its height in the late 1980s and early 1990s.

The globalisation tables on outbound tourism (R5) and media (R6) tell us something about the relation between global civil society and globalisation at the regional level. As last year, Europe predominates, but we can also see that East and South Asians have been travelling much more in the last decade, as well as doubling or tripling their television sets and cable subscriptions. In East Asia, this 'globalisation of peoples' has coincided with a strong growth in internationally oriented NGOs and INGOs (Table R16), but in South Asia it has not. It may be that what we are seeing in India in particular is globalisation without a concurrent growth in civility. Our figures on tolerance (see table R24b) show Indians to be less explicitly willing to tolerate as neighbours immigrants or people of a different race than most other nationals. The analysis of Hindu fundamentalism in Chapter 3, and of the development of South Asian television channels in Chapter 7, also seem to point in this direction.

A new set of data this year covers the distribution of NGOs in different cities. Again, Europe has the lion's share of these. The main cities where NGO and

Box 1.1: NGOs and CSOs

In this Yearbook, some authors use the expression 'non-governmental organisations' (NGOs) while others use 'civil society organisations' (CSOs), and Helmut Anheier and Nuno Themudo (Chapter 8) use both. Neither of these terms is easy to define. The original and widest meaning of NGO is simply that it is an organisation not belonging to a government and without a profit motive. Beyond this negative delimitation, there are numerous definitions and classifications, and there is little agreement. Salamon and Anheier (1992) distinguish between a legal, an economic/financial, a functional, and a structural/ operational approach to the definition; Najam (1996) on the other hand has tried to compile a 'police composite sketch' on the basis of the literature. The United Nations (url) accredits NGOs if they are registered as non-profit institutions in their home country, have been in existence for two years, and have a democratic decision-making structure.

The authors in this book who have chosen to use the term mostly do so in the widest and loosest sense. However, there are two reasons why some authors no longer find the term 'NGO' the most appropriate for the organisations they describe. First, it has, in common parlance at least, taken on the much more specific meaning of a rather institution-alised organisation, with fixed headquarters and paid staff, working in advocacy and service-delivery mainly in the fields of development, the environment, human rights, and humanitarian relief. Thus, the examples of NGOs most commonly quoted are Oxfam, Greenpeace, and Amnesty International. Some feel, therefore, that the associations of the term no longer express the richness and variety of organisations found in global civil society, including, in terms of structure, one-woman bedsit organisations and all-volunteer groups, or, in terms of activities, trade unions, churches, and cultural associations. They therefore prefer the term 'civil society organisations' (CSOs), which appear more inclusive of all these forms.

The second, related reason for rejecting the term NGOs is that it has, conceived in the narrow sense described above, come to be associated with a particular, neo-liberal, vision of global civil society, which we described last year as 'a way of minimising the role of the state in society, both a mechanism for restraining state power and as a substitute for many of the functions of the state' (Anheier, Glasius, and Kaldor 2001: 11; see also Chapter 2 in this volume for a similar conception). In relation to this conception, NGOs as a group are regularly accused of being tamed, bureaucratic, undemocratic, oblivious to cultural diversity, and unaccountable to their members and/or beneficiaries. For better or worse, the term CSOs does not—yet—carry all this negative baggage. Although it does not invalidate the substance of such criticism, some authors therefore prefer it as more neutral and politically correct alternative. The policy of this Yearbook is to let authors use whichever term they prefer, with whatever definition or connotations they bring to it.

INGO headquarters are concentrated in the South appear to be Buenos Aires, Nairobi, and Mexico City. As Chapter 9 by Saskia Sassen describes, cities like London, Buenos Aires, and Mexico City can in other ways, too, be considered as vibrant micro-sites of global civil society.

Our data also show an increase in parallel summits in 2001 compared with previous years, as well as an increase in the numbers participating. The data seem to suggest more grass-roots involvement than in previous summits. Although Europe is still the most important site of parallel summits, Southern regions are catching up, especially Latin America with 28 per cent of parallel summits compared with 30 per cent held in Europe and, to a lesser extent, Africa with 17 per cent. The predominant concern in 2001 has been social justice, expressed in the dominance of economic and development issues, as compared with earlier concerns about the environment, human rights, peace, or women. Finally, parallel summits have been much more concerned with networking among civil society groups and with raising public consciousness than with directly influencing formal

Table 1.1: Top 20 host cities of international and internationally-oriented non-governmental organisations	
City (country)	Number of organisations
1 Brussels (Belgium)	1,392
2 London (UK)	807
3 Paris (France)	729
4 Washington DC (US)	487
5 New York (US)	390
6 Geneva (Switzerland)	272
7 Rome (Italy)	228
8 Vienna (Austria)	190
9 Tokyo (Japan)	174
10 Amsterdam (Netherlands)	162
11 Madrid (Spain)	140
12 Stockholm (Sweden)	133
13 Buenos Aires (Argentina)	110
14 Copenhagen (Denmark)	108
15 Berlin (Germany)	101
16 Nairobi (Kenya)	100
17 Oslo (Norway)	95
18 Mexico City (Mexico)	87
19 Montreal (Canada)	86
20 Milan (Italy)	82

political institutions; 40 per cent of parallel summits in 2001 were not associated with official summits.

Our chronology of events, continued from the last Yearbook, once again shows the importance of global civil society activity in the South and the East. Although our information is, by no means, comprehensive since we depend on a voluntary network of global correspondents, the chronology does indicate the range and diversity of global civil society events in the South, involving, for example, women in Ethiopia concerned about violence against women, the Zapatistas in Mexico, anti-globalisation activists from a wide range of countries, anti-militarist activities in Asia, to name but a few. The growth of these activities is suggested by the fact that many organisations or new groups of organisations hold events for the first time, and those protests and actions which have been held before are seen to be more organised and to include a greater diversity of participants. What the chronology shows is a striking shift in the balance of global civil society events after

September 11 when most activities, world-wide, focus on anti-terrorist and anti-war activities.

Of course, the continued acceleration in the growth of global civil society was not a harmonious and universally celebrated coming-out party, nor was it a single event. While at some venues global civil society continued to meet with hostility and repression, in others it was uncritically celebrated, and in yet others the inequalities within global civil society became as glaring as those it exposed outside. The events at four global meeting places for civil society, which all convened between January and September 2001, can be used as illustrations of the characteristics and contradictions that attended global civil society's public arrival on the international scene.

The alternative forum: Porto Alegre

The first World Social Forum, held in Porto Alegre, Brazil during 25–30 January 2001, attracted approximately 11,000 people. It was held at the same time as the World Economic Forum being held in Davos, Switzerland, and its name consciously echoed the Davos meeting. In terms of numbers, this gathering was less spectacular than other recent parallel summits of global civil society have been (Pianta 2001: 178–9, 183). However, the Porto Alegre summit was a symbolic step forward in the history of parallel summits. In a way, this was the first truly parallel, rather than subordinate, summit of global civil society, deliberately held in a different place, with a different name, from the elitist Davos forum. The message of Porto Alegre was 'we have an alternative'. Instead of scaling the walls at Davos (which others were still doing as well), global civil society held its own alternative debates, proposing alternative policies, in the South, under the slogan 'another world is possible'. While some may have been sceptical about the utility of having a meeting in a different place, where power-holders could not be directly confronted, the formula was clearly a success in terms of empowering civil society groups. Participants called it a 'fertile and inspiring experience'. The next Porto Alegre summit in 2002 saw more than 68,000 visitors, and further regional and global meetings are now being organised, (see Box 1.2).

The 'co-opted' forum: Kyoto process, Bonn

The Earth Summit in Rio de Janeiro in 1992 can be seen as one of the birthplaces of global civil society.

The second World Social Forum held in Porto Alegre, Brazil, on 30 January–5 February 2002, may have been the largest gathering of global civil society to date. 68,000 registered participants from 131 countries, representing 5,000 associations, NGOs and local authorities, 3,000 journalists, and 800 members of parliaments have met in 28 major plenaries, 100 seminars, and 800 workshops. 40 per cent of the participants were women, 12,000 youths stayed in a city park, in a camp site named after Carlo Giuliani, the Italian youth killed by the police during the Genoa protests in July 2001. While Brazilians were by far the majority of people at the Forum, large contingents came from Latin America (Argentina in particular) and Europe (1,000 Italians, 700 French) and smaller groups from the United States (140 delegates) and from Africa (200 participants) (Fórum Encerrado em Clima de Festa 2002).

Participants included activists of social movements, political organisations, women's groups, representatives of all global campaigns, as well as environmentalists, peace activists, and smaller numbers of human rights campaigners, social economy organisations, development NGOs, and trade unions. The Brazilian organisers had a strong institutional profile, with a systematic involvement of the president of the State of Rio Grande do Sul, the mayor of Porto Alegre, and the leaders of the Workers' Party (PT), including Luis Ignacio Da Silva, known as Lula, candidate for the 2002 presidential elections. The Porto Alegre experience of participatory democracy in the local budgeting process has been a key issue, attracting interest from all over the world, with hundreds of local authorities planning the replicate it. The trade union CUT was also active, and a coalition of civil society organisations was responsible for the efficient organisation of the event.

The common analysis of global problems was the dominant theme of talks at the World Social Forum.

The shared understanding of the roots of poverty, inequality, underdevelopment, hunger, environmental degradation, wars, and human rights violations was remarkable, with activists of all continents sharing experiences, making links, and learning the relevance of new issues, in events of great impact, such as the largest plenary of the Forum featuring Noam Chomsky.

Much less attention was devoted to the diversity of strategies to address global problems and to the priorities of campaigns. Different approaches were visible, with the obvious division between North and South perspectives, but also with an emphasis on resistance from many North Americans and Asians, and greater attention to alternative projects from Europeans and Latin Americans.

The rejection of neo-liberalism and war emerged as the two key elements of the identity of the global movements gathered in Porto Alegre. In a final document agreed by hundreds of organisations, called the 'Call of Social Movements. Resistance to Neoliberalism, War and Militarism: for Peace and Social Justice', activists define themselves as a 'global movement for social justice and solidarity'. The first in the list of its objectives is 'democracy: people have the right to know about and criticize the decisions of their own governments, especially with respect to dealings with international institutions. Governments are ultimately accountable to their people. While we support the establishment of electoral and participative democracy across the world, we emphasise the need for the democratisation of states and societies and the struggles against dictatorship' (World Social Forum URL).

Mario Pianta, Professor of Economic Policy at the University of Urbino, attended the second World Social Forum.

It was 'unprecedented in . . . size, media resonance, and long-term impact on ideas and policies' (Pianta 2001: 174). Not only did the environmentalists turn out in great numbers and attract great media attention, they also had substantial influence on the three declarations and two treaties concluded at Rio (Arts 1998). These successes should be seen in the context of a wider acceptance of environmental values in society at large and hence also in political and business circles. Since Rio, the environmental

Table 1.2: Four global forums, 2001

Place and date	Civil society gathering	Official meeting	Relationship	Number of participants	Atmosphere
Porto Alegre 25–30 January	World Social Forum	World Economic Forum, Davos	Posing an alternative to elite forum	Approx. 11,000 people	Vibrant; constructive
Bonn, 16–27 July	Side events but no parallel forum	Conference of Parties to the UN Framework Convention on Climate Change	Lobbying; critiquing	Approx. 473 accredited NGOs, incl. Business Interest NGOs (BINGOs)	Specialist; co-opted?
Genoa 20–22 July	Demonstrations and debates but no parallel forum	G-8	Confrontational	Approx. 250,000 people	Marred by violence and repression but sophisticated demands
Durban, 28 August–1 September	NGO Forum World Conference Against Racism	World Conference Against Racism	Reflective of similar conflicts	Approx. 7,000 people representing more than 1,300 accredited NGOs	Marred by frictions and mutual accusations of racism

movement has often been described as 'further' in its development and its engagement with political and business elites than other groups in global civil society. Indeed, while green parties have been active in parliamentary politics, especially in Europe, since the 1960s and 1970s, they joined coalition governments in Belgium, France, Germany, and Italy for the first time in the late 1990s.

The commitments made in Rio, meanwhile, have since been subject to continuous back-pedalling from governments. The painfully negotiated Kyoto Protocol further specified, but also reduced, the commitments made with respect to greenhouse emissions in the Framework Convention on Climate Change (UNFCCC)

in 1992. While evidence on the effect of emissions on climate change piled up, governments went even further into reverse. The United States walked out on the protocol under the new Bush government, and the obligations were further watered down at the July 2001 meeting in Bonn in order to keep Australia, Canada, Japan, and Russia on side. Nevertheless, this meeting, which was considered to have saved Kyoto, was closed with 'exuberant applause' and hailed by Greenpeace as 'an historic landmark in the battle to protect the earth's climate' and by Friends of the Earth International (FOEI) as a 'victory for international cooperation, science and our common humanity' (Greenpeace 2001; FOEI 2001). It can be argued, however, that the intimate involvement of these organisations in the detailed negotiations, and the fear that nothing at all would be agreed after the US walk-out, caused them to lose sight of what had been lost over the years and to hail as a victory an agreement they would never have found acceptable ten years ago.

The environmental movement can be said to have been one of the most successful sectors in global civil society, as environmental considerations are now routinely taken into account in the decision-making by governments, intergovernmental organisations, and transnational corporations. However, some claim, in the light of what has happened to government commitments on green-house gas emissions over the last decade, that the environmental movement has been co-opted and tamed and has lost its teeth. Many former green activists have joined companies as their environmental advisers: something that can be hailed as a constructive move on the part of companies or criticised as a sign of co-option. According to Neera Chandhoke (Chapter 2), this development is merely indicative of a wider tendency of global civil society, which can operate only within the narrow margins set by dominant states and international capital; it can amend international structures but not transform them.

Even if one does not share her interpretation that global civil society is inherently unable to transform power structures, there is a lesson here for other parts of global civil society, namely, that apparent victories may have co-optive and demobilising effects, as also argued by Hakan Seckinelgin in relation to HIV/AIDS campaigning in Chapter 5. Young environmentalists appear, meanwhile, to be less attracted the traditional NGOs and to the details of intergovernmental negotiating processes. They prefer to bring their environmental concerns under the more radical umbrella of the anti-capitalist movement.

The confrontational forum: Genoa

The most eye-catching summit of 2001 was probably the G8 meeting and the parallel civil society rally that took place in Genoa, Italy in July. The meeting was overshadowed by violence, which caught the media's attention. The anti-capitalist movement acquired its first martyr, Italian Carlo Giuliani, who was shot in the chest by the Italian anti-riot police; approximately 200 others were injured.

Three types of action were employed in the streets of Genoa: violence by a small minority of so-called 'black blocs', who smashed windows and burned down offices and cars; peaceful manifestations by more than 200,000 so-called 'fluffy' participants; and systematic violence by the police during and after the demonstrations. It has been suggested that the Black Bloc had been infiltrated and encouraged by the Italian secret service in order to discredit the demonstrations and justify a crack-down. Whether this is true or not, it is a fact that on various occasions they were able to go about their burning and looting unhindered while the police focused on restraining non-violent demonstrators (Caldiron 2001: 204, Genoa Social Forum 2001: 212–13, Pietrangeli *et al.*: 2001).

During the demonstrations, the Italian police made 'indiscriminate assaults, including beatings with batons, on—amongst others—non-violent protestors (including minors), journalists reporting on the demonstrations, doctors and nurses who were clearly identifiable as such and providing medical assistance to demonstrators on a voluntary basis, and individuals unconnected to the demonstrations'. In the night after the official summit had ended, the police raided buildings occupied by the Genoa Social Forum, and started beating and abusing dozens of people, most of whom had been asleep. They arrested and detained hundreds, maltreating many of them, and deprived them of food, water, and sleep (Amnesty International 2001a: 10–12). According to protestors, the behaviour of the Italian police was comparable to police behaviour in Pinochet's Chile; indeed, one protester recounts that the police officer who beat him up was reciting a doggerel in praise of Pinochet (Longhi 2001). While other summits had already witnessed severe security measures and sometimes excessive violence in its handling of demonstrators, the Italian response set a new standard in all-out repression as a response to

> While other summits had already witnessed severe security measures and sometimes excessive violence in its handling of demonstrators, the Italian response set a new standard in all-out repression

the collective mobilisation of anti-capitalist sentiments we have seen in the last few years. Mario Pianta's prediction in *Global Civil Society 2001* that summits, particularly those concerning economic globalisation, would increasingly opt for 'a radical-isation of conflict with global civil society' seem to have been eerily accurate. (Pianta 2001: 192).

Perhaps Genoa was the last of these major confrontations. The organisers of high-level summits have adopted evasive tactics. The last World Trade Organisation (WTO) meeting took place in undemocratic Qatar, where unaccredited protestors were not allowed in; the next G8 meeting will be in a tiny mountain resort in Canada, where transport and accommodation will be a challenge for protestors. At the same time, members of the movement have apparently begun to put a higher premium on peaceful action: worldwide demonstrations against the WTO in November 2001 passed off peacefully, as did the 10,000-strong march against the World Economic Forum in New York in January 2002 (Protest.net URL; Anderson and Wright 2002). They have also begun to learn the value of the alternative venue, where attention to substantive issues is not undermined by physical confrontations.

While there is a price to be paid for this choice in lack of media attention, it is doubtful whether this is truly to be lamented when the focus of the media is so much on violence. What went almost unnoticed in Genoa was that serious issues were being debated in an increasingly sophisticated manner: the Tobin tax, proposals for which are being refined by thousands of local groups; Third World debt; the rights of migrants and refugees; and the opening of the European Union market to agricultural produce from outside. These debates may have found a more deserving and appropriate forum in Porto Alegre, where, moreover, the participants are less exposed to claims, for instance by the British development minister Clare Short, that they are Northern do-gooders, unable to understand Third World needs (Seabrook 2001).

Although the violence dominated the news, Genoa did provoke serious responses from politicians and from international institutions. The open letter of Guy Verhofstadt has already been mentioned. In France, the Health Minister, Bernard Kouchner, described the events at Genoa as a 'global kind of May 1968'. He anticipates a Tobin tax and global ethical investment. And the French Prime Minister, Lionel Jospin, welcomed 'the emergence of a citizens movement at the planetary level':

France denounces the violence by a tiny minority under the pretext of highlighting the evils of globalisation; but it is delighted to see the emergence of a citizens' movement at a planetary level, which wants a majority of men and women to share the potential benefits of globalisation between rich and poor countries ... We want to put in place a lasting system of regulation that makes the planet a common asset exploited in an equitable manner; we want to establish an international community as respectful of the environment as of different cultures and civilisations. This is the heart of the universal message France wants to carry round the world.
(Graham and Simonian 2001)

The uncivil forum: Durban

The World Conference against Racism in Durban, and its NGO counterpart, were mired in controversy from the beginning. To begin with, some South African civil society figures criticised the holding of the conference as 'a colossal waste of money which should be spent on housing and jobs' (Shepherd 2001). Moreover, two very controversial issues cast a shadow over both meetings: the legacy of slavery and whether reparations should be paid to its descendants, and the issue of Zionism and whether or not it is a form of racism. Whereas on the first issue there were strong divisions between states but a relative degree of unity within civil society, debate on the second issue became as vicious in the NGO Forum as in the official conference.

At the NGO Forum one incident followed another. A group of South African women interrupted the proceedings to complain that food and board had not been provided for them as promised by the African National Congress preparatory committee. A group of rabbis representing their own interpretation of Judaism were being shouted down by other Jewish delegates. They ended up marching in a demon-stration with the Palestinians (Shepherd 2001). After a chaotic and tense plenary NGO meeting from which various caucuses walked out, a controversial NGO Final Declaration, which characterised Israel as an apartheid state, was adopted through a questionable procedure, and many groups distanced themselves from it, although many Third World and Arab NGOs were pleased with the result (Shepherd 2001; Matas 2001). The European Caucus, when deciding how to respond to this statement, was accused of being 'run by the Jews or . . . paid by the Jews', and a 'Black European Caucus' split off from the main one after a meeting that ended in a shouting match (Harriford 2001).

While the furore over Zionism and anti-Semitism was widely reported in the international press, the Durban NGO Forum showed incivility in yet another way that was barely noticed. According to Immanuel Kant, the minimum precondition for a universal civil society is the right of hospitality, that is, the right to be treated politely by strangers and the duty to treat strangers politely (Kant [1795]1983). This right was reportedly violated by a group of international NGO representatives who failed to act in a hospitable way towards those who really represented the victims of global inequality. A group of citizens from Soweto, Johannesburg, mostly pensioners, decided to take the overnight train to Durban to tell the conference of their fight against electricity cuts in their homes by privatised energy companies. When they arrived the next morning, 'they knew that they could never afford the US$100 that it cost to get into the NGO Forum but they hoped to be able to sit down on the grass for a while and perhaps use the toilets. When they arrived the delegates panicked and the organisers of the Forum called the army and the police'. Scattered into the streets, they came across a trade union march against privatisation, and were later given food and shelter by local residents (Pillay and Pithouse 2001).

Of course, not all of the debates held, relationships forged, and manifestations organised in Durban were marred by intolerance and elitism. For Dalits, who were among the biggest delegations, and for Kurds, Tibetans, Roma and travellers, and indigenous peoples, it was an occasion to call attention to their cause, claim and proclaim solidarity, and forge new strategic alliances (Shepherd 2001). The final declaration of the NGO Forum, unlike the government declaration, endorsed the idea of reparations for slavery and made several specific suggestions for implementation even though it did not have the sort of moral legitimacy that such widely endorsed NGO declarations can usually claim, because of the controversial manner in which the declaration was adopted.

Nevertheless, if Porto Alegre displayed global civil society at its best, in Durban it showed its worst aspect: fractured, incapable of respectful dialogue,

> If Porto Alegre displayed global civil society at its best, in Durban it showed its worst aspect

and oblivious, even suspicious, of the causes of local grass-roots activists. As the opening of this chapter argued, global civil society is no longer just the romantic expression of 'the power of the powerless'. Parts of it are now included in global fora as relevant players. This entails risks of co-option, of importing the acrimony of 'real world' disputes into one's own ranks, and of becoming cut off from the local causes and activists global civil society is supposed to represent.

It was this global civil society, at times creative, brave, irreverent, inspiring, and effective, at times tamed, at times brutally repressed, and at other times fractious, sectarian, sterile, inward-looking, and elitist, but definitely a force to be reckoned with, which was confronted with the September 11 attack on the World Trade Center and its global repercussions.

September 11: Six Global Moments

The attacks on New York and Washington were nihilistic acts of violence. We shall never know the reasons for the attacks. As the Indian writer Arundhati Roy (2001) pointed out, the attackers left no suicide notes, so we are free to impose our own interpretations on these events. Even if they had left suicide notes, the notes would not necessarily have shed light on their motives. And even if we had some inkling of the motives, we still would not understand the deeper causes: what leads human beings to inflict such suffering on their fellows.

Such attacks could have taken place at any time since the development of aeroplanes and the construction of tall buildings. Terrorist attacks have taken place before: the Lockerbie disaster, for example, or the attacks on the American embassies in Kenya and Tanzania. There have also been state terrorism and large-scale massacres in Rwanda, Srebrenica, East Timor. What was unprecedented was the global resonance of the events of September 11. This was above all a global media happening, experienced by millions because the attacks were instantly broadcast, amplified, and commented upon. It was a global media happening both because of the reach of contemporary technology and because of the way in which the debates, protests, and struggles over global issues

Above: Bystanders witness the collapse of the first of the twin towers of the World Trade Center. © Klaus Reisinger/Editor/ Panos Pictures.

over the last decade gave meaning, albeit varied meaning, to September 11.

September 11 marked a particular moment in world history, a moment characterised by a new global consciousness and by a new set of social and political cleavages that no longer fit traditional territorially bound categories. Indeed, it was not one but many moments, reflecting a range of new preoccupations and dilemmas. Global developments in the preceding period conditioned the ways in which the events of September 11 were experienced—the character of these different moments. In *Global Civil Society 2001*, we identified different positions in global civil society, different strands of opinion on global issues. The groups and individuals that could be said to be participants in an emerging global public sphere understood what happened in terms of their experiences and standpoints in an ongoing global conversation. In what follows, we summarise these differences in terms of six global moments, six broad meanings of the events of September 11. Two were official moments, even though they had support from parts of global civil society, and four were global civil society moments.

The unilateralist moment

Javier Solana, the secretary-general of the Council of the European Union, has described the United States as a 'global unilateralist' (Solana 2002). The United States is the only country powerful enough to be an effective unilateralist, to be guided only by domestic politics. Other unilateralists remain in the world—China, India, Israel, Russia—but they are more vulnerable to international pressure.

September 11 was a specific moment in the evolution of American political culture. America is a country of migrants, many of whom or their parents or grandparents escaped from poverty or oppression and see themselves as part of the 'American dream'. For Americans, patriotism is understood as loyalty to a cause, not a tribe or a territory. In many parts of the world, people reacted to September 11 by saying 'now the US has experienced what we have experienced'. But that is not how Americans reacted. Many behaved as though this was the first time a tragedy on this scale had occurred and as though it was an attack on their cause.

To this generalisation about American political culture should be added the specific culture of the Bush administration. The end of the cold war represented a profound challenge to the way government and society is organised in the United States. For 50 years, the United States was organised on a more or less permanent war footing, which was intimately linked to political, economic, and cultural developments. Some people around President Bush are nostalgic for that period. In particular, among the defence and security advisers are people who gained their formative experiences during the Reagan years and who have been engaged in an intense debate about how to develop a new military role for the United States after the end of the cold war and to apply new developments in information technologies. September 11 seemed to confirm their security preoccupations.

During the 1990s, great efforts were expended in 'imagining' new 'worst-case scenarios' and new post-Soviet threats. With the collapse of the Soviet military-industrial complex, US strategists came up with all sorts of inventive new ways in which America might be attacked, through spreading viruses, poisoning water systems, causing the collapse of the banking system, disrupting air traffic control or power transmission. Of particular importance has been the notion of 'rogue states' that sponsor terrorism and acquire long-range missiles as well as weapons of mass destruction. These new threats emanating from a collapsing Russia or from Islamic fundamentalism are known as 'asymmetric' threats as weaker states or groups develop weapons of mass destruction or other horrific techniques to attack US vulnerabilities

not set as a dialogue programme

to compensate for conventional inferiority (see Freedman 1998). Although the planners never actually came up with a scenario like September 11, the term 'war on terrorism' was already circulating widely. Hence, what happened on September 11 and the subsequent anthrax scare seemed like a confirmation of these anticipations of horror.

After the end of the cold war, American military spending declined by one third, although spending on military research and development was largely sustained (SIPRI 2001). This was a moment when there was pressure to increase military spending as the newly designed systems came to fruition. It was also a moment of threatened recession, when increased public spending *à la* Reagan could be utilised to jump-start the economy. The advent of the Bush administration, with its distrust and rejection of international arrangements like the Kyoto Protocol, the International Criminal Court, and the protocol to the Biological Weapons Convention, as well as widely respected UN officials like Robert Watson (Chair, Intergovernmental Panel on Climate Change) and Jose Bustani (Director-General, Organisation for the Prohibition of Chemical Weapons), reinforced a world view of the rest against America. September 11 provided the moment for consolidating the notion of an inexplicable 'axis of evil' out to destroy the American way.

In retrospect, then, the reaction of the Bush administration, especially after 7 October when the air strikes began, should have been easy to anticipate. It was a reaction that expressed this way of thinking. First of all, the language of the Bush administration was the language of war and of territorially bound states. The parallel with Pearl Harbour was drawn immediately. Because the enemy had to be a state, Afghanistan was identified as the state harbouring Al Qaeda. But other rogue states, including Iraq and North Korea, may follow. The 'war on terrorism' was likened to the Second World War and the cold war. American military action was justified as self-defence. The polarising rhetoric of the war against terrorism magnifies the perceived power and reach of the terrorists; it gives them the respectable status of an enemy, it vests them with the role of an alternative

pole to the United States. It narrows the space for dissent, for those who oppose the terrorists and yet remain critical of American policy. 'You are either with us or against us', says Bush.

This is not just government rhetoric either. The American Council of Trustees and Alumni (ACTA), chaired by the Vice-President's wife Lynne Cheney, recently brought out a report, *Defending Civilization; How Our Universities Are Failing America and What Can be Done About It*, detailing over a hundred instances of 'unpatriotic incidents' alleged to have occurred at different universities, all mentioned by name, and insisting that they teach 'courses on the great works of Western civilization, as well as courses on American history, America's founding documents, and America's continuing struggle to extend and defend the principles on which it was founded' (Martin and Neal 2002: 8). Since ACTA is the largest private source of funding for higher education in the US, these denouncements and recommendations are not without consequences for the universities concerned.

Secondly, the global coalition constructed by the US administration in the aftermath of September 11 was an alliance of states on the cold war model. It was not, despite the claims of some of the allies, a multilateralist alliance, based on international principles. As in the cold war period, the criterion for membership in the alliance is support for America, not democracy or respect for human rights. Indeed, the 'war on terrorism' has provided a framework for states, both democratic and authoritarian, to introduce repressive legislation, allowing, for example, the detention for unspecified periods of suspected terrorists. It has also legitimised many 'dirty' wars in the name of the war against terrorism: the escalating Indo-Pakistan conflict; Israel's brutal action in the West Bank and Gaza; Russia's war in Chechnya; China's repression against Turkic-speaking Muslims; the repression of Islamists in Malaysia, Uzbekistan, or the Philippines, not to mention crack-downs on asylum-seekers in Australia and elsewhere. Thus, the American approach appears to have given the green light to these local wars on terror, amplifying local cleavages that are reproduced at the global level.

> The polarising rhetoric of the war against terrorism magnifies the perceived power and reach of the terrorists and narrows the space for dissent, for those who oppose the terrorists and yet remain critical of American policy

September 11: Egypt, United States. Egyptian Prime Minister Atef Abeid lashes out at human rights groups for 'calling on us to give these terrorists their "human rights"', referring to documented reports of torture and unfair trials. He says that, 'After these horrible crimes committed in New York and Virginia, maybe Western countries should begin to think of Egypt's own fight on terror as their new model.' US Secretary of State Colin Powell subsequently notes that 'we have much to learn' from Egypt's anti-terrorist tactics. Egypt is 'really ahead of us on this issue', Powell says.

September 12: Russia. Russian President Vladimir Putin declares that America and Russia have a 'common foe' because 'Bin Laden's people are connected with the events currently taking place in our Chechnya'.

September 13: Australia. Defence Minister Peter Reith cites the attacks in the United States to justify his government's effort to prevent asylum-seekers from entering Australia. His remarks come as his government successfully attempts to overturn a court decision that it had illegally detained hundreds of migrants from Afghanistan.

September 14: Israel. Israeli Defence Minister Benjamin Ben-Eliezer brags that 'it is a fact that we have killed 14 Palestinians in Jenin, Kabatyeh and Tammum, with the world remaining absolutely silent'. Prime Minister Ariel Sharon calls Palestinian Authority Chairman Yasser Arafat 'our Bin Laden'.

September 14: Kyrgyzstan. The Kyrgyz Ministry of Interior announces it has conducted a 'passport control regime' against 'pro-Islamic' activists in the southern part of the country.

September 15: Malaysia. Deputy Prime Minister Abdullah Ahman Badawi praises Malaysia's Internal Security Act (ISA), saying that the attacks of September 11 showed the value of the ISA as 'an initial preventive measure before threats get beyond control'. The ISA allows for arrest and indefinite detention without trial of anyone a police officer has 'reason to believe' has acted or is likely to act 'in any manner prejudicial to the security of Malaysia'.

September 18: Macedonia. Macedonian Prime Minister Ljubco Georgievski says he hopes that the attacks on the US will lead NATO to change its policy towards 'terrorism' in Macedonia.

October: Jordan. Jordan amends its penal code and press law, as Prime Minister Ali Abul Ragheb says, 'to cover all the needs that we are confronting now'. It allows the government to close down any publications deemed to have published 'false or libellous information that can undermine national unity or the country's reputation', and prescribes prison terms for publicising pictures 'that undermine the king's dignity' or information tarnishing the reputation of the royal family.

Finally, the form that military action took was also unilateralist in that it challenged a fundamental assumption of global civil society: that all human lives are of equal importance. The planners had argued that the response to these asymmetric threats was the so-called revolution in military affairs; the idea that, through the use of information technology, rogue states or states harbouring terrorists could be attacked with precision and discrimination from a distance by using aircraft and, in particular, cruise missiles. Such an approach had the advantage of not risking American casualties or the possibility of a domestic backlash against war, the so-called 'Vietnam syndrome'. Air strikes against a distant rogue state could be viewed as a form of political entertainment from the point of how the American public experience war through a television screen (Der Derian 2001). As well as air strikes, what might be called casualty-free war involves reliance on proxies, in this case the Northern Alliance. The strikes on Afghanistan were precise and they were effective in that they created the conditions for the fall of the Taliban and the capture of many Al Qaeda operatives, although not the leadership. But it is not possible to avoid mistakes or so-called 'collateral

October 11: China. Sun Yuxi, a spokesman for the Chinese Foreign Ministry, states that the Chinese government has 'conclusive evidence' proving that 'East Turkestan independent elements' have been involved in terrorist attacks and 'collude with international terrorist forces'. Yuxi added that 'opposing East Turkestan terrorism is also a component part of the international community's struggle against terrorism'.

October 24: India. The Indian government introduces the Prevention of Terrorism Ordinance (POTO), a modified version of the now-lapsed Terrorists and Disruptive Activities (Prevention) Act (TADA) of 1985, which facilitated the torture and arbitrary detention of minority groups and political opponents. POTO sets forth a broad definition of terrorism that includes acts of violence or disruption of essential services carried out with 'intent to threaten the unity and integrity of India or to strike terror in any part of the people'.

November 23: Zimbabwe. A spokesman for President Robert Mugabe states that six journalists for foreign-based media who have written stories on political violence in Zimbabwe will be treated as terrorists. 'As for the correspondents, we would like them to know that we agree with U.S. President Bush that anyone who in any way finances, harbors or defends terrorists is himself a terrorist. We, too, will not make any difference between terrorists and their friends and supporters.'

November 13: United States. President Bush gives a military order to institute military commissions which can arrest, try, convict, and even execute any foreign national designated by the president as a suspected terrorist or as aiding terrorists without a public trial, without access to a lawyer, without the presumption of innocence, and without the right to appeal except to the president himself. A few weeks later, Attorney General John Ashcroft explains 'to those who scare peace-loving people with phantoms of lost liberty, my message is this: Your tactics only aid terrorists, for they erode our national security and diminish our resolve. They give ammunition to America's enemies, and pause to America's friends'.

December 14: United Kingdom. The United Kingdom passes an anti-terrorism act that permits non-nationals to be detained without charge or trial indefinitely when the home secretary suspects a person to be a national security risk and an 'international terrorist'. Within days, immigration officials, backed by the police, raid homes in different cities to arrest people.

Sources: Amnesty International (2001b; 2001c); Human Rights Watch (URL); *Asia Times Online* (2002)

---

damage'. We do not know the extent of casualties but it is likely that the number of Afghan casualties, both civilian and military, is greater than the casualties on September 11. Moreover, in the aftermath of the fall of the Taliban, greater priority has been given to catching the remaining terrorist operatives in Afghanistan than to stabilisation and rebuilding a viable state. Most Afghans are deeply concerned still about personal security.

In the US as well as in other countries, unilateralism is not just a government policy: it commands widespread public support. Eighty seven per cent of

Americans supported the air strikes against Afghanistan when they started on 9 October; the same number continued to do so in January 2002 (CBS News 2001; 2002). A letter from Democratic Congressmen to President Bush on 2 April 2002 suggested that air strikes against Iraq had bipartisan support. Moreover, it is not just the US administration but also American civil society that has a tendency to privilege American lives. Enormous sums of money have been raised for the relatives of victims of September 11, and many fund-raising organisations are somewhat at a loss as to how to spend it (Inde-

Above: Taliban soldiers captured by the Northern Alliance. © Martin Adler/Aftonbladet/Panos Pictures.

pendent Sector 2001; Cater 2001). But there have been very few proposals to spend the money on more needy victims of violence in other countries. An important exception is the September Eleventh Families for Peaceful Tomorrows who have been supporting victims of the air strikes in Afghanistan, (Peaceful Tomorrows URL). Thus, alternative voices have been heard in US civil society too. As will be discussed in more detail below, they manifested themselves, among other things, in joint statements, demonstrations, campus debates, and editorials.

In Israel, too, nearly 86 per cent backed the military actions on the West Bank (Kafala 2002), and in India threatening language against Pakistan is fuelled by a Hindu nationalist base in civil society and in the media (see Chapters 3 and 7). As is often the case, hardline positions also thrive in diasporas; in the case of Israel this manifested itself, for instance, in a pro-military demonstration attended by tens of thousands in Washington DC (Knoll 2002).

The unilateralist approach cannot restore a world of geo-politics. The de-territorialisation of communities and social organisations as a consequence of easier travel and the information revolution cannot be reversed. The main consequence is to increase the real and perceived cleavages between rich and poor, Western and non-Western culture—cleavages which

are no longer territorial but exist side by side all over the world, in the inner cities of Europe and North America as well as in Afghanistan. It is likely to provide further succour to those who see a form of 'voice' in violence.

The multilateralist moment

As we showed in *Global Civil Society 2001*, global civil society is concentrated in certain areas of the world, particularly north-west Europe. It can be argued that one of the main impacts of global civil society has been in promoting multilateralism among certain states. These states, including Nordic and other European states, Canada, Costa Rica, and the new South Africa, have come to refer to themselves in the negotiations on the Landmines Ban Treaty and the International Criminal Court as 'like-minded', a term emanating from joint approaches by a smaller Western group to development and human rights policies in the 1970s. They are also sometimes described as 'globalising' states (Clark 1999) or 'post-modern' states (Cooper 2000) or, more negatively, 'international legal imperialists' (Anderson 2000: 101). We refer to this line of thinking as 'multilateralism'. As former Canadian foreign minister Lloyd Axworthy put it: 'The landmines campaign was the harbinger of the new multilateralism: new alliances among states, new partnerships with non-state actors, and new approaches to international governance' (Axworthy 1998: 452–3).

These states, together with some international institutions like the United Nations and many in global civil society, viewed the events of September 11 as an opportunity to put together a global justice agenda. In the immediate aftermath of September 11, in the period up to October 7, it was argued that the attacks had exposed global insecurity. What the destruction in New York and Washington showed was that no state can any longer insulate itself from attack; either we are all secure or we are all insecure. The United States, it was said, had to reverse its unilateralism; it could find security only through multilateral engagement. 'One illusion has been shattered on 11 September', said Tony Blair, the British prime minister, 'that we can have the good life of the West irrespective of the state of the rest of the world . . . the dragon's teeth are planted in the fertile soil of wrongs unrighted, of disputes left to fester for years, of failed states, of poverty and deprivation' (Blair 2001).

September 11 took place at a time when the so-called 'Washington consensus', the neo-liberal global agenda, was being questioned, when concern about financial crises in various parts of the world and doubt about standard recipes of transition and structural adjustment were being expressed, and when global institutions were beginning to respond to some of the critiques of the anti-capitalist movements. The promoters of human rights were coming to realise that social and economic rights cannot easily be disentangled from civil and political rights.

The recognition that global inequality needs to be redressed if globalisation is to succeed is beginning to make its way, albeit piecemeal, into the policies of European leaders. 'Tough on terrorism, tough on the causes of terrorism' is the sound-bite expression of this idea. France has attempted to take a civil society favourite, the proposal for a Tobin tax, into the Monterrey Financing for Development Summit, while the United Kingdom and the Scandinavian countries pushed for both a substantial increase in and untying of development aid (Ciesla 2001). While neither proposal

> **What the destruction in New York and Washington showed was that no state can any longer insulate itself from attack; either we are all secure or we are all insecure**

succeeded, President Bush unexpectedly announced a 14 per cent increase in US aid at Monterrey, saying: 'we work for prosperity and opportunity because they're right; it's the right thing to do . . . and because they help defeat terror' (Blustein 2002). The substance of the proposal was unimpressive, especially measured against US defence spending, and much less than the UN requested, but it nevertheless showed the Bush administration to be uncharacteristically open to European and civil society pressure.

The multilateralist position is not incompatible with support for the war on terror. On the contrary, while most global civil society activists condemned the unilateral approach of the Bush administration, most multilateral leaders supported the air strikes on Afghanistan and argued that the global coalition, established in the aftermath of September 11, was a form of multilateralism. In Germany, for example, the Chancellor called for a 'differentiated evaluation' of Russian policy in Chechnya, as though killings, atrocities, and displacements against a whole people were justified in the name of the 'war against terror' (Human Rights Watch URL). Some multilateralist states appear to be opposing the extension of the war to Iraq, however.

The peace moment

The most widely contested state policy has been the literal, military aspect of the 'war on terrorism'. Those who opposed the military aspects of the war included many in the peace movement who felt that earlier mobilisations in the cold war period had failed to dismantle the American military-industrial complex and to bring about the elimination of weapons of mass destruction.

They were joined by many more recent peace activists who were conscious of the ever-spiralling cycle of violence experienced in wars in Africa, eastern Europe, and even Northern Ireland and the Basque country. They greatly feared the immediate destructive effects of war as well as the longer-term consequences of the war. In addition, many activists from the anti-capitalist movement took on the anti-war issue, and for the first time, they linked up with Muslim communities. Thus, new synergies within global civil society are arising out of resistance to this new war.

Above: Muslim protesters at an anti-war rally in Trafalgar Square, London. © Marcus Rose/Panos Pictures.

Even before the 7 October attack on Afghanistan, for instance, a joint statement instigated by the international alliance of civil society organisations Civicus, and signed by 33 influential international and national groups, stated that 'we feel strongly that there is no purely military solution to the kinds of acts that we saw last week. Indeed, the blunt instrument of war may further intensify a cycle of violence and attract new recruits to terror' ('A Joint Civil Society Statement' 2001). Similar voices were heard in many countries. In Greece, Italy, Spain, and the United States pro-peace demonstrations were reaching levels of 10,000 and more demonstrators even in the weeks immediately after September 11 (Pax Protest 2001).

After the bombing of Afghanistan began, the anti-war mobilisation swelled, with tens of thousands of people demonstrating in Berlin, Cairo, London, and Madrid, and even higher numbers walking in two peace marches in Calcutta, India and Perugia, Italy. Smaller demonstrations took place in various cities in Australia, Brazil, Denmark, Greece, Indonesia, Japan, Kenya, Lebanon, New Zealand, Pakistan, South Korea, Sweden, Turkey, and the United States (Pax Protest 2001; 'Anti-War Protests' URL).

At the same time, new peace movements appear to arise out of some the more localised conflicts that are related to this global war: in India and Pakistan, for instance, or Israel and Palestine. This is especially significant in the case of the Israel-Palestine conflict, where the worsening war has provoked reactions not just within Israel and Palestine but also throughout the Middle East and Europe. The growing Israeli peace movement (see Box 1.4) has a potential to put pressure on the Israeli government but only if it can find a Palestinian partner ready to criticise terror as well as the war on terror; otherwise, it risks marginalising in the context of growing insecurity.

So far, the anti-war mobilisation has been only an immediate and ad hoc response, first to try to prevent a military reaction to the September 11 attacks, then to protest against the war in Afghanistan and then the Israel-Palestine war. But the 'war against terrorism', fluctuate though it may in intensity, enemies, and tactics, seems set to stay in place for a very long time. In this sense, it is more like the cold war than the Vietnam war. Whether the new anti-war mobilisation, which at present rather resembles the Vietnam protests, will adapt into a broader global social movement, capable of a sustained challenge of

THE STATE OF GLOBAL CIVIL SOCIETY   Marlies Glasius and Mary Kaldor

18

the war against terrorism, remains to be seen. In the context of polarisation, it will be easy to marginalise the peace movement, especially if it fails to offer convincing alternative approaches to dealing with terrorism. This is why working together with Islamic communities that could offer a political alternative to fundamentalism, and with human rights groups that offer a legal mechanism for dealing with terrorism, is so important.

The anti-capitalist moment

The new 'anti-capitalist movement' is our preferred term for what is often known as the anti-globalisation movement. Protestors at Seattle, Prague, or Genoa or the civil society groups that came together at the World Social Forum in Porto Alegre are not necessarily against global-isation. Rather, they are concerned about the unchecked spread of global capitalism. For them, the attacks of September 11 are viewed as a kind of wake-up call for the poor, down-trodden, and excluded, as well as an alarm bell for capitalist 'fat cats' and their government collaborators (see Update on the Anti-Capitalist Move-ment, pp. 387–8).

The significance of September 11, according to the anti-capitalist argument, was to be identified in the targets. The attackers chose to destroy the World Trade Towers—the most visible symbol of global capitalism. The other target was the Pentagon, which symbolised the role of the US administration either as the lackey of global capitalism (a reading confirmed by the close links between the Bush Administration and Enron as well as major oil companies) or as the other half of a capitalist-imperialist conspiracy. The hijackers may have been middle class and well-educated, and the goals of Al Qaeda may be religious rather than social. Nevertheless, ordinary people are attracted to extremist causes, so the argument goes, because of their exclusion from the benefits of globalisation, because they experience the breakup of their communities, the loss of livelihoods and hope for the future, and ever-worsening conditions of daily life.

To some extent, this argument is also an admission of the inadequacy of global civil society: the lack of access to, and representation at, a global level for victims of globalisation. On this line of

thinking, the attacks were a form of 'voice', a message that had no other form of expression than violence. Globalisation has weakened national forms of representation, it is argued, and yet global institutions have hardly any mechanisms for public accountability. Consequently we can talk about a global democratic deficit. Some argue that global civil society can be a 'functional equivalent' to democracy at a global level (Rosenau 1998: 40–1; see also Chapter 6). But global civil society itself, as the example of the Durban forum painfully illustrates, can be unequal and unrepresentative.

The political space in global civil society is increasingly occupied by Northern-based or Northern-dependent INGOs on the one hand, and religious and/or communalist groups on the other. The unregulated spread of global capitalism has often broken the power of traditional national social organisations like trades' unions or farmers organisations. The INGOs claim to represent the victims of globalisation but, in practice, they tend to be more accountable to donors than to beneficiaries (see Chapter 8 for a discussion of the pitfalls of INGO accountability). The religious and communalist groups are better at providing services as well as providing people with a group identity, but their value systems can lead to atrocities like the September 11 attacks, the recent communal violence in India, and the suicide bombing in Israel.

> The attackers chose to destroy the World Trade Towers—the most visible symbol of global capitalism

The anti-capitalists have some claims to being able to provide an alternative to 'tamed, co-opted' development NGOs, as well as fundamentalist manifestations of civil society. They question globalisation much more fundamentally than the multilateralists and their NGO counterparts, while by and large steering clear of populism and fundamentalism. After a brief period of disorientation brought on by the cancellation of the Washington IMF-World Bank summit, as well, possibly, as the momentary doubt whether fanatics within the movement itself could be responsible for the September 11 attacks, the demonstrations and campaigns of the anti-capitalist movement have continued, albeit in a less confrontational vein. Many in the anti-capitalist movement saw this stage of their struggle as an anti-war movement as well, pointing out that the American war in Afghanistan

Daily terror attacks on one hand and the use of brute military force against civilian populations on the other are just part of the horrors faced by Israelis and Palestinians over the past two years. Combined with the apparent lack of hope for a political solution, continued settlement activity, and economic decline they are radicalising both societies. Extremists on both sides are growing ever stronger and are dictating the political agenda. Their actions seem to be mutually reinforcing. Within the smouldering ruins of the Oslo peace process, however, an Israeli–Palestinian–international peace movement is struggling to give a voice to the vast majority of people in the region who crave peace but are being held hostage by the extremists.

The movement combines old and new actors and ideas. The main new element about the movement is that it is no longer limited to Israeli and international activists demonstrating their solidarity with the Palestinians. All three sides have come to realise that they need each other for support and legitimacy. Israeli peace activists and politicians who want to offer an alternative to the policy of force and settlements need to show that there is a partner on the other side. The same is true for Palestinians who have the courage to stand up to the politics of jihad. Even international activists seeking a deeper and more educated involvement by the US and Europe in the region need to show that there are Palestinians and Israelis who know the way out of this conflict and are prepared to fight for it.

Like the conflict itself, the movement is not symmetrical. While it is possible to speak of diverse and vibrant Israeli peace groups, this is less the case in the Palestinian territories. The space left between escalating Israeli violence, the Hamas-dominated political discourse, and the authoritarianism of the Palestinian Authority (PA) is too small for the articulation of a viable peace agenda. There is, however, a hard core of courageous Palestinian activists both within the PA establishment and in civil society who consistently argue for non-violent resistance.

The new movement is epitomised by the Peace Coalition established in July 2001. On the Israeli side it involves 24 groups, most notably Peace Now as well as the parliamentary opposition represented by the Meretz Party and the left wing of the Labour Party. On the Palestinian side the coalition involves the main secular/nationalist factions of the Palestinian Liberation Organisation (PLO) and is spearheaded by Sari Nusseibeh, the PA representative in Jerusalem. The coalition also has an international component with support from activists and municipalities in Europe, particularly Italy and the Netherlands. The coalition's platform is based on the following principles:

1. 'The adoption of a two state solution which guarantees the Israeli and Palestinian peoples the right to live in human dignity and security in their own independent states, along the 1967 boundaries. Israeli settlements will be removed from the Palestinian state.

2. The City of Jerusalem to contain two capitals for two states.

3. A just and equitable resolution to the Palestinian Refugee issue will be reached.' Peace Coalition (URL)

The coalition engages in three kind of activities: demonstrations, public diplomacy, and people's diplomacy. In February 2002 the coalition brought 20,000 people to the streets of Tel Aviv under slogans like 'the occupation kills us all' and 'get out of the territories, get back to normalcy'. It also organises regular vigils at the prime minister's office in Jerusalem and outside the Ministry of Defence.

The Coalition also promotes Israeli-Palestinian contacts. These contacts, which all but stopped

was a war of the richest nation on earth against the poorest nation on earth.

While actions against the WTO conference in Doha were not very noticeable, spread as they were over a number of cities, the protestors were out in force again at the European summit in Brussels on 13–14 December 2001. In a more anarchic vein, protests and riots forced two presidents to resign in a matter of

during the 18 months of the *Intifada*, are being resumed at various levels. There are semi-official contacts between experts involved in 'second track' and secret negotiations. There are also people-to-people contacts between civic activists, academics, and ordinary people , and finally there are contacts between moderate politicians on both sides.

The international peace activists are involved in various activities aimed at protecting civilians. These activities received prominent coverage during the April 2002 incursion by the Israeli Defence Force (IDF) into Palestinian cities and refugee camps. Many International activists stayed in the area to protect their Palestinian colleagues and to provide food, water, and medicine. Some of them suffered injuries, beatings, and arrest at the hands of the IDF.

The afore-mentioned Peace Coalition march in Tel Aviv was, among other things, expressing support to a group of reserve officers who signed a declaration refusing to serve in the occupied territories. The officers, while identifying themselves as Zionists committed to defending Israel, refused to serve in the territories 'for the purpose of dominating, expelling, starving and humiliating an entire people' (Seruv URL). This petition, signed so far by over 400 reserve officers and the broad support it received among Israelis (26 per cent, according to a recent poll published in *Haaretz*) is a qualitative new development. In the past, even the most ardent supporters of peace stopped short of calling for disobedience in the army. Since the latest incursion in the territories, at least 41 reserve officers have been jailed for refusing to participate in the operation, the highest number of such incidents in Israel's history (Seruv URL).

Apart from the well established human rights groups such as B'tselem (URL), which meticulously register and report human rights violations in the territories and regularly bring cases to the Israeli Supreme Court, there is a number of new radical Israeli groups. These groups largely attract younger

people and resemble in their tactics and approach the anti-capitalist movement. They call for direct action and civil disobedience and are mainly concerned with challenging the prevailing discourse and defending tolerance, pluralism, and secularism in Israeli society from the encroaching radicalisation, hardening, and racism. An example of these groups is Ta'ayush (URL), which works for cooperation between Arabs and Israelis on both sides of the Green Line (the border between Israel proper and the Palestinian territories occupied during the war of 1967). Ta'ayush organises convoys of supplies to Arab villages suffering under closure and occupation not only as an act of solidarity but as a way of exposing to Israelis the reality of the occupation.

Another such group is Green Line – Students Set the Border, which calls for an 'end to occupation for the sake of Israel's future'. In a pun on a typical settlement name, they pitched a tent in front of the Knesset called 'Ma'aleh Miyus', which translates as 'Upper Disgust' (*Haaretz*, 15 January 2002). This action reflects a sentiment shared by an increasing number of Israelis as they see how a small number of extremist settlers are hijacking the political discourse and dragging the entire country into war.

This box was written in April 2002 as the Israeli reoccupation of the main Palestinian population centres entered its third week, bringing death and destruction to innocent civilians. Regardless of the duration and outcome of this latest incursion, a critical moment for the new peace movement is a realisation on both sides that violence does not work. If Israeli Prime Minister Sharon's strategy of fire and brimstone fails, as predicted, to bring 'peace and security' to Israel, no force ever will. Likewise, many Palestinians are realising that suicide attacks are not only morally repulsive but also counter-productive.

Yahia Said, Centre for the Study of Global Governance, London School of Economics

weeks in Argentina, where bungled IMF policy was widely blamed for the country's economic woes (see Update on the Anti-Capitalist Movement, pp. 387–8). This and the collapse of Enron added new fuel to the

fire of the anti-capitalists, who turned out in their tens of thousands in Porto Alegre and New York in late January 2002 and at another EU summit in Barcelona in March 2002, as well as the World Bank/IMF meeting

Above: The protest march against the World Economic Forum held in New York in January 2002 passed off peacefully. © Teun Voeten / Panos Pictures.

in Washington, DC in April as well as a series of May Day demonstrations. The scene is familiar by now and, although the protestors do not seem to be getting the same publicity as before, they also seem to be becoming more respectable. In Barcelona, a quarter of a million people took to the streets, including the former mayor of Barcelona and other Socialist Party stalwarts. In Washington, DC, news coverage emphasised the non-violent nature of the protests, quoting police approval of their 'passionate but peaceful' character.

The 'Islamic' moment

While there is no single 'Islamic' doctrine, whether religious or political (see Chapter 3), there is a remarkable difference between Western interpretations of September 11 and those most current in the Muslim world. A Gallup poll held in nine Muslim countries showed that, while 67 per cent of people believed the September 11 attacks were morally unjustifiable, 61 per cent did not believe that the hijackers had been Arabs (Left 2002). The most common alternative explanation is that the Mossad and/or the CIA orchestrated the attack in order to justify a global crack-down on Islam.

The minority that did believe that Al-Qaeda was responsible might still interpret the attacks as understandable expressions of anti-Americanism, based on the desperate combination of everyday insecurity and the promise of religious fulfilment, even if they did not condone the attacks. The culture of blame propagated by authoritarian regimes such as Iraq and Syria against the US and Israel, laying every ill in their own societies at the door of these two demonised powers, contributes to this understanding. The anti-capitalist and the 'Islamic' interpretation of September 11 are related to each other: both emphasise the hegemony of smug Westerners in their steel and glass towers over the disempowered poor of the world, even though the former focus on economic injustice and the latter on cultural and political imperialism. The attacks occurred at a moment characterised by:

- the intensifying Al Aqsa Intifada in Israel/Palestine and the brutal Israeli response;

- continuing sanctions and air strikes against Iraq;
- the endless war in Chechnya;
- the nuclear confrontation between India and Pakistan, with Kashmir as a flashpoint;
- growing right-wing populism and hardline immigration policies among advanced industrial countries, especially Europe and Australia;
- repression of Islamists by pro-Western regimes such as Egypt, Tunisia, and Turkey; and
- failure to arrest war criminals responsible for the massacres in Srebrenica.

For those who are members of the Islamic community and, indeed, other non-dominant religions and cultures, the attacks of September 11 revealed the spread of identity conflicts and the perceived widespread discrimination against Islam in particular. In this view, September 11 formed the excuse for an intensified global manhunt on Muslims. September 11 underlined the global character of this perceived conflict of beliefs. The Huntington thesis of a 'clash of civilisations' is curiously caught in a territorial vision of the world; it is about the West versus the Islamic East, where borders are clearly demarcated and states represent different cultures (Huntington 1996). Yet what has become obvious is that the 'clash of civilisations', if there is such a phenomenon, is non-territorial. There are Islamic communities all over the world. Al Qaeda was not a state but a global network, not so very different in its form and infrastructure from the networks that characterise global civil society but feeding off the widely held belief that Muslims are victimised by the West, (see Figure 1.1).

On this line of thinking, it is from within civil society that attempts at healing or bridging or even refuting the existence of this clash have to be formulated. Religious groups and organisations have been especially active in this respect. In the wake of September 11, for instance, a group of young American Muslims set up Muslims Against Terrorism, which aims to 'honor the loss of the thousands who were senselessly killed by working to ensure that it never happens again. We stand, as Muslims, against all forms of terrorism in all parts of the world. We seek to increase awareness and understanding about

the true teachings of Islam, a religion that preaches peace, love of humanity and service to the community . . . Only through dialogue, cooperation, and mutual respect can we achieve the peace and justice the world so urgently needs' (Muslims Against Terrorism URL). Similar aims were behind an inter-faith statement entitled 'Deny Them Their Victory: A Religious Response to Terrorism', which was signed by close to 4,000 American religious leaders (Deny Them Their Victory URL), and the Arab League's initiative to invite Arab intellectuals to discuss the idea of a 'dialogue of civilisations' (see Chronology of Global Civil Society Events, p.379).

It is precisely this sort of dialogue about the nature and values of global civil society that Abdullahi AnNa'im advocates in Chapter 3:

> *a process of internal discourse within different constituencies of global civil society and dialogue between them, in order to promote an overlapping consensus about the normative content of their solidarity and cooperation . . . These prerequisite conditions include mutual respect and appreciation of cultural and contextual difference and the possibility of peaceful coexistence, as well as an appreciation of the need for consensus-building, instead of seeking to impose one's views on others.*
> (see p. 70)

He notes, however, that secular parts of global civil society must take seriously the concerns of their religious partners in such a dialogue instead of passively waiting for religious groups to adhere to secular standards of civility, that power relations condition its dynamics, and that the conditions for dialogue have not exactly been improved by the 'war on terrorism'.

Islamophobia has intensified since September 11, at least in western Europe and on the Indian subcontinent, as evidenced by the increased attacks on mosques and harassment of Muslims. Peculiarly, these attacks were specifically targeted against Muslim women, who are often perceived in the West as being oppressed by Islam and unable to stand up for themselves, proving the aggressors to be cowards as well as bigots. The attack on the Indian Parliament in Delhi in

Global civil society has a long way to go in fostering conditions for a global discourse in which Muslims feel at ease and able to participate on an equal basis

The infrastructure of Al Qaeda has many parallels with the infrastructure of international NGOs or civil society networks. What we know about Al Qaeda comes primarily from Western sources: evidence provided at trials of Al Qaeda associates and documents retrieved by the FBI and other Western agencies. This should be borne in mind when assessing information.

Al Qaeda is a cross-border network involving hybrid forms of organisation similar to those described in Chapter 8. Al Qaeda ('The Base') itself is a coalition involving a number of constituent organisations: the most well-known are the Egyptian groups Islamic Jihad and Jamaa Islamia (Islamic Group of Egypt) and the Groupe Islamique Armé (GIA) of Algeria, but there are also organisations from Pakistan, Chechnya, Sudan, Somalia, and the Philippines among others. These organisations come together in the Shura Majlis or Consultative Council, which has four committees: religious-legal, military, finance, and media. Al Qaeda is also involved in partnerships and different forms of cooperation with other Islamic terrorist groups, although this may be exaggerated by Western sources. Al Qaeda has many local branches, known in the West as 'operational cells', often linked to mosques and Muslim charities and NGOs. There are operational cells in more than 50 countries, including Western Europe and North America.

What holds the network together is the mission, just as is the case for networks like Jubilee 2000 or the Landmines Coalition. In the absence of traditional, vertical forms of organisation, individual commitment is a key organising tool. In this case, the mission is to restore to Islamic control the holy sites in the Middle East, especially the Al Aqsa Mosque in Jerusalem and the mosques in Mecca and Medina, and to attack the non-believers, literally Satans, America and Israel. In 1998, Al Qaeda established the 'World Islamic Jihad Against the Jews and Crusaders'. The constituent organisations are all signatories to the founding statement, which included the following fatwa:

The ruling to kill the Americans and their allies—civilians and military—is an individual duty for every Muslim who can do it in any country which is possible to do it, in order to liberate the Al Aqsa Mosque and the Holy Mosque (Mecca) from their grip, and in order for their armies to move out of all the lands of Islam, defeated and unable to threaten any Muslim.

Like global civil society groups, Al Qaeda has pioneered new forms of action. The main form of action is the 'raid'. In the last ten years before his death, the Prophet redefined the notion of a raid, which had been characteristic of pre-Islamic nomad groups, as part of *jihad*, to mean a raid aimed at the benefit of the whole community and not individual gain. Al Qaeda has resurrected the term and it was used to describe the attacks on the World Trade Center and other operations. In the founding statement quoted above, Al Qaeda calls on 'Muslim *Ulema*, leaders, youths and soldiers to launch a raid on Satan's US troops and the devil's supporters allying with them, and to displace those who are behind them so that they may learn a lesson'.

Two mechanisms are important in holding the network together and sustaining the mission. These are training camps and new forms of communication. The main training camps were in Afghanistan but there were, and perhaps still are, also training camps in Sudan, Pakistan, and Bosnia. The Americans in Afghanistan unearthed the Encyclopaedia of *jihad*, some 1,000 pages stored on computer diskettes, and the Manual of Military Studies of Jihad. Some courses are quite short—15 days—like staff training or summer schools for NGOs. As well as military training, the camps conduct courses in religious knowledge and theory of jihad, and training in operational principles: writing reports, using computers, fund-raising, and budgeting. Video cassettes seem to be widely used in the organisation: as a form of communication and propaganda (Bin Laden's speeches as well as those by favoured religious scholars); as a method of dialogue (the Americans seem uncannily to discover videos of discussions about proposed operations); for identifying targets and planning (this was very important in the Kenya and Tanzania embassy bombings, as emerged in the trials); and for demonstrating the success of actual operations and learning lessons. In the case of the bombing of the USS Cole in South Yemen, the Americans traced $5,000 provided to the local operational cell from Bin Laden. Like any good donor, Bin Laden had specified how he wanted his money to be used; reportedly, funds were specifically allocated to videoing the attack, although, in the end, this was not achieved, for technical reasons.

Al Qaeda has a range of funding sources. Bin Laden himself is personally very wealthy; his inherited fortune is estimated at $300 million and he owns a range of businesses, including banks, farms, and factories throughout the world. Nevertheless, the network seems to be engaged in perpetual fund-raising. First of all, operational cells appear to be self-sufficient. Members of the cells are mostly volunteers; their livelihoods are salaries or scholarships for students. They engage in their own fund-raising, which includes legitimate businesses, like home repairs or restoring second-hand cars, as is the case for one cell broken up in Germany, and criminal activity, such as credit card fraud (very frequent), burglaries and bank robberies, and kidnapping for ransom. In all Al-Qaeda statements, 'plunder' is frequently mentioned. In the founding statement, Al Qaeda calls on every Muslim 'to kill Americans and plunder their money wherever and whenever they find it'. It has suggested that this notion of plunder is ritualistic, linked to the concept of a raid. In the manual found in the car the hijackers left behind in Boston airport—two more copies have since been found by the FBI—it was written: 'If God grants you a slaughter, you should perform it as an offering on behalf of your mother and father, for they are owned by you . . . If you slaughter, you should plunder those you slaughter, for that is a sanctioned custom of the prophets'. Since the hijackers were all about to die, the emphasis on plunder must have been ritualistic. However, a ritualistic notion of plunder helps to justify and legitimise fund-raising.

The most likely explanation for the self-sufficiency of the operational cells is that, as with local branches of civil society networks, they are autonomous spontaneous groups, sympathetic to Al Qaeda but self-organised. Another explanation is security. The FBI argues that the way to catch Al Qaeda is to 'follow the money'. But if the cells are self-sufficient, it is much more difficult to trace financial links. Also, self-sufficiency helps to create a self-sustaining organisation. The cells appear to have a remarkable capacity to replicate themselves, even after being broken up by security services.

A second source of funding is banks and Islamic charities. The United States and its allies in the global coalition recently froze the assets of two banks, Al-Taqwa and Bakarat, that manage *hawala* transfers (non-recorded transfers of remittances). These transfers amount to some $5 billion–$6 billion annually. They are mostly legitimate: Gulf workers, for example, transferring money to their relatives. But the bank makes a 5 per cent commission and this can be used for transfers within the network. Bakarat seems to have branches in many countries but it is particularly important to Somalia, where it acts unofficially as the central bank. (It is not clear whether Al Qaeda exploited the informal nature of the *hawala* system to it own ends or whether these banks actively supported the organisation.) Likewise, Islamic NGOs like the Texas-based charity, the Holy Land Foundation for Relief and Development, or the International Islamic Relief Organisation (IIRO), are said by the FBI to be used both as methods for channelling funds and as a support infrastructure for terrorist activity.

Clearly, some groups are directly funded by Bin Laden through these mechanisms, which suggests that the mission is not always the only motive. According to the *Financial Times*, the Chechen warlord who executed the British telecommunications workers claimed he did it because his funding was in jeopardy. He said he could get more money from Islamic terrorist groups than as ransom from the telecommunications company. The group in Yemen, mentioned above, also received direct funding. Perhaps Bin Laden provides 'match funding' or 'start-up' funds.

Sources: Hirshkorn et al. (2001); Mneimneh and Makiya (2002); Halliday (2002); Lormel (2002); and *Financial Times* (various).

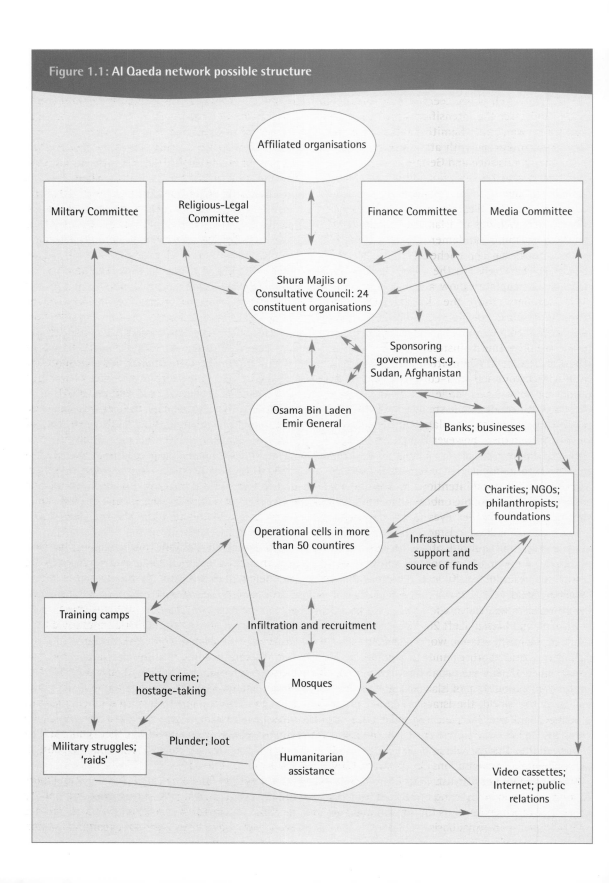

Figure 1.1: Al Qaeda network possible structure

Affiliated organisations

Miltary Committee

Religious-Legal Committee

Finance Committee

Media Committee

Shura Majlis or Consultative Council: 24 constituent organisations

Sponsoring governments e.g. Sudan, Afghanistan

Osama Bin Laden Emir General

Banks; businesses

Charities; NGOs; philanthropists; foundations

Operational cells in more than 50 countires

Infrastructure support and source of funds

Training camps

Infiltration and recruitment

Mosques

Petty crime; hostage-taking

Military struggles; 'raids'

Plunder; loot

Humanitarian assistance

Video cassettes; Internet; public relations

December 2001 and the worsening confrontation between India and Pakistan has generated widespread communal violence in the Indian state of Gujarat, in which police seem to have been complicit. And after the intensification of the Israeli-Palestine war, anti-Semitism has also been increasing in Europe with attacks on synagogues, particularly in France and Germany.

It must also be said, however, that dialogue initiatives have had some success in educating the Western public about the teachings of Islam and in distinguishing fundamentalist from mainstream approaches. The Koran is a best-seller in the West, and many people are now aware, for instance, that the Koran explicitly forbids suicide and that Al-Qaeda's conception of *jihad* is not shared by the mainstream of Muslim believers. While attempts at inter-religious and inter-cultural dialogue may have made some headway in fostering understanding of Muslims among secular and religious Westerners, however, it will be much more difficult to do the opposite: to gain back the confidence of Muslims concerning the good intentions of, and the ability to live together with, the unbelievers and Christians in the West, who in their eyes seek to dominate the world, as well as Jews in Israel and Hindus in India. The Gallup poll quoted above shows that the majority of the 10,000 respondents interviewed in Indonesia, Iran, Jordan, Kuwait, Lebanon, Morocco, Pakistan, Saudi Arabia, and Turkey considered the US to be 'ruthless, aggressive, conceited, arrogant, easily provoked and biased' (Left 2002).

If many in the Islamic world distrusted the rest of the world before and immediately after September 11, the war against Afghanistan, the detention without trial of Islamist 'suspects' in many parts of the world, the Israeli military actions in the West Bank and Gaza, and aggressive government rhetoric and communal violence in India can only have made things worse. The irony is that fundamentalist organisations like Al-Qaeda thrive in this environment of distrust. Global civil society has a long way to go in fostering conditions for a global discourse in which Muslims feel at ease and able to participate on an equal basis.

> For human rights groups, September 11 was a moment when international law might have been taken seriously, making possible effective responses, where feasible, to all such crimes in the future

The human rights moment

For human rights groups, what happened on September 11 was a crime against humanity, not very different from earlier crimes in Rwanda, Srebrenica, or Chechnya.

For these groups, this was a moment when international law might have been taken seriously, making possible effective responses, where feasible, to all such crimes in the future. Recent developments such as the arrest of Pinochet, the trial of Milosevic, and the agreement on the International Criminal Court made this seem like a real option. Such a legal response does not rule out military action to protect civilians and to arrest suspected criminals; but military action has to be sanctioned by the United Nations Security Council and to respect the framework of the laws of war (see for instance Robertson 2001).

Moreover, the suspects should be given criminal trials, preferably of an international nature and including judges from the Muslim world. There were proposals for the Security Council or the General Assembly to establish an ad hoc tribunal, as was done for the Yugoslav and Rwanda crises, to try suspected terrorists (see Neier 2002; Underhill 2001).

The thinking behind this argument is that terrorists, human rights violators, and criminals are best defeated by scrupulously upholding the rule of law instead of making martyrs out of them, and their values are best combated by holding these up to scrutiny in fair and high-profile trials that could truly be seen to be dispensing justice on behalf of the international community. An alternative rhetoric based on international law would have been a better way to marginalise the political pretensions of the terrorists. Had the terrorists been dubbed criminals rather than enemies, and been pursued by legally sanctioned means, even military, there could still be room for a truly global response and for political opposition and debate.

However, so far from being able to promote *more* respect for human rights as the most appropriate response to terrorism, human rights advocates everywhere have been fighting a rearguard action

Above: Members of Amnesty International getting ready for a demonstration in Islamabad. © Piers Benatar/Panos Pictures.

against rhetoric, legislation, and police and military actions that violated human rights and humanitarian law in the name of fighting terrorism. Some of the recent repressive measures are genuinely born out of government fears of terrorism; others are opportunistic attempts to use the anti-terrorist wave in order to thwart political opponents and stifle debate. Neither is anything new. In the past, both war-fighting and anti-terrorist action have gone hand in hand with human rights abuse, in Latin America, in Chechnya, in Egypt, but also in demo-cracies like Germany, Italy, Israel, and Spain. It is not surprising, then, when both are conflated into a global 'war on terrorism', that human rights should be at risk.

Human rights groups, both national and inter-national, have done important work in monitoring these developments and documenting how they violate international legal norms (see for instance Duffy 2001; Human Rights Watch URL; 2002; Amnesty International 2002). They have also strongly criticised the military tribunals at Guantanamo Bay. They have booked some victories in softening the new laws, for instance in India, and even softening some of the worst features of the military tribunals (Human Rights Watch URL).

However, the human rights movement is divided about the rights and wrongs of the war itself, as opposed to how it is to be conducted, and this has weakened its position. As Michael Ignatieff (2002) suggested in a recent article, the human rights movement 'will have to engage soon in the battle of ideas: it has to challenge directly the claim that national security trumps human rights. The argument to make is that human rights is the best guarantor of national security'. So far, the movement has not succeeded in countering the repressive logic of governments by persuading them, or at least public opinion, of the merits of the global justice approach, which would argue that less selective justice, more respect for civil and political as well as economic, social, and cultural rights, and resort where necessary to an international criminal court are the most appropriate medicine against terrorism.

Conclusion: Some Scenarios and Continued Reflection

The six global moments that we have described are overlapping and complementary as well as contradictory. It is possible to envisage different permutations of the responses these understandings generate. If we assume that what matters is the influence of global civil society on official policy, it is possible to outline four possible scenarios based on different permutations.

The unilateralist scenario

The first is the dominance of unilateralism, a scenario in which multilateral states are subsumed in the logic of the war on terror and forced to take sides, and in which the space for independent voices is narrowed drastically. This is a long-term war scenario in which terror justifies an extension of the war on terror and vice versa, and in which geo-politics rules internationally and repression increases domestically. As in all wars, non-violent dissent will be the loser. The various global civil society groups that criticise the war will be dubbed apologists for terrorism. Human Rights groups will be marginalised. Moreover, this global war with substitutable enemies can be indefinitely protracted. This scenario can be considered as the defeat of global civil society, which would be partly owing to its own weaknesses including, as outlined in this chapter and others, tendencies towards co-option, fractiousness, cultural arrogance, elitism, and inability to represent the victims of terror as well as the war on terror.

The bargain scenario

The second scenario is a bargain between the unilateralists and the multilateralists, one in which more economic equality is traded in exchange for a diminution of political, civil, and cultural rights. At the beginning of the cold war, European governments continued to receive American aid in exchange for support for anti-communism despite congressional disapproval of the European commitment to planning and welfare. In a similar way, we may see the United States agreeing to greater global economic redistribution and more global economic rules of the games in exchange for an anti-terrorist commitment that may well involve greater repression and continued cultural cleavages. This is also a long-term war scenario but tempered by greater economic equality. In this scenario, development NGOs and parts of the anti-capitalist movement are likely to be co-opted by the multilateral states, while more radical parts of the same movement, as well as peace and religious and human rights groups, are marginalised and muted by the polarisation of war.

The division scenario

The third scenario is a growing division between unilateralist states led by the United States, and multilateralist states led by the European Union. In this scenario, the multilateralists start to criticise the war on terror and the support for local wars on terror, and take on board some of the analysis of the peace, human rights, and religious groups. This is a scenario where the various global civil society groups do make alliances and are able to offer a dominant analysis that provides an alternative set of proposals for dealing with terror. But they are not able to win over dominant sections of society in the unilateralist states. In this scenario the multilateralists may succeed in restraining the wars on terror, although it may also lead to a new Atlantic conflict.

The utopian scenario

The final scenario is a utopian one in which the various interdependent efforts of global civil society to develop constructive responses to September 11 all come to fruition. It is a scenario where global civil society's efforts to cross the various cleavages in global society and to emphasis the advantages of a rule of law begin to influence public opinion in the unilateralist states. Growing American opposition to the Bush administration, coupled with campaign finance reform, an Israel-Palestine civil society partnership, and a South Asian citizens' movement might succeed in averting the worst catastrophes and change the respective regimes. In this scenario, people can be weaned from fundamentalism by constructive and respectful intercultural dialogue, terrorists are dealt with by legal means, and real inroads are made on global inequality.

The post-September 11 era may be the most dangerous period that those of us who were born after the Second World War, or perhaps after the Cuban missile crisis, have ever experienced. The voice of morality needs to be heard more than ever. Although, as we have tried to show, global civil society is heterogeneous, divided, often irrational, and sometimes uncivil, it is evident that the more optimistic scenarios outlined above do depend on a strong global civil society presence which allows for global public debate and deliberation and which gives greater priority to moral norms and values. They also depend on the quality of the actions and arguments deployed by global civil society, and the kind of alliances it suceeds in making.

Continuing reflection

The question we have posed about whether September 11 closed down global civil society or whether or it provided an opportunity for an even greater impact cannot be answered yet; but it will shape our discussions in this and future Yearbooks. In this year's report, we start with two conceptual essays, addressing in different ways the issue of the Northern bias of global civil society. For Neera Chandhoke, as discussed in Chapter 2, global civil society is identified with the NGOs that have flourished along with globalisation. She fears the role of global civil society as a form of co-option, of learning to live with globalisation, understood as the unrestrained spread of markets. Abdullahi AnNa'im is concerned in Chapter 3 with the spiritual dimension of global civil society. He argues that global civil society cannot be a meaningful concept to most people in the world if it does not take into account their religious identity and the role of religion in motivating them towards certain behaviour and alliances. Religious currents like the Gandhian tradition, liberal Islam, and liberation theology could greatly enhance the substantive morality and global appeal of global civil society, and help combat various forms of fundamentalism, but only if dominant secular discourses make a serious effort to accommodate them.

> The more optimistic scenarios for the future depend on a strong global civil society presence, which allows for global public debate and deliberation and which gives greater priority to moral norms and values

The three issue chapters all discuss in different ways the ethical influence of global civil society. In Chapter 4 on corporate social responsibility, Adele Simmons and Melanie Oliviero acknowledge divisions between 'outsiders' who are confrontational and 'insiders' who are accused of co-option and between Northern groups, who are closer to donors, and Southern groups, who are closer to the victims of irresponsibility, as well as the unresolved role of state regulation. Nevertheless, their combined impact has made tremendous strides towards making citizens in general, and corporate leaders in particular, recognise that businesses have social and environmental responsibilities. Hakan Seckinelgin describes in Chapter 5 how in the area of HIV/AIDS grass-roots movements initially succeeded in empowering people who had the disease, transforming them from victims into active citizens, and booking victories with respect to prevention, treatment, and care along the way. However, international approaches to the disease have since been institutionalised and bureaucratised, the availability of treatment in the North has led to demobilisation and loss of solidarity, and the future of the movement is in question. As articulated by Marlies Glasius in Chapter 6 on the International Criminal Court, global civil society has had a mixed record in making this negotiation process more democratic, but it made a particularly important contribution in strengthening the force of moral considerations in the state negotiations.

The three infrastructure chapters show the complex ways in which global civil society is adapting to its environment. James Deane, Njonjo Mue, and Fackson Banda describe in Chapter 7 a transformed landscape in traditional media, much more vibrant and open than it was ten years ago but also much more commercialised and focused on entertainment and consumption. This new scene is challenging civil society and the notion of a truly inclusive public debate in ways not foreseen in the days of censorship. Helmut Anheier and Nuno Themudo discuss in Chapter 8 the ways in which civil society is meeting the challenge of globalisation by exploring new organisational forms to accommodate global action. Chapter 9, by Saskia Sassen, looks at more informal manifestations of civil society action in global cities, and asks whether the experiences of the inhabitants of these cities are providing them with new identities that could be considered as forms of global, or at least transnational, citizenship. Part IV of the book, our Records on global civil society, opens with a discussion piece by Helmut Anheier and Sally Stares on the feasibility and desirability of constructing a global civil society index on the basis of existing data. This is followed by a data programme, a chronology of global civil society events of 2001, and updates on some of last year's chapters.

The resourcefulness and resilience of individuals and groups in global civil society suggest that new ways will be found to adapt to the post-September 11 context, although whether this will be creative and inclusive, defensive and confrontational, compromising and co-opted, civil or uncivil, is still to be determined. We understand our project of producing an annual report on global civil society as a reflexive enterprise. We hope this book will stimulate and provoke. We welcome critical responses. We want both our researchers and our readers to be part of a global public debate; we want to facilitate and to participate in the debate. Indeed, as we have argued, debate is the only way to counter the dangers that the world currently faces.

We would like to thank Amarjit Singh for research on this chapter and Helmut Anheier, Yahia Said, and Jill Timms for their comments.

References

Amnesty International (2001a). 'Italy: Genoa G8 Policing Operating of July 2001: Summary of Concerns'. London. 1 November.

— (2001b). 'United Kingdom: Rushed Legislation Opens Door to Human Rights Violations'. 14 December.

— (2001c). 'News Flash United Kingdom: Concern over Anti-Terrorist Arrests'. 19 December.

— (2002). *Rights at Risk: Amnesty International's Concerns Regarding Security Legislation and Law Enforcement Measures.* 18 January.

Anderson, Kenneth (2000). 'The Ottawa Convention Banning Landmines, the Role of International Non-governmental Organizations and the Idea of International Civil Society'. *European Journal of International Law*, 1/1: 91–120.

Anderson, Kevin and Ben Wright (2002). 'Eyewitness: Protest on Fifth Avenue'. *BBC News Online*. 3 February. http://news.bbc.co.uk/hi/english/business/newsid_17980 00/1798204.stm

Anheier, Helmut, Glasius, Marlies, and Kaldor, Mary (2001). 'Introducing Global Civil Society', in Helmut Anheier, Marlies Glasius, and Mary Kaldor (eds), *Global Civil Society 2001*. Oxford: Oxford University Press.

'Anti-War Protests from Around the World'. http://www.towsonactiongroup.org/antiwar.html

Arts, Bas (1998). *The Political Influence of Global NGOs: Case Studies on the Climate and Biodiversity Conventions*. Utrecht: International Books.

Asia Times Online (2002). 'Terror Crackdown Opportunism' Editorial. 10 January. http://www.atimes.com/editor/DA10Ba01.html

Axworthy, Lloyd (1998). 'Towards a New Multilateralism', in M. A. Cameron, R. J. Lawson, and B.W. Tomlin (eds), *To*

Walk Without Fear: The Global Movement to Ban Landmines. Toronto: Oxford University Press.

Blair, Tony (2001). 'Speech by the Prime Minister at the Lord Mayor's Banquet'. 12 November. http://www.number-10.gov.uk/news.asp?NewsId= 2997&SectionId=32

Blustein, Paul (2002). 'Bush Seeks Foreign Aid Boost; Plan Counters Overseas Critics'. *Washington Post*. 15 March.

B'tselem. http://www.btselem.org/

Caldiron, Guido (2001). 'Black Bloc, Nomadi No Copyright' [Black Block, Nomads Without Copyright], in *La Sfida al G8* [The Challenge to the G8]. Rome: Manifestolibri.

Cater, Nick (2001). 'Red Cross Resignation Highlights Charity Politics'. *Reuters Alertnet*. 1 November. http://www.alertnet.org/thefacts/reliefresources/318469

CBS News. (2001) 'Poll: United We Stand'. 9 October. http://www.cbsnews.com/stories/2001/10/09/opinion/m ain314059.shtml

— (2002). 'Poll: Support for War Stays Strong. 23 January. http://www.cbsnews.com/stories/2002/01/23/opinion/m ain325303.shtml

Ciesla, Eileen (2001). 'The Tobin Test: Meet the New Trial Balloon for Global Tax Advocates'. Guest Column. *National Review Online*. 14 December.

Clark, Ian (1999). *Globalisation and International Relations Theory*. Oxford: Oxford University Press.

Cooper, Robert (2000). *The Postmodern State and the World Order* (2nd edn). London: Demos/Foreign Policy Centre.

'Deny Them Their Victory: A Religious Response to Terrorism'. (2001) http://www.ncccusa.org/news/interfaithstatement.html. 14 September.

Der Derian (2001). *Virtuous War: Mapping the Military-Industrial-Media-Entertainment Network*. Boulder, CO: Westview Press.

Duffy, Helen (2001). *Responding to September 11: The Framework of International Law*. London: Interights. October. http://www.interights.org

'Fórum Encerrado em Clima de Festa' (2002). *Correio do Povo* (2002). 6 February. http://www.correiodopovo.com.br/

Freedman, L (1998). *The Revolution in Strategic Affairs* (Adelphi Paper 318). London: International Institute of Strategic Affairs.

Friends of the Earth International (2001). 'Kyoto Deal is Done'. Press Release, 25 July. http://www.foei.org/media/2001/25_july_bonn.html

Genoa Social Forum (2001). 'Stralcio dal Documento Presentato dal GSF alla Commissione Parlamentare il 6 Settembre 2001' [Summary of the Document Presented by GSF to the Parliamentary Commission on 6 September 2001], in *La Sfida al G8* [The Challenge to the G8]. Rome: Manifestolibri.

Graham, Robert and Haig Simonian (2001). 'Jospin Sees France as the Pilot of the G8 Protests'. *Financial Times.* 24 July.

Greenpeace International (2001). 'Greenpeace Hails Major Political Victory for the Climate'. Press Release, 27 July. http://www.greenpeace.org/~climate/

Halliday, Fred (2002). *Two Hours that Shook the World: September 11: Causes and Consequences.* London: Saqi Books.

Harriford, Erika (2001). 'The Death of the European Caucus'. Speech by Erika Harriford, read during a Day of Reflection on Durban and Beyond in Paris organized by CLEF and MAPP on 7 December. http://www.hri.ca/racism/analyses/harriford.htm

Hirschkorn, Phil, Gunaratna, Rohan, Blanche, Ed, and Leader, Stefan (2001). 'Blowback'. *Jane's Intelligence Review*, 1 August.

Human Rights Watch (2002). *Background Paper on Geneva Conventions and Persons Held by U.S. Forces.* New York. 29 January.

— (URL). *Opportunism in the Face of Tragedy: Repression in the Name of Anti-Terrorism.* http://www.hrw.org/campaigns/september11/opportunis mwatch.htm

Huntington, Samuel P. (1996). *The Clash of Civilizations and the Remaking of World Order.* New York: Simon & Schuster.

Ignatieff, Michael (2002). 'Is the Human Rights Era Ending?'. *The New York Times.* 5 February.

Independent Sector (2001). *A Survey of Independent Giving After September 11.* Washington, DC. 23 October. A Joint Civil Society Statement on the Tragedy in the United States' (2001). 21 September. http://www.civicus.org/main/server_navigation/ skeletons/Civicus_01/framework/index2.cfm

Kafala, Tarik (2002). 'Israelis Back Sharon'. *BBC News.* 8 April. http://news.bbc.co.uk/hi/english/world/middle_east/new sid_1916000/1916951.stm

Kant, Immanuel ([1795]1983). *Perpetual Peace, and Other Essays on Politics, History, and Morals.* Translated with introduction by Ted Humphrey. Indianapolis : Hackett Publishing Company.

Knoll, Jennifer (2002). 'Bush Welcomes Big Pro-Israel Rally'. *Reuters.* 15 April.

Left, Sarah (2002). 'Poll: Majority of Muslims Distrusts U.S.' *The Guardian.* 27 February.

Longhi, Vittorio (2001). 'Italy's Strategy of Tension'. *The Guardian.* 27 July.

Lormel, Dennis M (2002). *Statement for the Record.* Washington, DC: House Committee on Financial Services, Subcommittee on Oversight and Investigations, 1 February. http://www.fbi.gov/congress/congress02/ lormel021202.htm

Madmundo (2001). 'Les Deux Mondialisations Davos – Porto Alegre: un vis à vis special par satellite'. 2 February. http://www.madmundo.tv/francais/globaldiv/index.html

Martin, Jerry L. and Anne D. Neal (2002). *Defending Civilization: How Our Universities Are Failing America and What Can be Done About It.* Washington, DC: Defence of Civilization Fund, American Council of Trustees and Alumni. February.

Matas, David. (2001). 'Civil Society Smashes Up'. September. http://www.hri.ca/racism/analyses/matas.htm

Mneimneh, Hassan and Makiya, Kanan (2002) 'Manual for a "Raid"'. *New York Review of Books.* 17 January.

Muslims Against Terrorism. http://www.matusa.org/home.asp

Najam, A. (1996). 'Understanding the Third Sector: Revisiting the Prince, the Merchant, and the Citizen'. *Non-Profit Management and Leadership,* 7/2: 203–19.

Neier, Aryeh (2002). 'The Military Tribunals on Trial'. *New York Review of Books.* 14 February.

Pax Protest (2001). 'The Anti-War Movement is Growing Throughout the World'. 16 October. http://pax.protest.net/Peace/protest_numbers.html

Peace Coalition. http://www.peoples-peace-campaign.org/

Peaceful Tomorrows. http://www.peacefultomorrws.org

Pianta, Mario (2001). 'Parallel Summits of Global Civil Society', in Helmut Anheier, Marlies Glasius, and Mary Kaldor (eds), *Global Civil Society 2001.* Oxford: Oxford University Press.

Pietrangeli, Paolo with Roberto Giannarelli, Wilma Labate, and Francesco Martinotti in cooperation with Genoa Social Forum (2001). *Genova Per Noi. Immagini e Testimonianze sui Tre Giorni del G8.* [Genoa for us: Images and Testimony on Three Days of G8]. Video. Milan: Nuova Iniziativa Editoriale l'Unità, Milano.

Pillay, Pravasan and Pithouse, Richard (2001). 'The Durban March on the United Nations World Conference on Racism, South Africa'. *New Internationalist.* September. http://www.oneworld.org/ni/streets/durban/070901.htm

Protest.net (URL). 'Media Keeps Silent About Worldwide Demonstrations'. http://www.protest.net/view.cgi?view=2309

Robertson, Geoffrey (2001). 'There Is A Legal Way Out of This'. *The Guardian*. 14 September. http://www.guardian.co.uk/wtccrash/story/0,1300,551607,00.html

Rosenau, James (1998). 'Governance and Democracy in a Globalizing World', in Daniele Archibugi, David Held, and Martin Kohler (eds), *Re-Imagining Political Community: Studies in Cosmopolitan Democracy*. Stanford: Stanford University Press.

Roy, Arundhati (2001). 'The Algebra of Infinite Justice'. *The Guardian*. 29 September.

Salamon, L. M. and Anheier, H. K. (1992). 'In Search of the Non-Profit Sector, Part 1: The Question of Definitions'. *Voluntas*, 3/2: 125–51.

Seabrook, Jeremy (2001). 'Why Clare Short is Wrong'. *The Guardian*. 24 July.

Seruv. http://seruv.org.il/

SIPRI (Stockholm International Peace Research Institute) (2001). *SIPRI Yearbook 2001: Armaments, Disarmament and International Security*. Oxford: Oxford University Press.

Shepherd, George W. (2001). 'A New World Agenda for the 21st Century: The World Conference on Racism and Xenophobia in Durban, South Africa'. 26 October. http://www.hri.ca/racism/analyses/gshepherd.htm

Solana, Javier (2002). 'Global Security in a Changing Geopolitical Environment: the European Perspective'. Address at Seminar on War and Peace in the 21st Century An European Perspective. 12 January.

Ta'ayush. http://taayush.tripod.com/taayush.html

Underhill, William (2001). 'Trying Bin Laden'. *Newsweek*. 15 October.

United Nations (URL). 'Guidelines Association Between the United Nations and Non-Governmental Organizations'. http://www.un.org/esa/coordination/ngo/pdf/guidelines.pdf

Verhofstadt, Guy (2001). 'Open Letter: The Paradox of Anti-Globalisation', in *Open Letter on Globalisation: The Debate*. Laeken: European Council.

World Bank Group (2001). 'An Open Letter'. http://www.worldbank.org/html/extdr/openletter.htm 17 August.

World Social Forum (URL). 'Call of Social Movements. Resistance to Neoliberalism, War and Militarism: for Peace and Social Justice'. http://www.forumsocialmundial.org.br/eng/portoalegrefinal_english.asp

Chapter 2
THE LIMITS OF GLOBAL CIVIL SOCIETY

Neera Chandhoke

The Three Sector Fallacy

There is something about modern modes of analysis—a propensity to analyse phenomena in terms of discrete categories perhaps—which attracts theorists to additive modes of social science. Thus, they first subdivide areas of collective life into separate spheres, endow these domains with their distinct logics, distinguish them from each other, and then add them together to form a whole. Witness how modern social theory first separates the public and the private, views each of these spheres as possessing a different logic of thought and action, and then adds them together to form an entity called 'society'. The point is that, whereas in the process the public becomes the field of the rational, the private is conceptualised as the site of unreflective emotions and affections.

Now on the face of it there is nothing wrong with employing this strategy as a heuristic device. There is absolutely nothing wrong in conceptualising the different ways in which people make their own histories even if they may not make those histories very well. The idea that whereas the state is stamped mainly by the logic of coercion, the logic of the market is that of competition, is perfectly acceptable. We can also agree that there is a difference between the community and civil society. Community as social anthropologists tell us, represents personalised and face-to-face interactions. Relationships in civil society on the other hand are contractual.

What *is* problematic is the assumption that appears to underlie theorising in this mode, namely, that these domains of collective existence do not *influence* each other, or that they do not *affect* each other, or indeed that they do not *constitute* in the sense of shaping each other (Chandhoke 2001). This is something that additive social theorists tend to ignore. They should read Copernicus, who was to write about the astronomers of his day thus: 'With them it is as though an artist were to gather the hands, feet, head, and other members for his images

from diverse models, each part excellently drawn, but not related to a single body, and since they in no way match each other, the result would be a monster rather than man' (Kuhn 1962: 83). The same problem seems to bedevil additive social science, for in this genre no one category influences let alone constitutes others, no category is central to human life, and no category determines how we approach other categories of activity. The questions that immediately confront us in this connection are the following: do categories of collective existence *not* constitute each other? Equally, does not a single logic, that of power, underpin these categories and bind them together?

To put it plainly, the separation of collective human existence into mutually exclusive spheres of thought and action *elides* the way in which each of these domains is constructed by power, which spilling over arbitrary boundaries underpins the whole. Consider the feminist critique of the public-private dichotomy: if we conceptualise the household as the site of affection and emotions as different from the power-driven state or from the competition-ridden economy, we end up actually legitimising patriarchal power. For, as a microcosm of society, the household cannot but condense the tensions of the social formation, it cannot but be permeated by power.

Of course, power manifests itself in and through different avatars that apparently have nothing to do with each other. For instance, globalisation, which is legitimised by its defenders as the rationalisation of economic life, may seem diametrically opposed to, say, fundamentalist movements. On the face of it fundamentalist movements look as if they are a knee-jerk *reaction* to the globalising project and thus possessed of a different logic. But note that *both* of these projects manifest different forms of power, simply because both limit the endeavours of human beings to make their own lives with some degree of autonomy. This admittedly is difficult to fathom, simply because various forms of power not only appear as contradictory, oppositional, and diffused, but also happen to operate in invisible and intangible ways that escape the human gaze. Today theorists tell us and practitioners claim that it is difficult to decipher power since it does not originate from a single point. We have learnt that we can locate no meta-discourse but only the micro-politics of a power that is heterogeneous, dispersed, and even unpredictable. Nevertheless, power binds ostensibly autonomous institutions and practices in a myriad of ways, all of which constrain human autonomy and creativity and limit political initiatives. Power, in other words, *produces identifiable effects* even though its various manifestations do not always act in concert.

It is, however, precisely these insights that are at a discount when theorists suggest that civil society possesses a discrete and distinct *raison d'être* which marks it out as different as well as autonomous both from the state and from the market. Thus, civil society in contemporary political theory is often posed as an alternative to both the state and to the market. It simply emerges as the third sphere of collective life. Gordon White, for instance, conceptualises civil society as 'an intermediate associational realm between the family and the state populated by organisations which are separate from the state, enjoy autonomy in relation to the state and are formed voluntarily by members of society to protect or extend their interests or values' (White 1994: 379). Charles Taylor suggests that civil society is 'those dimensions of social life which cannot be confounded with, or swallowed up in, the state' (Taylor 1991:171). If Axel Honneth (1993: 19) thinks of civil society as 'all civil institutions and organisations which are prior to the state', Jeffrey Isaac (1993: 356) speaks of the sphere as 'those human networks that exist independently of, if not anterior to, the political state'. Above all, Jean Cohen and Andrew Arato in a rather well known definition, refer to a 'third realm' differentiated from the economy and the state as civil society (Cohen and Arato 1992: 18). In the hands of these two authors, civil society as a normative moral order is diametrically opposed to both the state and the economy.

The same kind of thinking is more than visible when it comes to global civil society. Many theorists seem to be of the view that global civil society represents a 'third sector', which can not only be distinguished from but which is an alternative to both the state-centric international order and the networks of global markets. Lipschutz, for instance, employs the concept of 'global civil society' to indicate a plurality of agencies such as social movements, interest groups, and global citizens. If the distinguishing feature of these organisations is that they defy national boundaries, the cornerstone of global civil society is constituted by the 'self-conscious construction of networks of knowledge and action, [and] by de-centred local actors, that cross the reified boundaries of space as though they were not there'. Global civil society actors, in other words, engage in practices that can possibly reshape the 'architecture' of international politics by denying the primacy of states or of their sovereign rights (Lipschutz 1992: 390). Other scholars are of the opinion that the anti-state character of global civil society is revealed through its projects, for example, through the promotion of values from below, which exist in tension with dominant statist conceptions of the state system (Falk, Johansen, and Kim 1993: 13–14). Or that global civil society moving beyond 'thin anarchical society' is in the business of inaugurating a post-foreign policy world (Booth 1991: 540).

In other words, contemporary thinking gives us a picture of a global civil society that seems to be supremely uncontaminated by either the power of states or that of markets. Moreover, many theorists believe that global civil society, consisting of transnational non-governmental organisations, political activists, social movements, religious denominations, and associations of all stripe and hue, from trade unions to business and financial groupings, can neutralise existing networks of power by putting forth a different set of values. Global civil society (GCS), it is said, represents 'a post realist constellation, where transnational associational life (TAL) challenges the conceit of the state system . . . GCS is touted as the antidote for the anarchical structure, inequality, and exclusions of the state system' (Pasha and Blaney 1998: 418).

Now, it is true that global civil society organisations have managed to dramatically expand the agenda of world politics by insistently casting and

> Contemporary thinking gives us a picture of a global civil society that seems to be supremely uncontaminated by either the power of states or that of markets

focusing widespread attention on issues such as human rights, the environment, development, and banning land mines. And all these issues, remember, have traditionally fallen within the province of state sovereignty. Global civil society actors have simultaneously challenged the new contours of the world economic order as mandated by the World Trade Organisation, the World Bank, and the International Monetary Fund: think of the protests against the global economic dispensation at Seattle in November 1999, at Prague in September 2000, and at Genoa in 2001. But to conclude from this that these actors have drawn up a blueprint for a new or an alternative global order, or indeed to assume that they are autonomous of both states and markets, may prove too hasty a judgement.

> Can global civil society provide us with a third and presumably an alternative way of organising international relations? Or is it bound by the same logic that characterises the other two systems?

This is not to say that global civil society can be *reduced* to the logic of the state-centric world order or to the workings of the global economy. All I wish to suggest is that we should treat with a fair amount of caution the assumptions that (a) global civil society is autonomous of other institutions of international politics, that (b) it can provide us with an alternative to these institutions, or (c) that it can even give us a deep-rooted and structural critique of the world order. Global civil society may well reflect the power constellations of existing institutions. To put it bluntly, should our *normative* expectations of civil society blind us to the nature of *real* civil societies whether national or global?

In this chapter I address the concept of global civil society by asking two questions. The first question has to do with the perennial preoccupations of political theorists, i.e., what are the implications of the development of global civil society for issues of representation and political agency? After all, civil society in classical political theory is conceptualised as the space where ordinary men and women through the practices of their daily life acquire political agency and selfhood. Do the organisations of global civil society enhance this empowering process or constrain it? The second question that I wish to explore is the following: to what extent can global civil society be autonomous of the state-centric world system and of

the system of markets? In other terms, can global civil society provide us with a third and presumably an alternative way of organising international relations? Or is it bound by the same logic that characterises the other two systems? Just one point here: I take it as given that both the international political and the international economic order are dominated by the countries of Western Europe and by the United States. Is it possible that actors from the same parts of the world dominate global civil society? In sum, rather than begin with the presupposition that global civil society constitutes a third, alternative sphere, we should perhaps explore the context of the emergence of the sphere itself in order to understand what precisely it is about. We may well find that it has thrown up genuine alternatives, or we may find that global civil society actors work within a particular historical conjunction: that of the post-cold war consensus among the powerful countries in the world. Let us see.

The Making of Global Civil Society

The idea of internationalism has, of course, been central to working-class politics since the end of the nineteenth century. In a parallel development Henri La Fontaine, who was awarded the Nobel Peace Prize in 1913, created the Central Office of International Associations in 1907 to link up non-governmental organisations (NGOs) in different countries. The United Nations institutionalised procedures for consulting with these organisations in 1945. It is estimated that whereas in 1948, 41 NGOs enjoyed consultative status with the Economic and Social Council of the UN, by 1968 the number had risen to 500. By 1992 we were to see the Economic and Social Council consulting 1,000 or more NGOs. If we add to this number NGOs that interact with other bodies of the United Nations, and which often participate directly in the proceedings, the number rises to tens of thousands (Korey 1998: 2). It is perhaps not surprising that global civil society has come to be dominated by NGOs, even though other

Above: Commemoration of the 1991 Santa Cruz massacre in Dili. © Irene Slegt/Panos Pictures.
Right: Frontline between the army and protesting students near the Indonesian Parliament. © Chris Stowes/Panos Pictures.

actors, such as political activists networking across borders and anti-globalisation movements, were playing an important role in this sphere. It is indicative of the power of the non-governmental sector that civil society has come to be identified with NGO activism both in influential tomes on civil society and in policy prescriptions of international institutions today. The discussion that follows therefore shifts between NGOs and other civil society actors, even as it recognises that NGOs play a larger-than-life role in global civil society.

It was, however, at the turn of the 1990s that we were to witness a veritable explosion of NGOs, which, networking across national borders, propelled critical issues onto international platforms. The power of global NGOs was first visible at the Earth Summit in Rio in 1992, when about 2,400 representatives of NGOs came to play a central role in the deliberations (Anheier, Glasius, and Kaldor 2001: 326). By putting forth radically different alternatives, by highlighting issues of global concern, and by stirring up proceedings in general, these organisations practically hijacked the summit. Subsequently, they were given a central role in the Committee on Sustainable Development created by the Rio Summit. At the 1994 Cairo World Population Conference, increasing numbers of international NGOs took on the responsibility of setting the agenda for discussions. And in 1995 this sector almost overwhelmed the Fourth World Conference on Women in Beijing. Almost 2,100 national and international NGOs, consisting largely of advocacy groups and social activists, completely dominated the conference (Anheier, Glasius, and Kaldor 2001: 328). Since then we have seen that international NGOs either participate directly in international conferences or hold parallel conferences, which incidentally attract more media attention than official conferences. And in the process they have won some major victories.

One of these major victories occurred when global NGOs launched a campaign to pressurise governments to draft a treaty to ban the production, the stockpiling, and the export of landmines. Almost 1,000 transnational NGOs coordinated the campaign through the Internet. The pooling and the coordination of energies proved so effective that not only was the treaty to ban landmines signed in 1997, but the International Campaign to Ban Landmines and its representative Jody Williams were awarded the Nobel

Peace Prize. The citation at the award-giving ceremony spoke of their unique effort that made it 'possible to express and mediate a broad wave of popular commitment in an unprecedented way'. A similar pooling of energies can be seen in the crusade that led to the 1998 Rome Statute on an International Criminal Court (see Chapter 6).

Other triumphs followed in the field of human rights: in the battle that led to the ousting of Soeharto in Indonesia in 1998, for instance. After the Indonesian military had massacred more than 150 participants in a funeral procession in Dili, East Timor, in 1991, transnational human rights organisations mobilised massively against the political abuses of the Soeharto regime. Under pressure from these organisations, Canada, Denmark, and the Netherlands froze economic aid to Indonesia, and the US, Japan, and the World Bank threatened similar measures. Soeharto appointed a National Investigation Commission, which issued a mildly critical report of the incident; and aid was resumed (Glasius 1999: 252–64). But Soeharto lost control of events as human rights groups in Indonesia and East Timor mobilised under global human rights organisations to criticise and publicise the violation of human rights. Opposition mounted even as Soeharto designated a national human rights commission, whose reports added to the general discontent. In 1996, even as the leaders of civil society in East Timor—Jose Ramos Horta and Bishop Ximenes Belo—were given the Nobel Peace Prize, the *Blitzkrieg* launched by global human rights organisations strengthened the general atmosphere of dissatisfaction, despite the intensified repression launched by the regime. In late 1997 the country was buffeted by an economic crisis and mass protests led to the resignation of Soeharto. Transnational human rights organisations had managed to spectacularly overthrow a regime on the grounds that it was not respecting the basic rights of its people.

In India the power of global civil society organisations was revealed in a different way. Soon after independence, a massive project was inaugurated to dam the gigantic Narmada River, which runs through the three States of Madhya Pradesh, Gujarat, and Maharashtra in western India. The Narmada Valley Development Project consists of 30 major dams, 135 minor dams, and 3,000 small dams. The largest dam is the Sardar Sarovar Project, which ultimately will submerge 92,000 acres of land, displacing and affecting more than 300,000 people, a majority of whom are tribals or forest dwellers. In the mid-1980s a number of voluntary organisations began to mobilise the tribals for better resettlement and rehabilitation policies, as the existing ones had been found sadly wanting. Even as these organisations linked up with international NGOs to pressure the government of India into granting better resettlement and rehabilitation for the displaced, in 1988 about 20 groups formed the Narmada Bachao Andolan (NBA) or the Save Narmada Movement. The NBA launched a massive struggle against big development projects and for the right of the people *not* to be displaced. At the same time, international NGOs such as the Environment Defense Fund and Oxfam began to lobby the World Bank and the Japanese government to withdraw from their commitments to fund the project. The World Bank, now under public scrutiny, laid down conditions for better resettlement policies, conditions that the Indian government refused to fulfil. In 1993 the government decided to ask the World Bank to withdraw from the project rather than face the embarrassment of having the Bank draw back on its own. Soon afterwards the Japanese government also retracted its funding commitments. Whereas most of the pressure against the dam was generated by the NBA, the matter would not have come to international attention in quite the same manner without the support of international NGOs, which publicised the issue and pressurised centres of power in the West, (Chandhoke 1997). That the Indian government

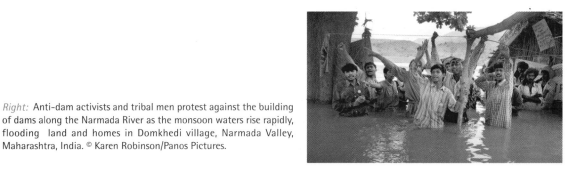

Right: Anti-dam activists and tribal men protest against the building of dams along the Narmada River as the monsoon waters rise rapidly, flooding land and homes in Domkhedi village, Narmada Valley, Maharashtra, India. © Karen Robinson/Panos Pictures.

THE LIMITS OF GLOBAL CIVIL SOCIETY Neera Chandhoke

has now decided to build the dam on its own, after the Supreme Court authorised it to do so in a judgement delivered on 18 October 2000, may point to the limits of political mobilisation in civil society.

However, the most dramatic manifestation of global civil society so far was to appear in what came to be known as the 'battle for Seattle'. At the end of November 1999, massive protests involving some 700 organisations and about 40,000 students, workers, NGOs, religious groups, and representatives of business and finance who were there for their own reasons brought the third ministerial meeting of the World Trade Organisation (WTO) in Seattle to a halt. The WTO was to set in motion a new multilateral round of trade negotiations. Collective anger at the relocation of industries to the Third World, at the unsafe and abusive work conditions in the factories and sweatshops found there, at environmental degradation, and at the widespread exploitation of working people, exploded in a series of angry demonstrations. Though large-scale protests against the WTO, the International Monetary Fund (IMF), and the World Bank were not new, what was new was both the scale of mobilisation and the intensity of protest. Angry demonstrations by student unions, environmentalists or 'tree huggers', economic and xenophobic nationalists, church groups, anarchists, protectionists, consumer groups, NGOs, and even business and financial groups were hailed by some scholars as 'globalisation from below' (Kaldor 2000) or as heralding a new internationalism.

There were two aspects of the 'battle for Seattle' that proved significant for the consolidation of global civil society. First, for the first time hitherto single-issue groups coalesced into a broad-based movement to challenge the way the world trade and financial system was being ordered by international institutions. Second, whereas in the late 1960s protest groups in the US and in Western Europe had targeted the state, at Seattle they targeted global corporations and international economic institutions. The protests

> As the upholders of an ethical canon that applies across nations and cultures, international actors in civil society now define as well as set the moral norms ...

themselves bore the mark of collective ire and resentment at the way in which globalisation that had been set in motion two decades earlier had exacerbated inequality and injustice. And matters did not stop here. Mass protests have become a regular feature of annual meetings of the World Economic Forum, the IMF and the World Bank, and the WTO. At the same time we have seen students across university campuses in the US demonstrate against the unethical practices of large corporations such as Nike, Reebok, the Gap, and Disney, which use cheap labour in the Third World. Novel methods and vocabularies of protests captured the attention of the international media and generated considerable excitement at the idea of renewed political activism. And the phrase 'global civil society' became an integral part of political, corporate, and technical vocabularies.

In sum, global civil society organisations have emerged as a powerful and influential force on the world stage, affecting as they do both domestic and international policies, deciding as they do the fate of some authoritarian governments at least, and laying down agendas as they do. They not only have the power of influencing international public opinion and mobilising it against policies that they consider undesirable, they do so in ways that are sensationally visible and therefore effective.

Arguably two factors have strengthened the mandate of these organisations. One, the informational revolution, has increased their capacity to collect, collate, select, and publicise information on a variety of specialised issues ranging from development disasters, to the environment, to the effect of WTO policies such a patenting, to human rights violations. In fact, governments often just do not possess the capacity to gather and assemble specialised information or mobilise public opinion in quite the same way as NGOs organised on a global scale can do.

> ... they command this kind of attention because they have access to the international media, they possess high profiles, and they put forth their ideas in dramatic ways

Moreover, the unprecedented and phenomenal revolution in information and communications often described as the 'third industrial revolution' has allowed organisations to network across the world through the fax, the e-mail, the Internet, and teleconferencing. Loosely structured movements have used the Internet to set up web sites that inform prospective participants about the timing of the meetings of international institutions, on the organisation of protests, and about transportation and accommodation. In fact we have witnessed a new phenomenon bursting onto the political scene: *cyber-space activism*. Via this form of activism, members of a group who may never see each other come together, through cyberspace, around issues that they consider important. Informational networks have allowed concerned organisations to gather and put together data on, for example, violations of human rights, muster opinion and activism around the issue, publicise information through the international media, and pressurise both national and international organisations to change both their mind and their manners.

The revolution in communications and information has allowed NGOs to form coalitions, as for instance the Conference of Peoples Global Action Against Free Trade, that held its first meeting in Geneva in May 1998, the Third World Network, which as a union of Third World NGOs is based in Malaysia, and the formation of the International Federation of Human Rights, a Paris-based transnational NGO, which consists of 89 human rights groups in 70 countries. In fact, the revolution has also facilitated a new phenomenon: the development of intermediary NGOs, which act as 'facilitators' to help voluntary organisations to find funds from donor agencies such as Action Aid (India) or Charity Aid Foundation (UK). Intermediate organisations are, in other words, involved in the channelling of money and information from one NGO to another or from donor agencies to NGOs.

Second, global NGOs have become influential simply because they possess a property that happens to be the peculiar hallmark of *ethical* political intervention: moral authority and legitimacy. And they possess moral authority because they claim to represent the *public* or the *general* interest against official- or power-driven interests of the state or of the economy. Though the idea that they are truly representative can be challenged as I suggest below, this is not to deny that NGOs have raised normative concerns in the domain of global civil society. As the upholders of an *ethical* canon that applies across nations and cultures, international actors in civil society now define as well as set the moral norms, which should at least in principle govern national and international orders. To put it differently, global civil society actors legislate and mandate a normative and thus a morally authoritative structure for the national and the international community. Because they lend moral depth to the agenda of global concerns and because they articulate a global and ethically informed vision on how states should treat their citizens, global civil society actors command the kind of attention that normally does not accrue to political activism within states. And they command this kind of attention because they have access to the international media, they possess high profiles, and they put forth their ideas in dramatic ways.

This as a matter of course has significant implications for our traditional concepts of state sovereignty. Traditionally states, pleading sovereignty and state security, have resisted any intervention by outside agencies,. Today global civil society actors act as the guardians of a morally informed consensus on the minimum that is due to human beings. As the keepers of a moral conscience that applies across borders, global civil society organisations question the monopoly of the nation state over the lives of its people. But they also challenge the workings of international institutions such as the World Bank, the IMF, and the WTO, as well as opposing the working of giant economic corporations. If the demonstrations at Seattle questioned the viability of economic arrangements set by international institutions, the charting of norms for, say, the banning of child labour, or exploitation of resources, or environmental protection, has mediated the operations of powerful economic corporations.

The Historical Context for the Emergence of Global Civil Society

The two factors set out above have certainly facilitated as well as legitimised the advent of global civil society actors as influential players on the world stage. However, the causes of this phenomenon have to be sought elsewhere, in the deeper structural changes that have occurred in the international political and economic order in the last two decades. And the major change that has taken place in the world system since the 1980s is of course globalisation. Now globalisation is difficult to characterise as it consists of a number of overlapping

Above: Children are taught to use an Apple laptop at Gatchi outstation, Arnhem Land, Australia. © Penny Tweedie/Panos Pictures.

and even conflicting projects. However, though it is increasingly difficult to define globalisation, the implications of this process—or, rather, of this series of processes—are increasingly clear. Globalisation has, for one, enabled the transmission of capital across the world as if national boundaries were non-existent. Correspondingly, through the processes of global-isation natural and national resources have been appropriated in the cause of capital. Local knowledge systems have been harnessed and patented for the same purpose. And flows of information and messages that tell people how they should think and what they should think have legitimised the process itself.

Therefore, despite the difficulty in capturing the essence of globalisation, we can accept that its core is constituted by a distinct phenomenon: capital's restless and relentless pursuit of profit across the world and across national borders. Today we see capital flitting across national borders as if they were just not there. But note that there is nothing natural or given in the processes of capital flows that ensure this much-needed erosion of state boundaries. In other words, globalisation demanded and demands sustained political intervention for one main reason.

Recollect in this context that the post-Second World War period was to widely disseminate and institution-alise the idea that the state should intervene in matters relating to the production and to the reproduction of the economy and of society. The interventionist state was to take many forms: the Soviet model of the state that commands the heights of the economy, the welfare state that looks after the basic needs of its people, the Keynesian state that regulates the market, or the developmentalist state in the post-colonial world that commandeers both material and human resources to offset the legacies of colonial underdevelopment.

Therefore, if capital more often than not originating in the West had to cross boundaries in order to pursue accumulation on the world scale, the state had to be rolled back from its hitherto legitimate tasks of regulating the market as well as providing social services to the people. In other words, the legitimisation of the ability of the market to regulate itself, as well as to provide for both growth and well-being, demanded the delegitimisation and the consequent withdrawal of the state from the market. The state had to be rolled back both to encourage the unhindered flow of capital and to enable the market to display its dynamics.

It was precisely this understanding that underpinned what came to be known as the neo-liberal agenda, or what John Williams termed the 'Washington consensus', which reined in the centres of power in the Western world in the late 1980s. The consensus manifested itself in the form of ten policy recom mendations, imposed on particularly debt-ridden Third World countries by international financial and lending institutions. Among these recommendations were the following: trade liberalisation, clearing all hurdles to foreign direct investment, privatisation, deregulation, strengthening property rights, and tax reforms. If we translate these economic imperatives into political terms, we find that the consensus dictated the following: (a) the state, particularly in Third World countries, should withdraw from the social sector; (b) the market should be freed from all constraints; and (c) people in civil society should organise their own social and economic reproduction instead of depending on the state.

Ironically, the idea that people in civil society should organise their own reproduction has emerged at exactly the same moment as globalisation has drastically eroded the capacity of the same people to order their own affairs. And reliance on the market for this purpose is inadequate, since the market, remember, has room for only those people who have something to sell and those who have something to buy. In other words, the market does not provide for those people who cannot participate in its transactions because they have nothing with which they can buy, or because they cannot find buyers for what they sell: labour, for instance. The unleashing of the market simply meant that massive sections of the people had to now fend for themselves in the sense of providing the conditions for their social reproduction.

It was in this particular historical conjunction that NGOs emerged on the horizon to take over functions hitherto reserved for the state, such as providing health and education, instituting income-generating schemes, creating safety nets, and encouraging people to be self-reliant. The space cleared by the rolling back of the state came to be known as 'civil society', and NGOs were transformed into the guardians of civil society even as they subcontracted for the state. To put it in stark terms, the emergence and the growing power of NGOs whether national or global has been actively facilitated by the Washington consensus.

The role of the non-governmental sector has been further strengthened by what came subsequently to be known as the post-Washington consensus. The mid-1990s were to witness a sharp swing in the mood of international trade and financial institutions. For the rhetoric of these institutions was to move away from an emphasis on a free and untrammelled market to the idea that both the market and the generic processes of globalisation had to be governed. The shift had largely to do with one main factor. Doctrines of free trade and unregulated markets had run into trouble ever since 1994, when Mexico was hit by financial devastation. The second financial crisis, which began when the government of Thailand devalued the bhat, and which then spread to the rest of East Asia, Japan, Brazil, and Russia in 1997 and 1998, impoverished millions, and generated rage and discontent. We saw an inkling of this dissatisfaction when Korean workers rose to defy the IMF. Many scholars saw these economic and financial crises as a consequence of unfettered globalisation, as a result of the working of the free and unregulated market (Rhodes and Higgot 2000). The neo-liberal agenda had after all failed to deliver the much-promised benefits of greater growth, stabilisation of financial markets, and political order. Income disparities had increased, the number of the poor had grown drastically, and people had been deprived of their livelihoods and security of life. A global economic order had been forged through globalisation without any prospect of justice, or democracy, or redistribution. And this posed problems for the defenders of globalisation. For if a system is widely perceived as unjust, it will necessarily engender resistance.

Therefore, whereas in the 1980s and the early 1990s free market liberalism had been left to private corporations, this strategy had to be rethought since it had proved counter-productive. In fact, as early as in 1995 the economist Paul Krugman had suggested

> The space cleared by the rolling back of the state became known as 'civil society', and NGOs were transformed into the guardians of civil society even as they subcontracted for the state

that the Mexican crisis marked the beginning of the deflation of the Washington consensus (1995: 31–5). The very idea that globalisation had rationalised capitalism came to be questioned because what we witnessed was the globalisation of a crisis. Consequently, the managers of international financial and economic institutions were to realise, somewhat late, what Marx had argued in the late nineteenth century: that there is nothing natural or self-regulating about markets and that they unleash their own oppressions. If markets were to endure they had to be controlled or, in the new parlance of international financial institutions, 'governed'. Alternatively, the dominant approach to development needed to be rethought, since neo-liberal policy prescriptions had not only failed, they had intensified dissatisfaction and hostility particularly in the countries of the Third World.

This realisation led to a radical shift in the rhetoric of globalisation: the replacement of the language of the market by that of governance, accountability, transparency, and democracy. And the World Bank, under the influence of the economist Joseph Stiglitz, known for his critique of the unfettered market, moved from a narrow economistic focus on development to what came to be known as the Comprehensive Development Framework. Even as policies of structural adjustment were replaced by notions of partnership between the Bank and borrowing governments, the language of the Bank shifted from macroeconomic theory that focused on economic growth to the recognition of the centrality of governance, albeit a notion of governance that was stripped of politics (Jayal: 1997). The shift was not radical inasmuch as the dominant themes of neo-liberalism continued to dominate the political imagination of most, if not all, of the international financial institutions. But now international financial institutions were to cushion neo-liberalism in a vocabulary that spoke of the regulation and the moderation of the processes of globalisation. In effect, these institutions opted for strategies of conflict management.

Perhaps the Bank had no choice. For global civil society actors in various demonstrations insisted that

> The idea that globalisation had rationalised capitalism came to be questioned. If markets were to endure they had to be controlled or, in the new parlance of international financial institutions, 'governed'

'Fifty Years is Enough', a slogan that overshadowed the golden jubilee of the Bank. Even as James Wolfensohn was appointed President in June 1995, he was faced with the need to restructure the policy of the World Bank in the face of sustained criticism by global civil society. In an attempt to legitimise the Bank, the President engaged global NGOs in dialogue and entered into collaborative ventures to reshape the policy prescriptions of the world body. The result was the adoption of a new language of sustainable development, preservation of natural resources, equitable development, and democratic development.

It is of some significance that some global civil society actors, who had earlier emerged on the political scene in and through the politics of protest, now became partners in decision-making activities. NGOs now attend the annual meetings of the World Bank and the IMF as special guests. In 1982 the World Bank had created a discussion forum in the shape of an NGO-World Bank Committee, which ensured the active involvement of the non-governmental sector in implementing projects. Now NGOs came to be involved in policy formulation. In 1996 the WTO General Council adopted guidelines that provided for increased contacts between the Secretariat and the NGOs. This of course raises an important methodological question: can we continue to call agencies that become a part of global decision-making structures 'civil society organisations' that supposedly challenge the workings of the global order? But more of that later.

In sum, in marked contrast to the earlier two decades that focused on the opening up of national borders to the free flow of global capital and the doctrines of free trade, the post-Washington consensus concentrates on the governance of these activities. For decision-makers recognised that the deep tensions that had been engendered by the processes of globalisation had to be managed if they were not to spiral out of control. To put it bluntly, international trade and financial institutions realised that the processes of globalisation could not be legitimised if they were left to private agencies such as corporate houses or to some 'invisible hand' of the market.

The post-Washington consensus was therefore to focus on three issues. First, globalisation was too important to be left to the unrestricted corporate world and should be mediated through 'governance' that ensured transparency, account-ability, capacity building, and safety networks. Second, the state needed to be replaced not so much by the market as by civil society organ-isations that represented the aspira-tions of the people and that strengthened democracy. This of course meant that the fields of the market and of non-market trans-actions were, in policy prescriptions, separated. Third, the new consensus opined that only a strong civil society under the guidance of NGOs can further democracy. Note, however, that this avatar of civil society is not marked by democratic contestation but by the building of 'social capital' and 'trust' among the inhabitants (Harriss: 2001). In effect, the earlier move away from the state to the market has now been replaced by a move away from the state to civil society based on networks of trust.

However, despite some changes in rhetoric, the post-Washington consensus continues to retain significant elements of the earlier neo-liberal consensus. For neither was the idea that a free market encourages democracy put aside, nor was the role of the state in institutionalising and realising democracy reconsidered. In the current dispensation, both a minimal state and a free market continue to provide the conditions of a strong and democratic civil society. More importantly, the international policy community now concentrates on the management of discontent, which has erupted in reaction to the liberalisation and the deregulation process that lies at the heart of globalisation (Higgot 2000: 138)

The post-Washington consensus, in other words, views protest and struggle, which happen to be an integral part of civil society, as problems that have to be resolved through managerial techniques. It still does not recognise that a democratic civil society is about struggling for a better world, that it is about politics and not only governance, that it is about visions and aspirations and not only about neutralisation of tensions. Nor does the present consensus address issues such as unequal power relations either in the world or within states. And

> The post-Washington consensus views protest and struggle, which happen to be an integral part of civil society, as problems that have to be resolved through managerial techniques

civil society continues to be identified, as in the earlier version, with NGOs. To put it differently, if earlier versions of neo-liberalism cleared the space for global civil society actors, the present consensus legitimises their activities. Con-versely, the activities of most if not all NGOs legitimise the post-Washington consensus, for instance by linking civil society to an apolitical notion of governance. All this, as argued below, has depoli-ticised the very concept of civil society. This of course requires some elaboration of what civil society is about.

What Does Civil Society Mean?

Now civil society has been subjected to considerable over-theorisation in the post-1989 era. The concept, never too clear at the best of times, has turned into the proverbial will-o'-the-wisp that eludes understanding. It has come to mean many things to many people: as the space of solidarity, as a project of projects, as the area of associational life, as a site of contestation, and as a third sector. This may not necessarily be a problem. For, as the editors of *Global Civil Society 2001* argue, multiple meanings of civil society can provide a space for dialogue (Anheier, Glasius, and Kaldor 2001: 12). On the other hand, when people come to this overlapping space armed with their own meanings of what civil society is about, we may find that such a dialogue becomes impossible. For any dialogue needs at the least a common referral as a starting point for an exchange of ideas. And such a referral can best be provided by classical political theory.

If we were to reach back into the annals of political theory to investigate the idea of civil society, it would look something like this. The concept of civil society signifies both a space and a set of values. As a space it is metaphorically located somewhere between the state, the market, and the family. Here people come together in projects of all kinds to make their collective histories. Histories are in turn made through the politics of affirmation as well as conflict-ridden encounters, the politics of solidarity as well as that of struggle. Civil society possesses no one characteristic, no one core, no one essential nature. Civil society is what its inhabitants make of it. It is a site where projects overlap, where they reinforce each other, and where they challenge each other. This is possible, for civil society, unlike pre-modern communities, allows its inhabitants to make their own lives and their own destinies perhaps independently, perhaps in concert with others, in some degree of freedom. For the values of civil society are those of freedom, accessibility, and publicness. On this ground alone no one is in theory barred from civil society, everyone is allowed entry into the sphere, and everyone—again in theory—is free to link with others to make their own histories even though these histories are not made, as Marx told us long ago, in conditions of their own choice. Thus is associational life born and thus is an activity called politics born.

For arguably, it is only when people in and through social associations translate their everyday experiences into expressed vocabularies, and it is only when people interpret the experiential through the prism provided by the expressive, that we see the birth of politics. Politics in the first sense is about translating the experiential into the expressive. As individuals bring their own world-views into social associations, they transcend individual beliefs into socially responsive and responsible political projects through dialogue as well as through contention. Conversely, politics is about interpreting the experiential in terms provided by the expressive. Consider, for instance, the women's movement. The movement was to gain shape and clarity only when some women—and some men— were to express their discontent with patriarchal structures of oppression in terms of feminism. In turn, feminist insights gave other women the tools with which they could interpret the injustice that was inflicted on them by patriarchy.

Politics is, in short, a two-way activity. It moves from what is experienced to the interpretation of these experiences in terms of specifically political categories such as feminism. In turn, political formulations allow other people to make sense of their experiences. What is important is that the activity is empowering inasmuch as, when ordinary men and women engage in political activity, they acquire agency, they recover selfhood, and they earn

> When ordinary men and women engage in political activity, they acquire agency, they recover selfhood, and they earn self-confidence. This is politics in the best Aristotelian tradition: politics as self-realisation

self-confidence. This is politics in the best Aristotelian tradition: politics as self-realisation.

Therefore, for most theorists of civil society, social associations are vital to collective life simply because they allow people to realise their selfhood through collective action. But note that social associations are significant only because membership in these groupings is voluntary as well as revocable. It is the individual who is the primary actor in civil society; social associations merely enable him or her to realise their own potential and their own projects. Social associations, in other words, are nothing but aggregates of individuals, which in turn reflect the wishes and the desires of their members.

It is this interpretation of civil society that finds it difficult to accommodate NGOs, for two reasons. First, though it is possible that individuals who come together in associations transform their association into an NGO, a number of important and influential NGOs are not created through this process. Global NGOs come in from the outside armed very often with their own ideas of what is wrong and what should be done to remedy the situation. At precisely this point the issue of representativeness arises to bedevil thinking on civil society. Second, the arrival of global NGOs onto the scene may carry important and not so positive implications for notions of political agency. For if they have their own ideas of what should be done and how should it be done, ordinary human beings who have experienced, say, injustice in their daily lives are denied the opportunity to frame their responses in their own terms. NGOs more often than not have their own programmes, they more often than not speak a highly specialised language that may well be incomprehensible for the inhabitants of the regions in which they operate, and they may well have their own ideas of what is politically permissible and what is not.

Ordinary individuals, it is evident, possess little opportunity to influence agendas that are formulated in far-off places. Associational activity at the global level tends therefore to acquire a life of its own, a life that is quite distinct from the everyday lives of the people who do not speak but who are spoken for.

Bluntly put, people are disempowered rather than empowered when highly specialised, professional, and more often than not bureaucratised civil society actors tell them what is wrong with their daily existence and how they should go about resolving the problems of their collective lives. In the process civil society may undergo both depoliticisation and disempowerment.

Admittedly, some global civil society actors have initiated novel ways of bringing the problems of everyday existence of poor and impoverished people of the Third World to international platforms and propelling them into the glare of the media spotlight. But can all this substitute for the activity we call politics? Let me put this differently: when individuals who are otherwise far too preoccupied in eking out a bare and minimum subsistence in adverse conditions come together and think through how to resolve their situation, they are empowered because they are politicised. And to be politicised is to acquire consciousness that collective endeavours offer possibilities of self-realisation. To be politicised is to be made aware that certain rights accrue to every human being by virtue of being human. It means that people who have been constituted as subjects and not as citizens by the policies of the state can rise to demand justice, equality, and freedom; to demand that the state delivers what it has promised in theory. Political activity simply makes for aware and self-confident human beings because these human beings acquire agency in and through politics. And thereby ordinary men and women make the transition from subject to citizen.

It is precisely this notion of politics that is devalued when global civil actors commandeer political initiatives and once again constitute human beings as subjects of political ideas arrived at elsewhere, or, worse, when they constitute individuals as consumers of agendas finalised elsewhere. For we must ask this uncomfortable question of even the most well-meaning of NGOs: *who* was consulted in the forging of agendas? *When*? And *how* where the local people consulted: through what procedures and through what modalities? Were they consulted at all? Do, in short, global civil society actors actually represent people, particularly of the Third World? Or are they self-styled spokespersons of people who do not have even a remote chance of influencing these agendas?

> We must ask this uncomfortable question of even the most well-meaning of NGOs: who was consulted in the forging of agendas?

Do these more often than not well-funded and often well-organised civil society actors actually speak from below? Or do they claim to do so in order to gain legitimacy?

Certainly cyber-savvy global activists are influential because they know the language that will win attention and perhaps applause. But it is precisely this that causes unease, for whatever happens to people who do not know any language that may have resonance in the world of international politics? What happens when ordinary human beings do not have access to computers through which civil society actors wage their battles? What happens when activists who feel passionately about certain crucial issues are not in a position to participate in acts of resistance at the annual meetings of the international financial institutions? And now consider the somewhat formidable range of issues that have been taken up by global NGOs. Today they dictate what kind of development should be given to Third World people, what kind of education they should receive, what kind of democracy should be institutionalised, what rights they should demand and possess, and what they should do to be empowered.

We have cause to worry. For what we see is the collapse of the idea that ordinary men and women are capable of appropriating the political initiative. What we see is the appropriation of political programmes in favour of the agenda of the global civil society actor. Frankly, it is unclear whether international NGOs strengthen or weaken the role of the community. First, NGO activism, which straddles national boundaries to create global coalitions, is no substitute for self-determining and empowering political action born out of specific experiences. Second, whereas the Third World State has proved notoriously non-responsive to the demands of civil society, it is also a fact that, at moments of crisis, this very civil society has mobilised to hold the state accountable. In December 2001, for instance, the streets of Buenos Aires were filled with agitating and agitated Argentinians who demanded the resignation of President Fernando de la Rua. Even as the country descended into financial chaos and anarchy, even as people banged pots and pans on their balconies, even as the streets of the city overflowed with crowds, and even as deadly riots took the lives of 30 people, the President had to resign. At some point he was held accountable.

To whom, we may ask, are the international NGOs accountable? Witness, for instance, the response of Lori Wallach, whose organisation Public Citizen orchestrated the battle for Seattle. In an interview published in *Foreign Policy*, she was asked the following question: 'You're referring to the idea of democratic deficits in multilateral organizations . . . Some people argue that nongovernmental organizations (NGOs) like yours also have a democratic deficit—that you also lack democracy, transparency, and accountability. Who elected you to represent the people at Seattle, and why are you more influential than the elected officials . . .?' The answer Ms Wallach gave was the following: 'Who elected Mr Moore? Who elected Charles Barshefsky? Who elected any of them?' (*Foreign Policy* 2000: 36). This, to put it mildly, is no answer simply because it evades the issue. In another question she was asked who Public Citizen is responsible to. 'Our members', she replied. 'How do they express their oversight?' 'Through their cheque-books', she replied, 'they just stop paying their membership dues' (2000: 39). Note that no longer are people expected to realise their selfhood in and through associational life, their participation is confined to the payment or withdrawal of membership dues.

We have cause for unease. For much of the leadership of global civil society organisations appears to be self-appointed and non-accountable to their members, many of whom are passive and confine their activism to signatures to petitions circulated via e-mail. Also note that, whereas we see huge crowds during demonstrations against the WTO or in alternative forums such as the World Social Forum, between such episodes activity is carried on by a core group of NGOs. It is possible that participants in demonstrations are handed a political platform and an agenda that has been finalised elsewhere. This is hardly either democratic or even political, it may even reek of bureaucratic management of participatory events. It may even render people, as suggested above, consumers of choices made elsewhere.

> No longer are people expected to realise their selfhood in and through associational life. Their participation is confined to the payment or withdrawal of membership dues

Moreover, as has been widely observed, international NGOs resist attempts to make their own functioning transparent even as they demand transparency and accountability from international financial organisations. Observers have commented that, since most global NGOs do not issue financial or activity reports or any declaration of objectives, it is difficult to gauge their nature (Scholte 2000: 119). Even if they do issue such statements, does this make their activities more transparent? And remember that it is precisely these organisations, whose own processes of decision-making are closed to public scrutiny, who happen to be in control of people's lives and destinies.

We also need to wonder how democratic the organisations of global civil society are given the great inequalities of resources between the North and the South. It is more than possible that Third World organisations get sidelined when it comes to the making of global agendas. For instance, Hart-Landsberg reports that influential groups such as Public Citizen and leaders of labour organisations in the US focused on keeping China out of the WTO at Seattle, citing exploitative working conditions and the unfair trade practices of the Chinese government. However, no independent movement of Chinese workers has called for international support for a campaign to keep China out of the world body. 'In fact, even organizations operating in Hong Kong that seek to promote independent labour organizing in China have refrained from supporting such a campaign' (Hart-Landsberg 2000:106).

To cite another example, environmental NGOs have persistently campaigned for lower emission levels in the atmosphere through control of polluting industries and vehicular traffic. In Delhi, at the beginning of the new millennium, 'polluting industries' were closed down and vehicles that did not meet the standard laid down were abandoned by a decision of the Supreme Court, which was under pressure from the environmental lobby. However, in the process people were condemned to homelessness, massive hardship, and unemployment (Delhi University 2001). The gap between the demands of environment-conscious NGOs and the need of the poorer sections of society was just too starkly visible. We discover dissonance in the way Third World activists envisage crucial matters and the way in which global civil society actors largely based in the West view them.

Certainly we need to acknowledge the outstanding services rendered by some global civil society organisations. We should be grateful that some of these groups have brought issues of crucial importance to the top of political agendas. Nevertheless, the domination of global civil society by organised and well-funded NGOs hailing from the West poses some very vexing questions for issues of political representation, political agency, and politics in general. They may even be a part of the project that seeks to disable activism in civil society and depoliticise it. Is it possible that NGOs perhaps unwittingly form an integral part of the same plan that characterises the state and the market? Is it possible that the same logic of power underpins the activities of international civil society actors?

Above: Dependence on US food aid in Mogadishu, Somalia.
© Crispin Hughes/Panos Pictures.

Global Civil Society Actors and International Politics and Economics

My second set of questions has to do with whether global civil society actors can counteract deep-rooted structures of global capitalism and the state-centric global order, or provide an alternative to the system. There is a much wider methodological issue that confronts us here: what is the relationship between civil society, whether national or global, and the other two domains of collective existence, namely, the state and the market. For, as suggested above, contemporary political theory tends to assume that different sectors of collective life can counter each other and perhaps even provide an alternative to each other because each of them has a specific *raison d'être*.

Let me begin this part of the argument by suggesting that civil society is not only constituted by the state and the market but also permeated by the same logic that underpins these two spheres. Recall, for a start, that civil society as a peculiarly modern phenomenon *emerges through the same historical processes that generate both the modern impersonal state and the modern market system.* These processes have to do with the separation of the economic and the political, the appropriation of the economy by a private class of proprietors, and the concomitant rise of the institution of private property. They have to do with the emergence of the notion of the autonomous individual and self-directed individualism. They have, further, to do with the dissolution of community as 'face to face' interaction and with the carving out of a space where individuals meet, in the words of Marx, as 'bearers of commodities'. Classical theory called this space 'civil society' which, peopled by legally autonomous individuals who may well be strangers to each other, was marked by impersonal and contractual relations. And all this carried its own problems, as the theorists of early modernity were to tell us in some detail.

For instance, Hegel, arguably *the* most distinguished proponent of civil society, in 1821 was to hail the propensity of modern civil society to enhance freedom in contrast to the 'unfreedom' of pre-modern societies (Hegel 1942) But at the same time he was profoundly ambivalent about the democratic potential of the sphere or of its capacity to institute ethicality in the Greek sense, or what he called

Sittlichkeit. For if the material context for the realisation of the self and for the recognition of rights is bourgeois or *bürgerliche* society, this, as he was quick to realise, carried its own momentum. Because even as modern life witnesses a dramatic expansion of the sphere of social interaction in civil society, this interaction is permeated deeply by the ethos of the capitalist market, that of self-serving and instrumental action. And this can pose a problem for the very reproduction of the sphere; it may well disintegrate under the influence of self-centred reasoning, which is the hallmark of the capitalist market system. In sum, Hegel was to teach us an important lesson: that civil society is shot through with the same power equations as the market, for it is constituted by the market system.

> Civil society as a peculiarly modern phenomenon emerges through the same historical processes that generate both the modern impersonal state and the modern market system

More significantly, there is another problem that confronts classical political theory: even as the market constitutes transactions in civil society, the market order presupposes a stable and sturdy civil society in order to function efficiently. Market relations simply need to be embedded in non-market relations in order to function with some measure of success. But not any kind of non-market relations, let me hasten to add, will do. Market transactions need disciplined, predictable, and socialised behaviour as a prerequisite for their successful operation. If Adam Smith put forth his theory of 'moral sentiments' in 1759 (Smith 1976) to accomplish this, a contemporary theorist such as Francis Fukuyama (1975) argues that capitalist accumulation needs the presence of trust. And James Coleman and Robert Putnam suggest that 'softer' social norms that guarantee expectation, such as social capital, should buttress economic transactions, *if* we want the domain of these transactions to expand (Coleman 1988: S95–S120; Putnam 1993; 1995). Civil society and the market, we realise, are dependent on each other; they need not provide an alternative to each other at all.

Therefore, whereas it is perfectly true that global civil society has critiqued the workings of the international economic order, is a critique of corporate managed globalisation, we are compelled to ask, the same as a critique of capital in search of global markets? The problem is that global civil society tends to be broad-based, comprising as it does many groups with divergent purposes and aims. Kaldor, for instance, accepts that only a few of the protestors at Seattle were actually against globalisation; the others wanted to reform international trade and financial institutions as well as make them accountable (Kaldor 2000: 112). And the same theme was echoed at the World Social Forum that met in Porto Alegre in Brazil in February 2002. The meeting, which was attended by 50,000 delegates and which was meant to be a parallel to the meeting of the World Economic Forum in New York, put forth the idea of an alternative world: 'Another world is possible', went the slogan. However, according to a newspaper report, 'delegates bristle at the WSF being called the "anti-globalisation" meet. They argue that they are not meeting here to register protests but to work out concrete proposals that will be superior to what will be floated at the New York meeting of the WEF' (*The Hindu*, 3 February 2002: 10).

Actually, the movement against globalisation can be split into (a) radical individuals and groups who oppose capitalism but are rather clueless as well as powerless when it comes to alternatives and (b) established NGOs that work at the margins to 'reform' the system. The latter would rather that the present system is reformed and made more accountable and humane. They consequently focus on institutional reform rather than on an alternative to the system. And the ones that are anti-capitalist globalisation and dream of a better international order are relegated to the fringes of global civil society, dominated as it is by professional bodies who now are partners in world decision-making forums.

Global civil society, it is evident, by and large prefers to work within the parameters of a system that has been found wanting by many critics both from the Third World and from the advanced capitalist world. Given the plural and somewhat contradictory nature of the protest movements, they can hardly provide us with an alternative system. In tandem with the post-Washington Consensus, some global civil society actors would humanise the capitalist system rather than think of another system that may be able to deliver justice and equity. Therefore, they may reform the neo-liberal platform but they are unable to map a new course. And the anti-capitalist globalisation groups are more romantic than pragmatic when it comes to alternatives. We seem to live in a world of disenchantment where activists either refuse to dream dreams of an alternative world system or are doubtful about what they want in its stead. For, as Scholte put it in the context of Seattle, 'halting a new round of trade liberalisation is not the same as building a better world order' (2000: 116). In the meantime liberalisation, privatisation, and exploitation of Third World resources continue to coexist with the rhetoric of human rights, environment, democracy, and what the World Bank now calls the Comprehensive Development Framework.

> Global civil society by and large prefers to work within the parameters of a system that has been found wanting by many critics both from the Third World and from the advanced capitalist world

When we come to the state-centric international order, we find that the relationship between states and global civil society is profoundly ambivalent. It is true that global civil society actors have through the techniques of 'naming and shaming' embarrassed individual states and even succeeded in overthrowing individual governments. But it is equally true that states are not at all ceding their power over matters that they consider crucial. Consider the response of the US to the mobilisation of international public opinion in the wake of the 11 September 2001 attacks on New York and Washington. Political activists were connecting via the Internet, peace marches dotted the landscape from Delhi to Washington to Berlin, and writers were authoring impassioned pieces on why the Bush government should not punish the innocent people of Afghanistan by bombarding the country. And yet the American government went ahead and declared war on Afghanistan, adding to the already considerable woes of the people of that country. The US, which incidentally claims to speak for the 'free world', refused to heed the voice of global civil society and proceeded to violate the freedom of the people of Afghanistan. The sovereignty of the US remained intact despite considerable criticism by civil society actors.

On the other hand, global civil society actors need states and their institutions to substantiate and codify their demands in law. Transnational organisations may critique the practices of states in, say, the field of

human rights, but they also require states to create political and legal frameworks that facilitate setting up of the rule of law, civil and political rights, or environmental protection. Women's groups can hardly demand, say, gender justice without the corresponding demand for state protection and the demand that states set up appropriate institutions for protection of women's rights. Alternatively, civil society groups fighting, say, violations of civil liberties will need the state to punish offenders. They simply will need human rights commissions, sympathetic judges, and a sensitive police to realise their objectives. I could cite a number of other such examples; the point, however, I hope is clear. Efforts in civil society will come to naught unless states codify these efforts in the form of law or regulations. In effect, what I am trying to suggest is that civil society actors will draw upon states both to redress violation of human rights and to reform civil society itself through enacting laws restricting sexual harassment in the workplace, for example. This again means—and this is a point that is not generally grasped by many current advocates of civil society—that states constitute the limits of civil society, as well as enabling political initiatives in global civil society. In effect, the very states that global civil society supposedly opposes *enable* the latter in the sense that only they can provide the conditions within which the civil society agenda is realised. In effect, vibrant civil societies require strong and stable states as a precondition to their very existence. After all, we hardly expect to find a civil society in countries like Afghanistan and Somalia, where the state itself leads a precarious existence as a result of the civil wars that have wrecked the countries and their polities. The shade of Hegel, who suggested that the state is a precondition for the existence of civil society, looms especially large here.

Finally, we should recall that not only Third World governments but also informed critics belonging to that part of the world argue that the values of global civil society reflect those held by a narrow group of influential states in the international order. Any attempt to institutionalise these values in states of the Third World, is seen as an imposition. This is particularly true of human rights, which are considered to be embedded in a set of norms and historical processes specific to

Western Europe and the US and therefore inappropriate for other societies. Incensed critics regard the imposition of human rights upon societies that may possess other notions of how relationships between individuals and governments should be arranged as an extension of imperialism. Whether these critiques are valid or invalid is not the issue here; the point is that global civil society actors, particularly human rights organisations, are seen as embedded within an ideology that is highly Euro-centric: liberal democracy. For even though some of these organisations have moved in the recent past to embrace ideas of social and economic rights, which for long have been seen as the preconditions of meaningful civil and political rights, it is the latter, not the former, that inform the consensus on human rights.

> Notions of governance remain devoid of politics as self-realisation even as global civil society fails to have an impact on the unequal distribution of global wealth

This really means that global civil society actors reflect the consensus that liberal democracy is the only form of democracy that remains of value in the aftermath of the fall of communism in 1989. Therefore, even as we accept that global civil society actors can launch, and have launched, a critique of the practices of some states, we must ponder upon whether, in doing so, they do not codify values that belong to another set of states. Can global civil society transcend the existing tension between the Western world and the Third World that permeates the international legal, political, and economic order? Or will it merely work within the parameters of a system that has already been laid down by a few powerful states? Can global civil society ever be truly global? Or is it fated, as national civil societies are, to function within the framework laid down by hegemonic states?

Conclusion

In sum, global civil society has managed to give a new vocabulary to the state-centric and market-oriented international order. The achievement is not meaningless, for at least international financial and trade institutions have become more responsive to public opinion, they have reformed earlier strategies of corporate managed globalisation, they have added issues of social concern to their agendas, and they have called for greater governance of globalisation. But notions of governance remain devoid of politics as self-realisation even as global civil society fails to have an impact on the unequal distribution of global wealth. In the meantime, the WTO concentrates on the widest and fastest possible liberalisation of the flow of goods across borders.

Therefore, the notion that global civil society can institutionalise normative structures that run counter to the principles of powerful states or equally powerful corporations, which govern international transactions, should be treated with a fair amount of caution. Of course, actors in global civil society have made a difference, as actors in national civil society make a difference. But they function as most human actors do, within the realm of the possible, not within the realm of the impossible. Ultimately, global civil society actors work within inherited structures of power that they may modify or alter but seldom transform. But this we can understand only if we locate global civil society in its constitutive context: a state-centric system of international relations that is dominated by a narrow section of humanity and within the structures of international capital that may permit dissent but do not permit any transformation of their own agendas.

References

Anheier, Helmut, Glasius, Marlies, and Kaldor, Mary (2001). *Global Civil Society 2001*. Oxford: Oxford University Press.

Booth, Kenneth (1991). 'Security in Anarchy: Utopian Realism in Theory and Practice'. *International Affairs*, 67: 527–45.

Chandhoke, Neera (1997). 'Politics of Peoples Rights' (Report of a Research Project funded by the Indian Council of Social Science Research, unpublished).

— (2001). 'The "Civil" and the "Political" in Civil Society'. *Democratization*, 8/2: 1–24.

Cohen, Jean and Arato, Andrew (1992). *Political Theory and Civil Society*. Cambridge, MA: MIT Press.

Coleman, J. S. (1988). 'Social Capital in the Creation of Human Capital'. *American Journal of Sociology* (Supplement), 94: S95–S120.

Delhi University (2001). 'Narratives of Displacement' (unpublished report). Department of Political Science. April.

Falk, Richard A., Johansen, Robert C., and Kim, Samuel S. (1993). 'Global Constitutionalism and World Order', in Richard A. Falk, Robert C. Johansen, and Samuel S. Kim (eds), *The Constitutional Foundations of World Peace*. Albany: SUNY Press.

Foreign Policy (2000). ' Lori's War'. Spring: 29–55.

Fukuyama, Francis (1995). *Trust: The Social Virtues and the Creation of Prosperity.* New York. The Free Press.

Glasius, Marlies (1999). *Foreign Policy on Human Rights: Its Influence on Indonesia under Soeharto.* Antwerp: Intersentia.

Harriss, John (2001). *Depoliticizing Development. The World Bank and Social Capital.* Delhi: LeftWord.

Hart- Landsberg, Martin (2000). 'After Seattle: Strategic Thinking About Movement Building'. *Monthly Review,* 52/3: 102–24.

Hegel, Georg W. F. (1942). *The Philosophy of Right* (trans. T.M. Knox). Oxford: Oxford University Press.

Higgot, Richard (2000). 'Contested Globalisation: The Changing Context and Normative Challenges'. *Review of International Studies,* 26: 131–53.

Honneth, Axel (1993). 'Conceptions of "Civil Society"'. *Radical Philosophy,* 64/Summer: 19–22.

Isaac, Jeffrey (1993). 'Civil Society and the Spirit of Revolt'. *Dissent,* Summer: 356–61.

Jayal, Niraja G. (1997). 'The Governance Agenda: Making Democratic Development Dispensable'. *Economic and Political Weekly,* 22 February: 407–12.

Kaldor, Mary (2000). 'Civilising Globalization: The Implications of the Battle of Seattle'. *Millennium: A Journal of International Studies,* 29/4: 105–14.

Korey, William (1998). *NGOs and the Universal Declaration of Human Rights.* New York: St Martin's Press.

Krugman, Paul (1995). 'Dutch Tulips and Emerging Markets'. *Foreign Affairs,* 74/4: 28–44.

Kuhn, Thomas (1962). *The Structure of Scientific Revolutions.* Chicago: University of Chicago Press.

Lipschutz, Ronnie (1992). 'Reconstructing World Politics: The Emergence of Global Civil Society'. *Millennium. A Journal of International Studies,* 21: 389–420.

Pasha, Mustapha Kamal and Blaney, David L. (1998). 'Elusive Paradise: The Promise and Peril of Global Civil Society'. *Alternatives,* 23: 417–50.

Putnam, Robert D. (1993). *Making Democracy Work: Civic Traditions in Modern Italy.* Princeton, NJ: Princeton University Press.

— (1995). 'Bowling Alone: America's Declining Social Capital'. *Journal of Democracy,* 6/1: 65–78.

Rhodes, Martin and Higgot, Richard (2000). 'Asian Crisis and the Myth of Capitalist Convergence'. *Pacific Review,* 13/1: 1–19.

Scholte, Jan Aarte (2000). 'Cautionary Reflections on Seattle'. *Millennium: A Journal of International Studies,* 29/1: 115–21.

Smith, Adam (1976). *The Theory of Moral Sentiments,* ed. D. D Raphael and A. L. Macfie. Oxford: Clarendon.

Taylor, Charles (1991). 'Civil Society in the Western Tradition', in E. Groffier and M. Paradis (eds), *The Notion of Tolerance and Human Rights: Essays in Honour of Raymond Klibansky.* Ottawa: University of Carleton Press.

White, Gordon (1994). 'Civil Society, Democratization and Development. (I) Clearing the Analytical Ground'. *Democratization,* 1: 375–90.

RELIGION AND GLOBAL CIVIL SOCIETY: INHERENT INCOMPATIBILITY OR SYNERGY AND INTERDEPENDENCE?

Abdullahi An-Na'im

Given the importance of religion for the vast majority of humankind, it is critical that conceptualisations of global civil society facilitate a positive engagement of religious perspectives. However, some understandings of religion are simply incompatible with the underlying rationale and purpose of global civil society. This chapter explores ways of promoting possibilities of consistency between the two. As I see it, this outcome depends on how each side of this relationship is understood and practised in each context rather than on any preconceived notion of what these ideas mean. I therefore propose a synergistic and interdependent model of the relationship between religion and global civil society whereby each is understood in a way that supports the other. The policy question for governmental and non-governmental actors on both sides of the issue is how to promote those mutually supportive understandings of religion and conceptualisations of civil society.

I discuss this thesis and explore its policy implications in three sections. First, I attempt to clarify some contrasting views on civil society in general with a view to relating these to a more inclusive range of definitions of global civil society. I also examine some of the difficulties of the *process* of such broader conceptualisations of global civil society. The second section analyses Gandhian and fundamentalist perspectives in order to highlight possibilities and challenges of the proposed approach. In the third section I discuss 'liberal Islam' and 'liberation theology' for a better understanding of the contextual dynamics of local and global civil society highlighted in the first two sections. In conclusion, I attempt to bring all the sections together and draw some policy implications.

A More Inclusive and Dynamic Understanding of Civil Society

I take as my point of departure the three propositions offered by Helmut Anheier, Marlies Glasius, and Mary Kaldor in *Global Civil Society 2001*. First, 'the spread of the term "global civil society" reflects an underlying social reality', an entity of transnational, national and local non-governmental actors who are engaged in negotiations and discussion about civil matters with governmental, intergovernmental, and other transnational actors at various levels and the business sphere. This network has become 'thicker', stronger, more durable, and more effective over the past decade (Anheier, Glasius, and Kaldor 2001: 4).

Second, global civil society 'both feeds on and reacts to globalisation', wherein the term 'globalisation' is used in three senses, namely, 'the spread of global capitalism', 'growing interconnectedness in political, social, and cultural spheres as well as the economy', and 'a growing global consciousness'. The impact of globalisation on global civil society can be measured according to various objective indices, such as the presence of transnational corporations, Internet usage, and action to promote respect for international human rights. The authors also assert, 'global civil society is best categorised not in terms of types of actors but in terms of positions in relation to globalisation' (Anheier, Glasius, and Kaldor 2001: 7).

The third proposition is that 'global civil society is both a fuzzy and a contested concept', which the authors attribute to its 'newness'. The other factor contributing to the fuzziness of the concept is that different groups within global civil society have different stakes in defining global civil society. For example, from an activist perspective civil society is more a matter of 'increasing the responsiveness of political institutions' than of 'minimising the role of the state' (Anheier, Glasius, and Kaldor 2001: 11).

I do not disagree with these reflections as such, but feel that they do not take us far in conceptualising global civil society. I also find it useful to take these remarks as my point of departure because they highlight some of the tensions I will be discussing in this chapter. My analysis of the relationship between religion and global civil society is premised on clarification of three relationships, namely, that between the *composition* and *function* of global civil society, between *space* and *place*, and between its *nature* and *operation*. Clarification of the relationship between the composition and the function of global civil society, what it is composed of and what it is supposed to do, should in turn lead to asking whether the present composition of global civil society is conducive to realising its objectives. Moreover, one should also take into account the relationship between space and place in order to appreciate how global civil society may operate in pursuit of its objectives.

Global civil society is supposed to be the space where people and transnational entities debate and negotiate the rules of their relationships, and pursue accountability for those rules, in furtherance of their respective concerns. But the physical location of actors conditions their perceptions of, and participation in, that process. That is what I mean by the relationship between space and place. Since people do not interact with transnational entities on an abstract conceptual plane, the question is where and how they actually participate in global civil society activities in the physical world. The nature and dynamics of these two relationships, in turn, affect the way global civil society operates in practice at any moment.

Understanding the nature and dynamics of these three relationships can be helpful in distinguishing between essential features of global civil society and some of its activities or manifestations. For example, the fact that some non-governmental organisations (NGOs) are now engaged in the provision of services that were traditionally supposed to be provided by the

> For global civil society to perform its role ... it has to have a minimum normative content ... the critical question is: by whom and how is that normative content to be determined?

state is a particular outcome of that process in specific place(s) rather than an essential feature of global civil society itself everywhere. To attribute this phenomenon to global civil society reflects a certain understanding of its composition and function as well as being an example of how global civil society operates in practice. But the need for the provision of medical and educational services and development assistance by local and international NGOs reflects a change in the role of the state under currently dominant free-marked ideology and economic power relations. Approaching issues from another standpoint, other actors will have a different understanding of the nature, role, and operation of global civil society. Conceptualisations of global civil society should therefore account for the impact of the physical location of its various constituencies on their respective objectives and possibilities of participation in the space it provides for collective action.

For global civil society to perform its role in this equation, it has to have a minimum normative content beyond its description as simply the non-governmental, non-profit 'third sector'. Otherwise, how would it set its own agenda and negotiating position in relation to other transnational entities? Since every analysis of global civil society must necessarily emanate from some implicit or presumed normative content, it is better to state that openly for debate instead of leaving it to the ideological or cultural bias of the analysis or actor. From my perspective, the critical question here is: by whom and how is that normative content to be determined? The true 'globalness' of global civil society requires a more inclusive sense of participants and process for this purpose. As I have argued in relation to the universality of human rights (An-Na'im 1992), one can of course begin with some *hypothesis* about the normative content of global civil society, but genuine universality has to evolve on the ground rather than being assumed or proclaimed on an abstract conceptual plane. The methodology I proposed for *constructing* the universality of human rights through an overlapping consensus among different constituencies about the normative content of global civil society, is to engage in an internal discourse within each of the constituencies and in a dialogue between them about elements of that content. The term 'overlapping' here indicates that consensus does not initially cover the whole field, but can grow to cover more common ground as participants engage in the process over time.

Accordingly, I suggest that global civil society can be seen as consisting of various actors with different objectives negotiating to broaden and deepen their overlapping consensus about the normative framework of their global association. This idea of overlapping consensus presupposes ideological and other differences, but also requires agreement on a core set of values for the negotiation process to achieve meaningful results. On the one hand, if there is no difference among various constituencies, there would be no need for an overlapping consensus. But that process is unworkable without agreement at least on the conditions necessary for the process of negotiation to continue, which include mutual respect and appreciation of cultural and contextual difference and the possibility of peaceful coexistence. Most importantly, all constituencies of global civil society must appreciate the need to construct an overlapping consensus over the normative content of their solidarity and cooperation rather than seeking to impose their own view of it on others. The considerations set out below appear to be relevant to this dynamic view of the process.

First, any definition needs to account for those aspects of civil life which are integral to the self-understanding and identity of members of a society. Hence, such a definition should provide for a space for such aspects of civil life that may not necessarily translate into objective indices that measure kinds of *linear* 'progress' that is suggested by the above-cited remarks of Anheier, Glasius, and Kaldor (2001). In relation to the subject of this chapter, for millions of people around the world social, political, and cultural issues are inextricably tied to perceptions of religious identity in local context as well as to a religious rationale of social institutions and behaviour.

Second, close attention needs to be paid to the contextual dynamics of the formation of networks and alliances, to the process of formation of the

> **Global civil society can be seen as consisting of various actors with different objectives negotiating to broaden and deepen their overlapping consensus over the normative framework of their global association**

entities that are taken as representative of global civil society. Any definition of global civil society needs to engage with questions of the politics of solidarity and alliance-formation, and needs to include the space for that engagement in contributing to conceptions of global civil society. Relevant issues include an appreciation of the role of religion in motivating people to forge alliances as well as their choice of allies and objectives. The purpose of such appreciation is to facilitate cooperation across religious and ideological divides around issues of shared concern rather than to simply acknowledge the difficulty of doing so on the basis of a presumed 'non-negotiability' of religion. The underlying concern should be about empowering believers to claim global civil society as their own medium of struggle for justice and human dignity.

Third, according to Anheier, Glasius, and Kaldor (2001: 7), 'global civil society is heavily concentrated in north-western Europe'. It is in this region of the world that the largest number of parallel summits has been held and a majority of international NGOs secretariats are located. Whatever may be the reasons for this, an exclusive focus on *certain types of facts*, whether economic indices, literacy, or Internet access, as representative of global civil society would inevitably suggest that global civil society is more 'evolved' in one part of the world than another. This may obscure a crucial dimension of the process of transnational alliance formation that directly bears upon any conception of global civil society, namely, how *differentials in power relations* between various actors in global civil society affect the agenda, strategies, and outcomes of their solidarity. I am therefore calling for an understanding of global civil society in which the struggle to define the term itself reflects the struggles to achieve a global civil society.

Fourth, this unbridgeable differential in power relations between developed and developing countries is manifested in a variety of ways that inhibit sustainable consensus building around issues of religion and global civil society. For example, severe resource limitations inhibit the ability of research institutions in Third World countries to fund studies of their own local and national civil society, let alone global civil society, or to support the participation of their local researchers in large-scale projects and international conferences. Whatever funding they are able to secure from foreign, 'donor' agencies and foundations has to be limited to the priorities of those sources. Western funding sources thus strongly influence decisions about what research issues of local significance are brought into the ambit of the international research community.

Moreover, research initiatives at the local level cannot be brought to the international academic and policy communities until they are *translated* into the terms of the dominant discourse of that framework. When such research requires understanding local forms of knowledge according to their own epistemologies, the translation process risks the loss of precisely that which makes a form of understanding contextually distinct. There is also always the risk that the international communities receiving this knowledge may find it difficult to understand what is being translated. Even when such knowledge reaches international academic

> The critical question is how to mediate the tension between the presumed exclusivity of religious communities and the requirements of inclusion, civility, and freedom of choice of civil society...

and policy communities, and is enriched by reflections and discussions there, that interactive 'final product' is likely to be translated *back* into its communities of origin and their local epistemologies. Issues of religion and religious identity are of course examined in relevant international scholarship, but the question is whether they are taken seriously in all their complexity in conceptualisations of global civil society.

Thus, conceptualisations of global civil society must take into account all aspects of civil life for different societies and communities around the world and with due regard to the impact of contextual and power-relations factors on the formation and dynamics of networks and alliances. It is from this perspective that I address the critical question for our purposes here, namely, how to mediate the tension between the presumed exclusivity of religious communities and their tendency to strictly enforce narrowly defined moral codes, on the one hand, and the requirements

Above: Friday dawn prayers, Gaza. © Chris Tordai/Panos Pictures.

of inclusion, civility, and freedom of choice of civil society, on the other hand. According to the proposed model for constructing an overlapping consensus over the normative content of global civil society, the mediation of this tension can happen through an internal discourse within religious communities and simultaneous dialogue with other constituencies. The challenge for those who engage in internal discourse within their own religious communities is how to promote understandings and practice of their religion that are more inclusive, civil, and voluntary, to enhance conformity with the essential qualities of global civil society. The corresponding challenge facing other constituencies of global civil society is how to cooperate with religious communities on that joint venture with due regard to the legitimate concerns of those communities.

The question whether some concerns are legitimate or not should itself be the subject of internal dialogue within religious communities and of dialogue with other constituencies. A practical guide for addressing this question is that the concerns of religious communities should be conceived in terms that are consistent with prerequisite conditions for the process of negotiation to continue, as noted earlier. Accordingly, for example, the political, economic, or security concerns of religious communities should be pursued through peaceful means rather than terrorist attacks and intimidation. Conversely, other constituencies must take the concerns of religious constituencies seriously and strive to address them. This is one the basic points I am trying to make regarding the terrorist attacks of 11 September 2001 on the United States in my discussion of Islamic fundamentalism in the next section. But the main conclusion of this first section is that the contingent possibilities of reconciliation between religious and other constituencies of global civil society must be actively sought by all sides, instead of passively waiting for religious persons and communities to succeed or fail the test of inclusion. In my view, this outcome is critical to the success of the global civil society project, whether seen as a matter of tactical cooperation or of reluctant partnership.

Global Civil Society and Religion: Possibilities and Challenges

I believe that religion and religious identity can be included in conceptualisations of global civil society precisely because current conditions of globalisation clearly show that religion everywhere is *socially constructed*, dynamic, and implicated in socio-economic and political power relations to varying degrees in different contexts. However, I also believe that a sharp dichotomy between the religious and the secular is not necessarily the best way of conceptualising the relationship between religion and the state or politics. I will first illustrate these remarks with a review of Gandhi's views on religion that promise a positive relationship with global civil society. In the second part of this section I will consider the challenge of fundamentalism to both the normative and the process aspects of the relationship between religion and global civil society.

Gandhi and civil society

Gandhi's views can provide a resource for more inclusive politics and a strong response to negative aspects of globalisation. The questions he struggled with included the notions of Indian identity that ought to be reflected in the Indian state in the context of competing conceptions of religious identity and spirituality. He also seriously considered issues of modernisation in relation to development and social justice. While Gandhi's ideas, and the movement that embodied them, preceded the current intensification of globalisation, they are relevant because similar questions clearly continue to be debated in different contexts, such as issues of the self-definition of peoples in post-colonial societies as well as matters concerning modernisation and development.

The significance of Gandhi's ideas for our purposes here can be highlighted through a discussion of two interrelated aspects of his assessment of civil society: first, his call for the secularisation of religion as a basis for civil society; and second, his view of civil society as a framework for mediating modernisation, where notions such as 'autonomy' and 'progress' are open to critique and examination. In exploring these aspects of Gandhi's thought, one can see that he sought to radically reframe three sets of relations that are central to the

> ...the mediation of this tension can happen through an internal discourse within religious communities and simultaneous dialogue with other constituencies

discourse of civil society, namely, those between the religious and the secular, between the individual and the social, and between the private and the public spheres.

The secularisation of religion

For Gandhi, religious and secular conceptions of self and society did not have to be defined in opposition to one another. As he understood it, religion was *secularisable* through a perception of religion as *spirituality*. Gandhi's notion of the 'spiritualization of politics' was based on 'the idea that the spiritual diffuses all aspects of everyday life, including the political, and should form the basis of the way humans live' (Young 2001: 337). He viewed the spiritual as the substratum that oriented *all* aspects of an individual's life, and insisted that religious expression was inseparable from the expression of cultural, political, and social values. Gandhi viewed religion and religious identity as neither the sole province of the individual nor *merely* as a basis for political or social action. He emphasised that religion offered the individual an ethic to live by and that religion could *itself* be the mode and medium of political action and expression.

Gandhi's reading of religion was thus not restricted to a set of either practices or personal beliefs or ultimately delimited by scripture. Indeed, for Gandhi, religion was a source of multiple possibilities, both the form and the content for social, political, and cultural identity and expression. 'His approach to religion was therefore profoundly ahistorical, uninhibited, and anti-traditionalist, and liberal and he made no attempt to read the scriptures and understand the religious traditions in their own terms' (Parekh 1997: 37). This flexible and unsystematic framework allowed Gandhi to incorporate insights from diverse religious, cultural, and philosophical traditions and to define religion as an expression of social, cultural, and political values (Young 2001: 346).

One can appreciate Gandhi's belief in the possibilities religion accords for both civil *action* and civil *existence* in a manner that is fully consistent with conceptualising civil society as the condition for possible political independence and autonomy. For the vast majority of humankind, to whom religion is an important dimension of their world view and source of normative guidance, the Gandhian notion of religion offers the possibility of full membership in, and engagement with, civil society, local, national, and global.

Gandhi's critique of modernisation

The articulation of civil society in Gandhi's thought can be seen as part of a discourse about the form of 'development' a society may take. 'In his ideal society, tradition, politics, economics, social relations, and autonomy are tightly linked, but with modernization [as he saw it in relation to the India of his time], he believes that any possible harmony is elusive' (Terchek 1998: 119). By emphasising duties over rights, he sought to transform relations between the individual and the social (Young 2001: 338). He criticised modernisation for diminishing 'the sense of duties individuals once carried for one another' and he sought 'a society of mutuality among people who know and care about each other and *who recognize the many debts they owe one another'* (Terchek 1998: 110; emphasis added).

Gandhi also questioned the distinction between the public and the private spheres whereby morality is traditionally conceived as belonging in the private sphere, and economic choice and political freedom in the public sphere. For him, 'the irony of the new freedom from traditional practices promised by modernity is that people now rely on unseen and unknown actors in more and more ways' (Terchek 1998: 109). He questioned whether the notion of autonomy associated with modernisation was genuine and whether it constricted and diminished the lives of any segment of the population. The moral costs of modernisation *had to be part of the calculation* about any supposed increase in autonomy that modernisation could deliver. 'Gandhi also reminds us that people have multiple needs that are affected by the economy, not just economic ones' (Terchek 1998: 109). Developments in the public sphere, such as those pertaining to economics and technology, have a strong impact on the private lives of the members of a society.

> Gandhi emphasised that religion offered the individual an ethic to live by and that religion could itself be the mode and medium of political action and expression

In my view, these are the sorts of insights about religion that can enhance the normative underpinnings of global civil society. But such synergy between the two cannot be realised without an effective and sustainable response to the challenge of fundamentalism, as illustrated by the rise of the Bharatiya Janata Party (BJP) in Gandhi's own India four decades after his assassination by a Hindu nationalist.

Gandhi's concerns about modernisation (read globalisation) and traditional understandings of religion appear to be fully justified in the light of the rise of Hindu fundamentalism in India since the early 1990s. The link between fundamentalism and globalisation was one factor in the rise of the Hindu nationalist BJP to national power, as suggested by studies of the factors that led to the demolition of the Babri mosque at Ayodhya (Shah 1991; Freitag 1996). Claiming that this mosque had been built on the site of the destroyed Ram temple (the birthplace of God Ram), Hindu nationalists had launched a political protest movement that culminated in the destruction of the Babri mosque on 6 December 1992 (Zaman 1999: n. 7). That event continues to fuel cycles of widespread communal tension and Hindu-Muslim riots up to the time of writing (March 2002). The destruction of the mosque was supported by a distinct subset of the Indian population who identified themselves as 'Hindu'. They included 'traders, small business people, and white collar workers, and those who formed part of the age cohort whose formative years occurred in the partition era'. These were the same groups that had 'been most threatened by the new economic liberalization initiatives aimed at greater privatization and increased global competitiveness' (Freitag 1996: 226–7).

As also emphasised in relation to Islam below, religious fundamentalism is the product of particular circumstances and not inherent to religion as such. Under such conditions, whether in India, Iran, or elsewhere, religious symbols and discourse are used by disadvantaged groups to mobilise politically against perceived internal or external threats to their identity. While such apprehensions should be appreciated, the question is whether fundamentalist understandings of religion can provide an appropriate

> The ideology of fundamentalism is inconsistent with an inclusive and civil global civil society, but that does not mean that the underlying concerns of fundamentalist movements should not be taken seriously

response to such threats. For our purposes here, I believe the ideology of fundamentalism is inconsistent with an inclusive and civil global civil society, but that does not mean that the underlying concerns of fundamentalist movements should not be taken seriously. This view assumes that global civil society is the medium for generating and implementing effective and sustainable responses to national and global problems. But global civil society would of course do that in ways that safeguard its own essential nature as both 'global' and 'civil'. In my view, *all* four responses by global civil society to 11 September 2001, discussed in Chapter 1 in this volume, (peace, economic, spiritual, and legal) are interdependent, each needing the other three for its own success. For my purposes here, neither will any of the other three work without the spiritual/religious, nor will the latter work without the former.

The challenge of religious fundamentalism

The problem with religious fundamentalist movements is their tendency to be totalitarian in seeking to mobilise all the resources of a society for the realisation of their own specific vision of the public good. Each form of fundamentalism possesses its own characteristic features and particular forms of discourse in relation to its own frame of reference. But the common problematic feature they all share is their negation of people's ability to make their own moral and political choices and to live accordingly. Thus, the main problem with any form of fundamentalism is that it repudiates a people's right to self-determination at a personal or collective, social, political, and/or economic level. It is from this perspective that I see all forms of fundamentalism as constituting a challenge to civil society, local, national, and global.

While focusing here on religious fundamentalism, I should emphasise that similar difficulties for civil society at the global and national level also arise from chauvinistic secular or nationalist ideologies. Another caveat is that I discuss the challenge of fundamentalist Islam because its supranational appeal and aspirations are particularly relevant to those of global civil society, without implying that fundamentalism is peculiar to Islam (Juergensmeyer 2000). I should also note here that the following critique applies to the failure of religious fundamentalists to adhere to the normative and process requirements of global civil society, without dismissing their underlying concerns as necessarily misconceived or exaggerated. Indeed, I strongly believe that taking those concerns seriously is essential for an effective response to the challenge of fundamentalism, as a matter of principle as well as for tactical reasons. It is necessary for civil society to address such concerns not only to deny fundamentalists the use of such grievances in mobilising political support for their own political ends but also because such issues are integral to what civil society is supposed to rectify in any case.

Islamic fundamentalism can be found in different stages of Islamic history, but always as an exceptional response to a sense of severe crisis, and never as the normal state of affairs (Al-Azm 1993–1994). As such, Islamic fundamentalists are both the product and the agents of social change, who seek to influence events at home and abroad in favour of their own vision of the public good. In relation to civil society concerns, these movements are problematic on two counts: the demand to implement *Shari'a* (traditional formulations of the normative system of Islam) at home, and an understanding of *jihad* as aggressive war that is inconsistent with peaceful international relations. While the first problem apparently relates to national civil society, it is conceptually and politically connected to the second problem that is more directly relevant to global civil society. Both aspects are equally relevant here because global civil society must be concerned with issues facing local or national civil society, albeit at a global plane of concept-ualisation and action.

Since Islamic fundamentalists seek to justify their claims as the legitimate exercise of the right of Muslim peoples to self-determination, their ideology should be judged by the validity of that claim. There are two aspects to this process, namely, the possibility of the verification of the claim of legitimate representation of the totality of national populations at home, and clear understanding of the realities of

global relations under which the right to self-determination can be realised. On the first count, Islamic fundamentalists must maintain a credible commitment to democracy at home so that Muslims can continue to express their support or opposition freely and without fear of violent retaliation. These movements must also respect the equal citizenship of non-Muslim nationals of the state because that is the only possible basis of peace, political stability, and economic development at home, and of acceptance in the international community abroad. In their relations with other countries, moreover, fundamentalists must accept the principles of the rule of law in international relations because that is also essential for peace, political stability, and economic development of their own country.

In my view, Islamic fundamentalism is unacceptable as a legitimate exercise of the collective right of Muslims to self-determination because of the inherent inconsistency of its essential precepts with the conditions under which this right can be realised in the modern context. It is clear that the internal and external context of claims of Islamic self-determination today is radically different from what it used to be in the pre-colonial era because all Islamic societies are now constituted into nation states which belong to global political and economic systems. They are all members of the United Nations and subject to international law, including universal human rights standards. None of these states is religiously homogeneous, politically insulated, or economically independent from the non-Muslim world. This drastic transformation of the internal and external context of self-determination is true everywhere in the Muslim world today.

It is neither legally permissible nor practically viable for fundamentalists to force other citizens of the state to accept and implement their view of *Shari'a* as a matter of state policy. At present, the vast majority of Muslims find it difficult to openly oppose its application, especially in view of their colonial history and current siege mentality. Nevertheless, I suggest, the idea of an Islamic state to enforce *Shari'a* is conceptually untenable, has no precedent in Islamic history, and is not practically viable in the modern context. The extreme diversity of views among schools

> Islamic fundamentalism can be found in different stages of Islamic history, but always as an exceptional response to a sense of severe crisis, and never as the normal state of affairs

> At present, the vast majority of Muslims find it difficult to openly oppose the application of Shari'a, especially in view of their colonial history and current siege mentality...

of Islamic jurisprudence means that whatever view is enforced by the state will violate the religious freedom of other Muslims, as well as the human rights of women and non-Muslims. This idea was never realised in over fifteen centuries of Islamic history, and cannot operate in the economic and political conditions of the world today (An-Na'im 1999).

In relation to global civil society in particular, Islamic fundamentalism poses a serious challenge to peaceful international relations because of its ideological commitment to an expansive view of *jihad*. The commonly accepted view among the majority of Muslims is that *Shari'a* both restricted the legitimate causes of the use of aggressive force in *jihad*, and strictly regulated the conduct of hostilities. But there are also strong differences of opinion as to the precise scope of those restrictions when judged by the realities of international relations today (An-Na'im 1988). To exploit this ambiguity, Islamic fundamentalists tend to take a more expansive view of legitimate *jihad* than the vast majority of Muslims.

It is possible to make a strong Islamic theological/legal argument, I believe, against aggressive *jihad* in the modern context (An-Na'im 1990: 141–60). However, while some Islamic countries are better than others in securing the necessary domestic conditions, it is clear that the 'space' allowed for free debate and dissent is not sufficient. Moreover, and without being apologetic for some of the most oppressive regimes that rule over Islamic societies today, I urge that one should also appreciate the significant impact of external factors on those domestic conditions. As is true of other parts of the world, an Islamic society tends to become defensive and conservative when it perceives itself to be under attack, especially when that perception also undermines belief in the rule of international law.

In particular, the manner and scale of the military retaliation by the United States against the terrorist attacks of 11 September 2001, and the failure of the international community to check that unilateral use of force, constitute a fundamental challenge to the rule of law in international relations. Moreover, the United States continues (at the time of writing) to violate the most basic requirements of international humanitarian law for so-called Taliban and Al Qaeda fighters it captured in Afghanistan, and even minimum protections of due process of law for those suspects within its own domestic jurisdiction (Neier 2002). Whether there is no international legality at all, or it is too weak to cope with the realities of global power relations, this situation encourages Islamic fundamentalist perceptions of *jihad* as the aggressive and unilateral use of violence for political ends (An-Na'im 2002). Unless this regressive situation is redressed effectively, the idea of a global civil society is untenable, at least from the perspective of Islamic communities throughout the world. Moreover, this state of affairs will hinder the realisation of the objectives of global civil society for other constituencies. As Marlies Glasius and Mary Kaldor report in Chapter 1 of this book, global civil society has been losing ground over human rights since 11 September.

The preceding discussion of Islamic fundamentalism, as an illustration of similar religious fundamentalism as well as chauvinistic secular or nationalist ideologies, is intended to emphasise the need for an effective response if the idea of global civil society is to be a viable and coherent concept for all those who take religion seriously. An effective response to the challenge of fundamentalism is one way of mediating tensions between religion and global civil society. Another approach to the same end is to promote and support understandings of religion that are more conducive to a positive relationship with global civil society. It is in this light that I now turn to a discussion of liberal Islam and liberation theology as understandings of religion that are more likely to be consistent with global civil society. However, I wish to emphasise again that the outcomes of such initiatives are always contingent on a variety of internal and external factors and processes, and should never be taken for granted.

> ...nevertheless, the idea of an Islamic state to enforce Shari'a is conceptually untenable, has no precedent in Islamic history, and is not practically viable in the modern context

Liberal Islam and Liberation Theology: Dialectics of the Local, Regional, and Global

As explained earlier, by questioning modernisation and subjecting it to examination and critique from his own Indian perspective, Gandhi made this notion relative to, and located within, a specific context. He reserved the right of his society to understand and adopt modernisation *on its own terms*. The same perspective can be applied to conceptualisations of global civil society.

I will now explore this issue through the experiences of two regional civil society movements that take religion seriously: liberal Islam in the Muslim world and liberation theology in Latin America. The first is about the possibility of responding to the challenge of fundamentalist Islam from an Islamic perspective; the second is a religious response to issues of economic justice and globalisation. These two thematic studies are related in that, while liberal Islam is a direct response to a particular form of fundamentalism, liberation theology is a response to the circumstances of injustice and disempowerment that can fuel fundamentalism.

Liberal Islam

The following discussion of liberal Islam/Islamic liberalism in relation to the triple problematic relationship of Islam, civil society, and global civil society will address the following questions in an integrated manner: Can there be a liberal Islam that does not conform to a particular Western understanding of liberalism and secularism? What is the contemporary context within which liberal Islam exists or can be expected to emerge? For instance, what is the role of the nation state and transnational movements in generating or sustaining liberal understandings of Islam in different parts of the world? Finally, how is liberal Islam shaped by the relationship between national identity and historical as well as current experiences with Islamic transnationalism? How does this phenomenon of Islamic globalism relate to globalisation and transnational forms of citizenship through a global civil society?

Liberal Islam and liberalism

Current discourse about liberal Islam is apparently concerned with its relationship to Western conceptions of liberalism and secularism. According to Dalacoura (1998: 192), Islamic liberalism cannot be neatly explained in the terms of Western liberalism. Although 'liberalism and Islamic liberalism are bound together in Middle Eastern societies, the implication is that secularism is not an essential prerequisite for liberalism ... liberalism and Islamic liberalism are two separate phenomena conceptually'. Nurcholish Madjid is also concerned with the relevance of secularism to conceptualisations of liberal Islam when he speaks of a revitalisation of Islamic thought. One of his proposals for a liberalisation of outlook is what he calls 'secularization', which he defines broadly as all forms of liberating development. 'This liberating process is particularly needed because the *umma* [global Islamic community] as a result of its own historical growth is no longer capable of distinguishing—among the values which they consider Islamic—those that are transcendental from those that are temporal' (Madjid 1998: 286).

This dual engagement of the historical and modern contexts of Islamic societies is integral to conceptualisations of liberal Islam as an interpretive approach that contrasts the historical context of the original formulation of religious doctrine to the modern context in which it is to be understood and applied. The proponents of liberal Islam are concerned with applying the insights and methodology of this historically contextual approach to contemporary issues in the Islamic world, with due regard to the central role of religion in the political culture of Islamic societies. Consequently, the terms in which the discussion of Islamic liberal thought must be framed, as well as the substantive aspects and tensions of that discussion, are clearly different from those of debates about liberalism in other parts of the world. But this difference should not be exaggerated either. For example, Islamic liberal thought cannot assume or presuppose Western conceptions of secularism, the nation-state, modernity, or civil society, while still having to deal with those conceptions within the present realities of globalisation and power relations. This negotiation of the liberal Islamic nation-state with secularism and the dynamics of the state's relationship with civil society can be briefly illustrated here with the cases of Tunisia and Turkey.

Abdelbaki Hermassi conceptualises contemporary Tunisian civil society as the result of several genealogies that are emerging from a different historical phase. 'The historical formation of civil society in Tunisia is best viewed in terms of an accumulation of consecutive layers, from the traditionalist associations through the colonialist and nationalist periods, to the corporatist associations and current diversification' (Hermassi 1995: 77). By traditional associations he means very old associations, such as groups that managed water distribution or administered religious charitable foundations (*awqaf*) and other philanthropic associations. The next layer of associational life emerged during the colonial encounter, like *al-Khalduniyyah*, a 'society' of civil character with a cultural orientation established by the modern elite created by French colonial rule. Another layer came with the creation of unions, political parties, professional associations, and art academies under the National Front that was in power in 1936. Eventually, 'the Destour Party [that led the country to independence] gradually established control over these organisations and created new ones in sectors where the party thought a supporting constituency would be crucial', including 'workers, peasants, businessmen, students, women, and youth' (Hermassi 1995: 77).

After independence these groups were brought under direct state control, under the aegis of a 'corporatist system of interest representation'. As a result of this primacy of the state over civil society, the latter had to be reclaimed by social actors in 'the absence of a free space for social and political expression' (Hermassi 1995: 78). The state forced these dissenting voices, including Islamic opposition groups, to seek alternative political arenas. This emergence of mass opposition movements led the government to re-evaluate its traditional hostility towards civil society organisations, with mixed results, as state authorities keep fluctuating between oppression and open engagement. What is interesting in Hermassi's sketch is that his historical understanding of the *lived* political culture of Islam is a framework that does not label political action exclusively as 'liberal' or 'conservative' but simply as a mode of legitimate intervention in claiming rights over a space. Whether one agrees or disagrees with that political action, its essential character as a civil act within *a* particular civil society cannot be denied.

> Some Islamist groups argue for a more inclusive secularism that does not relegate religion solely to the private sphere but grants it legitimacy as the basis of action in the public realm

Liberal Islam, the nation-state, and civil society

Maintaining that the emergence of liberalism presupposes and is inextricably linked to the modern state as an ideal type, Dalacoura (1998: 195) see the key question here as one of a balance between the two: 'Does the state develop into a modern formation in tandem with civil society? Or does it develop perpetually threatened by it or threatening it?'

Regarding this tripartite relationship in the case of Turkey, Binnaz Toprak challenges commonly held views about the relationship between secularism and fundamentalism. She asserts that those movements, often monolithically classified as 'Islamic funda-mentalism', are, indeed, *consistent* with liberal and progressive values. Pointing out that the plurality of Islamic political groups in Turkey covers a wide range of organisations, with a spectrum of political positions and beliefs, Toprak (1995: 95) writes, 'Indeed, militant Islam is a fringe movement within the larger context of a plethora of Islamic groups and organizations'.

The negotiations of these groups with the nation-state over claims to political space and action can be conceptualised as a form of civil society that calls into question the relationships among the nation-state, secularism, and religion. On the one hand, the state's strong promotion of secularism in Turkey has clearly enabled a political culture for the articulation for diverse voices, including those of the Islamist groups. On the other hand, some of these groups have launched their own challenge to aspects of the state, including secularism, on *religious* grounds as well as for excluding the rural uneducated majority of the population. Thus, these groups are arguing for a more inclusive secularism that does not relegate religion solely to the private sphere but grants it legitimacy as the basis of action in the public realm. Indeed, such deeply con-textual conceptions of secularism are necessary for a cultural legitimisation of human rights, regulating the relationship between religion and the state, and enhancing the moral depth of secularism (An-Na'im 2001).

In their assessments of civil society, both Toprak and Hermassi emphasise the fact that any thinking on civil society requires a simultaneous rethinking of the role of the nation-state and the lived meaning of secularism in various societies. In view of my emphasis on the relationship between local-national civil society and global civil society, only a genuinely pluralistic globalism will be able to guarantee a global civil society so that every voice, no matter how apparently insignificant, is included in that society. I now turn to the phenomenon of Islamic globalism for insights in this connection.

Islamic globalism and global civil society

Public discourse in the West often tends to equate Islamic globalism with pan-national fundamentalist networks. However, an assessment of Islamic globalism beyond this limited view shows that it can represent an alternative mode of forging social identity that, at the same time, draws upon and offers opportunities of response to globalisation. While not asserting particular conclusions about the long-term outcomes to conceptualisations of global civil society, I do believe that such social formations should be taken seriously as interlocutors and actors in the ongoing construction of global civil society.

> 'Lived Islam' in the diaspora necessitates negotiating the differences between Islamic communities and finding common ground by re-examining what Islam means in more inclusive ways ....

To clarify this point, I will argue that there is nothing in the phenomenon of Islamic globalism as such to make it inherently conservative or intolerant. Second, I will assess the relationship between Islamic globalism and globalisation by focusing on the nature and role of the Muslim diaspora. In this light, one wonders whether Islamic globalism today represents a notion of transnational citizenship, and what that means for conceptualisations of global civil society.

In the course of his exploration of how Islam has 'travelled' in the course of history, and continues to travel today, Mandaville states:

The multifaceted nature of identity has, under translocality, brought forth a diverse new set of political practices. These involve the possibility that any given individual may have ties and identity claims which pertain to more than one nation and state (or neither) . . . the activities of such individuals are not limited to a single political space, either in terms of territory or discourse. One's presence in a particular territorial state does not restrict one from engaging in transnational relations which seek to politicise a component of self-identity which is not 'of' the territory from which these activities emanate. (Mandaville 2001: 50–1, emphasis in original)

He also emphasises the diversity and continuity of the migrations of Muslims throughout their history, both within and across the borders of the Muslim world. Mandaville's argument is that the contemporary and *visible* form of Islamic globalism cannot be seen as an entirely new phenomenon, because it shares both historical continuities with Islam and modernity and a structural relationship with the interplay of capital.

One new aspect of Islamic globalism may be the shift in the nature and location of the recent Muslim diaspora experiences in Western Europe and North America which will probably have far-reaching consequences for Muslim views of themselves and of the 'other'. As Mandaville (2001: 127) observes, 'Muslims in diaspora come face to face with the myriad shapes and colours of global Islam, forcing the religion to hold a mirror up to its own diversity. These encounters often play an important role in processes of identity formation, prompting Muslims to relativise and compare their self-understandings of Islam'. As he explains: 'This process of relativisation allows Muslims to partake in a discourse of particularity, one in which their conception of religion is no longer universal ... this is also a space in which no particular conception of Islam is negated. Difference is negotiated rather than eradicated' (Mandaville 2001: 181). Thus, 'lived Islam' in the diaspora necessitates negotiating the differences between Islamic communities and finding common ground by re-examining what Islam means in more inclusive ways.

In this light, the case of the Muslim diaspora in the age of globalisation is extremely instructive as an *analogy* for understanding global civil society. As a result of accelerated globalisation, more and more communities are constantly negotiating how to share space and cooperate in pursuit of common concerns with more and more 'others'. What is new in these processes for most diasporic Muslim communities is that they encounter each other in a space that is neutral regarding difference *among* Muslim communities, though it may *not* be neutral in its perceptions of Muslim communities or Islam in general. Regardless of its reasons, which can include ignorance, indifference, or even prejudice, the nation-state in which diasporic Muslim communities exist is unlikely in its policies to privilege one Muslim community over another. Should similar conditions prevail in predominantly Islamic societies, through internal transformations and external influence that would provide the necessary space for global civil society to thrive and include such understandings of Islam? The analogy of Islamic globalism can also be instructive in challenging normative conceptions of global civil society that seek to define political action, state-society relations, and institutions in a manner that empties them of their specific local content. Only through recognition of this very specific content in its own historical context can the concept of global civil society be made meaningful for most people around the world.

Another form of Islamic globalism discussed by Mandaville is transnational Muslim organisations, offering possibilities of transnational citizenship, which question a conception of citizenship as an abstraction of the relationship between the individual and the state. By occupying a particular political *space* (in the sense of an agenda dealing with gender issues, human rights, religious and/or ethnic identity), which is not necessarily a specific *place*, these transnational social movements can provide an alternative definition of citizenship. The existence of such transnational groups is easily overlooked because they do not fall into the range of activities usually associated in dominant discourse with the political in the sense of addressing the state or even explicitly recognising its existence. Many such organisations, like Jam'at al-Tabligh, operate across and between bordered spaces, representing a diverse range of interests, often related to the sustenance or advancement of various ethnic and/or religious identities (Mandaville 2001: 16).

Such transnational organisations provide a notion of *participatory social-cultural citizenship* as an alternative understanding of citizenship itself. In the case of the Jama'at al-Tabligh, that participatory social-cultural citizenship is inextricably tied to religious identity in expressing a specific conception of religion as concerned simultaneously with an ethics of social action and questions of cultural identity. The notion of *participatory social-cultural citizenship* may be an effective way of thinking of different forms of participation of *individuals* in global civil society. For instance, the criteria of participation for organisations (and individuals) in global civil society need not be restricted to the exclusively secular, nor framed solely in terms of explicitly political issues.

> ... in this light, the case of the Muslim diaspora in the age of globalisation is extremely instructive as an analogy for understanding global civil society

Liberation theology

Liberation theology emerged as a movement in Latin America around 1968–71 in pursuit of radical structural change with the goal of liberating oppressive structures (MacLean 1999: 123; Turner 1994: 3, 9). According to one of its founders, the fundamental tenets of liberation theology combine the love of God with the urgency of solidarity with the poor (Gutiérrez, 1999: 27). Viewing the Latin American context as an 'unjust environment', this movement emphasised human agency in taking direct action to help the poor, and used a Marxist social analysis in working towards a socialist system that ultimately 'shares' [the] wealth (Fitzgerald 1999: 229; Turner 1999: 4). During the 1980s and 1990s, the movement evolved to encompass a more integrative social framework to include race, gender, culture, and ecological issues (Turner 1994: 5; Tombs 2001: 46–8).

Liberation theology is primarily an ecclesiastical movement with a focus on the liberation of the poor (Berryman 1987: 157; Duque 1995: 54). Its ideology is based on the assumption that oppressed peoples and classes are fundamentally in conflict with their oppressors who are the wealthy nations and oppressive classes (Gutiérrez 1973: 36). While the movement is by no means uniform, its various currents share the same three assumptions: that the majority of individuals live in a state of under-development and unjust dependence, that this state is sinful as viewed in Christian terms, and that it is the responsibility of the members of the Church to work to overcome this sinful state (Galilea 1979: 167). The same fundamental theme was also expressed as the 'preferential option for the poor', which was defined by Gutiérrez (1999: 27) in terms of 'solidarity with the poor and rejection of poverty as something contrary to the will of God'. This conception, which is the fundamental underlying theme of the whole movement, is linked to the work of grass-roots Christian communities and the evangelical mission of the Church (Gutiérrez, 1999: 19).

Liberation theology is a movement away from the metaphysical, and represents a paradigm shift from classical theology by focusing on and putting God's will into practice in solidarity with the poor, in contrast to the 'detachment and reflection' of traditional theology (Gutiérrez 1999: 28–9; Rowland 1999: 4). Instead of classic theology's reliance on philosophy, liberation theology uses social science analysis and seeks to link 'right action' with 'right thinking' (Richard 1991: 2; Williams 1998: 199). Whereas traditional Christianity frames the concept of utopia as being realised only through a direct act of God, liberation theology perceives it as a matter of practice. Gutiérrez also stresses the communitarian experience as essential to liberation practice, and that methodology is manifest in spirituality and one's life as a Christian. He links the relationship of Christian life and method to the ascending importance of Base Ecclesiastical Communities as agents of theological reflection (Gutiérrez 1999: 30). Resonating with Gandhian thought, liberation theology distinguishes between material poverty, which is 'the lack of economic goods necessary for a human life worthy of the name', and spiritual

poverty, 'an interior attitude of unattachment to the goods of this world' (Gutiérrez 1973: 204). From a Christian perspective, poverty is contrary to human dignity and against the will of God (Gutiérrez 1973: 291).

Through its use of social scientific analysis, liberation theology views the cause of poverty in Latin America as inequality in the system of power and ownership that inhibits access of the masses to participation in society (Boff 1979: 129). Liberation theologians have rejected conceptions of develpment theory as being based on the assumption that Third World countries were underdeveloped due to exclusively internal factors, or that the solution to end poverty was for these countries to 'catch up' by developing. Instead, they argue that massive poverty is not an accident. 'It is the result of *structures of exploitation and domination*; it derives from centuries of *colonial domination* and is reinforced by the present international *economic system*' (Dussel 1984: 89; emphasis in original).

The movement always had an ambivalent relationship with the Vatican. The Vatican's response has been consistently wary of the political role of liberation theology, especially its use of Marxism as a tool of social analysis, while at the same time apparently supporting the movement's agenda of social justice. To the Vatican, liberation theology's advocacy of an alternative church (the *iglesia popular* or people's church) is an affront to the official church (Gibelleni 1988: 46). Leading liberation theologians like Gutiérrez and Boff continue to insist that Marxism is used only as a conduit to understanding societal forms of oppression. But the Vatican and other critics hold that Marxism cannot be used for empirical analysis without regard for its critique of religion itself (Turner 1999: 203).

Liberation theology continues to be practised at the grass-roots level, and those who spearheaded efforts to further the movement during its inception continue to be prolific in their writings today. However, new strains have emerged and, although the underlying theme remains liberation from oppression, diverse perspectives within the movement have their own strong new agendas. Liberation theology has also lost large numbers of supporters due to changes in political, social, and religious circumstances throughout Latin America.

Commentators mention several factors as contributing to the decline of liberation theology in recent years, such as the perceived failure of Marxism,

Above: Demonstrators in Peru use religious imagery in their protest against the lack of help from the government when the savings scheme CLAE collapses. © Annie Bungerath/Panos Pictures.

conflict with the Vatican, and the rise of Pentecostalism. Another factor is the need to expand its social and political analysis to include such issues as race, gender, culture, and sexuality, as well as indigenous peoples and ecological concerns. The dilemma facing the movement now is that such diversification is necessary for it to remain relevant, but it also diminishes the clarity of its original focus (Tombs 2001: 53–6).

Finally, the religious situation in Latin America has become more pluralist, with the rise of Pentecostal churches that are posing a serious challenge to Catholicism as well as liberation theology (Tombs 2001: 55). The focus of liberation theology on a purely socio-economic analysis of conflict without addressing the dynamics of culture and religion may have contributed to Latin Americans turning to other religious movements (Moltman 1998: 74).

However, the strong focus on poverty and development linked liberation theology to other intellectual and political currents in the region, as well as to global trends. For example, Paulo Freire criticised the churches for failing to exercise their true prophetic function, and called on the churches to take sides in struggles for political liberation in order to avoid supporting repressive regimes. Freire also sees a relationship between black theology and Latin American liberation theology in that both have a political nature, both are aligned with the struggle of the oppressed, and both emphasise revolutionary praxis (Elias 1994: 145). Black North American liberation theology parallels Latin American liberation theology in that its leaders also deviated from the traditional theological paradigm. Latin American liberation theology reflected a move from developmentalism to liberation, while black theology reflected the passage from the ideal of integration to that of black power.

Other parallel theologies, including Asian, African, and feminist, have arisen out of struggles in reaction against the European and North American theological establishment that tended to assume that its theology was simply 'Christian' theology. African liberation theology differs from Latin American liberation theology with its focus on the problem of 'indigenization and the role of native African religions' (Ferm 1992: 3). In Asia, liberation theo-

logians face the challenge that Christianity is a minority religion. Each strain of theology is uniquely suited to its context, but all are linked by the preferential option for the poor. Dialogue between Latin American liberation theologians and feminist theologians has taken place mostly in the context of international ecumenical conferences, but dialogue has been rare, and it is argued that this dialogue is superficial and cautious (Vuola 1997).

The highly contextual nature of liberal Islam and liberation theology raises the question of how such localised forms of civil society can also function as part of global civil society. As briefly explained earlier, the exclusiveness of such local and regional associations is not necessarily inconsistent with their participation in global civil society provided they subscribe to a shared normative content. The idea of overlapping consensus requires unity of purpose and mutual respect for difference, not ideological and associational uniformity. But, as also emphasised throughout this chapter, this consensus building must take account of the 'unevenness' of political and institutional power relations between different regions of the world. The process of inclusion and incorporation of local or regional participants, like liberal Islam and liberation theology, should also be sensitive to the risks of serious cross-cultural misunderstandings which can be compounded by religious and cultural normative differences among all participants in global civil society.

> The idea of overlapping consensus requires unity of purpose and mutual respect for difference, not uniformity. But this consensus building must also take account of the 'unevenness' of global power relations

Concluding Remarks

The main question for this chapter is how concepts of global civil society can engage and encompass the centrality of religious and cultural identity for most people and communities throughout the world, including Western societies. Since this cannot mean the automatic inclusion of all forms of religious expressions, as some may be inherently inconsistent with the underlying rationale and purpose of global civil society, I have attempted to argue for a way of promoting possibilities of consistency between the two. The approach I proposed above is the development of a synergistic and interdependent model of the relationship between religion and global civil society, whereby understandings of religion are supportive of corresponding conceptualisations of global civil society and the latter are conceived in ways that are supportive of such understandings of religion. The policy question for this approach is how to promote conditions that are conducive to those mutually supportive understandings of religion and conceptualisations of civil society.

The analysis I presented in this chapter is based on the interplay between the composition and function or purpose of global civil society, the dynamics of specific place and space, and the impact of that on the way it operates in practice. Taking global civil society to be the space where people and transnational entities debate and negotiate the rules of their relationships and pursue accountability for those rules, in furtherance of their respective concerns, my analysis is also concerned with the relationship between space and place. The physical location of actors conditions their perceptions of the agenda and priority of global civil society as well as their ability to act in solidarity with others in pursuit of their own objectives.

Since any function or purpose of global civil society would necessarily presuppose a certain minimum normative content that cannot be presumed or expected to come about of its own accord, I am also concerned with the question of by whom and how that normative content is determined. Following an approach developed in relation to the universality of human rights, I propose a process of internal discourse within different constituencies of global civil society and dialogue between them, in order to promote an overlapping consensus about the normative content of their solidarity and cooperation. Full agreement on the subject may be lacking or insufficient at the beginning, but it cannot be promoted through a deliberate process without at least agreement on certain ground rules for the process of negotiation itself. These prerequisite conditions include mutual respect and appreciation of cultural and contextual difference and the possibility of peaceful coexistence, as well as an appreciation of the need for consensus-building,

> Power relations among different constituencies are critical for the ability of all constituencies, especially those based in the Third World, to participate in determining the function of global civil society

instead of seeking to impose one's views on others. If accepted, this proposition gives us the basis for assessing the 'candidacy' of various constituencies for membership in global civil society. This, of course, applies to secular ideological or philosophical as well as religious constituencies, because any of them can fail to live up to the minimum requirements of membership in global civil society. But religious constituencies happen to be my concern in this chapter.

I also highlighted in the first section several factors that affect the dynamics of membership in global civil society on the basis of above-mentioned minimum criteria, but emphasised the impact of differentials in power relations between constituencies based in developed countries and those located in the Third World. In my view, power relations among different constituencies are critical for the ability of all constituencies, especially those based in the Third World, to participate in determining the function of global civil society. These relations also condition the impact of location on the nature of the space it provides, as well as the practical operation of global civil society.

With regard to religious constituencies in particular, however, the ultimate question is how to mediate the presumed exclusivity of religious communities on the one hand, and the requirements of inclusion, civility, and freedom of choice of civil society on the other. According to the proposed model for promoting an overlapping consensus, this tension can be mediated through an internal discourse within religious communities and dialogue with other constituencies. For those engaged in internal discourse within their own religious communities the challenge is how to promote understandings and practice of their religion that are more inclusive, civil, and voluntary. But they cannot succeed without the cooperation and support of other constituencies of global civil society in addressing the legitimate concerns of those communities. The questions of which concerns are legitimate and how to address them should themselves be debated through the same process. I briefly illustrated this point by suggesting that the best response to the threat of international terrorism from a global civil society perspective is to uphold the rule of law in international relations while addressing the underlying grievances that motivate terrorists and their supporters. The main conclusion of the first section is that the contingent possibilities of reconciliation between religious and other constituencies of global civil society must be actively sought by all sides, instead of passively waiting for religious persons and communities to succeed or fail the test of inclusion.

The remaining sections in the chapter offered an elaboration and illustration of the main thesis presented in the first section. While Gandhi's approach to religion demonstrates possibilities of positive contributions to global civil society, in my view religious fundamentalism is clearly an unacceptable expression of religious beliefs. However, the main point of my discussion of Islamic fundamentalism is that possibilities of an effective Islamic response are contingent on a combination of internal and external conditions. The cases of liberal Islam and liberation theology represent regional manifestations of global civil society that are rooted in a religious discourse. Civil society is commonly understood in the context of nationalism and national boundaries, while the notion of global civil society seeks to add a transnational dimension through the existence of organisations, telecommunications networks, a public sphere where institutions sharing common goals and agendas cooperate in pursuit of shared objectives. The subsection on Islamic globalism raises the question of how this discourse of nationalism and transnationalism takes into account religion as a medium of both earlier and current forms of identify and experience. Does this phenomenon offer a basis for a transnational form of citizenship through a global civil society, and on whose terms? One possible contribution of religion to global civil society is that it can help mobilise believers in a moral and spiritual challenge to the globalisation of capitalism and consumerism, as illustrated by the case of liberation theology.

The general policy implication of my analysis is to challenge conceptions of global civil society as essentially defined by Western perspectives and experiences, and the assumption that what remains to be done is to develop the rudimentary or unsatisfactory forms of global civil society in other parts of the world according to that definitive model. In my view, these assumptions and their implications seriously undermine the true 'globality' of global civil society, which cannot be founded on universalising a region-specific formation as the most 'successful' embodiment of the concept. The effort should therefore be to conceptualise a more truly global civil society in terms of the actual social conditions of all parts of the world. Given the reality of drastic 'unevenness' and serious differentials in power relations among different regions of the world, valid conceptualisations of global civil society must therefore account for transnational and trans-regional, trans-cultural, and trans-religious contestations of its own premise and assumptions. But, in seeking to do so, one should be prepared to encounter developments and movements that challenge the premise or necessary implications of global civil society, as well as those that are more compatible with at least the core values and institutions of civil society.

I am grateful for the valuable research and editorial assistance of Rohit Chopra, Ph.D. candidate, Emory University, and the research assistance of Anupama Naidu of Emory School of Law. I have also benefited from the critical comments and useful suggestions of Marlies Glasius, Frank Lechner, and Neera Chandhoke.

References

Al-Azm, S. J. (1993–1994). 'Islamic Fundamentalism Reconsidered: A Critical Outline of Problems, Ideas and Approaches', Part I in *South Asia Bulletin*, 13/1-2 (1993), 93–121; Part II in *South Asia Bulletin*, 14/1 (1994): 73–98.

Anheier, Helmut, Glasius, Marlies, and Kaldor, Mary (2001). 'Introducing Global Civil Society', in Helmut Anheier, Marlies Glasius, and Mary Kaldor (eds), *Global Civil Society 2001*. Oxford: Oxford University Press.

An-Na'im, A. A. (1988). 'Islamic Ambivalence to Political Violence: Islamic Law and International Terrorism'. *German Yearbook of International Law*, 31: 307–36.

— (1990). *Toward an Islamic Reformation*. Syracuse, NY: Syracuse University Press.

— (1992) 'Introduction', in A. A. An-Na'im (ed.), *Human Rights in Cross-Cultural Perspectives: Quest for Consensus*. Philadelphia, PA: University of Pennsylvania Press.

— (1999). '*Shari'a* and Positive Legislation: is an Islamic State Possible or Viable?', in Eugene Cotran and Chibli

Mallat (eds), *Yearbook of Islamic and Middle Eastern Law*, Vol. 5. The Hague: Kluwer Law International.

— (2001). 'Synergy and Interdependence of Religion, Human Rights and Secularism'. *Polylog: Forum for Intercultural Philosophizing.* http://www.polylog.org/them/2/fcs7-en.htm

— (2002, forthcoming) 'Upholding International Legality Against Islamic and American *Jihad*', in K. Booth and T. Dunne (eds), *The Great Terror and Global Order.* London: Palgrave/Macmillan/St Martin's Press.

Berryman, P. (1987). *Liberation Theology: The Essential Facts about the Revolutionary Movement in Latin American and Beyond.* New York: Pantheon Books.

Boff, L. (1979). 'Christ's Liberation via Oppression: An Attempt at Theological Construction from the Standpoint of Latin America', in R. Gibelleni (ed.), *Frontiers of Liberation Theology in Latin America.* Maryknoll, NY: Orbis Books.

Dalacoura, K. (1998). *Islam, Liberalism and Human Rights.* London and New York: I. B. Tauris.

Dussel, E. (1984). 'Theologies of the "Periphery" and the "Centre": Encounter or Confrontation?', in G. Claude, G. Gustavo, and V. Elizondo (eds), *Different Theologies, Common Responsibility: Babel or Pentecost?* Edinburgh: T. & T. Clark Ltd.

Duque, J. (ed.) (1995). *Por una sociedad donde quedan todos.* San José, Costa Rica: Editorial Departamento Ecuménico de Investigaciones.

Elias, J. (1994). *Paulo Freire: Pedagogue of Liberation.* Malabar, FL: Krieger Publishing Co.

Ferm, D. W (1992). 'Third-World Liberation Theology', in D. Cohn-Sherbok (ed.), *World Religions and Human Liberation.* Maryknoll, NY: Orbis Books.

Fitzgerald, V. (1999). 'The Economics of Liberation Theology', in C. Rowland (ed.), *The Cambridge Companion to Liberation Theology.* Cambridge: Cambridge University Press.

Freitag, S. (1996). 'Contesting in Public: Colonial Legacies and Contemporary Communalism', in D. Ludden (ed.), *Contesting the Nation: Religion, Community, and the Politics of Democracy in India.* Philadelphia: University of Pennsylvania Press.

Galilea, S. (1979). 'Liberation Theology and New Tasks Facing Christians', in R. Gibelleni (ed.), *Frontiers of Liberation Theology in Latin America.* Maryknoll, NY: Orbis Books.

Gibelleni, R. (1988). *The Liberation Theology Debate.* Maryknoll, NY: Orbis Books.

Gutiérrez, G. (1973). *A Theology of Liberation.* Maryknoll, NY: Orbis Books. [Originally published in 1971 as *Teología de la liberación, Perspectivas.* Lima: CEP.]

— (1999). 'The Task and Content of Liberation Theology', trans. J. Connor in C. Rowland (ed.), *The Cambridge Companion to Liberation Theology.* Cambridge: Cambridge University Press.

Hermassi, A. (1995). 'Notes on Civil Society in Tunisia', in J. Schwedler (ed.), *Toward Civil Society in the Middle East? A Primer.* Boulder, CO and London: Lynne Rienner.

Juergensmeyer, M. (2000). *Terror in the Mind of God: The Global Rise of Religious Violence.* Berkeley: University of California Press.

Maclean, I. S. (1999). *Opting for Democracy: Liberation Theology and the Struggle for Democracy in Brazil.* New York: Peter Lang Publishing.

Madjid, N. (1998). 'The Necessity of Renewing Islamic Thought *and* Reinvigorating Religious Understanding', in C. Kurzman (ed.), *Liberal Islam.* New York, Oxford: Oxford University Press.

Mandaville, P. (2001). *Transnational Muslim Politics: Reimagining the Umma.* London and New York: Routledge.

Moltman, J. (1998). 'Political Theology and Theology of Liberation', in J. Reiger (ed.), *Liberating the Future: God, Mammon and Theology.* Minneapolis, MN: Augsburg Fortress.

Neier, A. (2002). 'The Military Tribunals on Trial', *The New York Review of Books*, 49/2 (14 February): 11–15.

Parekh, B. (1997). *Gandhi.* Oxford: Oxford University Press.

Richard, P. (1991). 'La Teología de la Liberación en la Nueva Coyuntura', *Pasos* 34/Marzo–Abril: 1–8, Segundo Epoca.

Rowland, C. (1999). *The Cambridge Companion to Liberation Theology.* Cambridge: Cambridge University Press.

Shah, G. (1991). 'Tenth Lok Sabha Elections: BJP's Victory in Gujarat'. *Economic and Political Weekly*, 21 December: 2921–4.

Terchek, R. J. (1998). *Gandhi.* New York, Oxford: Rowman & Littlefield Publishers.

Tombs, D. (2001). 'Latin American Liberation Theology Faces the Future', in S. E. Porter, M. Hayes, and D. Tombs (eds), *Faith in the New Millennium.* Sheffield, England: Sheffield Academic Press Ltd.

Toprak, B. (1995). 'Islam and the Secular State in Turkey', in C. Balim, E. Kalayciouglu, C. Karatas, G. Winrow, and F. Yasamee (eds), *Turkey: Political, Social and Economic Challenges in the 1990s.* London, New York, Cologne: E. J. Brill.

Turner, J. D. (1994). *An Introduction to Liberation Theology*. Lanham, MA: University Press of America, Inc.

— (1999). 'Marxism and Liberation Theology', in C. Rowland (ed.), *The Cambridge Companion to Liberation Theology*. Cambridge: Cambridge University Press.

Vuola, E. (1997). *Limits of Liberation*. Helsinki: Suomalainen Tiedeakatemia.

Williams, D. T. (1998). *Capitalism, Socialism, Christianity and Poverty*. Hatfield, Pretoria: J. L. Van Schaik Publishers.

Young, R. J. C. (2001). *Postcolonialisms: An Historical Introduction*. Malden, MA: Blackwell Publishers.

Zaman, H. (1999). 'The Taslima Nasrin Controversy and Feminism in Bangladesh: A Geo-Political and Transnational Perspective'. *Atlantis*, 23/2. 25th Anniversary Download Promotion. http://www.msvu.ca/atlantis/issues/V23_2/5.pdf

Part II: Issues in Global Civil Society

Chapter 4

WHO'S MINDING THE STORE? GLOBAL CIVIL SOCIETY AND CORPORATE RESPONSIBILITY

Melanie Beth Oliviero and Adele Simmons

Introduction

Green labels, eco-efficiency, life-cycle management, environmental and social reporting, triple bottom line, socially responsible investing, closed manufacturing processes . . . These expressions of corporate social responsibility (CSR) appear regularly in corporate publications, a phenomenon no one would have predicted 15 years ago. Global corporations did not wake up one morning and decide to become socially responsible citizens, however. They were instead awakened, sometimes roughly, by the concerted efforts of civil society organisations (CSOs), which can today boast a global reach equal to that of their corporate counterparts.

CSOs are uniquely qualified to monitor the enormous influence of the private sector on public life and they are taking on this challenge at a crucial time: global poverty and wealth disparity are increasing; child labour remains pervasive; and a growing amount of work is done in sweatshops. In this context the policies and actions of corporations have significant influence, for good or ill, through their business practices and their influence on governments and multilateral organisations.

Since multinational corporations are usually seen as the main actors in the global economy, most of what has been written about CSR provides accounts of how and why businesses are changing and what they can do to become more responsible. While there are case studies of how CSOs have promoted or demanded corporate responsibility, they have not been the focus of much systematic, independent research. Who are they? How do they work? What have they accomplished? What more can they do?

Definitive answers to these questions are elusive because so much basic research still needs to be done, but we know enough to suggest here a framework for further study and to sketch the impact of CSOs on both the policies and the practices of corporations, industries, and government. There are important differences among both the goals and the forms of action of CSOs. In this chapter, we draw attention to the distinctions between 'insiders' and 'outsiders' and between 'Northern' and 'Southern' CSOs. Insiders are those that work closely with corporations in helping to develop socially responsible programmes and policies; outsiders are sceptical that profit-seeking organisations can act responsibly, and tend to emphasise public pressure and government action. Northern CSOs generally act on behalf of others, whether dolphins or children, and exercise leverage in Northern centres of power; Southern CSOs tend to represent the victims of corporate behaviour more directly. Methods of protest range from direct action to consumer and investor behaviour, to partnerships and monitoring. We argue that global civil society needs to combine these varied types of organisation and forms of protest to be effective. In this chapter, we pay particular attention to monitoring, since this is a role that civil society is likely to play for some time.

The chapter concludes with a discussion of the power-and limitations-of civil society and of how CSOs work with governments and multilateral organisations in an effort to institutionalise corporate social responsibility. In particular, we address the debate about whether multinational corporations can be relied on to act responsibly voluntarily or whether there is a need for national and international legislation. We argue that what matters is a change in norms and ways of thinking. While formal regulation is important, not least to provide a tool for CSOs, even the best designed standards and codes will not work without a public commitment. And that is the job of civil society.

The historical view

Holding corporate players accountable for their actions in global economies is not a new idea. In 1787, Thomas Clarkson and eleven other men met in a Quaker bookshop in London to form a society to prohibit British companies and shipowners from participating in the slave trade, seeing this as a crucial first step in ending slavery throughout the world. Businessmen, clerics, and concerned men and women of all social classes were involved in the campaign and publicised the atrocities aboard the slave ships. Members of Parliament kept the issue in the public eye and writers spread word of a boycott of slave-grown products. By 1792, 400,000 people in Britain were boycotting slave-grown sugar. Legislation banning the British slave trade passed one House of Parliament in 1792, but the long war with France put everything on hold until both Houses agreed to ban the slave trade in 1807. Slavery in the British Empire came to an end in the 1830s, and Thomas Clarkson, who had assembled that first meeting 50 years earlier, was there to see it.

Another historical example is the work begun by Edmund Dene Morel a century later. In 1897, Morel, a minor official of a British shipping company and a freelance journalist, was in a position to observe ships from King Leopold's Congo load and unload in Antwerp. Rubber came off the ships; weapons went on. Discrepancies in the shipping figures Morel

Above: Congo reformers often pointed to the Berlin agreement of 1885, one of many broken promises regarding the treatment of Africans. Cartoon courtesy of Adam Hochschild.

collected for his articles eventually led him to King Leopold's dark secret: the king's rubber was extracted by forced labour, his colonial regime was sustained by mass murder, and the king (not the Belgian state) was the corporate profiteer. Belgian scholar Jules Marchal estimates that Leopold's profit, in today's dollars, amounted to $US1.1 billion.

In England, Morel launched what was to become the first international human rights movement of the twentieth century. He crafted his message to resonate with a wide constituency. He told British businessmen that Leopold's monopolistic practices denied them profits in the Congo. He recruited clergymen with his reliable and damning reports from missionaries. His publications informed public opinion and political debate and he was careful to portray the movement as above the partisan political and religious fray. He well understood the value of media attention, and worked hard to mobilise and inform journalists from Britain and abroad.

While Leopold's shrewd public relations campaign also had moments of success, in the end his efforts were undone by the facts. As a result of the labours of Morel and his civil society collaborators throughout the world, control of the Congo was transferred from the King to the Belgian government in 1908, and the most egregious abuses eventually came to a halt (Hochschild 1999).

Considered together, the two movements exemplify many of the components that we recognise in modern civil society campaigns: a coming together of different sectors of society, media coverage, a boycott, parliamentary debate, and reform legislation. The campaigns inevitably suffered from a lack of CSO infrastructure (each built networks of activists from scratch), the difficulty of educating a public unfamiliar with such campaigns, the dearth of enforcement and monitoring tools, and, of course, the lack of today's technology.

Corporate social responsibility: why corporations care

There are over 60,000 multinational corporations active today, with over 800,000 affiliates abroad (UNCTAD 2001). While different economists use different measures for determining the relative size of multinational corporations, at least 37 of the top 100 economies of the world are corporations (Wolf 2002). Some economists have found that the combined sales of the world's top 200 corporations are bigger than the combined economies of all but the 10 richest countries (Anderson and Cavanagh 2000, frontispiece). Needless to say, this represents enormous power in the hands of business.

Yet for all that—or perhaps because of it—a recent survey of European elites found that those surveyed trusted civil society organisations more than business, or government. Amnesty International, the World Wildlife Fund, and Greenpeace outranked the leading multinationals in Europe, and are among the top 15 most trusted organisations in the US. Respondents cared most about how businesses treat employees and the extent to which they are honest (Edelman PR Worldwide/Strategy One 2002). With this enhanced legitimacy, CSOs are well positioned to insist on responsible behaviour from corporations.

> In recent years, public opinion has embraced the concept that corporations have civic and social responsibilities. Corporations ignore these sentiments at some peril

In recent years, public opinion has embraced the concept that corporations have civic and social responsibilities. In a 1999 poll of 25,000 citizens in 23 countries, the Conference Board (URL)—a research, analysis, and information-sharing network—and the Prince of Wales International Business Leaders Forum—an international CSR advocate—found that two-thirds of those surveyed expected companies to do more than simply make a profit and obey the law (Environics International Ltd 1999). A recent Canadian poll found that 72 per cent of Canadians say business should pursue social responsibilities, not just profits, 80 per cent say government should set social responsibility standards, and most want pension funds invested in responsible companies (Canadian Democracy and Corporate Accountability 2002). The comparable US sampling finds 89 per cent of those asked expected the companies to do more than operate within legal boundaries and almost half had made purchasing decisions based on their view of a corporation's commitment to corporate citizenship (Weiser and Zadek 2000: 24). It is clear that corporations ignore these sentiments at some peril.

Most companies have statements of values and principles, but the interpretation of these statements and the extent to which they are followed vary widely. When it comes to corporate citizenship, the business world presents a broad continuum. On one end are those with little interest in the concept, some of whom, like the tobacco industry, persist in harmful practices even after being informed of the dangers or, like former Sunbeam Chief Executive Officer (CEO) Al Dunlop, run their businesses in keeping with the idea that 'you're not in business to be liked'. Many business leaders are coming to realise, however, that 'corporate social responsibility is not about being nice. The potential to limit expenditure, maintain or improve employee and community relations, control risk and promote reputation means that applying corporate social responsibility strategies is simply good business sense' (Kent 2001). In the middle of the continuum are the growing number of corporations that are in fact responsive to civil society pressure but are still unlikely to initiate change on their own. On the far end of the scale are those businesses, sometimes acting with only minimal prompting by civil society, whose leadership has changed practices throughout an industry. One thing is clear: any given company's commitment to the principles of CSR is directly dependent on its CEO's commitment.

The Aspen Institute's Business Leaders Dialogue in July 2001 (Aspen Institute 2001) discussed three types of corporate citizenship. The first includes those businesses that obey the law, operate in a transparent way, and focus on issues directly related to their business, in compliance with existing standards. Being a good corporate citizen at this level is not always easy, but the activity is clearly related to business and business strategy.

The second type of corporate citizen includes businesses that move beyond mere compliance to address issues in which there is a synergy between the business and society. Thus, when 80 tanneries in Bangkok joined forces to establish their own waste water treatment facility, there was certainly a direct environmental benefit, but the tannery owners also served their own bottom line by sharing treatment costs (Schmidheiny, Chase, and DeSimone 1997: 21).

The final type of corporate citizenship comprises businesses led by chief executives who address social and environmental issues that may seem to be far from, or even counter to, the interests of the corporation. These executives understand that the success of the world economy has a long-term impact on their business, and make efforts to understand the need to support public goods from clean air and a safe environment to human rights that provide the basic infrastructure that in turn allows corporations to operate safely and effectively. They are not afraid to speak out, even though their shareholders might question the appropriateness of doing so. When BP CEO John Browne called on businesses to address climate change, he was seen by some to be taking a position contrary to BP's short-term interest, though Browne himself understood the influence it would have on BP's long-term future. Under his leadership, BP has defined itself not as an oil company but as an energy company, a redefinition that incorporates renewables as well as oil.

This new view of corporate citizenship spreads daily. Business leaders brought together for the 2001 Aspen Institute's Business Leaders Dialogue 'voiced their deep seated concerns about the increasing alienation felt by many vis-à-vis the practices and culture propagated by globalisation. They felt strongly that businesses must attend to this alienation or risk facing the desperate actions of the many citizens who feel powerless to make change' (Aspen Institute 2001). This approach is reflected in new programmes in business schools from Korea to Costa Rica which are slowly beginning to offer elective courses on social and environmental issues and creating curriculum that engages communities directly (Beyond Grey Pinstripes URL). Another encouraging, if fledgling, development is the growing number of environmental entrepreneurs who have established small sustainable businesses in countries all over the world. Latin American business leaders are recognised annually by the World Resources Institute's New Ventures Forum for the part they play in this important new trend.

Despite the spreading faith in corporate good citizenship, investment analysts are notably unmoved. Corporate leaders have repeatedly complained that analysts, whose interpretations of a company's effectiveness influence stock prices, focus on quarterly earnings. The benefits of investments that are associated with corporate citizenship are not usually evident in the short term, and analysts are often hard-pressed to pay attention to much else; and reputational risk, a significant consideration in corporate board rooms, is not yet on the list of issues that concern analysts.

> Business leaders can have a substantial impact as unlikely allies when they speak up on issues such as climate change and working conditions. They can shift norms and gradually isolate those who do not participate

The corporate vanguard: business activists

There is perhaps no better indication of the inroads made by the notion of corporate social responsibility than the fact that many of the world's corporations have themselves adopted the language of CSR and in many cases formed social responsibility-oriented coalitions. Some, like the Business Environmental Leadership Council, focus on one particular issue while others take on a wide range of CSR problems. The number of these coalitions increases yearly, ranging from the Business Environmental Leadership Council, The Prince of Wales International Business Leaders Forum, and Business for Social Responsibility, to the Brazilian-based Instituto Ethos (URL) (see Box 4.1) and the Israeli group MAALA. 'Southern' corporations such as the Indian Bajaj Auto and the Saudi Dabbagh Group Holding are frequently partners to these efforts, but membership is heavily based in the industrial North, and multinationals such as Shell, Rio Tinto, and Deutsche Bank often provide leadership in several business coalitions simultaneously.

The 160 member-strong World Business Council for Sustainable Development (WBCSD URL), created to provide business input to the 1992 Rio Earth Summit, is among the most proactive of the business activist groups. Its members are drawn from more than 30 countries and 20 major industrial sectors, with a regional network of 35 national and regional business councils and partner organizations located primarily in the developing world. The WBCSD has been a leader in designing multistakeholder dialogue processes, with either an industry or an issue focus. For example, the WBCSD partnered with the World Resources Institute in 2001 to lead a multi-stakeholder process involving over 350 leading experts drawn from business, NGOs, governments, and accounting associations to develop the Greenhouse Gas Protocol, to 'promote internationally accepted greenhouse gas accounting and reporting standards through an open and inclusive process' (WBCSD/WRI 2001). The Protocol has been road tested by over 30 companies in nine countries.

In its 2001 report looking at market-driven sustainability, 'Sustainability through the Market:

Until recently few demands were placed on Brazilian companies to be socially responsible (Queiroz 2002). This has been changing, however, as interest in CSR has been growing (Collier and Waverley 2000), while there has also been a rise in the number of multinational companies locating there. For example, in 1999 a study sponsored by Catholic Relief Services, Oxfam-GB, Save the Children, and World Vision surveyed 300 of the most profitable businesses in the north-east of Brazil, one of the country's poorest regions. This found that nearly two-thirds of these businesses engaged in some sort of social activity (Mello 1999). This change is occurring against a backdrop of inequality and poverty as the richest 10 per cent of Brazilians receive 48 per cent of the national income, while the poorest 10 per cent receive only 1 per cent. Within this vast country, 81.3 per cent of the population live in urban areas and 22 per cent of Brazilians were estimated to be living below the poverty line, even though Brazil had the world's ninth largest gross national income in 2000 (World Bank URL).

One of the clearest expressions of the growing interest in CSR can be seen in organisations of Brazilian business leaders themselves. An example is the Ethos Institute, founded in 1998 by business-people to help companies understand their social responsibilities and incorporate responsible practices into their daily management. Today the Ethos Institute has 544 company members with a collective revenue of R$250 billion, 25 per cent of Brazil's GDP. The Institute's mission is to spread CSR through:

- *the production of guides*—focusing on how businesses can contribute to the community, for example to facilitate the rehabilitation of prisoners, to promote women's health, and to implement a programme of voluntary work;
- *the development of management tools*— including tools for developing an annual CSR report and balance, and the Ethos Indicators of CSR for companies to evaluate and monitor their activities (Ethos Institute 2001a);
- *research for understanding CSR in Brazil*— including a survey of 1,002 consumers about their perceptions of business responsibilities (Ethos Institute 2001b); and
- *promoting the UN Global Compact initiative in Brazil*—by being involved in its launch, providing businesses with information, and also as companies can sign up to the principles via the Ethos Institute

The example of the Ethos Institute demonstrates how Brazilian companies are increasingly recognising the need to consider obligations beyond minimum legal requirements. Furthermore, this example shows how businesses are beginning to respond to this need collectively, leveraging one another to raise standards across business sectors. An important link can be made between the growth of this interest and the rising numbers of multinational corporations locating in Brazil, bringing with them their own understanding of CSR, partly developed by the pressures and expectations of civil society. From within Brazil itself, it seems likely that civil society will increasingly contribute to both the global pressure on multinationals and the focus being given to CSR in Brazil, especially in view of the deep inequalities that the country continues to face.

Jill Timms, Centre for the Study of Global Governance, London School of Economics and Political Science

Seven Keys to Success', the WBCSD (2001) advocates that sustainability will be best achieved through 'a holistic approach, in which supply and demand are viewed as being part of a single system rather than separate entities'. In a recent paper, 'Shaping a Deal for the 2002 Johannesburg Summit', Claude Fussler, who coordinates the WBCSD's input into the World Summit on Sustainable Development, writes: 'Europe, North America and Japan cannot reach sustainability in a world that fails. They need to pioneer a more radical approach that provides sustainable development for all'. He stresses the need to focus on poverty eradication, education and capacity building, innovation and technology development, and the separation of 'economic growth and quality of life from the intense use of natural resources' (Fussler

2001). In addition to projects pertaining to its entire membership, the WBCSD carries out research and stakeholder initiatives in specific areas such as finance, mobility, cement, mining and minerals, and electric utilities.

These business-focused groups have helped to create a norm that reinforces those companies engaged in a variety of CSR practices. Their publications give visibility to companies that use best practices, and they sponsor partnerships that bring the views of CSOs into the boardroom.

'Outsider' CSOs often criticise corporate efforts as being deceptive window-dressing, worse than no action at all because they mislead the public. Most important, critics disagree with the presumption that global corporations with a conscience can mitigate the negative impact of globalisation. They argue that the aim of business is, first and foremost, to make a profit and, even if some companies behave responsibly, there will always be those who can make money by being negligent. Such critics insist that only regulation by governments and international institutions can ensure social responsibility.

CSO groups closer to the business world argue that the global economy is here to stay and laud the efforts of business activists as important steps towards a healthier, fairer world. Business activists believe that CSR practices benefit companies in the long run, if only by limiting exposure to reputational risk. It is clear that business leaders can have a substantial impact as unlikely allies when they speak up on issues such as climate change, sustainability and working conditions. The more business leaders are involved in CSR, the greater is the shift in norms, and the more isolated those who do not participate become.

Civil Society Involvement

Corporations pay attention to their role as corporate citizens largely in response to the pressures from, and resulting partnerships with, civil society. The extent of government involvement in setting standards for corporations is similarly a by-product of civil society activity. Who are the civil society actors? And what do they do?

> The South–North orientation is a problematic dimension to civil society activity: with the best of intentions, advocacy in the North might actually contravene the priorities of Southern actors, especially the workers

Who are the CSOs?

The number of civil society organisations involved in promoting corporate responsibility has increased dramatically in the last five years, and those who have had significant impact vary considerably in reach, tactics, and interests. Some are formally constituted as not-for-profit institutions, while others may be less formally structured, taking the shape of a grass-roots movement or becoming associated with existing social organisations such as faith groups or worker associations. As explored in Chapter 8, these organisational forms are becoming increasingly diverse, a fact which has had a significant impact on the way organisations operate and the actions they take. CSOs have used multiple tools and strategies, often at the same time, sometimes working collaboratively but more often independently. No one formula can be said to guarantee success, and yet success has not been elusive.

Large international CSOs tend to be Northern-based, but often operate in partnership with local branches or independent groups. Some organisations focus on a particular industry (e.g., mining, forestry, apparel), others target a single company (e.g., NikeWatch) or a specific issue (e.g., Transparency International, which concentrates solely on corruption). Many countries have CSOs that broadly represent consumers: For instance, the US-based Interfaith Center on Corporate Responsibility, funded by churches and synagogues, organises shareholders. Other organisations concentrate on a single constituency—children, workers, women—though they may have a broader base of support. Finally, some CSOs are associated with specific tactics, such as taking legal action, initiating direct action, promoting partnerships, or developing monitoring and/or certification processes.

How CSOs promote change

The vast majority of CSOs can be divided into two categories: outsiders and insiders. The outsiders see their role as stirring up public opinion, sometimes staging dramatic actions that place an issue on the public agenda. The insiders take advantage of public awareness, using it to work with governments and corporations to establish programmes for change. Sometimes a single civil society group will have it both ways, simultaneously working with one multi-national corporation to develop monitoring systems or strategies for sustainability and leading a world-wide campaign against another corporation. Often the two groups disparage each other. The insiders see the outsiders as obstructive, sometimes causing more harm than good; the outsiders dismiss the insiders as sell-outs—but change usually happens when there are effective groups working on both sides of the barricades.

The insiders need the outsiders to convey a message of urgency. The threat of direct action has kept many corporations at the table with insiders when discussions might otherwise have broken down. While outsiders force a company to agree to change, for example to reduce waste, insiders work over time with corporations to develop the specifics of a new packaging programme. Negotiating with corporations requires a certain level of trust, and the insiders who are negotiating need to be able to 'deliver' the outsiders, an assurance that the corporations will get something for their agreement. Sometimes CSOs informally agree on the roles that each will play in a specific campaign. Though we can describe a continuum of actions used by outsiders and insiders, it is important to understand that the civil movement

to increase corporate responsibility depends on the ability to use all, or any combination, of these actions.

There is a problematic dimension to civil society activity that must be recognised, however, and that is the South-North orientation. With the best of intentions, advocacy in the North might actually contravene the priorities of Southern actors, especially the workers. An anti-sweatshop campaign, for example, might persuade a company to move its operation rather than reform its practices, terminating jobs that workers desperately need even as they seek to improve conditions. Indeed, research shows that the priorities of sweatshop workers do not always coincide with the Northern demonstrators' demands (Global Alliance URL). Innumerable questions are raised by this dynamic: Should global standards apply in all cases? What weight should be given to local custom and practice? Does a family in Dacca that would starve but for their 12-year-old's income appreciate the demands of anti-child labour demonstrators in London? Can one ask villagers to save trees when selling firewood or harvesting lumber are their only sources of income? And who determines these answers? Northern-based CSOs? Local groups? The two, working in tandem? Should governments and corporations be part of the process? There are few unequivocal answers to these questions. What is important is that CSOs generate a broad-ranging debate. The tensions within civil society and among civil society, corporations, and governments need to be brought into the open so as to a provide a deeper

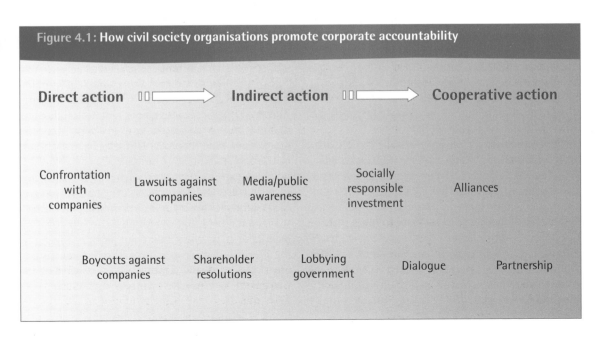

Figure 4.1: How civil society organisations promote corporate accountability

Direct action → Indirect action → Cooperative action

Confrontation with companies

Lawsuits against companies

Media/public awareness

Socially responsible investment

Alliances

Boycotts against companies

Shareholder resolutions

Lobbying government

Dialogue

Partnership

social understanding, which can lay the basis for better policies in the future. In Chapter 2 of this volume, Neera Chandhoke discusses in depth these tensions between global campaigns and local needs, posing questions about where agendas are set and what the implications of a developing global civil society are for issues of representation and political agency.

Direct action

Successful direct action campaigns work precisely because they attract the attention of the media and challenge the reputation and credibility of the corporation. And yet the media can be a fickle audience: a tactic used repetitively can fail to qualify as 'news'. Three examples—a sit-in and two boycotts—provide insight into the effectiveness of direct action.

In December 1996, Julia 'Butterfly' Hill, an Earth First volunteer, climbed into a redwood tree in California. Expecting to be there for three weeks, she settled in on a platform built among the branches of 'Luna' (as her tree came to be known), 51 metres above the ground. She was there for two years. When Hill finally came down, an agreement had been negotiated with Pacific Lumber to ensure the preservation of the tree and the surrounding forest. Civil society organisations made certain that Hill was as well provided for as possible, and a parade of visiting celebrities ensured regular press coverage. Pacific Lumber fed the publicity, sending security forces to harass Hill, dispatching helicopters to buzz her lofty position, and repeatedly threatening to cut Luna down with Hill in it (Hill 2000).

Sam LaBudde, an environmentalist who signed on as a cook on a tuna boat in 1989, recorded a videotape of dolphins being drowned and crushed by purse seine fishing nets. That tape launched the Save the Dolphin campaign in 1990, which included a broad-based boycott of tuna. The result was that the largest corporations in the industry—Starkist, Bumblebee, and Chicken of the Sea—now sell tuna labelled 'dolphin-safe', and laws governing tuna fishing are in force in the Eastern Tropical Pacific (Boycott News URL).

> Successful direct action works precisely because it attracts the attention of the media and challenges the reputation and credibility of the corporation – but a tactic used repetitively can fail to qualify as 'news'

While the efforts of international CSOs often win global headlines, lesser-known locally based groups are frequently the force behind successful direct actions. For some time, workers at Del Monte's Kenyan plantation had expressed a number of complaints against their employer: sub-standard worker housing, violence in protecting the facility from a perceived risk of theft, disregard for community needs and customs. Local CSOs organised around these issues and, teamed with Italian CSOs, launched a multinational boycott of Del Monte products in November 2000. The company responded swiftly, developing a consensus-building approach to management-employee relations, reviewing worker pay and all job descriptions, and instituting a new housing policy, leading to the cancellation of the boycott in March 2001.[1]

These examples attest to the power of direct action. Many corporations understand that bad publicity can have a long-lasting effect. Julia Hill's name has long been absent from the evening news, but people still remember that a young woman lived in a tree to fight Pacific Lumber. Boycotts of products not only have an impact on immediate sales but affect brand loyalty and consumer choice long after the action has been called off, as Del Monte was to see in the wake of the Kenyan action. Today, the mere threat of a widespread boycott can induce reform. Note, for example, the threatened boycotts of apparel companies in recent years. Once consumers were aware of working conditions in offshore apparel factories and direct action loomed, manufacturers accepted responsibility for the practices of even their subcontractors and set about instituting reforms.

At the same time, enforcing agreements that emerge from boycotts and occupations of company property can be difficult. Pacific Lumber cannot cut down Luna—that is something that cannot be hidden—but it is far more difficult to check that fishermen are abiding by the agreement to ensure dolphin-safe tuna. Fishing boats have been moved into areas not covered by the laws, and US owners have sold their fleets to companies

---

[1] *E-mail to the authors from Toby Kent, 12 March 2002.*

based in nations that have less enforcement capability. Furthermore, agreements are based on trust, and trust is often lacking after a long adversarial campaign. In order to ensure that reforms last, civil society has become involved in certification and monitoring (see the section on monitoring below).

Legal actions and formal complaints

Another route civil society groups have taken to confront companies directly is the legal system. In the last 20 years, lawsuits filed by CSOs have added considerable muscle to campaigns to hold corporations accountable for their actions in the social, political, and environmental arenas. In these suits, international CSOs are often the plaintiffs, though they sometimes organise the legal action for workers or other civil society actors affected by the targeted corporate policy or practice.

While the legal route can be costly and time-consuming, both the process and the outcomes have identified further tools that can be used to change corporate practice. Some court challenges proceed along the axis of constitutional law. For instance, according to a Report of the UN Special Rapporteur on Human Rights and the Environment (United Nations 1994), up to 100 national constitutions guarantee rights to a clean and healthy environment, or oblige the state to prevent environmental harm.

Court cases to test such constitutional provisions have been successful in holding companies accountable because of contractual arrangements they have made with governments. In a landmark decision in 1991, the Supreme Court of India ruled that every individual has the fundamental right to the 'enjoyment of pollution-free water and air'. As a result, the government, state-owned industries, and private companies can be held accountable for environmental degradation.[2] In 1993 in Costa Rica, the Supreme Court ruled that placing a dump in the plaintiff community's neighbourhood violated the right to a healthy environment.[3] As a result of a 1994 decision of the Philippine Supreme Court,[4] provisions of timber licences require logging corporations to respect Filipinos' right to a healthy environment.

Provisions of international law have also been invoked to expose corporations that violate universal norms and standards. Suits based on human rights treaties and International Labour Organisation (ILO) conventions have had some success in this respect. Several oil companies have been sued in domestic courts by national and international CSOs for violations of human rights in other countries. In June 2001, the US-based International Labor Rights Fund brought suit in US federal court on behalf of eleven villagers in Aceh, Indonesia, against the ExxonMobil Corporation for human rights abuses. The suit alleges that the multinational oil company, the largest in the world, provided barracks and equipment to state security services who kidnapped, murdered, and tortured villagers in the embattled Aceh region, where the company has a large natural gas field. The government and Aceh residents have been at odds over self-determination issues for decades.[5]

In order for cases derived from international law to enter most states' domestic legal systems, there must be enabling legislation. For example, the US Alien Tort Claims Act (a law dating from 1789) allows foreign plaintiffs to bring action against foreign defendants in cases of serious violations of international law. In the United Kingdom, courts have recognised that, in cases of human rights violations when the plaintiff cannot act in his own country, claims may be brought in the UK if the company has its headquarters there (the case

> While most legal actions can take years to adjudicate, they heighten activist, public and corporate awareness. Furthermore, court judgments can create precedents and provide interpretations of the law that have far-reaching implications

---

[2] *Subhash Kumar v. State of Bihar (India)AIR 1991 S.C.420.*

[3] *Constitutional Chamber of the Supreme Court (Costa Rica), Vote Number 3705, 30 July 1993.*

[4] *Minors Oposas v. Secretary of the Department of Environment and Natural Resources (Philippines) 33 I.L.M. 173, 1994.*

[5] *This case follows on the still pending cases brought by Burmese and US NGOs on behalf of Burmese nationals against the Unocal Corporation for torture, forced labour, and extrajudicial killing associated with the construction of a gas pipeline in violation of California's state constitution and unfair business practice law National Coalition Government of the Union of Burma (NCGUB) v. Unocal, Inc. (Myanmar), 176 F.R.D. 329 (C.D. Cal. 1997); John Doe I et al. v. Unocal Corp. (USA), 963 F. Supp 880 (C.D. Cal. 1997); John Doe I v. Unocal Corp. (USA), 110 F. Supp. 2d 1294 (C.D. Cal. 2000); John Doe I, et al. vs. ExxonMobil Corporation, ExxonMobil Oil Indonesia Inc., Mobil Corporation, Mobil Oil Corporation, and PT Arun Lng Co. (USA), U District Court, District of Columbia, 2001. While still on appeal, the rulings to date have validated the basis for the suits.*

concerned Cape plc for its 'duty of care' responsibilities to the employees of its South African subsidiary). These actions also address the question of liability on the part of a parent company for the actions of its subsidiaries or partners.

While most legal actions can take years to adjudicate, thus failing to generate the more immediate impact that can result from direct action campaigns,[6] they heighten awareness not only among civil society advocates and the public but within companies as well. Furthermore, court judgments can create precedents and provide interpretations of the law that have far-reaching implications.

Information and reputation

The publication by CSOs of reliable and specific information has been a powerful tool in promoting change, increasing public awareness and bolstering an array of direct and indirect civil society action. Information campaigns target a number audiences, from individual consumers to whole groups of stakeholders: a wide variety of 'green guides' inform the purchasing patterns of individuals or families, for instance, while certain organisations focus on uncovering and reporting information about the entire range of corporate activity so that stakeholders may insist on action en masse.

The not-for-profit Essential Information (URL), founded by Ralph Nader in 1982, publishes 'Multinational Monitor', a monthly that tracks corporate activity from a standpoint of social responsibility (Multinational Monitor URL). The annual 'Ten Worst Corporations' features reports on a selection of companies known to have engaged in abusive practices over the previous year, with an attempt to include in the list corporations that have exploited consumers, caused environmental harm, defrauded the government, disregarded labour rights, and so on.

> The publication of reliable and specific information has been a powerful tool in promoting change, increasing public awareness and bolstering an array of direct and indirect civil society action

Information based in scientific research can be a powerful tool. Building on a movement launched in Europe, scientists at the Union of Concerned Scientists (UCS) and Environmental Defense began in the 1990s to inform the American public of the extent to which antibiotic additives in animal feed fosters antibiotic resistance among human consumers. Some Americans began to seek out antibiotic-free poultry, and in February 2002 leading chicken producers Tyson Foods, Perdue Farms, and Foster Farms announced that they would remove most of the antibiotics used in their feed. Similarly, fast-food chains such as McDonald's and Wendy's announced they would no longer purchase poultry treated with Baytril, an antibiotic that is particularly important in human medical treatment. It is important to note, however, that several of the biggest poultry producers in the US were not parties to these decisions, and the scientists at UCS and Environmental Defense feel there is still much work to be done (UCS 2002).

The events following UNESCO's declaration of the Laguna San Ignacio in Mexico a World Heritage Site provide another example. Soon after the UN's decision, Mitsubishi Corporation and the Mexican government announced plans to use 62,000 acres of the reserve for a massive salt plant. The US-based National Resources Defense Council (NRDC) brought together an international coalition of environmentalists, fishermen, scientists, and consumer organisations. Scientists produced and validated information about the negative impact of the salt plant on the environment; economists demonstrated that there were better economic uses for the area. Armed with scientifically sound information, NRDC and its allies rallied more than a million consumers to write to Mitsubishi and an array of dignitaries to visit the site. Ultimately, representatives of Mitsubishi and the Mexican government agreed to meet with CSOs and to change their plans.

Of course, the effectiveness of any public education campaign depends in no small part on the

---

[6] *The United States Supreme Court accepted jurisdiction in 2001 of a case against the Shell and BP oil companies instigated in 1996, in which the plaintiffs argued that the two companies were consulted before two activists were tortured and murdered in Nigeria. The family of Ken Saro-Wiwa filed suit against Shell's complicity in the Nigerian security forces' brutality against Ogoni protesters and the execution of Ken Saro-Wiwa and eight others by a court proceeding under the military dictatorship in 1995 (Wiwa et al. v. Royal Dutch Shell, Case No. 96-8386, S. D. N.Y., 1996). Chevron has more recently been taken to court in 1999 over practices which violate human rights in Nigeria (Bowoto et al. v. Chevron Corporation), Case No. 99-2506 [N.D. Cal, 1999]. The cases continue to work their way through the legal system. On 28 February 2002, the Federal District Court rejected Shell's motion to dismiss the Saro-Wiwa case. The trial is moving forward to the discovery phase of evidence gathering.*

ability of its organisers to threaten the reputation of a corporation or industry. All too often, those in the corporate world will initiate real change only when the other option is real loss; and the loss of reputation generally translates into loss of revenue.

Investor action: socially responsible investing

Religious groups such as the Christian Scientists have long maintained investment portfolios that exclude companies or industries engaged in activities they deem morally untenable—the production of alcohol, cigarettes, military hardware. Investor action first gained widespread attention in the 1980s, though, when student activists in the United States began to demand that universities sell stock in corporations with South African operations, and the resulting campaign led to the withdrawal of more than 100 multinationals. Socially responsible investing (SRI) has evolved since, and it now takes two forms. The first focuses on negative screening—refusing to buy stock in companies associated with harmful practices—whereas the second involves actively seeking out stock in businesses known for good practices or for products that directly contribute to sustainability.

In the 1990s the amount of money invested with socially responsible funds skyrocketed in the United States, rising from $40 billion to $2.2 trillion between 1985 and 2000 according to the Social Investment Forum (Balmaceda and Larson 2000: 35). By 2000 one in every ten dollars invested in the United Kingdom and in the United States was linked to some kind of social criteria. An infrastructure of researchers, databases, and reports is now in place. Between 1995 and 1999, the Domini 400 fund, the best known of the US funds, recorded a total return of 575 per cent, outperforming the Standard and Poors 500, which returned 463 per cent in the same period. Since 1999, investors in the US have been able to track the Dow Sustainability Group Index, while investors in the UK can follow socially responsible companies on the FTSE4good index. The 1995 Pensions Act in the United Kingdom required that, as of 2000, pension fund trustees needed to take into account 'social, ethical and environmental issues' and to report annually on how they have done so, if at all (Cowe 2001: 8). Clearly the commitment of pension and other mutual investment funds to these issues significantly increases the impact of SRI. Moreover, these funds require reporting on social responsibility from all companies they invest in, whether or not they have come to the attention of civil society organisers.

Nor are social investment opportunities confined to the West. The United Global Unifem Singapore Fund was established in 1999 by the Singapore National Committee for UNIFEM, the UN fund for women, and UOB Asset Management, the largest unit trust fund manager in the country (SocialFunds 2002). It not only screens investments for women's equity but donates a third of its 1.5 per cent annual management fee to UNIFEM. The ability of CSOs to

Above left: Information campaign against the use of anti-biotics in animal feed, which increases anti-biotic resistance in human consumers. © Union of Concerned Scientists.

Above right: Laguna San Ignacio, famous for its gray whales, was saved from pollution by a massive salt plant when Mitsubishi was persuaded to withdraw its investment. © Frank Balthis.

shape investor action is perhaps one of the most powerful tools these organisations have. As shareholders direct more and more of their funds to corporations that meet certain CSR standards, corporate practices will change.

Investor action: shareholder resolutions

During the South Africa divestment campaign and the Vietnam War, shareholder initiatives calling for the withdrawal from South Africa or a cessation of the manufacture of chemicals such as napalm attracted considerable popular support and press attention. The Interfaith Center on Corporate Responsibility (ICCR), a major player in the South Africa campaign in the1980s, remains an active promoter of shareholder action on global issues, and each spring at the time of annual meetings attracts publicity for one or more of its main issues. The current priorities of the ICCR include issues of corporate governance and responsibility, environmental sustainability, global finance, international health, and militarism. Often the group's resolutions call simply for an implementation of a code of conduct or for the publication of information about a certain corporation's activities. In 2001, one resolution called on Citibank to report on its business in Myanmar; another called on BE Aerospace to implement the MacBride Principles, a set of fair employment guidelines, in its facilities in Northern Ireland. The ICCR is but one of a number of organisations in the US and Europe that focus public attention on corporate behaviour and demand that corporations explain and defend their practices in public. For example, Responsible Wealth, a network of influential and affluent Americans, uses shareholder resolutions to focus attention on fair taxes, a living wage, corporate accountability, and broader asset ownership. While few of the shareholder resolutions succeed, corporations will go to some lengths to head off such resolutions. The effect is both to change corporate practices and to restrain corporations from taking actions likely to provoke resolutions.

> The ability to shape investor action is one of the most powerful tools civil society organisations have. As shareholders direct more of their funds to corporations that meet certain standards, corporate practices will change

Partnerships

In the past decade, increasing numbers of CSOs and corporations have seen the wisdom of forming partnerships to advance social responsibility. Some are more successful than others, and many are fraught with tensions and difficulty. Partnerships vary in form, membership, and purpose. Some promote community development while others are designed to raise specific industry standards, monitor manufacturing processes, or certify that production methods entail no labour or environmental abuse. Many were set up after direct action was taken, or threatened, by civil society. McDonald's, for example, formed a waste reduction partnership with Environmental Defense after thousands of children mailed to the company the environmentally damaging Styrofoam 'clamshells' in which it formerly packaged its hamburgers. The partnership's effort has saved 200,000 tons of waste (McDonald's 2002).

Some civil society groups are critical of partnerships, taking the view that, if business is involved, the results cannot be good. They attack partnerships as business' way of coopting civil society in the globalisation process. CSO partners argue that multinational corporations are a permanent part of the landscape, and the more responsible corporate policies are, the better it will be for workers and the planet. A further argument is that partnerships develop extragovernmental standards, and the difficulties in passing and enforcing legislation in resource-strapped countries suggest that efforts to change norms without government involvement makes a difference and can ultimately lead to legislation.

Increasingly, partnerships involving CSOs are designed to bring about industry-wide reform. The mining industry provides one good example, as it is currently involved in one of the most comprehensive multi-stakeholder partnerships. Leaders in the mining industry concluded that access to both land and capital, essential to their work, was threatened because of the effective actions of local CSO groups worldwide. In April 2000, acting on behalf of the group of ten international mining companies that formed the Global Mining Initiative, the World

GLOBAL CIVIL SOCIETY AND CORPORATE RESPONSIBILITY   Melanie Beth Oliviero and Adele Simmons

Business Council for Sustainable Development (WBCSD) commissioned the International Institute for Environment and Development (IIED) to undertake an independent research and consultation process on the mining and minerals sector. The Mining, Minerals and Sustainable Development (MMSD) project brought together an unprecedented number of stakeholders, industry representatives, academics, government officials, and others. The project was supervised by an assurance group of 25 experienced individuals from different stake-holder groups and regions to safeguard the independence of the research. At the time of writing, the MMSD project aimed at having recommendations in place for the World Summit on Sustainable Development in Johannesburg in August 2002.

The mining and minerals project proved to be controversial and complex. In some regions and with some stakeholders there has been considerable engagement and a useful exchange of ideas. In other places and with other interest groups the response was much less positive, and in some cases there had even been an outright refusal to engage.

Governments have also taken the initiative. The concept of partnership was a favourite of the Clinton administration. The US President's Council on Sustainable Development brought together business, CSOs, and government agencies, and the council made a series of recommendations to each.

Pressing his luck, Clinton also convened apparel industry leaders, civil society groups, and trade unions in the short-lived Apparel Industry Partnership. The group, reborn as the Fair Labor Association (FLA), got off to a difficult start with the withdrawal of the Union of Needletrades Industrial and Textile Employees (UNITE) and a handful of other CSOs. Furthermore, it was shortly challenged by the creation of a Washington-based Workers Rights Coalition (WRC), a group widely support by students across the US and generally critical of any organisation that included industry representation. By 2002, however, the two groups had developed a relationship that, while not always easy, has allowed them to occasionally combine their efforts. The WRC has the independence to identify abuses and, if necessary,

> The partnership approach is still a work-in-progress. Again, it seems that both believers and sceptics among civil society organisations are necessary to ensure that a partnership brings significent reults

bring them to the attention of the public. At the same time, only the FLA has the capacity to establish monitoring systems and the relationship with corporations necessary to design and enforce remediation programmes. One hundred and seventy four universities have joined the FLA, in turn widening its scope by bringing some of their own licensees from outside the apparel industry to the organisations.

In the UK, the Blair government launched the Ethical Trading Initiative (ETI) in 1998, allying multinational companies with unions and CSOs. Rather than promoting a certification process, the Initiative applies best practices and develops internal monitoring and external verification procedures. It incorporates social and environmental benchmarks in published 'risk assessments', and members commit to business ethics, corporate responsibility, human rights, and workers' rights (including the end of child labour). The Body Shop, the International Confederation of Free Trade Unions, and Save the Children are among ETI's members.

At the multinational level, the World Bank has been a leader, a convener, and a partner. The Bank's Business Partners for Development now includes a network of 120 organisations, across 20 different countries, that aim to support and promote strategic examples of partnerships involving government, civil society, and business. The partnerships are voluntary, and the parties agree on mutual objectives, pool resources and share risk, and respond to community interests for a more efficient distribution of resources (Business Partnership Development 2002: 5). Local CSOs are key to these relationships because they bring an understanding of what is needed, know how to implement projects at local levels, command community respect, and can mobilise large numbers of people.

Partnerships between civil society and corporations are voluntary and based to some extent on trust. Both parties in the end move forward in an environment outside of government regulation. This approach leads to greater flexibility and generally a more informed perspective on the part of both civil society and business. Recent studies by the World Bank, The Conference Board, and international CSOs are helping to clarify when partnerships work best, what it takes to maintain an effective partnership, and what the added value of such partnerships is.[7]

Standard setting

Civil society is pushing the concept of partnership yet further, attempting to establish social reporting instruments comparable to the financial reporting instruments now standard throughout the world. Some CSOs are attempting to establish voluntary, industry-specific reporting mechanisms that measure the social and environmental performance of companies. Other CSOs labour to establish a process of social audits and the certification of auditors. A few CSOs propose an instrument that would transcend national boundaries and maintain a professional uniformity from country to country and business sector to business sector.

Coalition for Environmentally Responsible Societies (CERES) is the author of one standard-setting initiative. CERES, which came to prominence in the wake of the 1989 Exxon Valdez disaster in Alaska, is a coalition of environmentalists, corporate executives, and concerned citizens who have promoted an agenda for environmental sustainability. Its Global Reporting Initiative (GRI) emerged in response to the increasing number of examples of environmental and human rights abuses committed by corporations, incidents which have resulted in no penalty or even challenge by national or international agencies. The GRI, which is supported by major corporations and professional associations in the Americas, the European Union, Asia, and South Africa, is building a consensus for a voluntary standard of corporate reporting requirements that transcends specific industrial or geographic sectors (GRI 2000).

> Perhaps the most significant business-civil society interactions in the last decade have occured in developing valid and reliable systems for monitoring and certifying corporate performance

The international trade union movement plays a vital role in the drive for uniformity. In the area of workers' rights in particular, labour unions and the ILO are seeking to harmonise standards. The ILO is unique among intergovernmental agencies in that it is comprised of representatives from government, civil society (labour), and the private sector each with equal votes.

With so many kinds of groups working on social responsibility issues, tensions among them are inevitable. Conflicts arise not just between advocates of direct action and advocates of partnerships, but among rival local groups serving different constituencies, among international groups with different world views, and between advocates of international standards and communities for whom a corporate presence may mean the difference between a regular wage and hunger. One of the greatest challenges before civil society will always be to continually strike a balance among the legitimate needs of the various constituencies and audiences, while trying not to allow the inevitable tensions to stand in the way of getting important work done.

Monitoring: A Case Study of Civil Society in Action

Of course, having standards that reliably indicate social and environmental conditions is only the first step. The auditing process employed must also be a valid and reliable methodological approach. Perhaps the most significant business-CSO interactions in the last decade have occurred in developing systems for monitoring and certifying corporate performance. This section focuses on the monitoring methods that have evolved in response to civil society demands for corporate accountability. It also sounds the cautionary note that having a monitoring system in place does not necessarily mean that corporate practice is reliably and consistently regulated.

Why monitoring?

When one examines the phenomenon of global civil society, the parallels to the growth of multinational corporations in an integrated global economy are

[7] The World Bank's 'Learning to Partner: Engaging Civil Society' can be found at its website by clicking through to 'NGOs and Civil Society' and then to 'Key Documents' (World Bank URL). Information regarding The Conference Board's 'Innovative Public-Private Partnerships' series is available at the TCB website by clicking on 'Corporate Citizenship' and scrolling down to 'Publications' at http://www.conference-board.org. The International Labor Rights Fund, with other analysts, has explored a variety of approaches in a collection titled 'Workers in the Global Economy' which can be accessed on their website http://www.laborrights.org.

manifest. As companies operate through extensive production chains involving a series of suppliers, processors, and distributors, so are workers, consumers, rights advocates, and environmentalists from different countries similarly allied as stakeholders in these companies' operations. To the degree that private companies have a direct impact on air and water quality, the safety and health of workers, and the vitality of the local economy, it is in the public interest for companies to be held accountable.

Monitoring may take several forms, but at the core it is the delivery mechanism for the transparency so essential to any society that aspires to be open and free. The process usually focuses on two broad areas: working conditions, including freedom of association, and the environment. Effective monitoring depends primarily on three elements: agreed standards, usually set through consultation among CSOs, government, and a company or industry; a genuinely transparent and inclusive process; and monitors who have credibility with corporations as well as workers and their representatives.

Civil society has assumed a central role in monitoring the implementation of agreed standards. Global CSOs can, working with local counterparts, report on the extent to which companies or whole industries are enforcing codes and standards adopted in several countries. When developing countries are strapped for financial and human resources, they often do not have the capacity to monitor companies on a regular basis. Moreover, monitoring is still a work-in-progress and, as lessons are learned about how best to monitor the variety of corporations and industries in a number of countries, the flexibility of civil society is an advantage. While civil society is filling an important gap through its role in monitoring and standard setting, in a perfect world this work might be led by official international agencies or governments.

Monitoring of what?

How do we know that a company is following agreed-upon standards in carrying out its business operations? That question drives civil society activists concerned with the measurement of corporate behaviour. One need only to look at the Enron scandal in the United States to see that even institutionalised methods of accountability (e.g., compliance with domestic regulations and oversight by a board of directors) and the presence of an active and unfettered press can fail to prevent massive fraud and deception. Civil society faces a daunting task, not the least part of which is establishing what should be monitored and what constitutes corporate responsibility.

Standards, which include codes of conduct, certification schemes, laws, and regulations seeking to ensure socially responsible corporate practice, cover a variety of subject areas. Some standards are broadly generic, seeking to ensure adherence to certain measures of disclosure and reporting. Other standards are more specific, requiring multinational corporations to report that certain benchmarks have been met. Company codes of conduct, for example, have increasingly incorporated 'triple bottom line' accounting principles, measuring performance by social and environmental criteria, in additional to traditional financial parameters (Elkington 1998). It is important to keep in mind that such codes are voluntary pledges, however. The standards to which they aspire have, to date, been loosely defined. This has led to numerous efforts to develop more precise indicators that can measure social and environmental performance.

Most businesses publish a company code of conduct. These internal monitoring guidelines may be articulated as a set of values woven into company practices or explicitly embodied in formal documentation of company guidelines. Company codes of conduct typically address fundamental values such as freedom of association and the right to collective bargaining, rights codified in ILO conventions and international human rights treaties. But there remains a considerable distance between aspiration and achievement. Civil society pressure has closed the gap somewhat by insisting that the company's suppliers and subcontractors, often locally or regionally owned and managed factories, also recognise those basic rights. The challenge of monitoring working conditions in urban slums or

> Effective monitoring depends primarily on three elements: agreed standards; a genuinely transparent and inclusive process; and monitors who have credibility with corporations as well as workers

Above: A supermarket selection of certified products. © Denyse Kowalske.

remote rural areas remains but, thanks to CSOs, the responsibility for ensuring that monitoring takes place—even in remote locations—is increasingly a matter which multinational companies must address. Codes of conduct can also be industry-wide. The American Apparel Manufacturers Association created its Worldwide Responsible Apparel Production Certification Program (WRAP) in 1998 in the wake of heightened public scrutiny of sweatshop conditions in the apparel and footwear industries. As with many individual company codes, the focus is on standard labour practices such as forced labour, child labour, compensation and benefits, health and safety, and freedom of association. Other sectors have adopted similar frameworks, such as the chemical industry's Responsible Care plan (triggered by the Union Carbide disaster in Bhopal, India), and bilateral agreements such as the US-UK code governing their mining and extraction sectors.

While these industry codes specify core labour and safety issues addressed at the international level, multinationals routinely apply compliance with local laws as their standard—another practice with which civil society groups take issue. Many developing nations have weak judicial and legislative branches, and their laws do not meet international standards. The less rigorous labour requirements and lack of enforcement of international standards can be an effective recruitment tool for governments seeking foreign investment, and multinational corporations respond because using local law and practice as a benchmark can be advantageous to a company's financial bottom line (see Box 4.2). The competition among low-wage nations, in effect, has produced a 'race to the bottom', and a victory by any one state may not last long.

A monitoring system can also be established as a corollary to an independent set of standards mutually agreed upon by companies, CSOs (which may include employees), and/or government. A major difficulty lies in developing criteria that are scientifically valid. If the initial work is done without input from workers on the shop floor or members of the community, there is considerable danger that the monitoring process will not convey the true impact of corporate practice on working conditions or the physical environment.

The most common manifestation of such standards are certification schemes. The Forest Stewardship Council (FSC), for example, was founded in 1993 through the leadership of international CSOs such as the World Wildlife Fund and Greenpeace. Headquartered in Oaxaca, Mexico (soon to move to Europe), it has a presence in more than 50 countries. The certification targets both the management of the forest resource and the production of lumber. Certification is based on ten principles and criteria agreed upon by a broad constituency. They include conservation goals (e.g., selective cutting rather than clear cutting), preservation of wildlife habitat, and respect for the rights of indigenous peoples and the well-being of local communities.

Similarly, the Marine Stewardship Council targets the sustainability of managed fisheries and seeks to generate a market demand for certified products. The International Federation of Organic Agricultural Movements developed an accreditation programme in 1992 to qualify certifiers of organic products, a programme that has been credited with a huge increase of the market share of organic products. The Fair Trade Labeling Organizations International, which concentrates on cooperatives of small producers (e.g., coffee growers), targets importers and works to guarantee a minimum purchase price and advance partial payment to growers against future sales.

Certification works best where the products are marketed in economically strong consumer societies, but the process can be undermined by industry groups bent on confusing consumers. In response to the successful inroads of the Forest Stewardship Council, for example, three industry groups in Europe, Canada, and the US have established opposing and weaker standards, notable for their lack of transparency (Conroy 2001: 8).

Both civil society groups and corporations (particularly in the apparel industry) have raised concerns that certification falls short as an effective system for monitoring labour practices. Manu-

One notable case of civil society attacking the practice of placing production where wages are low and standards are lax is the 1999 lawsuit filed by a coalition of CSOs alleging abuses of apparel workers.

The US trade union, UNITE, and NGOs Global Exchange, Sweatshop Watch, and the Asian Law Caucus brought a suit against 18 apparel companies operating in the Mariana Islands in the western Pacific, a US protectorate, which in turn meant that the case would be tried in US courts. The companies, including Donna Karan and J. Crew, were accused of violating a law that prohibits the use of forced labour, and laws restricting overtime, and wrongly advertising their products as sweatshop-free, among other things. In two associated cases, class action suits have been filed involving 30,000 garment workers, most of them women from China, Philippines, and Bangladesh who were kept under conditions of indentured servitude. A settlement was reached with a majority of the companies which provides for compensatory payments and ongoing monitoring. The Gap, Levi Strauss, and Target, among other retailers, continue to contend that they should not be held responsible for the actions of subcontractors. The case is scheduled to go to trial before a US federal court in 2002.

facturers point out that they contract with thousands of different factories all over the world and it is impractical, if not impossible, to certify each one. CSOs know that certification of a factory does not prevent banned practices from being put back in place after the plant has passed muster.

Governments are also engaged in standard-setting and monitoring through both local laws and their obligation to ensure that organisations operating in a country are working within the framework of international agreements. A number of former Communist countries still have labour laws that are consistent with those sought by most international groups, while many other countries have very weak laws. The problem, however, is that many governments do not have the capacity or the will to enforce even existing legislation.

The impact of international laws and treaties varies from country to country. Governments can—and some do—implement ILO standards in domestic laws

that apply to companies, obliging them to comply. CSOs can strategically target government to act on behalf of society to hold companies accountable.

For example, women worker groups throughout Central America mobilised in the mid-1990s around a campaign for their own ethical code to apply to Export Processing (free trade) Zones. The Maria Elena Cuadra Women's Movement in Nicaragua secured some 30,000 signatories endorsing the campaign's list of labour and other human rights protections. These included non-discrimination provisions, health and safety standards, job security, rights to organise and bargain collectively, registration with the social security system, and respect for minimum wage and overtime laws. This effort culminated in the promulgation of a ministerial decree from the Nicaraguan Labour Ministry in 1998 adopting the code as law, and the next day all 23 *maquiladoras* (duty-free assembly-for-export factories in Mexico and Central America characterised by low wages and weak or non-existent environmental and labour regulations) in the zone signed an agreement to abide by the code. While this law covers only manufacturing for export, its existence provides an opening for further advocacy to extend the law's benefits to domestic market production.

As this review of monitoring mechanisms suggests, there are multiple routes to measuring corporate social responsibility—and therein lies another dilemma. The profusion of standards can create great confusion as well as opportunity for deliberate obfuscation. As Table 4.1 depicts, codes as varied as the United Nations 'Global Compact' and the international faith-based CSOs' 'Principles for Global Corporate Responsibility: Benchmarks' seek to track essentially the same things. And this comparison is only a snapshot; it is by no means exhaustive. Given the variability of these overlapping and often competing standards, it is important to recall that CERES's Global Reporting Initiative (described above) does not replicate existing approaches but aims to harmonise them under a single framework of reporting. The GRI is the inheritor of previous cross-sectoral efforts and appears to be the only one positioned to establish comparability among the myriad of approaches.

Monitoring by whom?

The monitoring of these multiple and various codes is performed by four different kinds of monitors: internal company personnel; external personnel hired to provide a monitoring service; external monitors who undertake independent evaluations; and public interest watchdogs.

Internal monitors

As most codes are self-imposed standards, companies consider monitoring compliance as an internal routine process. In recent years these issues have taken on a higher profile within companies and whole new divisions have been created. British Telecom-munications has a Corporate Reputation and Social Policy division, Shell has a Social Accountability Team, and Nike has a Vice President for Corporate Social Responsibility.

CSOs regard the claims of internal monitors as unreliable, however, arguing that, if companies are confident that they are meeting standards of accountability on labour, health and safety, and environmental protection, then they have nothing to lose and only positive reputation to gain if their findings are validated by an independent third party. Corporate claims that independent monitors would jeopardise trade secrets are hard to take seriously given the experience of the apparel industry, where rival companies often share the same subcontractor. Rather than fear violations of confidentiality, three major footwear manufacturers are even cooperating to assert their combined clout in empowering workers to press local factory owners to protect health and safety on the job (see Box 4.3).

Non-independent external monitors

In the face of demands from civil society for independent verification, corporations often hire an outside firm to perform the service. With the growth in awareness about CSR, a burgeoning industry has developed in the fields of social auditing, risk assurance, and needs assessment for a variety of environmental and social standards. Major financial accounting firms such as PricewaterhouseCoopers (PwC) and KPMG have viewed this as a natural extension of their auditing and consulting expertise. They offer advisory services on such issues as sustainability, global warming, and climate change,

and they perform assessments of supply chains and management systems.

CSOs see a number of problems with this approach to monitoring. Regardless of the fact that the auditing company has been brought in from outside, the hiring corporation still determines the terms of reference. Furthermore, a firm that is qualified to perform financial audits is not necessarily skilled at social auditing; social variables often cannot be reduced to a quantitative calculation. Finally, as the Arthur Anderson-Enron case shows, the desire to retain the corporation as a client compromises the chances of an independent investigation.

CSO scepticism of an auditing firm's ability to monitor social responsibility is based on more than theory. In 2000, a CSR researcher accompanying Pricewaterhouse-Cooper's auditors on inspection visits in China and Korea detailed a number of violations of labour laws and codes of conduct that the PwC team had overlooked (O'Rourke 2002). PwC failed to catch violations of wage and overtime, recommended a way to circumvent paying overtime wages, and failed to note that workers were exposed to hazardous chemicals with no shoes, gloves, or eye protection. They interviewed only workers identified by managers, and in some cases it was the managers who filled in wage and hour data in the PwC spreadsheets.

> True independence from the company being monitored, familiarity with local languages, and knowing when and where to conduct interviews, are some of the key factors in effective monitoring

Independent external monitors

As the PwC critique indicates, the criteria for effective monitoring are fairly well identified. True independence from the company being monitored, familiarity with local languages, and knowing when and where to conduct interviews, are just some of the key factors. Taking nothing at face value is equally important: The fact that factory workers have access to first-aid kits is meaningless, for instance, if the kits are empty.

For more specialised expertise, training is required. The UK-based Institute for Social and Ethical Accountability has established a set of professional credentials which a certified social auditor must possess. These process standards, known as the Accountability 1000 (or AA1000), have been derived

Table 4.1: Comparison of selected corporate social responsibility–related standards[a]

CSR-related issues referenced[b]	APEC Business Code of Conduct (Draft)	Caux Principles for Business	Global Reporting Initiative[c]	Global Sullivan Principles	OECD Guidelines for Multinational Enterprises	Principles for Global Corporate Responsibility	Social Accountability 8000 (SA8000)	UN Global Compact
Accountability								
Transparency	•	•	•	•	•	•	•	•
Stakeholders/stakeholder engagement	•	•	•		•	•		
Reporting								
Performance related to standard			•	•	•	•	•	•
Environmental performance			•		•	•		
Human rights issues			•				•	
Monitoring verification								
Performance related to standard		•					•	
Environmental performance		•		•	•			
Human rights issues			•			•	•	•
Standard applies to								
Company	•	•	•	•	•	•	•	
Business partners		•		•	•	•	•	
Business Conduct								
General CSR								
Compliance with the law	•	•		•	•	•	•	
Competitive conduct (e.g., price fixing, collusion, anti-trust)	•	•		•	•	•		
Corruption and bribery	•							
Political activities	•				•			•
Proprietary information/ intellectual property rights	•	•		•	•			
Whistleblowers					•	•		
Conflicts of interest						•		
Community Involvement								
Broad/general reference	•	•		•		•		
Community economic development		•			•	•		•
Employment of local and/or underutilised workers		•		•	•	•		
Philanthropy		•	•			•		
Corporate Governance								
Broad/general reference	•	•	•		•	•		
Rights of shareholders	•	•				•		

	APEC Business Code of Conduct (Draft)	Caux Principles for Business	Global Reporting Initiative[c]	Global Sullivan Principles	OECD Guidelines for Multinational Enterprises	Principles for Global Corporate Responsibility	Social Accountability 8000 (SA8000)	UN Global Compact
Environment								
Broad/general reference	●	●	●	●	●	●		●
Precautionary principle[d]			●		●	●		●
Product life cycle			●		●	●		
Stakeholder engagement on environmental issues					●	●		●
Appoint designated person or people with responsibility for environment/ provide employee training					●	●		
Establish environmental management system/environmental code of conduct					●	●		
Public policy on environmental issues	●				●			
Human Rights								
Broad/general reference	●	●	●	●	●	●	●	●
Health and safety		●	●	●	●	●	●	●
Child labour			●	●	●	●	●	●
Forced labour			●	●	●	●	●	●
Freedom of association/ collective bargaining			●	●	●	●	●	●
Wages and benefits (including 'living wage')		●	●	●			●	●
Indigenous peoples' rights	●	●	●			●		
Appoint designated person or people with responsibility for human rights						●	●	
Discipline				●			●	
Use of security forces			●					●
Working hours/overtime						●	●	
Marketplace/Consumers								
Broad/general reference	●	●	●		●	●		
Marketing/advertising		●		●	●	●		
Product quality and/or safety	●				●	●		
Consumer privacy					●			
Recalls					●			

	APEC Business Code of Conduct (Draft)	Caux Principles for Business	Global Reporting Initiative[c]	Global Sullivan Principles	OECD Guidelines for Multinational Enterprises	Principles for Global Corporate Responsibility	Social Accountability 8000 (SA8000)	UN Global Compact
Workplace/Employees								
Broad/general reference	•	•			•	•	•	
Non-discrimination		•	•	•	•	•	•	•
Training		•	•		•			
Downsizing/lay offs		•			•	•		
Harassment/abuse						•	•	
Child/elder care						•		
Maternity/paternity leave						•		

[a] The APEC Business Code of Conduct is an initiative of business leaders in the APEC countries. The Caux Principles for Business is proposed by the Caux Roundtable, a self-identified group of North American, European, and Japanese senior business executives. The Global Reporting Initiative is an outgrowth of the Coalition of Environmentally Responsible Economies (CERES), which is inclusive of NGOs, corporations, academicians, and other analysts. The Global Sullivan Principles are the US Reverend Leon Sullivan's contribution, modelled on the principles for divestment from apartheid South Africa. The OECD Guidelines for Multinational Enterprises is a product of the member states. The Principles for Global Corporate Responsibility: Benchmarks is the conceptualisation of the Interfaith Center of Corporate Responsibility (US), Taskforce on the Churches and Corporate Responsibility (Canada), and the Ecumenical Council for Corporate Responsibility (UK). The SA 8000 is the system devised by the Council on Economic Priorities, subsequently spun off and renamed Social Accountability International. The Global Compact is an initiative of the UN Secretary General's office.

[b] BSR did not approach the comparison of the standards with a pre-established list of topics. Rather, the list of issues included for comparison was developed in an iterative fashion, stemming from both the commonalties and differences in issues referenced by the selected standards. The main topic headings (e.g., Accountability, Business Conduct) are ordered alphabetically. With the exception of the first section on Accountability, within each main topic area 'broad/general reference' is always listed first, with the remaining issues listed in descending order based on the number of standards that reference the particular issue. Where multiple issues are referenced by the same number of standards, the issues are listed in alphabetical order.

[c] The Global Reporting Initiative (GRI) differs from the other standards compared in this chart in being a reporting standard with recommendations on what indicators companies should use in reporting social, environmental, and economic performance. It does not include recommendations for specific standards of performance, policies, or practices.

[d] For the purposes of this report, the 'precautionary principle' refers to the notion that the burden of proof for determining the environmental consequences of an action lies with the company to definitively prove environmental safety rather than environmental harm.

Source: Business for Social Responsibility (2000)

from a widely diverse consultative process. They stress that no social evaluation can be adequately undertaken without the full participation of all stakeholders—employees, vendors, consumers, communities, shareholders. To be accredited as a social auditor under the AA1000 system, an individual must master the skills of stakeholder dialogue (Institute of Social and Ethical Accountability URL).

Other groups, like the Canada-based Maquila Solidarity Network (URL), a solidarity and labour rights network, help provide local women's groups and workers' associations with specialised monitoring skills. The Asia Monitoring Resource Centre (URL) in Hong Kong, along with Hong Kong Christian Industrial Coalition (HKCIC) and the Chinese Working Women's Network (see Box 4.3) are involved in health and safety training with workers that includes code-related training. In Central America, the Commission for the Verification of Codes of Conduct (COVERCO Guatemala) and the El Salvador-based Independent Monitoring Group (GIMES), which have worked for major corporations in the apparel and coffee industries, have built local capacity for social auditing.

Another independent monitoring approach is exemplified by US-based Verité, which monitors the practices of subcontractors who fill production orders for multinational corporations at the end of the supply chain. Verité often works with locally based CSO partners in creating monitoring teams (Verité URL). Independent monitors go beyond the typical factory tour and examination of payroll records. They investigate living conditions, check the availability of food and water, and solicit information from workers at meetings held off-site, not in the factory. Unions also represent an experienced resource for workplace monitoring. They have established procedures for collecting and verifying worker claims, and as they are generally self-funded they are a cost-effective alternative in building capacity for social auditing.

Public interest watchdogs

In addition to professional monitors, civil society often benefits from the work done by public watchdogs,

investigators who operate with the cooperation of companies or more covertly. In some cases journalists monitor company practices in service of the public's right to know. The much-criticised corporate behaviour of Shell and Nike, for instance, first came to light as a result of media coverage, including biting satire in the syndicated US cartoon strip 'Doonesbury'.

Other civil society sectors have formed watchdog CSOs whose mission it is to track specific industries or even a single company. The Clean Clothes Campaign in Europe has ten autonomous national offices bridging coalitions of consumer organisations, trade unions, human rights and women rights organisations, researchers, solidarity groups, and activists. They monitor sweatshop complaints and other labour and human rights violations around the world.

Global civil society—or those parts with access to the necessary technology—can be galvanised in a matter of hours through information technology. CorpWatch, a US-based CSO, monitors lawsuits and direct action campaigns directed at companies. It functions as an Internet clearing house for information that can be accessed all over the world (CorpWatch URL).

Civil society activism has revealed the inadequacy of internal company approaches to monitoring, it has charted ways for responsible monitoring of corporate practice, and it has established the legitimacy of civil society actors as monitors. Equally important in raising standards for corporate behaviour has been the momentum CSOs have provided to lawmakers to incorporate and safeguard fundamental ILO standards and other international legal norms in local laws. Companies that resist transparency will continue to find ways to deny the findings of independent monitors' reports and dispute the necessity of remedial action, but if laws are established to codify codes of conduct this behaviour becomes much more difficult. Legislation, however, can be a deeply inadequate weapon if enforcement lags behind.

Ultimately the goal of voluntary approaches is to so routinise compliance that new norms can be made law with genuine cross-sectoral support. As Phil Knight, Nike's CEO and Chair, notes: 'A more effective

> Civil society also has other windows on corporate social responsibility issues in the form of public watchdogs: organisations as well as journalists who operate both with the cooperation of companies and more covertly

international regulatory framework can lead to distinct cost-savings...We believe in a global system that measures every multinational against a core set of universal standards using an independent process of social performance monitoring akin to financial auditing. This would bring greater clarity to the impact of globalisation and the performance of any one company' (Zadek 2001: 97).

Making a Difference?

Corporations that damage the environment, mistreat workers, or collude with military dictatorships increasingly have trouble doing business. Each day sees the commitment of more corporate resources to citizenship activities and more shareholder money in funds with social responsibility criteria. Civil society is often credited with establishing new norms, but determining the overall impact of CSOs on levels of corporate social responsibility is difficult. Governments, the third player in this powerful triangle, can through laws that they enforce ensure that standards are consistently applied to all businesses.

Civil Society: achievements and opportunities

While no one has yet attempted to assess the overall effect of the CSR movement, there are many indicators that demonstrate that corporations are acting more responsibly. Apparel companies have taken responsibility for the conditions in their subcontractor's plants, a development that was unthinkable ten years ago. The mining industry is taking verifiable steps toward sustainable development. Starting from virtually no measurable forest management as late as 1995, the rate of growth of certified forest acreage worldwide stands at nearly 70 million acres, or more than 5 per cent of working forests. The marketplace also provides a quantifiable measure of success: demand for certified forest products, for instance, is exceeding supply (Conroy 2001). Some financial institutions are playing a role as well: Deutsche Bank refused to provide financing for the Three Gorges Dam in China and, after completing an environmental

> Corporations that damage the environment, mistreat workers, or collude with military dictatorships increasingly have trouble doing business

impact review at the request of environmental CSOs, withdrew financing from an oil pipeline in Equador. A more indirect measure of the effect of CSOs is the number of new CSO networks that have strengthened the movement, reduced duplication of effort, and opened space for more strategic programming (see Box 4.4).

Ultimately what may win over the corporate world is the profit motive. Profits are affected by both negative and positive publicity, and in the case of the former it seems that, even if the publicity does not have a great impact on sales, it can still alter the corporate mindset. *The Economist* (21 April 2000) has reported that Shell did not actually suffer monetary loss over the boycotts in reaction to the Brent Spar and Ogoniland, Nigeria, incidents, but its corporate workforce was so demoralised and its reputation so badly tarnished that the company was moved to revamp its strategic processes, regardless. Today, Shell is considered by many to be a model of corporate citizenship. For a growing number of companies reputational risk is considered as important as the risk of fire or physical catastrophe (Cowe 2001: 6).

The argument that CSR is good for profits is a long way from being taken as self-evident in the corporate world, but the argument, once made almost exclusively by CSO leaders, is now heard even in some business circles. There is a growing body of evidence that that 'doing well by doing good' has been achieved at some corporations, that above-average social performance leads to above-average financial performance (Balmaceda and Larson 2000). Arguing that 'Corporate social responsibility is a serious business with serious implications for shareholders' (Cowe 2001: 6), a recent publication by the Association of British Insurers cites examples of companies that increased shareholder value while paying attention to principles of CSR (Cowe 2001: 31–4), and, in *Built to Last*, Collins and Porras (1994) claim that those companies that have effective programmes for corporate responsibility have a rate of return that is 9.8 per cent better than other companies over a ten-year period. The business press has begun to publish with increasing frequency articles confirming the correlation between good business practices (particularly in the environment) and financial success, drawing on new studies and exploring

For many, China represents all that is problematic about globalisation. Critics argue that the country's vast supply of cheap labour, lax enforcement of regulations, and suppression of labour and human rights make it both a magnet for socially irresponsible multinationals and a troubling model for developing countries seeking to attract foreign investors. Furthermore, traditional strategies of civic participation—political parties, free trade unions, and NGOs—continue to be controlled or blocked by the Chinese government.

Activists thus wonder whether production in China can be socially responsible or whether new strategies and mechanisms need to be developed to advance the rights of workers. Facing increasing pressure in the US and Europe, leading multinational corporations themselves are asking how they can manage their suppliers more responsibly in China, and how to guarantee that their workers are treated safely and fairly.

Towards these ends, a range of stakeholders have come together over the last two years to focus on improving workplace health and safety conditions in Chinese contract factories for major multinational footwear manufacturers. This cooperative effort has sought to support local participation in identifying and resolving problems inside the factories, and in advancing broader systems of monitoring and corporate accountability. Key participants include the Asia Monitor Resource Center (AMRC), Chinese Working Women Network (CWN), Hong Kong Christian Industrial Committee (HKCIC), Hong Kong Confederation of Trade Unions (HKCTU), representatives of adidas, Nike, and Reebok, managers of three Taiwanese contract factories (Pegasus, KTS, and Yue Yuen II) located in Guangdong Province, China, and factory employees.

Project coordinators from the US (including staff from the Labor Occupational Health Program at UC-Berkeley, the Maquiladora Health and Safety Support Network, and MIT) began the project with a series of interviews and needs assessments with workers, CSOs, and companies. They then conducted a four-day training programme to build the capacity of health and safety committees, and to involve shop-floor workers in identifying, evaluating, and controlling health and safety hazards. Each factory created or expanded a health and safety committee after the training, and began a series of initiatives inside the plant. The training was followed by a six-month evaluation and technical assistance process involving workers, managers, and outside stakeholders. The Hong Kong CSOs have played a critical role in supporting worker participation in the committees.

---

the issues from various perspectives (Goodman, Kron, and Little 2002: 26–40). Until this message carries the day, however, many corporations are still likely to stage continuous and crafty battle against the adoption or imposition of CSR principles.

While much civil society focus has been on individual corporations or specific industries, CSOs have also successfully lobbied for changes in policy, such as the British Pension Fund legislation and the US government's regulations relating to the energy efficiency of electrical appliances; civil society activity in India, Zimbabwe, Guatemala, and as many as 50 other countries has led to the enactment of new domestic laws adopting provisions of the International Code of Marketing of Breastmilk substitutes. In fact, the 1992 Infant Milk Substitute, Feeding Bottles and Infant Foods Bill adopted by India actually empowers watchdog groups, not just government or victims, to bring charges of violations. Most sustainable practices and workplace improvements can be effected by legislation that either broadly demands greater accountability, as in the case of labour law, or specifies outcomes, such as automobile fuel efficiency.

What civil society cannot do

The leverage civil society has is mostly limited to large and visible companies with brand names (Cowe 2001: 6) There are a host of corporations (e.g., financial services, 'no-name' manufacturers) that are not susceptible to public shaming through consumer-led action. In other cases, the corporation is so large

For example, AMRC and HKCIC helped monitor a union election in one factory, and are now providing training on how to run worker committees, and CWN staff have conducted follow-up assessments with workers at all three plants.

This initiative, while still young, has resulted in the creation of first-of-their-kind worker-management committees, including one committee supported by a democratically elected union. These committees are the first step in building systems for worker participation and monitoring health, safety, and environmental conditions inside the factories. The next step would be transferring this information to factory managers, brand managers, and CSOs outside the factories. Committees are working to develop new and safer mechanisms for workers to report and resolve problems, and new systems of corporate accountability.

There have been several keys to the progress of this initiative. First has been the participation and cooperation of different stakeholders who have taken risks to participate. Adidas, Nike, and Reebok pushed their Taiwanese contractors to participate and sat across the table from critics. The contractors risked opening their facilities to CSOs. And the CSOs risked PR exposure by working with the multinational corporations. In the end, all of the participants gained from the cooperation. Second has been the centrality of workers to the process. All of the stakeholders have agreed that building worker capacity is beneficial to improving conditions. The focus on worker empowerment has moved the process beyond past debates about codes and monitoring. Finally, the initiative has benefited from, and supported in a small way, the development of civil society actors in China. The increased connections between the CSOs and factory workers offer an interesting example of a potential way forward for civic participation in China.

This first phase of the project has focused squarely on capacity-building and learning. The longer-term vision is to build on these pilot initiatives to advance larger-scale efforts to develop systems of monitoring and worker participation. The experience of initiating and assisting health and safety committees in these three factories may be the basis for developing more extensive systems of worker participation and external processes of corporate accountability in China.

Dara O'Rourke, Assistant Professor, Urban Studies and Planning, Massachusetts Institute of Technology

that one division may be doing something praiseworthy while another is doing something questionable. BP, for example, is a leader on the issue of climate change, but its ARCO division advocates drilling in the Arctic refuge, which is unanimously opposed by environmental groups.

In still other cases, a CSR campaign aimed at a single company often stops there, failing to result in industry-wide changes of standards. The National Resources Defense Council (NRDC), for example, worked with Dow's Midland Michigan plant and achieved a significant reduction in emissions as well as the development of a new product recovered from the smoke. The NRDC was disappointed, however, when Dow did not institute the changes company-wide, a move which might have inspired other corporations to follow suit, and as a result they now enter into partnerships only in cases that are likely to lead to significant policy changes.

Furthermore, there are some CSR campaigns the public refuses to embrace. Americans continue to buy highly inefficient sports utility vehicles, manufacturers are unrepentant about making them, and elected representatives resist imposing higher gasoline taxes and increasing automobile fuel efficiency standards.

And even when corporations do respond, their efforts may not be enough to achieve true reform. The subcontractors of some multinationals are now required by their contracts to follow certain standards in terms of wages and working conditions. Subcontractors can evade those requirements, however, by

The fight against the aggressive marketing of infant formula by Nestlé and other manufacturers is one of the most prominent examples of cross-sectoral coalition building. The Nestlé Boycott, launched in the 1970s and continuing today, was a key factor in the development of the first-ever UN code to control inappropriate marketing practices. A North-South CSO network emerged to support code development, implementation, and monitoring. But, after 25 years of campaigning, the boycott is also a cautionary tale: Years of work can pay off, but patience is required.

Bottle feeding under poverty conditions—a lack of clean water, poor sanitation, illiteracy—can lead to contaminated, diluted infant food. Yet this deadly recipe competes with breast-feeding, and the World Health Organization (WHO) and UNICEF estimate that up to 1.5 million babies die every year as a result.

After years of advocacy by health professionals, consumer advocates, shareholders, and legislators, the International Code of Marketing Breastmilk Substitutes, developed under WHO and UNICEF, was adopted by the World Health Assembly (WHA) in 1981. The code focuses on marketing practices that contribute to the abandonment of breast-feeding. Advertising and promotion tactics are prohibited. Instructions and images on the labels for infant formula are also covered by the code. Even educational information must conform to code standards. But the code is not law; rather, it is a set of minimum requirements meant to be translated into national law.

Every WHA member state has endorsed the code at varying levels of commitment. Even the United States, the only country to vote against it in 1981, has supported recent WHA resolutions aimed at further implementation. To date, more than half the world's population lives in countries that have adopted laws which codify significant aspects of the standards.

This could never have been achieved without the efforts of the International Baby Food Action Network (IBFAN), a North-South CSO which has grown to include some 150 groups in over 90 countries. IBFAN translates code into law; trains government officials on implementation, coordinates monitoring efforts; and compiles a biennial

---

hiring out some of the work into homes or informal settings where conditions may be patently unsafe. And the subcontractor reform movement has thus far touched mostly products with daily relevance for Northern consumers, such as apparel and auto mobiles. The manufacturers of products more distant from the daily lives of consumers—i.e. elevators, freight cars, generators—have not been subject to similar scrutiny.

Moreover, dramatic announcements about the successes of civil society campaigns often mask important negative trends. The Free Burma Coalition announced its success in persuading two dozen US corporations to stop doing business in Myanmar at just about the same time as the US Commerce Department reported that the value of goods imported from Myanmar to the US had increased from $107 million in 1996 to $470 million in 2000 (*Chicago Tribune*, 6 January 2002).

Finally, many multinationals clearly remain wilfully oblivious to shifting attitudes among the general public. The US tobacco industry, for example, supports worthy youth programmes—but spends double its programme budget just advertising the programmes. More important, tobacco companies have no qualms about marketing cigarettes to people of any age in any country that will let them, in spite of the fact that the industry has spent billions of dollars settling suits which made public its early knowledge of the addictive nature of nicotine. If Philip Morris had been more attuned to the winds of change, it might not have publicised the findings of a 2000 report to the Czech government about the impact of smoking on health care costs. It is truly hard to believe that no one at the company understood the implications of a report that said that a cigarette smoking population would save the Czech government money because people who smoke die earlier than those who do not.

compendium of company practices and violations. It is organised as a decentralised network, and regional groups take leadership for selected tasks. This successful model has been followed by others such as the Pesticide Action Network and Third World Network (URL).

Yet, despite all this, Nestlé and other companies continue marketing practices designed to circumvent restrictions. 'Baby clubs' are still being established as conduits for promotional material, and contact with mothers is made through the Internet and toll-free hotlines offering 'infant feeding advice', even though the code prohibits direct contact with mothers. Hospitals and clinics are still supplied with, and encouraged to distribute, free supplies.

Change, often incremental, takes a long time and requires hard work. What is impressive is the ability of CSOs to keep the issue at the forefront of public health agendas. New models have emerged which increase the pressure on the companies: For example, Brazil recently passed a law requiring companies to remove pictures of babies, bottles, or toys from formula and baby food labels and to add warnings that the product is not to be used before a baby is six months old. It has been reported to IBFAN that both Gerber and Nestlé have complied.

A troubling footnote: soaring HIV rates in some Southern countries have provided an opportunity for manufacturers to claim that they are providing a service by donating formula and public education programmes as part of the effort to reduce virus transmission through the breast-milk of HIV-positive mothers. Nestlé is actively courting African health-care systems with funds for research and educational programmes. Meanwhile, IBFAN advocacy has contributed to the adoption of written recommendations by WHO, UNICEF, and UNAIDS that any donations must be made in conformity with code standards. CSOs such as IBFAN will surely need to monitor this complex health crisis with sensitivity so that it is not exploited for commercial gain.

Leah Margulies, public interest attorney, NGO representative to International Code of Marketing Breastmilk Substitutes negotiations, and former legal adviser to UNICEF's Baby Friendly Hospital Initiative.

Even so, the achievements of civil society to date are truly impressive and very encouraging. CSOs have trained a spotlight on crucial issues, changing public perceptions and expectations; effected changes in the practice of individual corporations; helped to establish industry-wide standards; and introduced significant policy changes around the world. But in the end no one sector can alone create the massive changes still necessary for a sustainable and just world. Effective local, state, and international laws are essential, and, while some new legislation has already been written (much of it the result of CSO action), more is needed. Governments must also stand behind and rigorously enforce these laws for them to have any real impact.

What governments must do

Unfortunately, the corporate or industry-wide changes that result from CSO action can be tempor-ary. A new CEO or a relaxation of regular monitoring can lead to backsliding. Ultimately, the impact of civil society groups is greatest when translated into legislation and international codes. In cases where change clearly involves additional costs, only a mandate from government can bring it about. Air bags, for example, add significantly to the cost of automobile manufacture, and it was only when governments required all manufacturers to add to their cost that air bags were installed in all automobiles. It is governments that can ensure that change is institutionalised and applied to all actors.

Governments must be willing and able to do their part, however, and many are not. Thus it becomes the task of CSOs to pressure governments to enforce and amend national and international law. An encouraging example is the evolution of the ILO Tripartite Declaration of Principles Concerning Multinational Enterprises and Social Policy (1977, amended 2000; ILO 2000) and the OECD Guidelines for Multinational

Enterprises (1976, updated June 2000; OECD 2000). While these codes are not so legally binding on companies or their officials as international criminal law, both have emerged as crucial precursors to international labour law that is binding on private actors.

Both the ILO and the OECD specifically incorporate respect for human rights as a fundamental tenet of their guidelines. Likewise, the UN's Universal Declaration of Human Rights holds that 'every individual and every organ of society' is obliged to uphold these rights, and parts of the Declaration have been recognised as legally binding on states. Significantly, applications that were originally non-binding on multinationals are evolving from voluntary standards to legal obligations. The UN Sub-Commission on the Promotion and Protection of Human Rights is currently working on a Draft Universal Human Rights Guidelines for Companies (International Council of Human Rights Policy 2002).

The UN's Global Compact, a high-profile voluntary initiative of the Secretary General, was established to reinforce joint governmental and private sector responsibility for human rights, as well as environmental and labour standards. This gives greater weight to voluntary promotion of universal standards, and complements the movement towards legally binding codes of the ILO and the OECD. The reactions of developing country governments have been mixed. Some embrace the association with the UN as providing legitimacy for the difficult task of demanding corporate accountability. Others fear that the compact is exclusionary of national policy, and may drive away investment. At a time when the UN itself seeks strategic partnerships with powerful players, the compact is a unique route for companies that are willing to make a commitment to corporate responsibility to get increased visibility.

At the regional and national levels, much more can be done. The UK and US governments have instituted a set of Voluntary Principles on Security and Human Rights covering the mining, extraction, and chemical industries, but other states have adopted regulations that go further. The Australian and New Zealand governments, for example, have a Procurement Agreement that includes ethical requirements. (Government of Australia 2002).

CSR can also be promoted by government incentives. Tax incentives can encourage the use of renewable energy, anti-bribery legislation can level

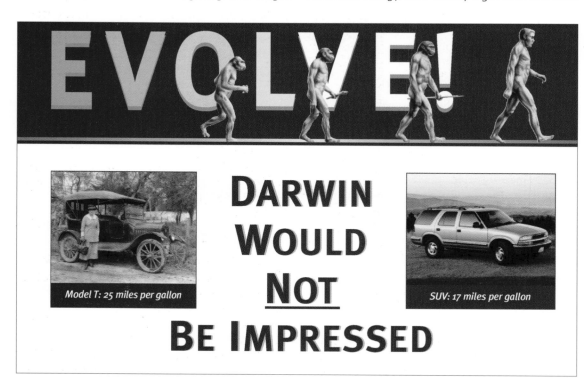

Above: The campaign targeting petrol-guzzling sports utility vehicles (SUVs) is not catching on in the US © Union of Concerned Scientists.

GLOBAL CIVIL SOCIETY AND CORPORATE RESPONSIBILITY   Melanie Beth Oliviero and Adele Simmons

the playing field for all businesses, and government regulations of pension fund investments can influence corporate behaviour. Trade agreements structured with social clauses are also a useful tool. One such agreement recently signed by the US and Cambodia increases the export quota of goods made in Cambodia by 14 per cent, contingent upon evidence that local labour laws are being honoured (USTR 2000). The need to harmonise domestic law with WTO rules is yet another opportunity for governments to lay down baseline standards for corporate practice.

Conclusion

Global civil society has made tremendous progress in the last decade, but the size of the problems at hand, already enormous, grows daily. 'Two thirds of the world's fisheries are being harvested beyond sustainability', reports Jonathan Lash of the World Resources Institute. 'Forest loss in poor regions is accelerating and soil degradation is widespread . . . The squalid slums of the sprawling cities of the poorest parts of the world are expanding by a million people a week' (Lash 2001: 1789). 1.2 billion people around the world currently live on less than a dollar a day.

To continue to be effective in addressing social responsibility issues, CSOs will need to continuously evolve, developing ever more sophisticated techniques, as they confront the resources at the disposal of multi-nationals. As discussed in Chapter 8, this is a matter of survival for the whole range of civil society groups as their organisational environment continues to be increasingly complex. CSOs already play a crucial role in setting standards and monitoring—no other sector has stepped forward to fill the obvious gap between regulation and reality on the shop floor—and that role will grow in years to come. It is imperative that CSOs find greater success in leveraging governmental action, particularly in the enforcement of existing domestic and international standards. They must also find ways to persuade legislators to institute and enforce social incentives and disincentives, and to play a role in international standard setting. The more laws and standards cross national borders, the more impact they will have.

> Civil society organisations must be careful not to lose their greatest source of leverage: the legitimacy that flows from the respect and trust that citizens place in them

CSOs would also benefit from better assessments of past campaigns, analyses of what has worked and what has failed. Alliances of all sorts, with other civil society groups, with companies, with scholars, and with government officials, add an inestimable volume of skills and resources to the fight, and may one day accumulate a critical mass for systemic change.

Finally, CSOs must be careful not to lose their greatest source of leverage: the legitimacy that flows from the respect and trust that citizens place in them. While standards within civil society groups are not uniform—and there have been examples of sloppy work—for the most part CSOs have maintained a high standard, relying on science to inform their work in health and the environment and the best data available in their work on labour conditions. Their strength lies in their ability to challenge the reputation of corporations; to continue in this role requires scrupulous attention to the reputation of civil society organisations themselves.

In the end, of course, social values and norms will have to change if the world is to become a safer, healthier place, and it is here that CSOs will always play one of their most important roles. Multinational corporations will not institute change, nor will governments legislate it, if the public does not care. By changing the way that people think about the world and their place in it, civil society organisations are creating the conditions under which human rights, environmental integrity, and social progress may be fully realised.

The authors wish to thank John Conroy, Emily Hauser, and Jill Timms for their valuable assistance.

References

Anderson, Sarah, and Cavanagh, John (2000). *Top 200: The Rise of Corporate Global Power*. Washington, DC: Institute for Policy Studies.

Asia Monitor Resource Center http://www.amrc.org.hk/home.htm

Aspen Institute (2001). *Aspen ISIB Business Leaders Dialogue*, 26–29 July. New York: Aspen.

Balmaceda, Mary and Larson, Todd (2000). 'Changing the Rules of the Game'. *Green@Work*, March–April: 35 ff.

Beyond Grey Pinstripes.
http://www.beyondgreypinstripes.org

The Boycott News.
http://www.geocities.com/CapitolHill/Lobby/3199

Business for Social Responsibility (2000). *Comparison of Selected Corporate Social Responsibility Related Standards*. San Francisco: Business for Social Responsibility, November. http://www.bsr.org

Business Partnership Development (2002). *Putting Partnering to Work*. Washington, DC: Business Partnership Development.

Canadian Democracy and Corporate Accountability Commission (2002). *The New Balance Sheet: Corporate Profits and Responsibility for the 21st Century: Final Report*. Ottawa: Canadian Democracy and Corporate Accountability Commission.

Collier, J. and Wanderley, L. (2002). 'Corporate Social Responsibility in Brazil: Pride or Prejudice?'. Second World Congress of ISBEE, Sao Paulo, Brazil 18 January. http://www.nd.edu/~isbee/papers/Collier.doc.

Collins, James C. and Porras, Jerry I. (1994). *Built to Last: Successful Habits of Visionary Companies*. New York: Harper Collins.

Cone Inc. (2002). 'Post-September 11th: Major Shift in American Attitudes towards Companies Involved with Social Issues – Press Release'. 15 January. http://www.coneinc.com/Pages/pr_8.html

The Conference Board. http://www.conference-board.org

Conroy, Michael E. (2001). *Can Advocacy-Led Certification Systems Transform Global Corporate Practices? Evidence, and Some Theory* (Working Paper Series No. DPE-01-07). Amherst: Political Economy Research Institute, University of Massachusetts.

CorpWatch http://www.corpwatch.org

Cowe, Roger (2001). *Investing in Social Responsibility: Risks and Opportunities*. London: Association of British Insurers.

Edelman PR Worldwide/Strategy One (2002). *Non-Governmental Organizations, the Fifth Estate in Global Governance: Second Annual Study of NGO and Institutional Credibility*. New York: The Conference Board.

Elkington, John (1998). *Cannibals with Forks*. Gabriola Island, British Columbia: New Society Publishers.

Environics International Ltd (1999). 'The Millennium Poll on Corporate Social Responsibility: Executive Briefing'. Toronto.

Essential Information. http//www.essential.org

Ethos Institute (2001a). *Indicadores Ethos de Responsabilidade Social Empresarial: Versao 2001 [Ethos Indicators of Business Social Responsibility: 2001 Version]*. Sao Paulo: Instituto Ethos.

— (2001b). *Responsibilidade Social das Empresas: Percepcao e Tendendias do Consumidor Brasileiro [Business and Social Responsibility: Perceptions and Trends of Brazilian Consumers]*. Sao Paulo: Instituto Ethos.

Fussler, Claude (2001). 'Shaping a Deal for the 2002 Johannesburg Summit'. Geneva: WBCSD: October 2001. 18 February. http://www.wbcsd.ch/newscenter/speeches/wssd/fussler-12-01.pdf

Global Alliance for Workers and Communities.
http://www.theglobalalliance.org

Goodman, Susannah Blake, Kron, Joan and Little, Tim (2002). 'The Environmental Fiduciary' (manuscript). Oakland, CA.

Government of Australia (2002). Department of Finance and Administration, Procurement Agreement. 14 April. http://www.finance.gov.au/ctc/publications/purchasing/international/australia_new_zealand_governme.html

GRI (Global Reporting Initiative) (2000). *Sustainability Reporting Guidelines*. Boston: GRI. http://www.globalreporting.org

Hill, Julia Butterfly (2000). *The Legacy of Luna*. San Francisco: Harper.

Hochschild, Adam (1999). *King Leopold's Ghost*. Boston: Houghton Mifflin.

ILO (International Labour Organisation) (2000). *Tripartite Declaration of Principles Concerning Multinational Enterprises and Social Policy*. Geneva: ILO.

Institute of Social and Ethical Accountability.
http://www.accountability.org.uk

Instituto Ethos de Empresas e Responsabilidade Social.
http://www.ethos.org.br

International Council of Human Rights Policy (2002). 'Beyond Volunteerism. Human Rights and the Developing International Legal Obligations of Companies'. Geneva. http://www.ichrp.org/107/1.pdf

Kent, Toby (2001). 'CSR Investment Is Not a Choice'. *Ethical Corporation Magazine*, November. 16 January. http://www.ethicalcorp.com/NewsTemplate.asp?IDNum=85

Lash, Jonathan (2001). 'Dealing with the Tinder as Well as the Flint'. *Science*, 294: 1789.

Maquila Solidarity Network
http://www.maquilasolidarity.org

Mazur, Jay (2000). 'Labor's New Internationalism'. *Foreign Affairs*, 79/1: 79–93.

McDonald's (2002). 'McDonald's Issues First Worldwide Social Responsibility Report – Press Release'. 15 April.

http://mcdonalds.com/corporate/press/corporate/
2002/04152002/index.html

Mello, S. (1999). 'Empresas e Responsabilidade Social: um
estudo no Nordeste do Brasil [Business and Social
Responsibility: A Study in the North East of Brazil]'.
http://www.rits.org.br/acervo/
acervo_pesquisa_detalhe.cfm?CA=1211.

Multinational Monitor.
http://www.essential.org/monitor/index.html

OECD (Organisation for Economic Cooperation and
Development) (2000). *Guidelines for Multinational
Enterprises* Paris: OECD.

O'Rourke, Dara (2002). 'Monitoring the Monitors: A
Critique of Corporate Third Party Labor Monitoring' in
Rhys Jenkins, Ruth Pearson and Gill Seyfung (eds)
*Corporate Responsibility and Ethical Trade: Codes of
Conduct in the Global Economy.* London: Earthscan.

Queiroz, A. (2001). 'Corporate Social Responsibility
Indicators: A Study from Brazil'. *MHC International
Monthly Feature*, April. 5 January.
http://www.mhcinternational.com

Schmidheiny, Stephen and Zorraquin, Federico (1996).
*Financing Change: The Financial Community, Eco-
efficiency and Sustainable Development.* Cambridge,
MA: MIT Press.

— Chase, Rodney, and DeSimone, Livio (1997). *Signals of
Change.* Geneva: WBCSD.

Schoenberger, Karl (2000). *Levi's Children: Coming to
Terms with Human Rights in the Global Marketplace.*
New York: Grove Press.

SocialFunds (2002). 'Asian Mutual Fund Sets New
Standard for Promoting Women's Issues'. Social Funds,
9 January 2001. 29 March. http:www.social
funds.com/news/article/cgi/article467.html

Thamotheram, Raj (ed.) (2000). *Visions of Ethical
Sourcing.* London: Financial Times Prentice Hall.

Third World Network. http://www.twnside.org.sg

UCS (Union of Concerned Scientists) (2002). 'Dramatic
Change Away from Antibiotic Use in Chicken Industry
– Press Release'. 11 February, 15 March 2002.
http://www.ucsusa.org/index.html

UNCTAD (United Nations Conference on Trade and
Development) (2001). 'World Investment Report'.
http://www.unctad.org/wir/pdfs/wir_tnc_top100.en.
pdf

United Nations (1994). Report on Human Rights and the
Environment. Geneva: UN.

USTR (United States Trade Representative) (2000). 'USTR
Announces Apparel Quota Increase for Cambodia –
Press Release'. 18 May.
http://www.ustr.gov/releases/2000/05/00-39.html

WBCSD (World Business Council for Sustainable
Development) (2001). 'Sustainability through the
Market: Seven Keys to Success'. Geneva.
http://www.wbcsd.ch/newscenter/reports/
2001/stm.pdf
(URL). http://www.wbcsd.org

WBCSD/WRI (World Resources Institute) (2001). *The
Greenhouse Gas Protocol.* Geneva: WBCSD/WRI.

Weiser, John and Zadek, Simon (2000). *Conversations
with Disbelievers: Persuading Companies to Address
Social Challenges.* New York: The Ford Foundation.

Wolf, Martin (2002). 'Countries Still Rule the World'.
Financial Times, 5 February.

World Bank. http://www.worldbank.org

Verité. http://www.verite.org

Zadek, Simon (2001). *The Civic Corporation.* London:
Earthscan.

Chapter 5

TIME TO STOP AND THINK: HIV/AIDS, GLOBAL CIVIL SOCIETY, AND PEOPLE'S POLITICS

Hakan Seckinelgin

Introduction

The largest international health related organisation, the World Health Organisation (WHO), has recently suggested that TB, malaria, and HIV/AIDS are the major causes of suffering around the world. However, the developing world is the location for most of these sufferings. The WHO has begun to relate the lack of health to poverty and underdevelopment. Recently, the Director-General of WHO, Dr Gro Harlem Brundtland, has posed the question 'why global health is now starting to come into focus as a serious political issue' (Brundtland 2001: 1), to which she has suggested two main answers. First, she argues, is 'the realisation of our common vulnerability to diseases in a globalised world' and second, 'the growing body of evidence linking ill health and the slow progress of economic development' (Brundtland 2001: 2). This view is also echoed in the World Bank: 'over and above its dramatic health impact, HIV/AIDS is also a major development problem. It threatens the economic and social growth and, even the stability itself of many nations'(World Bank 2002: 1)

Although both of these answers that Dr Brundtland gives are to be welcomed, they are symptomatic of the problematic nature of the general attitude of intergovernmental organisations towards disease. To regard these diseases as if they were just emerging as political issues or considering them under the new global awareness risks missing the point that most communicable diseases have been global for a long time. And the idea of diseases becoming political seems to imply that they do so only as states and international organisations are becoming much more involved in this area: thus, diseases are constituted as a matter of politics.

This chapter presents a different understanding of why the global politics of health is changing. History and people's sufferings matter. The WHO has identified a change, but it is not only based on, as it suggests, the realisation of global vulnerability to poverty-induced disease. I would argue that the change is coming from the increased dissatisfaction of people suffering from communicable diseases around the world with the existing global politics of health. In other words, the change is coming from the politics of people rather than the high politics of global governance of health. This politics of people and their networks is the material out of which an idea of global civil society can be formed. Brundtland's comments can be seen as responding to this grass-roots demand, albeit from the position of an intergovernmental organisation that conceives the world through a top-down understanding of events. The divergence between Brundtland's suggestion about the changing nature of this politics and my own account of it reflects the changing location of people in thinking about health. In the latter conception, people take active roles and initiatives in describing their needs and the appropriate health interventions, while in the former people are integrated into politics only as patients suffering from a disease. Their individual needs, depending on their socio-political conditions, are subsumed under the medical characteristics of a disease in terms of which the essential needs of patients are universally described.

The response to these conditions is gradually emerging. The WHO, for example, is responding to this change by creating new avenues of communication with civil society actors. In 2001 the WHO formed its first WHO Civil Society Initiative, headed by Eva Wallstam, who has given as one of the reasons for this move the advocacy role of civil society in the process, leading to adoption of the People's Health Charter *by* the People's Health Assembly in Dhaka 2000 (IFMSA 2001). The Assembly was a civil society initiative to bring people into the debate, observing that 'Governments and international organisations have largely failed to reach this goal [health for all], despite much rhetoric' (TWN 2002). The advocacy work persuaded the WHO to 'strengthen mutually beneficial relationships between WHO and civil society organisations (CSOs)' through this new initiative (Wallstam 2001: 3). Gro Harlem Brundtland recognises this from a wider perspective: she suggests that 'we (WHO) cannot expect there to be single entity in control, directing others with military precision . . . the work will be taken by a variety of groups'(Brundtland 2001: 3).

The WHO is involved in many partnerships with civil society and the private sector to deal with, for example, malaria under the Roll Back Malaria Programme. However, a tension remains in these relations as there is a danger of considering politics, *pace* Brundtland, only in terms of the changing institutional politics of the WHO and other similar organisations, and of the inclusion of new organisational forms into the global governance of health, and not in terms of emerging people's politics as a reaction to the entire relationship between health and the historical process (see also Chapter 2). In other words, if the inclusion of civil society in the global politics of health means giving these organisations a monopoly in dealing with a global disease, people and their particular needs will once more disappear from the discussion. Therefore, in order to resist the threat of depoliticisation, it is imperative to understand the essentially political nature of disease and the historical path that has created present conditions.

The following historical analysis argues that diseases have always been global in various forms that were political, and tries to present a change in what have been the global characteristics of health issues. The next section will present the way the global politics of health has evolved. This section also demonstrates the existing mechanisms within which civil society has engaged with HIV/AIDS. It will provide the grounds for the discussion of new phase in this process that has been marked by people's actions in recent decades. The discussion will move on to present civil society activity as *people's politics* that developed in response to HIV/AIDS and the globalisation of this politics to deal with the impact of the disease in the developing world. At the end of this section I discuss the structure of global civil society in this debate and articulate conclusions in relation to HIV/AIDS activism that have implications for civil society activity in health issues in general.

> The global politics of health is changing, but the change is coming from the politics of people rather than the high politics of global governance of health

History of Globalised Diseases

This section aims to give a summary account of the long history of globalised diseases while establishing the construction of the modern path to the present-day global politics of health. It is possible to consider the impact of the relationship between disease and globalisation under three headings: (1) the spread of diseases from one location to others by means of travel; (2) the relationship between various medical traditions to deal with unexpected diseases; and (3) the ascendancy of a particular understanding of medicine and its impact on disease. In reality these three paths have mostly merged and shaped each other according to socio-political contexts. Although various stages of the globality of disease have essentially occurred under different logics, it is the cumulative historical experience created by these stages together that ultimately informs global health politics. The manifestation of globalisation in the first stage is related to the logic of discoveries and encounters with the *exotic*. The second stage relates to the logic of permanent settlement of Europeans in newly discovered geographies. The third stage deals with the logic of colonialism. The aim in each stage is to demonstrate the larger concerns built into the globalisation of diseases and medicine through the historical process.

The spread of disease

The great discoveries around the globe by the Europeans from the fifteenth century onwards not only opened up new horizons for people and opportunities to get rich and win souls but became a conduit for the unintended spread of new diseases around the world. Although many infectious diseases were part of everyday life in geographically isolated populations, increased human contact created new scope for them to take hold in large communities. The expansion of human contact through travel and settlement in Africa, the Americas, and Asia facilitated the spread of diseases such as yellow fever, smallpox, syphilis, cholera, plague, and many other fevers around the world. The changing natural environment made travellers, settlers, and the natives of newly discovered geographies vulnerable to many diseases. It was not only those directly exposed but also those located within the larger geographies of empires, such as the Spanish and Portuguese, who became vulnerable to *new* diseases.

The spread of smallpox in Brazil and Mexico, for example, illustrates this process. The trans-infection of populations in the New World occurred immediately after the discovery of the Americas. The smallpox epidemics recorded from the late fifteenth century onwards in the New World were directly related to the European conquests. The epidemics lasted until the end of slave trade between Africa and Brazil in the early nineteenth century (Alden and Miller 2000). Climatic conditions, such as drought, and resulting famine may have been instrumental in the spread of the epidemics; it is clear, nonetheless, that the disease itself was introduced as a result of the workings of the Portuguese empire. The global interests in sustaining sugar plantations in Brazil with imported African slaves created a direct relationship, and thus a pathway for smallpox, between central Africa, where smallpox had been observed as an epidemic, and Brazil, where the pristine native population created the right conditions for long-term spread of the disease (Alden and Miller 2000: 208). The importance of smallpox in creating a 'a demographic catastrophe' in Mexico is also emphasised by McCaa (2000). In a similar fashion, it is suggested that syphilis, which spread through Europe after the discovery of the Americas, was transported to India in due course by Portuguese travellers. Syphilis seems to have arrived in Europe immediately after the discoveries of the Americas in the 1490s and spread throughout the continent. As Europeans travelled to the East it spread quickly to India in 1498, Canton in 1504, and Japan in 1512 (Boomgaard 1996: 49). Other diseases, however, made the journey back to Europe. Plague is believed to have originated in Asia and cholera to have travelled to Europe from Goa, where it was an epidemic from the mid-sixteenth century to the seventeenth (Pearson 1996: 23).

Looking at just a few specific infectious diseases that caused havoc around the world in the past presents us with a dynamic picture of the intensification of their impact as more and more people became introduced to new parts of the globe. This is not to say that these diseases did not exist before; it is clear that some of them were endemic in particular locations. The point is that the movement of people brought the movement of diseases with it. The rapid expansion of smallpox, cholera, plague, and syphilis demonstrates the logic of encounter. The diseases were either introduced to a new location or carried back to travellers' countries of origin.

> In order to resist the threat of depoliticisation, it is imperative to understand the essentially political nature of disease and the historical path that has created present conditions

Medical traditions

The relationship between people and disease is one of the important junctures between human beings and the nature within which they live. This relationship manifests a path on which people attempt to make sense of nature so as to improve their lives. The medical traditions around the world are in some ways attempts to make sense of human beings' location in their larger natural environment. Although there are many distinct medical traditions, such as the Chinese, Indian, Islamic, and Western, they have long influenced and exchanged knowledge and ideas with one another. Particularly in the time period starting with the great geographical discoveries, not only diseases were on the move: medical practices and understanding among various traditions *also* became exposed to each other in a much more unmediated manner. On the one hand, the European practitioners had to make sense of local diseases for which there were believed to be local remedies. On the other hand, the local healers had to understand the newly arrived European medical procedures such as bleeding. In other words, this was the period of observation, trial, and innovation that eventually spread throughout the vast mercantile networks.

In the case of smallpox in Brazil, Alden and Miller suggest that, towards the end of eighteenth century, inoculation had emerged as the effective way of dealing with it. The initial usage of the method, however, derived from elsewhere: inoculation was used by 'some Africans and technique spread from

Turkish sources to England'; and British slavers used the method in the Atlantic slave trade before the Portuguese were convinced of its usefulness (Alden and Miller 2000: 218). In Goa , the Portuguese encountered the local medical tradition and on many occasions fused Western and Indian medicine in order to solve problems. Of course, what is considered as local knowledge in Europe was, according to Pearson, already a fusion of 'Latin, Arabic, Greek and Hebrew knowledge' (1996: 21). Armed with this medical knowledge and understanding, the Europeans experienced newly encountered diseases such as cholera and malaria in India. Considering that Europeans were settling in new regions, it was natural for them to be curious about the way locals dealt with these diseases. As a result, some Indian medicinal drugs were sent to Europe (Correria-Afonso 1990). Some medical surgery techniques followed the same route (Patterson 1974). The history of the establishment and expansion of the Dutch East India Company (Verenigde Oostindische Compagnie–VOC) documents the existence of the extensive medical cross-fertilisation that took place in the East. The company 'during the 18th century had, on average, some 250–300 surgeons in Asia, of whom slightly over a 100 could be found in the Indonesian archipelago' (Boomgaard 1996: 43). It was this strong medical involvement and the establishment of clinics around the VOC factories which created the impetus for communication with the natives. Boomgaard (2000: 49) suggests that several drugs, as a result, became global in the sense that they travelled through the mercantile networks and were used to cure similar diseases around the world. One such cure, for example, was *radix China*: China root from Goa used against syphilis throughout a wide geographical area from Java to Europe.

Although the success of these medical cross-fertilisations may be uncertain, they suggest that, with the expansion of human contact through the networks of Western travellers, settlers' and missionaries' medical knowledge became a negotiated and tested substance. Once people from both sides were convinced of certain medical techniques or remedies, they become widely amalgamated with existing practices and some were transported throughout the vast geographies. Arguably, as the Europeans were becoming more settled in new regions and established their health systems with their hospitals and clinics, a relationship was established with the existing local knowledge. Medical practitioners from all sides observed each other's practice and began to negotiate their compatibility (Boomgaard 1996). The Hippocratic tradition that local medicine is central to the curing of endemic diseases encouraged the curious to treat other traditions equally. The logic of settlement further assumes a certain level of equality between settlers and locals. It was through this logic that medical substances from the East were introduced to Europe. Clearly this was to change rather rapidly through the eighteenth century due both to the changing medical understanding in Europe and to the changing political outlook.

Medicine can thus be considered as something which has been global for a fairly long time. The networks within which diseases and their medical knowledge became global-ised are important. Another aspect of the juncture between diseases and their global character presents itself during the period of colonisation in the nineteenth century.

> At the time of the great geographical discoveries not only diseases were on the move: medical practices and understanding among various traditions also became much more immediately exposed to each other

Politics of medicine

The changing conditions of colonialism throughout the eighteenth and nineteenth centuries, coupled with changing perceptions about the nature of medicine and disease, gradually altered the relationship between medicine and its globality. The nature of the relationship became related to the logic of colonial projects. This process gained pace as the political nature of European involvement transformed from maritime trade and trade posts to the establishment of overseas territories (Hobsbawm 1987). The sense of curiosity about local medical knowledge and practice that had accompanied their concerns for their health began to desert the Europeans. They became much more concerned with their long-term survival in what was described as 'fiercely malevolent tropics' (Arnold 1996: 7). This mode of thinking differs from that of the previous period in the sense that there was a major attempt by the colonising powers to deal with infectious diseases that were killing many Europeans, such as malaria, cholera, and sleeping sickness. The purpose of the medical concerns and the political expediency of colonialism had manifested itself as a merger between the two: 'for European doctors in the nineteenth century, tropical medicine and military medicine were nearly synonymous' (Curtin 1996: 99). Towards the end of the nineteenth century, the focus on tropical diseases reached a high point culminating in the founding of tropical medicine as a separate discipline in Britain. Many young British doctors, including Patrick Manson, who later became the founding father of tropical medicine, became interested in tropical diseases while serving in the British colonial project, whether as soldiers in India or in the West Indies, or as employees of administrative offices such as the Imperial Chinese Custom Services (Haynes 1996: 218). Haynes argues that research in these environments aimed to 'advance the mission of empire and establish Britain's reputation as a leader in a medical-scientific speciality' (1996: 219). These accounts demonstrate a change in the way diseases and medicine were now becoming global as a part of the expanding colonial empires, above all the British empire, but the work of the French physicians in the colonies was also 'influenced by military or paramilitary agendas' (Osborne 1996: 82).

However, it would be incorrect to assume this was happening only as a result of military might. The development of a particular understanding of tropical medicine based on the increased engagement with sanitary sciences and then the acceptance of the germ theory of diseases in Europe also contributed to the expansion of the globality of medical practices throughout the colonies. On the one hand, sanitation, Armstrong (1993: 396) suggests, was meant to differentiate between anatomical and environmental spaces whereby the traditional environments were more and more questioned, particularly by missionaries trying to demonstrate that African traditions were *unhealthy* for individuals. According to Butchart (1998: 75), for example, it was out of the sanitary divide that the image of Africa as 'dark with barbarism . . . savage customs' grew.

> In the interest of imperialism, only those diseases threatening the health of administrators, the military, and those natives working for the profits of colonial empires became the target of medical interventions

It was the success of finding out about the causes of malaria through germ theory that opened the next stage. It bolstered the methodological shift from 'diseases in the tropics', whereby the entire space within which a disease occurred was considered in dealing with them, to 'tropical diseases', in which particular diseases, such as malaria, were singled out and attempts made to solve them on their own (Worboys 1996: 199). The implication of this switch was important, as it meant that it was considered possible to eradicate single diseases through a focused effort. The possibility of eradicating a disease by controlling the environment within which the singular cause of the disease could be found meant that the colonial authorities were in a position to decide which diseases to engage with. This approach then became common-place in the interests of imperialism in Africa. Those diseases threatening the health of administrators, the military, and those natives who were working for the profits of colonial empires became the target of medical interventions (see Coast 2002).

In an attempt to solve sleeping sickness in Congo, the Belgian government, for example, focused on northern Congo as it was related to their interests in the rubber industry, but in a way that was top-down and focused directly on the cause of the disease without considering the larger context: by moving people to other areas they spread the disease to the rest of the region. In order to increase the efficiency of the mine workers who were suffering from unsuspected mental conditions, workers were exposed naked to 'the experimental chambers and heat tolerance tests' to simulate the conditions in the mines for observation by medical officers (Butchart 1998: 93). Arnold (1996: 8) suggests that 'non-whites continually informed the western understanding of the tropics and of the tropical diseases as clinical objects, as sources of epidemic danger, as sick or "shrinking workers" '.

In other words, the past is a narrative of expanding diseases and solutions for those diseases that were relevant to the concerns of the colonial powers without much reference to the stories of people and their needs and interests. The crucial condition for a medical problem to emerge as a global disease seems to be its impact on global power games. A similar link explains the disappearance of certain diseases from public discourse. The declining medical focus of the West on malaria and other tropical diseases despite the large numbers of people suffering from them can be related to the end of colonial interests. The colonial legacy also still remains in the politics of global diseases in the form of vertical health policies. Farley (1991: 13–30) argues that twentieth century medical effort in the Third World was an 'imperial tropical medicine' in terms of the definition and imposition of policies and the consequent 'non-involvement of the indigenous population'.

Despite the fact that today's global politics of diseases in relation to TB, malaria, and HIV/AIDS reflects these historically constructed policy structures, the global politics of diseases is changing. People's needs and interests are becoming more expressed and disease is rethought through the experience of people living with it. This process is creating spaces which are linked to the concept of civil society: people's needs are presented without reference to a grand design external to their livelihoods. The global spread of this attitude, and thus civil society, are creating the next stage of the relationship between diseases and their global appearance.

The next section looks briefly at the history of HIV/AIDS and how today it has been taken up as a cause by many civil society activists and organisations around the world.

AIDS and the Emergence of a Civil Society

The history of HIV/AIDS activism shows how people inspired changes in the conventional thinking of politicians and scientists, but it also demonstrates the limits of civil society. The emergence of HIV/AIDS patients, medical professionals, development workers, and others, whose values were challenged by the identification of HIV/AIDS, into civil society activism around HIV/AIDS has passed through several stages. It is clear that today there is a global awareness about HIV/AIDS, and the disease is one of the most recognised issues in the global arena. The disease has become a central policy issue

> The reaction to the epidemic in the absence of clear medical responses can be seen as the basis of an emerging civil society which in due course influenced international responses in the developing world

for NGOs and other civil society organisations over the last 20 years. Their work has helped to increase awareness of the disease in the developing world and has been instrumental in decreasing the stigma attached to it. In this process, however, the people living with HIV/AIDS in developing countries rarely come to the attention of a wider Northern public. In the absence of people's voices, their needs and expectations are assumed to be addressed in the activities of the metaphorical civil society that is NGOs (Seckinelgin 2002). Today, an analysis of the civil society developed over the last 20 years and the stages of its development presents a paradox for attempts at understanding the relationship between people and the disease. I will try to make sense of this paradox by following the development of civil society action from the identification of AIDS in 1981 in the US to the civil society action taking place in South Africa throughout 2001–2. The aim is not to give an exhaustive history but rather to understand why people made a difference and how they changed the international politics while they changed themselves to become a force for an institutionalised response to the disease internationally.

The search for the origins of HIV/AIDS has engaged the medical profession since the first recognition of AIDS in 1981. The debate around the origins of the disease is far from over, as new theories emerge from various perspectives (Hooper 1999). Despite the controversial discussions of origins, the relationship between AIDS (acquired immune deficiency syndrome) and HIV (human immunodeficiency virus) is clearly established. The identification of a disease in 1981 and its linkage to HIV a few years later was followed only in 1996 by a medical response in the form of a combination drug therapy. According to Christian Bastos (1999: 7), during the time lag between the identification of this disease and the arrival of a pharmaceutical response 'the social dimensions of the disease became more prominent, visible, and central'(1999: 7). Early on in the response, the realisation that a medical solution was not going to be available in the foreseeable future made treatment peripheral to the debates. The particular location of the disease in the gay community meant that people needed to deal with a social stigma that isolated infected people from the wider society. As a result a social struggle for recognition took place parallel to the struggle to get politicians at both local and federal levels to support people with the disease. The reaction of people to the epidemic in the absence of clear medical responses can be seen as the basis of an emerging civil society which in due course influenced the international responses to the disease in the developing world.

As the increased cases of *Kaposi's sarcoma* (KS) in the New York and *Pneumocystis carinii pneumonia* (PCP) in the Los Angeles gay communities became an issue in 1981, a discussion of a disease influencing a particular social group was established (CDC 1981). For a short while some scientists used the term 'gay-related immune deficiency' (GRID) to identify various symptoms that were proved to be lethal among gay men. The subsequent realisation that other groups such as drug users and certain minorities were susceptible only added to the prejudice. Although the usage of 'GRID' was dropped early on, as it was clear that drug users, haemophilia patients, and some ethnic groups were also vulnerable to the disease, the early epidemiology of the disease by and large located HIV/AIDS in a homosexual social environment. The disease was initially very difficult to accept even for the gay communities, as documented by Randy Shilts (1987). As gay men represented a marginalised and stigmatised group in the larger American society, no resources were made available to deal with the epidemic. The idea of a 'gay plague' exacerbated the negative attitude and imparted a very damaging image to the disease. This also meant that HIV/AIDS was located in the highly charged political context of the gay and lesbian movement in the US. In other words, HIV/AIDS became an issue led by the urban gay communities nearly as soon as it was diagnosed. In its designation as a disease, HIV/AIDS was related to particular social relations and their political struggle within the larger political debate in the United States of America. However, once people began to realise that the federal and local authorities in New York, San Francisco, Los Angeles, and other cities around the country were not responding to the crisis to meet

their needs, the debate turned to ways of taking the initiative to address the crisis (Perrow and Guillen 1990). HIV/AIDS rapidly become a political issue. Its politicisation meant that the importance of the social context of the disease was at the forefront of the debate. At the time, it also resisted the possible over-medicalisation of the disease, which happened in the 1990s. This particular story of the disease and its emergence within a particular social context has had both positive and negative impacts in the way it has become a global issue. Before we pursue this further, it is useful to understand the dynamics of this response.

Struggle for recognition

The particularity of people's response to HIV/AIDS was related to the general lack of understanding of the new disease and the unavailability of services to help people in the initial stages. The intensification of scientific debate is clear from the scientific discussion in the scholarly journals. Medical science responded promptly, but its approach was very slow to address the immediate needs of people who had HIV/AIDS. In the traditional structures of the profession, the initial reaction was to attempt to find an overall solution through lengthy research into every possible characteristic of the disease in order to identify the exact cause that would eventually lead to a cure. Clearly, this was and is needed; but while people are getting sick their needs are more pressing. In other words, the gap between the immediacy of people's needs and the systemic response from medicine and governmental agencies was substantial. HIV/AIDS testing based on standard protocols for sexually transmitted diseases (STD) was a major area of confrontation. It asked patients for contact numbers of people close to them. This was an impossible situation not only because it was related to sexual activities which were still illegal in some States but also because of widespread prejudice against homosexuals within the legal enforcement mechanisms. People could have faced criminal charges or lost their employment, stigmatised by a conservative society that considered the disease 'God's wrath' on homosexuals. The immediate needs essentially included anonymous testing procedures,

> People could have faced criminal charges or lost their employment, stigmatised by a conservative society that considered the disease 'God's wrath' on homosexuals

clinical procedures that would address opportunistic diseases taking hold of people as their immune systems were collapsing, and procedures to maintain the dignity of people while providing them help. Therefore, it was directly connected with overcoming the prejudices related to the two central issues of death and sex. People experiencing HIV/AIDS needed space both to voice their need to deal with HIV/AIDS through access to medicine and care, and to voice their pain and frustration in the face of losing their friends and family members. They also looked for some way of caring for their loved ones who were dying. The question of *how* to care affectionately for and recognise the dignity of someone who is dying from a sexually transmitted disease stirred up deeply held prejudices.

The above-mentioned gap between victims' need and the medical response combined with the platform provided by the gay and lesbian movement created the space for people to influence and give direction to the HIV/AIDS debate, particularly in the US, through turning their needs and frustration into a civil society platform. I will focus on only a few of them to point out the characteristics of the civil society at this stage. In Europe civil society was responding to the epidemic in the 1980s: in the United Kingdom the Terrence Higgins Trust was established as a charity in the in response to the HIV/AIDS epidemic in 1982. In France AIDES was established by a group of gay men and 'AIDS widows', who lost partners early in the epidemic, led by Daniel Defert to help others in similar situation in 1984 (Pollack, Paichler, and Pierret 1992; Caron 2001). However, the civil society reaction that was emerging in the US has come to inspire most of the activists around the world.

New York was the centre of the activity as it had a well-established urban gay community involved in politics. Individuals living with HIV/AIDS and their friends have been the most important force in stimulating the debate, such as Bobbi Campbell, who was the first HIV/AIDS case in San Francisco and a very vocal activist, writing a column in the San Francisco *Sentinel* about his experience of living with HIV/AIDS, or Phil Lanzaratta, who was the first publicly identified HIV/AIDS sufferer in New York,

appearing on television programmes and writing about his experience.

In this environment the gay community in New York stimulated the establishment of Gay Men's Health Crisis (GMHC) in 1982. GMHC was representative of the first generation of organisations, which also included San Francisco AIDS Foundation, Bay Area AIDS Consortium, AIDS Project LA, AIDS Foundation Houston, Minnesota AIDS Project, and Boston AIDS Action Committee. They were largely people's groups created to deal with the immediate threat posed to gay men by the disease and they were at the margins of, or initially outside, the existing civil society. They were providing whatever information was available on the disease, related to prevention and care that included housing, home help, emotional support, specialised transport services, to those who were sick. Many of these services were not available to HIV/AIDS patients; even those that were available were rarely provided as a result of prejudice in either the medical staff or other patients in clinics. They were also involved in community research in order to understand the needs of people and bring them to the organisation while lobbying for legal rights and more services. This was one of the milestones in the people's reaction to the disease. Another important step was the emergence of the People with AIDS Coalition in 1983 out of a meeting of HIV/AIDS patients in San Francisco. A meeting suggested by their physicians brought Bobbi Campbell and Dan Turner, who was also suffering from AIDS, to talk about their experience, which led the way to the establishment of People with AIDS (PWA), the first self-organisation of people with HIV/AIDS. In May 1983 they had their first ever candle-lit march behind the banner 'Fighting for Our Lives'.

The participation of people living with HIV/AIDS from San Francisco in the Fifth National Lesbian/Gay Health Conference in Denver, which included the Second National Forum on AIDS, was to bring people's voices into the debate in a radical fashion. This forum also included a New York-based group of people living with HIV/AIDS, the AIDS Network. The meeting in Denver expressed the frustration of people being treated as clients of organisations and patients without much contribution to make. In this meeting people from both sides of the US came together, shared their experiences

> The question of how to care affectionately for and recognise the dignity of someone who is dying from a sexually transmitted disease stirred up deeply held prejudices

This statement, written in June 1983 by the advisory committee of the People with AIDS Coalition, launched the People with Aids (PWA) self-empowerment movement.

The Denver Principles

We condemn attempts to label us as 'victims', a term which implies defeat, and we are only occasionally 'patients', a term which implies passivity, helplessness, and dependence upon the care of others. We are 'People With AIDS'.

Recommendations for All People

1. Support us in our struggle against those who would fire us from our jobs, evict us from our homes, refuse to touch us or separate us from our loved ones, our community or our peers, since available evidence does not support the view that AIDS can be spread by casual, social contact.
2. Not scapegoat people with AIDS, blame us for the epidemic or generalize about our lifestyles.

Recommendations for People with AIDS

1. Form caucuses to choose their own representatives, to deal with the media, to choose their own agenda and to plan their own strategies.
2. Be involved at every level of decision-making and specifically serve on the boards of directors of provider organizations.
3. Be included in all AIDS forums with equal credibility as other participants, to share their own experiences and knowledge.
4. Substitute low-risk sexual behaviors for those which could endanger themselves or their partners; we feel people with AIDS have an ethical responsibility to inform their potential sexual partners of their health status.

Rights of People with AIDS

1. To as full and satisfying sexual and emotional lives as anyone else.
2. To quality medical treatment and quality social service provision without discrimination of any form including sexual orientation, gender, diagnosis, economic status or race.
3. To full explanations of all medical procedures and risks, to choose or refuse their treatment modalities, to refuse to participate in research without jeopardizing their treatment and to make informed decisions about their lives.
4. To privacy, to confidentiality of medical records, to human respect and to choose who their significant others are.

To die—and to LIVE—in dignity.

and problems, and turned their frustrations into an active political agenda, The Denver Principles (see Box 5.1). This was one of the critical moments in the emergence of civil society activism: people decided to say 'no' to the way the system classified them, and they were articulating who they were and taking up the debate with the political and medical establishment.

From recognition to treatment

People's engagement with activism was further radicalised with the establishment of AIDS Coalition to Unleash Power (ACT UP) in 1987. This signalled a different phase in which, as the first generation of organisations became much more service-based, a new generation appeared. At the centre of ACT UP was the demand for treatment and access to drugs, claimed on the basis of the individual's right to life. Within a few weeks of its establishment, ACT UP targeted directly the federal Food and Drug Administration (FDA). They demanded the release of drugs 'that might help save our lives'. These demands were delivered on a flyer inviting people 'to Wall Street in Front of Trinity Church Tuesday March 24, 1987 for a Massive AIDS Demonstration'. Another flyer for the same event carried the statement 'AIDS is Everybody's Business Now'. The following day the *New York Times* reported that police officers arrested 16 homosexuals at an AIDS drug protest for blocking the traffic. This was the shape of things to come in HIV/AIDS activism. The aim was to pressure both government and the pharmaceutical industry through threats of political and sometimes financial protests in Wall Street while providing voice for PWAs. The interesting issue here is the role reversal between patients as victims and patients as political activists. This move was yet another stage taking the earlier transformation of patients into PWAs further and turning PWAs into policy advocates.

By providing anecdotal evidence, personal stories, and technical expertise on treatment issues, the activists challenged the federal authorities. Through this change the entire medical perspective that was focused mostly on finding a cure and ultimately producing a vaccine to remove the disease was challenged and transformed. People were voicing their immediate need for treatment as it was clear that, before finding a definitive cure for the disease, people needed to deal with their opportunistic infections and the impact on their lives. They were pushing companies and the FDA to alter their focus to include treatment and preventive medicine to address the needs of people who did not have time to wait for the long processes of finding curative medicine. The appearance of ACT UP and similar groups opened up the space for what is today referred to as 'treatment activism'. In this period activism changed the procedures of drug production and trials to accommodate the needs of people living with HIV/AIDS. The cumbersome and long drug trial processes of the FDA were pressured to change to accommodate the needs of people suffering from HIV/AIDS (see Young *et al.*1988). The target was to publicly challenge the authorities at all levels of the decision-making process around drug trials, political decisions about health and medical provisions, and those pharmaceutical companies said to conduct research in HIV/AIDS-related drugs (see Kramer 1987). The challenge was posed as an ongoing activist engagement with the FDA and others. The process was facilitated by strong support mechanisms: the Freedom of Information Act, used to get access to

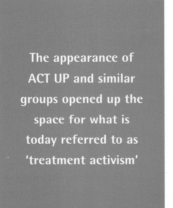

The appearance of ACT UP and similar groups opened up the space for what is today referred to as 'treatment activism'

both technical and political information available in the federal system, and the technical and scientific knowledge base created with the help of academics and medical practitioners. These gave the activists a strong grounding in the debates, enabling them to offer well-articulated scientific opinions. Also, most of this information was made public through publications such as *Body Positive* and *AIDS Treatment News*. It was becoming clear to the FDA and medical professionals that HIV/AIDS activists were far more informed and technically literate than had been assumed, and that they had to be consulted and brought into the debate (Friedman *et al.* 1992).

One of the early successes of the movement was the release of zidovudine-AZT, produced by Burroughs-Wellcome Company in limited quantities until it was approved by the FDA in 1987. The normal release protocol of FDA was cut short to made AZT available. Although the drug was used as a monotherapy for several years for HIV/AIDS-related problems, it proved to be controversial on many grounds; it was expensive and there were doubts about its benefits to patients. Activists campaigned successfully to reduce the price of AZT through protests targeting Wellcome, while the debate around the benefits and usefulness of the drug continued (Volberding *et al.*1990). According to Bastos (1999: 470), after ten years of activism the movement turned into a new phase around 1991 with increased specialisation of the activist organisations. Some of them, such as GMHC, were focusing more and more on services and trying to maintain financial sustainability. As the activists were winning some concessions relating to FDA procedures on drug release protocols, *and* influencing pharmaceuticals, more politically vocal groups were becoming aware of their ability to influence policy processes. A group called Treatment Action Group (TAG) broke from ACT UP and began to engage with the scientific community to contribute to the debate at the scientific level to influence future drug developments and releases by informing them about the experience of people with AZT. TAG also focused on monitoring scientific research, advocating new ways of thinking about drugs in the scientific community (Harrington 1994).

Treatment transformed

The next turning point arrived when the drug trials conducted during the early 1990s produced the highly active antiretroviral therapy (HAART) or 'cocktail therapy' method in 1996. A combination of three HIV-replication restraining enzymes created the cocktail that reduced the viral load, that is, the HIV virus produced in the body, which allowed patients to return to their everyday lives and take up jobs as their immune systems could be maintained by suppressing the viral reproduction. The therapy presented its own problems: its cost was and is very high. It also needs to be delivered under a very strict treatment regimen which, if not followed, will create drug-resistant strains. Nonetheless, the revolutionary developments made hope relevant for people with AIDS at the XI International AIDS Conference held in Vancouver in July 1996. Around 15,000 scientists, activists, politicians, and representatives of pharmaceuticals came together to discuss new developments. According to accounts of the conference, the event took place in an uncharacteristically optimistic mood despite warnings like that of Peter Piot, head of UN Programme on HIV/AIDS: 'There is hope, yes, but let's not exaggerate. Let's not switch from very dark pessimism to hype and over-optimism so we will have a hangover within six months or a year' (Maugh II 1996).

At this turning point, the civil society activism of the early days of ACT UP was no longer dominant; people's participation was mediated mostly by professional organisations that were dealing with policy-makers, pharmaceuticals, and the FDA. In other words, the increased communication with the authorities and the long sensitisation process undertaken through protests by the early 1990s had created a more welcoming environment for HIV/AIDS debate in the industrialised countries. This has also brought an increased funding for HIV/AIDS from central government. The possibility of treatment based on cocktail therapy that increased people's hopes for life greatly eased the accommodation of HIV/AIDS into the mainstream health systems. Therefore, even if civil society around the issue remains active, the concerns and the immediacy of needs are

> Funding gradually moved from grants to a competitive bidding process, which has created a confrontational relationship within civil society which had to transform itself into professional organisations ...

transformed. These successes of civil society are double-edged. The increased funding by the US federal government and other funding authorities gradually moved from grants to first-generation organisations to a competitive bidding process, which has created a confrontational relationship within civil society which had to transform itself into professional organisations. It has exacerbated the differences among organisations, focusing on different groups such as gay men, ethnic minorities, and women's organisations. The successful influence on the medical profession and on pharmaceutical companies also demobilised civil society. As the drugs became widely available in the North, an inevitable medicalisation of the disease removed discussions of HIV/AIDS from public discourse in the developed world. Some of the activists moved on to the international scene while some others 'got on with their lives'.

People's civil society activism established their central concerns as the main issue areas for the HIV/AIDS debate. It was clear that the disease needed to be discussed publicly in order to sensitise the larger communities that would be involved in prevention and care activities. The discussion of prevention needed to be explicit in order to reach people who in turn had to face entrenched prejudices about sexual behaviour. The nature of HIV/AIDS and resulting needs of PWAs for immediate medical attention influenced the traditional medical approach of looking at a disease and trying to cure it: the profession had to change its emphasis to look at palliative care for people that were becoming terminally ill from various opportunistic diseases.

The appearance of HIV/AIDS has been one of the most important determinants of the changing nature of globalisation in which people's need began to take precedence over the institutionalised politics of health. What Arno and Feiden call 'patient empowerment' has changed the relationship between the patient and the politics of health. They suggest that this change in response to AIDS 'eventually inspired broader changes as advocates for people with Alzheimer's, breast cancer, schizophrenia, and other diseases began to approach their diseases with new militancy' (Arno and Feiden 1992: 61). AIDS activism constructed as a social movement for people has inspired approaches to many other diseases and changed the way people think about their relationship to health policies. The idea of turning a disease into an issue of social movements has recently been considered one of the most important political moves to address issues of socio-political injustice implicit in the context of a disease.

As a result of the emergence of the cocktail therapy, some of the earlier activism strategies and institutional responses were subsumed under the medical possibilities. Also, the professionalisation of civil society has distanced people from the debate. This path through professionalisation, medicalisation, and demobilisation has had an inevitable impact on the way HIV/AIDS is now approached globally.

A Global Civil Society?

It is imperative to look at what has happened in the same period internationally in the developing countries, where the scope for activism has been limited, for various reasons. The internationalisation of the debate can be observed at two levels: (1) through the gradual institutionalisation of the HIV/AIDS issue on the agendas of the intergovernmental organisations; and (2) the response to the disease in various countries. The impact of the former on the latter has been an important part of the way civil society action is conditioned in the developing world.

International acceptance

Towards the late 1980s international organisations gradually came to accept HIV/AIDS as an international problem. In this internationalisation of the debate individuals and groups again made a considerable difference. One of the most memorable and important interventions came from the President of Zambia, Kenneth Kaunda, in 1987 when he announced that his son had died of AIDS and demanded that his fellow leaders around the world and in Africa in particular engage with the HIV/AIDS epidemic with an open mind (Foster and Lucas 1991: 38). Another important point was made by Dr Halfdan Mahler, the director of WHO in 1988, who stated

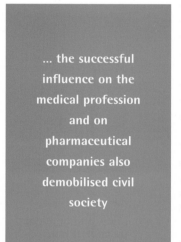

... the successful influence on the medical profession and on pharmaceutical companies also demobilised civil society

that 'I know that many people at first refused to believe that a crisis was upon us. I know because I was one of them' (Panos Institute 1988). Activist groups also played an important role in opening up the international fora for PWA participation in the debates; people's activism around HIV/AIDS was globalised too (Altman 2002: 70).

These perspectives were supported and stimulated by the individual experiences of medical professionals from the developing countries. Dr Jonathan Mann was one such professional who became a central figure in the debate to make a case for a comprehensive global approach to the epidemic that incorporated concerns for the developing world. For him it was clear from his experience in Zaire as the director of a project to follow up 'early cases of the disease in Europe that involved Africans' that the disease was an important social issue at a global scale (Mann 1986). It is possible to argue that it was political activism in the developed countries which pushed the disease into the international political arena. Attempts towards internationalisation and institutionalisation of the response to the epidemic were built by convincing professionals at the WHO that the epidemic was also affecting people in the developing countries and it was not only industrialised country problem based in gay communities (Gordenker et al. 1995: 42). This was a tall order considering that it was only on 1 January 1993 that the WHO removed homosexuality from its list of mental disorders.

The international debate was initiated by both the Northern activists and informed medical professionals who had experience of the disease in the developing countries. By hosting international conferences on HIV/AIDS, the WHO provided an important global space for people to come together and to discuss emerging issues and medical progress concerning HIV/AIDS. The meetings initially involved only medical professionals, health specialists, and policy-related participants; patients were not considered relevant participants. Gradually these international gatherings were pressured to open themselves to include people suffering from HIV/AIDS. It was in 1989 that ACT UP, with its counterparts in Canada, stormed the Fifth AIDS Conference in

Montreal. It was the first time PWA were in such fora. 'PWA Tim McCaskell grabbed the microphone and "officially" opened the conference "on behalf of people with AIDS from Canada and around the world"'(Goldberg 1998:1). In other words, activism was spilling over national borders and creating international links among various activist groups around the globe. Groups such as GMHC and ACT UP were providing know-how for civil society action in this area (Watney 1994). Activism in these areas allowed PWAs to assert their right to participate in the discussions that were central to their lives. Arguably, these events and activists' interventions were the roots of the global civil society action that was crystallizing around the issue of HIV/AIDS and PWAs globally. The main source of this expansion into the global must be seen as the values and beliefs people held in solidarity with others who were suffering from the same disease and who wished to voice their pain. The global perspective behind this deep-rooted camaraderie was very quickly institutionalised.

In 1987 the WHO established its Special Programme on AIDS, which became Global Programme on AIDS (GPA) and in 1996 the United Nations AIDS Programme, a specialised agency. Also around this time Perez De Cuellar, then Secretary-General of the United Nations, brought the issue to the General Assembly and called HIV/AIDS 'a global conflict' (Gordenker et al.1995: 41). From 1987 onwards, under Mann's directions through GPA, the WHO played an important role. NGOs were considered to be partners in this move. GPA has become the focal point for communication between intergovernmental policy discussions and NGOs that have moved to work in the South with people on HIV/AIDS. The changing attitude of the international fora somehow also reflects the gradual change of the perspectives of the governments of industrialised countries, which have become more open to engaging with civil society actors on the issue and to funding them. This is important as intergovernmental organisations have become central in influencing health policies in the developing countries.

This change is reflected in the special meeting of the United Nations General Assembly on AIDS in June 2001 that recommitted the international community to deal with the disease and created a Global Fund to direct funding for vaccine research and to help communities. Also, recent years have witnessed the expansion of the involvement of private sector and large philanthropic foundations in establishing HIV/AIDS programmes for vaccine research or care and prevention in the developing countries. For example, in 2001 Pfizer donated around $11 million to build a medical training centre in Uganda, while Merck is supporting local sensitisation campaigns such as *lovelife* in South Africa as a part of its involvement and, together with the Gates Foundation, is building research in Botswana.

HIV/AIDS in developing countries

It is important to look at the circumstances in the South during the same period. The following analysis follows a chronological sequence. Internationalisation, of course did not mean that the disease had emerged in the South for the first time. It already existed in the South, but it was now identified under the gaze of medical science and international politics. This view was rooted in the experience of industrialised countries in the North, and it had an important impact on the way the developing countries reacted to the disease.

Before the professionals arrived, the image of HIV/AIDS as a Northern homosexual disease was the only perspective available in the developing countries. This association of the disease with homosexuality in the Northern context created problems for various countries at the onset of the epidemic in the South. The early identification of patients in developing countries resulted in a very limited response from public policy-makers. The response in some countries mostly consisted of branding the disease as a foreign import from the West confined to high-risk groups such as gay men, while in other countries the existence of HIV/AIDS was denied altogether. In cultures that denied the existence of homosexuality, the public authorities could remain passive in relation to HIV/AIDS, which they constructed as an alien problem. The reaction of African governments was clear from the First International AIDS Conference in 1985, where no African government was present.

> AIDS activism constructed as a social movement has inspired approaches to many other diseases and changed the way people think about their relationship to health policies

This also points to a central difference in people's reaction: while in the developed world people themselves took the initiative, in the South the disease was initially articulated by outsiders rather than by people living with it.

The lack of local activism and the reluctance of governments to engage with HIV/AIDS meant that in many countries denial was the central problem in dealing with the disease. This problem was addressed by and large by existing religiously-based groups and services together with some NGOs already working in those countries. One of the first groups to provide AIDS services was the International Family Planning Agency, which distributed a manual on AIDS locally (Harper 1989). Another example is the Population and Community Development Association (PDA) in Thailand, founded by Mechai Viravaidya in 1974 to deal with development and birth control issues; it took on AIDS activism without any great difficulty. One of their advocacy projects, *Cabbages and Condoms Restaurants*, whose main aim was to make condoms an everyday issue, was easily adapted to HIV/AIDS activism. Their long-standing relationship with the government also allowed them to lobby the government to engage with the issue and to bring Buddhist monks into their project to disseminate information around the country. International funding agencies also got involved in funding HIV/AIDS-related programmes: for example, USAID and the Canadian International Development Agency (CIDA) supported prevention and sensitisation work in Senegal as early as 1985. The reluctance of governments to engage with HIV/AIDS as a policy issue made some NGOs wary of getting involved with this rather contentious issue. Nonetheless, church-based organisations and already existing NGOs presented themselves as important partners in the debate by utilising their existing cross-country networks. These groups focused on informing people about the disease and generally talking about prevention methods. Thus, the nature of civil society action was based on the already existing organisations and was within their existing interests. They were intervening to make people aware of the disease. Therefore, the emerging

> World Health Organisation meetings initially involved only medical professionals, health specialists, and policy-related participants; patients were not considered relevant participants

pattern was mostly based on considering people as patients rather than PWAs.

At the same time, the impact of the initial and sustained opposition to certain prevention methods, as well as the disbelief in such a complex disease among traditional communities by various faith groups, hindered early interventions. Respected community leaders had to assume the burden of talking about living with HIV/AIDS as a possibility and not as a cause of hopelessness. In Uganda, Rev. Gideon Byamugisha was the first practising priest in Africa to declare his HIV-positive status publicly to be able to educate people about the disease. At the international level the intervention of Kenneth Kaunda mentioned earlier was a very important turning-point in making some African countries take the issue seriously. Several countries in Africa, such as Uganda, Senegal and Kenya after it overcame its prejudice, demonstrated the key importance of political will and government leadership in dealing with the disease. The leadership provided by Yoweri Museveni, the President of Uganda, is a good example, while South African President Thabo Mbeki's continued denial of the link between HIV and AIDS represents a major failure of political leadership, with devastating impact on the disease. As AIDS-related deaths began to increase, traditional burial became a problem in many communities. The sheer numbers of dead made it impossible to observe the traditional ceremonies, which implied a lack of reverence for the dead. Burial societies begun to emerge to relieve the afflicted communities and turned the burial process into a community undertaking. Some of the names given to these societies in Uganda, such as *Twezikye*—'let's bury ourselves'—and *Munno mukabi*—'A friend in need'— echo people's reflections on their experiences.

Funding from external sources facilitated the creation of many local NGOs or sustained existing local initiatives. One such local initiative that has resulted in a major NGO in Uganda and in the region in general is the AIDS Support Organisation (TASO), which was established in 1987 by 16 volunteers who were personally affected by the disease, and led by Mrs Noerine Kaleeba, who, after losing her husband to AIDS in London, became aware of the absence of a service and advocacy organisation in Uganda. TASO today provides various services from medical help, counselling, and capacity building in communities around Uganda to training other NGOs working in Africa. In some countries such as Thailand, already existing NGOs and community groups have provided the avenues for interventions. Although the immediate reaction to the disease in 1984 was to ignore it as an alien homosexual problem, towards the end of 1980s the government was pressured by the medical profession and the press to engage with the disease more publicly (Ford 1994: 89). Today, information on HIV/AIDS is readily available around the world; most developing countries have either government or internationally supported HIV/AIDS information centres running programmes on HIV/AIDS sensitisation in their own countries. Some of these organisations also test people for their HIV status.

Towards local activism

Since the early 1990s the number of organisations working on HIV/AIDS-related issues in the developing countries has exploded. Many such organisations are either externally founded and funded or community initiatives supported by external funding. The civil society reaction to the disease in developing countries has been transformed by the emergence of local groups working in the HIV/AIDS area. In this changing environment the role of civil society in various countries is becoming much more pronounced. A new wave of activism from the South is emerging. Although it has both international and Northern components, the former seem to be supplementary to the voices of people from the South.

Northern groups are supporting the voices of the South in the way they are articulating their needs, as demonstrated for instance by the work of Johns Hopkins University in Rwanda and other countries (see Box 5.2). Organisations, some of them religiously based, are articulating the needs of people as they live through the disease according to their own conditions in which they live. In Uganda for instance, one diocese has developed a special prayer service dealing with HIV/AIDS (see Box 5.3). Religious institutions seem to have a

> While in the developed world people themselves took the initiative, in the South the disease was initially articulated by outsiders rather than by people living with it

significant impact as they are able to have access to the people in their everyday lives. Many organisations are bringing up issues that should be taken seriously but have not been focused on by the international fora. One such attempt, in Rwanda, is by a group called AVEGA 'AGAHOZO'. The group was established by women who were widowed after the 1994 genocide to help each other. The genocide was not the *only* cause of death for very large numbers of people but it *was* also at the root of the HIV/AIDS crisis in Rwanda. According to some, many women who survived the atrocities of the genocide were infected by the HIV virus as a result of systematic rape during the genocide. The problem is that these women have now begun to die, leaving behind children with no one to look after them. AVEGA tries to address this by asking its 25,000 members to adopt AIDS orphans, some of whom are HIV positive themselves. Other groups, such as THETA in Uganda, try to use already available resources, such as traditional healers, in the communities to build capacity in preventing, diagnosing, and treating HIV/AIDS (see Box 5.4).

Although these examples represent a new array of organisations in which HIV/AIDS-related programmes are adapted to local needs and available resources, they reflect a familiar pattern of civil society activity around the issue of sensitisation related to prevention and care. In other words, the main efforts in the field consist of prevention by providing more information to help effect a positive change in people's sexual behaviour. The issues around which civil society mobilises are, however, still articulated at the global level, not the local. As this external factor is also important in the funding of many local organisations, the relationship between global policy priorities and people's needs is difficult to balance. However, a different perspective on the issue is being forged by bringing PWAs into the debate. A transformation is emerging in the area of treatment as the availability of cocktail therapy since 1996 has created a new basis for discussion.

Transformation

The treatment action campaigns in Brazil, South Africa, and Thailand are particularly good examples of this change where an emergence of civil society

Johns Hopkins University/Centre for Communication Programs(JHU/CCP) works with several partnerships between the Northern partner and various groups from Africa to bring young people into the public debate about HIV/AIDS and to motivate youth towards a behavioural change in their sex lives, while overcoming the stigma associated with the disease. One aspect of this approach is a project called Africa Alive! (URL). It brings together a large number of national networks of public and private sector youth and AIDS organisations in Nigeria, Kenya, South Africa, Tanzania, Uganda, Zambia, and Zimbabwe. It uses methods that are entrenched in youth culture to foment change, such as football tournaments, music concerts, and popular cartoons. One important way of bringing the youth into the debate was constructed around the articulation of KUBA (Life Force-to be) as the symbol of HIV/AIDS in Rwanda. The following extract is taken from a JHU/CCP Rwanda documentation centre paper.

Kuba is the Design of Rwandan Youth: The prevention of STDs, including HIV and AIDS is as simple as A,B and C and where A stands for abstinence, B for Being faithful and C for the use of condom every time. In a workshop to develop youth-friendly materials, 44 young Rwandans (between ages 15–19) opted for KUBA as a way to prevent HIV and AIDS.

Meaning of KUBA: It stand for 'to be'. It is derived from three kinyarwanda words: Kwifata—abstinence; Ubudahemuka—Fidelity; Agakingirizo—Condom. KUBA is a memory-aide to encourage young people to make choices.

The KUBA Logo: Shape: The KUBA logo is a red ribbon tied into a star with three arms, one vertical and two horizontal. The vertical arm stands for Kwifata; the left for Ubudahemuka and the right for Agakingirizo: the three arms are joined together by a nought that signifies unity in purpose by young people. Meaning: The tied ribbons remind youth not to take anything for granted or open up to any risks (the logo was created by the active work of young people).

The project was launched by a series of concerts and public events where young people participated in the process. This approach clearly demonstrates a process through which a youth ownership is created for the project.

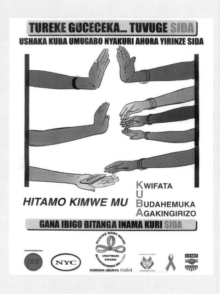

action in the sense of people taking control of their futures can be seen. In several countries PWAs launched their treatment campaigns with some support and expertise from the North. In Brazil, civil society activists persuaded the government to allow the generic production of otherwise expensive drugs, against the regulations of the World Trade Organisation. In the meantime generic drug production has also commenced in India and Thailand. The treatment action campaign in Thailand

Box 5.3: A prayer service for HIV/AIDS

In order to get its message across, the Archbishop Carey Regional Resource Centre of Namirembe, with the cooperation of Namirembe Diocese in Uganda, produced a special prayer service Liturgy for the World AIDS Campaign in 2000. The text of the service provides an innovative way of addressing the issues around the disease. Following are extracts from the core prayers in the Worship Service--Litany for Health:

Leader:
Let us now call the attention of God; of the health committee members, service prayers, educators policy officials, government and community leaders, volunteers and all those engaged in reproductive health improvement, HIV prevention and AIDS care, hygiene and sanitation, nutrition and general health situation among our children, youths adults that need our prayers and actions.

Part A

Leader 3:
Among our youths, girls in the age bracket 15–19 years are six times more infected with HIV than the boys in the same age group.
All: Oh God, hear our prayers and enable us to educate our people.

Part B

Leader 3:
There is widespread poverty at household level which drives women and men without physical, financial and spiritual resources to transact sex for gifts, for financial assistance, for shelter, for school fees and for goods.
All: Oh God, hear our prayers and enable us to overcome both material and spiritual poverty.

Part F

Leader 1:
Although people living with HIV/AIDS in the developed world can access Highly Active Anti-retroviral therapies which have made them live longer and more productive lives, millions of our friends in the developing world have little or no access to these drugs. Even drugs to treat opportunistic infections are scarce including simple pain killers like aspirin.
All: Oh God, build your world with cords of love that cannot be broken. Encourage those who have to give to those who do not have.

The prayer book is available from Bishop's office, Namirembe Diocese

Photo courtesy of Moses Matou.

persuaded the government in 2001 to produce generic drugs and make them available to PWAs. Thailand also decided to provide generic drug technology to African countries as a matter of solidarity with people suffering there (IRIN 2002). The success of the Treatment Action Campaign's lawsuit in South Africa in 2001 (see Box 5.5) forcing pharmaceuticals to lower their prices was a landmark in activism that has international ramifications. Gains made in South Africa through 2001–2 in persuading a reluctant government to make the drugs available to everyone in need in South Africa, primarily to prevent mother-to-child HIV transmission, are also significant in this civil society debate. In the process both local (AIDS Law Project and Treatment Action Campaign) and international NGOs (MSF and OXFAM) have been instrumental (Press Release 2002). It was a meeting point of activism for various civil society actors: international NGOs providing support for local activism as well as lobbying pharmaceuticals to

It is a national NGO initiated through partnership between TASO Uganda and MSF-Switzerland. It began in 1992 as a clinical study in Kampala evaluating with traditional healers(THs) the effectiveness of local herbal treatments for selected AIDS-related diseases. The success of this initiative transformed the project into an organisation working with THs in HIV/AIDS education, counselling and improved care. It is committed to promote traditional medicine to complement modern health care services and to work with THs as health educators. Some of THETA's work on herbal treatments for Herpes Zoster and chronic diarrhoea-opportunistic disease in AIDS patients showed significant improvement in patients on herbal treatments. THETA has also trained more than 356 healers including 58 who have been trained as trainers. While working towards these objectives, THETA also is leading a consortium of similar organisations in the region

Extracted from a THETA pamphlet

Above: An encounter between traditional healing and modern medicine. Photo courtesy of Joseph Tenywa, THETA.

lower the prices of particular drugs that could be used in the area, medical volunteers carrying out drug trials in local hospitals (Carter 2002), and legal professionals taking action against governments and companies. Moreover, the links between people involved in treatment action in different countries across continents accommodate a new way of conceiving global civil society, beyond the conventional international NGO perspective (Gomez-Pablos 2001). What is being witnessed in these actions is the revitalisation of civil society action, which in the North has become tamed and in the South has been mainly around organisational interventions based on global policies. Treatment action campaigns have made people's voices heard nearly for the first time on issues concerning their everyday existence. They have turned activism around and have brought people, PWAs, into the debate. This should be also seen as the result of people's frustration with the existing civil society interventions. A few central factors seem to have helped these efforts. The existence of enabling legal structures even in the absence of a willing government have proved to be central to the success of civil society action.

It is also clear that pressure on governments and international organisations from Northern civil society to support the Southern voices is important. For example, The Harvard Consensus Statement on Antiretroviral Treatment for AIDS in Poor Countries announced in April 2001 and signed by 148 academics provides parameters for making antiretroviral therapy immediately available to poor countries, while at the same time conducting carefully controlled clinical trials in order to determine the best practices for providing HIV/AIDS therapy in resource-poor settings (Harvard 2001). Included in the statement is a detailed cost estimate for delivering antiretroviral therapy as well as a proposal for how this treatment could be readily financed by resource-rich nations. The statement is the first authoritative declaration on the possibility of using available technology and resources in developing countries. It also calls upon wealthy countries, in partnership with poor ones, to establish a global HIV/AIDS Prevention and Treatment Trust Fund to provide both scientific and financial leadership to make antiretroviral therapy available in the areas of the world hardest hit by the epidemic. The importance of using 'existing and developing infrastructure, such as networks that have been developed for directly observed therapy for' TB and mother-to-child HIV transmission is recognised (Harvard 2001: 12–13). Furthermore, the statement places the debate in a moral context: 'The disparity in access to effective treatment between wealthy countries and developing countries is neither scientifically nor ethically justified at this time' (Harvard 2001: 4). This challenges the international political framework and the pharmaceutical industry by making the treatment issue central to the debate globally. The timing and the content of this intervention was very important particularly in terms of the civil society action against the pharmaceuticals in South Africa in April 2001. It seemed to have come as an expression of solidarity with the Treatment Action Campaign in South Africa while providing scientific and moral justification for further action.

The availability of treatment and its importance for influencing behavioural change are central to the debate in developing countries. This links two central issues for HIV/AIDS. The availability of treat-ment may be one of the missing ingredients to influence behavioural change promoted in the last decade through education campaigns. Treatment, in other words, can also be used as the grounds of preventive policies as it would remove the spectre of death as the only way out in the lives of PWAs.

> The impact of the initial and sustained opposition to certain prevention methods, as well as the disbelief in such a complex disease among traditional communities by various faith groups, hindered early interventions

Double standards remain

However, this connection and the importance of treatment for more than 36 million people in the developing world is jeopardised by the double standards prevailing between civil society action in the developed world and that in the developing world. Although a poster in Britain on 1 December 2001 said 'No One Has Been Cured', in the developed countries the disease has become a treatable chronic disease which no longer influences people's everyday lives as it did before. The high cost of the drugs has in developed countries resulted in the issue being incorporated into the medical system, while in developing countries treatment has been unavailable and interventions remain related to prevention and care: *drugs for us, condoms for you*. This particular problem points to a major tension between the needs of over 30 million people living

with HIV/AIDS and those who are able to discuss what *can be* or *cannot* be done for these people.

According to Paula Treichler (1999: 99), the mode of global civil society engagement took a form of 'A First World Chronicle' (see also Watney 1994). It suggests that the epidemic in developing countries was articulated through the vision of the developed world, formed around its own interests and priorities. This perspective came to public attention very directly in 2001 through the unfortunate statement of Andrew Natsios, director of USAID, one of the largest funders of civil society in the developing world. He suggested that Africans cannot keep time to administer HAART regimens: 'they do not use western means to tell time. They use the sun. These drugs have to be administered in certain sequences' (Attaran, Freeberg, and Hirsch 2001). This refusal to provide treatment on the basis of an assumed inherent weakness in people from certain geographical area nearly relocates the debate in the early nineteenth century moral framework. Paul Farmer *et al.* (2001: 405) argue that 'the response of the affluent countries and their institutions—from aid agencies, non-governmental organisations, and the pharmaceutical industry—has been insufficient (The death toll and increasing HIV incidence are the most eloquent rebuke to contrary assessments)'. After a long advocacy and service-based involvement of civil society in the developing world, the picture is not too optimistic (see Box 5.6). Therefore, it has become imperative for people to voice—indeed, shout—their needs, formulated as rights. The movement in relation to treatment is revitalising the socio-political struggle over AIDS through recontextualising the debate into the developing countries.

Conclusion

The way to deal with HIV/AIDS been shaped, brought into the public gaze, and integrated into the policy discussions as a result of civil society activism. However, today these areas are more or less taken to be the entry points for *top-down* technical policy interventions. The present state of affairs questions the past, which focused on long education and prevention campaigns largely based on

The Treatment Action Campaign (TAC) was launched on International Human Rights Day, 10 December 1998, by a group of ten activists, including Zackie Achmat, who chose the day to launch a fast to highlight the needs of people with HIV and AIDS in South Africa for medicine. The objective of the TAC is to campaign for access to treatment and, in particular, affordable medicines for people with HIV and AIDS. In the space of three years, it has grown from a handful of individuals to an organisation with 10,000 volunteers in South Africa but with wider respect and support both locally and internationally.

The TAC understands the complex array of issues that are linked to improving access to medicines. We realize that this campaign cannot be separated from campaigns around other global ills, such as poverty and the need for debt cancellation. The impoverishment of developing countries has impoverished health services and infrastructure. But the TAC also does not apologise for its bottom line: that medicines in mouths save the live of people with TB, HIV, and many other preventable diseases, and that, even whilst complex global issues are debated, lives can and must be saved.

Between 1999 and 2000 TAC's stature grew in a range of grass-roots campaigns. In October 2000, for example, a batch of generic medicines were imported in public defiance of Pfizer's patent on its anti-fungal drug Diflucan, causing an outcry about the price of many medicines that led Pfizer offering the drug free to the South African public sector. In 2001, the TAC helped to catalyse a global movement when it called for solidarity with South Africa's legal battle against 39 multinational pharmaceutical companies who had impugned South Africa's Medicines and Related Substances Control Act (90 0f 1997) through litigation that challenged its constitutionality and alleged that it violated intellectual property rights.

The TAC's legal strategy to win admittance to the court case as *amicus curiae* (friend of the court) fused with an advocacy strategy to bring to international public attention the need for affordable medicines—and the price of refusing them. Important alliances were built with organizations such as ACT-UP, Oxfam, the Consumer Project on Technology, and MSF. Between January and April 2001, an unprecedented civil society mobilization succeeded in bringing pressure on governments and the multinational pharmaceutical companies, and on 5 March, the first day of the case, demonstrations took place in 30 cities outside South Africa. This eventually led to the behind-the-scenes intervention of the UN Secretary-General, Kofi Annan, to try to persuade the companies to withdraw their challenge to South Africa's law.After the case was withdrawn on 18 April, the momentum of the campaign was sustained for much of the rest of the year and culminated in November 2001 when a ministerial meeting of the World Trade Organisation explicitly recognised that there are circumstances where public health and the need for affordable medicines takes priority over intellectual property rights.

TAC's success so far in this campaign has depended on ordinary people, particularly people with HIV, standing up and being participants in a global campaign—and not being relegated to victim

safe sex. These interventions seem to have been implemented generically without consideration of the conditions under which people are likely to change their behaviour in a given social context.

Jonathan Mann in 1996 discussed the previous decade, which saw the creation of a solidarity around AIDS as a global issue, and suggested that this perspective had been lost. He said 'For today, fragmentation, isolation and separation dominate the world of AIDS' (Mann 1999:1). The implication of this observation is central to understanding the role of civil society action in relation to AIDS. It points towards a major shift in the way civil society activism has developed. Mann pointed out the importance of deeply held values and beliefs that motivated people to participate in the AIDS movement early on and the resulting feeling of global solidarity; he went on, 'All that was intensifies our awareness of what we have

status. Television pictures of TAC members with the insignia of a new movement, the distinctive 'HIV-Positive' T-shirt, have given the fight for affordable medicines the face of the affected and infected. People with AIDS have narrated their own stories about loss of hope, dignity, and life. TAC volunteers who have died during these campaigns, such as Christopher Moraka and Sarah Hlalele, have begun a new roll of post-apartheid heroes, whose struggle has been for socio-economic equality. TAC's willing-

Above: Appeal for a demonstration demanding mother-to-child antiretroviral treatment in South Africa. The South African Constitution upholds the right to health. Poster courtesy of Tratment Action Campaign.

ness to defy unjust laws, particularly patents that make medicines prohibitively expensive, has raised public awareness in a way that has begun to change the culture and stigmatise profiteering from ill-health.

TAC's objective is to shift the way society, especially in the First' World, regards medicine. Until the last decades of the twentieth century, the greatest advances in public health came about as a result of social improvements—to which medicine contributed. But lately, the advent of preventable and treatable global epidemics, such as HIV, creates a new demand for medicine, both to save lives and to stem the consequences of diseases on society in terms of underdevelopment.

TAC believes that a broad movement of global civil society is needed to break barriers to access to affordable treatment, as well as to guarantee massively increased investment into Third World diseases and health services. But its global campaign is based on the premise that civil society must first be organized and empowered at a national level for these campaigns to work. That is why, on a daily basis, TAC volunteers teach each other about medicines and health, and activist train health workers and work with trade unions and churches and pursue a range of campaigns that target local issues as well as national and international issues.

In certain respects, the TAC movement mirrors the early struggles around AIDS in North America and Europe. There is one significant difference: TAC's activists come mostly from the poor.

Mark Heywood, Secretary, TAC

lost. For today, solidarity has become a virtually meaningless word . . . The more it is used, the emptier it feels . . . it sounds perfunctory . . . we immediately know and feel that something is wrong, discordant, disconnected, missing'(Mann 1999: 2). He further argued that 'it is now acceptable to think and live in isolation; people in the rich countries can receive treatment with whatever the latest and best science can provide; the North has resumed its limited,

"charity based" approach to international assistance against AIDS . . . the biomedical research establishment can pursue its course with diminished attention to pressing societal needs'(Mann 1999: 3). He suggested that the pre-AIDS status quo realities and relations in global health have reappeared and been reasserted. The foresight of this statement and its implications came to haunt the debate after more than a decade's work of global civil society in the

Box 5.6: Views from the field

The following are extracts from an Internet debate on the role of communications in the HIV/AIDS debate (Communication Initiative 2001). The participants are public health specialists and long-time HIV/AIDS workers from the field. The extracts here represent the views expressed by many PWAs and people working with the disease. They demonstrate the critical moment we are at.

Looking back over a decade, it seems to me from available statistics and experience from the field, that we have not made as much success in stopping the spread of HIV/AIDS especially among the youth.

If one take the issue of condoms, it is easy to say CONDOMIZE. This has failed to persuade people to use condoms because it [sex] takes place within a certain context. We have failed to get people to go BEYOND AWARENESS.

Please folks . . . we have got to start getting fund flows so that there are practical benefits SOON for PLWHA [People Living With HIV/AIDS] and others around the world who are in a health crisis.

developing world. His argument questions the existence of a global civil society that has the qualities of an earlier time, when people came first.

By way of conclusion, I want to reflect on the reasons for this discordance between the global civil society and civil society as people's action. The starting assumption of this chapter—that the change in the structure of the global politics of health is related to people's demands on the system—has been demonstrated by the case study of HIV/AIDS activism. However, this change, driven by people, is not unreservedly sustainable or positive in its long-term implications, as actions can turn into dominating frameworks. On the one hand, the idea of global civil

society seems to be relevant as long as one is looking at large structures that exist in global debates; on the other hand, a new people's politics is emerging from the South. It is the latter which is creating civil society activism that needs to be supported and sustained in order to significantly reorient the HIV/AIDS debate for the benefit of millions in the South. However, for this hope to be realised, the new activists need to understand the mechanisms that have created a certain stagnation after a successful engagement with the traditional systems in the last decade. I end by discussing the following three points in turn: (1) dangers of success, (2) institutionalisation, and (3) medicalisation.

Dangers of success

There is no doubt that the voices of PWAs were critical at every stage of the development of discussions around HIV/AIDS, and reformulated the debates on a new basis. Civil society has, for example, established 'safe sex' (Patton 1996) as a norm around the world. The campaigns around various preventive measures, particularly condoms, have become global common sense in thinking about sex. Establishment of access to care and treatment as a norm must be seen as another important area of success. But the early movement's achievement in anchoring the HIV/AIDS-related debates in civil society was a significant one. Only in its globalised and institutionalised form has this anchor in civil society become an encumbrance for people. The early success of HIV/AIDS activism in the United States established particular forms of engagement and delivery with sensitisation, prevention, and care as the model for interventions elsewhere. In other words, what civil society had created early on has now become a socio-medical perspective on intervention into other people's lives.

The adverse impact of this situation can be observed in relation to education and prevention programmes in the South. Pedzisani Motlhabane (2002) has argued that people are well informed about the disease, its sexual transmission, and methods of prevention. Therefore, their behaviour does not reflect a lack of knowledge but rather their social conditions, together with the failure to educate people in their own cultural and social contexts through their experience of the disease. Although a lot of time is spent on educating people to remove the stigma attached to the disease and induce behaviour change, at times the language used in relation to the AIDS issue exacerbated the stigma. According to Susan Reynolds Whyte (1997: 203), 'health information campaigns have made people aware of AIDS, and awareness itself is a source of uncertainty'. She argues that the information disseminated required people to distance themselves from their own understanding of both the disease and of what could be done for those suffering from it, creating a state of hopelessness as locally available medicine was deemed inappropriate for this foreign disease. This hopelessness is addressed by Tumi Tameii (2002) from the perspective of youth: she suggests that, although education programmes always try to target youngsters, they rarely include any youth member in their production, and as a result the target group is missed and pushed into a hopelessness leading to indifference (for work trying to overcome this see http://www.africadi.org).

Another example of this 'one size fits all' approach is related to one of the most heavily promoted prevention methods: condom use that would work if appropriate sexual behaviour could be sustained over an individual's life time. While millions of condoms are distributed as part of sensitisation and prevention programmes by hundreds of organisations, it is not clear how far the language of these programmes, mostly initiated by global civil society, relates to the context within which sexual habits are created and sustained. The question remains: does global civil society understand the social conditions disempowering people to use condoms, which include social stigma as well as poverty?

The language and the particular methods of global civil society need to be opened to debate, as the disease is generating many problems that have never yet been a part of the debate. One such problem is the increased numbers of AIDS orphans, counted in many millions. Because this problem has not arisen on a large scale in the developed world, the response to it and the future of these children have been not very widely discussed. As adults are either dead or not well enough to look after their children, grandparents are in charge of large numbers of children. In Rwanda many families are looked after by older children. As

a generation gap opens up between children and their communities, the children are not being trained in traditional livelihoods. When education is on the table, therefore, what is required is not only lessons on using condoms and yet more demonstrations of how devastating HIV/AIDS can be. Education should also mean addressing people's needs and it ought to be much more targeted, based on an in-depth understanding of communities and the resources available to them. This also means educating people who are mobilising resources and acting as facilitators of these interventions in both the North and the South. It requires a change in the way HIV/AIDS interventions are funded, with large sums of money given to cover the costs of known methods and areas of interventions.

> A new wave of activism from the South is emerging. Although it has both international and Northern components, they are supplementary to the voices of people from the South

Institutionalisation

Successes have become problems as they have been incorporated into the mechanisms of international organisations. The process initiated by activists to communicate the gravity of the situation around the world to international organisations was an important step that aimed at bringing the weight of the international politics to bear on the disease. Although internationalisation of HIV/AIDS put the debate on the global map, it located the debate in already existing international mechanisms that have been producing global inequalities and poverty. This meant that the progressive politics of people reflected in the earlier civil society action was left behind. This process has influenced the debate in two ways.

First, the debate was adapted to the traditional top-down approaches of these organisations in addition to becoming part of the wider global debate. The positive moves by the WHO, the World Bank, and others to engage with the disease may in the long run have had a certain negative impact on the spread of the disease as people's voices become less and less relevant in a debate dominated by the institutional wisdom of *expert* organisations trying to balance many interests that are not necessarily relevant to PWAs. The social and cultural contexts of the disease were subsumed within the top-down understanding that moved to 'help the patients'. The disease was constructed as an isolated medical condition that was devastating the South and needed intervention by medical and public health specialists. Civil society became relevant again only on a service-delivery basis, with minimal policy impact at the level of decision-making. This development has also led to NGOs working in development increasingly adopting HIV/AIDS into their mandate as an add-on, as there is a lot of money in the area, which is translated into generic interventions without much thought given to their impact. As a result one can argue that people have been further marginalised while the HIV/AIDS funding has become related to the survival of some organisations.

Second, when the influence of their policy experts was combined with their financial capacities, these organisations became the central actors in the debate. Their assumed expertise has taken precedence over the experiences and the needs of actually lived lives. The funding relations were able to dictate the style and the limits of programmes, which were usually more attuned to the changing interests of the experts. The debate around whether HIV-positive mothers should breast-feed their babies has been carried on without much attention to the social stigma attached to not breast-feeding. In a similar fashion, in the initial stages of the treatment debate experts and funders were uninterested in such interventions in the South since their perspective on the issue excluded the needs of people on the ground. This influenced many community organisations as they were pressured by their funding relations to get involved only in prevention

As funding is central to the survival of many community groups and NGOs, these organisations are finding themselves needing to move towards the international agendas. Moreover, as the focus and interests of international bodies are ever changing, their funding priorities are changing too, with adverse impact on community organisations. The pressure to survive in this environment is creating a short-term focus on unsustainable interventions, which eventually create distrust in communities. While most civil society action is based on these top-down policy

> Treatment action campaigns are a meeting point for various civil society actors: international NGOs providing support and lobbying pharmaceuticals, medical volunteers carrying out drug trials, and legal professionals taking action against governments and companies

approaches, some innovative activist groups are disenchanted as their main funders are withdrawing to move on to other topics and areas, leaving tasks unfinished and without much hope that they will be finished.

This analysis of institutionalisation suggests that the process has created a global civil society without much space for people in it; its recent development should be treated with caution. The initiatives for a vaccine and the Global Fund after the UN meeting on AIDS in 2001 have been welcomed. There is no doubt that both processes are important. But constructing these processes at the international organisational level has isolated *PWAs* from the discussion right from the beginning. They have the potential in their structures and decision-making processes to reproduce all the imbalances that are leading to global inequalities. These adverse conditions are further compounded by the policy agenda put forward by both the WHO and the World Bank (see Wolfensohn 2001), which considers the disease to be a political problem that can be best addressed within neo-liberal socio-economic relations. It is clear that already existing global market relations have exacerbated the disease as the spread of it seems to be more related to wealth differentials within a community than to absolute poverty: high incidences of migrant labour and prostitution, for instance, both frequent side-effects of inequality, tend to facilitate the spread of the disease (see Farmer 1999). The wisdom of this agenda therefore needs to be questioned by people that are creating the civil society action. Institutionalised civil society faces a major challenge as the financial power of these organisations makes it hard to resist to them.

Medicalisation

HIV/AIDS is a medical condition. Medicalisation is a particular form of institutionalisation through which the knowledge of and the resulting interventions for the disease shift from people's experiences and demands onto a technical level. It is in this process that people become patients and are, to a certain degree, disempowered. The characteristic institutional top-down approach has isolated the civil society discussions from the debate, as a result of which innovations in the debate have come mostly from medical science with targeted technical interventions. In this there has been a certain implicit assumption about the nature of the occurrences of the disease that has guided uniform policy formulations. As a result, a good deal of work is focused on medical interventions without consideration of larger issues.

Many medical interventions in the South have been focused on mother-to-child transmission. The established understanding of HIV/AIDS as a heterosexual epidemic in Africa seems to have justified a focus on women, in addition to the fact that the antenatal clinics provide easy access for women. However, this focus seems to ignore, to some extent, the role of men in the spread of the disease. It ignores the social relations between men and women in various societies as well as the potential impact of men who have sex with men. This has not only left the role of men in the story of the disease nearly untouched but also disregards the fact that the potential success of antenatal clinic interventions largely relies on engaging with the traditional role of men in communities, whose financial and social status is higher than women's in many communities. Women are usually unable to express their needs to, let alone discuss their HIV status with, their husbands, since doing so could terminate their marriages and force them out of their communities. Moreover, it is clear that capturing women is only the first step, as stopping transmission on one occasion does not necessarily result in behavioural change that influences transmission in further pregnancies.

Another aspect of this problem is related to the orphans: as mothers die the saved children face the social impact of HIV/AIDS. Therefore, it is imperative to combine medical intervention with social-economic concerns to address the problem of orphans and to create mechanisms of looking after them. As much as medical interventions are important, they confine the disease to hospitals rather than the family home and the communities where debate needs to take place.

> In the developed countries HIV/AIDS has become a treatable chronic disease, while in developing countries treatment has been unavailable and interventions remain related to prevention and care: drugs for us, condoms for you

This is not to suggest that medical interventions are not important, only that particular medical interventions that are not informed by the context of the disease are not achieving their aims. Another example is the practice of persuading people to have their HIV status tested, followed by initiating them in the use of condoms. In most cases, such communication with HIV clinics or medical staff, leading to the use of condoms, would be enough to cause stigmatisation and isolation. As argued by Sister Nambafu. 'many people are unwilling to acquiesce in a biomedical monopoly of certainty —specially when the consequences are so overwhelming' (cited in Whyte 1997: 214). Therefore, the medical push to get people tested without much attention to what happens to them after a mobile unit moves on to the next village in a rural area raises ethical questions. Knowing their HIV status will not necessarily help people to deal with the disease unless socio-economic conditions are addressed too.

The reluctance to provide treatment in the South after 1996 demonstrates a major problem, in many respects. As a medical intervention in the South, treatment was considered inappropriate because of its cost and the unavailability of required medical facilities. In itself this perspective demonstrated the top-down mentality that ignored the importance of treatment for prevention in the South, suggesting an implicit misconceived superiority on the part of Northern *experts*. The non-provision of treatment also meant that prevention methods were becoming much less convincing and effective after a decade of exposure which translated into a large increase in infection rates. Successful civil society actions in several countries have called for a change in perspective by pointing out that millions of people cannot wait for the vaccine while they are suffering now. The South African success story in bringing drugs to the people is remarkable; yet tension remains. The issue can be considered solved within the health system through the provision of drugs. But although making access to drugs a legal right is important, it is not enough to deal with the problem. The legal right to access and the availability of drugs in hospitals do not change the situation unless people are socially and economically empowered. Therefore, the problem is not solved merely by the universal provision of drugs to stop mother-to-child transmission. There is still need for active people's involvement in treatment to make sure that the issue is not lost through another medicalisation process. In order to sustain their voices in the debate people have to develop *their* arguments relating to larger social economic issues, such as the orphans that are suffering now and will suffer tomorrow unless they are given appropriate means to survive, or the sexual autonomy of women. Others may yet emerge as the disease becomes significant in countries such as Russia and China, whose cultural particularities that should inform the civil society debate.

We are at a critical moment that requires an important pause to rethink what has been done. In order to maintain its relevance, global civil society needs to think very hard about its continued relationship with internationalised top-down projects, that are creating uniformity, institutionalisation, and medicalisation, in order to find mechanisms for opening spaces for people to influence global health politics.

I would like to thank all the participants at the experts' meeting on the Role of Global Civil Society in Dealing with HIV/AIDS and other Infectious Diseases at the University of the Witwatersrand, Johannesburg, on 22–23 February 2002, and Jacquie Rubanga, James Deane, Laura Leonardi, Luciana Bassini, Pierre Claver, Betty Nabinye, Ndimbati, Deo Nyanzi, Warren Nyamugasira, Moses Matou, Rebecca Mukasa, Stephen Ochieng, Joseph Semujju, Brigitte Quenum, Shalita Steven, and John Rwomushana for discussing their experiences in the field and providing important insights to the debate. I would also like to thank Marlies Glasius and Karen Wright for commenting on the earlier versions of this chapter.

References

Africa Alive! http://www.africaalive.org

Alden, D. and Miller, J. C. (2000). 'Out of Africa: The Slave Trade and the Transmission of Smallpox to Brazil, 1560–1831', in R. I. Rotberg (ed.), *Health and Disease in Human History*. Cambridge: MIT Press.

Altman, D. (2002). 'Sexual Politics and International Relations', in L. Odysseos and H. Seckinelgin (eds), *Gendering the International*. New York: Palgrave.

Armstrong, D. (1993). 'Public Health Spaces and the Fabrication of Identity'. *Sociology*, 27 [PAGES].

Arno, S. and Feiden, K. L. (1992). *Against the Odds: The Story of AIDS Drug Development, Politics and Profits*. New York: HarperCollins.

Arnold, D. (1996). 'Introduction: Tropical Medicine before Manson', in D. Arnold (ed.), *Warm Climates and Western Medicine*. Atlanta: Rodopi.

Attaran, A., Freeberg, K.A., and Hirsch, M. (2001). 'Dead Wrong on AIDS'. *Washington Post*, 15 June.

Bastos, C. (1999). *Global Responses to AIDS: Science in Emergency*. Bloomington: Indiana University Press.

Boomgaard, P. (1996) 'Dutch Medicine in Asia, 1600–1900', in D. Arnold (ed.), *Warm Climates and Western Medicine*. Atlanta: Rodopi.

Brundtland, G. H. (2001). Fourth Meeting of the Global Roll Back Malaria Partnership. http://www.who.int/director-general/spe...h/20010418_RBMeetingwashington.en.html.

Butchart, A. (1998). *The Anatomy of Power: European Constructions of the African Body*. London: Zed Books.

Caron, D. (2001). *AIDS in French Culture: Social Ills, Literary Cures*. Madison: University of Wisconsin Press.

Carter, M. (2002). South African Activists Challenge State on Generics. http//www.aidsmap.com/news/newsdisplay2.asp?newsId=1370

CDC (Centre for Disease Control) (1981). '*Kaposi's* Sarcoma and *Pneumocystis* Pneumonia among Homosexual Men–New York and California'. *Morbidity and Mortality Weekly Report 30*, 25 (3 July): 305–8.

Coast, E. (2001). 'Colonial Preconceptions and Contemporary Demographic Reality: Maasai of Kenya and Tanzania'. Paper presented at the IUSSP Conference in London School of Hygiene and Tropical Medicine.

Communication Initiative (2001). The Communication for Development Roundtable. http://www.comminit.com/majordomo/roundtable/msg00010.html

Correria-Afonso, J. (1990). *Intrepid Itinerant: Manuel Godinho and his Journey from India to Portugal in 1663*. Bombay: Oxford University Press.

Curtin, D. (1996). 'Disease and Imperialism', in D. Arnold (ed.), *Warm Climates and Western Medicine*. Atlanta: Rodopi.

Farley, J. (1991). *Bilharzia: A History of Imperial Tropical Medicine*. Cambridge: Cambridge University Press.

Farmer, Paul (1999). *Infections and Inequalities*. Berkeley: University of California Press.

–, Léandre, Fernet, Mukherjee, Joia S., Claude, Marie Sidonise, Nevil, Patrice, Smith-Fawzi, Mary C., Koenig, Serena P., Castro, Arachu, Becerra, Mercedes C., Sachs, Jeffrey, Attaran, Amir, and Kim, Jim Yong (2001). 'Community-based Approaches to HIV Treatment in Resource-poor Settings'. *Lancet* 358: 404–9.

Foster, S. and Lucas, S. (1991*). Socioeconomic Aspects of HIV and AIDS in Developing Countries* (Department of Public Health and Public Policy. 3). London: London School of Hygiene and Tropical Medicine.

Ford, N. (1994). 'Cultural and Developmental Factors Underlying the Global Pattern of the Transmission of HIV/AIDS', in D. R. Phillips and Y. Verhasselt (eds), *Health and Development*. London: Routledge.

Friedmann, S. R. *et al.* (1992). 'Organising Drug Users Against AIDS', in J. Huber and B. E. Schneider (eds), *The Social Context of AIDS*. Newbury Park: Sage.

Goldberg, R. (1998). Conference Call: When PWAs First sat at the high table. http://www.actupny.org/documents/montreal.html

Gomez-Pablos, A. (2001). South Africa in AIDS Drug Fight (March 9). http://www.cnn.com/2001/WORLD/europe/03/09/inside.europe/

Gordenker, L., Coate, R. A., Jonsson C., and Soderholm, P. (1995). *International Cooperation in Response to AIDS*. London: Pinter.

Harper, M. (1989). 'AIDS in Africa-Plague or Propaganda?' *West Africa* (7–13 November): 2072–3.

Harvard (2001). The Harvard Consensus Statement on Antiretroviral Treatment for AIDS in Poor Countries. http://www.hsph.harvard.edu/hai/overview/news_events/events/consensus_aids_therapy.pdf

Haynes, D. M. (1996) 'Social Status and Imperial Service: Tropical Medicine and the British Medical Profession in the Nineteenth Century', in D. Arnold (ed.), *Warm Climates and Western Medicine*. Atlanta: Rodopi.

Harrington, M. (1994). 'The Community Research Initiative (CRI) of New York: Clinical Research and Prevention Treatments', in J. P. Van Vught (ed.), *AIDS Prevention Services: Community Based Research*. Westport, CT: Bergin and Garvey.

Hobsbawm, E. J. (1987). *The Age of Empire*. New York: Penguin Books.

Hooper, E. (1999). *The River: A Journey to the Source of HIV and AIDS*. New York: Little, Brown and Company.

IFMSA (International Federation of Medical Students Associations) (2001). WHO Civil Society Initiative. http://www.tripodent.nl/Jtroon/Aug01column3.htm

IRIN (2002). *HIV/AIDS News Weekly*, 62 (18 January). http//www.irinnews.org/Aidsreport.asp

Kramer, L. (1987). 'Taking Responsibility for Our Lives: Does the Gay Community Have a Death Wish?' *New York Native* (29 June): 37–40, 66–7.

Mann, J. *et al.* (1986). 'Surveillance for AIDS in a Central African City: Kinshasa, Zaire'. *Journal of the American Medical Association*, 225 (20 July): 3255–9.

– (1999). 'The Future of the Global AIDS Movement'. *Harvard AIDS Review* Spring. http://www.aids.harvard.edu/publications/har/spring_1999/spring99-7.html

McCaa, R. (2000). 'Spanish and Nahuatl Views on Smallpox and Demographic Catastrophe in Mexico', in R. I. Rotberg (ed.), *Health and Disease in Human History*. Cambridge, MA: MIT Press.

Maugh II, T. H. (1996). 'New AIDS Therapy Offers Hope at Forum–Health'. *Los Angeles Times* (8 July). http:/www.aegis.com/news/lt/1996/LT960704.html

Motlhabane, P. (2002). Presentation at the expert meeting on the Role of Global Civil Society in Dealing with HIV/AIDS and other Infectious Diseases. Witwatersrand University, Johannesburg , 22–23 February.

Osborne, M.A. (1996). ' Resurrecting Hippocrates: Hygienic Sciences and the French Scientific Expeditions to Egypt, Morea and Algeria', in D. Arnold (ed.), *Warm Climates and Western Medicine*. Atlanta: Rodopi.

Panos Institute (1988). *AIDS and the Third World*. London: Panos Institute

Patton, C. (1996) *Fatal Advice: How Safe-Sex Education Went Wrong*. Durham, NC: Duke University Press.

Patterson, T. J. S. (1974). 'The Transmission of Indian Surgical Techniques to Europe at the End of the Eighteenth Century'. *Proceedings of the XXIII International Congress of the History of Medicine*, 2 Vols. London: Wellcome Institute.

Pearson, M. N. (1996) ' First Contacts Between Indian and European Medical Systems: Goa in the Sixteenth Century', in D. Arnold (ed.), *Warm Climates and Western Medicine*. Atlanta: Rodopi.

Perrow, C. and Guillen, M. F. (1990). *The AIDS disaster: The Failure of Organisations in New York and the Nation*. New Haven: Yale University Press.

Pollack, M., Paichler, G. and Pierret, Y. (1992). *AIDS: A Problem for Sociological Research*. London: Sage.

Press Release (2002). Generic AIDS Drugs Offer New Lease on Life to South Africans. http//www.doctorswithoutborders.org/pr/2002/01-29-2002.shtml

Seckinelgin, H. (2002). 'Civil Society as a Metaphor for Western Liberalism'. *Global Society*, 16/4.

Shilts, R. (1987). *And the Band Played On: People, Politics, and the AIDS Epidemic*. New York: St Martin's Press.

Tameii, T. (2002). Presentation at the expert meeting on the Role of Global Civil Society in Dealing with HIV/AIDS and other Infectious Diseases . Witwatersrand University, Johannesburg , 22–23 February.

Treichler, P. (1999). *How to Have Theory in an Epidemic: Cultural Chronicles of AIDS.* Durham, NC: Duke University Press.

TWN (Third World Network) (2002). People's Health Assembly 2000. http//www.twnside.org.sg/title/pha2000.htm (visited 12 April 2002)

Volberding, P. A. *et al.* (1990) 'Zidovudine in Asymptomatic Human Immunodeficiency Virus Infection: A Controlled Trial in Persons with Fewer than 500 CD 4-Positive Cells per Cubic Millimetre'. *New England Journal of Medicine*, 322/14: 941–9.

Young, F. E. *et al.* (1988). ' The FDA's New Procedures for the Use of Investigational New Drugs in Treatment'.

Journal of the American Medical Association 259, no.15: 2267–70.

Wallstam, E. (2001). WHO Civil Society Initiative. IFMSA. http://www.tripodent.nl/Jtroon/Aug01column3.htm

Watney, S. (1994). Practices of Freedom: Selected Writings on HIV/AIDS. London: River Oram Press.

Whyte, S. R. (1997). *Questioning Misfortune: The Pragmatics of Uncertainty in Eastern Uganda.* Cambridge: Cambridge University Press.

Wolfensohn, J. D. (2001). Putting Africa Front and Centre. http://www.worldbank.org/html/extdr/jdwspo7/601.htm

Worboys, M. (1996). 'Germs, Malaria and the Invention of Mansonian Tropical Medicine: From "Disease in the Tropics" to "Tropical Diseases"', in D. Arnold (ed.), *Warm Climates and Western Medicine.* Atlanta: Rodopi.

World Bank (2002). World bank Intensifies Action Against HIV/AIDS. http://www.wbln0018.worldbank.org/HDNet/Hddocs.nsf/c840b6982d

EXPERTISE IN THE CAUSE OF JUSTICE: GLOBAL CIVIL SOCIETY INFLUENCE ON THE STATUTE FOR AN INTERNATIONAL CRIMINAL COURT

Marlies Glasius

The Rome Statute for an International Criminal Court ('the Statute'), which was adopted on 17 July 1998, provides for the establishment, in The Hague, of an international court that can prosecute individuals, from common soldiers to heads of state, for genocide, war crimes, and crimes against humanity. The Statute can be considered as a small revolution in international law and in the conduct of international relations, for two reasons. First, as will be discussed below, the International Criminal Court (ICC or 'the Court') will be an important step in the ongoing transition towards an international legal order that is less based on state sovereignty and more oriented towards the protection of all citizens of the world from abuse of power. Second, the input of global civil society in the process which led to the adoption of this Statute has been almost unprecedented in international treaty negotiations, rivalled only by its contribution to the Landmines Ban Treaty, concluded six months earlier. These two features are, of course, interrelated: the development of a more people-empowering international rule of law, and the emergence of a global civil society capable of contributing to such a rule of law, feed and drive one another.

International human rights law has, since its progressive codification after the Second World War, limited the state's absolute right to protect or abuse its citizens at will. However, these curbs on state abuse have too often been more symbolic than real. International human rights institutions now routinely condemn states' mistreatment of their citizens, designating any such treatment as a violation of human rights. However, the use of any sanctions to punish such treatment, or enforce improvement, is left to states, which, however, are too often reluctant to take the political risk, and to engage the resources that such action would involve. When they do take action, it is selective and politically motivated. International human rights law failed to prevent or punish genocides in Cambodia and East Timor, political murders and disappearances in Latin America, and numerous war crimes and human rights violations on the African continent. Only in the 1990s, in response to ethnic cleansing in Yugoslavia and genocide in Rwanda, were international tribunals established, as a placebo for more robust preventive action.

The establishment of the International Criminal Court is a more fundamental step towards removing the power to punish from the sole domain of governments. It is a modest step: the Court will have no police force and no powers of arrest, so it will still have to depend on states to actually deliver international criminals to it. Moreover, future Pol Pots, Pinochets, and Bin Ladens can be prosecuted only if their state of nationality has previously ratified the Statute or if they commit crimes in another state which has done so. It should not be concluded prematurely that such situations will never occur. Most Latin American states which evolved into military dictatorships in the 1970s had previously ratified human rights treaties. The rapid ratification of the Statute by countries which experienced gross human rights violations very recently, such as Nigeria, Sierra Leone, and Yugoslavia, shows that the present governments of these countries are willing to put their faith in the Court to deal with possible further violence in their own political future. Nevertheless, it would be naïve to believe that the establishment of the Court will prevent gross human rights violations from occurring in the twenty-first century. The significance of the Court lies in the fact that it is now clear that international law does not only have universal rules to protect human beings in principle, it has an instrument to punish individuals who gravely breach the rules, even if their own government is unwilling or unable to do so.

It appears that a majority of states are willing to throw their weight behind the idea of the Court: 120

states voted in favour of the Statute in Rome, and 139 have now signed it (although that does not mean ratification will necessarily follow). This means that they are prepared to sign away a small but essential part of their sovereign power in order to protect their future citizens against a possible situation where they may become unwilling or unable to prosecute genocide, war crimes, and crimes against humanity committed by their citizens or on their territory. Unfortunately, a minority of governments, including those of very big and powerful states such as China, India, and the United States, are not prepared to take out this insurance with the international community against their own future. This means that the selectivity that has characterised the enforcement of human rights so far, and the inequality between victims of human rights violations in different parts of the world that follows from it, will not be fully resolved by the establishment of the International Criminal Court—at least not yet.

> International law does not only have universal rules to protect human beings in principle, it now has an instrument to punish individuals who gravely breach the rules

Moreover, it is likely that the fundamental inequalities in resources and power between different parts of the world will also be reflected in the Court: while Northern states will put up most of the resources and play a substantial role in the Court's staffing, the perpetrators brought before the Court are likely to all be from the global South. The United States has already promised to put up a tremendous fight if any of its citizens is ever brought before the Court, but it may be assumed that the European states who are now such fervent supporters of the Court would also change their stance if the prosecutor ever found it necessary to indict one of their citizens. Whether the Court would be willing to take such a risk is doubtful. The refusal of the prosecutor of the Yugoslavia tribunal, Carla del Ponte, to seriously investigate whether NATO committed war crimes in its Kosovo campaign is not a promising precedent in this respect. On the other hand, it must be acknowledged that, while the hands of Northern governments are not clean, there also have been and will be many, many perpetrators of gross human rights violations in the South. Their victims now have a better chance to see these crimes acknowledged, condemned, and punished. The legal, political, and symbolic significance of the new Court has been the main focus of attention in the writing of legal scholars, diplomats, activists, and United Nations officials, proponents of the

Court, as well as those who think the erosion of state sovereignty has gone too far or has proceeded in the wrong direction. This chapter will make a different contribution by focusing on the global civil society input into the process of negotiating and drafting the Statute. It will examine the different angles from which civil society groups and individuals approached the idea of an ICC, their methods and forms and action, the influence they had on the Statute, and the nature and legitimacy of their contribution.

The next section will give a short history of international criminal courts and of the evolution of the idea of a permanent ICC to punish individuals who have committed grave crimes and are not prosecuted by their own state. The subsequent section describes what kinds of groups and individuals got involved in advocating an ICC and why they took an interest in the establishment of such a Court. The third section looks at the methods and forms of action used by global civil society in this effort. Three case studies will subsequently examine the influence of different sections of global civil society on a few of the Statute's provisions in some detail, and draw conclusions about their strengths and weaknesses. The conclusion will discuss whether, on the basis of the experience with the ICC, global civil society involvement in international law-making processes should be hailed as a contribution to the development of global democracy and global ethics.

Evolution of the International Criminal Court Idea

The first international trial designed to bring someone to justice for what would today be called crimes against humanity may have been that against a certain Peter von Hagenbach in 1474. An ad hoc international criminal tribunal of 28 judges from towns in Alsace, Rhineland, and Switzerland, with a presiding judge from Austria, tried and convicted him for murder, rape, and perjury, crimes which 'trampled under foot the laws of God and man', during his occupation of the town of Breisach on behalf of Charles, the Duke of Burgundy (Schwarzenberger 1968: 462–6).

The first proposal for a permanent international criminal court in modern times was made in 1872 by

Gustav Moynier of Switzerland, one of the founders of the International Committee of the Red Cross. Horrified by the atrocities committed by both sides in the Franco-Prussian war in 1870, he proposed the establishment of an international criminal court to deter violations of the Geneva Convention of 1864 and to bring to justice anyone responsible for such violations. However, governments showed little interest and many of the leading international experts on humanitarian law criticised the proposal as unrealistic (Bossier 1985: 283–4).

After the First World War, the Versailles treaty provided for ad hoc tribunals to try military officials of the Central Powers for breaching the laws of war, but Germany refused to hand anyone over for prosecution, and the Allies soon lost interest after the German Kaiser had been given asylum in the Netherlands (Von Hebel 1999: 16; Bassiouni 1999: 7). Proposals during the Second World War to set up a permanent international criminal court were rejected in favour of ad hoc international tribunals at Nuremberg and Tokyo, followed by Allied national military tribunals to prosecute nationals of the Axis powers. These were later criticised for imposing 'victor's justice' and for convicting people of crimes not previously formulated in laws (Bos 1999: 41)

Immediately after the Second World War, the international community was briefly united in drafting international rules that would help prevent atrocities occurring in the future. The Universal Declaration of Human Rights and the Genocide Convention were adopted in 1948. While there were also plans for an international criminal court, it missed the window of opportunity that closed with the onset of the Cold War. Between 1949 and 1954, the International Law Commission (ILC), a UN commission of legal experts, actually drafted a statute while also continuing to work on a code of crimes against the peace and security of mankind. The UN General Assembly shelved the idea, however, because of disagreement over the definition of aggression and other crimes (see Bassiouni 1999: 10–15 for a more detailed account).

The idea was kept alive, however, in various corners of global civil society. Non-governmental organ-isations (NGOs) like the International Law Association, which had concluded as early as 1926 that an ICC was 'not only highly expedient, but also practicable' (Von Hebel 1999: 17), the Association Internationale de Droit Penal, and the World Federalist Movement continued to propagate the court idea as a matter of principle. The independent UN experts of the International Law Commission, led by the Senegalese Doudou Thiam, continued to work on a code of international crimes, and individuals like Benjamin Ferencz, a former prosecutor of the Nuremberg tribunal, and M. Cherif Bassiouni, an Egyptian professor of criminal law, continued to devote academic treatises to the idea of a permanent court (Hall URL).

The watershed

In 1989, inspired by its Prime Minister Arthur Robinson, long a supporter of the idea of an international criminal court, Trinidad and Tobago formally proposed to the General Assembly the 'establishment of an international criminal court with jurisdiction to prosecute and punish individuals and entities who engage in, *inter alia*, the illicit trafficking in narcotic drugs across national borders' (UN 1989). The International Law Commission was again charged with drafting a statute for such a court. It seized enthusiastically upon this mandate, stretching it from framing the ICC merely as a drugs court to a court with jurisdiction over crimes against the peace and security of mankind (ILC 1993: esp. 30–60). In those years, work on the draft Statute proceeded quietly in the rarefied atmosphere of the International Law Commission, far from the political limelight, where many years were sometimes spent on the definition of a legal clause.

The ethnic cleansing in Yugoslavia and the genocide in Rwanda, and the subsequent Security Council decisions to establish ad hoc tribunals changed all this. The televised evidence of atrocities in Yugoslavia and Rwanda quite literally 'shocked the conscience of mankind'. In the aftermath of the Cold War, and through the activities of human rights organisations, the idea that perpetrators could and should be punished for these atrocities gained a foothold (Bassiouni 1999: 18–19)

> The International Law Commission seized enthusiastically upon this mandate, stretching it from designing a mere drugs court to a court with jurisdiction over crimes against the peace and security of mankind

GLOBAL CIVIL SOCIETY INFLUENCE ON THE STATUTE FOR AN INTERNATIONAL CRIMINAL COURT   Marlies Glasius

In 1993, the International Law Commission invited states to comment on a first draft, and in 1994, at lightning speed by its own standards, it had finished its work. It recommended that states now convene a conference to turn it into a binding treaty (ILC 1997: 26.) However, while a number of countries, mainly European and Caribbean, supported the idea of holding a conference as soon as possible, other members of the General Assembly demurred. It was decided that an ad hoc committee of state representatives should study and discuss the ILC draft first (UN 1994). A year later, the ad hoc committee converted itself into a preparatory committee (PrepCom), the difference being that this committee could actually draft text. At the end of the 1996 sessions, a date was set for the conference, a compromise between those states who wanted a conference as soon as possible and those who were in no rush at all: Rome, summer 1998.

While these first three years saw none of the main points of controversy resolved, they did see the emergence of a 'like-minded group' of countries who were in favour of swift establishment of a strong court. This group grew from a handful of state delegates, partly born out of personal friendships, to over 60 states in 1998 (interview Von Hebel). The formation, growth, and consolidation of this group was strongly encouraged by NGOs as a counterweight to the permanent members of the Security Council on the one hand and members of the Non-Aligned Movement on the other, both of which were reluctant to establish an independent court with supra-national powers (interviews Pace, Dicker).

Above: The Plenary meeting of the Rome Conference.
© United Nations.

The Rome Conference

The Rome Conference took place between 15 June and 17 July 1998. The draft text that was to be transformed, in Rome, into a definitive treaty contained more than 1,700 sets of brackets, representing competing proposals for the articles (Lee 1999: 13). Moreover, about 50 of the state delegations, mainly from developing countries, had not taken part in the preparatory committee meetings at all (Pace 1999: 193). The first two weeks in Rome were therefore mainly devoted to letting every state have its say; in the meantime coordinators of thematic working groups were informally trying to forge compromises (Von Hebel 1999: 36).

On the basis of these negotiations, the conference Bureau chaired by Canada published a first 'discussion paper' on 6 July, followed by a proposal narrowing down the options a few days later, and a final 'take-it-or-leave it' package deal in the night of 16 July, the day before the conference was to end.

The final session on the evening of Friday 17 July was very emotional. Two delegations proposed amendments to the final draft. India sought to include the use of nuclear weapons in the definition of war crimes and to deprive the Security Council of the power to refer cases to the court. The United States wanted the court to have jurisdiction only with the consent of the country of nationality of the accused. Reopening the debate on either of those issues would have meant missing the deadline for finalising a statute at this conference, and it might be a long, long time before the same momentum could be achieved again (Conso 1999: 471; interviews Van Boven, Van Troost). Norway introduced a motion to take no action on these amendments, which was overwhelmingly supported. After each of these votes, the delegates broke into applause, which, on the second occasion, turned into a rhythmic clapping that lasted for ten minutes (Benedetti and Washburn 1999: 26). At the final, formal plenary session, the Statute was adopted by secret vote, with 120 votes in favour, 7 against, and 21 abstentions (Lee 1999: 23–6).

Global Civil Society Players

Issue areas represented

Lawyers

The establishment of an International Criminal Court can be considered as a major step towards a more

The International Criminal Court officially came into existence on 1 July 2002, two months after 60 countries had ratified the Statute. However, it will be ready to function only after a prosecutor and judges have been elected, other essential staff has been appointed, and the relationship with the host state, the Netherlands, has been regulated. In the meantime, a new PrepCom of state delegates has come into being to prepare for the actual establishment of the court, working on more technical matters like detailed definitions of the crimes in the Statute and rules of procedure and evidence.

While most of these negotiations have been uncontentious, the United States attempted in various ways in 2000 to have the Statute reinterpreted so as to exempt officials from non-party states (read: American soldiers) from any possibility of prosecution. This global campaign by the US was met by an equally forceful counter-campaign by the NGO Coalition, and ultimately failed (Pace and Schense, 2002, forthcoming). In a peculiar last-minute gesture of commitment to the international community, Bill Clinton signed the ICC Statute on 31 December 2000, his last day in office. However, prospects for US ratification are bleak. There is even talk of the US 'unsigning' the Statute, a legal impossibility (Mufson and Sipress 2001). The US may in fact actively oppose the Court: Senator Jesse Helms has repeatedly tried to get the US

Congress to adopt a bill (nick-named the 'Bomb The Hague Bill') that would boycott any military cooperation with states, other than key US allies, that have ratified the Statute, and even allow the President to use 'all means necessary and appropriate' to release any Americans that might be held by the Court. Helms and others are likely to continue their efforts (CICC 2001).

The NGO Coalition continues to monitor the PrepCom negotiations, to counter US opposition to the Court, to raise global awareness of the ICC and press for ratification, and to give states technical assistance in adapting their laws according to their treaty obligations. The coalition hopes that the Court will be a reality in the summer of 2003.

The Alexander barracks in The Hague, designated site of the ICC. © Marlies Glasius.

accountable and people-centred international law. At the same time, though, drafting the rules for such a Court was a delicate but fascinating task from a strictly legal point of view: different areas of international law, including human rights law, humanitarian law, and the law of international institutions, and areas of domestic law like criminal law and extradition rules, all converged in a new way in the Statute. It is not surprising then that, from the beginning, the venture attracted a large number of lawyers. While the initial discussions by the ILC were barely noticed or monitored by anyone, the

quick transformation of the Yugoslavia tribunal from an idea into a working court excited and mobilised the legal profession.

Almost half of the 236 organisations represented in Rome were either legal-professional organisations, such as bar associations, or human rights NGOs. Other groups working for the ICC at the domestic level, at the PrepComs, and in Rome included a large number of women's organisations, peace and conflict resolution organisations, groups focused on global governance and strengthening the United Nations, and representatives of churches and religious organisations.

Human rights groups

Human rights organisations were particularly predominant. After decades of building an international human rights system at the regional and global levels, human rights experts began to realise that, while the body of law on human rights had become substantial, the scale of human rights violations in the world was not actually declining. 'Combating impunity' became a catch-phrase in the human rights idiom, but the experience in many Latin American and other countries even after their transition to demo-cracy was that it was not just legally but also politically, socially, and psychologically very difficult to prosecute perpetrators of human rights violations under previous regimes. Thus, the idea of recourse to an international criminal court came to be embraced by human rights groups. The Nuremberg and Tokyo tribunals, and the Yugoslavia and Rwanda tribunals, were considered as models to build on, but they were also seen as selective and wanting in impartiality as they had been set up by a few states to prosecute only in a few circumscribed situations. The ICC would be set up by the international community and have a global remit.

> Human rights experts began to realise that, while the body of law on human rights had become substantial, the scale of violations in the world was not actually declining

All the major international human rights organisations, including Amnesty International, Human Rights Watch, the International Commission of Jurists, and the Federation International des Ligues de Droits de l'Homme, were heavily involved in the ICC negotiations, but so were a host of regional and national organisations, including for instance the European Roma Rights Centre, the Arab Commission on Human Rights, the Argentinian Asamblea Permanente de Derechos Humanos, the Ligue Rwandaise pour la Promotion et la Défense des Droits de l'Homme, and the Cambodian Human Rights Task Force, as well as individual human rights professors, lawyers, and activists.

Establishing a criminal court rather than just holding states accountable required some adjustments of thought for human rights advocates. Their focus with respect to criminal trials had always instinctively been on safeguarding the rights of the defendant. Now, the rights of suspects, in effect enemies of human rights, the rights of victims, and the need to create an effective system capable of convicting perpetrators had to be balanced against each other. Amazingly, there was no tradition in human rights law of assigning criminal responsibility to individual perpetrators of violations. Building such rules from existing principles was the intellectual and political challenge of the ICC for human rights groups.

Women's groups

The women's groups were also particularly inspired by the example of the Yugoslavia tribunal in their work for an ICC. While in the past others had pointed out that women were particularly vulnerable to abuse in conflicts, the use of rape as a component of ethnic cleansing in the former Yugoslavia brought the issue to the fore (Steains 1999: 359). Although the statute of the Yugoslavia tribunal did not contain any gender-specific mandate, its functionaries recognised that an ostensibly gender-neutral justice system would in fact fail to address gender-specific abuses, and took on board some of the concerns of women's groups. An officer for gender issues was appointed within the prosecutor's office; and it was decided to allow rape victims to give testimony anonymously, and to seriously prosecute rape as a war crime, an issue to which the first prosecutor, Richard Goldstone, was particularly committed (Sharratt and Kaschak 1999: 12–13, 31, 54).

It was in their relations with the tribunal in The Hague that Yugoslav women and their European supporters had their first experience of inscribing women's concerns into humanitarian law, an experience they built on in New York and Rome. Other, more global, experiences included the World Conference on Human Rights in Vienna in 1993 and the Fourth World Conference on Women in Beijing in 1995 (Steains 1999: 360; Facio 1998: 1). These were not treaty-making conferences, however, and the challenge for women's rights groups was to take the progressive texts of these 'aspirational' final declarations into the 'mainstream big-boy venue of hard-core international law' of the ICC negotiations (interview Hall Martinez).

While some women's groups, such as Equality Now, had been involved since 1995, most were relative latecomers to the process. The Women's Caucus for Gender Justice was formed on the initiative of a small group of women's rights activists present at the February 1997 PrepCom, who realised that, without a much stronger effort, gender concerns were not going to be adequately represented in the negotiations. It quickly grew to be a coalition within a coalition, with more than 300 member organisations by the time of the Rome conference (Facio 1998: 1–3).

Like in Beijing and other fora, the feminist majority of women's groups in New York and Rome focused on women's rights encountered a vocal minority of 'family' groups supported by the Vatican and Arab states, whose preoccupation was to prevent any language that might be interpreted as facilitating abortion from entering the Statute (interviews Hall Martinez, Pace; REAL Women of Canada 1998a, b). The clash between these groups and the Women's Caucus will be discussed in more detail below in the case study on gender-specific crimes.

> A small but very active contingent of groups could be characterised as 'global governance' organisations, committed generally to promoting a more just and more democratic global order

Peace groups

The aims of the smaller peace contingent within the movement for an ICC were less clear. Two kinds of peace groups were represented. The first, typified for instance by the Nuclear Age Peace Foundation and the International Association of Lawyers against Nuclear Arms, were direct descendants of the nuclear disarmament movement of the 1980s, and their primary interest was in having the threat or use of nuclear arms designated as a war crime. As will be discussed below, they were largely unsuccessful in Rome.

The second, characterised by groups like International Alert or the Helsinki Citizens' Assembly, had roots in the same movement but had evolved in a different direction through direct involvement in the non-nuclear conflicts of the 1990s, in which abuse of civilians became a primary method of warfare. They were exploring solutions in the direction of grass-roots conflict resolution on the one hand and a more human rights-based approach on the other. Their interests in the Court were in fact very similar to those of the human rights groups (Kaldor 2001: 113–17; interview Pace).

Global governance groups

A small but very active contingent of groups could be characterised as 'global governance' organisations, committed generally to promoting a more just and more democratic global order. This included the World Federalists, various United Nations associations who propagate the idea of a strong United Nations while monitoring the organisation itself critically, and three interconnected part-international, part-Italian organisations with strong links to politicians, in all of which Emma Bonino (see Box 6.2) played an important role: Parliamentarians for Global Action, the Transnational Radical Party, and, especially, No Peace Without Justice (Benedetti and Washburn 1999: 22).

These groups were well-placed to make contributions to some of the less contentious issues in the Statute. An early paper by the World Federalist Movement, for instance, summarised state and NGO positions on how the Court might be financed, examined precedents concerning other international courts, and made a concrete proposal stressing that, while it might seem like a minor concern in negotiations, the Court would not be able to function successfully without adequate finance (Sweeney 1996). This paper appeared more than a year before states or the UN Secretariat produced anything on finance, and its usefulness was commented on by a number of delegates during the PrepCom meetings (Durham 2000).

Religious groups

Finally, a number of churches and religious groups were represented, including many mainstream Christian denominations but also Jewish, Bahai, Muslim, and Buddhist federations. At the end of the twentieth century, 'the century that has seen the killing of more humans by other humans than occurred in all the rest of our history put together' (Shriver URL), these members of religious groups began to reach a consensus around the need for more earthly justice to set beside eternal, divine justice. Their aim was, however, to go beyond mere punishment, from punitive justice to restorative justice, to help reconcile communities torn by violence and to inject a spiritual dimension into the ICC project. Most of these groups came together in a Faith-based Caucus (Shriver URL; Foundation Statement URL). They concerned them-

Box 6.2: **Individuals with multiple hats**

The negotiations for the International Criminal Court were marked by a good deal of cross-over between academics, NGO officials, and government representatives. These are just some examples of individuals who played important roles wearing more than one hat.

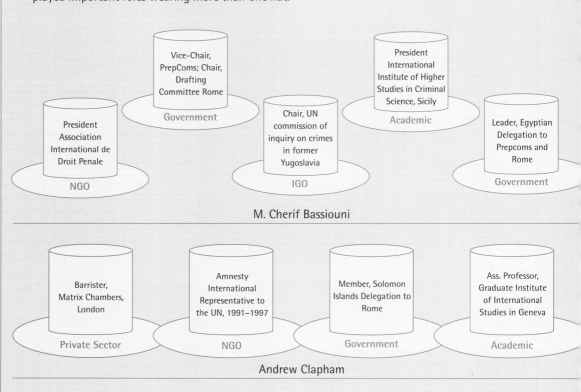

President Association International de Droit Penale — NGO

Vice-Chair, PrepComs; Chair, Drafting Committee Rome — Government

Chair, UN commission of inquiry on crimes in former Yugoslavia — IGO

President International Institute of Higher Studies in Criminal Science, Sicily — Academic

Leader, Egyptian Delegation to Prepcoms and Rome — Government

M. Cherif Bassiouni

Barrister, Matrix Chambers, London — Private Sector

Amnesty International Representative to the UN, 1991–1997 — NGO

Member, Solomon Islands Delegation to Rome — Government

Ass. Professor, Graduate Institute of International Studies in Geneva — Academic

Andrew Clapham

selves with the less political, more ethically oriented preamble and final clauses of the Statute, the wording of which, they felt, should have a spiritual dimension. According to the Samoan delegation, which coordinated the negotiations, 'Most of the concepts the Faith-Based Caucus espoused can be found in the final product, albeit in different language' (Clark and Slade 1999: 423–5).

Geographical representation

When the NGO Coalition for an International Criminal Court ('the Coalition') was founded in 1995, it consisted primarily of international organisations, usually with European or American headquarters, and a permanent representation at the United Nations in New York. However, a strong effort was made to involve national organisations from all regions in the Coalition, and with success. As explained above, Latin American organisations had a strong interest in the Court stemming from their own experience of living through dictatorships and the subsequent difficulties in bringing perpetrators of violations to justice. Indeed, most of the Latin-American organisations involved were (sometimes church-based) human rights organisations.

African organisations, mainly lawyers' and human rights groups, also apparently believed in the ICC as

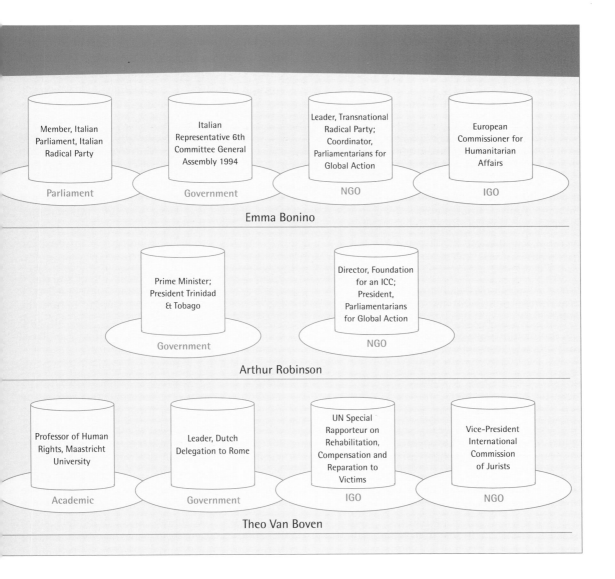

Member, Italian Parliament, Italian Radical Party

Parliament

Italian Representative 6th Committee General Assembly 1994

Government

Leader, Transnational Radical Party; Coordinator, Parliamentarians for Global Action

NGO

European Commissioner for Humanitarian Affairs

IGO

Emma Bonino

Prime Minister; President Trinidad & Tobago

Government

Director, Foundation for an ICC; President, Parliamentarians for Global Action

NGO

Arthur Robinson

Professor of Human Rights, Maastricht University

Academic

Leader, Dutch Delegation to Rome

Government

UN Special Rapporteur on Rehabilitation, Compensation and Reparation to Victims

IGO

Vice-President International Commission of Jurists

NGO

Theo Van Boven

part of a 'rule of law' solution to the wars and human rights abuses many of their countries had experienced. Their interest may also have been fuelled by the active involvement of African lawyers like the Senegalese Abdul Koroma, one of the most active members of the International Law Commission's sub-commission on the ICC (Krieger 1998), Cherif Bassiouni, and Richard Goldstone, and by the setting up of the Rwanda tribunal.

While a wide range of east and west European and North American organisations were also well-represented, there was little interest from organisations in North Africa and the Middle East or from Asia. Indeed, not a single Asian NGO produced a paper during the three years of PrepCom negotiation (Durham 2000). Some groups were represented in Rome, and interest has grown since then, particularly in Bangladesh, the Philippines, and Egypt, but the activities have not been comparable to other regions. The weakness of global civil society participation from these two regions is in keeping with the figures on membership in international NGOs published in *Global Civil Society 2001* (Anheier, Glasius, and Kaldor 2001: 6–7). It may be related to the corresponding weakness in the development of international law, and in particular human rights law, in the same regions. A glance at the ratification record of existing human rights

GLOBAL CIVIL SOCIETY INFLUENCE ON THE STATUTE FOR AN INTERNATIONAL CRIMINAL COURT   Marlies Glasius

145

treaties—for instance, the International Covenant on Civil and Political Rights or the Convention Against Torture—shows that, regardless of their official ideology, states in North Africa and the Middle East and Asia are least likely to become parties (see Record 8 in Part IV of this Yearbook). Many Asian human rights groups have tried unsuccessfully for years to set up an Asian human rights system. It is not surprising, then, that their enthusiasm for setting up an even more forceful human rights implementation mechanism, one that their governments would be even less likely to participate in, was lukewarm. The situation in the Middle East and North Africa is even bleaker. In many of the countries in this region, there is not enough political space for human rights groups to operate freely, let alone to campaign for a Court that might have the authority to bring leaders of their governments to justice for human rights abuses.

> Despite the loose formal structure of the Coalition and the wide variety of its members' views, it was extremely effective in its coordinating role

At the time of writing, Cyprus and Tajikistan were the only countries in the vast region between Morocco and Japan to have ratified the Statute, while, by contrast, 26 European, 12 sub-Saharan African, and 11 Latin American countries had become parties to the Court. This uneven development confirms the idea, posed in the opening paragraph of this chapter, that global civil society and the international rule of law are interdependent, and need each other to be able to develop further.

The Coalition

When the UN General Assembly decided, in December 1994, not to take the ILC's draft Statute straight to a treaty-drafting conference but instead to consider it further in an ad hoc committee, the five or six NGOs following the proceedings were disappointed and shocked, in particular by the excessive willingness of states they considered progressive to compromise. A phone call between William Pace, Executive Director of the World Federalist Movement, and Christopher Hall, legal adviser of Amnesty International, who had both been observers, resulted in an invitation to a number of groups to discuss the formation of an NGO Coalition (interview Pace). At that meeting, on 10 February 1995, the NGO Coalition for an International Criminal Court (CICC) was founded as 'a broad-based network of NGOs and international law experts' (*ICC Monitor 1* URL).

The Coalition was given a loose structure. Although there were a coordinating organisation and a coordinator, a steering committee, and ordinary members, no formal decision-making structure was agreed. Moreover, the Coalition chose initially to formulate no common position except 'to advocate for the creation of an effective, just and independent International Criminal Court', and to be no more than a conduit of information between NGOs, state representatives, and the general public, and a resource for coordination between NGOs. On the Sunday before the Rome Conference, the Steering Committee of the Coalition did adopt a list of 'Basic Principles' (CICC 1998*a*).

The self-appointed Steering Committee initially consisted almost exclusively of human rights groups, including Amnesty International, the Federation International des Ligues de Droits de l'Homme, Human Rights Watch, the International Commission of Jurists, and the Lawyers' Committee for Human Rights. Coordination, however, was given to the World Federalist Movement. The legal and human rights groups were already developing strong opinions on specific aspects of the international criminal court, and neither too much agreement nor open competition between them would have been good for the image of the Coalition. The World Federalists merely advocated the idea of an ICC in principle as part of the vision of a 'just world order through a strengthened United Nations' to which they are committed (World Federalist Movement URL). They were considered neutral enough to be trusted by a whole range of NGOs (interviews Pace, Dicker, Van Troost).

The level of recognition of the Coalition's role by state representatives and United Nations officials was probably unprecedented. The chairman of the PrepComs and many other official delegates took the participation of NGOs in the proceedings for granted, and the Coalition was their first point of contact with them (see for instance Bos 1999: 45–6). Before the Rome Conference, the Coalition coordinator was actually asked by the United Nations to organise the accreditation of NGOs to the Conference, a unique form of self-regulation not attempted before at international conferences (Pace 1999: 209). By the time of the Rome Conference, the NGO Coalition for an International Criminal Court had grown into a network of over 800 organisations, 236 of which sent one or more representatives to Rome. Thus, the Coalition delegation was far bigger than any state delegation.

Despite the loose formal structure of the Coalition and the wide variety of its members' interests, it was extremely effective in its coordinating role. In order to be as effective as possible, it split into three types of groups: regional caucuses, who lobbied state representatives from their own regions; thematic caucuses on gender justice, victims, children, peace, and a faith-based caucus; and twelve working groups on different parts of the draft Statute. The last of these shadowed the corresponding working groups of state representatives on different sets of articles and made daily reports available to NGOs and state delegates (Pace and Thieroff 1999: 394).

Through the Latin-American regional caucus, for instance, wavering delegates from Mexico and Peru were pushed toward more progressive positions, partly through debates in their domestic newspapers (On The Record 1998e).

Special themes that cut across various parts of the Statute were tackled by thematic caucuses. Members of the Victims Rights Working Group, the Children's Caucus, and the Women's Caucus all worked together intensively to improve the position of witnesses in the proceedings of the Court. They worked to afford victims better protection, the right to have their own say, rather than being just an instrument of the prosecution, and the right to reparation. According to two state delegates who later wrote on the subject, they played a vital role in the formulation of the relevant articles (Van Boven 1999: 83–9; Steains 1999: 384–7).

The daily reports of the twelve shadow teams on different parts of the Statute allowed all NGOs and the smaller state delegations to keep abreast of all the sub-negotiations even if they could not physically attend (CICC-TR 1998). They also maintained close relations with the chairs of the official working groups, most of whom represented states that were strong proponents of the ICC as well as often being personally committed to the Court (Pace 1999: 207–8).

The loose structure and lack of cumbersome procedures of the Coalition undoubtedly contributed to its flexibility and effectiveness. However, this came at the expense of internal democracy. It was not clear how members, other than those represented in the—non-elected— steering committee, could shape or change its policies. As the case study on weapons of mass destruction will show, this lack of internal mechanisms, in combination with the dominating role of human rights groups, made it very difficult for other members to enlist the Coalition in its causes.

> Global civil society and the international rule of law are interdependent, and need each other to be able to develop further

Methods and Forms of Action of the Campaign for an ICC

The organisations and individuals involved in the campaign for an international criminal court mainly undertook the following forms of action:

- Lobbying state and intergovernmental representatives
- Writing expert documents, reports, and journal articles
- Convening seminars and conferences
- Disseminating the Court ideal to a wider audience
- Seeking and giving financial support for Southern NGO and expert participation in the debates
- Providing experts and interns to smaller and poorer government delegations.
- Street action

Lobbying

Lobbying took place at the official PrepComs and in Rome, of course, but also in a wide range of other fora. Organisations sought meetings with officials of their national Justice, Foreign Affairs, and Defence departments, trying to awaken interest in and support for the Court. They were always a presence at intergovernmental conferences, such

Map 6.1: Global action on the International Criminal Court

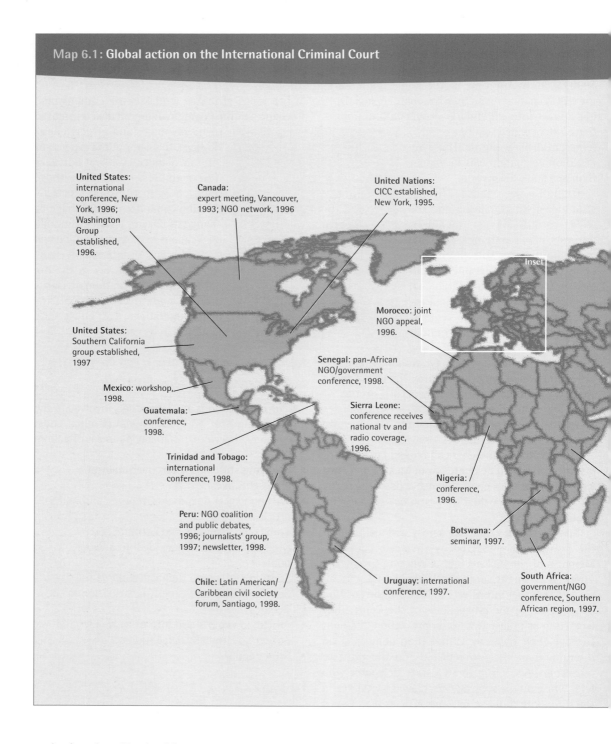

United States: international conference, New York, 1996; Washington Group established, 1996.

Canada: expert meeting, Vancouver, 1993; NGO network, 1996

United Nations: CICC established, New York, 1995.

United States: Southern California group established, 1997

Mexico: workshop, 1998.

Guatemala: conference, 1998.

Trinidad and Tobago: international conference, 1998.

Peru: NGO coalition and public debates, 1996; journalists' group, 1997; newsletter, 1998.

Chile: Latin American/ Caribbean civil society forum, Santiago, 1998.

Morocco: joint NGO appeal, 1996.

Senegal: pan-African NGO/government conference, 1998.

Sierra Leone: conference receives national tv and radio coverage, 1996.

Nigeria: conference, 1996.

Botswana: seminar, 1997.

Uruguay: international conference, 1997.

South Africa: government/NGO conference, Southern African region, 1997.

Inset

as the American Heads of State summit in Santiago de Chile in 1998. Many of these intergovernmental conferences, such as the Southern African Development Cooperation meeting of Justice Ministers in South Africa in 1997, a Caribbean conference in Trinidad and a pan-African conference in Dakar in 1998, were in fact co-organised by governments and NGOs.

The informal meetings at Cherif Bassiouni's International Institute for the Higher Criminal Sciences

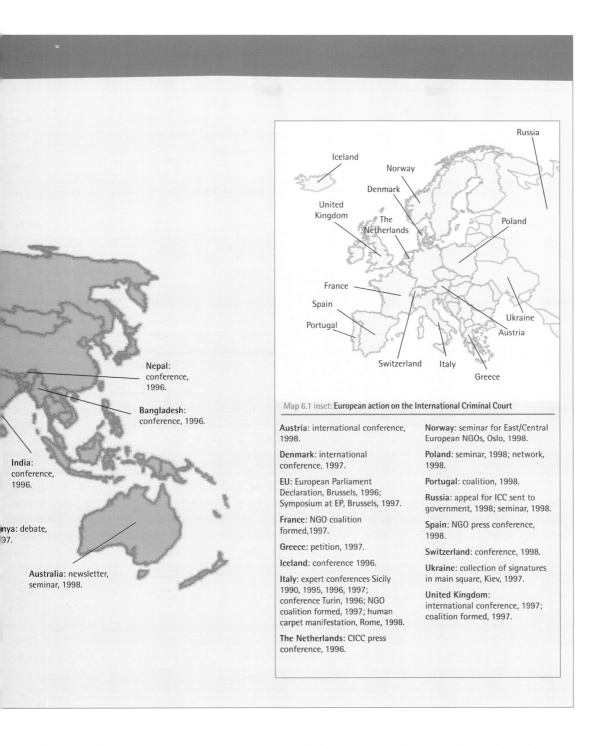

Map 6.1 inset: **European action on the International Criminal Court**

Nepal: conference, 1996.

Bangladesh: conference, 1996.

India: conference, 1996.

...nya: debate, ...97.

Australia: newsletter, seminar, 1998.

Austria: international conference, 1998.

Denmark: international conference, 1997.

EU: European Parliament Declaration, Brussels, 1996; Symposium at EP, Brussels, 1997.

France: NGO coalition formed, 1997.

Greece: petition, 1997.

Iceland: conference 1996.

Italy: expert conferences Sicily 1990, 1995, 1996, 1997; conference Turin, 1996; NGO coalition formed, 1997; human carpet manifestation, Rome, 1998.

The Netherlands: CICC press conference, 1996.

Norway: seminar for East/Central European NGOs, Oslo, 1998.

Poland: seminar, 1998; network, 1998.

Portugal: coalition, 1998.

Russia: appeal for ICC sent to government, 1998; seminar, 1998.

Spain: NGO press conference, 1998.

Switzerland: conference, 1998.

Ukraine: collection of signatures in main square, Kiev, 1997.

United Kingdom: international conference, 1997; coalition formed, 1997.

in Sicily provided another very important forum for NGO lobbying. At these meetings, which took place between PrepCom sessions, a select group of NGO representatives as well as mainly 'pro-court' state representatives were invited to discuss and thrash out further details of the future Court. According to a participating diplomat, these meetings 'were extremely instrumental. No difference was made there between state delegates and NGOs, we were all there as experts. It was very informal, there was lots of sunshine, good food, that had an impact on the negotiations, there was more space, we had fun, it was pleasant, relaxed. It was an instrument for taking further steps' (interview).

Conference lobbying and domestic lobbying were coordinated: 'When national delegations or portions thereof (e.g. specific ministries) needed reinforcement, or when concerns arose that a delegation might be compromising key principles, the Coalition contacted ministers, parliamentarians, and media in the capital through its national networks. This type of conference-to-capital coordination has been a goal of NGOs at many conferences; for many of us its effective implementation in Rome was a first', writes CICC coordinator William Pace (Pace and Thieroff 1999: 395). Lobbying state representatives was the main purpose of most organisations in coming to Rome, as evidenced by the fact that, very unusually, there was no separate NGO Forum to the Conference.

Producing expert documents

At the same time, a great deal of specialist documentation was produced by individuals and organisations involved in the ICC process. This took two main forms: journal articles in especially legal journals by individuals (sometimes written by the staff of NGOs—Christopher Hall of Amnesty was particularly prolific—but more often by academics), and reports by NGOs. Both had the primary aim of informing and influencing a specialist public of NGOs, academics, and state representatives on specific sub-themes, promoting certain alternatives over others with reference to precedent, legal argument, or political realities (see Lyonette URL for an extensive bibliography of the ICC). According to the Dutch delegation leader to Rome: 'The papers of the four or five bigger organisations, Amnesty, Human Rights Watch, International Service for Human Rights, Lawyers Committee for Human Rights, International Commission of Jurists, have been extremely helpful, that was real quality input. They were very good, and they made an impact' (interview Van Boven).

Convening conferences

One of the most prevalent forms of action in the years leading up to the Rome conference was the organisation of national and international confer-

ences, expert meetings, public debates, seminars, symposia, and workshops. Such meetings were organised all over Europe, in Southern and West Africa, South Asia, North, South, and Central America, and the Caribbean.

There was less activity elsewhere in Asia and in North Africa and the Middle East, which is in line with the figures on civil society participation from these regions in Rome. Indeed, in many of these countries there is no tradition of government tolerance for public debates about the country's foreign policy.

The conferences were often either organised by NGOs or academic institutions or co-organised by these and the national governments. They were characterised by an intermingling of officials with the NGO and academic communities and by high-level legal debates rather than political confrontations. Some were regional or international in character, but even the national meetings often boasted one or more international guests, drawn from the ranks of the NGO Coalition, the Yugoslavia and Rwanda tribunals, or the academic community.

Thus, a global specialist debate about the ICC, involving academics, NGO advocates, practising lawyers, and state officials, was going on in the years leading up to the Rome conference, through the numerous expert conferences, the Sicilian retreats, and the law journals and NGO publications, as well as in the official PrepCom meetings.

Dissemination to a wider audience

While most of these meetings and the longer NGO reports and law journal articles on the ICC were aimed at an already informed specialist audience, the idea of an international criminal court was also disseminated to a much wider public. A strong effort was made by organisations at the national and sometimes even local level to attract the attention and support of the press for the ICC. The general aims of the court and its consequences for the country in question were explained at press conferences and by putting together media kits.

At the same time, 'big name' international lawyers guest-authored articles, even in local newspapers,

> A strong effort was made by organisations at the national and sometimes even local level to attract the attention and support of the press for the ICC ...

particularly in the United States but also in Botswana, for instance (see for instance Bassiouni 1996; Nanda 1996; *ICC Monitor 6* URL).

Other organisations gathered signatures from celebrities, including the Dalai Lama, Queen Noor of Jordan, Jean-Bertrand Aristide of Haiti, and former US President Jimmy Carter, in favour of the Court, and published these in an appeal in the *International Herald Tribune* and *Le Monde* (Busdachin URL).

Big membership organisations like Amnesty International and the World Federalist Movement, and some of the churches including the Quakers and Mennonites, disseminated the ideas behind the Court to their millions of members.

A hybrid between the mass media and the specialist publications were dedicated newsletters, as came out in Australia and Peru, as, on the international level, was the Coalition's own *ICC Monitor*, which kept interested audiences abreast of the developments in articles that avoided or explained specialist legal jargon.

At the Rome conference, no fewer than three daily news teams set up camp. The Coalition transformed its two-monthly *Monitor* into a daily newsletter, the InterPress Service published a series of its *Terra Viva* newspaper, as it does at all major UN conferences, and the Advocacy Project, an NGO that specialises in activist newsletters, produced *On The Record*, which was also e-mailed to about 4,000 subscribers. According to one participant, 'numerous delegations awaited with interest and enthusiasm the "new highlights" from these news sources' (Almeida 1999: 15).

Seeking and use of funding

The Coalition and its constituent organisations needed, of course, to raise funds for their activities to support the establishment of the Court. Initially, the World Federalist Movement went tens of thousands of dollars into debt, and relied largely on volunteer labour by graduate students, in setting up the Coalition. Later, the Ford Foundation, the MacArthur Foundation, and the European Union, as well as some governments, made grants both to the Coalition and to some of its constituent organisations.

The money thus raised was used especially to take more Southern NGOs and academics to New York and Rome, and to a lesser extent to prepare and disseminate campaign material (Facio 1998: 2, 4; interviews Pace, Donat-Cattin, Hall Martinez).

The participation of other relevant experts was made possible by funding channelled through civil society: thus, the presence of high-level officials from the Yugoslavia and Rwanda tribunals was made possible by an external grant applied for by the Coalition (interview Pace).

The coordination, research, and lobbying efforts of the Coalition and its members were mainly self-funded, however, by member donations, by the use of volunteers including many students and academics, and by finding ways of allocating staff and resources from other departments and projects to the ICC (interviews Pace, Dicker, Hall Martinez, Burroughs).

> ... the general aims of the court and its consequences for the country in question were explained at press conferences and by putting together media kits

Provision of experts and interns

Another type of activity that supported the process of negotiations, and particularly the fuller participation of Southern governments in the process, was the provision of legal experts and interns from civil society to the state delegations. This allowed them to be present at more parallel meetings as well as helping to develop their legal arguments. Some governments, such as those of Canada and Costa Rica, included NGO representatives in their delegations as a gesture of goodwill. Others, including those of Bosnia, Trinidad and Tobago, Sierra Leone, Senegal, Burundi, and Congo, relied on a technical assistance programme by the NGO No Peace Without Justice to augment the size and expertise of their delegations. Other countries engaged the services of domestic—Germany, the Netherlands, and the US—or foreign—Samoa, the Solomon Islands—professors of law as delegation members. Needless to say, this kind of expertise would not be as neutral and malleable to government positions as the contributions of professional diplomats. These 'experts on loan' came with independent views, which influenced the delegations from within. Andrew Clapham, the lawyer engaged by the Solomon Islands, for instance, sought, ultimately without success, to make it possible to indict not just individuals before the Court but also companies (Saland 1999: 199). It seems most likely that he acted on his own judgement, not on government instructions, in this respect.

Street action

Finally, some more direct actions were organised in relation to the ICC. Amnesty International and No Peace Without Justice were two organisations that took on many of these actions aimed at attracting the attention of the general public. Amnesty's Croatian section organised a demonstration in 1996, and its Ukrainian section collected signatures in Kiev's main square (Wolf URL). In Rome, Amnesty International organised an open-air manifestation, a 'human carpet' to represent the victims of genocide, war crimes, and crimes against humanity on 4 July, and No Peace Without Justice undertook a 24-hour vigil outside the conference building on 16 July, waiting to celebrate or mourn the final outcome of the meeting (*ICC Monitor 10* URL). Such actions were few and far between, however: for every demonstration, there were dozens of conferences on the ICC.

An epistemic community

In terms of militancy and visibility, the ICC campaign formed a sharp contrast to other recent global civil society manifestations, such as the demonstrations in Seattle, Genoa, and Porto Alegre. As Benedetti and Washburn (1999: 25) write, 'NGOs . . . had learned to accept a great deal in the institutional culture and style of international treaty conferences, which many of them had previously inclined to ignore. This included matters of procedure, timing, access to documents, decorum, and even dress'. If these people were representing the 'wretched of the earth', they certainly did so in less dramatic fashion than those bashing at the gates in Seattle and Genoa. However, the fact that they had adopted the style, procedures, and clothing of state delegates does not mean that they were being co-opted on substance.

The methods of most members of global civil society involved in the ICC campaign, and their interaction with state representatives, are charact-

> 'Experts on loan' came with independent views, which influenced the delegations from within

eristic of what Peter Haas and others have termed an 'epistemic community': 'The epistemic community members' professional training, prestige, and reputation for expertise in an area highly valued by society or elite decision makers accord them access to the political system and legitimise or authorize their activities' (Haas 1992: 17). An epistemic community consists of more than technocrats, however: 'Unlike members of a profession or discipline, who seldom limit themselves to work that is closely congruent with their principled values, members of an epistemic community tend to pursue activities that closely reflect the community's principled beliefs and tend to affiliate and identify themselves with groups that likewise reflect or seek to promote these beliefs' (Haas 1999: 19).

The match between the ICC actors and what Haas *et al.* have called epistemic communities is not perfect. These authors describe groups of 'typically under thirty-five people' with highly homogeneous beliefs (Adler and Haas 1992: 380). The ICC groups consisted of hundreds, perhaps thousands, of people, and fell into different sub-groups according to their profession, their moral and technical priorities, and their preferred methods. While they placed much emphasis on informing and persuading state representatives, they devoted attention to informing a wider public as well, and, while their relations with state delegates were mostly cordial, they did not hesitate to expose and condemn official behaviour

Above: 'Human carpet' demonstration by Amnesty International in Rome representing the victims of genocide, war crimes and crimes against humanity. © Amnesty International.

they did not like. Nevertheless, seeing the global civil society activities with regard to the Court as those of an epistemic community, credited with expertise and imbued with moral values, helps to understand them and their influence. The next section will look at three case studies to examine in detail how the different actors operated and what gave them influence.

Influence on the Statute

Global civil society attempted to influence almost all aspects of the Statute, ranging from its general principles and its relations with states to its composition to jurisdiction rules, definition of crimes, rules relating to prosecution and trial, and financing. Some of the areas in which global civil society had an impact have already been mentioned. This section provides some detailed and comparative illustrations of the arguments used by civil society groups in favour of certain provisions, the strategies they used to get these implemented, and the circumstances under which they succeeded and failed, in three particular cases.

The independent prosecutor

This subsection discusses how prosecutions can be initiated before the Court. The 1994 draft of the International Law Commission listed only two ways in which an investigation could be initiated (or 'triggered', as it came to be called). States parties could lodge a complaint, alleging that a crime had been committed, or the UN Security Council could refer a matter to the Court. Unlike in domestic criminal law systems, the Court's prosecutor could not institute any investigations him- or herself.

Civil society proposals and arguments
The NGOs and individuals constituting the NGO Coalition were united in insisting on a third 'trigger': the prosecutor should be able to institute his or her own proceedings. In fact, this independence of the prosecutor was the single biggest issue on the agenda of the Coalition and many of its constituent organisations. An Amnesty International repres-

> Independence of the prosecutor was the single biggest issue on the agenda of the Coalition and many of its constituent organisations

entative called it *a 'collective bottom line'* (interview Van Troost). According to the Argentine state delegate Silvia Fernàndez de Gurmendi, an early and active member of the like-minded group who chaired the negotiations on this issue and had frequent contact with NGOs, 'Non-governmental organizations led a strong campaign in favor of conferring such power as an essential feature of an independent, credible Court. The issue became a central point in the discussions' (Fernandez de Gurmendi 1999: 177).

As an alternative to the prosecutor's own initiative, it was suggested that individuals, and perhaps also NGOs, might lodge complaints, as they do under various human rights treaties. NGOs also pointed to the practice of the European Court of Human Rights, the Inter-American Court of Human Rights, and domestic courts in this respect (ICJ 1995; HRW 1996; Pax Romana 1996).

One of the main reasons why NGOs insisted on extending the prosecutor's powers was that they feared very few cases would come to the Court if only the Security Council and states could trigger proceedings (AI 1994: 28; ICJ 1995). They pointed out that, in existing human rights treaties, states very rarely lodge complaints against each other because it strains relations, and they would not be likely to do so under the Statute either. The Security Council has likewise been selective in using its powers in response to grave crimes (AI 1994: 28).

When a state or the Security Council does act, it is likely to be wholly or partially politically motivated. NGOs argued that limiting prosecutions in this manner would compromise the perceived impartiality and legitimacy of the Court as well as its effectiveness (AI 1994: 28; EN 1995; ELSA 1996: 2).

State negotiations
In August 1995, a few states, including Austria, Greece, the Netherlands, Norway, and Switzerland, began to voice the idea of a prosecutor initiating proceedings on his or her own behalf. They did so in very cautious terms, saying for instance that the prosecutor's role was 'too narrow' and needed to be 'more active' and that 'possible enhancement of the prosecutor's role needed further examination' (UN 1995c). An even smaller number of states,

including Chile and the Czech Republic, made the further-reaching suggestion that individuals, victims, and/or NGOs should be able to trigger a procedure (UN 1995*a*, *b*). In April 1996 the support for such views was still so weak that a UN Press Release (UN 1996) stated: 'Speakers were almost unanimous in opposing the granting of powers to the prosecutor of the court to initiate an investigation on his own, based on information received, without the consent of the States concerned.'

In August 1997, in order to overcome some objections, Argentina informally proposed that the Prosecutor might be allowed to pursue his own investigations subject to the permission of a pre-trial chamber of judges (Fernàndez de Gurmendi 1999: 183). This became a formal Argentine-German proposal in April 1998, and remained in the draft that went to the Rome conference. However, the entire article was in square brackets, which meant some states objected, and the whole text might yet be struck.

Although there was significant opposition, it was becoming increasingly clear in Rome that the majority of states favoured some form of own initiative (Fernàndez de Gurmendi 1999: 186; Wilmshurst 1999: 134). Despite the majority view in favour, rumours abounded in the last day or two of the conference that the independent prosecutor might yet be sacrificed to placate US opposition (interview Dicker). However, the final Draft Statute of 17 July essentially incorporated the Argentine-German proposal, giving the Prosecutor the right to investigate cases on his own initiative, subject to the permission of a pre-trial chamber. This was accepted by the Conference.

Civil society strategies and influence

It is impossible to say for certain that it was the civil society campaign which tipped the balance in favour of the independent prosecutor. This is the strong belief of many activists, however, and it appears to be shared by state delegates who were closely involved in the negotiations, like Silvia Fernandez de Gurmendi of Argentina and Theo Van Boven of the Netherlands. The latter called this 'the most important point on which the NGOs booked success'

> In response to rumours in the final days of the conference that the independent prosecutor might be dropped, mixed teams of major human rights NGOs were formed to approach specific delegations

(Fernandez de Gurmendi 1999: 177; interview Van Boven).

The NGOs in the Coalition contributed to the adoption of the prosecutor's power to investigate on his own initiative in various ways. First, they proposed the even more radical idea: that victims and/or NGOs might institute proceedings by lodging a complaint. This proposal moved the previously most radical proposal of having an independent prosecutor closer to the middle of the spectrum of opinion. According to a member of the NGO Coalition, 'it was clearly understood by the majority of the Coalition that it was unlikely for States to agree to individuals having the capacity to initiate proceedings. However, such a "radical" suggestion made the prospect of an independent Prosecutor appear more acceptable and less threatening than that of individual citizens "triggering" the Court. An independent Prosecutor was thus seen as a less extreme option' (Durham 2000). The credibility of this tactic was strengthened by the fact that a few states also referred to this option, so threatening to others, early on in the negotiations.

NGOs also made a contribution, before and during Rome, to the substance of the debate by combating the arguments of opponents of an independent prosecutor. In particular, they constantly rebutted the arguments of the most prolific opponent of the prosecutor's initiative, the United States. On 22 June, for instance, the United States submitted a position paper about the prosecutor. On 24 June, the US-based Lawyers Committee for Human Rights hit back with a document rebutting the arguments as well as drawing attention to inaccuracies in the US paper (United States 1998; LCHR 1998).

Third, all through 1997, the Coalition pressed the like-minded group of states to assert itself and show its hand by formulating its guiding principles. In December 1997 it finally did so, and the prosecutor's initiative was one of those principles (Pace 1999: 206; Benedetti and Washburn 1999: 21, 23).

A related activity of the Coalition was not so much to convince state delegates that an independent prosecutor was desirable as to make those who already thought so believe that it was also politically possible. This was done by demonstrating the existing support for the position and, consequently, continuing to build on it. Despite the fact that they had a stake in a certain outcome, this 'barometer' function of the Coalition was apparently credible in the eyes of state delegates. On 23 June, for instance, NGO representatives reported for the first time that a majority now favoured the prosecutor's initiative, with Brazil, Mexico, Venezuela, France, and Syria having recently shifted into that direction. They also candidly reported that Kenya had moved in the opposite direction (Haq 1998; 'On The Record 1998b).

A particular form this took was to transpose the statements made by delegates into virtual votes on different positions towards the end of the Rome Conference. This showed that 61 states explicitly expressed their approval of the prosecutor's initiative in the opening statement to the conference (CICC-TM 1998). On 10 July, 76 per cent of the 80 states speaking were in favour of the prosecutor's initiative, and four days later 83 per cent of 76 states took this position (CICC 1998b, c). According to Richard Dicker of Human Rights Watch, 'that bit of work, of accurately recording and putting together immediately where each state stood on the major issues, was the single greatest contribution of the NGOs. Each state might have done it, except they didn't really have the capacity. We spent late nights . . . getting it out into the newsletter, getting it to the delegates, and they faxed it to their capitals, that was crucial, stiffening the resolve by accentuating the number of states that wanted an effective independent court' (interview Dicker).

Finally, in response to rumours in the final days of the conference that the independent prosecutorial powers might be dropped, 'the major international human rights groups then formed mixed swat-teams, Human Rights Watch, Amnesty, the ICJ, Lawyers Committee, to approach specific delegations with this message, so it didn't come from one particular group by itself, it was a very important theme for all of us' (interview Dicker).

Gender-specific crimes

The original ILC draft paid no explicit attention to the gender dimensions of any of the areas of law it covered. This reflected the existing state of humanitarian law and international criminal law, as codified in the The Hague and Geneva Conventions and the statutes of the ad hoc tribunals for Yugoslavia and Rwanda. The practices and jurisprudence of these tribunals between 1995 and 1998 were beginning to change this situation, however, and provided inspiration for the demands of the women's rights groups united in the Women's Caucus for Gender Justice (Steains 1999: 359).

Gender concerns related to many parts of the Statute. This subsection will focus on only one of them: inclusion of a sub-paragraph on gender-specific crimes, including forced pregnancy, in the definition of war crimes and crimes against humanity. 'Forced pregnancy' is the term used for a practice, within the context of war or crimes against humanity, of raping a woman and then keeping her confined so she is forced to carry the baby to full term. This practice occurred as part of a programme of ethnic cleansing in the war in Bosnia.

Other concerns of the women's groups, including a reference to gender in a general non-discrimination clause, the definition of gender, a gender dimension to the definition of slavery, the inclusion of persecution on the basis of gender as a component of crimes against humanity, and protection for and gender-sensitive treatment of victims and witnesses, will not be dealt with here. All of these concerns, however, came to be reflected in the final Statute in a way that either completely or partially satisfied the Women's Caucus.

> Forced pregnancy became the most contentious gender issue at Rome, with the Vatican and other opponents arguing that making it a crime implied a state obligation to permit abortion

Civil society proposals and arguments

In a paper for the December 1997 PrepCom, the Women's Caucus first proposed a separate sub-paragraph on sexual and gender crimes in the definition of war crimes, which was to include 'rape, sexual slavery, forced prostitution, forced pregnancy, forced sterilization and other sexual or gender violence or abuse'. It recommended this extra paragraph, partially based on the prosecutorial practices of the Yugoslavia and Rwanda tribunals, because 'sexual and gender violence are severe and particular and their particularities should not be lost by mainstreaming.

Where not explicit, they are too often ignored, even today' (WC 1997).

Anti-abortion groups like REAL Women of Canada voiced objections to the inclusion of forced pregnancy as a war crime, arguing that the term had been used by the American Civil Liberties Union in a US lawsuit as meaning 'forcing women to continue pregnancy against their will for the purpose of serving the state's declared interest in preserving unborn human life', i.e. to describe an anti-abortion law or policy (REAL Women of Canada 1998a). They also generally opposed the use of the term 'gender' in the Statute, predicated on the idea that it might 'provide protection for "other genders" including homosexuals, lesbians, bisexuals, transgendered, etc.' (REAL Women of Canada 1998b).

State negotiations

Early proposals relating to the definition of crimes made scant reference to rape as an 'outrage on personal dignity' and none to other gender-related crimes. This changed with a joint proposal in February 1997 by New Zealand and Switzerland to include rape directly as a war crime. The United States, however, favoured a much more restrictive definition of war crimes, and the whole text remained bracketed. At the same time, 'rape, other sexual abuse and enforced prostitution' were included, unbracketed, as a crime against humanity (Hall 1998: 127–8). In December 1997, a special sub-paragraph on 'rape, sexual slavery, enforced prostitution, enforced pregnancy, enforced sterilisation, and any other form of sexual violence' was included in the draft text on war crimes for Rome, without brackets, that is, reflecting widespread consensus among states, despite an objection from the Vatican to 'enforced pregnancy' (Steains 1999: 364–6).

This became the most contentious gender issue at Rome, with opponents, including the Vatican and some Catholic and Arab states, arguing that making enforced pregnancy a crime implied a state obligation to permit abortion. Proponents of the clause, including many Western states but also conflict states like Bosnia and Rwanda and Muslim states such as Azerbaijan and Turkey, argued that it was meant to codify a terrible crime, such as witnessed in Bosnia, and had nothing to do with viewpoints on abortion (Steains 1999: 366). Bosnia issued a paper documenting the practice and calling for the retention of enforced pregnancy as a separate crime in the Statute, and lobbied other Muslim countries on the

issue (Oosterveld 1999: 39; 'National Abortion Laws', 1998d).

After three weeks in Rome, an informal working group was formed, chaired by an Australian delegate, to bring the two sides closer together and to try to define forced pregnancy in a mutually satisfactory way. The definition that came out of these negotiations in the final week of the conference was as follows: 'The unlawful confinement of a woman forcibly made pregnant, with the intent of affecting the ethnic composition of any population or carrying out other grave violations of international law. This definition shall not in any way be interpreted as affecting national laws relating to pregnancy.' The second sentence was clearly inserted to protect the anti-abortion laws of the objecting countries (Steains 1999: 366–8). The sub-paragraph was then included in the definitions both of war crimes and of crimes against humanity.

Civil society strategies and influence

The first proposal to make rape and other sexual and gender crimes punishable as war crimes, made in February 1997 by Switzerland and New Zealand, was taken over almost verbatim from a paper by the International Committee of the Red Cross, reflecting developments in the Yugoslavia tribunal in particular (Hall 1998: 127–8; ICRC 1997). The Women's Caucus was just beginning to be formed at that time, and probably did not play a significant role.

By the time these proposals were being refined and finalised in the December 1997 PrepCom, the Women's Caucus was fully operational, and it made inclusion of sexual and gender crimes one of its five lobbying issues for this PrepCom (Axel, Marrow, and Martinez URL). The sub-paragraph adopted then, which was substantially more comprehensive than the earlier proposals, mirrors exactly the wording proposed by the Women's Caucus in its preparatory paper, and it can safely be assumed to have been proposed at its instigation. The preservation of this clause, however, over strong opposition to forced pregnancy in particular, probably owed more to the strong advocacy of Bosnia, which had the moral high ground on this issue, and the patient but tough negotiating by Australia than to the Women's Caucus, although its statement in Rome that 'this will not affect national abortion laws' ('National Abortion Laws', 1998), may have been helpful.

The Women's Caucus was highly visible in Rome. One of the main reasons for its success was probably its sheer numbers: it had between 12 and 15 people at Rome at all times and, with more than 300 member organisations, it could legitimately claim to be representing a global women's movement (Facio 1998: 3–4). The delegation, moreover, included both women from conflict areas and experts on the 'hard-core legal stuff' (interview Hall Martinez). While the former could speak with moral authority about violations of women's rights, the latter could invoke emerging precedents in national and international law.

Finally, the Women's Caucus was able, due to its large numbers and energy but also its natural advantage in often—but by no means inevitably!—finding allies in female state delegates, to get many states on its side. One member of the Caucus mentions Australia, Bosnia, Canada, Costa Rica, Mexico, the Netherlands, European countries generally, South Africa for ten Southern African countries, and Sweden among the countries the Caucus had very good relations with: a formidable list (interview Hall Martinez).

The right-to-life groups arrived on the scene even later than the Women's Caucus. They came not just with an anti-abortion agenda but more generally with anti-feminist and anti-homosexual concerns. They lobbied and worked together with the Vatican and Catholic and Arab countries. Their links with the Vatican gave them a privileged position: they were given their own office in the conference building in Rome, while all other NGOs had to share one room and very few state delegations had offices (interviews Pace, Hall Martinez). According to one source, moreover, it was rumoured that the Pope personally placed phone calls to leaders of Latin American countries on the issue of forced pregnancy (interview Hall Martinez).

Their main tactics were to equate use of the term 'gender' with en-dorsement of homosexuality—an argument strengthened by the fact that 'gender' is difficult to translate into other languages, including Arabic—and use of 'enforced pregnancy' with support for the right to abortion. This probably had some impact in the last PrepCom and early in Rome, but it was countered by the tactic of states sympathetic to the gender clauses negotiating an agreed definition

to both terms to allay fears of such interpretations. Once such definitions had been agreed, their role was pretty much played out and, although the Women's Caucus might have preferred slightly different definitions, it cannot be said that 'pro-family' groups had a noticeable influence on the wording of the Statute.

Indiscriminate weapons

In 1997, a number of groups involved in the ICC process formed the Weapons Systems Caucus, later renamed 'Peace Caucus', which aimed to 'make the Statute as restrictive as possible in regard to nuclear weapons, landmines, and other weapons inflicting indiscriminate harm and unnecessary suffering, including blinding laser weapons'. It was a small caucus, consisting of about ten groups, many of which were also members of the anti-nuclear Abolition 2000 Network (Burroughs and Cabasso 1999: 470).

Civil society proposals and arguments

The ideal outcome the Peace Caucus aimed for, as elaborated in a proposal for the December 1997 PrepCom, was to have both a general prohibition of weapons that caused 'superfluous injury or unneces-sary suffering' or were 'inherently indiscriminate' and a specific list of prohibited weapons, including expanding bullets, chemical and biological weapons, landmines, and the threat or use of nuclear weapons (Weapons Systems Caucus 1997).

Its fall-back position was to have only a general prohibition of weapons that cause unneces-sary suffering or are inherently indiscriminate, as also proposed by the Red Cross. Its third choice was to have at least an incomplete list of prohibited weapons, with a reference to future expansion (Burroughs and Cabasso 1999: 471; ICRC 1997).

The 'superfluous injury or unne-cessary suffering' phrase was based on language in the Hague Conventions and Protocol I to the Geneva Conventions, the 'inherently indis-criminate' phrase on the humanitarian law principle that a distinction must be made between the treat-ment of combatants and that of civilians. For the

> The Peace Caucus might have done better to abandon their ideal of explicit nuclear weapons language, instead pushing hard for a general prohibition clause and attempting to make this a Coalition principle

prohibition of the threat or use of nuclear arms, the Caucus referred to the 1996 Advisory Opinion by the International Court of Justice, and for landmines to the Landmines Ban Treaty (Weapons Systems Caucus 1997). It did not explicitly defend the need for other weapons to be on the list, reflecting the fact that, while there was some interest in landmines and other weapons, the activism of the Peace Caucus was primarily anti-nuclear (interviews Pace, Burroughs).

State negotiations

Inclusion of the use of certain weapons as a war crime was first seriously discussed in February 1997. The United States proposed listing biological and chemical weapons and expanding bullets. Syria proposed the threat or use of nuclear weapons. New Zealand and Switzerland put forward a proposal, once again based on the ICRC paper, that no specific weapons be listed but that the use of weapons 'of such a nature as to cause superfluous injury or unnecessary suffering or being inherently indiscriminate' be prohibited. In December 1997, the US and New Zealand-Switzerland options were maintained. Canada suggested a compromise option including the weapons listed by the US plus 'such other weapons or weapons systems as become the subject of a comprehensive prohibition pursuant to customary or conventional international law'. The Philippines proposed a fourth option with both a general prohibition and a longer list of weapons, including nuclear weapons and landmines (Ware 1997). This whole text, with all the options in brackets, went to Rome.

The Non-Aligned Movement (NAM) adopted a position a month before Rome that made explicit prohibition of nuclear weapons one of its key objectives for the ICC (Burroughs and Cabasso 1999: 471). However, while India continued to pursue this objective, the unity of the NAM was much weakened at the Rome Conference by the defection of many states to the like-minded group (Benedetti and Washburn 1999: 31, 33). Like-minded leaders like the Scandinavian countries and Canada were timid, not only on nuclear arms but even on landmines (On The Record 1998a, c). The credibility of India's anti-nuclear stance was, moreover, much weakened by the fact that it had carried out its own nuclear tests only a month earlier. Many NGOs and state delegates believed that India's real objective was to wreck the Statute rather than to insert anti-nuclear language (Jaura 1998; interview Pace).

When the first Bureau proposal was presented on 6 July, it still included the short US list of weapons, the longer list including nuclear weapons and landmines and, as a third option, the general prohibition. It was becoming clear that a majority of countries were prepared to sacrifice nuclear weapons, with 57 states in favour of option 1, 25 for option 2, and 6 for option 3 (CICC 1998b). The next Bureau proposal included only this option, i.e. prohibition of biological and chemical weapons and expanding bullets, with a reference to future expansion to other weapons that 'become subject of a comprehensive prohibition'.

However, worse was to come. Some states argued that, if nuclear weapons were not expressly included, then biological and chemical weapons, 'poor man's weapons', ought not to be included either. In the last week of the conference, in closed negotiations the Dutch chair of the working group on nuclear weapons succumbed to this line of argument, reportedly pursued by the Arab states, and, in what he refers to as a 'Solomonesque' solution, deleted the explicit reference to biological and chemical weapons, leaving only expanding bullets, poison weapons, and poisonous gases and analogous materials, relegating all other weapons which might be subject to prohibition to a future annex, yet to be negotiated (Von Hebel and Robinson 1999: 116; Burroughs and Cabasso 1999: 471–2). This is the formulation used in the final Statute. The poisonous weapons phrase, based on an old (1925) treaty, can be read as meaning 'chemical weapons', but it is harder to read biological weapons into it as well (Burroughs and Cabasso 1999: 471–2).

On the evening of 17 July, India proposed an amendment to the Statute to reinstate biological, chemical, and nuclear weapons. However, as described earlier in this chapter, reopening the negotiations at this point was seen as ruining the prospects for a Statute, and a no-action motion by Norway, opening the way to adoption of the Statute, was overwhelmingly supported.

Civil society strategies and influence

The Rome Statute does not advance the state of international law on weapons of mass destruction; indeed, it might be argued that the exclusion of biological weapons sets it back. There are, however, many provisions in the Statute which may be used indirectly to prosecute the use of such weapons, such as those prohibiting attacks on civilians, and military attacks that have 'clearly excessive' effects on civilians in relation to the military goal (Burroughs and Cabasso 1999: 472; interviews Von Hebel, Pace). Nevertheless, the efforts of the Peace Caucus must be considered almost entirely unsuccessful.

The Peace Caucus had a difficult mission because its main objective, the explicit criminalisation of nuclear weapons, was 'at odds with the aim of obtaining support or at least tolerance of the Statute from the nuclear weapons states' (Burroughs and Cabasso 1999: 471). The introduction of an option including landmines and nuclear weapons by the Philippines in December 1997 may have been orchestrated by the Caucus (Ware 1997), but, as one of its members put it, he went to Rome knowing 'there was just no way nuclear arms were going to be explicitly made a crime' (interview Burroughs). According to the NGO Coalition's coordinator, 'peace groups understood that a hard push for nuclear weapons would undermine the overall cause, so they backed off' (interview Pace).

The Peace Caucus's second option, a general clause prohibiting weapons that are 'inherently indiscriminate' or cause 'unnecessary suffering', was not realised either. This was partly because it was only a small Caucus. The Coalition and most of its participants avoided the topic of weapons of mass destruction because they were more interested in human rights issues and because it was seen as a potential conference wrecker (Burroughs and Cabasso 1999: 474). In fact, the Coalition's 'Basic Principles' (CICC 1998a) incorporate concerns on gender, children's rights, and victims, but nothing on weapons of mass destruction. The groups in the Peace Caucus might have done better to abandon their ideal of explicit nuclear weapons language, instead pushing hard for a general prohibition clause and attempting to make this a Coalition principle. However, it might have been difficult to push this through within a Coalition that was generally more interested in human rights issues and disinclined to jeopardise the Statute for other reasons. Another problem for the Peace Caucus was that, in these negotiations, it had few allies among states. Unlike in the case of the independent prosecutor, the 'barometer' function of the Coalition actually worked against it by showing that a strong majority of states was prepared to accept the short weapons list of the US. Moreover, it strongest ally, India, was not perceived by other states as a bona fide negotiating partner and, in particular, it lacked

credibility with respect to its stance on nuclear weapons.

The groups in the Peace Caucus do, however, bear some responsibility for not jealously guarding the draft language on biological and chemical weapons. It is true that this was lost in closed negotiations, but they never made much of a case for these weapons either. In fact, they may even have made things worse by arguing that including these weapons, but not nuclear ones, amounted to 'criminalizing the poor man's weapons of mass destruction', an argument also put forward by states (*On The Record*, 1998c).

A comparison

The campaign to get an independent prosecutor and the effort to get gender-specific crimes, in particular forced pregnancy, into the Statute had a successful outcome, and this can at least partially be ascribed to the activities of the relevant civil society actors. The attempt to get the use of indiscriminate weapons prohibited, on the other hand, largely failed. What did these efforts have in common, and how did they differ?

The people involved in all three issues could claim to have extensive expertise on the subject matter in question. They each appealed to legal precedents to strengthen their position, as well as using ethical arguments for changing the law to combat existing practices. The Women's Caucus also brought experiential expertise in the form of women from conflict areas. This expertise, extolled by state delegates, was obviously a great source of strength for civil society in relation to the ICC process (Bassiouni 1999: vi; Steains 1999: 361; interviews Van Boven, Von Hebel).

The mainstream human rights groups who led the initiative with respect to the independent prosecutor were also veteran conference-goers, with a history and an infrastructure to support the lobbying effort. While the Women's Caucus also had much conference experience, they were relative newcomers to this particular treaty-making process. Their ceaseless lobbying efforts appear to have occasionally irritated state delegates. This does not seem to have substantially impaired their influence, however. While the Peace Caucus also included experienced lawyers, they were people who were used to being excluded from state decision-making, as the atmosphere at arms conferences is usually much less conducive to NGO participation (Burroughs and Cabasso 1999: 475–6). Possibly as a result of this, they did not make effective strategic choices during the conference. While having three different options in mind, they continued to be seen as pushing the most radical anti-nuclear option even though they themselves recognised before the conference began that there was no possibility of its being adopted. This position even caused them to use rhetoric on the equivalence of different weapons of mass destruction which was used by states with the opposite aims, i.e. to exclude more types of weapons.

Both the campaign on the independent prosecutor and the Women's Caucus drew strength from their sheer numbers. As seen above, almost half of the civil society delegation consisted of human rights and legal groups, for whom the independent prosecutor was one of the highest priorities on their agenda. The Women's Caucus, while substantially smaller, also had between 12 and 15 representatives in Rome at all times. The Peace Caucus had only between five and ten.

The independent prosecutor issue, moreover, was supported by the overwhelming majority of civil society representatives, with virtually no overt opposition from within. This was not the case with gender issues and forced pregnancy in particular. As seen above, groups supporting these issues were battling with a small but very vocal group of opponents from within civil society. It is doubtful how much this hurt them, however, as the anti-abortion minority could not credibly claim to be committed to a strong Court in principle, and was seen by state representatives as attempting to 'obfuscate the issue' and 'an unfortunate departure

from the generally constructive role played by NGOs throughout the Conference' (Steains 1999: 368). The Coalition as a whole, moreover, did include in its basic principles a commitment 'to ensure that all aspects of its work take gender concerns into account' (CICC 1998a). The Peace Caucus did not have to deal with the same level of vocal opposition, but neither was it able to get the same explicit support. Most of the Coalition partners appear to have viewed it with caution or indifference.

The efforts for an independent prosecutor and for a gender crimes clause both managed to get a large number of states on side. In the case of the independent prosecutor, this support was actually demonstrated in figures by the 'virtual vote' efforts. What the figures do not show is what kind of states supported these two campaigns: many of these were prime movers in the like-minded group. The Peace Caucus had relatively few allies. The 'virtual vote' actually worked against it by showing the lack of state support. Moreover, the states it did have on its side—India and to a lesser extent the Arab states—were generally seen as conference wreckers, not constructive negotiating partners.

Finally, the campaigns for an independent prosecutor and for gender-specific crimes could be said to have displayed a high level of vigilance. The independent prosecutor even had its own monitoring team. When there was a realisation that the independent prosecutor proposal was in danger in the final negotiations with permanent members of the Security Council, a rapid and coherent response was developed in the form of the

Table 6.1: Global civil society's sources of strength

Issues	Sources of strength					
	Substantive expertise	Process expertise	Numerous global civil society representatives	Internal unity of global civil society	State allies	Vigilance
Independent prosecutor	+	+	+	+	+	+
Gender-specific crimes	+	+ −	+	−	+	+ −
Indiscriminate weapons	+	−	−	+ −	−	−

'mixed teams'. The Peace Caucus, in contrast, did not realise in time that one of its principles, albeit not its highest priority, was being compromised away.

The Contribution to Democracy and Ethical Principles in International Law-making

The intense involvement of global civil society in the negotiations for an international criminal court was viewed as very positive by those individuals who played a role in it, as well as by many state delegates. The virtue of such involvement is not self-evident, however. It is clear that global civil society was influential in these negotiations, but was it legitimate? This concluding section will consider this legitimacy along two dimensions: global civil society's contribution (1) to democracy and (2) to ethical principles.

Democracy

According to Adriaan Bos, the Dutch chair of the ICC negotiations until Rome, global civil society involvement 'fills in gaps arising from a democratic deficit in the international decision-making process' (Bos 1999: 44–5). Although international law-making has never been a democratic process, there is an increasing sense among national and international diplomats that, as more decisions have moved up to the international level, international decision-making and international law-making in particular ought to be democratic. This idea is related to a more general recognition by political thinkers that, while more states have been converted to parliamentary democracy, the onset of globalisation has eroded the substance of democratic participation and choice (see for instance Held 1995; McGrew 1997; Scholte 2001; Anderson 2000). The view, widely echoed among state delegates as well as activists involved in the ICC process, that civil society involvement somehow made the ICC process 'more democratic' than pure state deliberations would have been, should probably be seen in this context. However, at first sight, this is a peculiar notion: the activities of NGOs, students, academics, and

> The present enthusiasm of officials from governmental and intergovernmental institutions is partly based on their own crisis of legitimacy and the hope that global civil society can provide it for them

journalists cannot be said to have much to do with democracy in the traditional, literal sense of 'rule by the people' or 'majority rule'. In that sense, state delegates might actually come closer to being 'democratic' now that most states have multi-party elections, even though diplomats are not elected and international issues such as the ICC are not exactly electoral themes in most countries. It is on this basis that some dismiss the claim that global civil society brings democracy to international decision-making processes.

Kenneth Anderson, for instance, under the trenchant headline 'But who elected the international NGOs?', criticises both the Landmines Ban Coalition and the ICC Coalition on this basis. He correctly points out that the present enthusiasm of officials from governmental and intergovernmental institutions is partly based on their own crisis of legitimacy and the hope that global civil society can provide it for them. He also points out, again correctly, that most NGOs are 'not very often connected, in any direct way, to masses of "people"' and that in domestic contexts they are not usually seen as a 'substitute for democratic processes' (Anderson 2000: 112–18).

However, such critics cannot move beyond lamenting the perceived loss of democracy—the loss really is just perceived here, as international law-making was never democratic—because they cannot conceive of democracy in any other than representative and territorial terms. Democracy on a planetary scale is literally unimaginable to them (see Anderson 2000: 115–16). Therefore, the only recipe they have is to return decision-making power to the level of the nation-state. This notion is not only unimaginative and backward-looking; it also fails, as will be elaborated below in the subsection on ethical principles, to understand the possible gains, the liberating potential, of moving up to the supranational level.

More imaginative responses are possible, and necessary, to give the global *demos* a more substantive sense of participation in the development of decisions that affect it. Global civil society has been conceptualised as a 'functional equivalent' (Rosenau 1998: 40–1) or 'alternative mechanism' (Scholte 2001: 15) for democratising global governance. Such conceptions suggest that global civil society can make the following contributions to enhancing democracy:

- fostering deliberation (Scholte 2001: 16);
- developing alternative proposals (Falk 1998: 323; Pianta 2001: 171–2);
- promoting access/giving voice to unheard groups (Scholte 2001: 16);
- improving transparency for and accountability to a wider public (Keane 2001: 43–4; Falk 1998: 328; Scholte 2001: 16–17); and
- diminishing power distortions among states (Falk 1998: 322).

To what extent did the sections of global civil society involved with the international criminal court fulfil these aspirations?

Deliberation

First of all, did global civil society contribute to the airing and deliberation of different viewpoints in relation to the Court? The idea of deliberative democracy is that proposals can be debated on their merits through rational arguments rather than on the basis of representation of interests. This aspect of democracy is therefore related to the ethical contribution discussed below. There are two components to this question: whether global civil society made the official state debates more deliberative and less focused on narrow interests, and whether there was a form of deliberative decision-making going on within global civil society. On the first count, the answer is clearly 'yes'. There is no doubt that the numerous conferences and seminars, the Sicilian retreats, academic articles, and NGO position papers contributed to a global, albeit specialist, debate on the merits of the international criminal court, which informed and influenced the ultimate decision-making by state delegates.

On the second count, of internal deliberation, there is rather more doubt. The NGO Coalition for an ICC was inclusive and tolerant in principle and in practice. A very wide range of groups who supported the broad goal of a 'just, effective and independent court' joined the Coalition. This included even the small minority of 'family-oriented' groups who were

opposed to the aims of the Women's Caucus, unless it became clear that they were generally hostile to the idea of a strong Court. They were met with irritation by most NGOs and many state delegates, but tolerated, accredited, and given access to the same facilities as others (interviews Pace, Hall Martinez; Facio 1998: 5). Some of these groups themselves on the other hand 'did not play by the rules' according to one activist, for instance circulating lobbying materials without institutional affiliation (which was against UN rules) and dumping Women's Caucus documents in the waste-paper basket (interview Hall Martinez). However, it must also be said that the Coalition did not favour extensive internal deliberation. As Burroughs and Cabasso (1999: 474) write,

> Lack of space and time for open and free deliberation can have consequences for the legitimacy and creativity of global civil society, and hence for its influence in the long term

'there was no thorough debate, still less any formal collective decision-making, among all participating NGOs. Partly this was for practical reasons, because of the number of NGOs, the cumbersome internal decision-making procedures of some NGOs, and the onslaught of events, and partly because it was deemed too divisive to get into controversial matters. Partly, too, the NGO Coalition lacked the kind of culture of consensus reflecting commitments to social transformation, non-violence, and representation of popular demands.'

The Coalition emphasised pluralism rather than internal democracy and chose to take few common positions. Admittedly, the Steering Committee, and the Coordinator in particular, had good reasons for such an approach, having 'experienced the break-downs and break-ups of NGO steering committees' all too often, and it was a matter of 'amazing grace' that this Coalition survived such pressures (Pace 1999: 208). However, the few common positions taken, and even informal understandings about the priorities, were crucial, as leading state delegates often chan-nelled their consultation with NGOs through the Coalition (interview Bos).

These decisions did not come about through genuine deliberation among all or most members of the Coalition, and it must be said that, in terms of internal deliberative democracy, the Coalition was wanting. While in the case of the ICC this does not seem to have detracted at all from its effectiveness, such lack of space and time for open and free deliberation can have consequences for the legitimacy as well as the creativity of global civil society, and hence for its influence, in the long term.

Alternative proposals

Global civil society produced thousands of pages of text developing different proposals in relation to the ICC. It is clear that these academic submissions and NGO position papers had an impact on the negotiations. However, they had no official status. Therefore, states often copied these papers, or passages from them, and introduced them as their own. In this respect, it would be desirable if civil society involvement could be taken one step further in future negotiations, allowing NGOs and individuals to introduce proposals in their own name: not only does their work deserve to be credited, it may also be assumed that the actual authors of certain positions can be expected to be their most effective defenders. A limit might be imposed on such powers by requiring that at least one state co-sponsor the proposal so as to prevent the flooding of negotiations with proposals which do not stand a chance among states.

Access and voice

The ICC Coalition met the challenge of including representation from the global South at least as well as their more colourful global civil society counterparts on the streets of Seattle and Genoa, and perhaps better. It also represented the interests of the under-represented, including victims of war crimes and human rights violations, and women and children in particular, securing better protection for these groups than they might otherwise have had. It must be said, however, that this representation was often rather abstract. Many of the civil society representatives were well-heeled, university-educated cosmopolitans with little direct experience of violence. There were also more grass-roots representatives, including for instance women from Afghanistan and the grandmothers of the Plaza de Mayo, Argentina, but it appears that their presence served a symbolic purpose rather than actually involving them in the negotiations. This emphasis on expertise rather than experience was perhaps inevitable in this law-making process, but it is to be hoped that, when the Court is up and running and dealing with actual rather than abstract violations, the direct representation of victims will become more of a reality.

> Many of the civil society representatives were well-heeled, university-educated cosmopolitans with little direct experience of violence

Transparency, accountability and public education

While, as discussed above, the internal transparency of decision-making within the Coalition left something to be desired, civil society involvement certainly did succeed in making the official decision-making process more transparent: for its members, for journalists, and, through them, for a wider interested audience and even for delegates of smaller states. Funnily enough, the fact that the final conference took place at a UN building in Rome with which most delegates were unfamiliar, contributed to this transparency, making it very difficult for them to slink off into remote rooms for secret meetings (interview Donat-Cattin). It is unlikely that international negotiations will ever be entirely open, just as at the domestic level, for instance, Cabinet meetings remain confidential. The working method of the Coalition— forming teams to monitor negotiations on different parts of the Statute, debriefing friendly state delegates after informal meetings, and keeping 'virtual vote' tallies on crucial issues—was very effective, however. It took the potential for making international negotiations transparent to its limits, and it is an example worth following in other fora.

Redressing inter-state power imbalances

Many of the ways in which global civil society contributed to the ICC process also served, deliberately or accidentally, to empower smaller and poorer states in the process and to give them a more equal footing with traditionally powerful states. The documents produced by individuals and NGOs helped to educate them with respect to the issues involved. The provision of interns and legal experts swelled their delegations in quality and quantity. The monitoring, by the NGOs, of both public and, as far as possible, secret negotiations, in terms of both the substance of the debate and the numbers in favour of certain positions, made the process more transparent and easier to follow for such states.

In sum, global civil society did well on injecting deliberation and transparency into the negotiations, but not quite so well on fostering internal democracy and transparency. Its alternative proposals were taken seriously and contributed to the process. The Coalition was wide-ranging and inclusive in nature, and succeeded well in representing the interests of the oppressed, although there was little direct representation of victims. Monitoring and education activities made the process much more transparent, which also had a positive effect on the position of smaller and poorer states.

Ethical principles

The most valuable contribution of global civil society to the international criminal court, however, was not the dimension of increased democracy but the dimension of morality and idealism. It furthered the goal of achieving a particular type of court, a Court that takes, as the introduction to this chapter characterises it, 'a fundamental step towards removing the power to punish from the sole domain of governments'. This is not universally considered as progress. Unilateralists fundamentally object to it. Kenneth Anderson calls it 'international legal imperialism' and accuses international lawyers in general, and those involved in the landmines and ICC campaigns in particular, of an unreasoned 'fundamentally religious and mystical' belief in the supremacy of international law (Anderson 2000: 114). While he attacks these beliefs from the left, his position, and that of most opponents of the Court, belongs to the larger category that *Global Civil Society 2001* termed the 'rejectionist' or 'sovereignist' position towards globalisation held by traditional leftists, right-wing unilateralists, and nationalists alike (Anheier, Glasius and Kaldor 2001: 9–10; Kaldor 2001: 130–2).

The ethical project of global civil society described in this chapter embraces the supportive and reformist position, focusing on a globalisation of the rule of law. It is undoubtedly based on a belief, but not an unreasoned belief. It is predicated on the twentieth-century experience with powerful states unaccountable to any higher powers. The genocides, war crimes, and crimes against humanity that states have committed over the past century far outstrip any misdeeds that global institutions, fallible though they be, have ever performed. While only one of many avenues, drafting international human rights and humanitarian law and, even more importantly, creating institutions that can help implement such law is seen by lawyers and activists in this field as their contribution to preventing such crimes in future.

Olivier de Frouville has described the essence of the 'ethical project' of the ICC campaign in terms of George Scelle's doctrine, which holds that, in international law-making, each state has a double function: to defend its own national interests but also the global public interest, or interest of humanity (Frouville 2000: 271–2). It was the continual strengthening and encouragement of states, and tendencies within states, towards the latter interest that was the contribution of global civil society. According to Adriaan Bos, the Dutch chair of the negotiations up until Rome, 'the aims of the NGOs and the like-minded group were completely parallel' (interview Bos). William Pace, the NGO Coalition coordinator, agrees with this assessment, 'with the caveat that some like-minded group delegates were willing to achieve much less, NGOs pressed for greater specificity and strength . . . The official line is often quite good, but in personal negotiations in many instances they go in with a *Realpolitik* idea, and they would have allowed a very weak, US-controlled ICC' (interview Pace). Richard Dicker of Human Rights Watch also stresses that, while expertise was very important, the 'strategic vision' civil society brought to the negotiations, 'stiffening the resolve by accentuating the number of states that wanted an effective independent court', was crucial (interview Dicker).

It was through this contribution that what Canadian Foreign Minister Lloyd Axworthy has termed 'the New Diplomacy' could prevail, rather than the traditional lowest common denominator approach to treaty-making (Pace 1999: 206–7). The alliance of civil society and progressive states enjoyed a double advantage over the opponents of the Court

> The alliance of civil society and progressive states enjoyed a double advantage over the opponents of the Court by having an informal but robust agreement both on the goal and on the means

by having an informal but robust agreement both on the goal—a just, independent, and effective Court—and on the means—forming a common front between NGOs and states in favour of such a Court, which simultaneously boosted the status of civil society and strengthened the resolve of states in the negotiations (Frouville 2000: 274). Against this common front, the divided, unilateral strategies (natural to a sovereignist position) of the enemies of the Court—India and the United States in particular—for the most part failed.

I would like to thank everyone I have interviewed for their valuable time and insights, and Abdullahi AnNa'im, Mary Kaldor, Zdenek Kavan, Simone Remijnse, and Jill Timms for their thoughtful comments on earlier drafts.

References

Adler, Emanuel and Haas, Peter M. (1992). 'Conclusion: Epistemic Communities, World Order, and the Creation of A Reflective Research Program', in Peter M. Haas (ed.) *Knowledge, Power and International Policy Coordination.* Columbia, SC: University of South Carolina Press.

AI (Amnesty International) (1994). *Establishing a Just, Fair and Effective International Criminal Court.* London: AI.

Anheier, Helmut, Glasius, Marlies, and Kaldor, Mary (2001). 'Introducing Global Civil Society', in Helmut Anheier, Marlies Glasius, and Mary Kaldor (eds), *Global Civil Society 2001.* Oxford: Oxford University Press.

Almeida, Iris (1999). 'Civil Society and the Establishment of the International Criminal Court', in Maureen McCarthy and Patricia Brown (eds), *Civil Society Engaging Multilateral Institutions: At the Crossroads.* Montreal: Proceedings from the First Forum.

Anderson, Kenneth (2000). 'The Ottawa Convention Banning Landmines, the Role of International Non-governmental Organizations and the Idea of International Civil Society'. *European Journal of International Law,* 11/1: 91–120.

Axel, Donna K., Marrow, Mary Winston, and Hall Martinez, Katherine. 'Women's Caucus on International Cooperation'. *ICC Monitor* Special Edition. gopher://gopher.igc.apc.org/00/orgs/icc/ngodocs/monitor/se/wc%09%09%2B

Bassiouni, M. Cherif (1996). 'An Idea Whose Times Has Come'. *Chicago Tribune.* 18 June.

— (1999). *A Draft International Criminal Code and Draft Statute for an International Criminal Tribunal.* Dordrecht: Martinus Nijhoff.

Benedetti, Fanny and Washburn, John. (1999). 'Drafting the International Criminal Court Treaty: Two Years to Rome and an Afterword on the Rome Diplomatic Conference'. *Global Governance,* 5: 1–37.

Bos, Adriaan (1999). 'The International Criminal Court: Recent Developments', in Herman A.M. von Hebel, Johan G. Lammers, and Jolien Schukking (eds), *Reflections on the International Criminal Court: Essays in Honour of Adriaan Bos.* The Hague: TMC. Asser Press.

Bossier, Pierre (1985). *From Solferino to Tsushima: History of the International Committee of the Red Cross.* Geneva: Henry Dunant Institute.

Burroughs, John and Cabasso, Jacqueline (1999). 'Confronting the Nuclear-Armed States in International Negotiating Forums: Lessons for NGOs'. *International Negotiation,* 4: 457–80.

Busdachin, Marino. 'ICC Appeal Gathers Hundreds of Signatures'. *ICC Monitor* 3. gopher://gopher.igc.apc.org/00/orgs/icc/ngodocs/monitor/Three/petition %09%09%2B

CICC (Coalition for an International Criminal Court) (1998a). 'Basic Principles for an Independent, Effective and Fair International Criminal Court'. gopher://gopher.igc.org/00/orgs/icc/ngodocs/rome/basicprinciples.txt

— (1998b). 'The Numbers; NGO Coalition Special Report on Country Positions'. *The Rome Treaty Conference ICC Monitor.* Special Report, 10 July. gopher://gopher.igc.org/00/orgs/icc/ngodocs/rome/numbers.txt

— (1998c). 'The Virtual Vote, NGO Coalition Special Report on Country Positions on L. 59'. 13 July. http://www.igc.apc.org/icc/rome/html/team_rep/virtual_vote.html

— (2001). 'Congress Backs Away from Passing Strong Anti-ICC Legislation; Remaining Language Reveals Softer Yet Continued U.S. Opposition to the ICC'. Press Release. 21 December.

CICC-TM (Coalition for an International Criminal Court, Trigger Mechanisms and Admissibility Team) (1998). 'Draft Summary of Country Positions on Article 10–20, Based on Opening Statements in the Plenary'. Report #2. 22 June. http://www.igc.apc.org/icc/rome/html/team_rep/trigger/22JUNE.html

CICC-TR (Coalition for an International Criminal Court NGO Teams, Team Reports) (1998). 15 June–17 July. http://www.igc.org/icc/rome/html/rome_other.html

Clark, Roger S. and Slade, Tuiloma Neroni (1999). 'Preamble and Final Clauses', in Roy S. Lee (ed.), *The International Criminal Court: The Making of the Rome Statute; Issues, Negotiations, Results*. The Hague: Kluwer Law International.

Conso, Giovanni (1999). 'Looking to the Future', in Roy S. Lee (ed.), *The International Criminal Court: The Making of the Rome Statute; Issues, Negotiations, Results*. The Hague: Kluwer Law International.

Durham, Helen (2000). 'The Role of NGOs in Creating the International Criminal Court Statute' (Ph.D. thesis). Melbourne: University of Melbourne.

ELSA (European Law Students Association) (1996). 'Trigger Mechanisms (the Role of the Prosecutor)' (Working Paper). Brussels: ELSA.

EN (Equality Now) (1995). 'Recommendations for the Draft Statute for an International Criminal Court'. New York: EN. April.

Facio, Alda. (1998). 'The Rome Diplomatic Conference: A Report'.

Falk, Richard (1998). 'The United Nations and Cosmopolitan Democracy: Bad Dream, Utopian Fantasy, Political Project', in Daniele Archibugi, David Held, and Martin Köhler (eds), *Re-Imagining Political Community: Studies in Cosmopolitan Democracy*. Stanford: Stanford University Press.

Fernàndez de Gurmendi, Silvia A. (1999). 'The Process of Negotiations', in Roy S. Lee (ed.), *The International Criminal Court: The Making of the Rome Statute; Issues, Negotiations, Results*. The Hague: Kluwer Law International.

'Foundation Statement of the Faith-Based Caucus for an International Criminal Court' (n.d.). http://www.igc.org/icc/html/faith.html

Frouville, Olivier de (2000). 'La Cour Penale Internationale: Une Humanité Souveraine?'. *Les Temps Modernes*, 55/610: 257–88.

Haas, Peter M. (1992). 'Introduction: Epistemic Communities and International Policy Coordination', in Peter M. Haas (ed.), *Knowledge, Power and International Policy Coordination*. Columbia, SC: University of South Carolina Press.

Hall, Christopher Keith. 'History of the ICC, Part II: From Nuremberg to the PrepComs'. *ICC Monitor* 7. gopher://gopher.igc.apc.org/00/orgs/icc/ngodocs/monitor /seven/history2%09%09%2B.

— (1998). 'The Third and Fourth Sessions of the UN Preparatory Committee on the Establishment of an International Criminal Court'. *American Journal of International Law*, 92: 124–33.

Haq, Farhan (1998). 'Momentum Builds Behind Powerful Prosecutor'. *Terra Viva*. 23 June.

Held, David. (1995). *Democracy and the Global Order: From the Modern State to Cosmopolitan Governance*. Cambridge: Polity Press.

HRW (Human Rights Watch) (1996). *Commentary for the Preparatory Committee on the Establishment of an International Criminal Court*. New York: HRW. August.

ICC Monitor 1. 'ABC of the ICC'. gopher://gopher.igc.apc.org/00/orgs /icc/ngodocs/monitor/one/abcs_icc%09%09%2B

ICC Monitor 6. 'Regional Reports'. gopher://gopher.igc.apc.org/00/orgs/icc/ ngodocs/monitor/six/regional%09%09%2B

ICC Monitor 10 . 'NGO Activities at Rome Conference'. gopher://gopher.igc. apc.org/00/orgs/icc/ngodocs/monitor/ten/ngo%09%09%2B

ICJ (International Commission of Jurists) (1995). *The International Criminal Court* (Third ICJ Position Paper). Geneva: ICJ. August.

ICRC (International Committee of the Red Cross) (1997). 'War Crimes: Working paper prepared by the ICRC for the Preparatory Committee for the Establishment of an International Criminal Court'. New York. 13 February.

ILC (International Law Commission) (1993). *Yearbook of the International Law Commission* 1990 Vol. I, Summary Records of the forty-second session. New York: United Nations.

— (1997). *Yearbook of the International Law Commission* 1994 Vol. II, Part 2, Report of the Commission to the General Assembly on the work of its forty-sixth session. New York: United Nations.

Jaura, Ramesh. (1998). 'India Thumbs Nose at "European" Court'. *Terra Viva*. 17 July.

Kaldor, Mary (2001) 'A Decade of Humanitarian Intervention: The Role of Global Civil Society', in Helmut Anheier, Marlies Glasius, and Mary Kaldor (eds), *Global Civil Society 2001*. Oxford: Oxford University Press.

Keane, John. (2001). 'Global Civil Society?', in Helmut Anheier, Marlies Glasius, and Mary Kaldor (eds), *Global Civil Society 2001*. Oxford: Oxford University Press.

Krieger, David (1998). 'The Nuremberg Promise and the International Criminal Court'. Nuclear Age Peace Foundation. December. http://www.wagingpeace .org/articles/nuremberg.html

LCHR (Lawyers Committee for Human Rights) (1998). 'Response to US Concerns Regarding the Proposal for a Proprio Motu Prosecutor'. New York: LCHR. 24 June.

Lee, Roy S. (1999). 'Introduction: The Rome Conference and Its Contributions to International Law', in Roy S. Lee (ed.), *The International Criminal Court: The Making of the Rome Statute; Issues, Negotiations, Results*. The Hague: Kluwer Law International.

Lyonette, Louis-Jacques. 'International Criminal Court: Resources in Print and Electronic Format'. http://www.lib.uchicago.edu/~llou/icc.html.

McGrew, Anthony (1997). *The Transformation of Democracy? Globalization and Territorial Democracy*. Cambridge: Polity Press.

Mufson, Steven and Alan Sipress (2001). 'U.N. Funds In Crossfire Over Court—Exemption Sought For U.S. Troops'. *Washington Post*. 16 August.

Nanda, Ved (1996). 'World Needs a Court for World Crimes'. *Denver Post*, 18 August.

On The Record (1998a). 'Canada Slammed by Peace Activists for "Timidity" on Landmines'. Vol. 1, No. 4. 18 June.

On The Record (1998b). 'Support Growing for an Independent Prosecutor; Make or Break Issue for NGO Coalition' Vol.1, No.7. 23 June.

On The Record (1998c). 'Special Analysis of the ICC Statute 1 (Defining Crimes)'. Vol. 1, No. 8. 26 June.

On The Record (1998d) 'National Abortion Laws will not be Undermined by Inclusion of Forced Pregnancy as a Crime Against Humanity, Pledges Women's Caucus'. Vol.1, No. 9 (29 June).

On The Record (1998e). 'Strong Lobbying Efforts of Latin American NGOs Impacted the Rome Conference'. Vol.1, No. 23, Part 2 (27 July).

Oosterveld, Valerie L. (1999). 'The Making of a Gender-Sensitive International Criminal Court'. *International Law FORUM du droit international*, 1/1 (February): 38–41.

Pace, William R. (1999). 'The Relationship between the International Criminal Court and Non-Governmental Organizations', in Herman A.M. von Hebel, Johan G. Lammers, and Jolien Schukking (eds), *Reflections on the International Criminal Court: Essays in Honour of Adriaan Bos*. The Hague: TMC Asser Press.

— and Thieroff, Mark (1999). 'Participation of Non-Governmental Organizations', in Roy S. Lee (ed.), *The International Criminal Court: The Making of the Rome Statute; Issues, Negotiations, Results*. The Hague: Kluwer Law International.

Pace, William and Schense, Jennifer (2002, forthcoming). 'The NGO Coalition's Contribution to the Making of the Elements of Crime and Rules of Procedure', in Roy S. Lee (ed.), *The Making of Elements of Crime and Rules of Procedure: Issues, Negotiations, Results*. New York: Transnational Publications.

Pax Romana (1996). 'Commentaries to the Draft Statute of the International Permanent Criminal Court (IPCC)'. Barcelona: Pax Romana. 28 March.

Pianta, Mario (2001). 'Parallel Summits of Global Civil Society', in Helmut Anheier, Marlies Glasius, and Mary Kaldor (eds), *Global Civil Society 2001*. Oxford: Oxford University Press.

REAL Women of Canada. (1998a) 'The International Criminal Court – World Nightmare'. *REALity Newsletter*, 16/9. http://www.real women ca.com/html/newsletter/1998_May_Jun/Article_9.html .

— (1998b) 'Canada Courts Disaster With World Court'. *REALity Newsletter*, 16/10. http://www.realwomenca.com/html/newsletter/1998_July_Aug/Article_1.html

Rosenau, James (1998). 'Governance and Democracy in a Globalizing World', in Daniele Archibugi, David Held, and Martin Köhler (eds), *Re-Imagining Political Community: Studies in Cosmopolitan Democracy*. Stanford: Stanford University Press.

Saland, Per (1999). 'International Criminal Law Principles', in Roy S. Lee (ed.) *The International Criminal Court: The Making of the Rome Statute; Issues, Negotiations, Results*. The Hague: Kluwer Law International.

Scholte, Jan Aart (2001). Civil Society and Democracy in Global Governance (CSGR Working Paper No.65/01). *Warwick University: Centre for the Study of Globalisation and Regionalisation*.

Schwarzenberger, Georg (1968). *International Law as Applied by Courts and Tribunals. Vol. II: The Law of Armed Conflict*. London: Stevens & Sons Limited.

Sharratt, Sara and Kaschak, Ellyn (1999). *Assault on the Soul: Women in the Former Yugoslavia*. New York: Haworth Press.

Shriver, Donald W. 'The International Criminal Court: Its Moral Urgency'. *ICC Monitor* 7. gopher://gopher.igc.apc.org/00/orgs/icc/ngodocs/monitor/seven/ shriver%09%09%2B

Steains, Cate (1999). 'Gender Issues', in Roy S. Lee (ed.), *The International Criminal Court: The Making of the Rome Statute; Issues, Negotiations, Results*. The Hague: Kluwer Law International.

Sweeney, Daniel Mac (1996). *Prospects for the Financing of an International Criminal Court* (WFM/IGP Discussion Paper). August.

UN (United Nations) (1989). Request for the Inclusion of a Supplementary Item in the Agenda of the Forty-fourth session, International Criminal Responsibility of Individuals and Entities Engaged in Illicit Trafficking in Narcotic Drugs and Across National Frontiers and Other Transnational Criminal Activities: Establishment of an International Criminal Court with Jurisdiction over Such Crimes, Letter dated 21 August 1989 from the Permanent Representative of Trinidad and Tobago to the United Nations addressed to the Secretary-General, 21 August 1989. Doc. A/44/195.

— (1994). Resolution Adopted by the General Assembly, Establishment of an International Criminal Court, 9 December 1994. Doc. A/RES/49/53.

— (1995a). 'Power of Security Council to Refer Cases to Proposed International Criminal Court Debated in Ad Hoc Committee'. Committee on International Criminal Court, First Session, 4th Meeting (PM). 4 April.

— (1995b). 'Security Council's Right to Refer Cases to Proposed International Criminal Tribunal Discussed In Ad Hoc Committee'. Committee on International Criminal Court, First Session, 5th Meeting (AM). 5 April. Press Release L/2717

— (1995c). 'Committee Turns to Jurisdictional Issues Affecting Proposed Criminal Court'. Committee on International Criminal Court, Resumed First Session, 23rd Meeting (PM). 18 August. Press Release L/2738.

— (1996) 'Preparatory Committee on International Criminal Court Concludes First Session'. 12 April. Press Release L/2787.

United States (1998). 'The Concerns of the United States Regarding the Proposal for a Proprio Motu Prosecutor'. Department of State (22 June).

Van Boven, Theo (1999). 'The Position of the Victim in the Statute for an International Criminal Court', in Herman A.M. von Hebel, Johan G. Lammers, and Jolien Schukking (eds), Reflections on the International Criminal Court: Essays in Honour of Adriaan Bos. The Hague: TMC Asser Press.

Von Hebel, Herman (1999). 'An International Criminal Court–A Historical Perspective', in Herman A.M. von Hebel, Johan G. Lammers, and Jolien Schukking (eds), Reflections on the International Criminal Court: Essays in Honour of Adriaan Bos. The Hague: TMC Asser Press.

— and Darryl Robinson (1999). 'Crimes within the Jurisdiction of the Court', in Roy S. Lee (ed.), The International Criminal Court: The Making of the Rome Statute; Issues, Negotiations, Results. The Hague: Kluwer Law International.

Ware, Alyn (1997). 'Preparatory Committee on the Establishment of an International Criminal Court (ICC PrepCom), December 1–12 1997: Report on War Crimes and Weapons Systems'. http://www.ialana.org/site/affairs/rel_icc.html

WC (Women's Caucus for Gender Justice in the International Criminal Court) (1997). Recommendations and Commentary For December 1997 PrepCom On The Establishment of An International Criminal Court, United Nations Headquarters December 1–12, 1997. December.

Weapons Systems Caucus (1997). 'Proposal of the Weapons Systems Caucus'. New York: Weapons Systems Caucus. http://www.ialana.org/site/affairs/index.html

Wilmshurst, Elizabeth (1999). 'Jurisdiction of the Court', in Roy S. Lee (ed.), The International Criminal Court: The Making of the Rome Statute; Issues, Negotiations, Results. The Hague: Kluwer Law International.

Wolf, Val. 'Amnesty International Campaign Update'. ICC Monitor Special Edition. gopher://gopher.igc.apc.org/00/orgs/icc/ngodocs/monitor/se/ai%09%09%2B

World Federalist Movement. http://www.worldfederalist.org/ ABOUT_WFM / About WFM.html.

Interviews

Bos, Adriaan. Dutch Delegation Leader and Chairman of PrepComs, 26 November 2001.

Burroughs, John. Executive Director, Lawyers Committee on Nuclear Policy, 5 December 2001.

Dicker, Richard. Legal Officer, Human Rights Watch, 6 December 2001.

Donat-Cattin, David. Program Officer for International Law and Human Rights; Former President of the European Law Students Association, 5 December 2001.

Hall Martinez, Katherine. Deputy Director, International Program, Center for Reproductive Law and Policy, 4 December 2001.

Pace, William. Coordinator of the NGO Coalition for an International Criminal Court, 3 and 17 December 2001.

Van Boven, Theo. Dutch delegation leader to the Rome Conference, 28 November 2001.

Van Troost, Lars. ICC Project Coordinator, Amnesty International, 27 November 2001.

Von Hebel, Herman. Member, Dutch delegation to PrepComs and Rome Conference, 26 November 2001.

Part III: Infrastructure of Global Civil Society

Chapter 7

THE OTHER INFORMATION REVOLUTION: MEDIA AND EMPOWERMENT IN DEVELOPING COUNTRIES

James Deane with Njonjo Mue and Fackson Banda

The emergence, health, and diversity of civil society depend on access to information on key issues that affect people's lives and the capacity of people and organisations to have their voices heard in the public and political arena.

The role of the information technology revolution and its implications for global civil society have been well documented in this respect, including in the first Global Civil Society Yearbook (Naughton (2001); see also Castells (1998)). The potential of the Internet and mobile telephony in particular to provide unprecedented access to information and knowledge, and their record in providing new ways for geographically disparate people to form communities of common interest, to communicate, organise, and make their voices heard is widely acknowledged. This information revolution—complex, unevenly distributed, creating new divides while narrowing others, but undoubtedly transformative—has overshadowed a broader, more pervasive information revolution that is less understood and certainly less documented.

For much of humanity, particularly the 2 billion people on the planet earning less than two dollars a day, access to information through these new communication technologies remains a distant (though not impossible) prospect. For most people in most developing countries, it is rapidly changing media which provide the information, perspective, and analysis which enable them to make sense of their world and which enable them to engage as citizens in their society; which provide an increasingly important means of making their voices heard; which increasingly facilitate horizontal and interpersonal communication and debate, and which provide mechanisms for the formulation of identity and the creation of community spaces. Conversely, it is the media that are often most instrumental in creating new forms of social and political division in society, in depoliticising public debate, in fostering tension and conflict between countries and communities.

Over the last decade, and the last five years in particular, media in most developing countries have undergone a revolution in their structure, dynamism, interactivity, reach, and accessibility. This has had a profound impact on and for civil society in these countries, and very mixed implications for the inclusiveness and character of public debate, particularly in relation to the exposure of public and political debate to the voices, concerns, and perspectives of the poor and marginalised in these societies.

Independence, plurality, and accessibility of media constitute fundamental constituents of an environment which facilitates social change. The role of the media in fostering democratic inclusion, in underpinning social and political change, in economic development, and in empowering marginalised communities is well documented (Sen 1999; Besley and Burgess 2000; Hamelink 1994; Lush 1997; Westoff and Bankole 1999; Dreze and Sen 1989). The vibrancy, intensity, and effectiveness of civil society, particularly in developing countries, are intimately related to the freedom and pluralism of the media. Civil society depends heavily on people having access to information and having channels to voice issues of concern in the public arena. If civil society organisations are to effect positive change they need to articulate their arguments in the public arena and subject their arguments to public debate. While there are plenty of examples of civil society organisations exerting influence in closed and oppressive regimes where the media are tightly controlled, free and genuinely plural media clearly provide the opportunity and foundation for the kind of inclusive public debate where civil society perspectives can be aired, heard, and themselves tested by debate in the public arena. Freedom and pluralism of the media are both a product and an engine for an inclusive, genuinely civil society.

This chapter examines some of the changes in the media over the last decade, particularly in developing countries, and provides a broad examination of some of the implications for public debate, free expression, and civil society, at both the national level and the international and global levels. It argues that, in terms of how most people on the planet access information and knowledge on the issues that affect their lives, and how most people articulate and make their feelings heard in national and international public debates, the changes in structure, content, ownership, and access within the 'traditional' media in the last five years have been equally if not more profound than those occurring among the new technologies. While changes in the global media and increased concentration of the media internationally have been the subject of substantial comment (e.g. McChesney and Herman 1997; Gerbner, Mowlana, and Schiller 1996; Mediachannel URL), changes in the media within developing countries have received substantially less attention. This chapter argues that the implications of these changes for civil society are extremely contradictory.

> State control and influence over the media in most countries defined political and social discourse and fundamentally constrained the emergence of non-governmental and civil society actors

Out with the Old: The Former Status Quo

Little more than a decade ago, the principal way in which most people on the planet accessed information from beyond their immediate communities was from their governments, mainly in the form of state-owned and controlled monopoly media. Throughout the Soviet Union and most of its sphere, government control of media was total. In China, the same situation applied. Throughout much of Africa and much of the rest of Asia, post-independence governments invested heavily in their radio broadcasting and press infrastructures as key tools of nation building. In these countries, governments were keen to assert strong control and monopoly ownership of the media, in part to guard against fragmentation of the media along ethnic, tribal, or political lines, and in part in order to maximise political control over their peoples. In many countries media systems were either inherited from the former colonial powers and in several media infrastructure was non-existent, either because it had not been established or because radio stations, for example, had suffered wholesale demolition by the outgoing colonial governments.

Throughout four decades in which aspirant presidents sought to take power by making their first coup objective the commandeering of their nation's broadcasting station, governments protective of their power have kept jealous control of 'their' media systems. The degree of control exerted over the media was generally closely linked to the autocracy of the government in power but, even in democracies such as India, governments insisted on monopoly control of the broadcast media. The print media, generally with a much smaller reach and limited principally to urban populations, were less controlled. In Latin America, tight control of the media was less often exercised through direct government ownership and more often by privately owned media whose owners' interests were closely allied to those in power or, at a minimum, served the interests of a small and wealthy elite. Much of this control took place in the context of a Cold War where the superpowers and their client states exercised definitive influence on who was in government and how long they remained in power. Much of the information available to people through the media was similarly defined by that context.

This chapter is not designed to provide a detailed analysis of the history of the media over the last 50 years, and there are many examples of non-Western countries which have a long tradition of free and open media, as well as cases of Western countries seeking to keep a tight a rein on freedom of the media. But its starting point is that, for much of the post-Second World War period, the vast majority of people on the planet had access only to information from the media to which their governments allowed them access. Although the complexity and penetration of social, community, and other informal and non-media information networks should not be underestimated, state control and influence over the media in most countries defined political and social discourse and fundamentally constrained the emergence of non-governmental and civil society actors.

In many countries, state control of the media remains extremely powerful. While China, for example, is witnessing increasing diversity and energy within its media, the Chinese media continue to operate under a tight regimen controlled by government (Sun 2001). And, as this chapter argues, where state control in the media has declined, commercial and corporate control of the media has taken its place. However, for most developing countries the end of the Cold War has prompted an information revolution every bit as important as the digital information revolution.

Freedom, Choice . . . and Money

Since the fall of the Berlin wall and the end of the Cold War, and in tandem with other processes, there has been a rapid, widespread liberalisation of media in general and of broadcast media in particular.

Pressures on governments to liberalise their media take a number of forms. The fall of many one-party systems of government across Africa, parts of Asia, in eastern Europe, the former Soviet Union, and elsewhere in the 1980s led to the coming to power of many governments committed to ending state media control. These embarked on a rapid liberalisation of media, some of them from a genuine belief in the importance of free and plural media in ensuring democratic, inclusive societies, often combined with the belief in the importance of a free flow of information as a prerequisite for the effective functioning of a free market economy. The trend towards more open media systems is among the trends documented in Chapter 2, including the weakening of nation states, the advance of the free market philosophy, and the rise of democratic globalism.

Most governments have also understood that maintaining a monopoly over their citizens' access to information in the wake of satellite, Internet, mobile telephony is no longer possible. An increasingly well-informed, powerful, and pervasive civil society has reinforced that reality. This has been combined with the huge international information flows which underpin the global economy and the importance for most governments of being part of that economy. For poorer countries, these factors are reinforced by pressure from donors and other international actors, with countries refusing to liberalise media and

guarantee media freedoms finding donor funding and loans withdrawn.

The net result has been that in areas formerly dominated by state-controlled media systems, particularly in much of Africa and Asia, only a few countries have retained full state control of their media. Liberalisation, particularly of broadcast media, has often been partial, haphazard, and evolutionary rather than revolutionary, but it has nevertheless been transformative. In other regions, such as in large parts of Latin America, which has a long tradition of community media and where government control of media has tended to be more complex, the transformation has tended to be less dramatic.

> Liberalisation, particularly of broadcast media, has often been partial, haphazard, and evolutionary rather than revolutionary, but it has nevertheless been transformative

The most immediate consequence of these changes has been far greater freedom of information and expression. Liberalisation and diversification, particularly in Africa and Asia, have transformed both print and broadcast media from a largely government-owned, monopolistic, and uncreative media environment to a more dynamic, popular, democratic, creative, commercial, and complex one.

Print Media

The print media have, despite their sometimes limited readership, played a critical role in providing internal scrutiny of governments, and a free press has become increasingly regarded as both a precondition for and major indicator of democracy, effective and sustainable development, and good governance (Roth 2001). Media freedoms remain under constant pressure and attack, but the general trend is of an increasing number of print titles in many countries, and, while numbers rise and fall rapidly, particularly during election periods, many have been able to sustain themselves financially and have retained a genuine political independence from government.

The international image of print media in developing countries has tended to be shaped by fiercely independent, courageous journalists battling to retain their professional integrity in the face of an often brutal state and exposing corruption and wrongdoing. There are many astonishing and inspirational examples of this, ranging from the bombed *Daily News* in Zimbabwe continuing to publish independently of the government despite sustained and violent intimidation, to journalists such as P. Sainath (author of *Everyone Loves a Good Drought*) who spends several months of each year travelling in and reporting from India's rural villages for the *Times of India* (Sainath 1996). Throughout much of Africa, independent newspapers have played central roles in guaranteeing and nourishing new democratic systems.

These courageous examples and individuals are, however, just one side of a coin, the flip side of which is print media which sees themselves increasingly serving a metropolitan business and political elite augmented by a lifestyle agenda catering for a burgeoning middle class. Journalists wanting to invest time in investigative stories, or wanting to report on stories concerning the poor, or who want to invest in serious and more objective analysis underlying conflict are finding themselves both a minority and increasingly struggling for the attention and respect of their editors and proprietors. As Neera Chandoke points out in Chapter 2, 'the market . . . has room for only those people who have something to sell and those who have something to buy'. The evolution of the media is characterised increasingly by a generalised lack of interest in the fate of those who can neither buy nor sell the products they are advertising, even though these constitute the large majority of the populations of their countries.

Proprietors are in turn becoming more and more remote and impersonal as print media, even in the poorest countries, become more concentrated in the hands either of international (global and regional) media conglomerates or of narrow party political interests. India, for example, has seen a major shift in the attitude of press proprietors. Once greatly respected for their commitment to journalistic integrity, democratic principles, and professional ethics, newspapers are, according to a recent report by the UK Department for International Development, 'increasingly treated as commercial brands, their independence made suspect by collaborative ties with the state-owned media' (Roth 2001).

> Journalists wanting to invest time in investigative stories or wanting to report on stories concerning the poor are increasingly struggling for the attention and respect of their editors and proprietors

Print media in most developing countries are also becoming more parochial in their views. Twenty-five years ago, media in developing countries were engaged in a fierce debate and attempt to create a New World Information and Communication Order (NWICO), where media in developing countries could free themselves from dependence on Northern news sources and create their own common news-gathering and exchange systems. They would source their news increasingly from other developing countries through information exchange, news agencies, and other mechanisms designed to improve South-South communication. While the credibility of the NWICO perished many years ago, largely because its ideals were undermined by government attempts to use the new initiative to control, rather than facilitate, new information flows, the extent to which these ideals have been abandoned is stark.

In an increasingly globalised world, editors find it increasingly difficult to interest their readers in stories which are not explicitly locally, nationally, or regionally relevant, or are following a global news agenda (generally set in the North). Reporting of stories from Africa in the Asian print media, for example, is rare, despite the many shared issues of trade, debt, and other globally relevant issues. Meanwhile the major international agencies, such as Reuters, are increasingly focusing their reporting on the lucrative business and economic reporting markets, while their news reporting (like those of other major international agencies such as Associated Press and Agence France Presse) continues to follow a heavily Northern-focused agenda. Developing country news services, meanwhile, such as the Inter Press Service and Gemini News Service, are struggling partly because of falls in donor funding which helped subsidise them, and particularly because major developing country media are increasingly being bought up by international conglomerates, many of whom have their own—again, Northern-focused—features services.

Many optimists in the 1980s foresaw a flowering of a new age of media pluralism and public debate as new media began to flourish in the new political dispensation of the end of the Cold War. Media freedom has increased, but while a political environment exists which enables more open public debate in the media, the liberalised commercial media are often unwilling to facilitate or contribute to such debate. As the World Bank points out, in Hungary before 1989 the relatively relaxed regime allowed many dissident writers to have their work published in ways that could stimulate public debate, but these same writers are now finding it increasingly difficult to get their work published in a profit oriented free market (World Bank 2001). That situation pertains in many other former one-party states.

There is a further trend towards the sensational and media dividing along ethnic or religious lines. Senegal, for example, has recently witnessed the emergence of a generation of highly populist and salacious print titles clearly modelled on the British tabloid papers (Diop 2001). The titles of these newspapers leave little doubt of their content: *Le Populaire*, *Le Tract (The Pamphlet),* and *Le Scoop* deal with sex, crime, the freakish, and gossip. In Nigeria, a country with a very rich tradition of public interest journalism and where journalists are often held in high public esteem for their role in restoring democracy to the country, increasing concern is being expressed at the emergence of 'ethnic journalism' with media reporting and journalism increasingly fragmenting along Christian and Muslim fault-lines.

The salaries and status of journalists in society have often increased substantially following liberalisation, but in some of the poorest countries journalism continues to be a desperately difficult profession, both politically and economically. In Guinea Bisseau, for example, journalists operate not only in a hostile political environment but also with poor equipment and even poorer salaries. The editor-in-chief on one (government) paper, *No Pintcha*, earns approximately 240 FF per month in a country where a 5kg bag of rice costs between 1,250 and 1,400 FF (Diallo 2001).

Despite this, and although most media continue to serve a metropolitan elite, print media are the most important credible way of informing and stimulating public debate on key development issues, particularly the complex, contested, and often technical issues of globalisation. However, an ugly combination of increased concentration of ownership, a growing focus on business and lifestyle agendas, editors' lack of interest in supporting investigative or specialist journalism on social or development issues is fatally undermining the extent to which publics in many developing countries have access to, and the means to sensibly interpret, issues of globalisation, or have access to the issues facing the poor in their countries. Even for those editors who want to cover these issues in more detail, there is a growing shortage of credible, independent, developing country-focused news and analysis of global issues.

The print media more than any others have the capacity to provide explanation, reporting, analysis, and opinion on complex issues that affect their readers' lives. Print provides a medium which can deal with complexity unlike any other. But, although literacy rates have increased substantially over the last three decades, even in some of the poorest countries access to newspapers continues to be constrained by relatively low literacy rates. Even in India, which has one of the richest newspaper publishing industries in the world, national literacy levels are still as low as 51 per cent.

The print media in most developing countries are more free and more diverse than a decade ago, and have played a central role in the political evolution of many countries. But there are major questions as to whether, given their increasing obsession with commercial advantage, they are becoming more plural or are able to inform public and political debate to the extent that democratic societies require.

> Print media are the most important credible way of informing and stimulating public debate on key development issues, particularly the complex, contested, and often technical issues of globalisation

The Rebirth of Radio and a New Oral Tradition?

Changes in the print media, which have a long tradition of providing independent journalism including in several one-party states, are less pronounced than those in the broadcast sector. It is the broadcast media, particularly radio, which have undergone the greatest transformation in many countries, with competition ushering in a new environment of choice and creativity in programming, with many new private and (to a much lesser extent) community-owned radio and television stations rapidly establishing audience dominance over old state-run broadcasting systems.

In the radio sector, liberalisation has led to three main trends. The first of these is the flourishing of a new generation of commercial, generally independent FM radio stations. From Uganda to Zambia, Sri Lanka to Nepal, and in the large majority of countries formerly controlled by one party states, a plethora of new mostly privately run and heavily commercially oriented stations has emerged. Dependent entirely on advertising for their funding and emerging most rapidly in the 1990s, these have often been criticised by civil society organisations in their countries for their general avoidance of public debate and political discussion. Many commercial FM stations carry little or no news, or relay brief news from an international news provider such as the BBC (thus providing little or no local analysis or news). Programming, at least in the early stages of liberalisation, typically consists of often Western-originated music programming. Some early FM stations in Africa, such as Capital Radio in Uganda, won praise from civil society organisations for their range of programmes and particularly, in the case of Capital Radio, for the development of innovative health and sex education programming, such as Capital Doctor, which was a global pioneer in addressing the issue of HIV/AIDS and stimulating public discussion and dialogue on the issue.

However, the apolitical, non-news and music-based content of many radio stations led civil society organisations to complain increasingly that liberalisation was leading to a commercialisation and privatisation of the airwaves, with content being defined entirely by a consumer-oriented, advertising-dependent, urban-focused, and generally youth lifestyle agenda. There was little or no investment in news or analysis of global or national political developments and very little exposure or reference to the rural, marginalised majorities in these countries. While the FM stations were successful in rapidly gaining an often eager audience through more dynamic, engaging, and popular programming, they had a very poor early record in addressing issues of public concern.

This trend towards an urban, consumer-oriented agenda was further reinforced by the second key trend in this sector, with state broadcasting systems plunging into crisis. The loss of monopoly effectively involved a loss of incentive by governments to invest in state broadcasting systems. These have mostly tended to try to reinvent themselves as commercial broadcasters, supplementing dwindling government

MEDIA AND EMPOWERMENT IN DEVELOPING COUNTRIES   James Deane with Njonjo Mue and Fackson Banda

Box 7.1: Women and the media

Women continue to suffer marginalisation in and from communication networks, and evidence of the scale of sexual harassment and discrimination within the media itself in Africa (and elsewhere) is growing. When in 1995 UNESCO sponsored a global media monitoring project to explore the representation of women in 71 countries, it found that women made up just 17 per cent of all interviewees in the news worldwide. Women interviewees were much more likely to be lay voices, even on topics which were very woman-focused. Male interviewees were more typically interviewed as voices of authority. Twenty-nine per cent of all female interviewees were portrayed as victims of crime or accidents compared with just 10 per cent of male interviewees. A follow-up worldwide study in 2000 has found similar results and these are relatively consistent across regions (Spears and Seydegart 2001). Similar findings have been repeated in many national studies. A further twist in the story is the split in news coverage between urban and rural concerns, the latter receiving comparatively little attention. In one Kenyan study, rural women featured in a tiny fraction of news coverage and a striking 76 per cent of rural women who appeared in the media were portrayed as criminals or victims. Liberalisation of radio and television has also prompted major concerns about the increasing objectification of women in society through advertising and highly sexualised content. Counterbalancing some of these trends is the prominent role played by the women in the new media environment, including in societies, such as in Pakistan and elsewhere in South Asia, where women are particularly prominent as editors and owners of news organisations.

subsidy with advertising income. In doing so they have followed the same content agenda as the commercial sector. They have tended to cut back on both content and infrastructure, with the most common and critical consequence being the reduction of transmitting capacity to rural areas, a decrease in language programming with a shift to mainstream language programming, a decrease in programming aimed, for example, at education, health, environmental, or agricultural support, and,

Above: Community radio station broadcasting from a bedroom in Somaliland. © Hamish Wilson/Panos Pictures.

with some exceptions, an unwillingness to invest in programming which provided a voice for rural communities in national debate. There are very few examples of former state broadcast monopolies successfully transforming themselves into genuinely public service broadcasters.

A third, more positive, trend is the increasing investment and flourishing of community radio internationally. Originally strongest in Latin America, community radio is growing very rapidly in much of Africa and some parts of Asia. West Africa has 450 radio stations, the vast majority of which have been formed in the last decade, and South Africa has more than 100. Community radio is by most definitions taken to mean radio which is substantially owned and/or formally controlled by a community and is not run for private profit. The flourishing of community radio, although facilitated by and generally dependent on government liberalisation of the airwaves, is also being driven by much lower start-up costs as the price of transmitters and other radio equipment falls. All the equipment required to establish a community radio station can be acquired for less than $20,000 (and a very

basic set up could be established for a tenth of that amount). Although facing problems of sustainability, with several examples of donor-funded community radio stations being initiated and then collapsing after initial investment, organisations such as AMARC (World Association of Community Broadcasters) are facilitating a major growth in this area. Community stations, such as Radio Sagarmatha in Nepal, have grown to the extent they have become increasingly professional, national, and commercial entities, blending their original commitment to community issues and public debate with a commercial business plan. In some cases original community radio organisations have abandoned their roots and transformed themselves entirely into commercial, advertising-driven organisations.

These trends, which were set in motion in the 1990s, reflect a complex picture of privatisation and commercialisation of the airwaves with a small window also being opened to the community sector. More recently, however, a new, largely unpredicted trend has emerged which is offering major new opportunities for public debate: the rise of the talk show. Talk-based radio, involving free-ranging studio

The last ten years have seen unprecedented changes on the media landscape across southern Africa. These changes have been occurring at two interconnected levels: the global and the local. In part, these have been a function of greater political pluralism across various nation-states. Also, foreign media moguls, such as the Cable News Network (CNN), the British Broadcasting Corporation (BBC), and others have taken advantage of this situation to export international capital to finance many of the local-foreign media ventures that the sub-region has begun to witness. Locally, there have been organic media formations, such as community or alternative radio, private FM radio stations, and other initiatives which, nevertheless, have ended up looking to foreign financiers for their sustainability. For instance, UNESCO has been in the forefront of supporting community radio initiatives across southern Africa, from Malawi's Dzimwe Community Radio, through Namibia's Katutura Community Radio Station, to Zambia's Mazabuka Community Radio Station. For all its efforts, UNESCO has been accused of failing to sustain such radio stations, with the result that most of them end up operating as though they were private, commercial stations.

The global level
The liberalisation of the media industry and the attendant commercialisation and privatisation of hitherto state media have had a profound effect upon local media spaces. The 1990s have seen the transnationalisation of major world media, such as CNN, the BBC, Bloomberg, and others, as a consequence of such satellite broadcasting services as Multichoice Kaleidoscope in South Africa. Multichoice has set up agents throughout the African continent, with thousands of subscribers shifting to this multi-channel television and radio broadcasting service.

The print media, such as *The Mail and Guardian* and *Mmegi*, are also beginning to regionalise, reaching out to such countries as Zambia, Zimbabwe, and Kenya, cultivating in the process a regional media entertainment consumer network. As a consequence, many people in many nations are now exposed to much foreign content across different genres. It would appear that it is mostly those with the wherewithal who can afford such continent-wide satellite broadcasting and regional newspapers. This seems to be a common or homogenising factor. It is not far-fetched to argue that an elite is emerging that may well be 'delocalised' from its local cultural roots, basically united in common, cosmopolitan lifestyles, values, and world-views.

But this has raised questions about the importance of local content as a counter to any possible undesirable influences on the local cultures of the consumers of such media products.

Perhaps, given the rate at which South Africa's Multichoice Kaleidoscope is developing on the continent, there is growing concern that this economic powerhouse might, in fact, be on the verge of becoming one of the main exporters of media products to the rest of Africa. M-NET, SABC Africa, e-TV, Africa-to-Africa, and other South African channels are beginning to make great inroads into several countries. In fact, SABC Africa prides itself on being 'the pulse of Africa', almost as though it were setting itself forth as the essence of African broadcasting.

Furthermore, this global trend in media has resulted in a realignment of the local media landscape. There appear to be emerging state-private media business alliances. For instance, the Zambia National Broadcasting (ZNBC) has entered into strategic partnerships with M-NET, African Broadcasting Network (ABN), TV Africa, and Sandon Television to bring entertainment-based television

discussions, phone-ins, political interviews, as well as interviews with celebrities combined with music, are becoming some of the most popular programming for FM broadcasters. Although few FM radio stations have the resources to invest in significant independent news-gathering operations,

talk shows are opening up new spaces for political and public debate, and through debate to public engagement. They are, according to Muthoni Wanyeki, director-general of FEMNET in Africa, leading to 'reinvention of the African oral tradition' (Wanyeki 2000). New radio stations, such as Monitor

James Deane with Njonjo Mue and Fackson Banda   MEDIA AND EMPOWERMENT IN DEVELOPING COUNTRIES

programming to Zambian audiences of the ZNBC TV. The same trend is true of Malawi, which has just introduced locally produced television services, as well as Mozambique, Botswana, Zimbabwe, Lesotho, Namibia, and Swaziland.

The local level

As noted above, the southern African sub-region has experienced a process of deregulation in which the media industry has essentially been opened up to private capital. Thus, the state media have begun to face stiff competition from their private counterparts for audiences.

However, purely private, commercial media are themselves coming into competition with so-called community or alternative media. With more defined audiences, community or alternative media are becoming more pronounced as agents of social and political change across the continent, although most of them are turning out to be purveyors of popular entertainment rather than serious political communication. Over 80 community radio stations have been given licences by South Africa's Independent Communications Authority of South Africa (ICASA). The Ministry of Information and Broadcasting Services in Zambia has given out over ten licences to private FM radio stations, some of which, although not necessarily owned or controlled by communities, claim to be *community* stations.

Even with all these unprecedented changes on the ground, however, little has happened in terms of consistent, coherent, and comprehensive policy frameworks to deal with the ever-evolving media scenario. This policy laxity has extended to the so-called new media, such as the Internet and e-mail services.

On the contrary, new laws and policies seem to be an attempt at *re-regulating* the media industry with a heavier hand. In Zambia, efforts to set up an independent broadcasting authority have not succeeded, with both the state and private broadcasting arenas largely filled on the basis of political caprice. In Zimbabwe, though the Broadcasting Authority of Zimbabwe (BAZ) has been established under the Broadcasting Services Act 2001, there is suspicion that the state's purported desire to finalise the drafting of the frequency map which will allow more private broadcasters to obtain frequencies is not likely to open up the airwaves in ways that will promote independent broadcast journalism.

Indeed, the process of re-regulation is taking place in other, more subtle ways, such as harassment of journalists, tolerating policy gaps, removal of advertising from private media, etc.

Conclusion

The future of free media is bleak in most countries in southern Africa, with the exception of South Africa. Even *there*, the highly commercialised nature of mostly urban-based South African media seems to be working against poor people's access to these media to make their perspectives and views known to the political and public policy-making elites, but this seems to be somewhat mitigated by the mushrooming of community media initiatives. The entertainment media industry, on the other hand, seems to have a bright future. The so-called 'liberalisation' of the media industry has worked to promote largely foreign music-and-movie media outlets. Local news, especially that which focuses on political issues and events, on community or private FM radio stations has met with state censure.

Fackson Banda

FM in Kampala, are emerging which are specifically devoted to talk-based radio. Although still heavily urban-based and oriented, and with very limited access and reporting from non-urban areas, these are creating new channels and opportunities for public debate in general and for civil society organisations in particular to have their voices heard in the public arena.

The complexity and potential of radio as a reborn medium in many developing countries is further augmented by other technological developments, particularly the potential of the Internet to enable resource-poor radio stations to access and exchange content, and the telephone which, through phone-ins, is making radio a much more horizontal and interactive medium. Audio files are easily digitised and, although there are major constraints caused by poor levels of connectivity and capacity to take advantage of these technologies, there are several projects which are seeking to use the technology to improve coverage of development issues by FM and community radio stations.

Despite this, the gap between rich and poor, rural and urban is huge. While the community radio movement is providing empowering new forms of information and communication, this movement is patchy and many governments (such as Zimbabwe) are refusing to grant licences to community media. More broadly, governments in much of the developing world appear content to allow a burgeoning of the FM radio sector provided that the limited geographical reach of FM radio transmitters makes them a principally urban phenomenon. Walk more than a few miles outside of the urban centres in most countries and this radio revolution might never exist.

While liberalisation in the radio sector is a dominant trend globally, it is far from a universal one. India, the largest democracy in the world, has proved particularly reluctant to license independent radio stations outside of the monopoly Doordarshan network, despite its deregulation of satellite television.

Governments generally are much less willing to grant licences to short- or medium-wave radio stations which have the capacity to reach rural areas and are proving fiercely—and effectively—protective of their broadcasting monopoly in rural areas where, for many, their political power base rests. The decline in investment in state-run broadcasting systems, including the closing or breaking down of transmitters, the cutting of minority language services, and lack of investment in appropriate content, means that rural areas are becoming increasingly, rather than decreasingly, marginalised from public and political debate. The urban-rural divide is intensifying in media, and in doing so reflects a similar divide in civil society, with most civil society organisations also being very heavily an urban phenomenon. Together with other more conventionally understood characteristics of the 'digital divide' such as the lack of access to tele-

phony and Internet by the rural and the poor, this marginalisation is becoming increasingly stark.

Religious organisations have also responded to broadcast liberalisation with alacrity. Mostly US-based or funded fundamentalist religious organisations broadcast to large parts of the developing world. Religious organisations have also been quick to take advantage of new broadcast licences, sometimes with the help of strongly religious governments or government leaders. In Zambia, the first independent radio station was a Christian one; and, of six supposedly independent community radio stations recently granted radio licences, four are owned and controlled by the Catholic Church.

Liberalisation is also leading to a strengthening and increasing dependence on international news networks, particularly the BBC. The BBC has always been a much valued and respected news source in much of the developing world, and its value has generally risen in inverse relationship with the credibility of local news sources. The less plural, the more controlled the national media, the more people turn to sources such as the BBC for their news and information. It is perhaps curious that, at a time of increased freedom, the BBC is on the whole thriving, reporting steadily increasing audiences for its radio output on the BBC World Service and through its strategy of becoming in effect a national broadcaster by securing national FM licences for its broadcasts. The success of the BBC's continuing building of audiences at national level reflects no longer principally a lack of freedom in most of the countries it works in, but the inability or unwillingness of local broadcasters to access and provide news and information to their audiences in a detailed way. Although the picture is complex and in some countries the BBC is suffering significant audience losses while in others achieving major gains, countries where the BBC's audience share tends to be low, such as in Uganda, tend to be those where domestic news sources and the domestic broadcast environment do provide sufficient, locally relevant news and information.

The key to addressing the challenges of providing public interest radio in a liberalised and commercialised environment lies in creating intelligent, flexible, and creative regulatory environments which encourage diversity and genuine pluralism. There are, however, very few examples where such regulation has been successfully developed and applied.

Television: Consumerism, Conflict, and an End to Boredom

The transformation in media content following liberalisation is seen nowhere more graphically than in television. Although Malawi opened its first ever television station only in 2000, and television signals are available to just 70 per cent of Kenyans, global access to television has grown massively in the last decade. It remains, however, a minority medium, particularly when compared with radio, and for rural areas in Africa and Asia (but to a much lesser extent in much of Latin America) television penetration remains very limited. In terms of where its content is principally targeted and for whom it is produced, rural populations generally could be on another planet.

An increasingly competitive, commercial, ratings-hungry television industry is clearly not restricted to the developing world, but the rate and scale of change in the television industry and consequent implications for public debate and social change are particularly intense in much of the South. As with radio, a little over a decade ago most governments monopolised television. State ownership and control of the media was (and in several countries still is) a fundamental pillar of oppression, disenfranchisement, and control. This has changed and for many people

its passing is celebrated almost as much for an end to boredom as an end to state control of their lives. Commercial television has, if nothing else, created television that is more dynamic, entertaining, and far more popular than the state-controlled fodder that preceded it.

Perhaps the most dramatic change in the television industry anywhere on the planet has occurred in South Asia, with the introduction of mostly Indian-based satellite television. South Asian governments have proved very reluctant to surrender control of the broadcast media, even in India, where the birth of the satellite revolution has been rooted. But satellite television has been licensed and in a decade has transformed television, has had major repercussions for culture, regional political relations, economic development, and political debate, and has impinged on almost all other aspects of life on the sub-continent.

The Zee TV and Rupert Murdoch-owned Star TV networks first started broadcasting in the early 1990s. These channels, and others such as Sony TV, Gemini, and Sun, are based in India but have a footprint across the South Asian region and beyond. They have revitalised media in much of the region, throwing down a gauntlet to traditional, staid programming of the monopoly broadcaster Doordarshan through a dynamic, energetic, and massively popular mix of lifestyle, music, movies,

Box 7.3: The satellite revolution and civil society

The satellite revolution in South Asia has played an important role in extending the bounds of civil society and the forum for public debate...If the new satellite media have contributed to the development of civil society, they have done so largely on the terms of the commercial entrepreneurs. Public feedback on these developments has been largely confined to the columns of a small number of newspapers and the activities of non government organisations...Television programmes have generated huge volumes of correspondence, sometimes on a scale which producers have found impossible to process, but there are few organisations representing the viewer and listener in a more systematic way...

It is not sufficient... to argue that the state has an important role to play in safeguarding the public interest. In the interest of the development of civil

society, equal stress also needs to be placed on the development and reflection of public opinion on media issues... There is much to learn from the experiences of other South Asian countries, though as yet regional awareness is surprisingly low, except among a handful of media and development professionals. It is too early yet to talk of regional public opinion, but beyond the need to develop a more critical public opinion in individual countries, the regional character of the new media also requires a regional public response. With many South Asians now watching the same programmes, those [who] produce them, often only with Indian audiences in mind, need to be made aware [o]f the wider public and their reactions.

Extract from Page and Crawley (2000b: 386–388).

MEDIA AND EMPOWERMENT IN DEVELOPING COUNTRIES   James Deane with Njonjo Mue and Fackson Banda

Box 7.4: Media trends in eastern Africa

Recent developments in eastern Africa reflect the complex and contradictory character of political and social trends that have affected many other parts of the continent. Since 1990, most countries in the sub-region have undergone a far-reaching political transformation, mostly by replacing former one-party regimes with nominal multiparty democracies. Freedom of expression, press freedom, and media diversity have become critical indicators of the health or otherwise of democratic transition in the sub-region.

On the whole, the transformation of the media landscape over the last decade has been impressive. The political transitions from monolithic one-party rule, as well as external and internal pressures on governments of eastern African countries for constitutional and legal reforms—including calls to 'free the airwaves'—have substantially changed radio and television broadcasting regulation and ownership in the sub-region. Where governments previously retained broadcasting as the preserve of the state and the ruling party, now all have accepted the establishment of independent, private broadcasters and in some cases community radio stations.

Most countries in the regions now have a nascent private broadcast sector and citizens now have access to alternative voices. But as a recent Panos Eastern Africa publication points out, 'While it is easy to track quantitatively the number of new broadcasters, it is less easy to assess qualitatively their ownership, content and meaning to their audiences. The real impact of independent, private broadcasters on access to and dissemination of information in the sub-region is as yet unknown, as is the potential role of regulation in directing the development of broadcasting so that it brings real and widespread benefits' (Wanyeki 2000:).

Thus, while media freedom has undoubtedly advanced, the record of the media in contributing to more informed, inclusive, and democratic societies in the sub-region is much more mixed. New FM radio stations are beginning to emerge, creating a highly populist, music-based programming while, at least in some cases, also providing new ways for people rarely heard in public domains to have their say through live debates and phone-in discussions. But many more of the media emerging in the region are heavily advertising-dependent and consumer-oriented, and have limited interest in highlighting issues of concern to people in the rural areas. Indeed, one of the greatest challenges emerging from the way media are

and news. Zee TV in particular has met with huge success through its adaptation of a general entertainment formula to the Hindi language, a process which has become known as 'Hindigenisation'.

However, both the popularity and the content of these new Hindi language entertainment channels are, according to David Page and William Crawley (2000a) , giving rise 'to apprehensions that the culture of Bollywood is swamping other national cultures and even destroying the ideological boundaries of the nation state'. It is also creating a new 'lingua franca' for the region, a hybrid of English and Hindi developed particularly by Zee TV.

At a time of increased international tensions in the region, satellite television is leading to markedly increased suspicion and resentment of India among other populations in the region. The dominance of Hindi channels such as Zee and Star is having increasingly significant political as well as cultural

repercussions, particularly feeding tensions and public resentment of India in Pakistan. Reporting and analysis by Indian-based satellite news organisations of Kashmir and the Kargil crisis are widely perceived as being biased, nationalistic, and often inflammatory. Reporting on the satellite channels, which are widely accessed in Pakistan, is pushing a heavily patriotic and nationalistic Indian line on what is a regional medium. This has substantially exacerbated public suspicion in Pakistan; and satellite broadcasts were prohibited recently by the Pakistan government from being relayed on cable channels. The names given to programmes on the conflict, such as *The Big Fight*, further contribute to this feeling. The role of the satellite television media in fuelling conflict between these new nuclear powers, and their unwillingness to provide a space and a voice to independent, peace-oriented views, are a source of increasing alarm within civil society in the region.

developing in the region is the dichotomy between metropolitan areas—with a diversity of print, electronic, and new media—and the rural areas, which have largely remained neglected and where government propaganda remains the only source of news and information.

Governments in the sub-region have also been reluctant to loosen their grip over state broadcasters. In spite of campaigns by civil society groups to have these transformed into public broadcasters representing all the viewpoints in society, all state broadcasters in the sub-region have remained mouthpieces for the ruling party. The distinction between public and government broadcasting is not widely recognised and there is little clear policy articulation of the necessity for retained public service broadcasting and of a revisited role in this respect for the public broadcaster.

New information and communications technologies and transnational satellite broadcasting are so far available only to those with disposable income in urban areas. The implications of technological convergence are as yet unknown. But the likely impact on the region of the international trend towards the consolidation of media ownership can be inferred from the case of the Nation Media Group, which owns the largest circulation daily in east and central Africa, the only regional weekly newspaper, and radio and TV stations in Kenya and Uganda, and which has plans to rapidly expand its dominance. This highlights issues of regulation of cross-media ownership, which has not been regarded as a priority by regulators in the sub-region.

Print media continue to play an important part in creating democratic space in the region, but are hampered by draconian legislation, some dating to colonial rule, which severely restricts media freedom and exposes journalists to harsh punishments for transgression and therefore promotes self-censorship.

As the media landscape in eastern Africa changes rapidly, the key challenges remain those of providing regulatory frameworks that can cope with the rapid developments, providing content that is relevant to the context and developmental challenges of the sub-region and enhancing the capacity of journalists to provide professional and quality services in one of the fastest-growing sectors in the sub-region, to enable it to play its historic role in the promotion and entrenchment of democracy, good governance, and development in this part of the world.

Njonjo Mue

While there are some attempts by satellite television to address these issues (Star TV started but has since discontinued a regular letter from Pakistan), the overwhelming sense is of a regional media giant acting as a national and narrowly patriotic broadcaster. Nor is this confined to relations between India and Pakistan. Nepal and Bangladesh are barely featured in this South Asian regional medium. 'Zee TV has probably done more to harm Nepal-India relations at the people level than anything else in recent times . . . satellite television, instead of bringing people together is polarising them', according to Kunda Dixit, editor of the *Nepali Times* (Page and Crawley 2000b, 386–388).

Liberalisation of television is, as with radio and print, a principally urban-focused phenomenon. Sixty per cent of South Asians live in rural areas and here access to television, while beginning to spread rapidly, nevertheless continues to be limited.

The social and political reverberations caused by satellite television have perhaps been felt even more strongly in the extraordinary global and regional prominence achieved by Al Jazeera television in the wake of 11 September 2001. Al Jazeera ('The Peninsula') was launched in 1996 with $137 million of funding provided by the Qatari emirate with the express purpose of modernising and democratising Qatar. It rapidly developed a reputation for outspoken, independent reporting, and equally quickly became the most popular television news station throughout the Middle East and beyond. It claims 35 million viewers.

Al Jazeera has become famous through its coverage of Afghanistan and its exclusive broadcasts of tapes provided by Osama bin Laden. However, it is not just the quality and independence of its journalism that has marked it out but also its free-ranging studio discussions and phone-ins, some of them resulting in loud shouting arguments with often extremist positions. It has upset not only the US but also many political leaders in the Arab world and has been banned from Saudi Arabia. Tunisia, Morocco, and Libya recalled their ambassadors to Qatar, and Jordan closed the station's bureau after a programme critical of the Amman government.

Popular it may be, but a lucrative business proposition it was not. Advertisers were wary of being associated with controversy and Al Jazeera generated only $15 million in advertising revenue in 2000, compared to $93 million by LBC, Lebanon's entertainment network (Zednick 2002). It was creeping slowly towards commercial sustainability before 11 September and is still reliant on Qatari funding, but since then its revenues have escalated rapidly. Nevertheless, it is difficult to imagine it establishing the kind of reputation that it has if it had been established with principally commercial objectives.

Television remains the least plural and least democratic of all media, with ownership continuing to be concentrated in the hands of the few. In Latin America, television has long been a far more pervasive medium than in much of the rest of the developing world, with even some of the poorest communities having access to television, and ownership has long been tightly controlled by extremely powerful private companies generally with strong links to government. In this sense, the changes in Latin America have been less dramatic than elsewhere. In Brazil, 80 per cent of the population, amounting to 90 million people, have access to television, and glamorous soap operas have been credited with helping to reduce fertility rates as poor families aspire to the exclusive lifestyles they see on television and have smaller families as a result.

Latin America is also the home and international inspiration of a host of community and participatory communication initiatives, many of which use television to give voice and expression to people otherwise marginalised, but these are principally found outside the mainstream television infrastructure. The Brazilian initiative *TV Maxam-bomba*, for example, uses video to record the experiences of local people, appraises what is done by grass-roots or com-munity organisations, and brings information necessary to the understanding of people's rights. It

also produces videos on local culture and programmes for children, with more than 100 videos being produced since its inception in 1986 (Gumucio-Dagron 2000).

There are also increasing numbers of cases where television has proved itself to be the most effective way of stimulating social change. In South Africa, the most popular television soap opera is *Soul City*, a high-quality drama series which also has a very explicit social remit. Dealing with issues of domestic violence, HIV/AIDS, diarrhoeal diseases, and urban violence, it has become one of the most respected examples in the world of a communication initiative which can inform, engage, and entertain while having a demonstrable and proven impact in achieving change. Three out of four viewers watched the most recent series of *Soul City*.

> Commercial television has, if nothing else, created television that is more dynamic, entertaining, and far more popular than the state-controlled fodder that preceded it

Why This Matters

All of the above amounts to a series of complex, contradictory trends which have major implications for social inclusion and public debate. First of all, they raise major issues of access to information which enables people, particularly poor and marginalised peoples, to make sense of their lives, especially in the context of an increasingly complex and globalised society; and second, they raise issues of voice, the role and potential of the media to provide a channel and space for the voices and perspectives of those most affected by these issues, in terms both of reporting from the poor and of providing a voice or space for civil society.

Access to information is being transformed. There is a major and growing gulf between information accessible and relevant to the rich and the poor, the urban and the rural. Despite new media freedoms, the liberalised environment has led to a decline in both the inclination and the capacity of media to cover complex, contentious, technical issues such as those relating to globalisation and poverty. The media are becoming increasingly fragmented and politically partial, and the decline of state-run media infrastructures is, along with a welcome loss of control over information, leading to the emergence of an information vacuum for an increasing number of communities. Despite this, the

Participatory approaches to development are now very popular with international development agencies, to the point where they are enshrined in the 'Poverty Reduction Strategy Paper' (PRSP) process that now underpins the dialogue between the World Bank/IMF and most of their client countries. Yet participatory approaches to development are meaningful only if the poor and marginalised truly have an effective voice in the process, and the necessary information and knowledge to exercise informed choice. In too many cases, the 'participatory' dimension of the PRSP process is pro forma: a handful of consultations with prominent local NGOs and others with whom the governments and international agencies feel comfortable. Even when the views and concerns of the poorest are actively solicited, as in the World Bank's 'Voices of the Poor' project, the mechanisms for inserting those views and concerns into the national poverty-reduction strategy process are often weak, and the ability of the poor and marginalised to play a meaningful role in the debate is weakened by their lack of access to information.

Poverty is not just a lack of material resources. The poor often lack access to vital information that can shape their lives. They lack information about their rights and about government services to which they are entitled; about strategies for combating illness; about the economic choices facing their communities and the consequences of these choices. In these information-poor environments, markets perform badly, government institutions are inefficient and unresponsive, and the poor are disempowered by both lack of effective voice in public debates and lack of information about the challenges and choices facing them. Economic, social, and political elites dominate the flow of information and the shaping of public debates and choices.

A participatory approach to development is, therefore, meaningful only if it directly and actively addresses the challenge of creating information-rich environments where the poor have access to information and voice, where a variety of views can be heard on public issues, where public institutions can be held accountable. Creating information-rich societies means not simply increasing the *quantity* of information; the focus needs to be on increasing the quality, diversity, and relevance of information as a tool in improving the lives and livelihoods of the poor. The role of independent media, both commercial and non-commercial, is crucial to this task.

Kerry McNamara, formerly Senior Knowledge Management Officer, World Bank

traditional media remain the principal source of information for much of humanity on issues outside their community and are likely to continue to do so for decades to come. Taken as an average, every African household has a radio, whereas only 1 per cent have access to the Internet. Internet access, while growing rapidly, is still accessed by only 3 per cent of Brazilians. (See Record 7 in Part IV of this Yearbook.)

The potential of media to act as a conduit for perspectives and a voice for the poor is growing, both through the emergence of community radio and through other forms of broadcasting. Discussion programmes on new FM radio stations are creating new and unprecedented spaces for public debate and an increased political vibrancy, and these provide major new opportunities to place issues of public concern onto public agendas. However, this goes hand in hand with a lack of resources and the emergence of a new journalism culture which is uninterested in providing in-depth reports and analysis of major development, international, or social issues, and where journalists rarely venture out of the major cities. There are many journalists who remain committed to covering public interest issues, but they increasingly operate within a media culture that neither encourages nor values their work.

In the context of globalisation, these trends are particularly acute. The challenge of global inclusion is to ensure that decisions that affect peoples' lives are subject to debate by those whose lives they affect. That means a much stronger, not weaker, public understanding and engagement on issues of globalisation. The media in most developing countries, despite the early promises and optimism of liberalisation and the growth

In March 2000, a group of senior editors, publishers, and directors of training institutions from developing countries gathered at the Global Knowledge Forum and mapped out an agenda for creating a free and plural media. This is a summary of their recommendations.

1. Policy: To create an effective policy environment that nurtures a free, independent and pluralistic media

Analysis: Society benefits from free, independent, and pluralistic media. But to achieve this, a supportive policy environment is required, and it must be proactively encouraged by public and private sectors, the international community and multilateral agencies.

Action:
- Promote, consolidate and effectively enforce freedom of information legislation.
- Encourage independent voluntary complaints procedures based on industry codes of ethics, and including representation from other sectors of civil society.
- Promote independent public service broadcasting.
- Develop independent media support agencies (voluntary or statutory) which provide assistance through loans and subsidies, and/or other measures such as postal rate or connectivity cost reductions (e.g. the Media Development and Diversity Agency being established in South Africa).
- Encourage the private sector to support socially useful communication initiatives.
- Make licensing and regulation policies for broadcast media transparent and open.
- Implement effectively legislation that already exists in these areas.

2. Ownership and Control: To prevent excessive concentration of media power, much of it located in the North

Analysis: An increasing concentration of power in media ownership, internationally and within some countries, works directly against plurality. It leads to more homogeneous content, reducing spaces for the expression of a diversity of views. New information technologies pose an additional challenge because they are outside existing systems of accountability. The implications of creating such systems are complex, but this remains a key global issue.

Action:
- Do research to map and monitor the economic and power relationships emerging among global media and communications conglomerates.
- Introduce or strengthen anti-monopoly legislation or measures to prevent the emergence of private or state monopolies.
- Seek dialogue between transnational media groups, the telecommunications industries and local communities.
- Explore creating voluntary codes of conduct at the global level.
- Support existing proposals to organise an International Congress on Media and Communications similar to the UN Social Summit.

of new media freedoms, appear decreasingly, rather than increasingly, equipped to play this role.

These issues also raise significant questions on the sustainability and health of democracy and democratic culture, and the capacity of people to hold their governments to account; but they go deeper than this. Arguably there has never been a greater opportunity or a more critical time for open public debate. This is true in terms of issues of globalisation but encompasses wider development processes and

3. Content: To create dynamic and locally relevant content to counteract North–South information imbalances

Analysis: While developing countries need a media that is open, ensures access, and encompasses new technologies, the most crucial aspect is content. Strong and imaginative content can be compelling and, given commitment, can attract and expand audiences. It should be developed and promoted in local languages, and be focused on community needs as expressed by the communities themselves.

Action:
- Create space for locally generated content through a variety of measures (which could include legislation).
- Strengthen public service media such that the choice is not solely between private media and government media.
- Foster the ability of communities to operate and control their own media.

4. Skills: To build human capacity and skills within the media of developing countries.

Analysis: To strengthen the media sector a significant investment in human resources and technical infrastructure is required. Only in this way will poorer societies gain greater control of their own media, and therefore greater control over their future. A coalition of various actors—public, private, local, regional, and global—is needed to enable this investment to take place.

Action:
- Invest in training and professional standards of journalism.
- Provide training in the use of new technologies as an urgent priority for the media sector as a whole.

- Develop skills to interpret information in ways that are relevant to developing countries.
- Promote investigative reporting skills and techniques among journalists.
- Design training programmes that are customised, relevant and appropriate to local needs.
- Build stronger, professional South-focused information and news networks.

5. Technology: To combine old and new technologies creating imaginative synergies between the two.

Analysis: The use of hybrids and applications that arise from the integration of new and old technologies offer exciting, cost effective and empowering forms of communication. In this way 'old' technologies can be reinvigorated, and advantage can be taken of their wider reach. An example: in Sri Lanka, radio and television programming are being used to demystify the Internet so that those without access know and understand the potential power and advantages of the newer technology. New media advantages, including the ability to be small scale, low cost, community oriented and beyond the control of censorship clearly add value.

Action:
- Actively support efforts to upgrade media industry technological capacity at grass roots level.
- Identify and encourage innovative uses of new technology. Learning experiences need to be shared.
- Support specific initiatives which combine the power and flexibility of new technologies with the reach of more traditional media.
- Promote a legislative and policy environment which favours multiple media approaches.

strategies which are increasingly premised on issues of popular consultation, ownership, and debate. Much current mainstream development thinking (especially from the World Bank and donors committed to new sets of international development targets aimed at halving poverty by the year 2015) stresses the importance of ownership, holding that countries should shape and drive their own development agendas and that these agendas should be informed by the 'voices of the poor'. Poverty reduction strategy

Above: A Zambian family displays its primary source of outside information. © Nick Robinson/Panos Pictures.

papers (PRSPs) which form the centrepiece of current development thinking and strategic planning are founded on this premise. This cannot happen in an environment where publics and particularly the poor have so little information on the issues that affect their lives (see Box 7.5).

Nor has liberalisation yet led to a true diversity in media ownership. The globalisation, concentration of ownership, and increasingly profit-oriented nature of the international media have been well documented, but less documented are continuing patterns of media power taking place at the national level. The ceding of state control of media has been far from universal, and even in more liberalised media environments state ownership and influence often remains pervasive. According to a World Bank survey of 97 mostly developing countries, the largest media firms were owned either by governments or by private families, with government ownership being more pervasive in broadcasting than in the print media. It argued that 'government ownership of the media is generally associated with less press freedom, fewer political and economic rights and, most conspicuously, inferior social

outcomes in the areas of education and health' (Djankov *et al.* 2001: 1).

Media freedom and media liberalisation have only rarely resulted in media pluralism. This is a global trend, but one which is particularly acute in poorer countries where those with most to win or lose from political and public debate—the poor and marginalised—have least access and least representation in mainstream media.

Freedom of expression is just one essential component of a plural media. Genuine media pluralism also implies a diversity of ownership, including media which explicitly serve a public or community interest; media that are accessible by and intelligible (particularly in relation to issues of literacy and language) to all citizens, media that reflect diversity of public opinion, and particularly that give and reflect expression of the marginalised (often a majority in many developing countries) in society. According to these criteria, the global trend is moving away from, not towards, real media pluralism.

What Is To Be Done?

Analysing a communication environment as complex and fast-moving as the one outlined above is a great deal easier than identifying clear-cut policy responses to it. At the least, in the context of this book, the issue of public access to information in developing countries should preoccupy civil society organisations a good deal more than it does. Freedom of information and expression remains the primary concern for journalists around the world and most governments on the planet still have much to do to guarantee such freedom.

Beyond that, however, while much attention is rightly focused on the concentration of ownership of media in the North, genuine global inclusion depends also on the emergence from within the fascinating media liberalisation maelstrom of a stronger public interest media in the South. The most obvious solution to this—the creation of intelligent, flexible regulatory frameworks for media—is a highly sensitive issue among journalists who have fought for years to escape the clutches of government control. It is clear that a range of policy responses is required of which regulation is just one. It is beyond the remit of the authors of this article to outline any specific blueprint for change since these should emerge from debate and dialogue within countries, but it is clear that the drift away from public interest media will continue and probably accelerate without concerted action by civil society and by the media themselves.

Outlined in Box 7.6 is a set of conclusions and recommendations that a group of senior editors, publishers, and directors of print, radio, and television organisations as well as media training institutions produced at a meeting convened at a forum organised by the Panos Institute under the auspices of the Global Knowledge Partnership in 2000. They illustrate some of the policy and media responses that many media organisations, including some large mainstream institutions, would like to see happen. Other opportunities, such as the forthcoming World Summit on the Information Summit in 2003 and 2005, may also provide important opportunities for advancing thinking and action on these issues.

The rapidity and scale of the transformation of media internationally, particularly within developing countries, over the last decade demonstrates the power and influence of the mostly economic pressures shaping the new media environment. There are many within the media who are struggling in the teeth of these pressures to retain the media's critical public interest role, but the evidence is that they are losing. While governments clearly have a major role to play in creating a legal and policy environment for free and plural media, the media generally remain distrustful and cautious about strong government action in the area of the media. In this context, civil society has a major role to play in putting pressure on both media and government in creating and supporting more public interest-oriented media. It also has much to lose if media continue to develop in ways that serve the private interest and ignore the public interest. With 2 billion people in the world still living in absolute poverty, the public interest, and the role of the media in serving it, has never been as important.

References

Besley, R. and Burgess, R. (2000). 'Does Media Make Government More Responsive? Theory and Evidence from Indian Famine Relief Policy' . LSE working paper. http://econ.lse.ac.uk/staff/rburgess/wp/mediaf.pdf

Castells, M. (1998). *The Information Age: Economy, Society, and Culture*. Oxford: Blackwell.

Diallo, M. A. (2001). 'When a Journalist is "Worth" Less than a Bag of Rice'. *Media Actions*, 26 (April–June). Panos West Africa.

Djankov, S., McLiesh, C., Nenova, T., and Shleifer, A. (2001). *Who Owns the Media?* (Working Paper No. 2620). Washington, DC: World Bank.

Diop, Jean Meissa (2001). 'Senegal: Sex, Blood and Gossip on the Front Page'. *Media Actions*, 26 (April–June). Panos West Africa

Dreze, J. and Sen, A. (1989). *Hunger and Public Action*. Oxford: Clarendon Press.

Gerbner, G., Mowlana, H., and Schiller, H (eds) (1996). *Invisible Crises: What Conglomerate Control of Media Means for America and the World*. Boulder, CO: Westview Press.

Gumucio-Dagron, A. (2000). *Making Waves: Stories of Participatory Communication for Social Change*. New York: Rockefeller Foundation

Hamelink, C. J. (1994). *Trends in World Communication: On Disempowerment and Self-empowerment*. Penang, Malaysia: Southbound Third World Network.

Lush, D. (1997). 'The Role of African Media in the Promotion of Democracy and Human Rights'. Paper commissioned by the Swedish Ministry of Foreign Affairs for the Partnerships Africa Conference, Stockholm, 25–27 June.

Mediachannel. http://www.mediachannel.org

McChesney, R.W. and Herman, E. S. (1997). *Global Media*. New York: Continuum Publishing Group.

Naughton, J. (2001). 'Contested Space: The Internet and Global Civil Society', in Helmut Anheier, Marlies Glasius, and Mary Kaldor (eds), *Global Civil Society 2001*. Oxford: Oxford University Press.

Page, D. and Crawley, W. (2000a). 'Satellites and South Asia'. *Himal Magazine*, 13/12. http://www.himalmag.com/dec2000/coverfile.html

— (2000b). *Satellites over South Asia: Broadcasting, Culture and the Public Interest*. New Delhi: Sage Publications India.

Roth, C. (2001). *The Media and Good Governance: Developing Free and Effective Media to Serve the Interests of the Poor*. London: Department for International Development.

Sainath, P. (1996). *Everyone Loves a Good Drought*. New Delhi: Penguin India.

Sen, A. (1999). *Development as Freedom*. New York: Random House.

Spears, George and Seydegart, Kasia (2001). Who Makes the News? *Global Media Monitoring Project 2001*. London: World Association for Christian Communication.

Sun, Wanning (2001). 'The Politics of Compassion: Journalism, Class Formation and Social Change in China'. *Media for Development*, Issue 3. London: World Association for Christian Communication. http://www.wacc.org.uk/publications/md/md2001-3/wanning_sun.html

Wanyeki, L. M. (ed.) (2000). *Up in the Air? The State of Broadcasting in Eastern Africa*. Kampala, Uganda: Panos Eastern Africa.

Westoff, C. and Bankole, A. (1999). *Mass Media and Reproductive Behaviour in Pakistan, India, and Bangladesh* (Demographic Health Surveys Analytical Report No. 10). Maryland: Macro International Inc..

Zednick, Rick (2002). 'Perspectives on War: Inside Al Jazeera'. *Columbia Journalism Review*, March/April. http://www.cjr.org/year/02/2/zednik.asp

Chapter 8

Organisational Forms of Global Civil Society: Implications of Going Global

Helmut Anheier and Nuno Themudo

Introduction

Global civil society includes a vast and diverse set of organisations, associations, networks, movements, and groups whose overall contours and the forces that shape them we are just beginning to fathom (Anheier, Glasius, and Kaldor 2001; Keane 2001). Global civil society organisations (CSOs) range from large-scale charities with hundreds of staff to transnational volunteer-run networks with no real expenditures at all; from non-profit corporations with franchises in numerous countries to 'virtual' associations with no identifiable location; from single-issue campaign groups and professional service providers to voluntary organisations offering humanitarian assistance; from democratically run organisations to autocratic sects; from anti-globalisation groups and environmental movements to Christian revival groups and trade unions; and from philanthropic foundations with multi-billion-dollar endowments to savings clubs among migrant communities spread across different countries.

These examples illustrate that CSOs vary in structure, governance, formality, and the scale and scope of their operations and revenue. Importantly, they also show that CSOs include many more forms than the term 'non-governmental organisation' (NGO) suggests, and the organisational repertoire of global civil society goes well beyond what more narrow interpretations suggest (e.g., Grimond 2002). Yet, whatever their name or form, in their totality CSOs make up the organisational infrastructure of global civil society. The purpose of this chapter is to throw light on some of the principles underlying the various forms CSOs take in an effort to understand more about the roles they play in a globalising world.

In this chapter we use insights from organisation and management theory to examine this organisational infrastructure. Organisation theory shows that form matters to the way we organise and manage (Williamson 1985; Aldrich 1999) and for the structure and dynamics of the societies we live in (e.g., Castells 1996; Meyer et al. 1997). 'Organisational form' is a somewhat technocratic term for those characteristics of an organisation that 'identify it as a distinct entity and, at the same time, classify it as a member of group of similar organisations' (Romanelli 1991: 81–2). Organisational form is more than formal organisational structure, and includes resource types, governance, accountability, organisational culture, informal structures, and external relations.

For example, service providing and advocacy NGOs are both part of the larger category 'non-profit organisations' and share similar governance and accountability structures, but they differ in terms of activities, output, cost and revenue structure, and, most likely, in their inter-organisational relations. The Internet organisation One World, dedicated to free information access, may differ from other 'dot-causes' in terms of professionalism and decision-making structure (see Clark and Themudo forthcoming), but they share the same crucial resource, i.e., the Internet, that makes their existence possible.

In contrast to more established fields in politics (e.g., party systems), social policy (welfare systems) or the economy (e.g., specific industries like petroleum, electronics, or insurance markets), the organisational infrastructure of global civil society is less settled and in a state of flux, with new forms emerging and others becoming less frequent. This accounts for the somewhat 'fluid', even 'ephemeral' nature of some types of organisations and network forms that observers like Clark and Themudo (forthcoming) and Lindenberg and Dobel (1999), among others, report. As communication costs plummeted internationally in the 1990s, network forms of organisation (Powell 1990) emerged among CSOs and are, as we suggest below, becoming a signature element of global organising.

Network forms emerge, for example, when national affiliates of international non-governmental organisations (INGOs) increasingly cooperate and coordinate their activities outside the conventional headquarter-subunit structure, and develop lateral relations both locally and internationally. In this sense, Oxfam India may be more closely involved with, for example, Save the Children India, World Vision India, other Indian NGOs, local UNICEF branches, local governments, and social movement networks than with Oxfam International headquarters in London. We therefore use the term 'organisational form' in a broader sense as 'organised and structured action' rather than applying it to formal, singular organisations only. Thus the term covers networks, coalitions, partnerships, and social movements in addition to more conventional forms such as NGOs and other non-profit organisations.

The case of Jubilee 2000 helps illustrate what we mean by organisational form (see Box 8.1). Indeed, by examining its form we can identify the reasons for the organisation's success and difficulties in mounting a global advocacy campaign on the rather difficult issue of debt cancellation for developing countries.

From an early stage, Jubilee 2000 adopted a social movement form, with little central coordination, dispersed resources, and decentralised information management. As it grew rapidly, Jubilee 2000 soon encountered conventional organisational problems such as overreach, lack of central coordination, mission dilution, and 'scapegoating' (see Anheier 1999). Moreover, its decentralised information system failed to detect such problems early on and divergent strategies began to take root leading to the movement sending mixed signals to their audience. The movement had quickly become global but without a global governance and management structure that reconciled emerging tensions between national and global. These problems reduced the movement's cohesion and, ultimately, we believe, its effectiveness and legitimacy. Marlies Glasius (Chapter 6), in describing the CSO coalition that lobbied for the formation of the International Criminal Court,

ORGANISATIONAL FORMS OF GLOBAL CIVIL SOCIETY   Helmut Anheier and Nuno Themudo

Box 8.1: The challenge of success – Jubilee 2000

Jubilee 2000 started in 1996 as a partnership of UK development NGOs. It grew very quickly into a large international movement campaigning for debt cancellation for poor countries. In 1998 in Birmingham it gathered about 50,000 people in a human chain around a G7 meeting (Bauck 2001). From the outset, Jubilee 2000 avoided a formal structure and instead preferred to adopt the structure and identity of a social movement (Jubilee 2000 UK URL). This structure gave Jubilee 2000 a great fluidity and ability to grow. Rather than growing as a single organisation, it encouraged similar groups to form in other countries with little central oversight. There was almost no standardisation of message or philosophy. This growth by replication rather than internal expansion bypassed limitations of central coordination capacity of the founding group and enabled a very fast growth of the movement. Albeit limited, their achievements were substantial in a very difficult area where many NGOs had campaigned for years without much success. The Jubilee movement form was a key ingredient of its success, enabling the mobilisation of around 24 million people worldwide within a relatively short period of time (Jubilee 2000 UK URL).

Eventually, however, North-South tensions began to emerge within the movement. Some Southern-based groups such as Jubilee South and Jubilee South Africa began to openly question the positions of Northern Jubilee 2000 members, which they perceived to be too narrow to really address global inequality problems. Alongside a North-South rift there were also strong conflicts between moderate and radical members at the national levels in, for example, the US Jubilee 2000 (Bauck 2001). These conflicts transpired in their campaigning exposing an increasing internal rift. The result of the antagonism was an erosion of legitimacy for the overall movement (Bauck 2001). Today Jubilee 2000 UK has turned into Jubilee Debt Campaign but much of its dynamism appears to have withered.

While the movement form facilitated a very fast growth of support for the cause, its lack of formal decision-making and governance structures also led to a difficulty in coordinating the various interests in the movement. Jubilee 2000 had a global presence but not global governance. What was a very appropriate organisational form for some purposes in a given context (e.g., to get 24 million people to sign a petition worldwide) was less appropriate for other purposes and contexts (e.g., to sustain a global advocacy campaign over a long period).

'Launched in 1961 by British lawyer Peter Benenson, Amnesty International has today more than 1,000,000 members, subscribers and regular donors in more than 140 countries and territories. The organisation's nerve centre is the International Secretariat in London, with more than 320 members of staff and over 100 volunteers from more than 50 countries around the world.

The movement consists of more than 7,500 local, youth & student, and professional Amnesty International groups registered at the International Secretariat plus several thousand other youth & student groups, specialist groups, networks and co-ordinators in nearly 100 countries and territories throughout the world. There are nationally organised sections in 56 countries, and pre-section co-ordinating structures in another 23 countries and territories worldwide . . .

Rapid action for prisoners and others . . . is mobilised by the Urgent Action (UA) network made up of more than 80,000 volunteers in some 85 countries' (Amnesty International URL).

---

presents interesting decision-making and transparency issues that resulted from the coalition's organisational form.

Thus, forms that are appropriate for specific purposes (e.g., expansion and organisational growth) in certain environments (e.g., Europe) can be disabling for different purposes and phases (e.g., consolidation or retrenchment) as well as environments (e.g., global or transnational). Choice matters in two other important aspects as well: organisational legitimacy and impact. If CSOs challenge the accountability of other social actors, they must themselves be accountable (Edwards 1999). Otherwise, their ability to be effective advocates in supporting democratisation or addressing North-South power imbalances, among other issues, will be limited. Moreover, as seen in the Jubilee 2000 example, one single movement can achieve much and may have significant impact on global governance, which suggests that the organisational forms CSOs take is closely related to their capacity for effecting change.

While forms typically develop more or less 'organically' over the life cycle of organisations, they can also experience fundamental changes and major redesigns (Greiner 1972; Aldrich 1999). For example, Amnesty International underwent frequent reorganisation as it grew to a presence in over 100 countries in just over 40 years and evolved from a small volunteer-run group to a transnational organisation with a highly complex governance structure (Anheier and Themudo 2002) with members in over 140 countries (see Box 8.2). Likewise, in recent years most of the large international relief and development

NGOs have undergone profound form changes that go beyond the reorganisation of their structure to involve changes in mission and culture as well (Lindenberg and Dobel 1999; Korten 1990). We suggest that the reason why many NGOs finds themselves in more or less 'constant reorganisation' is closely related to the environment in which they operate. To explore this further, we will take a look at the relationship between form and environment.

Forms Old and New

We understand 'global civil society' as the socio-sphere 'located *between* the family, state, and market and operating *beyond* the confines of national societies, polities, and economies' (Anheier, Glasius, and Kaldor 2001: 17, emphasis in original). Next to individual values and activities, organisations are a major element of global civil society. Taken together, the forms they take make up part of a modern 'institutional laboratory' that, along with transnational corporations and governments, is creating the organisational infrastructure of a globalising world.

While no comprehensive data are available for the full range of CSOs, it is fair to conclude that they have experienced a broad and significant expansion in recent years. Figure 8.1 tracks INGOs and intergovernmental organisations from 1900 and shows that their number began to accelerate in the 1970s, with increasing growth rates after 1990. When we take a look at changes in the composition of INGOs by form characteristics in terms of membership-

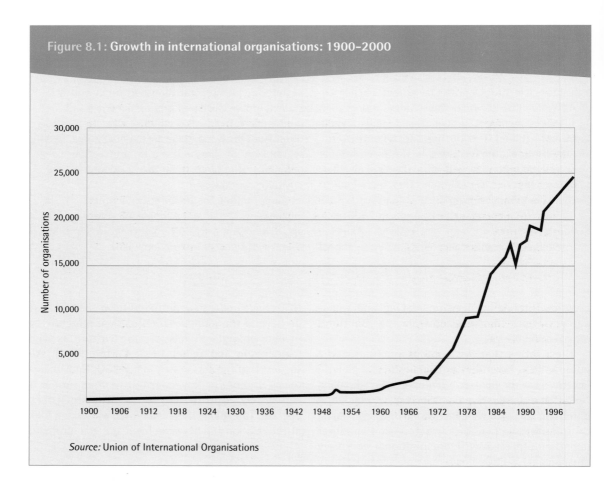

Figure 8.1: Growth in international organisations: 1900–2000

Source: Union of International Organisations

based versus non-membership-based organisations, several striking results emerge over the 20-year period from 1981 to 2001 (Table 8.1).

As readily indicated by the upward trend in Figure 8.1, the number of known INGOs increased from about 13,000 in 1981 to over 47,000 by 2001. The number of INGOs reported in 1981 would make up just under 28 per cent of the stock of INGOs 20 years later. The most numerous forms are the category 'internationally-oriented national organisations' with a share of around 40 per cent over the two decades. This includes 'national organisations with various forms of international activity or concern such as research, peace, human rights, development or relief' (UIA URL), e.g., NGOs like Human Rights Watch that have mainly a national presence (USA) but with an international or global orientation. Other examples include Article 19, Minority Rights Group or the German relief organisation Bread for the World.

Of the various forms listed in Table 8.1, only the small group of federations of international organisations, typically umbrella organisations linked to the UN system, seem to have declined in absolute numbers over the 20-year period. Conversely, the frequency of all other forms has increased in absolute terms since 1981. Yet some forms have increased more than others. Among those that experienced absolute growth but relative decline are membership organisations which saw their share go down—a trend most pronounced for regional ones limited to particular political or geographical regions (e.g., EU, Africa).

By contrast, what seems to have expanded in both absolute and relative terms is what the Union of International Associations (UIA) classifies as 'organisations of *special form*'. Their share of all INGOs has increased from 7 per cent in 1981 to 15 per cent in 2001 with their absolute numbers growing by more than five times in the same period. UIA (URL) describes

Types	1981 Number	%	1991 Number	%	2001 Number	%
International organisations						
Federations of international organisations	45	0	39	0	37	0
Universal membership organisations	370	4	427	2	475	2
Intercontinental membership organisations	859	9	773	4	1,063	4
Regionally oriented membership organisations	2,991	31	3,381	19	4,782	19
Organisations of special form	680	7	1,970	11	3,631	15
Dependent bodies						
Org's emanating from places, persons, bodies	1,010	10	1,656	9	2,328	9
Subsidiary and internal bodies	391	4	511	3	1,417	6
Religious orders and secular institutes	n/a		753	4	903	4
National bodies (claiming wider relevance)						
Internationally oriented national organisations	3,443	35	7,867	44	9,606	39
Organisational substitutes						
Autonomous conference series	n/a		449	3	555	2
Total	9,789	100	17,826	100	24,797	100
Dead, inactive, and unconfirmed bodies						
Recently reported bodies– not yet confirmed	539	15	941	16	472	2
Dissolved or apparently inactive organisations	1,212	34	2,323	40	3,834	17
Currently inactive non-conventional bodies	1,769	50	2,545	44	17,995	81
Total	3,520	100	5,809	100	22,301	100
Total recorded	13,309		23,635		47,098	

The form characteristics are based on the classification of the UIA and were especially computed for the purposes of this chapter. We thank Nadia McLaren and Anthony Judge at the Union of International Associations for making the data available and for conducting a special analysis exploring form differences among the many thousands of organisations in the UIA data bases.

Source: Union of International Associations

organisations with special form as international organisations 'whose formal characteristics would raise fundamental questions if they were allocated to any of the preceeding types' in Table 8.1. They include foundations and funds, financial organisations, information networks, certain types of educational and training organisations, exile and diaspora organisations, and, significant for our purposes here, 'discontinuous' bodies, and hybrids such as 'informal quasi-organisations'. Thus, there is a growing number of organisations that no longer fits standard classifications of INGO forms—forms that are neither conventional membership organisations nor typical NGOs but somewhere in between or altogether different.

Next to 'special forms', dependent bodies, too, have expanded in absolute and relative terms when taken together. These are organisations that are dependent on some other organisations or are subsidiaries thereof, be they secular or religious. Examples would be national chapters of Amnesty International or organisations linked to the Catholic Church that are international in focus. The growth of dependent bodies from 14 per cent of all classified INGOs in 1981 to 19 per cent in 2001 suggests that existing INGOs are growing not only in numbers but also in organisational scale by creating subsidiaries in an increasing number of countries. They are becoming federations of *national* organisations.

Finally, the relative share of INGOs classified as 'dissolved or apparently inactive' and 'currently inactive non-conventional body' has increased significantly over the last two decades. Nearly 18,000 strong in number 'currently inactive non-conventional bodies' make up the largest classification category in 2001, a major increase over 1991 even when data coverage is taken into account. Whatever the finer points of definitions and measurement criteria might be in distinguishing active from inactive organisations, together with the other category of 'organisations of special form' the figure in Table 8.1 suggests a dramatic conclusion: a very large proportion of existing CSOs fall outside conventional classification criteria. They do not fit clearly into previously defined forms, i.e., 'conventional bodies',

> There is a growing number of organisations that no longer fits standard classifications—forms that are neither conventional membership organisations nor typical NGOs, but somewhere in between or altogether different

which suggests that a high rate of form differentiation and innovation has taken place especially in the past ten years.

The fact that many of these non-conventional bodies are either 'currently inactive' or 'apparently inactive' suggests that they are less regular and less permanent than typical INGOs. It reflects the 'fluidity' of some organisational forms in the emerging organisational infrastructure of global civil society. Indeed, many of the organisations classified as currently or apparently inactive may still exist and could potentially be mobilised, if necessary.[1]

The latter is particularly the case for social movement organisations, like environmental groups that organise around specific issues and entities associated with particular events such as alternative summits.

Of course, the data reported in Table 8.1 are limited to INGOs and exclude many organisational forms that do not register on the 'radar screen' of official statistics, as would be the case for many Internet-based organisations or very small, informal, grass-roots organisations such as immigrant networks and diaspora organisations (see Chapter 9) and various small religious groups (see Chapter 3). Nonetheless, the results that emerge from Table 8.1 seem indicative of a general empirical pattern: *CSOs have expanded in number both within existing and into new forms.*

What forces and factors are behind this trend? Our answer involves two arguments, one pertaining to the organisational environment in which CSOs operate, the other to the constraints of existing forms. Put differently, one relates to the larger environment in which civil society organisations operate and emphasises new and growing needs and opportunities. The other focuses on the constraints and dilemmas civil society organisations face in this environment. While the former pushes CSOs toward expansion, the latter propels them towards innovation.

---

[1] *Moreover UIA's tracking techniques may not work as well for organisational forms that are less institutionalised and resemble movements and networks, which are less likely to respond to official surveys.*

First, the *expansion of CSOs within existing forms* is possible in an environment that seems to have significantly expanded or opened up in recent years. The capacity of the environment to accommodate CSOs appears not to have reached its limits, and CSOs do not yet amount to collective numbers that threaten their survival, given the resources available. This is shown by the historical growth of INGOs in Figure 8.1, which has not yet seem to have peaked or reached some kind of equilibrium. Organisational theorists use the term 'carrying capacity' (Aldrich 1999) to refer to the size of a population of organisations a given environment can support with the resources available. For example, how many 'Jubilee 2000's, 'Amnesty International's or 'GreenPeace's can there be relative to available resources (members, finance, causes)? We suggest that, whatever that number, CSOs do not seem to have reached some critical size yet (see Figure 8.1), although, as we argue below, competition for financial resources is increasing among professionalised INGOs in particular (Foreman 1999).

Second, the expansion of CSOs in new and emerging forms, i.e., the special and non-conventional forms in Table 8.1, reflects less the limitations in the overall carrying capacity than the constraints inherent in existing forms that prevent them taking full advantage of the opportunities that are presenting themselves in an increasingly global environment. To be sure, the carrying capacity for some forms and sectors may be reaching a limit, implying greater competition among forms and forcing innovations and differentiation among organisations such as Northern-based development and relief NGOs. For example, ActionAid is experimenting with moving its headquarters from the UK to the South (probably India or South Africa) in an attempt to differentiate itself from typical 'Northern NGOs'. This is partly related to a shift in donor preferences to fund NGOs in the South as well as the belief that such a move will make ActionAid more effective and more accountable to their Southern constituencies.

As we will show below, there is a frequent mismatch between existing forms and the complexity of the organisational environment in which CSOs operate. For conventional CSOs, this mismatch creates tensions and problems of all sorts and, ultimately, incentives for new forms and other organisational innovations. Thus, *we suggest that the tension between needs and opportunities on the one hand and the constraints of existing organisational forms on the other create a push towards differentiation and innovation. Over time, these processes lead to the development of new forms.*

Opportunities and Constraints

Form changes are often responses to changes in the environment in which organisations operate. Indeed, organisational theorists like Hannan and Freeman (1989) suggest that the array of organisational forms existing at any point in time is a product of responses to prior environmental conditions. Moreover, they argue that current form changes are a function of both environmental variations and the capacity of existing and emerging organisations for innovation. Forms that offer competitive advantages over others are more likely to be selected by new and existing organisations for maximising their sustainability, while other forms become less frequently used (Aldrich 1999). Thus, understanding form developments in global civil society organisations requires a look at both the larger environment in which they operate, e.g., globalisation, and the responses of existing and emerging organisations in reaction to these changes, with a particular emphasis on innovation and growth.

Organisations can typically choose their forms from a range of options in terms of legal status, governance, and accountability, and management models relative to their activities and objectives. For some organisations these choices are straightforward while for others they are complex and unpredictable.

Clearly, globalisation changes the organisational task environment for many CSOs, and going global entails dealing with the challenge of increasing complexity and unpredictability (see Bartlett and Ghoshal 1997). Indeed, some analysts suggest that 'global trends challenge civil society organisations

> The environment for existing forms of civil society organisations seems to have significantly expanded or opened up in recent years, and its capacity to accommodate them appears not to have reached its limits

to rethink their mandate, mission and strategies' (Edwards, Hulme, and Wallace 1999: 134).

Opportunities

The organisational environment for CSOs has expanded in recent decades, particularly since 1989, and offers greater opportunities for organising across borders than before, in terms of both resources and access to centres of influence (Clark 2001; Dichter 1999; Edwards 1999; Lindenberg and Dobel 1999; Kriesberg 1997). Along this with we suggest that the global environment for organising over the last decade has been characterised by:

- an opening of political opportunities outside and beyond conventional national politics, due to the end of the Cold War and to a superpower, the US, in favour of a minimalist, liberal state; the rise of a 'New Policy Agenda' pushing for the global spread of liberal economics and democratic governance, which emphasises the role of civil society and sees INGOs ever more part of an emerging system of global governance and welfare (Edwards and Hulme 1995);
- the development of international forms of government and interstate and inter-regional coordination, from the UN system to the European Union and from Mercosur to ECOWAS (Kriesberg 1997);
- major reductions in the cost of communication, in particular for telecommunication and Internet access, which increases information sharing while reducing coordination costs overall (Clark 2001; Naughton 2001; Warkentin 2001). The development of communications technologies has decreased the costs of organising and thus increased the carrying capacity of the organisational environment;
- generally favourable economic conditions in major world economies since the late 1940s and a considerable expansion of populations living in relative prosperity (Hirschman 1982; Kriesberg 1997);
- a value change over the last 25 years in most industrialised countries that emphasises individual opportunities and responsibilities over state involvement and control (Inglehart and Abramson 1995); and

- a major expansion of democracy across most parts of the world, with freedom of expression and associations granted in most countries (Linz and Stepan 1996; Diamond 1997). The 'thickening' of the international rule of law since the 1970s has greatly facilitated the growth of global civil society organisations (see Keck and Sikkink 1998) (see also Records 8 and 9).

It is this opening of a transnational and increasingly global 'organisational space' and the greater recognition of cross-border needs (e.g., environmental protection, human rights) that has provided, and continues to provide, the opportunity for CSO development and growth. This opening has led to the rise in the economic importance of private, non-profit organisations in social services, health care, education, and culture (Salamon et al. 1999), which resulted in large-scale national non-profit sectors that increasingly operate across borders (Anheier and List 2000; Anheier 2002). While none of these social factors alone, be they political, sociological, economic, or technological, could have brought about the expansion in organised global civil society, it is the combination of these factors that made it possible.

We can easily see that the combination of opportunities appears stronger in some parts of the world than in others. The combination of factors and the strength of each seem more pronounced in OECD countries, and it is here that we also find the centres of global civil society (Anheier, Glasius, and Kaldor 2001; see also Records 16–29). By contrast, in other areas we find different scenarios, and some factors are typically weaker, making their combination less forceful. In Africa or Latin America economic and political conditions have been much less favourable than in countries of the OECD, and in parts of central Asia and the Middle East value changes may have been regressive rather than progressive in terms of human rights and tolerance, thereby reducing the 'space' for CSOs.[2]

Different combinations of these factors will create opportunities for CSOs and encourage different globalisation options and the adoption of different organisational forms. Cheaper communications, for example, will encourage greater

---

[2] *This is not a claim about the quality or 'health' of civil society in those regions. It is a simpler claim that the organisational environment in some regions is more supportive of CSOs than in others, particularly in their ability to globalise and link up with CSOs in other regions.*

networking but will tend to do so more in countries where communication technologies are already widely available and accessible. Middle class confidence is not growing equally across the globe, and concern for 'global goods' such as the environment or cultural heritage are less potent in some parts of the world than in others (Kaul, Grunberg, and Stern 1999).

Constraints

The social forces that bring new needs and open up opportunities also imply constraints, challenges, and dilemmas for civil society organisations. These challenges ultimately raise the question of what kind of organisational form is best suited for CSOs working in complex task environments. Typical organisational dilemmas revolve around questions of ownership, governance and accountability, organisational structure in terms of decentralisation and centralisation, internal democracy, and the type of organisational culture. The evolving interplay of opportunities and constraints creates a need for organisational innovations.

For international NGOs some of these dilemmas are amplified by the significant growth they experienced in recent years both as a form and also frequently as individual organisations (Anheier and Themudo 2002; Lindenberg 1999; Meyer et al. 1997; UIA url). To address global problems and issues, NGOs have themselves grown into global entities (Young 1992) and increasingly 'network' and operate transnationally (see Tarrow 2001). Not surprisingly, this growth, fuelled by the many new opportunities that have opened up, brings with it new organisational challenges (Clark 2001; Lindenberg 1999; Young 1992). Specifically:

- By growing into global entities and by becoming transnational in character, CSOs also incorporate, and must address, the complexity and diversity of the political, economic, and cultural environments in which they operate.
- By networking transnationally, they also relate to diverse constituencies and stakeholders, which can lead to contradictions that entail complex political dilemmas (see Chapter 2).
- By working in multiple jurisdictions, they must develop ways of managing tensions and conflicting requirements that stem from the intricacies of different legal and fiscal systems.

- By incorporating and dealing with different organisational, national, and religious cultures and value systems, they acquire the need to develop some common base and understanding to make communication and decision-making possible (see Chapter 3).
- At the governance level, critical challenges develop from the need to remain accountable to a dispersed membership base, and have boards that reflect the diversity of the organisation in structure and composition.
- Similarly, at the transnational level, governance structures must outline responsibilities as well as oversight and enforcement mechanisms across various parts and locations of the organisation.
- At the managerial level, CSOs face problems associated with increased organisational size in more competitive funding environments, which can increase management and administrative costs to hitherto unknown levels, creating the potential of frictions with members, the board, and other stakeholders (Anheier 2000).

From Bureaucracies to Network Organisations

Managing the tensions arising from the organisational environment in which CSOs operate becomes critical for sustainability and survival (Fowler 1997). The pressures created by these tensions may trigger a large-scale search for organisational forms capable of handling such challenges and constraints, as suggested by the categories 'special form' and 'non-conventional bodies' in Table 8.1. We can assume that at some point the carrying capacity of the global environment for CSOs will reach a critical stage, particularly in terms of resources, and encourage a search for forms that could transform, even revolutionise, the organisational infrastructure of global civil society.[3] At present, however, it appears that we have some way to go before reaching this point, but there are clear indications of form transformations, as we will see below.

Since the industrial revolution of the eighteenth and nineteenth centuries, organisational history has

[3] See Aldrich (1999) and Romanelli (1991) on the general background of organisational theory, in particular on form emergence and survival.

seen three major epochal developments that cut across the constraints of existing forms. The first, identified by Max Weber ([1924] 1997; see Perrow 1986), was the full development of the modern bureaucracy, a major innovation that made the nation state and the industrial corporation possible. With a premium on stability, predictability, responsibility, and the long term, bureaucracies were efficient tools of administration and production. State agencies, industrial giants, and even charities and religious organisations became bureaucratic organisations.

The second major organisational innovation of the industrial era involved, according to Chandler (1962; 1990), a fundamental shift from hierarchical relationships organised along functional activities (e.g., accounting, marketing, production) to multi-divisional coordination within modern firms. This shift was first noticed in the US and Germany where expansion and product diversification placed costly strains on the conventional hierarchical or unitary structure. Corporations divided their operations into divisions, with each responsible for a different product or geographical region and each organised along functional lines. Organisations changed from a unitary, hierarchical U-form to a more decentralised, multi-divisional or M-form. Decentralisation allowed parts of the organisation to be managed as relatively autonomous subunits along functional lines. The adoption of the M-form began as a slow process that nonetheless revolutionised the organisational landscape of modern industry within 50 years. In 1929 fewer than 2 per cent of the 100 largest non-financial companies in the US had adopted the M-form; by 1979, 84 per cent had adopted it (Aldrich 1999).

Whereas bureaucracies brought certainty of performance and increased volume (scale economics), the multi-divisional form allowed for the combination of scale and scope economics.[4] This development made possible hitherto unknown levels of national and international expansion. Economies of scale require integration and centralisation as core management tasks while economies of scope imply coordination of decentralised, semi-autonomous units (Chandler 1990). The multi-divisional form was able to combine both centralisation and decentralisation imperatives, reaping the benefits of both scale and scope economies, which made it attractive not only to corporations but also to public agencies and non-profit organisations, and helped pave the way for new public management (Ferlie 1996).

Yet for organisations operating in complex environments greater decentralisation also requires greater predictability in the way organisational units relate to each other. This, however, may ultimately push organisations towards greater formalisation in the way they manage internal information flows and decision-making (Hatch 1997; Scott 1998) and thereby increase rather than decrease the costs of organising. Decentralisation and formalisation therefore stand in some tension with each other, and this tension puts pressure on information management and decision-making, which becomes the crucial nexus in the relationship between central (e.g., the headquarter) and decentralised units 'in the field' (Perrow 1986; Pugh 1997).

While most information is generated in decentralised units, it passes upwards in the organisational hierarchy for processing by central management before being passed down in the form of directives. Central management, however, is typically confronted with a limited capacity for processing information and for translating it into actionable decisions, particularly across national, legal, and cultural boundaries (Bartlett and Ghoshal 1997). The result is an information overload of central managers (Day et al. 2001). In such conditions, efficient decision-making should rest closer to where the information is collected (Dawson 1996). This, however, implies yet further decentralisation, which, in turn, increases the cost of information management and the transaction costs of decision-making and coordination throughout. As a result, most CSOs like corporations and state agencies are in a more or less constant

> The tension between needs and opportunities on the one hand and the constraints of existing organisational forms on the other create a push towards differentiation and innovation into new forms

---

[4] By divisionalising, production firms can combine the gains from manufacturing products in large quantities (e.g., shampoo) with the gains from producing related products (e.g., detergent, washing-up liquid) based on cost sharing. Scope economics applies to production as well as to service provision and sales markets.

struggle to find the right balance between decentralisation and centralisation (see Clark 2001; Lindenberg and Dobel 1999).

One strategy to find a balance between form and environment is the relational or network organisation, which constitutes the third epochal form development. While the shift from functional to multi-divisional forms was based primarily on scale and scope economies, the relational form is fuelled primarily by transaction cost considerations, i.e., the costs of 'organising and doing business' (see Williamson 1985). Pressures to minimise transaction costs encourage form innovations and the evolution of forms based on inter-organisational cooperation (Powell 1990; Thompson 1991), and, ultimately, to some form of disaggregated complex organisation (Day and Wendler 1998; Day et al. 2001). In particular, in competitive, global markets, higher-scope economies combined with lower communication costs (i.e., reduced transaction costs) to provide strong incentives for outsourcing activities to networks of suppliers, producers, and distributors. The result has been the increased role for 'relational' forms, such as the network organisation, and extensive production and distribution chains criss-crossing the globe (Dicken 1998; Held et al. 1999). It is important to see that the network form is by no means limited to the world of transnational business. According to Wainwright (2001), the network organisation and other non-hierarchical forms have long been used in civil society by, for example, the women's movement and the anti-Vietnam War movement. In this context, a key driver of the network form was its emphasis on equality and individual autonomy in relations.

> Most civil society organisations like corporations and state agencies are in a more or less constant struggle to find the right balance between decentralisation and centralisation

Relational forms are somewhat 'fluid' organisations particularly suited for highly variable task environments. Without central coordination for everyday management tasks and operations, decisions are made at the local levels with a minimum of costs for consultation and negotiation. Adaptability is maximised when undertaken by small independent units rather than large bureaucratic

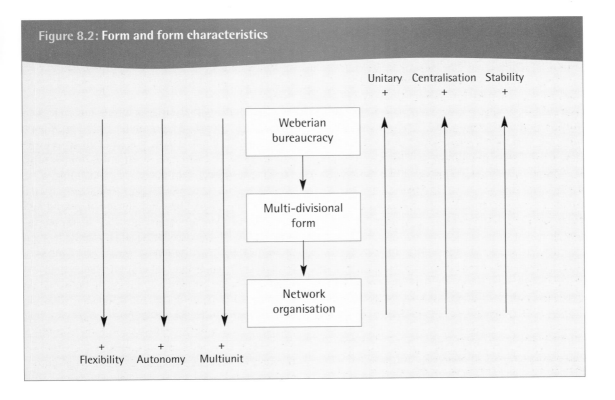

Figure 8.2: **Form and form characteristics**

organisations. By implication, lack of coordination can reduce opportunities for scale economies and also invite 'free riding'. The nature of networks can lead to difficulties in sharing development costs as well as brand and knowledge management sharing, i.e., activities that require some form of collective action and common identity.

This network form constrains identity formation, collective action, and perhaps even the legitimacy of the organisation speaking with one voice. But on balance, and on largely economic grounds, the global organisational environment for CSOs would favour the network form with decentralised and autonomous units. There is some empirical evidence to support this claim. Using data from the Union of International Associations, Smith (1997) found that between 1973 and 1993 the number of coalitions (a form of network organisation) increased from 25 per cent to 40 per cent of the total number of INGOs observed. The number of coalitions Smith observed in the UIA database rose in absolute and relative terms.

Figure 8.2 summarises the evolutionary relationship between form characteristics from the nineteenth-century bureaucracies to twenty-first-century network organisations. We are not claiming that network forms are better or 'more evolved' than hierarchical, unitary forms. There are many successful unitary or M-form CSOs operating at global level (e.g., Human Rights Watch; see Clark 2001). There are many advantages to the centralisation of activities, as we discuss throughout this chapter. We are, however, suggesting that the general historical trend identified in the organisational literature for firms (e.g. Day et al 2001; Powell 1990) has some correspondence with the evolving form of civil society organisations. What, then, will be the major organisational innovations of global civil society in contrast to existing forms, structures, and management practices?

Organisational Dynamics

Most organisations that populated nascent global civil society, let's say some 100 years ago, were basically membership and non-membership organisations modelled on the Weberian model of bureaucracy. They included scholarly associations, the International Chamber of Commerce, the Red Cross Federation, and various political party alliances such as the Socialist International. Non-membership organisations like the Catholic Church[5]

too, were outgrowing their late medieval past and developed into formal bureaucracies at local, national, and international levels resembling the modern state administration. Some organisations like some national Red Cross societies or the Salvation Army incorporated distinctive military elements in their organisational design and structure.

As well, INGOs with observer status at the UN from the 1950 onwards were rather conventional bureaucracies, and largely indistinguishable in their structure from national organisations and perhaps even state agencies. Yet, as suggested above, the growth of CSOs into more global organisations has brought new challenges and opportunities to experiment with multi-divisional and network forms that push them away from the model of nineteenth-century bureaucracies. CSOs like Amnesty International or Action Aid are engaged in ongoing processes of reorganisation so as to capitalise on the new opportunities and respond to the new environmental challenges. These reorganisations are quests for innovations in organisational forms that are more suitable to the complex task environment of a globalising world than bureaucracies and multi-divisional forms, or variations thereof, are at present. To untangle the organisational dynamics of global civil society, we put forward four main propositions.

Proposition 1. *The symmetry between environment and form is difficult to achieve and maintain for CSOs in a globalising world, which encourages diversity and innovation.*

As it expands, global civil society is incorporating different elements and is becoming itself more diverse as a result (Table 8.1). It is not difficult to provide examples of the diversity in organisational forms existing in global civil society. For example, Care International is an NGO with over 10,000 professional staff. Its US affiliate alone has income of around $US 450 million. Not surprisingly, its structure is very professionalised. Friends of the Earth (FoE) is a confederation of 66 member organisations, some of which are very large (FoE-UK has 10 per cent of total membership) and others very small (see Box 8.3). The World Conservation Union is a CSO that brings together 735 NGOs, 35 affiliates, 78 states, 112 government agencies, and some 10,000 scientists and experts from 181 countries

---

[5] *We say that the Catholic Church is a non-membership organisation because its members have no democratic voting power in the organisation's governance. We discuss this distinction below.*

Box 8.3: Friends of the Earth – Global federation

Friends of the Earth International (FoE) is a federation of 61 groups with an international secretariat and an executive committee to oversee the operations between biennial General Assembly meetings. It is a federation of membership organisations, i.e., its membership base is primarily organisational; individual members join at the national level. Together the FoE federation of member organisations combines about 5,000 local groups and 1 million members. FoE is highly decentralised network of autonomous organisations. About half of the member organisations use the name FoE, others prefer names in local languages.

Entry into the federation is a very strict process based on wide criteria, with internal democracy at its centre. Applicant organisations must be membership-based and have clear internal democratic procedures, including a representative board. They must also be independent from religious and political affiliations, dedicated to national and international issues, and work on more than one environmental area. After a first administrative screening, applications are submitted to the International Executive Committee (IEC) that meets three times a year. If considered suitable, the IEC will then submit the application to the General Assembly for final approval. Normally some 50 organisations apply and only one or two are approved.

Biennially, a week-long General Assembly of representatives of member organisations decides on the policies and activities of the federation. All member organisations have the same vote. The General Assembly elects a nine-member Executive Committee, which meets four times a year.

Sources: Interviews and FoE (URL)

---

in a unique worldwide partnership (IUCN URL). Alcoholics Anonymous is a volunteer-run NGO. OneWorld.net is an Internet-based NGO dedicated to providing free information for development.

Organisational theory (Hannan and Freeman 1989; Aldrich 1999) suggests that organisational forms will be *as diverse as the environment that supports them* and that organisations are more sustainable if they adapt to specific environmental conditions, i.e., a niche. This symmetry between environmental niche and form is more difficult to achieve when organisations face not one but multiple, complex environments, as is the case for CSOs with activities across the globe. Critical elements include:

- *Funding sources.* CSOs raise funds from a wide variety of donors (e.g., individual members and sympathisers, foundations, and bilateral and multilateral agencies) and other sources (sales, fees, and charges) that spread across different countries and that typically involves a geographical separation of contributors and beneficiaries (Edwards and Hulme 1995; Hansmann 1996).
- *Staff, members, and volunteers.* CSOs typically hire staff from a number of different countries, and recruit members and volunteers from sometimes even larger number of countries and regions. Care International, for example has 10,000 employees, 9,000 of whom are nationals of the countries in which they work (Care UK URL).
- *Diversity of missions.* From the preservation of wetlands to the promotion of micro-credit, from working with recycling in the North to supplying humanitarian assistance in conflict areas, CSOs are concerned with a multiplicity of issues and missions. Depending on local conditions, within the same organisation different parts of the mission may be emphasised at the expense of others. For example Southern parts of environmental CSOs notmally pay greater attention to development aspects of environmental protection than their Northern counterparts (Clark 2001; Princen and Finger 1994). Similarly the importance of class, caste, or gender relations will vary in different cultures, with immense implications for management.
- *Need to be locally responsive, conform to national regulations, and be globally relevant.* CSOs work with very different beneficiaries who

have different views of a 'good society' and require very different tasks and management models. The local-national-global link requires skilful handling of needs, resources, and expectations. Being able to linking the local with the global is essential for the effectiveness of global CSOs (see Edwards, Hulme, and Wallace 1999).

- *Varying costs of communications and organising*. Different parts of the world have very limited access to new information technologies. This 'digital divide' requires CSOs to organise in different ways in different areas. The extent and intensity of networking forms will vary dramatically between North and South (Clark and Themudo forthcoming).

These factors interact to create the diverse, multiple local and global organisational environments that CSOs face. As a consequence, in CSOs operating across the globe the principle of symmetry is difficult to achieve and maintain, as they need to organise differently in different locations depending on their portfolio of products, markets, geography, or culture (Bartlett and Ghoshal 1997). For example, FoE is highly decentralised in Sweden, where it has a long history and faces a culture of association and participatory democracy; at the same time, it is much more centralised in a country like Colombia, where it faces a generally antagonistic government, a small membership base, and limited participation (interviews at FoE International).

Such diversity generates both intra-organisational and inter-organisational differentiation. For example, there are differences in individual membership rights between organisations but also within different national branches of the same organisations. Variations exist because of historical and legal conditions that influence the type of governance structure that is chosen in each national chapter of the INGO. In most national branches, GreenPeace members do not have voting power. For example, the board of GreenPeace US is self-appointed and members have no voting rights. In Spain, however, members have voting rights and elect GreenPeace Spain's board democratically (GreenPeace Spain url) because national law requires most NGOs to be 'associations'. In contrast to GreenPeace, most FoE national branches are strongly committed to internal democracy, and members have voting power. In Canada, however, FoE members do not vote, and the national

branch has a self-appointed board (Anheier and Themudo 2002). Such diversity is promoted not by the global mission, which is fairly homogeneous, but by national variations of historical and regulatory conditions as well as different cultural interpretations of that global mission.

Proposition 2. *CSOs are becoming more similar and dissimilar at the same time.*

Despite the remarkable diversity that characterises CSOs we also observe common characteristics and patterns of similarity, which organisational theory refers to as 'isomorphism' tendencies (Powell and DiMaggio 1991). In terms of internal structure, CSO forms cluster around various models of federation, a version of the multi-divisional form. Specifically, the need to balance pressures towards centralisation and decentralisation, economies of scale and scope, flexibility and adaptability appears to translate into a widespread adoption of the *federation*[6] as an organisational form. Lindenberg and Dobel (1999) found this tendency among large INGOs dedicated to relief and development. Young *et al.* (1999) found a similar tendency among international advocacy NGOs. In terms of external relations, economic and political pressures encourage inter-organisational collaboration in the form of partnerships and coalitions—examples of the network organisation described above. Together, federations, partnerships, and network structures seem to emerge as signature elements of organised global civil society.

At the same time, the trend toward coordination rather than the hierarchical control of semi-autonomous units has become more pronounced in recent years. In particular, decreases in transaction costs act as centrifugal tendencies in global civil society organisations and encourage a move away from global hierarchies (unless central units control the resource environments). The result has been a trend towards 'operational downsizing' where organisations concentrate on their 'core activities' and contract out auxiliary activities (see Day and Wendler 1998; Powell 1990). So for example many Northern development NGOs have grown in size and resources in the past two decades but they have reduced their operational involvement in the South,

[6] We use the term 'federation' as originally understood by Handy (1988; 1989) as organisations based on the principle of subsidiarity, whereby power ultimately rests with the local units rather than the coordinating centre. As such it includes both 'federations' and 'confederations' in Lindenberg and Dobel's (1999) and Clark's (2001) typologies.

preferring instead to sub-contract operational activities to Southern NGOs. Northern NGOs for their part concentrate on fund-raising, capacity building, and advocacy (Edwards 1999; Lewis 2001). On the other hand, small organisations may still need to globalise some of their activities but their reduced size may prevent them from setting up a federation structure across many different countries. Instead some organisations have chosen to network and collaborate across borders, thus taking advantage of some of the opportunities of globalisation.

These trends foster inter-organ-isational cooperation. In terms of service delivery, many North-South NGO partnerships have sprung up in recent years. Oxfam International, for example, has over 3,000 partner organisations in the South (Clark 2001). This partnership push is a North-South division of labour based on 'inter-organisational' co-operation and contracting rather than vertical expansion of Northern NGOs. The resulting division of labour is based as much on efficiency as on normative pressures exerted by donors that stipulate NGO collaboration and partnership as a precondition for funding.

In international campaigning, coalitions have become a common organisational form (Smith 1997). Coalitions are a more structured form of transnational advocacy networks (Keck and Sikkink 1998). The recent success and visibility of coalitions such as the Coalition for an International Criminal Court (see Chapter 6), Coalition to Stop the Use of Child Soldiers (Box 8.4), Campaign Against Landmines, International Action Network on Small Arms, Jubilee 2000, and the Climate Action Network clearly demonstrate the wide use of this organisational form for global organising, which further encourages its use for advocacy campaigns more generally.

Other factors, too, encourage similarities among CSO forms. The absence of some global regulations of CSOs significantly reduces legal standardisation when compared with the national level. Yet Meyer *et al.* (1997) point to more subtle ways in which CSOs are becoming more alike. This is the development of a 'world culture' and organisational blueprints that at the global level give greater legitimacy to some

> Typical organisational dilemmas evolve around questions of ownership, governance and accountability, organisational structure in terms of decentralisation and centralisation, internal democracy, and the type of organisational culture

forms of organising (typically Western forms) than to others such as Chinese or Indian. Clark (2001) has argued that US civil law practices and tax regulations have spread to other parts of the world (e.g., central and eastern Europe) and helped policies that encourage 'enabling frameworks' for civil society.

We suggest that a growing group of international professionals transmits the development of a world culture. Members of this group may have studied at similar universities, learned the same professional skills, and share similar knowledge irrespective of their world-views and values. As a result, they may run organisations in similar ways.

Another powerful set of iso-morphic tendencies derives from the global funding environment. CSOs' resource dependency on a limited set of funders increases the possibility of external influence on organisational form (see Pfeffer and Salancik 1978). There are indications that competition for scarce funding is increasing for global civil society (Foreman 1999; Lindenberg and Dobel 1999). At the core of the greater competition for resources is the fact that in some fields, such as development and humanitarian relief, the growth of INGOs seems to have surpassed the expansion of resources available to them, either from private (donations and dues) or public (government grants and contracts) sources. Such conditions increase environmental uncertainty, which leads organisations to imitate those they perceive to be successful, resulting in greater homogeneity (see Powell and Dimaggio 1991).

Moreover, intense competition between CSOs for global funding, which is provided by very few major donors, provides strong pressures for isomorphism not only among CSOs but also between CSOs and funding agencies (intergovernmental organisations, governments, and foundations). NGOs face strong pressures for bureaucratisation and the imposition of reporting requirements to suit donors rather than beneficiaries (Edwards and Hulme 1995). Competition need not necessarily lead to isomorphism as donors can, and often do, encourage innovation and diversity among CSOs. However, there has been a general trend for donors to emphasise efficiency over

'The Coalition to Stop the Use of Child Soldiers was formed in June 1998 to advocate for the adoption of, and adherence to, national, regional and international legal standards (including an Optional Protocol to the Convention on the Rights of the Child) prohibiting the military recruitment and use in hostilities of any person younger than eighteen years of age.

The Coalition was founded by six international NGOs—Amnesty International, Human Rights Watch, the International Save the Children Alliance, Jesuit Refugee Service, the Quaker United Nations Office, Geneva, and International Federation Terre des Hommes—and later joined by Defence for Children International, World Vision International, and regional NGOs from Latin America, Africa, Asia and the Pacific. The Coalition has also established partners and national coalitions which are engaged in advocacy, campaigns and public education in nearly 40 countries . . . The Coalition has established and maintained active links with UNICEF, the International Red Cross and Red Crescent Movement, UNESCO, UNHCR, UNHCHR and the Special Representative of the UN Secretary-General for Children and Armed Conflict.

. . . the Coalition has established partners and national coalitions in nearly 40 countries. These local campaigns have been organised in different ways, in some places formally constituted in others through loose networks of organisations and individuals. They bring together international, regional and local human rights and children's rights non-governmental organisations, humanitarian and developmental agencies, peace and disarmament groups, veterans' associations and youth movements, teachers and students, religious groups and trade unions, academics and other interested individuals. Together we number more than 500 organisations. These committed organisations and individuals have been the very heart of the Coalition's campaign and a critical factor in its success.' (CSC URL)

The CSC is one example of a relational organisational form. The CSC is extremely fluid, as demonstrated by the variety of organisations that compose it and the different structures used in different local contexts. Globally its form is a hybrid of a coalition, a joint venture, and a federation. A number of INGOs got together to create a *new*, separate organisation to pursue their common interest in the subject of child soldiers. The founding INGOs are the 'owners' of the organisation. The founding organisations retain control through the steering committee, setting the CSC's mission and directing the organisation. The CSC has no power over the founding organisations. So as well as being a coalition the CSC has formal elements of a joint venture. It also establishes or accepts local and regional coalitions as part of the larger CSC family. Some of these local elements have representation at the governance level, being more than simply 'sections'.

CSC is also very much like an international federation. Despite having an international secretariat staffed by only four people, it maintains an organisational structure with a global level (secretariat),

---

innovation (Riddell 1999; Salm 1999), thus promoting isomorphism.

Alongside competition, pressures for isomorphism can equally come from increased collaboration, such as in the case of partnerships among CSOs and between CSOs and state or business (Tuckman 1998). Inter-organisational collaboration can produce 'co-evolutionary arrangements' whereby collaborating organisations jointly adapt to environmental changes through division of labour, mutual learning, and the diffusion of best practices. In this way, current efforts of capacity building of CSOs both by donors and by CSOs themselves provide an important vehicle for isomorphism.

Some authors have expressed fears that some CSOs are becoming increasingly like state agencies and form a quasi-state sector allied with official donor agencies in complex public-private partnerships (e.g., Edwards and Hulme 1995; Smith and Lipsky 1993). Others fear that CSOs are becoming more like businesses (e.g., Dichter 1999; Edwards 1999; Weisbrod 1998) as intense competition for foundation and government grants drives them to exploit alternative sources such as related and unrelated business income to support their mission.

ORGANISATIONAL FORMS OF GLOBAL CIVIL SOCIETY   Helmut Anheier and Nuno Themudo

regional level (e.g., Asia), and national levels. Each level is itself a coalition involving various other organisations. The international secretariat helps create and coordinates the various coalitions on the lines of a federation. However, the original founders did not become units of the new organisation, as would be the case in a 'true federation'. And the national coalitions do not fully elect the board or steering committee. They have some representation at the board level, which they share with the founding organisations. Sometimes the CSC behaves as a global federation of national and international NGOs. Some national NGOs become members at the global level and vote for the secretariat. Sometimes the founding board members play a very important role and the CSC behaves like a coalition or joint venture. Sometimes, however, board members are not very active and the CSC behaves like a federation or multi-divisional organisation. All this ambiguity and flexibility allows the CSC to be very adaptive and so far it has been very effective in its advocacy. The ambiguous nature of the CSC's organisational form manifests itself in its ability to be different things in different circumstances. Is it a network/coalition or a federation? Or is it a federation of networks? Maybe a coalition of coalitions? What unites this loose structure is the clear commitment to a goal (banning the use of child soldiers across the globe) and the coordinating role of the steering committee enabling adaptive local action.

There is some evidence that public and private agencies partly adapt to CSOs, with corporate social responsibility as perhaps the best example (see Chapter 4). But because of resource dependency it seems that, by and large, CSOs have been doing most of the adapting while trying to obtain funding. This challenge of adapting to both funders and very diverse local conditions is why flexible intra- and inter-organisational forms (i.e., federations, partnerships, and coalitions) are so prevalent in global civil society.

Dealing with globalisation is the single most important concern of multinational enterprises (Micklethwait and Wooldridge 1996). The degree of globalisation varies with respect to (1) the proportion of activities undertaken that are international (as opposed to national), measured by the income of foreign affiliates compared with domestic income; and (2) the number of countries in which the organisation either conducts activities or obtains resources and revenue. At low levels of 'globalisation' CSOs develop an awareness of international issues. Some of a CSO's activities are concerned with scanning and monitoring the international environment for threats and opportunities (e.g., funding). As globalisation increases further it establishes increasingly formal relations with organisations from a wider range of countries. It may even join a formal international coalition/network or enter into partnership agreements with foreign organisations. At the highest levels of globalisation it becomes a global organisation either by creating franchises or by setting up foreign affiliates.

What is the impact of changes in the level of globalisation on organisational form? When developing into transnational organisations, most INGOs tend to adopt a multi-level structure that involves local, national, and international components. As mentioned above, multinational NGOs work in different cultural, political, and economic settings, often with very different problems and organisational tasks. Environmental variations across local chapters and national societies are high, which suggests that a decentralised mode is best suited for achieving results locally. Decisions should be made at levels where expertise and knowledge are greatest—which may not necessarily be at the central level at all. At the same time, local resources are unevenly distributed, and task requirements do not match available support, requiring resource redistribution across different parts of the organisation. In situations where tasks and resources vary across geographically dispersed organisations, a federal form is best. In this model, the main purpose of the central body is twofold: first, to maintain diversity and expertise at appropriate levels, and second, to coordinate among units and to take on collective action vis-à-vis third parties. This is typically done with a division of labour between local and non-local tasks.

At the global level, the organisational form is determined by the need for affiliate self-determination, economies of scale, resource acquisition, protection of global brand, pressures for global accountability, scale of impact, and technology (Lindenberg and Dobel 1999). Unitary or corporate models facilitate coordination and help maintain a single clear brand identity. On the other hand, weakly coordinated networks maximise organisational autonomy and adaptation to local conditions.

INGOs must find a balance between centralisation and decentralisation, standardisation and flexibility. According to Foreman (1999: 179), 'advancements in communications, increased social mobility, and greater competition for resources will tend to push an NGO toward centralising its control and increase standardisation among its domestic members. [T]he diversity and instability of the working environment . . . will encourage an NGO to decentralise decision making to its domestic member organisations to increase flexibility and adaptability. [These pressures] must be balanced within the context of an NGO's organisational culture, history, and mission to determine the appropriate governance structure'.

Increasing globalisation of activities leads to an increase in the complexity of organisational task environment. The reason for this is a general understanding that internationalisation represents an increase in the scope of the organisation's activities (see Hatch 1997). Generally speaking, increasing globalisation of organisational activities leads first to an increase in complexity and in the scope rather than the scale of organisational activities, which then leads to pressures toward decentralisation and formalisation. At the same time, reductions in the costs of communications lead to downsizing and greater demands for coordination, which favours 'networking' rather than 'controlling'.

On the other hand, globalisation may also allow for greater economies of scale, which would strengthen the centre's position vis-à-vis its geographically dispersed units. However, to the extent that globalisation produces economies of scale, greater integration and centralisation will counter some of the pressures towards decentralisation and coordination. Of course,

> One strategy to find a balance between form and environment is the relational or network organisation, a somewhat fluid form particularly suited for highly variable task environments

globalisation of organisational activities is not the only determinant of organisational form. Technology, mission, resource environment, or legal frameworks will influence form choice.

Proposition 4. *Form constraints encourage innovations and the creation of hybrid and relational forms.*

Hybridisation implies the combination of elements of two different organisational forms to generate a third form (Romanelli 1991). This combination entails an effort to maximise the strengths of both forms while minimising the impact of their weaknesses. Global civil society tends to encourage the emergence of hybrid forms, for several reasons. First, the global organisational environment is very diverse and changing, and rewards flexibility and adaptation. Because they combine selected elements of two or more forms, hybrid forms tend to provide the flexibility needed. Second, to be successful, global CSOs must often combine elements borrowed from public agencies as well as business. This need places global CSOs in a naturally 'hybrid environment' between the state and commerce. Third, the global organisational environment with its combination of national and international cultures and ways of organising displays tensions that require a hybridisation of national and international organisational forms such as the federation.

Hybridisation involves two main processes: recombination and refunctionality. 'Recombination' involves the introduction of new elements into an existing organisational form. Global CSOs have adopted many elements from their state funders. For example, the 'log-frame' approach to project planning and implementation was developed for the public sector and is now widely used by INGOs in their development projects (Riddell 1999). On the other hand, non-profits are increasing creating commercial enterprises (Weisbrod 1998) such as charity shops, mail-order catalogues, or Fair Trade products. As they do so they find themselves increasingly relying on private sector management tools such as marketing, benchmarking, franchising, branding, and other corporate management tools.

INGOs have also pioneered elements that are now being introduced into other organisational forms. Participatory processes in development projects were developed by NGOs and are now widely employed by public agencies. The term 'reverse agenda' suggests that NGOs are influencing aid policy (ODI 1995; Lewis 2001). Increasingly, businesses use methods developed by NGOs to evaluate social impact (see Lewis 1998; Zadek and Gatwood 1995) and social responsibility (see Chapter 4).

'Refunctionality' means the relocation of one form in a different context, e.g., the migration of for-profit providers into fields previously populated primarily by non-profits, as in social services. The loss of legitimacy of the state implied by the 'New Policy Agenda' (Edwards and Hulme 1995; Lewis 2001) allowed NGOs to move further into the development-service delivery field, which used to be dominated by the public agencies. Similarly, NGOs are increasingly moving into the provision of credit, entering an area currently occupied mainly by business.

However, it would be premature to claim that the recent growth of CSOs was, in organisational terms, the sole result of recombination and refunctionality rather than a linear, quantitative expansion along the trajectory local-national-international. The figures in Table 8.1 suggest that both processes have been taking place, but that the expansion of existing forms has been the primary locus of this growth. At the same time, as shown above, innovation towards hybrid forms is taking place, indicative of qualitative changes in the composition of organisational forms across different branches and segments of the economy, both private and public, locally, nationally, transnationally, etc. (see Box 8.4).

The process of hybridisation and innovation at global level has already been extensive, and some organisations look more like patchworks of different structures networking with other structures united by some shared goals but at the same time competing in other fields. Some authors describe these organisational developments as the constitution of multi-member global 'organisational families' (Lindenberg and Bryant 2001).

> In formal organisations, two basic forms have emerged: the 'global democracy' model and the 'global federation' model, each with different implications for internal democracy and North-South relations

To address North-South imbalances of power, some INGOs have tried a number of organisational form innovations. For example, the World Rainforest Movement has experimented with placing power in Southern units by setting up its international secretariat in Uruguay and a powerful fundraising 'Northern Office' in the United Kingdom (WRM URL). The World Social Forum is trying to develop a ring structure with rotating headquarters where any country member organisation can become the headquarters for a period of time (WSF URL). The main objective of this organisational form is to build local capacity and create a more egalitarian relationship among parts of the organisation. Panos is another example of a CSO trying to develop a similar ring structure with rotating headquarters.

In terms of internal governance, some INGOs such as Amnesty International have created a 'global democracy' form by varying the number of representatives from a member country according to the size of that country's membership, avoiding the typical 'one country, one representative' governance system of federations. Other INGOs like FoE have created a governing board election system that gives a majority to Southern members even though Southern countries contribute fewer resources and members to the organisation.

Because information is critical for advocacy, communications technologies have a profound impact on organisational form in this field. One example is the emergence of 'dot-causes', Internet-based advocacy organisations (Clark and Themudo forthcoming). By using the Internet, these virtual organisations represent a radical breakthrough. Their flexibility, informality, and rejection of hierarchy (see Box 8.5) make them ideal vehicles for organising anti-globalisation movements (Clark and Themudo forthcoming) as well as other movement organisations such as the Anti-Landmines Campaign.

In most cases, however, few 'pure' innovations occur, and it is frequently the hybridisation and the importation and modification of ideas from different circumstances, or the pursuit of analogous problem-solving techniques from quite different sectors and

SEI is a civil society organisation dedicated to mobilising support for the anti-global capitalism movement. Its primary location is on the Internet and so it has been called a 'dot-cause' (Clark and Themudo forthcoming). Its organisational form embodies an anarchic disdain of structure and leadership.

> Who is in charge of Subversive Enterprises, Int'l.? No one . . . Each member of Subversive Enterprises, Int'l. is responsible for their own actions, and their own leadership . . . No one is higher than anyone else. No one is lower than anyone else. We are a network, not a bureaucracy. Feel free to consider yourself a member right now . . . The only reason this 'organisation' was formed, was that we hoped that individuals like yourself (-selves) might be more encouraged to take action if you knew that there were others out there like you, with similar interests and goals. You want to start you own chapter/branch/franchise of Subversive Enterprises, Int'l.? Go right ahead. We would prefer that your agendas be somewhat compatible with ours, but anything goes. (Subversive Enterprises International URL)

SEI's members are not organised into any form of hierarchy. Instead they are organised as a fluid network of autonomous individuals and possibly groups (chapters) that change depending on the circumstances. The main organisational 'glue' is the similar interests among individuals belonging to the network and the technology that permits their coordination.

contexts, that lead to innovative approaches. For example, venture philanthropy imports the idea and analogous investment approach from the field of finance into the field of philanthropy. Under this approach, instead of making a grant, donors 'invest' in CSOs for specified 'social returns'.

Impact of Organisational Forms

The organisational dynamics explored above have important implications for global civil society, in particular for effectiveness and sustainability, internal and external democratisation and accountability, and North-South tensions.

Variety of organisational form is essential for the sustainability of the infrastructure of global civil society. This form variety provides an insurance against environmental changes that can threaten some parts and elements of the infrastructure while leaving others to thrive and yet others unaffected. Diversity can also lead to greater overall effectiveness, as it constitutes a laboratory for social experimentation that leads to learning and improvement. The development of more appropriate forms to a given mission and task environment can lead to more effective organisations. At the same time diversity can be very wasteful in terms of organisational efficiency. Many experiments fail and best practices are not shared. So the drive to increase efficiency can in fact lead to reduced diversity, particularly when competition is intense and donors value short-term cost-efficiency and certainty over long-term effectiveness and innovation that might involve risks. In this scenario, competitive pressure and donor influence help select forms and generalised best practices that are efficient but potentially less effective, and isomorphic niche-seekers rather than diverse innovators.

Democratisation is the second critical area of impact. Some suggest that economic globalisation is leading to a democratic deficit at the global level (e.g., Boggs 2001), and question whether current organisational forms do indeed address 'the need to bring greater democracy to global civil society' (Keane 2001: 43). Ownership and the structure of decision-making in CSOs are critical issues in this respect.

Two major 'ownership' clusters seem to have emerged among CSOs: membership-based organisations and non-membership, or supporter-based, organisations, each with important implications for decision-making, accountability, and legitimacy (Anheier and Themudo 2002). Simply put, membership-based organisations give their members the right to vote in organisational governance. Non-membership organisations often refer to their individual donors as 'members' (e.g., GreenPeace) but they do not give them any governance role. In a strict sense, non-membership non-profit organisations are non-proprietary organisations and have no owners as such (Hansmann 1996). However, even though many CSOs are legally either associations or corporations, each category leaves significant room for 'quasi-ownership' among different stakeholders, i.e., board, management, clients and users, and members, including donors. In the case of non-membership CSOs, decision-making is not based on democratic principles but on the relative influence (e.g., financial resources, legitimacy) of different stakeholders (Pfeffer and Salancik 1978). The contribution of this type of CSO to democratisation is increased pluralism of society generally. This may involve giving voice to otherwise excluded groups and taking up emerging issues that turn out to be critical—e.g., the environment—but accountability remains weak (Edwards and Hulme 1995) and legitimacy claims are easily questioned (Hudson 2000; Hudson and Bielefeld 1997).

> Membership organisations have the greatest potential for democracy and accountability. Non-membership organisations can contribute to increased pluralism, but accountability remains weak and legitimacy claims are easily questioned

Membership organisations have the greater potential for democracy and accountability (Yeo 2002). By providing formal mechanisms for the representation of different groups, they reinforce notions of citizenship and enhance the democratic potentials in society (Selle and Strømsnes 1998), performing a role of 'schools of democracy' (Putnam 1995). Some authors argue that the accountability of membership-based organisations to the grass roots distinguishes them from corporate, non-membership NGOs that are ever more similar to the business sector (see Uphoff 1995). However, there are also some pitfalls. Because some members are more committed than others, all democratic membership organisations have to address the tension between the free riding of uncommitted members and tendencies towards elite control by core activists. Most members participate by paying dues only and leave the organising to a dedicated few (Lansey 1997; Putnam 1995). The latter stand in danger of developing into an elite that dominates the organisation, thereby undermining democratic ideals.

Using UIA data, Anheier, Glasius, and Kaldor (2001) show that membership of INGOs increased between 1990 and 2000. However UIA's definition of membership does not distinguish between membership based on voting rights and membership in the sense of general support (e.g., GreenPeace, WWF). Trends of decreasing membership in traditional CSOs such as trade unions (Clark 2001) and cooperatives (Yeo 2002) suggest that much of the growth in membership numbers may take place in supporter-based CSOs rather than membership CSOs. If confirmed, this apparent shift from member-based to supporter-based CSOs suggests a challenge for their potential impact on global democratisation. This challenge is made all the greater by the low active participation of most members in membership-based CSOs.

North-South tensions are a third critical area of CSO impact. How equal are the relationships between Northern and Southern parts of the same organisation or between Northern and Southern organisations working in partnership or within coalitions? Vianna (2000) describes a risk of 'neo-imperialism' in the tendency of some Northern NGOs to determine the agendas of Southern NGOs, due to their privileged access to centres of power and resources (see also Chapter 2). Similarly, Hudson (2000) and Lister (2001) suggest that Northern NGOs claim legitimacy for 'representing' Southern NGOs and tend to speak on behalf of Southern CSOs without proper consultation, with partnership being little more than rhetoric in practice. Indeed, for Lewis (2001) partnership often becomes a vehicle for 'one way' influence in exchange for resources. Likewise, advocacy coalitions see power not equally distributed, and Northern members have typically greater voice and influence (see Princen and Finger 1994; Vianna 2000). In this respect, is the reality of North-South relations among CSOs best described as hierarchy or partnership?

Within global CSOs, the distribution of power between headquarters and national affiliates is critical for addressing this question. On global issues, international secretariats tend to speak on behalf of national affiliates, which, in turn, influence organisational decision-making at the international level. In formal CSOs, two basic forms emerged: the 'global democracy' model and the 'global federation' model, each with different implications for internal democracy and North-South relations.

The 'global democracy' form, used for example in Amnesty International, gives equal voice to individual members. But because most global CSO members reside in the North, in particular Europe (Anheier, Glasius, and Kaldor 2001), the principle of 'one individual member, one vote' can lead to an over-representation of the North at the global level. By contrast, the 'global federation' form gives representation on a 'one country section, one vote' basis. This form is used for example by FoE. It can give greater weight to Southern voices and help to address internally some North-South power imbalances. However, a country representation means that countries with fewer members (normally Southern) have the same voting power as countries with more members (normally Northern). As a result, individual members from the South have greater power than members in the North, an imbalance politically made more sensitive by the reliance of most CSOs on funds provided by Northern sections.

It appears that global civil society is incapable of overcoming global power inequalities such as the North-South difference within conventional forms. It is here that we can expect innovation and new form developments to take place over the next few years. Much of this experimentation will be aided by the factors mentioned above, in particular lower communication costs. Some innovations are already happening, such as split headquarter functions, ring structure, and Southern majorities on boards that force CSOs out of established forms and introduce new structures and elements to address North-South power differentials.

> Organisational form variety is essential for the sustainability of the infrastructure of global civil society, as it provides an insurance against environmental changes that can threaten some parts of the infrastructure

Concluding Comments

Underlying our discussion of organisational forms in global civil society is the realisation that being global is different. Being global is more than an increase in scale of national work. It is qualitatively different from being national. Being global is different because there are fewer 'tested and proven' forms available for working globally than is the case for national and transnational CSOs.

The absence of an international legal framework, mixed messages about resource dependencies, and unresolved issues of internal democracy and accountability to multiple stakeholders may sooner or later drive CSOs to seek alternative forms at global level. Mimetic isomorphism resulting from increased competition for scarce funding may be encouraging global CSOs to be more like transnational corporations and less like international state agencies modelled on some modernised version of the UN system. There is some support for this hypothesis. Over a decade ago, Korten (1990) argued that many NGOs were simply 'public sector contractors' behaving like bureaucratic businesses that work for government. More recently, Dichter (1999: 52) argued that many NGOs 'have taken on aspects of the current commercial zeitgeist', while Edwards (1999: 263) claimed that there is a trend 'among NGOs everywhere to internalise market values and dilute the links to a social base'. *The Economist* (29 January 2000: 25–8) made a similar observation and suggested that 'NGOs are also looking more and more like businesses' as they get larger. Clearly, this trend, if true, will have wide-ranging implications for global civil society.

Donors play an important role in this trend. In terms of isomorphism, donors can evaluate CSOs on their efficiency and promote the adoption of best practices. In terms of diversity and innovation, donors can evaluate the innovativeness of different funding proposals and provide 'seed' funding for pilot projects. Donors can also create more flexible systems so that a greater variety of organisations can benefit from funding. Unfortunately, it appears that, so far, official donor agencies continue to emphasise cost-efficiency rather than innovation (Riddell 1999). At least for development NGOs, this preference has promoted isomorphic tendencies in organisational form (e.g., federation), objectives (e.g., self-help), and operations (e.g., logical framework evaluation). While this trend can increase efficiency and even impact effectiveness, it can also signal wide co-option and vulnerability once funding preferences shift.

How can global CSOs escape these pressures, which are likely to strengthen with increased competition? One approach, as suggested above, would be for global CSOs to become in fact socially responsible businesses or modernised quasi-state agencies. This would solve some of the democratic and accountability dilemmas CSOs face, and it may also contribute to resource stability. It would not, however, make them necessarily more effective and innovative organisations, and other stakeholders and influences would take hold. In any case, they would be more part of global capitalism and governance systems, and likely to lose the special functions civil society institutions have by providing the (often fragile) counterbalance to the dominating forces of state and market.

> Because being global is new and uncertain, global civil society must experiment with different forms and explore different models of governance, accountability, decision-making, and resource generation and distribution

Indeed, one suggestion, the world-polity/culture theory (Meyer *et al.* 1997), sees INGOs very much in the light of what could be called a 'precursor organisation' for global, i.e. Western, capitalism and forms of governance. According to Boli (2000: 3), INGOs are 'the primary organisational form through which transnational (world) culture is developed, elaborated, and propagated in the world polity', paving the way for other organisational forms to take hold. If this theory is right, the organisational form and dynamics of global civil society will have vast implications for a globalising world.

A different approach would be to seek innovative ways for CSOs to develop from within existing forms. Their ability to do so will rest partly on attracting resources with fewer strings attached (see Edwards and Hulme 1995; Fowler 1997). But it will also rest on CSOs' ability to seek innovative governance models that break away from the constraints inherent in conventional forms. They must also be able to 'practice what they preach' and seek greater internal democracy and equality in North-South relations. In other words, because being global is new and uncertain, global civil society must experiment with different forms and explore different models of governance, accountability, decision-making, and resource generation and distribution. Importantly, donors should provide room for such

experimentation, allowing some experiments to go wrong so that innovative breakthroughs can occur.

We have described some such past innovations (bureaucracy, multi-divisional form, network organisation) and some of the forces behind form developments (carrying capacity, isomorphism). We can only speculate what the future form of global civil society infrastructure will look like. Yet, whatever the contours of CSOs in 30 or 50 years' time will be, they are likely to be as different from conventional NGOs today as the industrial giants of the early twentieth century are from present transnational network organisations. Future CSOs will also most likely be as different from each other as the European Union is from the League of Nations. These are stark contrasts, we admit, but we nonetheless suggest that epochal transformations are beginning to take hold. Having expanded both within and outside existing forms, future increases in CSO numbers are likely to lead to an innovation push in the way global civil society is organised.

We thank John Clark, Marlies Glasius, and those who attended presentations of earlier versions of this chapter at LSE for their valuable comments, and Nadia McLaren and Anthony Judge for data access.

References

Aldrich, H. (1999). *Organizations Evolving*. London, Thousand Oaks: Sage.

Amnesty International. http://www.amnesty.org

Anheier, H. (ed.) (1999). *When Things go Wrong: Failures, Bankruptcies, and Breakdowns in Organizations*. Thousand Oaks, CA: Sage.

Anheier, H. K. (2000). *Managing Nonprofit Organisations: Towards a New Approach* (Civil Society Working Paper 1). London: Centre for Civil Society, London School of Economics.

— (2002). 'The Third Sector in Europe: Five Theses' (Global Civil Society Working Paper 12). London: Centre for Civil Society, London School of Economics.

— and List, R. (2000). *Cross-border Philanthropy: An Exploratory Study of International Giving in the United Kingdom, United States, Germany and Japan.* West Malling, Kent: Charities Aid Foundation; London: Centre for Civil Society, London School of Economics.

—, Glasius, M., and Kaldor, M. (2001). 'Introducing Global Civil Society', in Helmut Anheier, Marlies Glasius, and Mary Kaldor (eds), *Global Civil Society 2001.* Oxford: Oxford University Press.

— and Themudo, N. (2002). 'On the Governance and Management of International Membership Organisations' (Global Civil Society Working Paper). London: Centre for Civil Society, London School of Economics.

Bartlett, C.A. and Ghoshal, S. (1997) 'The Transnational Organization', in Derek S. Pugh (ed.), *Organization Theory: Selected Readings* (4th edn). London: Penguin Books.

Bauck, A. (2001). 'Oxfam and Debt Relief Advocacy'. Case study written at the Daniel J. Evans School of Public Affairs, Washington University, Seattle.

Boggs, C. (2001). 'Economic Globalization and Political Atrophy'. *Democracy and Nature*, 7: 303–16.

Boli, J. (2001). 'Thoughts on Transnational Civil Society'. Document prepared for the conference on Transnational Civil Society, Hauser Center, Harvard University, 22–4 January.

Care UK. http://www.careinternational.org.uk/aboutcare.html

Castells, M. (1996). *The Rise of the Network Society.* Oxford: Blackwell.

Chandler, A. (1962). *Strategy and Structure: Chapters in the History of American Industrial Enterprise.* Cambridge, MA: MIT Press.

— (1990). *Scale and Scope: The Dynamics of Industrial Capitalism.* Cambridge, MA: Harvard University Press.

Clark, J. (2001). 'Trans-national Civil Society: Issues of Governance and Organisation'. Issues paper prepared as background for a seminar on Transnational Civil Society, London School of Economics, 1–2 June.

— and Themudo, N. (forthcoming). 'Linking the Web and the Street: Internet-based "Dot-causes" and the "Anti-globalisation" Movement' (Global Civil Society Working Paper). London: Centre for Civil Society, London School of Economics.

Dawson, S. (1996). *Analysing Organisations.* London: Macmillan.

Day, J. and J. Wendler (1998). 'The New Economics of Organisation'. *McKinsey Quarterly*, No. 1: 4–18.

—, Mang, P., Richter, A., and Roberts, J. (2001). 'The Innovative Organisation: Why New Ventures Need More than a Room of their Own'. *McKinsey Quarterly*, No. 2: 20–31.

Diamond, L. (ed.) (1997). *Consolidating the Third Wave Democracies: Themes and Perspectives.* Baltimore, MD: Johns Hopkins University Press.

Dichter, T. (1999) 'Globalisation and its Effect on NGOs: Efflorescence or a Blurring of Roles and Relevance?', *Nonprofit and Voluntary Sector Quarterly*, 28/4 Supplement: 38–58.

Dicken, P. (1998). *Global Shift: Transforming the Global Economy.* London: Chapman.

Edwards, M. (1999). 'Legitimacy and Values in NGOs and Voluntary Organizations: Some Sceptical Thoughts', in D. J. Lewis (ed.), *International Perspectives on Voluntary Action: Reshaping the Third Sector.* London: Earthscan.

— and Hulme, D. (eds) (1995). *Beyond the Magic Bullet: NGO Performance and Accountability in the Post-Cold War World.* London: Macmillan.

—, —, and Wallace, T. (1999). 'NGOs in a Global Future: Marrying Local Delivery to Worldwide Leverage'. *Public Administration and Development*, 19: 136–77.

Ferlie, E. (ed.) (1996). *The New Public Management in Action.* Oxford: Oxford University Press.

Foreman, K. (1999). 'Evolving Global Structures and the Challenges Facing International Relief and Development Organizations'. *Nonprofit and Voluntary Sector Quarterly*, 28/4 Supplement: 178–97.

Fowler, A (1997). *Striking a Balance: A Guide to Enhancing the Effectiveness of NGOs in International Development.* London: Earthscan.

Friends of the Earth. http://www.foei.org

GreenPeace Spain. http://www.greenpeace.es

Greiner, L. (1972). 'Evolution and Revolution as Organizations Grow'. *Harvard Business Review*, 50: 37–46.

Grimond, J. (2002). 'Civil Society', in The Economist, *World in 2002.* London: The Economist.

Handy, C. (1988). *Managing Voluntary Organisations.* Harmondsworth: Penguin.

— (1989). *The Age of Paradox.* Boston: Harvard Business School Press.

Hannan, M. and Freeman, J. (1989). *Organizational Ecology.* Cambridge, MA: Harvard University Press.

Hansmann, H. (1996). *The Ownership of Enterprise.* London: The Belknap Press of Harvard University Press.

Hatch, M. J. (1997). *Organisation Theory: Modern, Symbolic and Postmodern Perspectives*. Oxford: Oxford University Press.

Held, D., McGrew, A., Goldblatt, D., and Perraton, J. (1999). *Global Transformations: Politics, Economics and Culture*. Cambridge: Polity Press.

Hirschman, A. (1982). *Shifting Involvements: Private Interest and Public Action*. Princeton, NJ: Princeton University Press.

Hudson, A. (2000). 'Making the Connection: Legitimacy Claims, Legitimacy Chains and Northern NGOs' International Advocacy', in D. J. Lewis and T. Wallace (eds), *New Roles and Relevance: Development NGOs and the Challenge of Change*. Hartford: Kumarian.

Hudson, B.A. and Bielefeld, W. (1997). 'Structures of Multinational Nonprofit Organisations'. *Nonprofit Management and Leadership*, 8/1: 31–49.

Inglehart, R. and Abramson, P. (1995). *Value Change in Global Perspective*. Ann Arbor: University of Michigan Press.

IUCN (World Conservation Union). http://www.iucn.org/2000/about/content/index.html

Jubilee 2000 UK. http://www.jubilee2000uk.org

Kaul, I., Grunberg, I., and Stern, M. (eds) (1999). *Global Public Goods: International Cooperation in the 21st Century*. Oxford: Oxford University Press.

Keane, J. (2001). 'Global Civil Society?', in Helmut Anheier, Marlies Glasius, and Mary Kaldor (eds), *Global Civil Society 2001*. Oxford: Oxford University Press.

Keck, M. and Sikkink, K. (1998). *Activists Beyond Borders: Advocacy Networks in International Politics*. Ithaca: Cornell University Press.

Korten, D. (1990). *Getting to the 21st Century: Voluntary Action and the Global Agenda*. West Hartford, CT: Kumarian Press.

Kriesberg, L. (1997). 'Social Movements and Global Transformation', in J. Smith, C. Chatfield, and R. Pagnucco (eds), *Transnational Social Movements and Global Politics: Solidarity Beyond the State*. Syracuse, NY: Syracuse University Press.

Lansey, J. (1997). 'Membership Participation and Ideology in Large Voluntary Organisations: The Case of the National Trust'. *Voluntas*, 7: 221–40.

Lewis, D. J. (1998). 'Nonprofit Organisations, Business and the Management of Ambiguity: Case Studies of "Fair Trade" from Nepal and Bangladesh'. *Nonprofit Management and Leadership*, 9/2: 135–52.

— (2001). *The Management of Non-governmental Development Organisations: An Introduction*. London: Routledge.

Lindenberg, M. (1999). 'Declining State Capacity, Voluntarism, and the Globalization of the Not-for-profit Sector'. *Nonprofit and Voluntary Sector Quarterly*, 28/4 Supplement: 147–67.

— and Dobel, J. P. (1999). 'The Challenges of Globalization for Northern International Relief and Development NGOs'. *Nonprofit and Voluntary Sector Quarterly*, 28/4 Supplement: 2–24.

— and Bryant, C. (2001). *Going Global: Transforming Relief and Development NGOs*. Bloomfield, CT: Kumarian Press.

Linz, J. J. and Stepan, A. (1996). *Problems of Democratic Transition and Consolidation*. Baltimore, MD: Johns Hopkins University Press.

Lister, S. (2001). 'The Consultation Practice of Northern NGOs: A Study of British Organizations in Guatemala'. *Journal of International Development*, 3: 1071–82.

Meyer, J., Boli, J., Thomas, G., and Ramirez, F. O. (1997). 'World Society and the Nation State'. *American Journal of Sociology*, 103: 144–81.

Micklethwait, J. and Wooldridge, A. (1996). *The Witch Doctors: What The Management Gurus Are Saying, Why it Matters and How to Make Sense of it*. London: Heinemann.

Naughton, J. (2001). 'Contested Space: The Internet and Global Civil Society' in Helmut Anheier, Marlies Glasius, and Mary Kaldor (eds), *Global Civil Society 2001*. Oxford: Oxford University Press.

ODI (Overseas Development Institute) (1995). 'NGOs and Official Donors' (Briefing Paper No. 4). London: ODI.

Perrow, C. (1986). *Complex Organizations: A Critical Essay* (3rd edn). London: McGraw-Hill.

Pfeffer, J. and Salancik, G. (1978). *The External Control of Organizations: A Resource Dependence Perspective*. London: Harper & Row.

Powell, W. (1990). 'Neither Market nor Hierarchy: Network Forms of Organization'. *Research in Organizational Behaviour*, 12: 295–336.

— and DiMaggio, P. (1991). 'The Iron Cage Revisited: Institutional Isomorphism and Collective Rationality in Organisational Fields', in W.W. Powell and P. DiMaggio (eds), *The New Institutionalism in Organisational Analysis*. Chicago: Chicago University Press.

Princen, T. and Finger, M. (1994). *Environmental NGOs in World Politics: Linking the Global and the Local*. London: Routledge.

Pugh, Derek S. (ed.) (1997). *Organization Theory: Selected Readings* (4th edn). London: Penguin Books.

Putnam, Robert D. (1995). 'Bowling Alone: America's Declining Social Capital'. *Journal of Democracy*, 6: 65–78.

Riddell, R. (1999). 'Evaluation and Effectiveness in NGOs', in D. Lewis (ed.), *International Perspectives on Voluntary Action: Reshaping the Third Sector*. London: Earthscan.

Romanelli, E. (1991). 'The Evolution of New Organizational Forms'. *Annual Review of Sociology*, 17: 79–103.

Salamon, L., Anheier, H., List, R., Toepler, S., and Sokolowski, W. (eds) (1999). *Global Civil Society: Dimensions of the Nonprofit Sector*. Baltimore, MD: Institute for Policy Studies, Johns Hopkins University.

Salm, J. (1999). 'Coping with Globalization: A Profile of the Northern NGO Sector'. *Nonprofit and Voluntary Sector Quarterly*, 28/4 Supplement: 87–103.

Scott, W. R. (1998). *Organizations: Rational, Natural, and Open Systems* (4th edn). Upper Saddle River, NJ: Prentice Hall.

Selle, P. and Strømsnes, K. (1998). 'Organised Environmentalists: Democracy as a Key Value'. *Voluntas*, 9: 319–43.

Smith, J. (1997). 'Characteristics of the Modern Transnational Social Movement Sector', in J. Smith, C. Chatfield, and R. Pagnucco (eds), *Transnational Social Movements and Global Politics: Solidarity Beyond the State*. Syracuse, NY: Syracuse University Press.

Smith, S.R. and Lipsky, M. (1993). *Nonprofits for Hire: The Welfare State in the Age of Contracting*. Cambridge: Harvard University Press.

Subversive Enterprises International. http://www.geocities.com/Heartland/2484/intro.htm

Tarrow, S. (2001). 'Transnational Politics: Contention and Institutions in International Politics'. *Annual Review of Political Science*, 4: 1–20.

Thompson, G. (ed.) (1991). *Markets, Hierarchies and Networks: The Coordination of Social Life*. London: Sage.

Tuckman, H. (1998). 'Competition, Commercialism, and the Evolution of Nonprofit Organization Structures' in B. Weisbrod (ed.), *To Profit or Not to Profit: The Commercial Transformation of the Nonprofit Sector*. Cambridge; New York: Cambridge University Press.

UIA (Union of International Associations). http://www.uia.org/uiadocs/orgtyped.htm

Uphoff, N. (1995) 'Why NGOs Are Not a Third Sector: A Sectoral Analysis with Some Thoughts on Accountability, Sustainability and Evaluation', in M. Edwards and D. Hulme (eds), *Beyond the Magic Bullet: NGO Performance and Accountability in the Post-Cold War World*. London: Earthscan.

Vianna, A. (2000). 'The Work of Brazilian NGOs on the International Level'. Discussion paper prepared for the seminar 'Transnational Civil Society', London School of Economics, 1–2 June.

Wainwright, H. (2001). Paper presented at the seminar 'Meaning and Value of the Concept of Civil Society in Different Cultural Contexts', London School of Economics, 28–9 September.

Warkentin, C. (2001). *Reshaping World Politics: NGOs, the Internet, and Global Civil Society*. Lanham, MD: Rowman & Littlefield Publishers.

Weber, M. ([1924] 1997) 'Bureaucracy', in Derek S. Pugh (ed.), *Organization Theory: Selected Readings* (4th edn). London: Penguin Books.

Weisbrod, B. (ed.) (1998). *To Profit or Not to Profit: The Commercial Transformation of the Nonprofit Sector*. Cambridge; New York: Cambridge University Press.

Williamson, O. E. (1985). *The Economic Institutions of Capitalism: Firms, Markets, Relational Contracting*. London: Collier Macmillan.

WRM (World Rainforest Movement). http://www.wrm.org.uy

WSF (World Social Forum). http://www.forumsocialmundial.org.br/eng/index.asp

Yeo, S. (2002). *Membership and Mutualism* (Report of the Centre for Civil Society). London: London School of Economics.

Young. D. (1992). 'Organizing Principles for International Advocacy Associations'. *Voluntas*, 3: 1–28.

—, Koenig, B.L., Najam, A., and Fisher, J. (1999). 'Strategy and Structure in Managing Global Associations'. *Voluntas*, 10: 323–43.

Zadek, S. and Gatwood, M. (1995). 'Social Auditing or Bust?', in M. Edwards and D. Hulme (eds), *Beyond the Magic Bullet: NGO Performance and Accountability in the Post-Cold War World*. London: Earthscan.

Chapter 9

GLOBAL CITIES AND DIASPORIC NETWORKS: MICROSITES IN GLOBAL CIVIL SOCIETY

Saskia Sassen

Globalisation and the international human rights regime have contributed to the creation of operational and legal openings for non-state actors to enter international arenas that were once the exclusive domain of national states. Various, often as yet very minor, developments signal that the state is no longer the exclusive subject of international law or the only actor in international relations. Other actors—from NGOs and indigenous peoples to immigrants and refugees who become subjects of adjudication in human rights decisions—are increasingly emerging as subjects of international law and actors in international relations. That is to say, these non-state actors can gain visibility in international fora as individuals and as collectivities, emerging from the invisibility of aggregate membership in a nation-state exclusively represented by the sovereign.

One way of interpreting this is in terms of an incipient unbundling of the exclusive authority over territory and people that we have long associated with the national state. The most strategic instantiation of this unbundling is probably the global city, which operates as a partly denationalised platform for global capital and, at the same time, is emerging as a key site for the most astounding mix of people from all over the world. The growing intensity of transactions among major cities is creating a strategic cross-border geography that partly bypasses national states. The new network technologies further strengthen these transactions, whether they are electronic transfers of specialised services among firms or Internet-based communications among the members of diasporas and interest groups.

Do these developments contribute to the expansion of a global civil society? These cities and the new strategic geographies that connect them and bypass national states can be seen as constituting part of the infrastructure for global civil society. They do so from the ground up, through multiple microsites and microtransactions. Among them are a variety of organisations focused on trans-boundary issues concerning immigration, asylum, international women's agendas, anti-globalisation struggles, and many others. While these are not necessarily urban in their orientation or genesis, they tend to converge in cities. The new network technologies, especially the Internet, ironically have strengthened the urban map of these trans-boundary networks. It does not have to be that way, but at this time cities and the networks that bind them function as an anchor and an enabler of cross-border struggles. These same developments and conditions also facilitate the internationalising of terrorist and trafficking networks; it is not clear how these fit into global civil society.

Global cities are, then, thick enabling environments for these types of activities, even though the networks themselves are not urban per se. In this regard, these cities help people experience themselves as part of global non-state networks as they live their daily lives. They enact global civil society in the micro-spaces of daily life rather than on some putative global stage.

The Ascendancy of Sub- and Transnational Spaces and Actors

The key nexus in this configuration is that the weakening of the exclusive formal authority of states over national territory facilitates the ascendancy of sub- and transnational spaces and actors in politico-civic processes. These are spaces that tended to be confined to the national domain or that have evolved as novel types in the context of globalisation and digitisation. This loss of power at the national level produces the possibility of new forms of power and politics at the sub-national level and at the supra-national level. The national as container of social process and power is cracked (P. Taylor 2000; Sachar 1990). This cracked casing opens up a geography of politics and civics that links subnational spaces. Cities are foremost in this new geography.

The density of political and civic cultures in large cities localises global civil society in people's lives. We can think of these as multiple localisations of civil society that are global in that they are part of global circuits and trans-boundary networks .

The organisational side of the global economy materialises in a worldwide grid of strategic places, uppermost among which are major international business and financial centres. We can think of this global grid as constituting a new economic geography of centrality, one that cuts across national boundaries and increasingly across the old North-South divide. It has emerged as a transnational space for the formation of new claims by global capital but also by other types of actors. The most powerful of these new geographies of centrality at the inter-urban level bind the major international financial and business centres: New York, London, Tokyo, Paris, Frankfurt, Zurich, Amsterdam, Los Angeles, Sydney, Hong Kong, among others. But this geography now also includes cities such as Sao Paulo, Shanghai, Bangkok, Taipei, and Mexico City. The intensity of transactions among these cities, particularly through the financial markets, transactions in services, and investment, has increased sharply, and so have the orders of magnitude involved.

Economic globalisation and telecommunications have contributed to produce a space for the urban which pivots on de-territorialised cross-border networks and territorial locations with massive concentrations of resources. This is not a completely new feature. Over the centuries cities have been at the intersection of processes with supra-urban and even intercontinental scaling. Ancient Athens and Rome, the cities of the Hanseatic League, Genoa, Venice, Baghdad, Cairo, Istanbul, each has been at the crossroads of major dynamics in their time (Braudel 1984). What is different today is the coexistence of multiple networks and the intensity, complexity, and global span of these networks. Another marking feature of the contemporary period, especially when it comes to the economy, is the extent to which significant portions of economies are now de-materialised and digitised and hence can travel at great speeds through these networks. Also new is the growing use of digital networks by a broad range of often resource-poor organisations to pursue a variety of cross-border initiatives. All of this has increased the number of cities that are part of cross-border networks operating on often vast geographic scales. Under these conditions, much of what we experience and represent as the local level turns out to be a micro-environment with global span.

The new urban spatiality thus produced is partial in a double sense: it accounts for only part of what happens in cities and what cities are about, and it inhabits only part of what we might think of as the space of the city, whether this be understood in terms as diverse as those of a city's administrative boundaries or in the sense of the public life of a city's people. But it is nonetheless one way in which cities can become part of the live infrastructure of global civil society.

The space constituted by the worldwide grid of global cities, a space with new economic and political potentialities, is perhaps one of the most strategic spaces for the formation of transnational identities and communities. This is a space that is both place-centred in that it is embedded in particular and strategic cities, and trans-territorial because it connects sites that are not geographically proximate yet are intensely linked to each other. It is not only the transmigration of capital that takes place in this global grid but also that of people, both rich—i.e., the new transnational professional workforce—and poor—i.e., most migrant workers; and it is a space for the transmigration of cultural forms, for the re-territorialisation of 'local' subcultures. An important question is whether it is also a space for a new politics, one going beyond the politics of culture and identity while likely to remain at least partly embedded in it. One of the most radical forms assumed today by the linkage of people to territory is the loosening of identities from their traditional sources, such as the nation or the village. This unmooring in the process of identity formation engenders new notions of community of membership and of entitlement.

Immigration is one major process through which a new transnational political economy is being constituted, one which is largely embedded in major cities in so far as most immigrants are concentrated in

> Global cities and the new strategic geographies that connect them and bypass national states can be seen as constituting part of the infrastructure for global civil society

major cities. It is, on my reading, one of the constitutive processes of globalisation today, even though not recognised or represented as such in mainstream accounts of the global economy. It becomes, in more and more cities, part of a massive demographic transition towards a growing presence of women, native minorities, and immigrants in the population.

Global capital and immigrants are two major instances of transnationalised actors that have cross-border unifying properties internally and find themselves in conflict with each other inside global cities. The leading sectors of corporate capital are now global in their organisation and operations. And many of the disadvantaged workers in global cities are women, immigrants, people of colour—men and women whose sense of membership is not necessarily adequately captured in terms of the national, and indeed often evince cross-border solidarities around issues of substance. Both types of actors find in the global city a strategic site for their economic and political operations. We see here an interesting correspondence between great concentrations of corporate power and large concentrations of 'others'.

In brief, large cities in both the global South and the global North are the terrain where a multiplicity of globalisation processes assume concrete, localised forms. A focus on cities allows us to capture, not only the upper, but also the lower circuits of globalisation. These localised forms are, in good part, what globalisation is about. Further, the thickening transactions that bind cities across borders signal the possibility of a new politics of traditionally disadvantaged actors operating in this new transnational economic geography. This is a politics that arises out of actual participation by workers in the global economy, but under conditions of disadvantage and lack of recognition, whether as factory workers in export-processing zones or as cleaners on Wall Street.

> The space constituted by the worldwide grid of global cities, a space with new economic and political potentialities, is perhaps one of the most strategic spaces for the formation of transnational identities and communities

Peoples' Networks: Micro-Politics For and Against Global Civil Society

The cross-border network of global cities is a space where we are seeing the formation of new types of 'global' politics of place which contest corporate globalisation. The demonstrations by the anti-globalisation movement signal the potential for developing a politics centred on places understood as locations on global networks. This is a place-specific politics with a global span. It is a type of political work deeply embedded in people's actions and activities but made possible partly by the existence of global digital linkages. These are mostly organisations operating through networks of cities and involving informal political actors, that is, actors who are not necessarily engaging in politics as citizens narrowly defined, where voting is the most formalised type of citizen politics. Among such informal political actors are women who engage in political struggles in their condition as mothers, anti-globalisation activists who go to a foreign country as tourists but to do citizen politics, undocumented immigrants who join protests against police brutality.

We can identify at least four specific types of these politics in terms of their objectives or focus: anti-capitalism, women, migrants, and anti-trafficking. One of their characteristics, especially of the first three types, is that they engage in 'non-cosmopolitan' forms of global politics. Partly enabled by the Internet, activists can develop global networks for circulating not only information (about environmental, housing, political issues, etc.) but also political work and strategies. Yet they remain grounded in very specific issues and are often focused on their localities even as they operate as part of global networks. There are many examples of such a new type of cross-border political work. For instance, the Society for Promotion of Area Resource Centres (SPARC; see Table 9.4), started by and centred on women, began as an effort to organise slum dwellers in Bombay to get housing. Now it has a network of such groups throughout Asia and some cities in Latin America and Africa. This is one of the key forms of critical politics

Name	Description	Website address
50 Years Is Enough	50 Years Is Enough was founded in 1994, the year of the 50th anniversary of the Bretton Woods conference, by a group of US organisations . '50 Years Is Enough' was chosen as the slogan to express the belief that the type of development that the World Bank and the IMF promote should not be allowed to continue. The 50 Years Is Enough Network aims at increasing the awareness of the US public, the media, and policy-makers of change at the Bretton Woods institutions. It aims at the same time to limit the power of these institutions and to promote a public exploration of new structures that could deliver relevant and appropriate assistance.	http://www.50years.org/
Third World Network	The Third World Network(TWN) is an independent non-profit international network of organisations and individuals involved in issues relating to development, the Third World, and North-South issues. Its objectives are to conduct research on economic, social, and environmental issues pertaining to the South; to publish books and magazines; to organise and participate in seminars; and to provide a platform representing Southern interests and perspectives at international fora such as the UN conferences and processes. The TWN's international secretariat is based in Penang, Malaysia. It has offices in Delhi, India; Montevideo, Uruguay (for South America); Geneva; London; and Accra, Ghana. The Third World Network has affiliated organisations in several Third World countries, including India, the Philippines, Thailand, Brazil, Bangladesh, Malaysia, Peru, Ethiopia, Uruguay, Mexico, Ghana, South Africa, and Senegal. It also cooperates with several organisations in the North.	http://www.twnside.org.sg/
International Third Position	The International Third Position is defined as a world view which rejects and transcends the wisdom of the modern world so as to become the political creed of the twenty-first century. The Third Position views international finance as one of the greatest evils of the modern world, and thus hostile to its own programme. It supports the idea of popular rule, the preservation of the environment, the replacement of the banking system and usury by a sound money system, an alternative to both socialism and capitalism based on the widespread diffusion of property, and supports a worldwide revolution. It is organised all over the world, bringing together like-minded organisations, groups, and individuals who share its aims.	http://dspace.dial.pipex.com/third-position/

that the Internet can make possible: a politics of the local with a big difference in that these are localities connected with each other across a region, a country, or the world. Although the network is global, this does not mean that it all has to happen at the global level.

Table 9.4 contains a list of organisations concerned with women's issues and often very local concerns but which are nonetheless part of global networks.

I will also focus on two very different types of networks which have, however, similarly been enabled by the technical infrastructure of globalisation. They are organised terrorist networks and trafficking organisations.

Anti-capitalist organisations

Tables 9.1 and 9.2 briefly present a few organisations dedicated to fight, criticise, and expose various aspects of globalisation and capitalism generally. Most of them have been formed only recently. Table 9.1 contains three particular examples, and Table 9.2 a more general list of these organisations. Together they show the variety of issues, some broad and some very narrow, that are bringing people together in struggles and work against global corporate capital and other sources of social injustice. This has clearly emerged as an important anchor for cross-border peoples' networks. Many of these organisations are or might become micro-elements of global civil society.

Women

Women have become increasingly active in this world of cross-border efforts. This has often meant the potential transformation of a whole range of 'local' conditions or domestic institutional domains—such as the household, the community, or the neighbourhood, where women find themselves confined to domestic roles—into political spaces. Women can emerge as political and civic subjects without having to step out of these domestic worlds. From being lived or experienced as non-political or domestic, these places are transformed into micro-environments with global span. An example of this is MADRE, an international organisation presented in Table 9.3. In Table 9.4 we list a variety of organisations concerned with women.

> Life in global cities helps people experience themselves as part of global non-state networks. They enact global civil society in the micro-spaces of daily life rather than on some putative global stage

What I mean by the term 'micro-environment with global span' is that technical connectivity links even resource-poor organisations with other similar local entities in neighbourhoods and cities in other countries. A community of practice can emerge that creates multiple lateral, horizontal communications, collaborations, solidarities, supports. This can enable local political or non-political actors to enter into cross-border politics.

Migrants

There are a growing number of organisations addressing the issues of immigrants and asylum-seekers in a variety of countries (see Table 9.5).

The city is a far more concrete space for politics than the nation. It becomes a place where non-formal political actors can be part of the political scene in a way that is more difficult, though not impossible, at the national level. Nationally politics needs to run through existing formal systems, whether the electoral political system or the judiciary (taking state agencies to court). To do this you need to be a citizen. Non-formal political actors are thereby more easily rendered invisible in the space of national politics. The space of the city accommodates a broad range of political activities—squatting, demonstrations against police brutality, fighting for the rights of immigrants and the homeless—and issues—the politics of culture and identity, gay and lesbian and queer politics. Much of this becomes visible on the street. Much of urban politics is concrete, enacted by people rather than dependent on massive media technologies. Street-level politics make possible the formation of new types of political subjects that do not have to go through the formal political system.

It is in this sense that those who lack power and are 'unauthorised' (i.e. unauthorised immigrants, those who are disadvantaged, outsiders, discriminated minorities, can in global cities gain presence, vis-à-vis power and vis-à-vis each other (Sassen 1996: Ch. 1). A good example of this is the Europe-wide demonstrations of Kurds in response to the arrest of Öcalan: suddenly they were on the map not only as an oppressed minority but also as a diaspora in their

Table 9.2: More social justice networks – in brief

Name	Brief description	Web address
People's Global Action	A global instrument for communication and coordination against the global market.	http://www.nadir.org/nadir/initiativ/agp/
Development Gap	Research, resource, and networking organisation addressing structural adjustment and trade liberalisation issues.	http://www.developmentgap.org/
Jubilee South	A coalition of debt cancellation movements from across the global South.	http://www.jubileesouth.net/
A SEED	Targets the structural causes of the environment and development crisis, it campaigns against the international financial institutions and 'free' trade agreements.	http://www.aseed.net/
Corporate Watch	Monitors transnational corporations' social, ecological and economic practices.	http://www.corpwatch.org/
The American Federation of Labor-Congress of Industrial Organizations	Aims at bringing social and economic justice by enabling working people to have a voice on the job, in government, in the global economy, and in their communities. Since the late 1990s it has changed its position on immigrants and now seeks to organise them and to work across borders.	http://www.aflcio.org/home.htm
Continental Direct Action Network	Consists of autonomous US locals working to overcome corporate globalisation. Has the potential to go transnational.	http://cdan.org/
Alliance for Democracy	A movement to restore populist democracy over corporations. Has the potential to go transnational.	http://www.afd-online.org/
Global Exchange	Global Exchange is a research, education, and action centre dedicated to advocating and working for political, economic, and social justice on a global scale.	http://www.globalexchange.org/
International Forum on Globalization	An alliance of 60 leading activists to stimulate new thinking, joint activity, and public education in response to the global economy.	http://www.ifg.org/

Name	Brief description	Web address
JustAct	JustAct offers programmes that link students and youth in the US to organisations and grass-roots movements working for sustainable and self-reliant communities around the world.	http://www.justact.org/home/index.html
Project Underground	Carries out focused campaigns against abusive extractive resource activity.	http://www.moles.org/
Phase1	A radical left group of Switzerland engaged in the struggle against racism, sexism, and capitalism.	http://www.phase1.net/
Youthactivism organisation	Dedicated to the young women and men around the world taking action for a more just and democratic world.	http://www.youthactivism.org/
Student Environmental Action Coalition	Network of progressive orgs and individuals aimed at uprooting environmental injustices through action and education.	http://www.seac.org/
Seattle Youth Involvement Network	Promotes youth voice through civic involvement, leadership training, and decision-making.	http://www.seattleyouth.org/
WTO Watch	WTO Watch is a website on trade and globalisation.	http://www.wtowatch.org/
A-Infos	A project coordinated by an international collective of revolutionary anti-authoritarian, anti-capitalist activists, involved with class and believing in revolution as necessary to bring a new classless social order.	http://www.ainfos.ca/
World Bank Bonds Boycott	An international grass-roots campaign building political and financial pressure on the world.	http://www.econjustice.net/wbbb/who_we_are.htm
SEEN	Aimed at steering the financial investments of wealthy countries away from support for fossil fuels.	http://www.seen.org/pages/issues.shtml
La Lutta Media Collective	A group of activists, artists, educators, and professionals united to promote a greater level of social awareness.	http://www.lalutta.org

Table 9.3: MADRE and its sister organisations

Name	Description	Website address
MADRE	MADRE works to support women who are organising against attacks on their rights and resources. Since 1983, it has worked in partnership with community-based women's organisations in conflict areas worldwide to address issues of health, education, economic development, and other human rights. It provides resources and training for its sister organisations and works to empower people in the US to demand changes to unjust policies. It develops programmes to meet immediate needs in communities hurt by US policy and supports women's long-term struggles for social justice and human rights. MADRE's international human rights advocacy programme aims to make international law relevant and accountable to the people it is meant to serve. It brings women who work for social change at the community level into the process of creating and improving international law by providing the training and resources for them to advocate for their rights. It serves as a bridge between its sister organisations so that they can join forces on international campaigns and share ideas and strategies to strengthen their work for social justice in their home countries.	http://www.madre.org
K'inal Antzetik	In Chiapas, a cooperative of indigenous women weavers.	http://www.laneta.apc.org/kinal/
Q'ati't	In Guatemala, equips women maquila workers to document and combat human rights abuses in factories where they work.	
Wangky Luhpia	In Nicaragua, supports programmes combating violence against women, drug addiction, illiteracy, and malnutrition.	
Ibdaa	In the in Deheishe refugee camp in Palestine, enables children to develop the skills and political vision to build a future for themselves and their community.	http://www.dheisheh-ibdaa.net/
Benimpuhwe	An association of Rwandan women who pulled together in the wake of the genocide to support each other and to rebuild their lives.	

Table 9.4: More women's organisations – in brief

Name	Description	Website address
SPARC	The Society for Promotion of Area Resource Centres (SPARC) was registered as a society and trust in 1984. Since then, it has worked with the urban and rural poor, especially women, with the aim of helping them to organise themselves, develop skills, and create sustainable processes and institutions in order to participate in decisions which affect their lives. SPARC's philosophy is that a key element of such capacity building is learning from one's experiences and those of others. Thus, peer-based capacity building is a thread running through all of SPARC's activities. SPARC works closely with women's collectives. Savings and credit is frequently the entry point for these interactions. Though the amount of money circulated by these groups may be small, this activity allows women to extricate themselves from the clutches of exploitative moneylenders. SPARC's capacity- building work with these groups enables them to handle monetary transactions, analyse economic options, and prepare budgets	www.sparcindia.org
The Network of East-West Women (NEWW)	An international communication and resource network founded by women across the US and the former Yugoslavia	www.neww.org
The Association for Women Rights in Development	An international organisation committed to achieving gender equality	www.awid.org
Women Living Under Muslim Law	An international network providing support for all women whose lives are conditioned by laws and customs said to derive from Islam	www.wluml.org
Alternative Women in Development	A working group struggling to bring a feminist analysis to economic and social issues affecting women.	www.geocities.com/ altwid.org
The Global Fund For Women	An international network of women and men committed to a world of equality and social justice.	www.globalfundfor women.org
Women's Environ-ment and Development Organization	An international organisation working to increase women's visibility, roles, and leadership nationally, regionally, and internationally	www.wedo.org/
Women Human Rights Net	A partnership of women's human rights organisations around the world; provides links to organisations and explanations of systems and strategies for women's human rights work.	www.whrnet.org
Black Women's Website Against Racist Sexual Violence	A point of reference for information on black, ethnic minority, immigrant, migrant, and refugee women in Britain who have suffered rape, racist sexual assault, or other forms of violence and harassment, including women seeking asylum after being raped in their country of origin.	www.bwrap.dircon. co.uk/

Immigrant communities in many different parts of the world have formed home-town associations of various kinds over the last two centuries. But today we are seeing a very specific type of home-town association, one directly concerned with socio-economic development in its communities of origin and increasingly engaging both governmental and civic entities in sending and receiving countries in these projects. These home-town associations are becoming micro-level building blocks of global civil society.

In the particular case of the Mexican immigrant community in the US, home-town associations were formed already in the 1920s and 1930s; but there was little if anything in the way of development efforts. These were often a one-shot affair and then the association would disappear. In the 1960s a whole series of new associations were formed. This corresponded partly to a generational renewal and the increase of immigration. But it is particularly in the 1980s and 1990s that these associations grew stronger and proliferated. This is partly because there are now 3 million Mexican nationals settled permanently in the US.

But it is also partly because globalisation and the new types of transnationalisms that are emerging have created enabling environments for the types of projects these associations are launching.

Today more than 400 home-town clubs and associations of Mexican immigrants have been counted in the US. The largest single concentration of Mexican home-town associations in the US is in Los Angeles. The second largest is in Chicago, the particular focus here.

According to the Mexican Consulate of Chicago, there are seven federations of home towns organised according to state of origin. In Chicago, a total of 125 home-town clubs constitute these seven federations. There are several researchers working on these home-town associations in Chicago (Gzesh and Espinoza 1999; Pizarro 2001; Bada 2001). A growing number of these are working on infrastructure and development projects in their communities of origin, with several more probably uncounted, working quietly and unnoticed on small projects. This is a new development; there is no precedent in the Mexican community of such cross-border socio-economic development projects.

In their research on one particular federation of home towns, the Federation of Michoacan Clubs in Illinois, Gzesh and Espinoza (1999) made the following major findings.

1. The formation of Mexican home-town associations in the US is a grass-roots response to the stresses placed on communities undergoing rapid change in a globalising society. Mexicans from Michoacan residing in Illinois have an ethic of community responsibility that transcends national boundaries.
2. The 14 Mexican home-town associations which make up the Illinois Federation of Michoacan Clubs

own right, distinct from the Turks. This signals, for me, the possibility of a new type of politics centred in new types of political actors. It is not simply a matter of having or not having power. These are new hybrid bases from which to act. Tables 9.5 and 9.6 present organisations that are largely focused on a variety of issues of powerless groups and individuals. Some are global and others national. While powerless, these individuals and groups are acquiring presence in a broader politico-civic stage .

The case of the Federation of Michoacan Clubs in Illinois (USA) described in Box 9.1 illustrates this mix of dynamics. These are associations of often very poor immigrants which are beginning to engage in cross-border development projects and in that process are mobilising additional resources and political capital in both their countries of origin and of immigration.

Terrorists

But the city and the infrastructure for global networks also enable the operations of militant, criminal, and terrorists organisations. Globalisation, telecommunications, flexible loyalties and identities facilitate the formation of cross-border geographies for an increasing range of activities and communities of membership. The evidence that has come out since

depend entirely on volunteer work and voluntary contributions from their members. They have developed high standards of accountability and serve as a model of international, grass-roots philanthropy.

3. Mexican immigrants who form home-town associations are often from rural communities which have lost jobs and population during the economic restructuring of Mexico over the past two decades. The projects they undertake in their communities of origin are intended to mitigate those problems and preserve community life. Projects completed by contributions from Illinois-based Michoacan clubs include construction and repair of bridges, roads, schools, and churches, as well as water systems and recreational facilities in their communities of origin.

4. The Michocacan home-town associations in this study have developed along similar paths, which likely reflect a common experience among Mexican immigrant home-town associations across the US.

The organisational base for the Illinois Michoacanos has been the home-town-level association; immigrants from a single community of origin often work together or live in the same community. These associations often start as soccer clubs or organisations that raise money to support town-specific religious festivals in the home towns or in the US, and are run entirely by volunteer labour. With time, these associations have come to take on social and economic development projects in their communities of origin, working in conjunction with Mexican local, state, or federal government entities through various 'matching' programmes.

The home-town clubs eventually formed state-wide federations (i.e. all of the home-town clubs from Michoaca operating in Illinois) to increase their co-ordination, the scale of the projects which they can undertake, and their leverage with Mexican government officials. These are in turn seeking relationships with other entities in the US and Mexico which share common interests in community and job development in a globalising economy.

These developments in the immigrant community in the US parallel developments in Mexico, where there is now a local movement searching for alternative ways to promote development at the local level in a political system which has been historically highly centralised. Further, there is a concurrent development of new transnational politics in which migrant organisations along with other new political actors can play an important role in the construction of more democratic ways of promoting local development in Mexico.

Sources: the Mexico-US Advocates Network URL; Pizarro 2001; Bada 2001.

the terrorist attacks of 11 September 2001 have made it clear that the global financial system also served their purposes and that several major cities in Europe were key bases for the Al Qaeda network. Many militant organisations set up an international network of bases in various cities. London has been a key base for the Sri Lanka's Liberation Tigers of Tamil Eelam's international secretariat, and cities in France, Norway, Sweden, Canada, and the US are home to various of their centres of activity. Osama Bin Laden's AlQaida terrorist organisation is known to have established a support network in Great Britain, run through an office in London called the 'Advice and Reformation Committee', founded in July 1994, which is likely to have closed by now. (For more details Box 1.5 on page 24).

Traffickers

Another example of illegal networks is those concerned with human trafficking, a major source of income for criminal organisations, often mixed in with trafficking in drugs and arms. Large cities are crucial spaces both in the input (recruitment) and in the output (insertion of the trafficked person in the destination country labour market) process of trafficking. Cities such as Bangkok, Lagos, Moscow, Kiev, are key sites for the top organisers from where

Name	Description	Website address
The Platform of Filipino Migrant Organisations in Europe	The Platform of Filipino Migrant Organisations in Europe was established during a Europe-wide Conference in Athens in November 1997, marking 30 years of Filipino migration experience in Europe and celebrating the Centennial of Philippine independence. Its 120 delegates representing 75 organisations, national and Europe-wide networks from 14 countries in Europe, developed a Migrant Agenda which aims at equality of rights in Europe and for participative development in the Philippines. The Migrant Agenda is addressed to both the Philippine and European governments and envisages migrants themselves as key actors and participants in the development of Europe and the Philippines. Priority concerns of the Platform also include the sectors of women, youth, and second generation seafarers and the undocumented migrants.	http://www.platformweb.org/
Kalayaan	Kalayaan actively campaigns for basic workers' rights for overseas domestic workers of all nationalities and for an end to their current irregular immigration status in the UK and Europe. Established in 1987, Kalayaan is an independent coalition of people and organisations that includes migrant and immigrant support organisations, trade unions, law centres, and concerned individuals. Its work also addresses the practical needs of overseas domestic workers by providing initial advice to domestic workers about their immigration status, assisting overseas domestic workers in finding emergency housing, and running English classes. It also provides free legal advice sessions so that workers can make informed decisions and obtain their unpaid wages, passports, and other belongings from former employers.	http://ourworld.compuserve.com/homepages/kalayaan/home.htm
The Chinese Staff and Workers' Association	Founded in 1979, CSWA is the only organisation in New York that brings together Chinese immigrant workers of all trades. It began as a small mutual assistance group and has grown into an organisation of over 1,000 members, with centres in Manhattan and Brooklyn. It aims at guaranteeing the rights of its members in the workplace and in the communities where they live, to challenge the sweatshop system, to counter racism and sexism, and to work for social and economic. Most of its members are low-income Chinese workers-including garment, domestic, restaurant and construction workers, women and men, young and old, union and non-union. Together they have developed a model of organising that brings Chinese workers together to claim their voice in shaping the priorities, laws, policies, and values of the community in which they live, and beyond.	http://www.cswa.org

The Iranian Refugees' Alliance	A community-based organisation to promote the rights of Iranian refugees in the US.	www.irainc.org
The Ethiopian Community Development Council	Serves the community of immigrants and refugees through a wide range of activities locally and regionally in the Washington, DC, metropolitan area a well as nationally and in Ethiopia.	www.ecdcinternational.org
The African Service Committee	Provides health, legal, and social services to all Africans and Middle Eastern and French-speaking Caribbean immigrants and refugees in the US.	www.africanservices.org
The Refugee Resource Group	Protects and promotes rights of refugees, migrant workers in Pakistan.	www.rwcz.tripod.com
The African Service Committee	Provides resettlement assistance to new Africans arrivals throughout the New York metropolitan area.	http://www.africanservices.org/
The Filipino Youth in Europe	Operating out of The Netherlands, pursues the development of a Europe-wide network with youth and other organisations in the Philippines and Europe.	
The Commission for Filipino Migrant Workers (CFMW)	Works in partnership with the Filipino migrant community in Europe and aims to develop migrant empowerment and capacity building.	www.cfmw.org
Immigrant Workers Resource Center	Located in Massachusetts, the centre is aimed at building the capacity of all immigrant workers to defend and protect their rights in the workplace, in their unions, and in society.	http://www.communityworks.com/html/mgd/iwrc.html
Korean Immigrant Workers Advocates (KIWA)	A non-profit workers centre organising low-wage Korean immigrant workers of Los Angeles' Koreatown.	www.kiwa.org
Mission for Filipino Migrant Workers	Established in Hong Kong, the centre assists migrant workers who are in distress.	www.migrants.net
New York Asian Women's Center	Acts as a vehicle for placing the concerns of Asian women and children on the agenda in New York City.	www.nyawc.org
A Ta Turquie	Seeks to strengthen links between the Turkish community in France and the host society.	www.ataturquie.asso.fr

Table 9.6: Mail-order bride services	
Apex Visa Services	http://www.hervisa.com
Goodwife.com	http://www.goodwife.com
Mail-orders bride.com	http://www.tourrussia.com
Heart of Asia	http://www.heart-of-asia.org
A pretty woman	http://aprettywoman.com
Kiss.com	http://www.kiss.com
Romancium.com	http://www.romancium.com
Beautiful Russian Women Net	http://www.beautiful-russian-women.net
Mail Order Bride Guide	http://www.mailorderbrideguide.com
Mail Order Brides 4U	http://www.mailorderbrides4u.com

they are able to control the whole process up to its final destination, whereas the other categories of personnel, usually lower-level actors, enforcers, debt collectors, etc., operate in the major destination cities, New York, Los Angeles, Paris, London, etc.

In recent years other forms of 'trafficking', particularly in women and minors , have developed through the use of the Internet. Bride traffickers, for example, advertise through catalogues on the Internet operating mainly in the US (in particular New York, Los Angeles, Miami) as well as in the countries where women are recruited: the Philippines, the former Soviet Union, and south-east Asia. According to the International Organisation for Migration (1999), nearly all the mail-order bride services, especially those in the former Soviet Union, are under the control of organised crime networks (see Table 9.6).

Anti-trafficking

In turn, there has been an increase of counter-networks for anti-trafficking programmes in the areas of trafficking prevention, protection, and assistance for victims, and prosecution of traffickers (see Table 9.7). Much of this effort is centred in non-governmental organisations. Insofar as the numbers of peoples and organisations, the geographic scope and the institutional spread of these anti-trafficking efforts are all growing, they are becoming a significant component of global networks, both constitutive of and enabled by global civil society.

The Forging of New Political Subjects

The mix of focused activism and local/global networks represented by the organisations described in the preceding section creates conditions for the emergence of at least partly transnational identities. The possibility of identifying with larger communities of practice or membership can bring about the partial unmooring of identities referred to in the first section. While this does not necessarily neutralise attachments to a country or national cause, it does shift this attachment to include trans-local communities of practice and/or membership. This is a crucial building block for a global civil society that can incorporate the micro-practices and micro-objectives of people's daily lives as well as their political passions. The possibility of transnational identities emerging as a consequence of this thickness of micro-politics is important for strengthening global civil society; the risk of nationalisms and fundamentalisms is, clearly, present in these dynamics as well.

A growing number of scholars concerned with identity and solidarity posit the rise of transnational identities (Torres 1998; R. Cohen 1996; Franck 1992) and trans-local loyalties (Appadurai 1996: 165). This

Table 9.7: Anti-trafficking organisations

The Global Alliance Against Traffic in Women	Aimed at ensuring that the human rights of migrant women are respected and protected by authorities and agencies.	http://www.inet.co.th/org/gaatw
Anti Slavery International	Aimed at eliminating slavery in all its forms through awareness raising, lobbying of governments and international bodies and public campaigning.	http://www.antislavery.org
The Initiative Against Trafficking in Persons	Established as a project of the Women's Rights Advocacy Program (WRAP) to combat the global trade in persons.	http://www.hrlawgroup.org /site/programs/Traffic.htm
Asian Women's Human Rights Council	An Asia-wide network of women's human rights programmes, centres, organisations, and individuals with coordinating offices in Bangalore, India and Manila, Philippines.	http://www.awhrc.org
Coalition to Abolish Slavery and Trafficking (CAST)	Established to address the special needs of trafficked persons, and related issues, within the context of a network of non-profit human service providers.	http://www.trafficked-women.org
Fundacion ESPERANZA	An NGO in Colombia working on the issue of trafficking in the Latin American region. Their work mainly focuses on prevention, reintegration, and documentation.	http://www.fundacionesperanza.org.co
La Strada	La Strada group is an international programme which operates in the Netherlands, Poland, Bulgaria, Ukraine, and the Czech Republic. La Strada focuses on prevention of traffic in women, support of victims of traffic in women, influencing legislation, and disseminating information on the issue.	http://www.ecn.cz/lastrada

literature provides us with a broader conceptual landscape within which we can place the more specific types of organisations and practices that concern us here. Following Bosniak (2000: 482) we can find at least four forms taken by trans-nationalised identity claims.

One is the growth of European-wide citizenship said to be developing as part of the European Union (EU) integration process, and beyond the formal status of EU citizenship (Soysal 1994; Howe 1991; Isin 2000; Delanty 2000). Turner (2000) has posited a growing cultural awareness of a 'European identity'. This is clearly a different condition from that represented by the activist and diasporic networks described in the second section, which include some European-wide organisations but with a very specific, particularistic focus, notably immigration issues. In contrast, European identity entails a diffuse sense of belonging on a semi-continental level.

A second focus is on the affective connections that people establish and maintain with one another in the context of a growing transnational civil society (J.

Cohen 1995; Lipschutz 1996; Lister 1997). Citizenship here resides in identities and commitments that arise out of cross-border affiliations, especially those associated with oppositional politics though it might include the corporate professional circuits that are increasingly forms of partly de-territorialised global cultures (Sassen 2001). These identities and commitments can be of an elite and cosmopolitan nature or they can be very focused and with specific objectives, such as those of many of the licit organisations described in the preceding section. MADRE and its worldwide affiliates is a good example. Many aspects of the global environmental movement as well as the human rights movement are actually rather focused and illustrate these emergent cross-border identities in that these activists tend to identify more strongly with the global movement than with their national state. There are elements of this also in many of the women's organisations we presented earlier. Table 9.8 lists some very diverse organisations that capture some of the features of an emergent transnational sense of one's community of membership and to some extent an often key part of one's sense of identity.

> A key dynamic becoming evident among some of the organisations we studied is a shift away from the type of bi-national experience that most of the migration literature on the subject describes, towards a more diffuse condition of globally constituted diasporic networks

A third version is the emergence of transnational social and political communities constituted through trans-border migration. These begin to function as bases for new forms of citizenship identity to the extent that members maintain identification and solidarities with one another across state territorial divides (Portes 1996; Basch, Schiller, and Szanton-Blanc 1994; Smith 1997; Soysal 1994). These are, then, identities that arise out of networks, activities, ideologies that span the home and the host societies. A key dynamic becoming evident among some of the organisations we studied is a shift away from the type of bi-national experience that most of the migration literature on the subject describes, towards a more diffuse condition of globally constituted diasporic networks. The orientation ceases to be confined to one's community of residence and one's community of origin, and shifts towards multiple immigrant communities of the same nationality or ethnicity wherever they might be located. The

Internet has played a crucial role in making this possible. It is, perhaps, this type of network that best captures the notion of diasporic networks as enabling participation in and contribution to global civil society (see Table 9.9 for examples). Though of a very different sort from those described here, diasporic networks can enable the formation of international organised terrorism and certain types of ethnic-based cross-border trafficking networks (Sassen 2000).

A fourth version is a sort of global sense of solidarity and identification, partly out of humanitarian convictions (Pogge 1992). Notions of the ultimate unity of human experience are part of a long tradition. Today there are also more practical considerations at work, as in global ecological interdependence, economic globalisation, global media and commercial culture, all of which create structural interdependencies and senses of global responsibility (Falk 1993; Hunter 1992; Held 1995; Sassen 1996). Table 9.8 lists some possible examples of this kind of organisation.

Towards Denationalised Citizenship Practices and Identities

How do we interpret these types of developments in ways that help us understand their implications for global civil society? One way is to explore what it tells us about modern nation-based citizenship in so far as the existence of a global civil society requires the possibility of an at least partial reorientation towards objectives that are not exclusively geared towards one's nation-state. Yet global civil society would be severely weakened if it were to become completely disconnected from the substantive notion of citizenship as a complex condition predicated on formal rights and obligations configured in ways that negotiate individual and shared interests and needs.

Most of the scholarship on citizenship has claimed a necessary and exclusive connection to the national state, thereby neutralising the meaning and significance of the types of citizenship practices and emergent

Table 9.8: Organisations promoting transnational identity based on activities

Name	Description	Website adress
The International Association for Cross-Cultural Psychology (IACCP)	It has a membership of over 500 persons in more than 65 countries with the aim of facilitating communication among persons interested in cross-cultural psychology.	http://www.fit.edu/ft-orgs/iaccp/
International Tobacco Control Network	Its aim is to serve all those active in tobacco control, cancer control and public health.	http://www.globalink.org
The International Association of Refugee Law Judges	It fosters recognition that protection from persecution is an individual right established under international law, and that the determination of refugee status and its cessation should be subject to the rule of law.	http://www.iarlj.nl/
International Criminal Defence Lawyers Association	Founded with the core goal of ensuring a full, fair and well organised defence in the proceedings of the ad hoc tribunals and the future International Criminal Court.	http://www.hri.ca/partners/aiad-icdaa/
World Business Council for Sustainable Development (WBCSD)	A coalition of 125 international companies united by a shared commitment to the environment and to the principles of economic growth and sustainable development.	www.wbcsd.ch
Water Partners International	Addresses water supply and sanitation needs in developing countries. Promotes innovative and cost-effective community water projects.	www.water.org
50 Years is Enough	See Table 9.1 for details	www.50years.org
MADRE	An international women's human rights organisation, see Table 9.3 for details.	www.madre.org

identities present in the variety of organisations described in the preceding sections. The transformations afoot today raise questions about this proposition of a necessary connection of citizenship to the national state in so far as they significantly alter those conditions which in the past fed that connection (for a good description of these conditions see Turner 2000). If this is indeed the case, then we need to ask whether national conceptions of citizenship exhaust the possible range of experiences and aspirations that today denote citizenship. It is becoming evident that, far from being unitary, the institution of citizenship has multiple dimensions, only some of which might be inextricably linked to the national state (Isin and Turner 2002).

The context of this possible transformation is defined by the two major, partly interconnected conditions discussed in the preceding sections. One is the change in the position and institutional features of national states since the 1980s resulting from various forms of globalisation, ranging from economic privatisation and deregulation to the increased prominence of the international human rights regime. Among the consequences of these developments is the ascendance of sub-national and

Table 9.9: Diaspora organisations

Name	Description	Website adress
The Council of Hellenes Abroad	An historic international movement that unites Hellenes worldwide under one, non-profit, non-governmental organisation with its permanent headquarters in Thessaloniki, Greece	http://www.saeamerica.org/
The Hungarian Human Rights Foundation (HHRF)	Formed to alert the public opinion and political leadership of the United States and other Western countries to the gross human rights violations against national minorities in Romania. The Foundation is now working on behalf of the ethnic Hungarians who live as minorities in Croatia, Serbia, Slovenia, Slovakia and Ukraine, as well as in Romania itself.	http://www.hhrf.org
BADIL	A Palestinian NGO that works to find solutions to the residency problems of the Palestinian diaspora.	www.badil.org

transnational spaces for politics. The second is the emergence of multiple actors, groups, and communities partly strengthened by these transformations in the state and increasingly unwilling automatically to identify with a nation as represented by the state. Again, it is important to emphasise that the growth of the Internet and linked technologies has facilitated and often enabled the formation of cross-border networks among individuals and groups with shared interests that may be highly specialised, as in professional networks, or involve particularised political projects, as in human rights and environmental struggles or the diasporic networks and immigrant organisations described above. This has engendered or strengthened alternative notions of community of membership. These new experiences and orientations of citizenship may not necessarily be new; in some cases they may well be the result of long gestations or features that were there since the beginning of the formation of citizenship as a national institution, but are only now evident because strengthened and rendered legible by current developments.

One of the implications of these developments is the possibility of post-national forms of citizenship (Soysal 1994; Feldblum 1998; see multiple chapters in Isin 2000). The emphasis in that formulation is on the emergence of locations for citizenship outside the confines of the national state. The European passport is, perhaps, the most formalised of these. But the emergence of a re-invigorated cosmopolitanism (Turner 2000; Nussbaum 1994) and of a proliferation of trans-nationalisms (Smith 1997; Basch, Schiller, and Szanton-Blanc 1994) have been key sources for notions of post-national citizenship. As Bosniak (2000) has put it, there is a reasonable case to be made that the experiences and practices associated with citizenship do, to variable degrees, have locations that exceed the boundaries of the territorial nation-state. Whether it is the organisation of formal status, the protection of rights, citizenship practices, or the experience of collective identities and solidarities, the nation state is not the exclusive site for their enactment. It remains by far the most important site, but the transformations in its exclusivity signal a possibly important new dynamic.

There is a second dynamic becoming evident that, while sharing aspects with post-national citizenship, is usefully distinguished from it in that it concerns specific transformations inside the national state which directly and indirectly alter specific aspects of the institution of citizenship (Sassen 2003). These transformations are not predicated necessarily on a relocating of citizenship components outside the national state, as is key to conceptions of post-national citizenship. Two instances are changes in the law of nationality entailing a shift from exclusive allegiance to one nation-state to dual nationality, and enabling legislation allowing national courts to use international instruments. These are transformations inside the national state. More encompassing changes, captured in notions of privatisation and shrinking welfare states, signal a shift in the relationship of citizens to the state. Similarly, the widespread constitutionalising of the right to take one's government to court for failure to fulfil its obligations has also changed the relationship of citizens to their national states in the sense that they create a legally sanctioned possibility of separation of interests.

These and other developments all point to impacts on citizenship that take place inside formal institutions of the national state. It is useful to distinguish this second dynamic of transformation inside the national state from post-national dynamics because most of the scholarship on citizenship has failed to make this distinction. The focus has almost exclusively been on post-national citizenship, either by opposing or accepting it or by interpreting these trends as post-national. In my own work (Sassen 1996; 2003) I have conceptualised this second dynamic as a de-nationalising of particular aspects of citizenship to be distinguished from post-national developments.

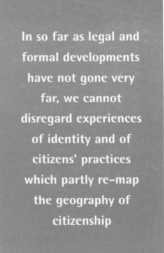

In so far as legal and formal developments have not gone very far, we cannot disregard experiences of identity and of citizens' practices which partly re-map the geography of citizenship

The materials presented in this chapter on global cities and activist/diasporic networks fall into this second type of conception of changes in the institution of citizenship. These are mostly not post-national in their orientation: they are either sub-national, or they are about third issues where shared nationality, as in immigrant organisations, is the bonding element but the objective may have little to do with national issues per se. Further, they do not scale at the national level, in so far as they constitute micro-politics or micro-initiatives enacted in sub-national spaces that are part of cross-border networks connecting multiple such sub-national spaces.

Though often talked about as a single concept and experienced as a unitary institution, citizenship actually describes a number of discrete but related aspects in the relation between the individual and the polity. Current developments are bringing to light

and accentuating the distinctiveness of these various aspects, from formal rights to psychological dimensions. These developments also bring to the fore the tension between citizenship as a formal legal status and as a normative project or an aspiration. Again, current conditions have led to a growing emphasis on claims and aspirations that go beyond the formal legal definition of rights and obligations. The last few years have witnessed a renewed determination by multiple organisations and individuals to play a role in this changed world. Many of the groups mentioned here do not necessarily have a particularly strong sense of gratitude to either their country of origin or that of immigration. Others have a generalised critical stance towards the major trends evident in the world, including their countries of origin, which also reorients their sense of attachment. As Mary Kaldor (2001) has repeatedly found in her research on wars, people, and soldiers in particular, are no longer prepared or expected to die for their country. But as Srebrenica has shown, they are not quite ready to die for global ideals either. It suggests that the building blocks for global civil society are to a considerable extent micro-sites in people's daily lives.

For the development of notions of citizenship that can strengthen global civil society directly, it is important to question the assumption that people's sense of citizenship in liberal democratic states is fundamentally and exclusively characterised by nation-based frames. Non-formal identities and practices need to be taken into account along with formal developments such as European Union citizenship and the growth of the international human rights regime. In so far as legal and formal developments have not gone very far, we cannot disregard experiences of identity and of citizens' practices which partly re-map the geography of citizenship. This deconstruction of citizenship feeds notions of citizenship not based on the nation-state, whether understood in narrow political terms or broader sociological and psychological terms. The growing prominence of the international human rights regime has played an important theoretical and political role in strengthening these conceptions even as it has underlined the differences between citizenship rights and human rights.

Recently there have been several efforts to organise the various understandings of citizenship one can find in the scholarly literature: citizenship as legal status, as possession of rights, as political activity, as a form of collective identity and sentiment (Kymlicka and Norman 1994; Carens 1989; Kratochwil 1994; Conover 1995; Bosniak 2000). Further, some scholars (Turner 1993; C. Taylor 1994; see also generally Van Steenbergen 1994) have posited that cultural citizenship is a necessary part of any adequate conception of citizenship, while others have insisted on the importance of economic citizenship (Fernandez Kelly 1993) and yet others on the psychological dimension and the ties of identification and solidarity we maintain with other groups in the world (Conover 1995; Carens 1989; Pogge 1992). (See in this regard also Record 23 and 27 in this volume).

This pluralised meaning of citizenship, partly produced by the formal expansions of the legal status of citizenship, is today contributing to the expansion of the boundaries of that legal status even further. One of the ironies is that, in so far as the enjoyment of rights is crucial to what we understand citizenship to be, it is precisely the formalised expansion of citizen rights which has weakened the 'national grip' on citizenship. Notable here is also the emergence of the human rights regime partly enabled by national states. Again, it seems to me that this transformation in nation-based citizenship is not only due to the emergence of non-national sites for legitimate claim-making, i.e. the human rights regime, as is posited in the post-national conception. I would add two other elements already, alluded to earlier, which concern changes internal to the national state.

First, and more importantly in my reading, is the strengthening, including the constitutionalising, of civil rights which allow citizens to make claims against their states and allow them to invoke a measure of autonomy in the formal political arena that can be read as a lengthening distance between the formal apparatus of the state and the institution

> Through new forms of citizenship practise new understandings of what citizenship is about and can aspire to are being constituted. Cities and cross-border networks are two key sites for this type of engagement

of citizenship. Instances that capture this are lawsuits filed by citizens against particular state agencies, notably the police and the Immigration and Naturalization Service in the case of the US. The implications, both political and theoretical, of this dimension are complex and in the making: we cannot tell what will be the practices and rhetorics that might be invented.

Second, there is the granting, by national states, of a whole range of 'rights' to foreign actors, largely and especially economic actors— foreign firms, foreign investors, international markets, foreign business people (see Sassen 1996: Ch. 2). Admittedly, this is not a common way of framing the issue. It comes out of my particular perspective about the impact of globalisation and denationalisation on the national state, including the impact on the relation between the state and its own citizens, and between the state and foreign actors. I see this as a significant, though not widely recognised development in the history of claim-making. For me the question as to how citizens should handle these new concentrations of power and 'legitimacy' that attach to global firms and markets is a key to the future of democracy. My efforts to detect the extent to which the global is embedded and filtered through the national (e.g. the concept of the global city) is one way of understanding whether this might enable citizens, still largely confined to national institutions, to demand accountability of global economic actors through national institutional channels rather than having to wait for a 'global' state. Herein would also lie a key element for participation in, and the further constituting of global civil society through sub-national initiatives that are part of cross-border dynamics or issue-oriented global networks.

These new conditions may well signal the possibility of new forms of citizenship practices and identities that can allow large numbers of localised people and organisations to become part of global civil society. New understandings of what citizenship is about and can aspire to are being constituted through these practices. Cities and cross-border networks are two key sites for this type of engagement. After the long historical phase that saw the ascendancy of the national state and the scaling of key economic dynamics at the national level, we now see the ascendancy of sub- and transnational spaces. The city is once again today a scale for strategic economic and political dynamics. Many of the disadvantaged concentrated in cities can become part of this global civil society even as they remain confined to their localities and to some extent absorbed by problems and struggles that are not cosmopolitan.

The author thanks the Centre for the Study of Global Governance for its support and Isabel Crowhurst for her excellent research assistance.

References

Anheier, Helmut, Glasius, Marlies, and Kaldor, Mary (eds) (2001). *Global Civil Society 2001*. Oxford: Oxford University Press.

Appadurai, Arjun (1996). *Modernity at Large*. Minneapolis: University of Minnesota Press.

Bada, Xchotil (2001). 'Mexican Hometown Associations in Chicago: Engaging in Development Back Home' (unpublished thesis). Chicago: MAPS Program, University of Chicago.

Basch, Linda, Glick Schiller, Nina, and Szanton-Blanc, Cristina (1994). *Nations Unbound: Transnationalized Projects and the Deterritorialized Nation-State*. New York: Gordon and Breach.

Bosniak, Linda S. (2000). 'Universal Citizenship and the Problem of Alienage'. *Northwestern University Law Review*, 94: 963–982.

Braudel, Ferdinand (1984). *The Perspective of the World*. London: Collins.

Carens, Joseph H. (1989). 'Membership and Morality: Admission to Citizenship in Liberal Democratic States', in Roger W. Brubaker (ed.), *Immigration and the Politics of Citizenship*. Lanham, New York, and London: University Press of America (with the German Marshall Fund of the US).

Cohen, Jean (1995). 'Interpreting the Notion of Global Civil Society', in M. Walzer (ed.), *Toward a Global Civil Society*. Providence, RI: Berghahn Books.

Cohen, Robin (1996). 'Diasporas and the Nation-State: From Victims to Challenges'. *International Affairs*, 72/3: 507–520.

Conover, Pamela Johnston (1995). 'Citizen Identities and Conceptions of the Self'. *Journal of Political Philosophy*, 3/2: 133–165.

Delanty, Gerard (2000). 'The Resurgence of the City in Europe?: The Spaces of European Citizenship', in Engin Isin (ed.), *Democracy, Citizenship and the Global City*. London and New York: Routledge.

Falk, Richard (1993). 'The Making of Global Citizenship', in Jeremy Brecher and Tim Costello (eds), *Global Visions: Beyond the New World Order*. Boston: South End Press.

Feldblum, Miriam (1998). 'Reconfiguring Citizenship in Western Europe', in Christian Joppke (ed.), *Challenge to the Nation-State*. Oxford: Oxford University Press.

Fernandez Kelly, Maria-Patricia (1993). 'Underclass and Immigrant Women as Economic Actors: Rethinking Citizenship in a Changing Global Economy'. *American University. International Law Review*, 9/1: 151–169.

Franck, Thomas M. (1992). 'The Emerging Right to Democratic Governance'. *American Journal of International Law*, 86/1: 46–91.

Gzesh, Susan and Espinoza, Victor (1999). *The Federation of Michoacan Clubs in Illinois*. Chicago: Chicago-Michoacan Project, Heartland Alliance for Human Needs and Human Rights.

Held, David (1995). *Democracy and the Global Order: From the Modern State to Cosmopolitan Governance*. Cambridge: Polity Press.

Howe, Stephen (1991). 'Citizenship in the New Europe', in Geoff Andrews (ed.), *Citizenship*. London: Lawrence and Wishart.

Hunter, David B. (1992). 'Toward Global Citizenship in International Environmental Law'. *Willamette Law Review*, 28/3, (Summer 1992): 547–563.

International Organisation for Migration (1999). http://www.iom.int/en/what/main_MR_new.shtlm

Isin, Engin F. (ed.) (2000). *Democracy, Citizenship and the Global City*. London and New York: Routledge.

Isin, E. and Turner, B. (eds) (2002). *Handbook of Citizenship Studies*. London: Sage Publications

Kaldor, Mary (2001). *New Wars and Old Wars: Organized Violence in a Global Era*. Cambridge: Polity Press.

Kratochwil, Friedrich (1994). 'Citizenship: On the Border of Order'. *Alternatives*, 19/4: 485–506.

Kymlicka, Will and Norman, Wayne (1994). 'Return of the Citizen: A Survey of Recent Work on Citizenship Theory'. *Ethics*, 104: 352–81.

Lipschutz, Ronnie (with Judith Mayer) (1996). *Global Civil Society and Global Environmental Governance: The Politics of Nature from Place to Planet*. Albany, NY: SUNY Press.

Lister, Ruth (1997). *Citizenship: Feminist Perspectives*. Basingstoke: Macmillan.

Mexico-US Advocates Network, Heartland Alliance for Human Needs and Human Rights, Chicago. http://www.mexus@msn.com

Nussbaum, Martha (1994). 'Patriotism and Cosmopolitanism'. in Joshua Cohen (ed), *For Love of Country: debating the limits of patriotism*, Boston: Beacon Press.

Pizarro, Maria (2001). 'Chicago's Mexican Hometown Associations and Transnational Politics' (unpublished thesis). Chicago: School of Social Services, University of Chicago.

Pogge, Thomas (1992). 'Cosmopolitanism and Sovereignty'. *Ethics*, 103: 48–75.

Portes, A. (1996). 'Global Villagers: The Rise of Transnational Communities'. *American Prospect*, 7/25: 74–77.

Sachar, A. 1990. 'The Global Economy and World Cities', in A. Sachar and S. Oberg (eds), *The World Economy and the Spatial Organization of Power*. Aldershot: Avebury.

Sassen, Saskia (1996). *Losing Control? Sovereignty in an Age of Globalization* (The 1995 Columbia University Leonard Hastings Schoff Memorial Lectures). New York: Columbia University Press.

— (2000). 'Women's Burden: Countergeographies of Globalization and the Feminization of survival'. *Journal of International Affairs*, 53: 503–24.

— (2001). *The Global City: New York, London, Tokyo*. Princeton, NJ: Princeton University Press, (New Ed.)

— (2003). *Denationalization: Territory, Authority and Rights in a Global Digital Age*. Princeton, NJ: Princeton University Press. (Under contract)

Smith, Robert C. (1997).'Transnational Migration, Assimilation and Political Community', in Margaret Crahan and Alberto Vourvoulias-Bush (eds), *The City and the World*. New York: Council of Foreign Relations.

Soysal, Yasemin Nohuglu (1994). *Limits of Citizenship: Migrants and Postnational Membership in Europe*. Chicago: University of Chicago Press.

— (1997). 'Changing Parameters of Citizenship and Claims-Making: Organized Islam in European Public Spheres'. *Theory and Society*, 26: 509–27.

Taylor, Charles (1994). 'The Politics of Recognition', in Amy Gutmann (ed.), *Multiculturalism: Examining the Politics of Recognition*. Princeton: Princeton University Press.

Taylor, Peter (2000). 'World Cities and Territorial States under Conditions of Contemporary Globalization'. *Political Geography*, 19/5: 5–32.

Torres, Maria de los Angeles (1998). 'Transnational Political and Cultural Identities: Crossing Theoretical Borders', in Frank Bonilla, Edwin Melendez, Rebecca Morales, and Maria de los Angeles Torres (eds), *Borderless Borders*. Philadelphia: Temple University Press.

Turner, Bryan S. (ed.) (1993). *Citizenship and Social Theory*. London: Sage Publications.

— (2000). 'Cosmopolitan Virtue: Loyalty and the City', in Engin Isin (ed.), *Democracy, Citizenship and the Global*

Part IV: Records of Global Civil Society

INTRODUCING THE GLOBAL CIVIL SOCIETY INDEX

Helmut Anheier and Sally Stares

Introduction

In *Global Civil Society 2001* (Anheier 2001: 229), we suggested that future editions of the Yearbook explore the possibility of developing an index that would summarise the major contours of global civil society. Such an index would allow for a comparative ranking of countries and regions in terms of their participation and inclusion in global civil society. The index would fit well into the existing range of international indices like the Human Development Index (HDI) developed by the United Nations Development Programme (UNDP) (2000), the Corruption Perception Index developed by Transparency International (1999–2000), or the growing number of quality of life measures that complement more conventional economic measures such as per capita income. Yet, more importantly, as we will argue below, the index would fill a serious gap in empirical globalisation research and provide critical information alongside other measures of globalisation that are typically based on trade and investment statistics.

Indices are summary measures that try to gauge complex, abstract phenomena by combining several measurements or indicators into a single number. Much methodological expertise and statistical finesse is typically invested in the development of indices, but the underlying assumption is simple: any indicator is a simpler yet more systematic representation of the reality it tries to measure. From this, however, follows a fundamental challenge: how can we be sure that simplicity is not distortion, and how can we know that resulting patterns reflect reality and not the way we measured and calculated? Statisticians use the terms 'validity' and 'reliability' to describe the quality of measurement.[1] Thus, a global civil society indicator should be a valid and reliable representation of actually existing global civil society as opposed to the ideals associated with it (see Kaldor, forthcoming).

Complex phenomena such as development, power, social inequality, or quality of life require several indicators to measure the various dimensions or components they have. For example, the HDI (see for example UNDP 2000) uses three main indicators that through a statistical transformation are combined into a single index: life expectancy at birth, educational attainment, and income. For each indicator, and for the index as such, questions about validity and reliability arise that have to be addressed with the help of methodological tools and statistical techniques as well as in more qualitative, interpretative ways. Thus, index construction is a demanding task, particularly for measures taken across a wide range of countries, cultures, and circumstances. The critical question, therefore, becomes: what theoretical deficit or policy issue would lead us to expect that such an index would make a useful contribution to our understanding of globalisation and in the end play a fertile role in developing policies?

Why A Global Civil Society Index?

The Global Civil Society Index (GCSI) proposed here has to avoid becoming, in the critical judgement of McGillivray (1991:1467), 'yet another redundant composite inter-country development indicator' that is ultimately of little use for theory and policy analysis. In essence, there have to be deeper substantive reasons for developing an index of global civil society, reasons that go beyond the fleeting interest of knowing how some countries fare in relation to others.

We suggest that there are three such reasons, each related to key theoretical and policy problems of global civil society. The first addresses the socio-genesis of global civil society in relation to economic globalisation and the development of the international rule of law; the second refers to the

---

[1] *'Validity' is the extent to which an indicator measures the range of meanings associated with it (e.g., does the measure in fact measure what it is supposed to measure?), and 'reliability' refers to the technical aspects of measurement (e.g., would we obtain similar results under similar circumstances?).*

interplay between nations and other geographical and organisational units over time, and the emergence of supra and transnational units such as global organisations or global cities and regions; and the third deals with the normative content that underlies the concepts of global civil society and that, at least partially, carries over into the index. We will discuss each in turn.

In Anheier, Glasius, and Kaldor (2001) we suggest that global civil society exists in the context of two other complexes: economic globalisation (e.g., finance, production, trade, population mobility, cultural diversity and diffusion, and communication) and international law (treaty ratification, human rights, etc). Yet the strength, direction, and development of the relationships among these three complexes still need to be empirically tested in a systematic way (see Figure I.1), in particular in their over-time dimensions. While researchers like Held *et al.* (1999) and others have proposed measures for globalisation, no such systematic work has been done on the 'thickening' of the international rule of law and, critical for our purposes here, on global civil society. In essence, while research on globalisation and global civil society has become conceptually rich, empirical work has not kept up with this development. An index could push the field forward and bring theoretical thinking closer to testable proposition.

While the first reason emphasised the need for broader empirical explorations of globalisation across countries and regions, and over time, the second takes up the issue of fundamental shifts in what methodologists call 'units of analysis', such as regions, organisations, or individuals. Much comparative empirical work on globalisation faces a significant problem in that the aggregation of these individual units follows the rather conventional method of using political units such as 'country', i.e. the nation state , rather than social and economic units that would be more appropriate for the analysis of global, international, and transnational phenomena (see Anheier 2001).

We hypothesise that emergent network units and aggregation levels such as global cities, globalised regions, globalised organisations, federations, and groups will become ever more important in the future. Of course, state and country will remain important actors as well as useful statistical units, and the argument here is not to replace them. Rather, our suggestion is to track the emergence of new units and aggregation levels, and to monitor the shift from conventional categories such as country to unconventional ones.

To do so, however, will require some form of yardstick. In other words, what is needed is an index that shows to what extent 'country' and other aggregation levels are meaningful categories for aggregation in measuring the development of globalisation and global civil society over time. Thus, the challenge will be to develop the GCSI at different aggregation levels that go beyond the confines of the nation state. Even though the results and ranking reported further below are at the country level, we intend to develop measures for use of the GCSI at regional and other levels as well.

The third reason why the index would be needed involves a different set of issues from the aggregation problem, but points to a similar solution. Numerous scholars have commented on the normative bases of the concept of civil society that range from overtly political projects of NGO activities to combat global capitalism (see Desai and Said 2001) and Neo-Tocquevillian approaches to increase 'social capital' in a fight against social exclusion (e.g., Putnam 2000) to more implicit normative thinking like Küng's 'global ethic' (1998) or Shaw's 'awareness of a common worldwide human society' (2000: 12).

In this context, the promise of the index is to make the normative aspects of the various indicators explicit. The strategy in developing a set of alternative indicators would be to offer a range of options that vary in their normative base. As a result, researchers would be able to identify empirically where and how much normative elements 'matter' for the overall index. For example, instead of using a measure of cosmopolitan values close to Küng's (1998) global ethic like a deeply felt concern for humankind, a more 'neutral' value such as tolerance could be used

Figure I.1: Global civil society and globalisation

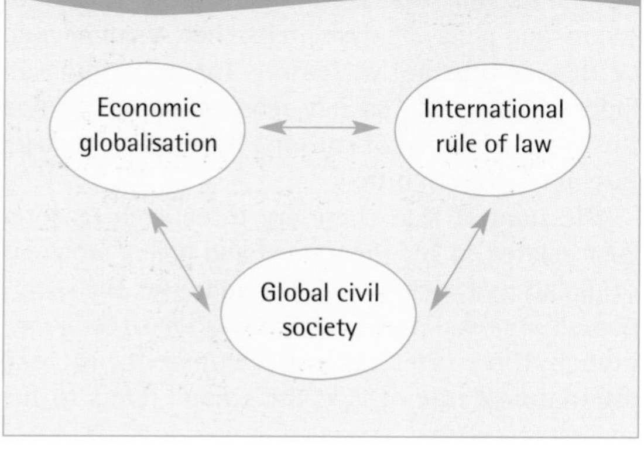

Economic globalisation

International rule of law

Global civil society

instead. Moreover, instead of using a general indicator of NGO density across all fields and activities (see below), a disaggregated measure could focus on those supporting particular positions or causes. By developing and testing alternative measures that vary in their normative content, we will be able to gauge to what extent they lead to different results and hence have the potential to distort or inform the debate. Even though we will further below present the GCSI for a basic set of indicators only, the intent is to let users choose from a menu or inventory of indicators over time.

Indices, Indicators, Measures, and Data

The development of the GCSI follows the initial operationalisation proposed in *Global Civil Society 2001* (Anheier 2001: 225–7). By 'global civil society' we depict the socio-sphere of ideas, values, organisations, networks, and individuals located primarily outside the institutional complexes of family, market, and state and beyond the confines of national societies, polities, and economies. This operational definition includes two fundamental units of analysis:

- *individuals*, and their ideas, values, identities, opinions, and actions; and
- *organisations*, including associations and networks of many kinds.

While the latter makes up the infrastructure of global civil society, the former gives it meaning and agency (individual action). We are looking for indicators for each unit that are closely linked to global civil society, and seek to aggregate the resulting data at the national level but also, in the future, at alternative aggregation levels more in line with the intent of the index, such as cities, agglomerations, and regions. Figure I.2 shows the flow of the index construction, which is based on the more detailed operationalisation of global civil society presented in Anheier (2001: 225–8). The flow chart in Figure I.2 follows each unit of analysis and selects indicators along various sub-dimensions:

- the *organisational infrastructure* of global civil society, as measured by the density of international NGOs and associations over a given population (see Record 16);

- the *civility* of individuals, as a measure of cosmopolitan values such as 'tolerance' (R24), and possibly also 'democratic values' (R25), or 'hospitality' (R27); and

- the *participation* of individuals, as measured by membership in, and volunteering for, global civil society organisations (R28); and the participation of individuals in political action (R29).

The Global Civil Society Index would be a composite measure of separate component indicators, each measuring a distinct aspect, but unlike the HDI it would cover two units of analysis: organisations and individuals. Specifically, *infrastructure* would refer to the density of international NGOs and associations in a particular country (see Castells 1996; Dicken 1998; Held *et al.* 1999). In the initial index results presented below, the infrastructure measure reports on organisation-based data provided by the Union of International Associations (1905–1999/2000). *Civility* would be a combined measure of cosmopolitan values such as tolerance (see

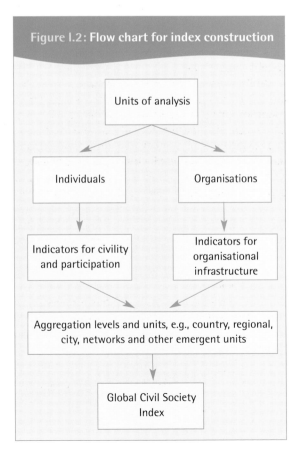

Figure I.2: **Flow chart for index construction**

Units of analysis

Individuals

Organisations

Indicators for civility and participation

Indicators for organisational infrastructure

Aggregation levels and units, e.g., country, regional, city, networks and other emergent units

Global Civil Society Index

Kaldor, forthcoming; Shaw 2000). Data for these measures are from individual population surveys like the World Values Survey (Inglehart, Basañez, and Moreno 1998) and the European Values Survey (Halman 2001). *Participation* would be a measure of individual involvement in, and voluntary work for, organisations, associations, or networks related to global civil society and political action (see Keck and Sikkink 1998), and would complement organisation-based indicators, and link the global civil society to measures of social capital (Dasgupta and Serageldin 2000).

There are two basic ways to construct an index: a priori-additive and scaling. The first approach takes the indicators as given, using theoretical knowledge and measurement assumptions to guide index construction. The Human Development Index is an example of such an approach. The second approach is more cautious in first proposing a theoretical measurement model that is then tested empirically against the data structure. In this case, we use confirmatory factor-analytic methods (Jöreskog 1973) to examine the extent to which the data reflect or 'fit' the structure of the model specified. In constructing the GCSI, we make use of both approaches, and indeed, as we will show below, we use both as a way of cross-validation.

The a priori-additive approach to constructing the GCSI relates the observed score for each indicator to its overall range. Specifically, for a given indicator I, the normalised value is calculated as follows:

$$I_i = \frac{\text{Observed score} - \text{minimum score}}{\text{Maximum score} - \text{minimum score}}$$

Depending on the number of indicators used, and assuming equal weights for each, the GCSI becomes:

$$GCSI = \frac{1}{k} \sum I_{(i=1,k)}$$

Box I.1 uses Finland for a detailed example to show how the GCSI is calculated following the a priori-additive approach of the HDI (see Ivanova, Arcelus, and Srinivasan 1999).

We tested the GCSI at the country level, using information from three basic data sources: the organisational database of the Union of International Associations, the individual-level data from the World Values Survey, and equivalent data from the European Values Survey. We included 176 countries overall[2] but as the 33 countries for which we have complete information in Table I.1 suggest, in many cases data coverage was rather limited, with 46 per cent of the

necessary information missing. Clearly, improving data coverage becomes a central challenge for the index, and at present the GCSI is available primarily for developed countries.

Several methodological issues are worth noting. In the HDI approach, each of the three indicators carries equal weight, and they are presumed to be equally important both from a measurement perspective and in theoretical terms. What is more, indicators are expected to have positive co-variations with each other but are treated as independent, additive elements with no cross-cutting links between indicators and constructs. With the help of the factor analysis below we have, however, moved away from this assumption and include the membership indicator for both the participation and the infrastructure construct. The result is a somewhat more elaborate way of calculating the index, as shown for Finland in Box I.1.[3]

A final point worth noting is the choice of maximum and minimum values used to re-scale the components of the overall index. We have simply taken the maximum and minimum of the observed values, so that our scale summarises available information only. Yet it is not necessary to choose these end points, and other 'markers' are possible as well. In constructing the HDI, UNDP sets its maximum and minimum values according to some hypothetical expectations, e.g., adult literacy, which stretches from 0 to 100 per cent though no country reports either 0 or 100 percentage points. These issues point to a more general theoretical question on whether it is possible to define 'perfect' global civil society at one extreme and 'perfect' lack of global civil society at the other.

The second approach tries to measure global civil society as an unobserved construct with multiple indicators, using statistical scaling techniques such as confirmatory factor analysis. In contrast to the additive approach presented above, the scaling approach is a form of hypothesis testing whereby a model is tested against available data. Figure I.3 presents the basic input model for the various components that are hypothesised to make up global civil society. We employed the programme AMOS 4,[4]

---

[2] See Yearbook website for full information:
http://www.lse.ac.uk/depts/global/yearbook

[3] For the purpose of index construction and cross-validation, we had to take a somewhat different approach from the one taken by the final HDI calculations. Specifically, we re-normalised the resulting scale so that the final index ranges between 0 and 1 to enable comparison with the rankings generated by the factor-analytic approach presented below. By contrast, the HDI score is the simple average of its three components. However, in future years, and for purposes of over-time comparison across countries and other units, GCSI scores will not be re-normalised, and we will report simple averages (see Table I.1).

[4] © James L. Arbuckle, SmallWaters Corp.; see also Arbuckle and Wothke (1999).

Table I.1: Component Indicators and GCSI scores, by country, 2000

| Country | Indicators | | | | | GCSI–score HDI-style | | |
	Political participation	Membership of civil society groups	Membership density of INGOs	Tolerance towards immigrants as neighbours	Encourage tolerance in children	Simple average score	Re-normalised score	Country ranking
Argentina	0.25	0.00	0.45	0.92	0.55	0.38	0.13	25
Austria	0.46	0.68	0.70	0.74	0.58	0.90	0.53	10
Belarus	0.06	0.45	0.45	0.61	0.58	0.44	0.17	24
Belgium	0.82	0.66	0.70	0.64	0.84	1.11	0.70	6
Bulgaria	0.11	0.16	0.60	0.41	0.33	0.28	0.04	32
Chile	0.14	0.04	0.53	0.76	0.67	0.37	0.12	27
Croatia	0.25	0.42	0.66	0.55	0.44	0.56	0.27	22
Czech Republic	0.60	0.60	0.62	0.55	0.41	0.80	0.45	13
Denmark	0.81	0.87	0.77	0.79	0.89	1.29	0.84	4
Estonia	0.10	0.31	0.78	0.51	0.56	0.51	0.23	23
Finland	0.61	0.82	0.76	0.68	0.80	1.11	0.70	5
France	0.86	0.36	0.51	0.75	0.84	0.91	0.54	9
Germany	0.49	0.47	0.45	0.84	0.55	0.71	0.38	16
Greece	0.57	0.47	0.64	0.55	0.19	0.67	0.35	19
Hungary	0.01	0.26	0.64	0.47	0.46	0.34	0.10	28
Iceland	0.52	0.97	1.00	0.99	0.83	1.35	0.88	2
Ireland	0.54	0.56	0.77	0.74	0.68	0.94	0.56	8
Italy	0.65	0.40	0.49	0.63	0.64	0.74	0.41	14
Latvia	0.20	0.29	0.69	0.81	0.54	0.58	0.28	21
Lithuania	0.18	0.12	0.65	0.43	0.30	0.31	0.07	31
Luxembourg	0.54	0.59	0.98	0.85	0.69	1.09	0.68	7
Mexico	0.29	0.05	0.33	0.34	0.58	0.22	0.00	33
Netherlands	0.76	0.97	0.66	0.93	0.98	1.32	0.86	3
Poland	0.16	0.22	0.47	0.43	0.72	0.38	0.12	26
Russian Fed.	0.13	0.29	0.28	0.78	0.50	0.33	0.09	30
Slovakia	0.42	0.65	0.65	0.45	0.29	0.69	0.37	18
Slovenia	0.24	0.51	0.77	0.64	0.55	0.71	0.38	17
Spain	0.36	0.28	0.53	0.82	0.74	0.63	0.32	20
Sweden	1.00	1.00	0.71	1.00	1.00	1.50	1.00	1
Switzerland	0.52	0.41	0.73	0.80	0.72	0.87	0.51	11
Ukraine	0.14	0.32	0.33	0.67	0.46	0.33	0.09	29
United Kingdom	0.71	0.44	0.52	0.65	0.73	0.83	0.48	12
United States	0.80	0.24	0.30	0.80	0.75	0.71	0.39	15

which is useful for carrying out estimation tasks on sparse input data, as is the case here. Avoiding both listwise and pairwise deletion of cases based on missing data, AMOS uses all available information (see Anderson 1957). The estimates are displayed in Figure I.4.[5] In particular it tells us:

- the relative strengths of relationships between each of the indicators and latent constructs (weights or 'loadings');
- the amount of variance in each of the indicators accounted for by the model;
- the relative strengths of relationships between the constructs of GCS (co-variances); and

[5] *Further statistical information about the model may be found at http://www.lse.ac.uk/depts/global/yearbook.*

INTRODUCING THE GLOBAL CIVIL SOCIETY INDEX   Helmut Anheier and Sally Stares

1. Calculating the civility index

This index consists of two indicators; here we combine information on

- the proportion of people who would not object to having immigrants or foreign workers as neighbours (R24b), and
- the proportion of people who say that tolerance is an important quality to encourage in children (R24a).

As a first step we calculate Finland's scores on each of the two normalised indicators.

$$\text{Neighbours index} = \frac{0.855 - 0.605}{0.972 - 0.605} = 0.681$$

$$\text{Tolerance (children) index} = \frac{0.826 - 0.430}{0.923 - 0.430} = 0.803$$

To calculate Finland's score on the civility index we add these two scores together, and re-normalise the scale so that the civility index stretches from 0 to 1.

$$\text{Civility index} = \frac{(0.681 + 0.803) - 0.08}{2.00 - 0.08} = 0.731$$

2. Calculating the participation and infrastructure indices

These indices are linked through a common indicator, so we calculate Finland's scores on participation and infrastructure together. The reason for this procedure is based on the results of the confirmatory factor analysis below, which suggested the indicator 'membership in global civil society associations' is highly related to both the participation and the infrastructure constructs. Therefore we take account of this dual relationship in calculating the GCSI using the additive approach presented here. The individual measures are:

- the percentage of the Finnish population who are members of at least one of four civil society organisations (a community action group, a Third World or human rights movement, a peace movement, or an environmental group) (R28);
- the average proportion of Finns willing to take political action for or against a particular cause (the arithmetic mean of proportions of Finns who would be willing to sign a petition, join a boycott, attend a lawful demonstration, take part in an unofficial strike, and/or occupy a building) (R29); and
- membership density of INGOs (how many INGOs have one member or more in Finland, per million Finnish population) (R16).

We adjust the membership density index by applying a logarithmic transformation because the distribution of its scores appears highly skewed, and biased towards small countries. The majority of countries have very low scores and a few countries have very high scores; by using the logarithm of membership density we improve the quality of the scale by removing most of the skew and some of the bias.

As a next step we compute Finland's scores on each of the three normalised indicators.

$$\text{Voluntary CS membership index} = \frac{79.96 - 5.74}{96.06 - 5.74} = 0.891$$

$$\text{Political participation index} = \frac{0.22 - 0.04}{0.33 - 0.04} = 0.621$$

$$\text{INGO membership density index} = \frac{\log_e(829) - \log_e(2)}{\log_e(5819) - \log_e(2)} = 0.756$$

To calculate Finland's score on infrastructure and participation, we simply sum the three component scores and renormalise the scale.

$$\text{Infrastructure and participation index} = \frac{(0.819 + 0.621 + 0.756) - 0.66}{2.71 - 0.66} = 0.749$$

3. Calculating the Global Civil Society Index

To calculate Finland's GCSI score, we combine the scores on infrastructure, participation, and civility. Since two of the components are already combined in a double-score, we give the civility index half the weight of this double-score index.

$$\text{Global civil society index} = \frac{[(\text{infrastructure and participation}) + 0.5\,(\text{civility})] - \text{min. of GCS index scale}}{\text{max.} - \text{min. of GCS index scale}}$$

$$\text{GCS index for Finland} = \frac{[0.749 + 0.5\,(0.731)] - 0.22}{1.50 - 0.22} = 0.698$$

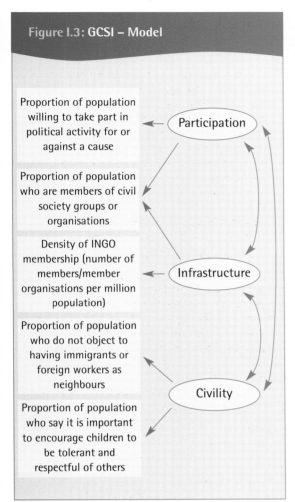

Figure I.3: GCSI – Model

Proportion of population willing to take part in political activity for or against a cause

Proportion of population who are members of civil society groups or organisations

Density of INGO membership (number of members/member organisations per million population)

Proportion of population who do not object to having immigrants or foreign workers as neighbours

Proportion of population who say it is important to encourage children to be tolerant and respectful of others

Participation

Infrastructure

Civility

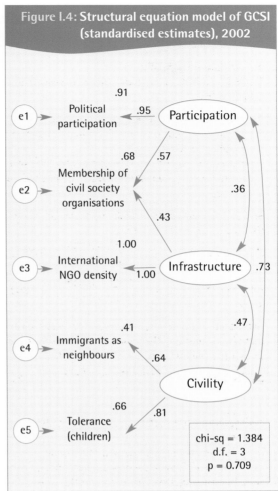

Figure I.4: Structural equation model of GCSI (standardised estimates), 2002

chi-sq = 1.384
d.f. = 3
p = 0.709

- the overall goodness of fit of the model based on the (null) hypothesis that the model fits the data perfectly. The actual test statistic follows a chi-square distribution, with a conventional p-value of greater than 0.05 needed for failing to reject the null hypothesis, and infer that the model is a good fit.[6]

The input model for the estimation specified no constraints on the co-variances between latent dimensions. Means of all error terms are set to zero, and we constrain the error variance of political participation

and membership density to small sizes to identify the model, assuming that both indicators are almost perfectly measured. In earlier steps in the analysis, it became clear that membership in civil society organisations loads on two constructs, i.e. participation and infrastructure. Therefore, we specified membership as a shared indicator. We constrained the means and variances of latent dimensions to 0 and 1 respectively in order to define metrics for the estimates. In general, we kept the model as 'free' as possible, and only constrained estimates where necessary for purposes of identification and simplicity.

To arrive at the final rankings we compute scores on each of the three latent factors, using the factor score weights derived by AMOS, and calculate the overall GCSI score from these (Table I.2).

---

[6] The goodness-of-fit test should be interpreted with some degree of caution. The relatively small number of cases used in the estimation procedure increases the likelihood of a type-II error, i.e. failing to reject the null hypothesis when it is actually false. As we add more observations over time, we will have to track how the goodness of fit statistic changes as sample size increases.

Country	Infrastructure score	Civility score	Participation score	GCS index factor score	Country ranking
Argentina	0.28	0.33	0.20	0.19	25
Austria	0.60	0.44	0.45	0.50	12
Belarus	0.27	0.22	0.10	0.09	29
Belgium	0.61	0.70	0.78	0.76	6
Bulgaria	0.47	0.00	0.06	0.07	30
Chile	0.38	0.34	0.10	0.20	24
Croatia	0.55	0.19	0.23	0.26	23
Czech Republic	0.50	0.28	0.55	0.43	15
Denmark	0.69	0.80	0.80	0.86	3
Estonia	0.71	0.23	0.08	0.29	22
Finland	0.68	0.64	0.62	0.70	7
France	0.35	0.69	0.78	0.64	8
Germany	0.28	0.41	0.46	0.34	18
Greece	0.53	0.11	0.49	0.33	19
Hungary	0.52	0.09	0.00	0.10	28
Iceland	1.00	0.78	0.56	0.88	2
Ireland	0.70	0.54	0.51	0.61	9
Italy	0.32	0.45	0.59	0.44	14
Latvia	0.59	0.33	0.18	0.32	20
Lithuania	0.54	0.02	0.11	0.12	27
Luxembourg	0.97	0.62	0.51	0.77	5
Mexico	0.11	0.16	0.23	0.05	31
Netherlands	0.55	0.88	0.79	0.83	4
Poland	0.30	0.28	0.15	0.16	26
Russian Fed.	0.05	0.20	0.14	0.00	33
Slovakia	0.54	0.11	0.39	0.29	21
Slovenia	0.69	0.32	0.24	0.38	16
Spain	0.37	0.50	0.34	0.37	17
Sweden	0.61	1.00	1.00	1.00	1
Switzerland	0.64	0.57	0.48	0.59	10
Ukraine	0.12	0.15	0.14	0.01	32
United Kingdom	0.37	0.55	0.65	0.53	11
United States	0.07	0.59	0.72	0.45	13

Our intent in taking two different though complementary routes was to make cross-validation possible. How similar or dissimilar are the two indices? Even a cursory look at the country rankings in Tables I.1 and I.2 suggests that the two approaches lead to very similar results, with only some countries changing ranks but no major 'reshuffling'. This impression is graphically supported by the rather close realignment of both scores presented in Figure I.5, and it finds statistical support in various measures of associations.[7]

As a result of this comparison, we suggest, subject to further testing across different units of analyses and more observations, that the HDI-style approach may be preferable on the grounds that it is simpler and more intuitive in its meaning and actual calculation than the factor-analytic model of unobserved constructs.

---

[7] *Pearson correlation = 0.983 (p<0.01); Kendall's tau = 0.883 (p<0.01); and Spearman's rho = 0.979 (p<0.01), by the near perfect fit obtained (R-squared = .97).*

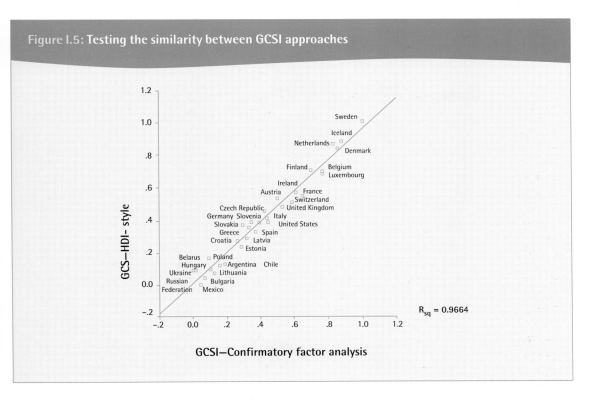

Figure I.5: Testing the similarity between GCSI approaches

Validating the Global Civil Society Index

We have argued that reliability and validity are two critical aspects of measurement quality. Unfortunately, the relatively small sample size limits the full exploration of both when applied to the GCSI and its component parts, but we can offer at least some preliminary results. In terms of reliability, Cronbach's alpha is a widely-used measure of the internal consistency of a scale, based on average inter-item correlations. For the five indicators that are part of the GCSI, the alpha value of 0.8047 is sufficiently high to let us conclude that the scale has internal consistency.

A more detailed analysis in Table I.3 shows the various alpha values for the scale on the assumption that each item would be deleted in turn. Table I.3 indicates that all items contribute well to the scale. However, the reliability analysis is limited in the sense that Cronbach's alpha assumes a unidimensional measurement space, which the factor analysis has shown not to be the case. To compensate for this, an alternative approach would be to take the squared multiple correlation coefficients as proxies for

reliability for each variable. This suggests that the 'neighbours' indicator in the civility construct performs least well, at 0.41, whereas membership density performs best (although the error variance for this indicator was set to near 0 in order to make the model work).[8]

What can we say about validity? Among the various approaches available, construct validity is a commonly used way to gauge this aspect of the measurement quality of indices like the GCSI. In essence, construct validity examines the extent to which the results of a 'new' index differ from the patterns obtained from related and well-established existing measures within a system of theoretical relationships. In this case, using country as the unit of analysis, we relate the GCSI to different measures of development, assuming that 'size' of global civil society is closely linked to the extent to which countries meet the needs of their people. To this end, we test how the distribution of GCSI scores differs from established measures for

[8] *If more indicators were added to the GCSI, then the squared multiple correlation would be a better judgement, as error variance would have to be less constrained. This would also allow us to calculate Cronbach's alpha for each dimension of the index. What is more, if the number of cases could be increased, split-half methods and related reliability tests become feasible.*

INTRODUCING THE GLOBAL CIVIL SOCIETY INDEX   Helmut Anheier and Sally Stares

249

Table I.3: Reliability analysis of GCSI (HDI-style)

Item	Scale mean if item deleted	Scale variance if item deleted	Corrected item-total correlation	Alpha if item deleted
Political participation	2.3626	.3943	.6618	0.7475
Membership of civil society organisations	2.3449	.3778	.7423	0.7142
Membership density of INGOs	2.1858	.5637	.3943	0.8177
Tolerance towards immigrants as neighbours	2.1130	.5227	.5657	0.7785
Encourage tolerance in children	2.1771	.4812	.6434	0.7538

human development (the HDI) and economic development (GDP). The expectation is that the GCSI should reveal a regular pattern with the other two indices whereby countries ranking high in terms of human and economic development would also rank higher on global civil society measures (Figure I.6).[9] Both versions of the GCSI are plotted against values for GDP and HDI, using the most recent data available in each case. Different versions of the GCSI are represented by squares and triangles and plotted on the vertical axis to gain an idea of how 'different' they are. The various scatterplots in Figure I.6 show that the two GCSI versions yield patterns that correspond closely to the overall distributional properties of related indices. In each case, we have fitted regression lines to suggest the relationship between the scales. Specifically, both versions of the GCSI correlate moderately to strongly with both GDP and HDI. There is not much to separate the patterns they generate, although the factor-analytic approach gives slightly higher correlations.

The relationship between GCSI and HDI does not seem to be linear, and the GCSI discriminates more among countries at the top end of HDI scale than HDI itself does. An example is the difference between the US and the Netherlands, where both score highly on HDI (both HDI = 0.93), but in terms of GCSI the Netherlands scores much higher than the US . The values for individual indicators suggest that the greatest difference between these two countries is found in membership of civil society groups. Of course, some of these patterns may change as data for more countries are added to the model and as the mechanics of the scale are further developed.

There are also indications that the relationship between the GCSI and GDP is not linear, but this may not be a firm conclusion. The results are somewhat distorted by outliers (e.g., Luxembourg and the US have high GDP values but relatively low GCSI scores, while Iceland and the Netherlands rank lower in terms of GDP but higher on the GCSI).

Both sets of graphs in Figure I.6 suggest that the GCSI is also measuring something different from both economic and human development. While it correlates with both, indicating construct validity, it also points to the theoretical issues raised earlier (see Figure I.1), and the relationship between global civil society and other dimensions of globalisation.

---

[9] *It should be stressed that the purpose here is not to test any theory or hypothesis but to explore whether an indicator produces systematic results.*

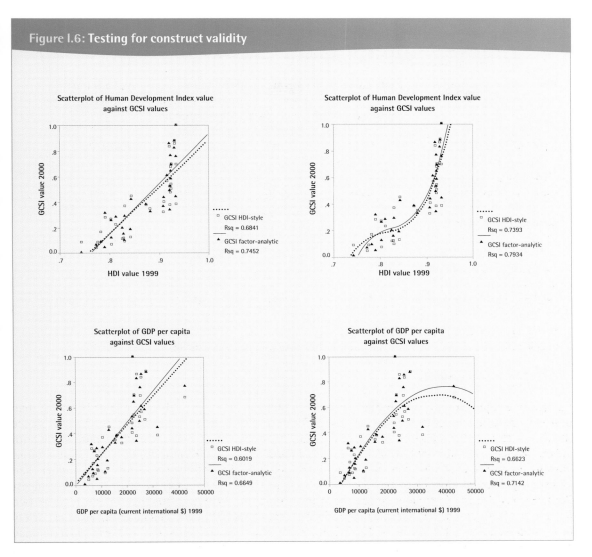

To explore this aspect, we test for theoretical or predictive validity of the GCSI using correlation and regression analysis. As in the case of construct validity, the aim is not to test theory but to see whether the index yields empirically systematic and conceptually fruitful relationships.

The correlation coefficients show that the relationships among global civil society, economic globalisation, and the international rule of law are somewhat surprising and certainly warrant closer inspection. Important for our purposes here are not so much the specific insights that can be gained from the results presented in Figure I.7, but the promise that more refined work of this type holds for our theoretical understanding of the role global civil society plays in

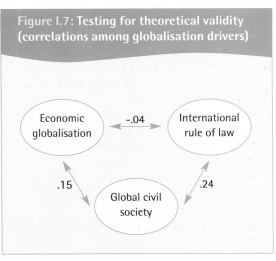

Figure I.7: Testing for theoretical validity (correlations among globalisation drivers)

Table I.4a: Estimates for linear regression model predicting globalisation

	Unstandardized coefficients b	Standard Error	Standardized coefficients Beta	t- statistic	p
(Constant)	6.803	35.799		.190	.851
International rule of law (number of treaties ratified)	.743	1.696	.056	.438	.667
Economic globalisation (trade in % of GDP,1999)	.059	.046	.160	1.289	.214
Global civil society (GCSI, HDI-style)	38.206	6.249	.796	6.114	.000

Dependent Variable: globalisation (A.T. Kearney/Foreign Policy Magazine Globalisation Index ™)

Table I.4b: Model summary

R	R Square	Adjusted R Square	Std. Error of the Estimate
.858	.737	.693	7.01600

Table I.4c: Analysis of variance

	Sum of Squares	df	Mean square	F-ratio	p
Regression	2482.917	3	827.639	16.814	.000
Residual	886.037	18	49.224		
Total	3368.955	21			

the globalisation process relative to other 'drivers.' Of course, some of the measures used in Figure I.7 are rather crude and need further refinement, in particular the measure for International Rule of Law, which is based on the number of international treaties a country has ratified.

Another test of theoretical validity is to use the GCSI as a predictor of some generalized globalisation variable.[10] The regression analysis presented in Table I.4 underscores the predictive value of the GCSI. The results show the GCSI to be a better predictor of overall globalisation, as measured by the A.T. Kearney/Foreign Policy Magazine (2000) Globalisation Index™, than

[10] The same cautious note about data quality has to be raised for overall globalisation indices like the A.T. Kearney/Foreign Policy Magazine Globalisation Index™, which to our knowledge remains unexamined in its statistical and measurement properties.

either International Rule of Law or Economic Globalisation. Preliminary as these results are, they suggest that the GCSI could potentially add an important dimension to our understanding of globalisation, and that its introduction into the empirical discourse in globalisation research carries significant potential.

Conclusion

This introduction to the global civil society index could do little more than provide some of the theoretical and methodological rationale for its development, present two different approaches to index construction, explore its measurement properties and quality, and hint at its potential for informing research on globalisation. Of course, fuller testing of the index is still to be achieved, and we will report on progress made in future editions of the Yearbook. Nonetheless, we could make a case for the more parsimonious version of the GCSI, with the added advantage that its construction follows the well-known, intuitive index construction, popularised by the HDI. We hope that this similarity in approach will add to the wider acceptance and use of the index developed here.

What are the next tasks in developing the GCSI? To a large extent, these reflect some of the basic issues we raised at the beginning and that led us to move forward with the idea of the GCSI in the first place. For one, we need to explore the application of the GCSI approach to non-conventional aggregation levels such as cities, regions, and supra-locational or non-contiguous units. Thus, a key challenge is to address the applicability of the index to the emergent units of globalisation rather than remaining locked in a nation-state framework, however important countries might be as a unit of analysis.

What is more, the normative content of global civil society requires, as argued above, a broader inventory of alternative measures and indicators than we have been able to test and present so far. Clearly, the challenge to explore new aggregation units and levels is closely related to the need for a wider repertoire of indicators. Expanding the range of potential indicators across a broader and more diverse set of countries is one of the key challenges for making sure that the GCSI will help fill the theoretical and empirical gap we discussed at the outset.

Finally, the GCSI relies significantly on data taken from population surveys like the World Values Survey or the European Values Survey. While these surveys have their strengths, they also have limitations in terms of periodicity and country coverage, in addition to aspects like sample restrictions in some developing countries. More critically, the organisational database provided by the Union of International Associations has no equivalent in population surveys when it comes to data quality. Indeed, much of the missing data problem for estimating the GCSI is due to the still limited coverage of international opinion surveys for units other than nation states.

Therefore, there is a great need not only to create an inventory of measures and indicators for the GCSI but also to put in place a database that covers a larger number of countries and other aggregation levels more fully and more regularly than is the case at present. Ideally, the global civil society index requires a global civil society survey at the individual and organisational level to bring out its full potential for researchers, policy-makers, and practitioners alike.

References

Anderson, T.W. (1957) 'Maximum likelihood estimates for a multivariate normal distribution when some observations are missing'. *Journal of the American Statistical Association*, 52: 200-203.

Anheier, H. (2001). 'Measuring Global Civil Society', in Helmut Anheier, Marlies Glasius, and Mary Kaldor (eds), *Global Civil Society 2001*. Oxford: Oxford University Press.

— , Glasius, Marlies, and Kaldor, Mary (2001). 'Introducing Global Civil Society', in Helmut Anheier, Marlies Glasius, and Mary Kaldor (eds), *Global Civil Society 2001*. Oxford: Oxford University Press.

Arbuckle, James L. and Wothke, Werner (1999). *AMOS 4 User's Guide*, Chicago: Marketing Dept., SPSS Inc., SmallWaters Corporation. http://www.smallwaters.com/amos/

A.T. Kearney/Foreign Policy Magazine (2002). *Globalisation Index 2002*. http://www.atkearney.com/main.taf?site=1&ta=5&b=4&c=1&d=42. See also www.foreignpolicy.com

Castells, Manuel (1996). *The Rise of Network Society*. Oxford: Blackwell.

Dasgupta, P., and Serageldin, I. (2000). *Social Capital: A Multifaceted Perspective*. Washington, DC: World Bank.

Desai, Meghnad and Said, Yahia (2001). 'The New Anti-Capitalist Movement: Money and Global Civil Society', in Helmut Anheier, Marlies Glasius, and Mary Kaldor (eds), *Global Civil Society 2001*. Oxford: Oxford University Press.

Dicken, Peter (1998). *Global Shift: Transforming the World Economy*. London: Chapman.

Halman, Loek (2001). *European Values Survey*. Tilburg University, Netherlands: WORC.

Held, David, McGrew, Anthony, Goldblatt, David, and Perraton, Jonathan (1999). *Global Transformations*. Cambridge: Polity Press.

Inglehart, R., Basañez, M., and Moreno, A. (1998). *Human Values and Beliefs: A Cross-Cultural Sourcebook: Political, Religious, Sexual, and Economic Norms in 43 Societies: Findings from the 1990–1993 World Values Survey*. Ann Arbor: University of Michigan Press.

Ivanova, I., Arcelus, F. J., and Srinivasan, G. (1999) 'An Assessment of the Measurement Properties of the Human Development Index'. *Social Indicators Research*, 46: 157–79. Kluwer Academic Publishers

Jöreskog, Karl G. (1973). 'A general method for estimating a linear structural equation system', in A. S. Goldberger and O. D. Duncan (eds), *Structural Equation Models in the Social Sciences*. New York: Seminar Press.

Kaldor, Mary (forthcoming). *Global Civil Society*. Cambridge: Polity Press.

Keck, Margaret E. and Sikkink, Kathryn (1998). *Activists Beyond Borders*. Ithaca, NY: Cornell University Press.

Küng, Hans (1998). *A Global Ethic for Global Politics and Economics*. Oxford: Oxford University Press.

McGillivray, M. (1991) 'The Human Development Index: Yet Another Redundant Composite Development Indicator?'. *World Development*, 19: 1461–8.

Putnam, Robert D. (2000). *Bowling Alone: The Collapse and Revival of American Community*. New York: Simon & Schuster.

Shaw, Martin (2000). *Theory of the Global State: Global Reality as an Unfinished Revolution*. Cambridge: Cambridge University Press.

Transparency International (1999–2000). *The 2000 Corruption Perceptions Index* (CPI). http://www.transparency .org/cpi/2000/cpi2000.html (see also http://www.gwdg.de/~uwvw/ for previous years and http://www.transparency.org/cpi/2001/methodology.html for background methodology)

UNDP (United Nations Development Programme) (2000). *Human Development Report 2000: Human Rights and Human Development*. New York: United Nations. http://www.undp.org/hdr2000/english/book/back1.pdf

Union of International Associations (1905–1999/2000). *Yearbook of International Organizations*. Munich: K. G. Saur.

For more detailed information on the results of the index construction, see http://www.lse.ac.uk/depts/global/yearbook

DATA PROGRAMME

Note On Data

Relation to data programme Global Civil Society 2001

We have updated the information presented in the 2001 edition of the Yearbook wherever possible. Most records similar to those in the 2001 data programme represent more recent, more comprehensive or more accurate figures. The tables on tolerance, membership and volunteering, and participation in political action have not substantially changed, but they have been reproduced because they are part of the Global Civil Society Index calculations. We present more data in a graphical format (e.g. Record 3: Students abroad, Record 8b and 8c: Cumulative ratification) in order to make the findings more immediately apparent, and thus more user-friendly.

We have added new indicators where they appeared to be valuable, sometimes presenting a departure from the indicators presented last year. Notable additions this year are Record 14 on Emissions (replacing last year's Energy record), Record 15 on Crime (where rather than reproduce the same outdated crime data, we have asked an expert to reflect on the significance and the limitations of such data), Record 19 on meetings, Record 22 on networks, Record 25 on value attached to democracy, and Record 26 on confidence in institutions.

For some elements of last year's data programme, we have not been able to gain updated or equivalent data for this edition of the Yearbook. Thus, we have decided not to reproduce the data on migrant labour, trade in cultural goods, languages, concern about humankind, environmental concern, and leadership of international NGOs. These data remain available on our website at http://www.lse.ac.uk/depts/global/yearbook/outline.htm.

Sources and explanatory notes

Brief references to sources are found at the end of each record. All major terms used in the records are briefly defined in the Glossary. As will become clear, comparative information is not available for some countries and variables. A blank entry indicates that the data are not available, not comparable, or otherwise of insufficient quality to warrant reporting. To improve readability of the data and to facilitate interpretation, each record is preceded by a brief description of the information presented and points to some of the key findings.

Time periods

Dependent on data availability, data are reported for 1991 and 2001 or the closest years possible.

Countries

Countries in these tables are independent states with more than 100,000 inhabitants. Country names are used for the sake of brevity and common usage. It is not the intention of the editors to take a position with regard to the political or diplomatic implications of geographical names or continental groupings used.

China, Hong Kong, Macao, Taiwan, and Tibet

Hong Kong became a Special Administrative Region (SAR) of China in 1997 after formal transfer from the UK. Macau became a Special Administrative Region (SAR) of China in 1999 after formal transfer from Portugal. Data for China before these dates do not include Hong Kong and Macao; thereafter they generally do unless otherwise stated. Tibet was annexed by the People's Republic of China in 1949. Data for Tibet are included in those for China and Tibet. Taiwan became the home of Chinese nationalists fleeing communist rule on the mainland and claims separate status from China. No data are given for Taiwan, which is not recognised by the United Nations as an independent country.

Czechoslovakia

Czechoslovakia ceased to exist (by UN terms) on 31 December 1992. Its successor states, the Czech Republic and the Slovak Republic, became UN members in 1993. As no fruitful comparisons can be made, no 1990 data are given for Czechoslovakia.

Ethiopia and Eritrea

Eritrea became independent from Ethiopia in 1993. Data for Ethiopia until 1993 include Eritrea, later data do not.

Germany

The Federal Republic of Germany and the German Democratic Republic were unified in 1990. Data for 1990 and 1991 concern only former West Germany (FRG), later data include both.

Indonesia and East Timor

The Indonesian occupation of East Timor ended in late 1999. After a transitional period under the authority of the United Nations, East Timor became independent on 20 May 2002. All data for Indonesia and East Timor include East Timor unless otherwise indicated. All data for Indonesia also include Irian Jaya (West Papua), the status of which has been in dispute since the 1960s.

Israel and the Occupied Territories

Data for Israel generally include both the occupied territories and territories administered by the Palestinian Authority. In Records 16–20 they include territories identified by INGOs as 'Palestine', 'Cisjordania', 'Gaza', 'Jerusalem', and 'West Bank'.

Morocco and the Western Sahara

The Western Sahara (formerly Spanish Sahara) was annexed by Morocco in the 1970s. Unless otherwise stated, data are generally amalgamated for 'Morocco and the Western Sahara'.

USSR

The Union of Soviet Socialist Republics (USSR) dissolved in 1991 into Armenia, Azerbaijan, Belarus, Georgia, Kazakhstan, Kyrgyzstan, Republic of Moldova, Russian Federation, Tajikistan, Turkmenistan, Ukraine, and Uzbekistan. 1990 and 1991 data for the Russian Federation concern only the Russian Federation, except where they are indicated to concern the USSR.

Yemen

Yemen and Democratic Yemen (formerly both UN members) merged under the name 'Yemen' in 1990. Data from 1990 onwards concern the unified country.

Yugoslavia

The Socialist Federal Republic of Yugoslavia dissolved in 1991 into Bosnia and Herzegovina, the Republic of Croatia, the Republic of Slovenia, the former Yugoslav Republic of Macedonia, and the Federal Republic of Yugoslavia. For 1990, data for Yugoslavia include all the constituent States. For later dates, Yugoslavia includes data for 'Yugoslavia' or 'Serbia and Montenegro' or aggregates thereof.

Aggregations

Where possible we present data for groups of countries (by region and economy) as well as for individual countries. These groups are generally classified according to World Bank definitions. The aggregations are weighted differently depending on information availability. To give an example, in R1 we present figures for trade as percentage of GDP. The aggregate figure for South Asia is calculated as the sum of trade for Afghanistan, Bangladesh, Bhutan, India, Maldives, Nepal, Pakistan and Sri Lanka, divided by the sum of GDP for those countries, and multiplied by 100 to generate a percentage, i.e.

Trade as % GDP for South Asia =

$$\frac{\text{Afghan trade} + \text{Bangladeshi trade} + \ldots}{\text{Afghan GDP} + \text{Bangladeshi GDP} + \ldots} \times 100$$

By contrast, in R7 the aggregates we present are simple averages. Taking the example of 'main telephone lines per 1000 inhabitants', to calculate the aggregate figure for South Asia we sum the ratios 'mainlines per 1000 inhabitants' in Afghanistan, Bangladesh, Bhutan, India, Maldives, Nepal, Pakistan and Sri Lanka, and divide this figure by the number of countries in this region (eight), i.e.

Average no. mainlines per 1000 pop. for South Asia =

$$\frac{\text{Mainlines per 1000 pop. in Afghanistan} + \text{in Bangladesh} + \ldots}{\text{Number of countries in South Asia}}$$

Each country's contribution to the regional figure is given equal weight using this method of aggregation.

Record 1 Global economy

This table presents data on the globalisation of domestic economies using three indicators: total trade; stock of foreign direct investment; and receipts of overseas development assistance. All three indicators are expressed as a percentage of GDP, and the table also reports changes over time between 1990 and 1999, the latest figures available. The table shows the extent to which different national economies are part of the emerging global economy, and where economic growth or contraction processes have been most pronounced over the last decade in this respect. The table confirms that economies are becoming increasingly interconnected, a process that coincides with the emergence of global civil society. It shows significant increases in trade and direct investments, and decreases in overseas development assistance between 1990 and 1999.

| | Trade | | | Foreign Direct Investment | | | Official Development Aid* | | |
| | Total trade in % GDP | | % change | Inward plus outward FDI stock in % GDP | | % change | Aid in % GNI | | % change |
Country	1990	1999	1990–1999	1990	1999	1990–1999	1990	1999	1990–1999
Afghanistan				0.2	1.0	400.0			
Albania	38	41	8.4	0.0	18.9		0.5	12.8	2,320.8
Algeria	48	51	5.4	2.4	3.5	45.8	0.4	0.2	-56.8
Angola	60			13.2	121.1	817.4	3.3	13.1	298.5
Argentina	15	21	42.3	10.7	28.9	170.1	0.1	0.0	-76.9
Armenia	81	71	-13.1	0.0	24.4		0.1	7.4	8,144.4
Australia	34			35.2	54.1	53.7			
Austria	78	91	16.2	8.9	20.4	129.2			
Azerbaijan		84		0.0	92.0			4.7	
Bahamas				67.5	88.2	30.7	0.1		
Bahrain	222			31.8	132.2	315.7	4.0	1.0	-75.0
Bangladesh	20	32	60.2	0.5	1.7	240.0	6.8	2.5	-62.8
Barbados	101	106	4.9	11.2	15.0	33.9	0.2	-0.1	-152.9
Belarus	90	127	39.9	0.0	8.4		0.5	0.1	-82.7
Belgium & Luxembourg**	145	153	5.0	48.0	205.8	328.8			
Belize	125	107	-14.5	18.1	41.4	128.7	7.6	6.6	-13.9
Benin	41	45	10.2	8.6	24.9	189.5	14.8	9.0	-39.6
Bhutan	61	75	23.9	0.6	0.8	33.3	17.6	16.1	-8.7
Bolivia	47	44	-4.8	21.3	57.2	168.5	11.8	7.0	-40.8
Bosnia & Herzegovina		90		0.0	7.6			22.8	
Botswana	106	61	-42.6	51.9	33.1	-36.2	4.0	1.1	-73.3
Brazil	15	22	47.1	8.5	23.2	172.9	0.0	0.0	0.0
Brunei				0.8	2.8	250.0	0.1	0.0	-100.0
Bulgaria	70	96	37.5	0.5	20.6	4,020.0	0.1	2.1	2,575.0
Burkina Faso	38	41	6.1	1.5	6.1	306.7	12.0	15.5	29.1
Burundi	36	27	-24.0	2.6	5.4	107.7	23.6	10.5	-55.5
Cambodia	19			13.4	19.4	44.8	3.7	9.0	142.4
Cameroon	37	49	31.6	10.7	16.6	55.1	4.2	5.0	19.1
Canada	52	84	62.0	34.5	58.5	69.6			
Cape Verde	56	74	30.3	1.7	18.5	988.2	31.7	23.7	-25.2
Central African Republic	42	41	-3.5	7.6	16.7	119.7	17.1	11.3	-33.7
Chad	42	47	11.5	17.3	30.1	74.0	18.1	12.4	-31.5
Chile	66	56	-14.6	33.8	74.2	119.5	0.4	0.1	-69.4
China & Tibet***	32	41	29.5	7.7	33.4	333.8	0.6	0.2	-59.3
Colombia	35	37	5.3	9.7	25.5	162.9	0.2	0.4	56.5
Comoros	51	67	29.9	7.2	14.1	95.8	18.2	11.1	-38.7
Congo, Dem. Rep.	59			4.0	5.9	47.5	10.5	2.5	-75.9

Record 1 continued	Trade			Foreign Direct Investment			Official Development Aid*		
	Total trade in % GDP		% change	Inward plus outward FDI stock in % GDP		% change	Aid in % GNI		% change
Country	1990	1999	1990–1999	1990	1999	1990–1999	1990	1999	1990–1999
Congo, Rep.	99	148	49.2	20.3	26.9	32.5	9.4	8.4	-10.0
Costa Rica	76	101	32.9	26.1	44.1	69.0	3.3	-0.1	-102.1
Côte d'Ivoire	59	82	39.2	9.3	32.2	246.2	7.5	4.3	-42.6
Croatia	164	89	-45.8	0.0	25.3			0.2	
Cuba				0.0	0.4				
Cyprus	109	93	-13.9	20.8	24.1	15.9	0.7	0.6	-19.1
Czech Republic	88	129	46.8	4.3	34.3	697.7		0.6	
Denmark	67	70	4.5	12.4	42.4	241.9			
Djibouti	134			1.3	6.9	430.8	23.7	14.2	-39.9
Dominican Republic	78	69	-10.7	8.1	25.2	211.1	1.5	1.2	-20.8
Ecuador	60	63	4.6	15.2	32.5	113.8	1.7	0.8	-50.3
Egypt	53	40	-23.4	26.0	19.8	-23.8	12.9	1.8	-86.5
El Salvador	50	62	23.9	5.5	15.3	178.2	7.4	1.5	-79.8
Equatorial Guinea	102	188	85.0	19.4	112.0	477.3	49.2	3.5	-92.9
Eritrea		89		0.0	0.0			19.5	
Estonia		159		0.0	53.2		0.3	1.6	519.2
Ethiopia	20	43	112.9	1.6	14.4	800.0	15.0	9.9	-33.7
Fiji	130	131	1.4	37.1	67.5	81.9	3.7	2.0	-47.3
Finland	47	67	41.4	12.1	41.3	241.3			
France	43	50	14.3	18.5	41.8	125.9			
Gabon	77	83	8.5	23.0	39.0	69.6	2.5	1.3	-49.6
Gambia	131	117	-10.9	11.3	30.6	170.8	34.0	8.6	-74.8
Georgia		73		0.0	7.0			8.4	
Germany	53	57	8.6	16.4	32.6	98.8			
Ghana	43	84	96.6	5.4	19.0	251.9	9.7	8.0	-18.3
Greece	47	44	-6.7	17.9	18.1	1.1	0.0		
Guatemala	46	46	1.1	22.7	17.7	-22.0	2.7	1.6	-39.2
Guinea	62	45	-27.0	2.5	6.9	176.0	11.0	7.0	-36.6
Guinea-Bissau	47	70	48.1	3.3	14.1	327.3	55.1	25.7	-53.4
Guyana	143	206	44.6	0.0	93.6		61.3	4.3	-93.0
Haiti	45	40	-11.4	5.0	5.2	4.0	5.7	6.1	7.0
Honduras	76	100	30.9	12.5	22.5	80.0	15.7	15.6	-0.6
Hungary	60	108	80.3	2.3	43.1	1,773.9	0.2	0.5	152.4
Iceland	67	72	7.0	3.5	10.9	211.4			
India	17	27	57.3	0.6	3.8	533.3	0.5	0.3	-26.7
Indonesia	49	62	26.0	34.0	47.8	40.6	1.6	1.7	5.0
Iran	46	38	-17.3	1.8	2.3	27.8	0.1	0.2	66.7
Iraq				0.0	0.0		0.1		
Ireland	109	161	47.6	17.0	67.1	294.7			
Israel & Occupied Territories	80	81	1.2	7.8	25.4	225.6	2.7	0.9	-65.7
Italy	39	49	24.3	10.5	25.2	140.0			
Jamaica	108	107	-0.6	18.1	55.8	208.3	7.1	-0.3	-104.8
Japan	21	19	-7.5	7.1	6.7	-5.6			
Jordan	155	105	-31.8	15.7	21.7	38.2	23.3	5.4	-76.7
Kazakhstan		85		0.0	51.9		0.4	1.1	200.0
Kenya	57	56	-2.5	9.1	10.0	9.9	14.7	2.9	-79.9

258

Country	Trade Total trade in % GDP 1990	1999	% change 1990–1999	Foreign Direct Investment Inward plus outward FDI stock in % GDP 1990	1999	% change 1990–1999	Official Development Aid* Aid in % GNI 1990	1999	% change 1990–1999
Korea, Dem. Rep.				3.0	18.7	523.3			
Korea, Rep.	59	77	30.3	2.9	13.4	362.1	0.0	-0.0	-150.0
Kuwait	103	84	-18.3	19.9	7.5	-62.3	0.0	0.0	0.0
Kyrgyzstan	79	99	26.0	0.0	23.1			22.7	
Laos	36			1.4	42.8	2,957.1	17.3	21.1	21.8
Latvia	97	104	7.9	0.0	30.6		0.0	1.6	5,066.7
Lebanon	118			1.9	5.5	189.5	7.5	1.2	-84.2
Lesotho	138			24.9	262.7	955.0	13.8	2.8	-79.7
Liberia				219.4	1039.5	373.8			
Libya				1.7	3.7	117.6	0.1		
Lithuania	113	90	-20.1	0.0	19.9		0.0	1.2	4,033.3
Macedonia	62	97	57.1	0.0	6.2			8.0	
Madagascar	44	57	30.7	3.4	7.2	111.8	13.6	9.8	-28.0
Malawi	60	70	16.7	10.2	25.1	146.1	28.6	25.1	-12.0
Malaysia	147	218	48.5	30.3	87.9	190.1	1.1	0.2	-82.9
Maldives	130			17.4	30.5	75.3	17.0	9.5	-44.1
Mali	51	61	19.7	2.4	17.7	637.5	20.0	14.0	-30.1
Malta	184			20.1	67.8	237.3	0.2	0.7	373.3
Mauritania	106	88	-17.5	5.9	11.0	86.4	22.0	23.6	7.2
Mauritius	138	133	-3.6	6.2	12.4	100.0	3.4	1.0	-70.7
Mexico	38	63	63.9	8.7	17.9	105.7	0.1	0.0	-83.3
Moldova	66	115	72.9	0.0	28.8			8.5	
Mongolia	64			0.0	14.6			25.4	
Morocco & Western Sahara	59	64	9.2	4.0	16.9	322.5	4.2	2.0	-52.8
Mozambique	44	49	11.3	2.0	22.4	1,020.0	42.4	3.2	-92.5
Myanmar	7			0.7	4.0	471.4			
Namibia	120	116	-3.0	87.1	50.7	-41.8	5.1	5.7	11.0
Nepal	32	53	67.5	0.3	2.0	566.7	11.5	6.7	-42.2
Netherlands	113	116	2.9	59.8	115.8	93.6			
New Caledonia	53	46	-13.4	2.1	2.8	33.3	12.0	10.3	-14.0
New Zealand	55			33.2	75.9	128.6			
Nicaragua	71	122	71.5	11.4	48.1	321.9	33.7	33.0	-2.0
Niger	37	38	3.7	14.0	27.1	93.6	16.4	9.4	-42.5
Nigeria	72	79	9.1	62.2	70.5	13.3	1.0	0.5	-50.5
Norway	75	72	-3.6	20.1	46.4	130.8			
Oman	83			16.3	15.8	-3.1	0.7		
Pakistan	39	35	-9.3	5.4	18.0	233.3	2.7	1.2	-54.1
Panama	72	74	2.7	119.5	140.3	17.4	2.0	0.2	-92.3
Papua New Guinea	90	87	-3.1	49.3	53.7	8.9	13.3	6.3	-52.6
Paraguay	73	60	-17.9	10.1	23.2	129.7	1.1	1.0	-4.8
Peru	30	32	7.3	4.3	16.4	281.4	1.6	0.9	-42.7
Philippines	61	101	66.7	7.7	17.4	126.0	2.9	0.9	-70.2
Poland	48	59	21.2	0.4	18.1	4,425.0	2.4	0.6	-73.1
Portugal	73			16.6	31.8	91.6			
Qatar				0.8	18.3	2,187.5	0.0		
Romania	43	64	50.1	2.2	16.5	650.0	0.6	1.1	76.2

259

Country	Trade Total trade in % GDP 1990	1999	% change 1990–1999	Foreign Direct Investment Inward plus outward FDI stock in % GDP 1990	1999	% change 1990–1999	Official Development Aid* Aid in % GNI 1990	1999	% change 1990–1999
Russian Federation	36	74	106.2	0.0	6.7		0.0	0.5	1,100.0
Rwanda	20	27	35.7	8.2	12.5	52.4	11.3	19.2	69.3
Samoa	96			5.6	27.8	396.4	31.5	12.9	-59.0
Sao Tome & Principe	87	119	37.2	0.8	2.5	212.5	104.2	65.1	-37.5
Saudi Arabia	82	68	-17.8	23.2	21.1	-9.1	0.0	0.0	-50.0
Senegal	56	72	28.8	5.6	17.3	208.9	14.9	11.4	-23.2
Sierra Leone	49	34	-30.5	0.0	0.2		7.9	11.3	43.1
Singapore	397			97.2	155.1	59.6	-0.0	0.0	-100.0
Slovakia	62	128	106.8	0.6	16.1	2,583.3	0.0	1.6	4,000.0
Slovenia	158	109	-30.7	5.3	15.9	200.0		0.2	
Solomon Islands	120			33.0	52.8	60.0	21.8	12.6	-42.4
Somalia	48			0.0	4.3		59.1		
South Africa	43	48	12.2	22.7	64.7	185.0		0.4	
Spain	36	56	57.4	16.6	39.5	138.0			
Sri Lanka	68	78	14.1	8.6	14.5	68.6	9.3	1.6	-82.7
St. Lucia	157	126	-19.5	75.7	119.4	57.7	3.3	4.2	27.5
St. Vincent & the Grenadines	143	123	-13.9	25.0	158.2	532.8	8.0	5.3	-33.7
Sudan				0.4	9.7	2,325.0	6.5	2.8	-57.8
Suriname	56			0.0	0.0		19.9	8.1	-59.3
Swaziland	153	205	34.4	43.6	53.5	22.7	5.9	2.2	-63.4
Sweden	60	82	37.7	26.9	80.1	197.8			
Switzerland	72			43.9	103.8	136.4			
Syria	55	69	25.2	1.6	6.5	306.3	5.9	1.5	-74.4
Tajikistan		132		0.0	10.4			6.6	
Tanzania	50	41	-17.5	2.2	11.2	409.1	28.8	11.3	-60.6
Thailand	76	102	34.9	10.1	19.4	92.1	1.0	0.8	-12.6
Togo	79	70	-10.7	17.2	39.1	127.3	16.3	5.2	-68.2
Trinidad & Tobago	74	93	26.3	41.7	95.0	127.8	0.4	0.4	5.1
Tunisia	94	86	-8.6	59.1	57.2	-3.2	3.3	1.2	-63.1
Turkey	31	50	62.4	0.9	5.3	488.9	0.8	-0.0	-101.3
Turkmenistan		104		0.0	31.9			0.7	
Uganda	27	34	28.6	0.1	20.4	20,300.0	15.8	9.2	-41.6
Ukraine	56	104	85.3	0.0	10.8		0.3	1.3	312.9
United Arab Emirates	106			2.5	5.3	112.0	0.0	0.0	0.0
United Kingdom	51	53	5.1	44.2	76.6	73.3			
United States	21			14.9	24.1	61.7			
Uruguay	42	38	-9.7	12.5	10.8	-13.6	0.6	0.1	-81.4
Uzbekistan	77	38	-50.6	0.0	6.0			0.8	
Vanuatu	123			71.9	141.0	96.1	30.6	16.3	-46.9
Venezuela	60	37	-37.3	7.2	26.4	266.7	0.2	0.0	-75.0
Vietnam	60			3.6	55.6	1,444.4		5.0	
Yemen	44	84	91.7	3.9	16.1	312.8	9.1	7.4	-18.9
Zambia	72	63	-12.9	30.0	58.4	94.7	16.0	20.8	30.5
Zimbabwe	46	91	99.1	2.4	22.7	845.8	4.0	4.7	16.3

Record 1 continued	Trade			Official Development Aid*		
	Total trade in % GDP		% change	Aid in % GNI		% change
Region	1990	1999	1990–1999	1990	1999	1990–1999
Low income	37	50	33.5	1.9	2.2	17.4
Middle income	42	55	31.8	0.7	0.4	-38.6
Low & middle income	41	54	32.1	1.1	0.8	-28.7
East Asia & Pacific	52	70	35.0	0.9	0.5	-37.6
Europe & Central Asia	46	77	66.1	0.2	1.0	390.5
Latin America & Caribbean	26	34	30.7	0.5	0.3	-37.5
Middle East & North Africa	69	57	-17.4	2.57	0.9	-66.5
South Asia	22	30	37.1	1.5	0.7	-51.0
Sub-Saharan Africa	53	60	12.5	6.4	4.1	-36.4
High income	38	*43*	*11.9*	0.0	0.0	0.0
World	39	52	34.2	0.3	0.2	-32.1

Where data for a particular year are not available, figures are taken from the year before or after as an estimate. These figures, and estimates based on them, are presented in italics.

Figures for FDI change as newer data are acquired (data for 1990 may be different in different versions of World Investment Report)

*Official Development Aid includes both official development assistance and official aid.

**Data for Hong Kong and Macao are not included in this table.

***FDI data is not supplied for Belgium and Luxembourg individually; figures for trade for Belgium and Luxembourg together are therefore estimates calculated by LSE and are not attributable to the World Bank.

Sources: World Bank, World Development Indicators 2001, CD-Rom; UNCTAD, FDI/TNC database; World Investment Report 2001: Promoting Linkages

Record 2 Global trade

Following Record 1, this map offers a simplified and consolidated view of trade flows among major world regions for 1999. It shows the unevenness of economic globalisation as measured by trade flows. Flows between three high income industrial economies (USA, Japan and EU) and six low or middle income regions are shown, where the thicker the arrow, the greater the flow of trade. Trade flows which constitute 0.1% world trade or less are omitted from the map.

Direction of flow (export region → import region)	Amount of trade in % world trade
East Asia & Pacific → USA	2.3
East Asia & Pacific → EU	1.7
East Asia & Pacific → Japan	1.6
East Asia & Pacific → Latin America & Caribbean	0.3
East Asia & Pacific → Middle East & North Africa	0.2
East Asia & Pacific → South Asia	0.2
East Asia & Pacific → Europe & Central Asia	0.2
Within East Asia & Pacific	1.6
EU → USA	3.5
EU → Europe & Central Asia	2.8
EU → East Asia & Pacific	1.0
EU → Latin America & Caribbean	1.0
EU → Middle East & North Africa	1.0
EU → Japan	0.7
EU → Sub-Saharan Africa	0.5
EU → South Asia	0.3
Within EU	24.6
Europe & Central Asia → EU	2.3
Europe & Central Asia → USA	0.3
Within Europe & Central Asia	1.2
Japan → USA	2.3
Japan → East Asia & Pacific	1.5
Japan → EU	1.3
Japan → Latin America & Caribbean	0.3
Latin America & Caribbean → USA	3.1
Latin America & Caribbean → EU	0.7
Within Latin America & Caribbean	0.7
Middle East & North Africa → EU	0.8
Middle East & North Africa→ East Asia & Pacific	0.4
Middle East & North Africa → USA	0.3
Middle East & North Africa → Japan	0.2
Within Middle East & North Africa	0.2
South Asia → EU	0.3
South Asia → USA	0.2
Within South Asia	0.0
Sub-Saharan Africa → EU	0.5
Sub-Saharan Africa → USA	0.2
Within Sub-Saharan Africa	0.2
USA → EU	2.7
USA → Latin America & Caribbean	2.5
USA → East Asia & Pacific	1.0
USA → Japan	1.0
USA → Middle East & North Africa	0.3
USA → Europe & Central Asia	0.2

USA

= data for these countries not included on this map

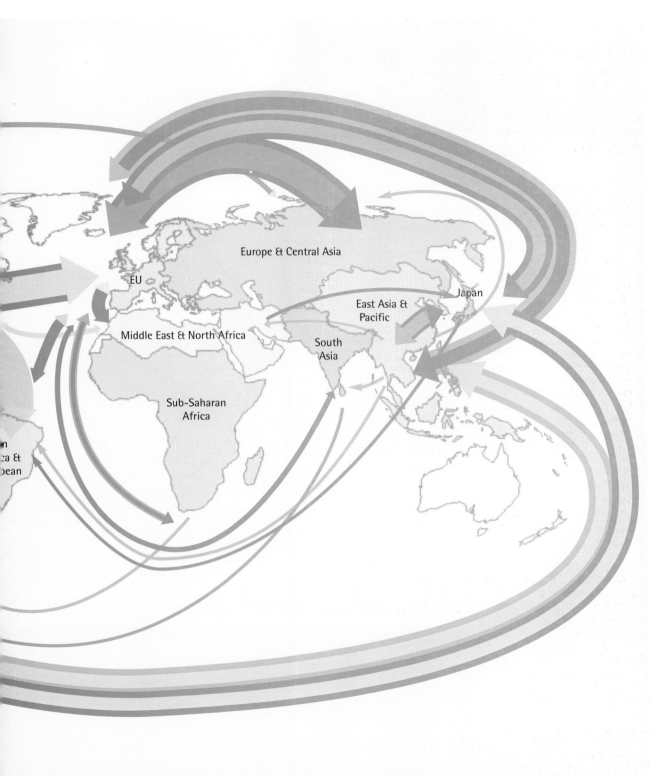

Europe & Central Asia

EU

Middle East & North Africa

Sub-Saharan
Africa

South
Asia

East Asia &
Pacific

Japan

Sources: Map produced by Ben Cracknell © based on information from World Bank, *World Development Indicators 2001* (CD-Rom), restructured by Sally Stares, map template MapInfo ©

Record 3 Students abroad

This map shows the numbers and flows of students from one country to another, within and between major world regions for the academic year 1998-99. Widths of arrows represent numbers of students studying abroad. Information for this record is collected from hosting countries only (so figures should be interpreted as absolute minimum numbers), and no data are available for some major countries known to send significant numbers of students abroad, including China, India, Brazil, Pakistan, Bangladesh, Nigeria, and Egypt. Students are major transmitters of knowledge and ideas, and interlocutors among cultures. A growing practice of studying abroad may therefore be one catalyst of the emergence and spread of global civil society.

Direction of flow (region of origin → host region)	Number of students
Africa → Asia	4,288
Africa → Europe	127,390
Africa → North America	33,202
Africa → Oceania	2,580
Africa → South America	3
Within Africa	19,993
Asia → Africa	1,909
Asia → Europe	234,632
Asia → North America	326,049
Asia → Oceania	89,941
Asia → South America	54
Within Asia	397,168
Europe → Africa	2,424
Europe → Asia	12,868
Europe → North America	76,563
Europe → Oceania	10,546
Europe → South America	26
Within Europe	435.579
North America → Africa	6,396
North America → Asia	3,074
North America → Europe	38,229
North America → Oceania	3,306
North America → South America	459
Within North America	57,362
Oceania → Africa	102
Oceania → Asia	616
Oceania → Europe	3,056
Oceania → North America	4,425
Oceania → South America	no data
Within Oceania	7,601
South America → Africa	75
South America → Asia	781
South America → Europe	21,567
South America → North America	28,286
South America → Oceania	654
Within South America	201,509

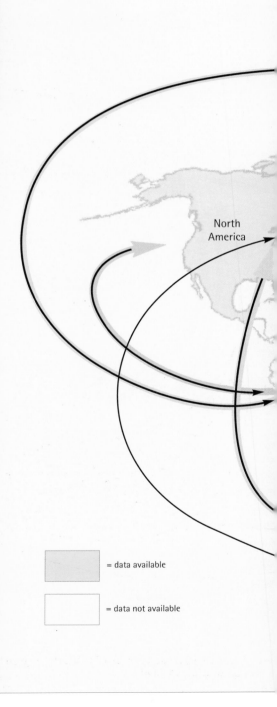

North America

= data available

= data not available

Record 4 Transnationality of top 100 TNCs

This table lists the name and global headquarter country for the 100 largest non-financial corporations, and then presents data on their size and foreign share of assets, sales, and employment for 1999. In addition, the table shows the ranks and degree of transnationality of each TNC, with the most transnational companies at the top, where higher index numbers (and lower rank numbers) indicate an overall greater extent of transnationality. The table suggests the importance of TNCs and the globalised economy they create as one major reference point for the development of global civil society—from activists protesting against certain corporate practices and the emergence of corporate cultures, to the growing numbers and influence of highly mobile groups of managers and professionals working for TNCs.

Ranking by: Transnationality Index* Corporation	Country	Assets			Sales			Employment			TNI (%)
		Foreign	Total	% Foreign	Foreign	Total	% Foreign	Foreign	Total	% Foreign	
1 Thomson Corporation	Canada	13.6	13.8	98.6	5.5	5.8	94.8	37,000	40,000	92.5	95.4
2 Nestlé SA	Switzerland	33.1	36.8	89.9	45.9	46.7	98.3	224,554	230,929	97.2	95.2
3 ABB	Switzerland	27.0	30.6	88.2	23.8	24.4	97.5	155,427	161,430	96.3	94.1
4 Electrolux AB	Sweden	9.1	9.8	92.9	13.9	14.5	95.9	84,035	92,916	90.4	93.2
5 Holcim (ex Holderbank)	Switzerland	12.5	13.6	91.9	7.3	8.1	90.1	36,719	39,327	93.4	91.8
6 Roche Group	Switzerland	24.5	27.1	90.4	18.1	18.4	98.4	57,970	67,695	85.6	91.5
7 British American Tobacco Plc	United Kingdom	22.0	26.2	84.0	16.5	18.1	91.2	104,223	107,620	96.8	90.7
8 Unilever	United Kingdom/ Netherlands	25.3	28.0	90.4	38.4	44.0	87.3	222,614	246,033	90.5	89.3
9 Seagram Company	Canada	25.6	35.0	73.1	12.3	11.8	104.2				88.6
10 Akzo Nobel NV	Netherlands	10.2	12.0	85.0	12.6	15.4	81.8	55,100	68,000	81.0	82.6
11 Nippon Mitsubishi Oil Corporation (Nippon Oil Co. Ltd)	Japan	31.5	35.5	88.7	28.4	33.9	83.8	11,900	15,964	74.5	82.4
12 Cadbury-Schweppes Plc	United Kingdom	7.1	8.0	88.8	5.3	6.8	77.9	29,835	37,425	79.7	81.9
13 Diageo Plc	United Kingdom	28.0	40.4	69.3	16.4	19.0	86.3	59,852	72,479	82.6	79.4
14 News Corporation	Australia	23.5	38.4	61.2	12.9	14.3	90.2	24,500	33,800	72.5	78.3
15 L'Air Liquide Groupe	France		10.5		4.6	6.1	75.4		29,000		76.9
16 Glaxo Wellcome Plc	United Kingdom	11.8	16.8	70.2	11.8	13.8	85.5	44,976	60,726	74.1	76.6
17 Michelin	France		17.3		11.9	13.8	86.2		130,434		73.8
18 BP	United Kingdom	39.3	52.6	74.7	57.7	83.5	69.1	62,150	80,400	77.3	73.7
19 Stora Enso OYS	Finland		16.2		10.0	10.7	93.5		40,226		72.5
20 AstraZeneca Plc	United States	7.2	19.3	37.3	14.3	15.1	94.7	48,300	58,000	83.3	71.6
21 TotalFina SA	France		77.6		31.6	39.6	79.8	50,538	74,437	67.9	70.3
22 ExxonMobil Corporation	United States	99.4	144.5	68.8	115.5	160.9	71.8	68,000	107,000	63.6	68.0
23 Danone Groupe SA	France	9.5	15.1	62.9	8.9	13.4	66.4		75,965		67.8
24 McDonald's Corporation	United States	12.1	21.0	57.6	8.1	13.3	60.9	260,000	314,000	82.8	67.1
25 Alcatel	France	17.7	34.0	52.1	16.4	23.2	70.7	85,712	115,712	74.1	65.6
26 Coca-Cola Company	United States	18.0	21.6	83.3	12.4	19.8	62.6		37,000		65.2
27 Honda Motor Co. Ltd.	Japan	24.4	41.8	58.4	38.7	51.7	74.9		112,200		64.7
28 Compart Spa	Italy		18.6		8.0	11.8	67.8	25,177	36,916	68.2	63.8
29 Montedison Group	Italy		16.7		7.9	11.5	68.7	21,181	29,550	71.7	62.2
30 Volvo AB	Sweden		17.7		13.4	15.1	88.7	28,630	53,600	53.4	61.4
31 Ericsson LM	Sweden	10.6	23.8	44.5	20.4	25.3	80.6	59,250	103,290	57.4	60.9
32 BMW AG	Germany	27.1	39.2	69.1	26.8	36.7	73.0	46,104	114,952	40.1	60.9
33 Bayer AG	Germany	18.2	31.4	58.0	20.3	29.2	69.5	64,100	120,400	53.2	60.2

US$ billions and number of employees, 1999

US$ billions and number of employees, 1999

Ranking by: TNI* Corporation	Country	Assets Foreign	Total	% Foreign	Sales Foreign	Total	% Foreign	Employment Foreign	Total	% Foreign	TNI (%)
34 Rio Tinto Plc	Australia/ United Kingdom	7.4	12.1	61.2	5.3	9.3	57.0	16,829	26,938	62.5	60.2
35 Philips Electronics	Netherlands	22.7	29.8	76.2	31.8	33.5	94.9		226,874		59.9
36 BASF AG	Germany	17.1	30.0	57.0	22.5	29.5	76.3	46,455	104,628	44.4	59.2
37 Bridgestone	Japan	7.0	15.7	44.6	11.6	18.3	63.4	70,000	101,489	69.0	58.9
38 Renault SA	France		46.4		23.9	37.6	63.6		159,608		58.2
39 Crown Cork & Seal	United States	7.2	11.5	62.6	3.9	7.7	50.6		35,959		57.5
40 Canon Electronics	Japan	12.3	25.4	48.4	18.0	25.7	70.0	42,787	81,009	52.8	57.1
41 Siemens AG	Germany		76.6		53.2	72.2	73.7	251,000	443,000	56.7	56.8
42 Sony Corporation	Japan		64.2		43.1	63.1	68.3	115,717	189,700	61.0	56.7
43 Royal Dutch/Shell Group	Netherlands/ United Kingdom	68.7	113.9	60.3	53.5	105.4	50.8	57,367	99,310	57.8	56.3
44 Motorola Inc.	United States	23.5	40.5	58.0	18.3	33.1	55.3	70,800	128,000	55.3	56.2
45 Volkswagen Group	Germany		64.3		47.8	70.6	67.7	147,959	306,275	48.3	55.7
46 Robert Bosch GmbH	Germany		20.9		18.5	28.0	66.1	96,970	194,889	49.8	55.3
47 Cemex SA	Mexico	7.0	11.9	58.8	2.5	4.8	52.1		20,902		54.6
48 Johnson & Johnson	United States	19.8	29.2	67.8	12.1	27.5	44.0	49,571	97,806	50.7	54.2
49 Aventis	France		39.0		4.7	19.2	24.5		92,446		54.0
50 IBM	United States	44.7	87.5	51.1	50.4	87.6	57.5	161,612	307,401	52.6	53.7
51 DaimlerChrysler AG	Germany	55.7	175.9	31.7	122.4	151.0	81.1	225,705	466,938	48.3	53.7
52 Hewlett-Packard	United States		35.3		23.4	42.4	55.2	41,400	84,400	49.1	53.1
53 Royal Ahold NV	Netherlands	10.0	14.3	69.9	23.3	33.8	68.9	59,428	308,793	19.2	52.7
54 Elf Aquitaine SA	France	18.8	43.2	43.5	25.7	35.8	71.8		57,400		51.7
55 Repsol-YPF SA	Spain	29.6	42.1	70.3	9.1	26.3	34.6		29,262		51.6
56 Texaco Inc.	United States		29.0		25.2	35.0	72.0		18,443		51.2
57 Mitsubishi Motors Corporation	Japan	7.0	25.4	27.6	16.8	29.1	57.7		26,749		51.2
58 Suez Lyonnaise des Eaux	France		71.6		9.7	23.5	41.3	150,000	220,000	68.2	49.1
59 Mannesmann AG	Germany		57.7		11.8	21.8	54.1	58,694	130,860	44.9	48.9
60 Dow Chemical Company	United States	13.3	33.5	39.7	14.5	25.9	56.0	21,850	51,012	42.8	46.2
61 AES Corporation	United States	10.2	20.9	48.8	2.1	3.3	63.6		14,500		45.5
62 Peugeot SA	France	15.6	39.8	39.2	24.4	37.8	64.6	50,300	165,800	30.3	44.7
63 Usinor	France	7.4	15.6	47.4	7.0	14.5	48.3	22,395	64,118	34.9	43.5
64 Viag AG	Germany		34.2		11.1	19.6	56.6	41,723	81,809	51.0	43.3
65 Veba Group	Germany	15.1	55.8	27.1	24.5	39.1	62.7	49,590	131,602	37.7	42.4
66 Du Pont (E.I.) de Nemours	United States	14.8	40.8	36.3	13.3	26.9	49.4	36,000	94,000	38.3	41.3
67 ENI Group	Italy	20.9	44.3	47.2	11.4	29.1	39.2		72,023		40.9
68 Nissan Motor Co. Ltd.	Japan		59.7			58.1			136,397		40.7
69 Texas Utilities Company	United States	17.3	40.7	42.5	6.8	17.1	39.8	8,590	21,934	39.2	40.4
70 Procter & Gamble	United States	10.7	32.1	33.3	18.4	38.1	48.3		110,000		40.3
71 Matsushita Industrial Co. Ltd.	Japan	13.9	72.5	19.2	34.0	68.9	49.3	143,773	290,448	49.5	39.3
72 Fujitsu Ltd.	Japan	15.3	42.3	36.2	17.5	43.3	40.4	72,851	188,573	38.6	38.4
73 Telefónica SA	Spain	24.2	64.1	37.8	9.5	23.0	41.3		127,193		38.0
74 Hutchison Whampoa Ltd.	Hong Kong, China		48.5		2.1	7.1	29.6	21,652	42,510	50.9	38.0

US$ billions and number of employees, 1999

Ranking by: TNI*

Corporation	Country	Assets Foreign	Total	% Foreign	Sales Foreign	Total	% Foreign	Employment Foreign	Total	% Foreign	TNI (%)
75 General Electric	United States	141.1	405.2	34.8	32.7	111.6	29.3	143,000	310,000	46.1	36.7
76 Metro AG	Germany	7.2	19.1	37.7	17.3	44.1	39.2	55,571	171,440	32.4	36.4
77 Ford Motor Company	United States		273.4		50.1	162.6	30.8	191,486	364,550	52.5	36.1
78 Carrefour SA	France	12.3	33.7	36.5	14.3	37.7	37.9		297,290		34.7
79 Chevron Corporation	United States	20.1	40.7	49.4	9.7	35.4	27.4	9,426	36,490	25.8	34.2
80 Vivendi SA	France		79.3		16.7	39.1	42.7		275,591		34.0
81 Fiat Spa	Italy	15.2	80.4	18.9	16.5	45.2	36.5	98,589	221,319	44.5	33.4
82 Toyota Motor Corporation	Japan	56.3	154.9	36.3	60.0	119.7	50.1	13,500	214,631	6.3	30.9
83 General Motors	United States	68.5	274.7	24.9	46.5	176.6	26.3	162,300	398,000	40.8	30.7
84 Petróleos de Venezuela SA	Venezuela	8.0	47.3	16.9	13.3	32.6	40.8		47,760		29.8
85 Mitsubishi Corporation	Japan	24.6	78.6	31.3	15.8	127.3	12.4	3,437	7,556	45.5	29.7
86 Mitsui & Co. Ltd.	Japan	17.3	56.5	30.6	57.8	118.5	48.8		31,250		29.1
87 Merck & Co.	United States	9.1	35.6	25.6	7.0	32.7	21.4	23,824	62,300	38.2	28.4
88 Marubeni Corporation	Japan	10.8	54.2	19.9	31.9	99.3	32.1		8,618		26.0
89 Lucent Technologies	United States	7.2	32.1	22.4	12.2	38.3	31.9	36,000	153,000	23.5	25.9
90 Wal-Mart Stores	United States	30.2	50.0	60.4	19.4	137.6	14.1		1,140,000		25.8
91 Edison International	United States	8.1	35.0	23.1	1.0	9.2	10.9		19,570		24.3
92 Toshiba Corporation	Japan	7.1	53.8	13.2	17.5	54.2	32.3	46,500	190,870	24.4	23.3
93 Atlantic Richfield	United States		26.3		2.0	12.5	16.0		16,600		23.3
94 RWE Group	Germany	10.9	57.4	19.0	7.9	35.1	22.5		155,576		22.9
95 Southern Company	United States	9.6	38.4	25.0	1.5	11.6	12.9	6,928	32,949	21.0	19.8
96 Hitachi Ltd.	Japan	14.6	91.5	16.0	15.4	77.7	19.8		323,827		17.9
97 Sumitomo Corporation	Japan	15.0	47.6	31.5	12.6	103.5	12.2		33,057		16.1
98 Nissho Iwai	Japan	9.1	38.5	23.6	12.9	68.7	18.8		18,446		15.8
99 Itochu Corporation	Japan	12.4	55.9	22.2	18.4	115.3	16.0		40,683		13.7
100 SBC Communications	United States		83.2			49.5			204,530		12.9

*TNI = Transnationality Index (average of the ratios of foreign to total assets, sales and employment).

Where data for part of the TNI are unavailable, they are estimated to enable calculation of TNI (such estimates of assets, sales or employment are not included in this table).

List includes non-financial TNCs only.

Definitions of 'foreign' are not straightforward for some TNCs; see notes accompanying this information in World Investment Report for for more details.

Source: UNCTAD, World Investment Report 2001: Promoting Linkages, Annex B (website: http://www.unctad.org/wir/contents/wir01content.en.htm)

Record 5 Air travel and international tourism

This record offers data on air transport and international tourism for 1990 and 1999, and also presents the percentage change for this time period. Record 5b shows in-bound and out-bound tourism for major world regions in 1998/1999. The bars in the map represent numbers of departures and arrivals per capita (exact figures are given alongside the graphics) for low and middle income regions, plus three high income areas: Canada and US, the EU and Japan. The massive expansion of tourism and air transport establishes connections among different cultures and peoples, and creates economic as well as social ties. Air travel also facilitates global activism. Obviously, any possible decline in air travel after 11 September 2001 is not recorded here.

Record 5a

Country	Air transport Passengers carried 1990 Total (thousands)	Per capita	1999 Total (thousands)	Per capita	% change in total 1990-1999	International tourism Inbound tourists 1990 Total (thousands)	Per capita	1999 Total (thousands)	Per capita	% change in total 1990-1999	Outbound tourists 1990 Total (thousands)	Per capita	1998 Total (thousands)	Per capita	% change in total 1990-1998
Afghanistan	241	0.02	140	0.01	-41.9	8	0.00	4	0.00	-50.0					
Albania			20	0.01		30	0.01	39	0.01	30.0			18	0.01	
Algeria	3,748	0.15	2,937	0.10	-21.6	1,137	0.05	755	0.03	-33.6	3,828	0.15	1,377	0.05	-64.0
Angola	452	0.05	531	0.04	17.5	46	0.00	45	0.00	-2.2			3	0.00	
Argentina	5,369	0.17	9,192	0.25	71.2	1,930	0.06	2898	0.08	50.2	2,398	0.07	4,592	0.13	91.5
Armenia			343	0.09				41							
Australia	17,553	1.04	30,007	1.58	70.9	2,215	0.13	4459	0.24	101.3	2,170	0.13	3,161	0.17	45.7
Austria	2,532	0.33	6,057	0.75	139.2	19,011	2.46	17467	2.16	-8.1	8,527	1.10	13,263	1.64	55.5
Azerbaijan			572	0.07				63					343	0.04	
Bahamas	1,090	4.27	1,719	5.73	57.7	1,562	6.13	1540	5.13	-1.4					
Bahrain	771	1.57	1,307	2.08	69.5	1,376	2.81	1991	3.18	44.7	147	0.30			
Bangladesh	1,044	0.01	1,215	0.01	16.4	115	0.00	173	0.00	50.4	388	0.00	992	0.01	155.7
Barbados	0	0.00				432	1.68	512	1.92	18.5					
Belarus			212	0.02				355					969	0.09	
Belgium	3,133	0.31	9,965	0.97	218.1	5,147	0.52	6369	0.62	23.7	3,835	0.38	7,773	0.76	102.7
Belize						88	0.47	157	0.71	78.4					
Benin	76	0.02	84	0.01	10.0	110	0.02	152	0.02	38.2	418	0.09	420	0.07	0.5
Bermuda						435		354		-18.6	102				
Bhutan	8	0.00	31	0.02	283.8	2	0.00	7	0.00	250.0					
Bolivia	1,238	0.19	1,873	0.23	51.3	254	0.04	410	0.05	61.4	242	0.04	298	0.04	23.1
Bosnia & Herzegovina			60	0.02				89							
Botswana	101	0.08	144	0.09	42.3	543	0.44	740	0.49	36.3	192	0.15	460	0.31	139.6
Brazil	19,150	0.13	28,273	0.17	47.6	1,091	0.01	5107	0.03	368.1	1,188	0.01	4,598	0.03	287.0
Brunei	307	1.19	808	2.51	163.2	377	1.47	964	2.99	155.7	246	0.96			
Bulgaria	1,907	0.22	735	0.09	-61.5	1,586	0.18	2472	0.31	55.9	2,395	0.27	2,592	0.32	8.2
Burkina Faso	137	0.02	147	0.01	7.8	74	0.01	218	0.02	194.6					
Burundi	8	0.00	0	0.00	-100.0	109	0.02	15	0.00	-86.2	24	0.00	16	0.00	-33.3
Cambodia						17	0.00	368	0.03	2064.7			41	0.00	
Cameroon	284	0.02	293	0.02	3.0	89	0.01	135	0.01	51.7					
Canada	20,601	1.50	24,039	0.79	16.7	15,209	1.11	19557	0.64	28.6	20,415	1.49	17,640	0.58	-13.6
Cape Verde	177	0.52	252	0.61	42.6	24	0.07	52	0.12	116.7					
Central African Republic	130	0.04	84	0.02	-35.6	6	0.00	10	0.00	66.7					

269

Air transport / International tourism

Country	Air transport Passengers carried 1990 Total (thousands)	Per capita	1999 Total (thousands)	Per capita	% change in total 1990-1999	International tourism Inbound tourists 1990 Total (thousands)	Per capita	1999 Total (thousands)	Per capita	% change in total 1990-1999	Outbound tourists 1990 Total (thousands)	Per capita	1998 Total (thousands)	Per capita	% change in total 1990-1998
Chad	93	0.02	84	0.01	-10.1	9	0.00	43	0.01	377.8	24	0.00	10	0.00	-58.3
Chile	1,364	0.10	5,188	0.35	280.4	943	0.07	1626	0.11	72.4	768	0.06	1,351	0.09	75.9
China & Tibet*	16,596	0.01	55,853	0.04	236.5	10,484	0.01	27047	0.02	158.0	2,134	0.00	8,426	0.01	294.8
Colombia	5,267	0.15	8,665	0.21	64.5	813	0.02	841	0.02	3.4	781	0.02	1,140	0.03	46.0
Comoros	26	0.05				8	0.02	24	0.04	200.0					
Congo, Dem. Rep.	207	0.01				55	0.00	53	0.00	-3.6					
Congo, Rep.	239	0.11	132	0.05	-44.7	33	0.01	25	0.01	-24.2					
Costa Rica	467	0.15	1,055	0.27	126.0	435	0.14	1027	0.26	136.1	191	0.06	330	0.09	72.8
Côte d'Ivoire	200	0.02	260	0.02	29.7	196	0.02	301	0.02	53.6	2	0.00	5	0.00	150.0
Croatia	113	0.03	833	0.18	634.7	7,049	1.56	3443	0.74	-51.2					
Cuba	1,138	0.11	1,259	0.11	10.7	327	0.03	1561	0.14	377.4	12	0.00	55	0.00	358.3
Cyprus	814	1.19	1,337	1.72	64.3	1,561	2.29	2434	3.13	55.9	228	0.33		0.54	82.9
Czech Republic	1,096	0.11	1,853	0.18	69.1	7,278	0.71	16031	1.56	120.3	3,510	0.34			
Denmark	4,840	0.94	5,971	1.13	23.4	1,838	0.36	2023	0.38	10.1	3,929	0.76	4,972	0.94	26.5
Djibouti	131	0.26				33	0.07	21	0.03	-36.4					
Dominican Republic	718	0.10	10	0.00	-98.6	1,305	0.18	2649	0.32	103.0	137	0.02	354	0.04	158.4
Ecuador	763	0.07	1,387	0.11	81.9	362	0.04	509	0.04	40.6	181	0.02	330	0.03	82.3
Egypt	3,239	0.06	4,620	0.07	42.6	2,411	0.04	4489	0.07	86.2	2,012	0.04	2,854	0.04	41.8
El Salvador	525	0.10	1,624	0.26	209.4	194	0.04	658	0.11	239.2	525	0.10	868	0.14	65.3
Equatorial Guinea	14	0.04	0	0.00	-100.0										
Estonia			302	0.21				950					1,659	1.16	
Ethiopia	620	0.01	861	0.01	38.9	79	0.00	91	0.00	15.2	89	0.00	140	0.00	57.3
Fiji	433	0.60	525	0.65	21.2	279	0.39	410	0.51	47.0	61	0.08		0.10	27.9
Finland	4,450	0.89	6,050	1.17	35.9	1,572	0.32	2700	0.52	71.8	1,169	0.23	4,743	0.92	305.7
France	35,964	0.63	49,691	0.84	38.2	52,497	0.93	73042	1.24	39.1	19,430	0.34	18,077	0.31	-7.0
Gabon	398	0.43	423	0.35	6.2	109	0.12	194	0.16	78.0	161	0.17			
Gambia						100	0.11	91	0.07	-9.0					
Georgia			159	0.03				384					433	0.08	
Germany	22,147	0.28	54,550	0.67	146.3	17,045	0.21	17116	0.21	0.4	56,261	0.71	82,975	1.01	47.5
Ghana	188	0.01	304	0.02	61.7	146	0.01	373	0.02	155.5					
Greece	6,135	0.60	6,267	0.59	2.2	8,873	0.87	12000	1.13	35.2	1,651	0.16	1,935	0.18	17.2
Guatemala	156	0.02	506	0.05	224.5	509	0.06	823	0.07	61.7	289	0.03	391	0.04	35.3
Guinea	41	0.01	59	0.01	41.6	49	0.01	27	0.00	-44.9					
Guinea-Bissau	21	0.02	0	0.00	-100.0										
Guyana	146	0.20	70	0.09	-51.7	64	0.09	66	0.09	3.1					
Haiti	0	0.00				144	0.02	147	0.02	2.1					
Honduras	610	0.13				202	0.04	371	0.06	83.7	196	0.04	202	0.03	3.1
Hungary	1,363	0.13	1,944	0.19	42.6	20,510	1.98	12930	1.29	-37.0	13,596	1.31	12,317	1.22	-9.4
Iceland	760	2.98	1,350	4.87	77.8	142	0.56	263	0.95	85.2	142	0.56		0.83	59.9
India	10,862	0.01	16,005	0.02	47.3	1,707	0.00	2482	0.00	45.4	2,281	0.00	3,811	0.00	67.1
Indonesia	9,223	0.05	8,047	0.04	-12.8	2,178	0.01	4700	0.02	115.8	688	0.00	2,076	0.01	201.7
Iran	5,633	0.10	8,277	0.12	47.0	154	0.00	1174	0.02	662.3	788	0.01	1,450	0.02	84.0
Iraq	702	0.04	0	0.00	-100.0	748	0.04	51	0.00	-93.2	239	0.01			

Country	Air transport — Passengers carried 1990 Total (thousands)	1990 Per capita	1999 Total (thousands)	1999 Per capita	% change in total 1990–1999	International tourism — Inbound tourists 1990 Total (thousands)	1990 Per capita	1999 Total (thousands)	1999 Per capita	% change in total 1990–1999	Outbound tourists 1990 Total (thousands)	1990 Per capita	1998 Total (thousands)	1998 Per capita	% change in total 1990–1998
Ireland	4,812	1.37	11,949	3.18	148.3	3,666	1.04	6511	1.73	77.6	1,798	0.51	3,053	0.82	69.8
Israel & Occupied Territories	2,004	0.44	4,033	0.68	101.3	1,063	0.24	2275	0.38	114.0	883	0.20	2,983	0.52	237.8
Italy	19,750	0.35	28,049	0.49	42.0	26,679	0.47	36097	0.63	35.3	16,152	0.28	19,352	0.34	19.8
Jamaica	1,004	0.42	1,670	0.65	66.4	989	0.42	1248	0.49	26.2					
Japan	76,224	0.62	105,960	0.84	39.0	3,236	0.03	4438	0.03	37.1	10,997	0.09	15,806	0.12	43.7
Jordan	964	0.30	1,252	0.26	29.9	572	0.18	1358	0.28	137.4	1,143	0.35	1,347	0.29	17.8
Kazakhstan			667	0.04											
Kenya	794	0.03	1,358	0.05	70.9	814	0.03	943	0.03	15.8	210	0.01	300	0.01	42.9
Korea, Dem. Rep.	223	0.01	59	0.00	-73.3	115	0.01	130	0.01	13.0					
Korea, Rep.	15,685	0.37	31,319	0.67	99.7	2,959	0.07	4660	0.10	57.5	1,561	0.04	3,067	0.07	96.5
Kuwait	966	0.45	2,130	1.15	120.6	15	0.01	77	0.04	413.3	195	0.09			
Kyrgyzstan			312	0.06				69					32	0.01	
Laos	115	0.03	197	0.04	70.9	14	0.00	270	0.05	1828.6					
Latvia			199	0.08				489					1,961	0.80	
Lebanon	572	0.21	719	0.21	25.7			673					1,650	0.49	
Lesotho	56	0.03	1	0.00	-97.7	171	0.10	186	0.09	8.8					
Liberia	34	0.02													
Libya	1,803	0.42	571	0.11	-68.4	96	0.02	40	0.01	-58.3	425	0.10	650	0.13	52.9
Lithuania			250	0.07				1422					3,241	0.88	
Luxembourg	409	1.07	843	1.96	105.9	820	2.15	789	1.83	-3.8					
Macedonia			488	0.24											
Madagascar	424	0.04	635	0.04	49.7	53	0.00	138	0.01	160.4	34	0.00	35	0.00	2.9
Malawi	120	0.01	112	0.01	-6.7	130	0.01	150	0.01	15.4					
Malaysia	10,242	0.57	14,985	0.69	46.3	7,446	0.42	7931	0.36	6.5	14,920	0.84	25,631	1.20	71.8
Maldives	9	0.04	344	1.22	3558.5	195	0.90	430	1.52	120.5	21	0.10		0.14	85.7
Mali			84	0.01				44	0.01	83	0.01	88.6			
Malta	598	1.66	1,421	3.66	137.8	872	2.42	1214	3.13	39.2	122	0.34		0.43	36.9
Mauritania	223	0.11	187	0.07	-15.9										
Mauritius	520	0.49	831	0.72	60.0	292	0.28	578	0.50	97.9	89	0.08	143	0.13	60.7
Mexico	14,341	0.17	19,263	0.20	34.3	17,176	0.21	19043	0.20	10.9	7,357	0.09	9,637	0.10	31.0
Moldova			43					19			49	0.01	28	0.01	-42.9
Mongolia	616		225	0.09	-63.5	147		159		8.2					
Morocco & Western Sahara	1,580	0.06	3,392	0.12	114.7	4,024	0.16	3824	0.13	-5.0	1,202	0.05	1,480	0.05	23.1
Mozambique	280	0.02	235	0.01	-16.0										
Myanmar	319	0.01	537	0.01	68.5	21	0.00	198	0.00	842.9					
Namibia	455	0.33	201	0.12	-55.8	213	0.15	560	0.32	162.9					
Nepal	679	0.04	583	0.03	-14.2	255	0.01	492	0.02	92.9	82	0.00	122	0.01	48.8
Netherlands	8,559	0.57	19,741	1.25	130.6	5,795	0.39	9881	0.63	70.5	9,000	0.60	13,560	0.86	50.7
New Zealand	5,866	1.75	8,892	2.37	51.6	976	0.29	1607	0.43	64.7	717	0.21	1,166	0.31	62.6
Nicaragua	130	0.03	59	0.01	-54.7	106	0.03	468	0.09	341.5	173	0.05	422	0.09	143.9
Niger	76	0.01	84	0.01	10.0	21	0.00	39	0.00	85.7	18	0.00	10	0.00	-44.4

271

Air transport
Passengers carried

International tourism
Inbound tourists
Outbound tourists

Country	1990 Total (thousands)	1990 Per capita	1999 Total (thousands)	1999 Per capita	% change in total 1990–1999	1990 Total (thousands)	1990 Per capita	1999 Total (thousands)	1999 Per capita	% change in total 1990–1999	1990 Total (thousands)	1990 Per capita	1998 Total (thousands)	1998 Per capita	% change in total 1990–1998
Nigeria	965	0.01	668	0.01	-30.8	190	0.00	739	0.01	288.9	56	0.00			
Norway	8,929	2.11	15,020	3.38	68.2	1,955	0.46	4481	1.01	129.2	2,667	0.63	3,120	0.70	17.0
Oman	853	0.48	1,933	0.79	126.7	149	0.08	502	0.20	236.9					
Pakistan	5,180	0.05	4,972	0.04	-4.0	424	0.00	429	0.00	1.2					
Panama	266	0.11	933	0.33	250.8	214	0.09	431	0.15	101.4	151	0.06	211	0.08	39.7
Papua New Guinea	931	0.25	1,102	0.23	18.3	41	0.01	70	0.01	70.7	66	0.02	63		
Paraguay	273	0.06	232	0.04	-15.1	280	0.07	272	0.05	-2.9	264	0.06	318	0.06	20.5
Peru	1,816	0.08	1,900	0.08	4.6	317	0.01	944	0.04	197.8	329	0.02	616	0.02	87.2
Philippines	5,639	0.09	5,004	0.07	-11.3	1,025	0.02	2171	0.03	111.8	1,137	0.02	1,817	0.02	59.8
Poland	1,501	0.04	2,141	0.06	42.6	3,400	0.09	17950	0.46	427.9	22,131	0.58	49,328	1.28	122.9
Portugal	3,505	0.35	7,325	0.73	109.0	8,020	0.81	11600	1.16	44.6	2,268	0.23	2,425	0.24	6.9
Qatar	771	1.70	1,307	2.35	69.5	136	0.30	451	0.81	231.6					
Romania	1,322	0.06	980	0.04	-25.8	3,009	0.13	3209	0.14	6.6	11,247	0.48	6,893	0.31	-38.7
Russian Federation	128,761	0.87	18,600	0.13	-85.6			18496			4,150	0.03	11,711	0.08	182.2
Rwanda	8	0.00				16	0.00	2	0.00	-87.5					
Samoa			92	0.58		48	0.30	85	0.54	77.1					
Sao Tome & Principe	22		34		50.2	4		5		25.0					
Saudi Arabia	10,312	0.67	12,329	0.63	19.6	2,209	0.14	3700	0.19	67.5					
Senegal	148	0.02	103	0.01	-30.3	246	0.03	369	0.04	50.0					
Sierra Leone	30	0.01	19	0.00	-36.0	98	0.02								
Singapore	7,046	2.34	15,283	3.90	116.9	4,842	1.61	6258	1.60	29.2	1,237	0.41	3,745	0.98	202.7
Slovakia			111	0.02				822	0.16	975	0.18	18.6	188	0.04	414	0.08	120.2
Slovenia			556	0.28		650	0.34	884	0.44	36.0					
Solomon Islands	69	0.22	98	0.23	40.8	9	0.03	13	0.03	44.4					
Somalia	88	0.01				46	0.01	10	0.00	-78.3					
South Africa	5,365	0.15	7,374	0.17	37.4	1,029	0.03	6253	0.15	507.7	616	0.02	3,080	0.07	400.0
Spain	21,652	0.55	33,559	0.84	55.0	34,085	0.87	51772	1.30	51.9	10,698	0.27	13,203	0.33	23.4
Sri Lanka	892	0.05	1,422	0.08	59.4	298	0.02	436	0.02	46.3	297	0.02	518	0.03	74.4
St. Lucia						141	1.08	261	1.79	85.1					
Sudan	454	0.02	390	0.01	-14.0	33	0.00	39	0.00	18.2	203	0.01	200	0.01	-1.5
Suriname	133	0.33	194	0.47	46.5	46	0.11	54	0.13	17.4	55	0.14			
Swaziland	53	0.07	12	0.01	-76.6	263	0.34	319	0.35	21.3					
Sweden	11,403	1.33	12,933	1.46	13.4	1,900	0.22	2595	0.29	36.6	6,232	0.73	11,422	1.29	83.3
Switzerland	8,603	1.26	16,209	2.26	88.4	13,200	1.93	10800	1.51	-18.2	9,627	1.41	12,213	1.70	26.9
Syria	613	0.05	668	0.04	9.0	562	0.05	1386	0.09	146.6	1,041	0.08	2,750	0.18	164.2
Tajikistan			156	0.03				511							
Tanzania	292	0.01	190	0.01	-35.0	153	0.01	450	0.01	194.1	301	0.01	150	0.00	-50.2
Thailand	8,201	0.15	15,951	0.26	94.5	5,299	0.10	8651	0.14	63.3	883	0.02	1,412	0.02	59.9
Togo	76	0.02	84	0.02	10.0	103	0.03	99	0.02	-3.9					
Trinidad & Tobago	1,285	1.06	1,112	0.86	-13.5	195	0.16	336	0.26	72.3	254	0.21	250	0.19	-1.6
Tunisia	1,313	0.16	1,923	0.21	46.4	3,204	0.39	4832	0.52	50.8	1,727	0.21	1,526	0.16	-11.6
Turkey	4,337	0.08	10,097	0.15	132.8	4,799	0.09	6893	0.10	43.6	2,917	0.05	4,601	0.07	57.7

Country	Air transport — Passengers carried 1990 Total (thousands)	Per capita	1999 Total (thousands)	Per capita	% change in total 1990–1999	International tourism — Inbound tourists 1990 Total (thousands)	Per capita	1999 Total (thousands)	Per capita	% change in total 1990–1999	Outbound tourists 1990 Total (thousands)	Per capita	1998 Total (thousands)	Per capita	% change in total 1990–1998
Turkmenistan			220	0.05				*300*					357	0.08	
Uganda	116	0.01	179	0.01	54.7	69	0.00	*238*	*0.01*	244.9					
Ukraine			891	0.02				7500					8,241	0.16	
United Arab Emirates	1,686	0.84	5,848	2.29	246.9	633	0.31	2481	0.97	291.9					
United Kingdom	47,114	0.82	68,235	1.15	44.8	18,013	0.31	25740	0.43	42.9	31,150	0.54	50,872	0.86	63.3
United States	464,574	1.82	634,365	2.26	36.5	39,363	0.15	48491	0.17	23.2	44,623	0.18	56,287	0.20	26.1
Uruguay	318	0.10	728	0.22	128.6	1,267	0.41	2139	0.65	68.8			654	0.20	
Uzbekistan			1,658	0.07				*272*							
Vanuatu	19	0.12	86	0.45	364.9	35	0.23	51	0.27	45.7	6	0.04		0.06	100.0
Venezuela	6,847	0.35	4,690	0.20	-31.5	525	0.03	587	0.02	11.8	309	0.02	524	0.02	69.6
Vietnam	89	0.00	2,600	0.03	2821.3	250	0.00	1782	0.02	612.8			168	0.00	
Yemen	671	0.06	731	0.04	8.9	52	0.00	*88*	*0.00*	69.2					
Yugoslavia	3,668	0.36				1,186	0.12	152	0.01	-87.2					
Zambia	407	0.05	42	0.00	-89.7	141	0.02	456	0.04	223.4					
Zimbabwe	601	0.06	567	0.05	-5.6	605	0.06	2328	0.19	284.8	200	0.02	213	0.02	6.5

International tourism

Region	Inbound tourists 1990 Total (thousnads)	Per capita	1999 Total (thousands)	Per capita	% change in total 1990–1999	Outbound tourists 1990 Total (thousands)	Per capita	1998 Total (thousands)	Per capita	% change in total 1990–1998
Low income	12,966	0.01	29,365	0.01	126.5			33,972	0.02	
Middle income	136,571	0.06	223,020	0.09	63.3	118,014	0.05	189,960	0.07	61.0
Low & middle income:										
East Asia & Pacific	30,457	0.02	58,837	0.03	93.2	23,210	0.01	46,785	0.03	101.6
Europe & Central Asia	59,439	0.12	99,660	0.20	67.7	87,991	0.18	126,738	0.26	44.0
Latin America & Caribbean	33,354	0.08	48,755	0.10	46.2	17,289	0.04	28,720	0.06	66.1
Middle East & North Africa	17,932	0.07	26,885	0.09	49.9	16,180	0.07	16,300	0.06	0.7
South Asia	3,004	0.00	4,481	0.00	49.2	3,503	0.00	6,258	0.00	78.6
Sub-Saharan Africa	7,052	0.02	17,850	0.03	153.1					
High income	308,084	0.41	412,769	0.51	34.0	274,192	0.37	380,583	0.47	38.8
World	461,483	0.09	668,484	0.11	44.9	458,115	0.09	670,815	0.11	46.4

Data on inbound and outbound tourists refer to number of arrivals and departures, not number of people.

Per capita estimates (aggregate and individual country level) are calculated by the LSE research team using UN population figures.

Where data for a particular year are not available, figures are taken from the year before or after as an estimate. These figures, and estimates based on them, are presented in italics.

*Data for Hong Kong and Macao are not included in this table.

Sources: World Bank, World Development Indicators 2001 (CD-Rom); Population Division of the Department of Economic and Social Affairs of the United Nations Secretariat, World Population Prospects: The 2000 Revision, www.un.org/esa/population/demobase

USA & Canada
Inbound 0.22
Outbound 0.24

Latin America & Caribbean
Inbound 0.10
Outbound 0.06

= data for these countries not
included on this map

Sources: Map produced by Ben Cracknell © based on information from World Bank, *World Development Indicators 2001* (CD-Rom); Population Division of the Department of Economic and Social Affairs of the United Nations Secretariat, World Population Prospects: The 2000 Revision, www.un.org/esa/population/demobase, restructured by Sally Stares, map template Map Info©

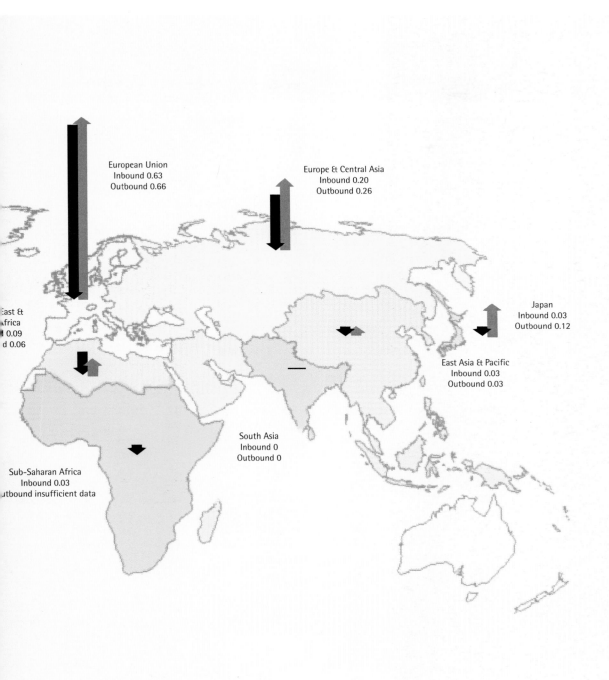

European Union
Inbound 0.63
Outbound 0.66

Europe & Central Asia
Inbound 0.20
Outbound 0.26

Japan
Inbound 0.03
Outbound 0.12

East &
Africa
0.09
d 0.06

East Asia & Pacific
Inbound 0.03
Outbound 0.03

South Asia
Inbound 0
Outbound 0

Sub-Saharan Africa
Inbound 0.03
utbound insufficient data

Record 6 Media

This table shows the daily newspaper circulation, the number of radios, television sets, and cable subscribers per thousand people in each country, for 1990 and the latest available year. It gives an indication of people's exposure to different media, although it does not show the diversity of sources, and ownership, within each medium.

Country (figures are per thousand of population)	Daily newspapers 1990	1996	% change 1990–1996	Radios 1990	1997	% change 1990–1997	Television sets 1990	1999	% change 1990–1999	Cable television subscribers 1995	1999	% change 1995–1999
Afghanistan	10	5	-52	106	124	17	8	14	64	0.0		
Albania	41	36	-14	175	217	24	86	113	32			
Algeria	51	38	-26	232	241	4	73	107	46	0.0		
Angola	12	11	-9	28	54	92	6	15	145			
Argentina	123	123	0	671	681	1	249	293	18	135.1	163	21
Armenia				174	224	29	202	238	18		0	
Australia	302	293	-3	1,263	1,378	9	520	706	36	0.0	30	
Austria	350	296	-16	617	753	22	473	516	9	124.2	139	12
Azerbaijan				19	23	18	195	254	31		0	
Bahamas	137	99	-28	537	744	38	224	243	9			
Bahrain	58	112	94	549	545	-1	424	406	-4		9	
Bangladesh	6	9	45	45	50	12	5	7	43			
Barbados	116	200	72	875	891	2	265	287	9			
Belarus	286			252	296	17	267	322	21			
Belgium	201	160	-20	768	792	3	446	523	17	359.4	370	3
Belize				577	594	3	143	183	28			
Benin	0	2	909	90	110	22	5	11	126	0.0		
Bhutan				48	60	25		20		0.0	0	
Bolivia	61	55	-9	661	676	2	113	118	4	3.4	5	52
Bosnia & Herzegovina				172	249	44		112				
Botswana	14	27	90	117	156	33	16	20	30			
Brazil	43	40	-7	393	444	13	212	333	57	8.3	15	86
Brunei	39	70	79	265	303	14	241	637	164	0.0	53	
Bulgaria	466	257	-45	439	543	24	250	408	63		29	
Burkina Faso	0	1	305	26	33	28	5	11	99			
Burundi	4	3	-13	62	71	14	1	15	1,464			
Cambodia		2		107	128	20	8	9	17			
Cameroon	7	7	-4	143	163	14	23	34	43			
Canada	209	159	-24	1,052	1,047	0	627	715	14	265.3	273	3
Cape Verde				173	180	4	3	5	67			
Central African Republic	1	2	163	68	83	21	4	6	35			
Chad	0	0	-17	241	242	0	1	1	12	0.0		
Chile	103	98	-5	344	355	3	206	240	16	34.1	45	32
China & Tibet	42			322	334	4	155	292	88	28.5	47	66
Colombia	57	46	-20	173	560	223	118	199	69	3.4	16	354
Congo, Dem. Rep.	2	3	37	207	375	81	1	2	90			
Congo, Rep.	8			112	124	11	6	13	123	0.0		
Costa Rica	102	94	-8	279	271	-3	221	229	3	16.5	19	16
Côte d'Ivoire	8	17	115	145	164	13	60	70	16	0.0	0	
Croatia	49	115	136	228	336	47	215	279	29	11.0	42	286
Cuba	78	118	52	341	355	4	206	246	20	0.0		

Country figures are per thousand of population	Daily newspapers			Radios			Television sets			Cable television subscribers		
	1990	1996	% change 1990–1996	1990	1997	% change 1990–1997	1990	1999	% change 1990–1999	1995	1999	% change 1995–1999
Cyprus	115	114	-1	357	437	23	177	*157*	*-11*	0.0		
Czech Republic	772	254	-67	769	803	4		487		46.1	90	95
Denmark	352	309	-12	1,021	1,140	12	535	621	16	228.0	250	10
Djibouti				79	84	6	43	*47*	*9*	0.0		
Dominican Republic	32	52	61	169	178	5	84	*96*	*15*	15.8		
Ecuador	80	70	-12	323	420	30	85	*205*	*140*	3.9	*16*	*319*
Egypt	46	40	-12	320	324	1	107	183	71			
El Salvador	53	48	-9	412	464	13	92	191	108	*4.5*	45	896
Equatorial Guinea	6	5	-14	418	429	3	9	*116*	*1,261*	0.0		
Eritrea					317			16				
Estonia		174		433	692	60	344	555	61	12.5	76	507
Ethiopia	2	1	-24	196	196	0	2	6	136	0.0		
Fiji	37	52	41	582	640	10	15	110	641	0.0		
Finland	558	455	-18	994	1,489	50	494	643	30	160.0	180	13
France	208	218	5	887	937	6	540	623	15	22.7	*43*	*91*
Gabon	21	29	41	172	182	6	45	251	459		8	
Gambia	2	2	-20	160	168	4		3				
Georgia				458	555	21	201	*474*	*135*	0.0	3	
Germany	304	311	2	964	948	-2	526	580	10	193.2	226	17
Ghana	13	14	6	228	238	4	16	115	603			
Greece	123			417	478	15	193	480	149	0.0	1	
Guatemala	22	33	52	67	80	19	53	*61*	*15*	18.0	*28*	*58*
Guinea				42	47	13	7	44	532	0.0	*0*	
Guinea-Bissau	6	5	-12	39	44	12						
Guyana	60	50	-17	486	498	2	35	*65*	*84*			
Haiti	7	3	-61	45	55	24	5	*5*	*11*			
Honduras	41	55	35	387	395	2	72	95	31	7.6	*8*	*7*
Hungary	237	186	-22	604	687	14	416	448	8	135.3	159	18
Iceland	510	537	5	781	952	22	316	520	64	*4.5*		
India				79	121	53	32	75	135	17.2	37	115
Indonesia	29	24	-18	148	157	6	61	143	133	0.0		
Iran	28	28	0	245	265	8	66	157	138	0.0		
Iraq	36	19	-47	214	229	7	72	*83*	*15*			
Ireland	169	150	-11	620	699	13	294	406	38	133.0	*171*	*29*
Israel & Occupied Territories	258	290	13	460	519	13	259	328	26	160.1	189	18
Italy	106	104	-2	789	880	12	419	*488*	*16*	0.0	3	
Jamaica	64	62	-3	428	482	13	136	*189*	*39*	54.8	*99*	*80*
Japan	587	578	-2	895	960	7	609	719	18	87.3	*125*	*44*
Jordan	71	58	-18	239	288	20	76	83	9	0.0	*0*	*248*
Kazakhstan				250	395	58	216	238	10			
Kenya	14	9	-33	87	104	20	15	*22*	*43*			
Kiribati				207	211	2	9	23	144	0.0		
Korea, Dem. Rep.	244	199	-18	127	147	16	16	55	239	0.0		
Korea, Rep.	280			1,012	1,033	2	210	361	72	156.3	150	-4
Kuwait	252	374	49	821	663	-19	433	480	11			

figures are per thousand of population Country	Daily newspapers 1990	1996	% change 1990–1996	Radios 1990	1997	% change 1990–1997	Television sets 1990	1999	% change 1990–1999	Cable television subscribers 1995	1999	% change 1995–1999
Kyrgyzstan	7	15	114	105	112	7	18	*47*	*160*			
Latvia	75	247	230	528	710	34	370	741	100		67	
Lebanon	88	107	21	886	908	2	349	*351*	*1*	0.2	*1*	*743*
Lesotho	12	8	-34	33	49	50	6	16	174			
Liberia	14	12	-13	225	274	22	18	*28*	*54*			
Libya	16	14	-12	224	243	9	96	*136*	*42*	0.0		
Lithuania	215	93	-57	407	514	26	328	420	28	27.0	62	131
Luxembourg	374	325	-13	628	682	9	359	*389*	*9*	323.5	*323*	*0*
Macedonia	29	21	-28	189	206	9	173	250	45			
Madagascar	4	5	12	189	198	5	19	*22*	*17*			
Malawi	3			244	250	3		3				
Malaysia	110	158	44	431	419	-3	148	174	18	0.0	*5*	
Maldives	14	20	42	117	125	6	24	*38*	*57*	0.0		
Mali	1	1	2	47	54	14	9	*12*	*28*	0.0	*0*	
Malta	152	129	-16	522	673	29	323	549	70	98.9	198	100
Mauritania	0	0	-15	146	151	4	15	96	562			
Mauritius	76	75	-1	363	368	1	170	230	35			
Mexico	135	97	-28	260	325	25	150	267	78	13.1	*16*	*19*
Moldova		60		553	740	34	281	297	6	7.1	18	152
Mongolia	73	27	-63	138	151	9	66			2.8	*11*	*286*
Morocco & Western Sahara	13	26	97	214	241	13	102	165	62	0.0		
Mozambique	6	3	-47	37	40	8	3	*5*	*78*			
Myanmar	17	10	-40	83	95	14	3	7	158	0.0		
Namibia		19		133	144	8	22	*38*	*71*			
Nepal	8	11	44	36	39	10	2	*7*	*246*	0.0	3	
Netherlands	301	306	2	907	981	8	480	600	25	376.8	387	3
New Zealand	291	216	-26	923	989	7	442	518	17	0.4	77	18,559
Nicaragua	47	30	-37	260	278	7	65	69	6	22.9	*41*	*77*
Niger	0	0	-46	60	69	17	11	27	142			
Nigeria	18	24	35	194	224	15	36	68	87			
Norway	610	588	-4	792	916	16	422	648	53	155.3	184	19
Oman	38	29	-24	577	598	4	657	575	-13	0.0		
Pakistan	17			96	104	9	26	119	360	0.1	*0*	*38*
Panama	98	62	-36	232	300	29	172	192	12	11.4		
Papua New Guinea	13	15	16	74	95	27	2	13	433			
Paraguay	39	43	10	173	182	5	52	205	293	7.3	*15*	*113*
Peru	0	0	1	252	273	8	96	147	53	1.9	*14*	*639*
Philippines	54	79	46	142	159	12	49	110	123	5.8	9	61
Poland	128	113	-12	433	522	21	265	387	46	70.5	122	73
Portugal	45	75	65	228	304	33	186	560	202	5.8	*60*	*926*
Qatar	165	130	-21	425	450	6	392	*846*	*116*	44.8	*89*	*99*
Romania	271			287	319	11	194	312	61	57.3	129	126
Russian Federation		105		372	418	13	365	421	15	68.9	23	-67
Rwanda	0			74	102	38	0	*0*	*-74*			
Samoa				463	1,047	126	39	*52*	*33*	1.3	*3*	*171*

Country (figures are per thousand of population)	Daily newspapers 1990	1996	% change 1990–1996	Radios 1990	1997	% change 1990–1997	Television Sets 1990	1999	% change 1990–1999	Cable television subscribers 1995	1999	% change 1995–1999
Sao Tome & Principe				278	275	-1		227				
Saudi Arabia	36	57	58	291	321	10	250	263	5			
Senegal	7	5	-23	113	142	25	36	41	14			
Sierra Leone	3	4	73	223	253	13	10	13	30	0.0	0	
Singapore	282	360	28	589	682	16	341	308	-10	6.9	53	669
Slovakia	246	185	-25	485	967	99		417		74.5	122	64
Slovenia	152	199	31	350	407	16	275	356	29	110.6	151	36
Solomon Islands				119	141	19		14		0.0		
Somalia	1	1	2	37	48	30	12	14	17			
South Africa	38	32	-15	303	333	10	97	129	32			
Spain	89	100	13	301	333	11	388	547	41	10.2	13	30
Sri Lanka	32	29	-11	200	209	5	35	102	189	0.0		
St. Lucia				746	740	-1	187	362	94	48.3		
St. Vincent & the Grenadines		0		660	688	4	142	228	61		23	
Sudan	25	27	7	255	271	6	73	173	136	0.0	0	
Suriname	100	122	23	663	726	10	138	237	72	0.0	5	
Swaziland	14	26	81	151	164	8	19	113	500	0.0	..	
Sweden	526	445	-15	873	932	7	466	531	14	212.9	221	4
Switzerland	456	337	-26	827	1,000	21	397	518	30	330.0	357	8
Syria	17	20	14	256	277	8	60	66	10			
Tajikistan	47	20	-57	113	142	26	189	328	74			
Tanzania	3	4	50	195	279	43	2	21	1,235			
Thailand	81	63	-22	189	233	23	108	289	167	3.5	2	-32
Togo	3	4	25	210	218	4	6	22	253	0.0		
Trinidad & Tobago	78	123	57	513	535	4	331	337	2			
Tunisia	42	31	-27	192	143	-26	77	190	146			
Turkey	71	111	56	159	180	13	230	332	44	6.5	11	71
Turkmenistan				218	277	27	191	201	5			
Uganda	2	2	11	113	127	13	11	28	158			
Ukraine	251	54	-78	792	884	12	328	413	26		16	
United Arab Emirates	136	156	15	268	345	28	91	252	176			
United Kingdom	388	329	-15	1,389	1,435	3	432	652	51	24.3	53	117
United States	250	215	-14	2,116	2,146	1	772	844	9	239.5	246	3
Uruguay	232	293	26	605	606	0	388	531	37	21.9	105	377
Uzbekistan		3		343	458	33	181	276	52			
Vanuatu				293	348	19	9	12	28	0.0		
Venezuela	144	206	44	475	470	-1	177	185	5	4.6	26	459
Vietnam	8	4	-52	104	107	3	39	184	369	0.0		
Yemen	17	15	-13	27	64	132	274	286	4			
Yugoslavia	35	107	207	279	297	6	176	273	55			
Zambia	13	12	-3	88	121	38	34	145	327			
Zimbabwe	21	19	-12	84	102	21	26	180	585	0.0		

Region (figures are per thousand of population)	Radios			Television sets			Cable television subscribers		
	1990	1997	% change 1990–1997	1990	1999	% change 1990–1999	1995	1999	% change 1995–1999
Low income	127	157	24	42	85	104	*6.27*		
Middle income	331	360	9	169	279	65	29.36	45	52
Low & middle income:									
East Asia & Pacific	291	302	4	129	252	96	27.65	47	69
Europe & Central Asia	385	446	16	286	370	29	*34.89*	50	43
Latin America & Caribbean	353	419	19	170	272	59	19.3	*30*	*53*
Middle East & North Africa	258	272	5	113	175	55			
South Asia	79	113	43	28	71	155	14.39	36	152
Sub-Saharan Africa	168	201	20	26	*43*	70			
High income	1,255	1,289	3	569	693	22	144.83	*160*	*11*
World	397	420	6	185	268	45	46.44	*59*	*26*

Data for Hong Kong and Macao are not included in this table.

Where data for a particular year are not available, figures are taken from the year before or after as an estimate. These figures, and estimates based on them, are presented in italics.

Sources: UNESCO, Culture and Communication Statistics Team (2002); World Bank, World Development Indicators 2001 (CD-Rom)

Record 7 Communication

This table shows the number of telephone mainlines and mobile phones per 1,000 people and the number of international out-going call minutes per mainline subscriber (but not for mobile phones, which probably explains the downturn in many countries) for 1991/1995 and 1999. It also gives the number of estimated Internet users as a percentage of the population. It is an indication of the growing extent to which people communicate with each other across distances.

Country	Main telephone lines as % population			Cellular mobile telephone subscribers as % population			International outgoing telephone traffic minutes per mainline			Estimated Internet users as % population
	1991	2000	% change	1995	2000	% change	1991	2000	% change	2000
Afghanistan	0.2	0.1	-43.5							
Albania	1.3	3.9	207.9	0.1	0.8	1,166.7	481.9	468.4	-2.8	0.3
Algeria	3.4	5.7	65.7	0.0	0.3	1,300.0	183.5	86.3	-53.0	0.2
Angola	0.8	0.5	-29.3	0.0	0.2	900.0	121.2	508.5	319.6	0.3
Argentina	9.5	21.3	124.4	1.0	16.3	1,567.3	32.3	56.1	74.0	6.8
Armenia	15.8	15.2	-4.1	0.0	0.5	4,800.0				0.9
Aruba	28.5	37.2	30.4	2.1	14.6	593.4				5.8
Australia	46.6	52.5	12.7	12.4	44.7	260.1	72.7	135.8	86.8	43.9
Austria	42.9	46.7	8.8	4.8	76.2	1,496.4	192.0	299.8	56.1	36.9
Azerbaijan	8.6	10.4	20.6	0.1	5.6	6,850.0		35.0		0.2
Bahamas	30.1	37.6	25.0	1.5	10.4	604.8				4.4
Bahrain	19.8	25.0	26.1	4.8	30.1	532.6	616.4	818.8	32.8	6.0
Bangladesh	0.2	0.4	63.6		0.2		35.6	89.4	150.8	0.0
Barbados	30.2	43.7	44.7	1.8			297.0			2.2
Belarus	16.3	26.9	65.0	0.1	0.5	700.0		65.0		1.7
Belgium	41.1	49.8	21.3	2.3	52.5	2,163.4	200.9	304.9	51.7	26.4
Belize	11.2	14.9	32.7	0.7	7.0	872.2	271.0	268.0	-1.1	2.5
Benin	0.3	0.9	174.2	0.0	0.9	4,450.0	170.2	318.4	87.1	0.2
Bermuda	63.9	87.0	36.1	10.0						
Bhutan	0.5	2.0	302.0							0.0
Bolivia	3.0	6.1	101.0	0.1	6.7	5,046.2	48.7			1.4
Bosnia & Herzegovina	14.0	10.3	-26.7	0.0	3.0	7,325.0				0.1
Botswana	2.5	9.3	276.8		12.3		775.3			0.8
Brazil	6.9	18.2	165.4	0.8	13.6	1,542.2	16.3	21.0	29.1	5.0
Brunei	15.0	24.5	63.4	12.6	28.9	129.1	434.9			1.2
Bulgaria	24.6	35.0	42.7	0.3	9.0	3,488.0	33.1	38.2	15.3	5.2
Burkina Faso	0.2	0.5	136.8		0.2		114.4	199.5	74.3	0.1
Burundi	0.2	0.3	66.7	0.0	0.2	2,300.0	174.4	145.0	-16.9	0.0
Cambodia	0.0	0.2	500.0	0.1	1.0	614.3		310.9		0.0
Cameroon	0.4	0.6	82.9	0.0	1.0	4,800.0	405.4	296.0	-27.0	0.1
Canada	57.9	67.7	16.8	8.8	28.5	222.7	127.5	347.3	172.3	42.8
Cape Verde	2.6	12.6	387.3		4.5		217.8	125.5	-42.4	2.0
Central African Republic	0.2	0.3	44.4	0.0	0.1	366.7	316.0	474.8	50.3	0.0
Chad	0.1	0.1	85.7		0.1		410.6	292.5	-28.8	0.0
Chile	7.9	22.1	179.1	1.4	22.2	1,510.1	54.0	63.8	18.1	11.6
China & Tibet*	0.7	11.2	1,452.8	0.3	6.6	2,169.0	52.1	10.7	-79.5	0.8
Colombia	7.4	16.9	129.3	0.7	5.3	650.7	31.9	39.8	24.8	2.2
Comoros	0.8	1.0	23.5							0.3
Congo, Dem.Rep.	0.1	0.0	-55.6	0.0	0.0	50.0				
Congo, Rep.	0.7	0.8	1.4	0.0	2.4	5,850.0				0.0
Costa Rica	10.6	24.9	134.8	0.6	5.2	828.6	91.8	80.7	-12.1	6.7

Country	Main telephone lines as % population			Cellular mobile telephone subscribers as % population			International outgoing telephone traffic minutes per mainline			Estimated Internet users as % population
	1991	2000	% change	1995	2000	% change	1991	2000	% change	2000
Côte d'Ivoire	0.7	1.8	165.7	0.1	3.0	2,940.0	270.7	163.1	-39.7	0.1
Croatia	18.6	36.5	95.9	0.7	23.1	3,020.3	104.4	135.9	30.2	4.7
Cuba	3.1	4.4	38.9	0.0	0.1	200.0	35.5	74.0	108.4	0.5
Cyprus	44.6	64.7	45.1	6.9	32.1	365.4	260.3	436.3	67.6	15.8
Czech Republic	16.6	37.8	128.1	0.5	42.4	8,925.5	65.6	93.0	41.7	10.7
Denmark	57.3	72.0	25.5	15.8	63.1	300.2	136.9	182.8	33.5	43.1
Djibouti	1.2	1.5	28.8	0.0	0.0	100.0	757.6	466.9	-38.4	0.2
Dominican Republic	5.6	10.5	86.3	0.7	8.3	1,045.8				
Ecuador	4.7	10.0	113.7	0.5	3.8	710.6	48.8	81.4	66.7	1.4
Egypt	3.4	8.6	157.9	0.0	2.1	21,300.0	33.6	34.1	1.6	0.7
El Salvador	2.5	10.0	297.2	0.2	11.9	4,837.5	346.2	222.1	-35.8	0.8
Equitorial Guinea	0.4	1.4	275.0	0.0						0.1
Eritrea	0.4	0.8	105.1				39.4	94.1	138.7	0.1
Estonia	21.2	36.3	71.4	2.1	38.7	1,787.8	135.2	149.4	10.5	25.6
Ethiopia	0.3	0.4	37.0		0.0		66.6	57.9	-13.1	0.0
Fiji	6.1	10.6	73.5	0.3	6.8	2,314.3	236.6	217.6	-8.1	0.9
Finland	54.0	55.0	1.8	20.1	72.0	258.9	79.1	164.3	107.7	43.9
France	51.1	57.9	13.4	2.3	49.3	2,092.4	78.9	145.2	84.1	15.3
Gabon	2.7	3.2	17.8	0.4	9.8	2,545.9	653.9	565.6	-13.5	1.2
Gambia	1.1	2.6	143.8	0.1	0.4	230.8	247.3	192.2	-22.3	0.0
Georgia	10.2	13.9	35.9	0.0	3.4	8,375.0		60.2		0.4
Germany	43.9	61.1	39.2	4.6	58.6	1,187.9	106.0	183.7	73.2	29.0
Ghana	0.3	1.2	290.0	0.0	0.6	1,500.0	144.8	184.8	27.6	0.1
Greece	40.8	53.2	30.2	2.6	55.7	2,035.2	59.2	140.1	136.8	12.4
Guatemala	2.2	5.7	158.4	0.3	6.1	1,940.0	118.7	192.4	62.1	0.7
Guinea	0.2	0.8	315.8	0.0	0.5	5,200.0	703.5	285.9	-59.4	0.1
Guinea-Bissau	0.6	0.9	47.6				215.7	270.8	25.5	0.1
Guyana	2.0	7.9	299.0	0.2	4.6	2,986.7	567.4	234.8	-58.6	0.5
Haiti	0.7	0.9	30.9		0.3					0.1
Honduras	1.8	4.6	156.1	0.0	2.4	5,875.0	328.3	144.0	-56.1	0.6
Hungary	10.9	37.3	242.1	2.6	30.2	1,064.9	133.9	55.6	-58.5	7.2
Iceland	52.2	70.1	34.2	11.5	78.3	579.0	153.4	195.4	27.4	60.8
India	0.7	3.2	377.6	0.0	0.4	3,400.0	31.8	16.2	-49.0	0.5
Indonesia & East Timor	0.7	3.1	336.1	0.1	1.7	1,472.7	77.2	37.7	-51.2	0.7
Iran	4.4	14.9	238.6	0.0	1.5	4,933.3	31.4	21.1	-32.8	0.4
Iraq	3.6	2.9	-18.8							0.1
Ireland	29.7	42.0	41.3	4.4	65.8	1,401.1	260.5	786.2	201.8	27.5
Israel & Occupied Territories**	26.2	34.8	32.5	5.9	49.5	745.0	81.6	323.4	296.2	18.8
Italy	40.7	47.4	16.6	6.8	73.7	977.9	52.9	100.9	90.8	23.3
Jamaica	5.6	19.9	257.2	1.8	14.2	686.7	321.4	144.2	-55.1	3.1
Japan	45.4	58.6	29.1	9.3	52.6	464.0	20.6	34.6	68.0	37.2
Jordan	6.0	9.3	54.9	0.2	5.8	2,434.8	158.4	277.1	75.0	2.6
Kazakhstan	8.5	11.3	32.9	0.0	1.2	3,966.7	2.1	57.3	2,619.5	0.4
Kenya	0.8	1.1	28.0	0.0	0.4	4,100.0	112.6	74.5	-33.8	0.7
Korea, Dem. Rep.	3.9	4.6	18.3							
Korea, Rep.	33.6	46.4	38.2	3.6	56.7	1,457.4	15.9	48.5	204.5	34.6

Country	Main telephone lines as % population			Cellular mobile telephone subscribers as % population			International outgoing telephone traffic minutes per mainline			Estimated Internet users as % population
	1991	2000	% change	1995	2000	% change	1991	2000	% change	2000
Kuwait	23.3	24.4	4.7	7.0	24.9	257.2	180.1	340.5	89.0	7.6
Kyrgyzstan	7.5	7.7	3.4		0.2		3.2	61.6	1,807.1	1.1
Laos	0.2	0.8	341.2	0.0	0.2	666.7	95.7	206.6	116.0	0.1
Latvia	24.4	30.3	24.3	0.6	16.6	2,705.1	3.1	78.9	2,438.2	9.7
Lebanon										8.4
Lesotho	0.7	1.0	49.3	0.1	1.0	1,566.7	1,562.4	1,612.6	3.2	0.1
Liberia	0.1	0.2	75.0							0.0
Libya	5.0	10.8	118.0							0.2
Lithuania	22.0	32.1	46.0	0.4	14.2	3,442.5	3.3	33.2	912.1	6.2
Luxembourg	49.2	75.0	52.5	6.5	86.1	1,224.8	860.5	984.9	14.5	22.9
Macedonia	14.9	25.5	70.6	0.1	5.7	11,340.0	75.9	172.5	127.4	4.9
Madagascar	0.3	0.3	21.4	0.0	0.4	3,900.0	89.9	166.2	84.8	0.2
Malawi	0.3	0.4	33.3	0.0	0.5	1,075.0	257.5	217.2	-15.6	0.1
Malaysia	9.9	19.9	101.0	5.0	21.3	326.4	97.4	193.1	98.3	17.0
Maldives	3.5	9.1	160.9	0.0	2.8	28,300.0	216.1	227.7	5.3	2.0
Mali	0.1	0.4	150.0	0.0	0.1	800.0	446.0	358.0	-19.7	0.1
Malta	38.6	52.2	35.2	2.9	29.2	908.3	115.3	210.6	82.7	10.2
Mauritania	0.3	0.7	132.3		0.3		464.1	476.0	2.6	0.1
Mauritius	6.0	23.5	292.8	1.1	15.1	1,336.2	234.3	124.6	-46.8	7.3
Mexico	6.9	12.5	81.8	0.7	14.2	1,850.7	84.8	152.7	80.0	2.7
Moldova	11.4	13.3	16.8	0.0	3.2	15,750.0		73.6		1.2
Mongolia	3.3	5.6	70.9	0.0	4.5	11,225.0	8.6	34.9	307.3	1.2
Morocco & Western Sahara	2.0	5.0	152.8	0.1	8.3	7,409.1	169.0	171.9	1.7	0.7
Mozambique	0.4	0.4	18.9		0.3		146.8	261.7	78.2	0.2
Myanmar	0.2	0.6	166.7	0.0	0.0	200.0	16.9	43.8	158.8	0.0
Namibia	4.0	6.3	55.2	0.2	4.7	1,930.4	649.8	562.7	-13.4	1.7
Nepal	0.4	1.2	231.4		0.0		140.4	97.6	-30.5	0.2
Netherlands	47.6	61.8	29.8	3.5	67.0	1,825.0	141.9	286.5	101.9	45.8
New Zealand	43.5	50.0	15.0	10.1	56.3	460.5	107.2	339.9	217.2	39.0
Nicaragua	1.3	3.1	145.7	0.1	1.8	1,680.0	289.8	321.0	10.8	1.0
Niger	0.1	0.2	58.3		0.0		261.6	184.3	-29.5	0.0
Nigeria	0.3	0.4	43.3	0.0	0.0	200.0	170.1	117.9	-30.7	0.1
Norway	51.4	53.2	3.5	22.5	75.1	234.3	140.6	234.3	66.7	52.6
Oman	6.4	8.9	39.2	0.4	6.5	1,651.4	266.0	519.0	95.1	3.5
Pakistan	1.0	2.2	125.0	0.0	0.3	733.3	30.5	32.4	6.4	0.9
Panama	9.4	15.1	60.9	0.3	14.5	5,461.5	143.9	121.2	-15.8	3.2
Papua New Guinea	0.9	1.4	50.0	0.1	0.2	150.0	590.4	370.2	-37.3	2.7
Paraguay	2.8	5.0	79.9	0.3	14.9	4,424.2	107.5	124.2	15.6	0.7
Peru	2.5	6.7	173.1	0.3	5.0	1,500.0	54.3	57.6	6.1	1.5
Philippines	1.0	4.0	284.6	0.7	8.4	1,072.2	192.0	44.5	-76.8	2.5
Poland	9.3	28.2	203.0	0.2	17.4	9,057.9	33.1	61.8	86.6	7.3
Portugal	27.3	43.0	57.6	3.4	66.5	1,832.8	69.4	118.5	70.6	24.9
Qatar	19.4	26.8	37.8	3.4	20.2	502.7	475.9	892.7	87.6	6.2
Romania	10.5	17.5	65.7	0.0	11.2	27,875.0	10.6	43.3	307.6	4.5
Russian Federation	15.0	21.8	45.1	0.1	2.2	3,600.0	3.5	29.4	741.4	2.1
Rwanda	0.2	0.2	21.1		0.5					0.1

Country	Main telephone lines as % population			Cellular mobile telephone subscribers as % population			International outgoing telephone traffic minutes per mainline			Estimated Internet users as % population
	1991	2000	% change	1995	2000	% change	1991	2000	% change	2000
Samoa	2.6	4.7	83.3		1.7		703.4	1,196.2	70.1	0.3
Sao Tome & Principe	0.9	3.1	244.4							4.1
Saudi Arabia	8.9	13.7	54.7	0.1	6.4	6,977.8	326.7	323.4	-1.0	1.4
Senegal	0.7	2.2	232.3	0.0	2.6	13,050.0	293.7	243.0	-17.3	0.4
Sierra Leone	0.3	0.4	21.9		0.3		90.5	278.7	208.0	0.4
Singapore	35.6	48.5	36.0	8.8	68.4	675.3	347.9	538.3	54.7	44.6
Slovakia	14.4	31.4	118.3	0.2	20.5	8,826.1	18.4	95.4	417.2	12.9
Slovenia	22.9	38.6	68.5	1.4	61.2	4,367.9	76.3	192.9	152.8	31.1
Solomon Islands	1.5	1.8	19.7	0.1	0.3	333.3	309.9	389.8	25.8	0.6
Somalia	0.2	0.2	-11.8							
South Africa	9.5	11.4	19.7	1.4	19.0	1,298.5	58.8	99.8	69.6	5.5
Spain	34.1	42.1	23.4	2.4	60.9	2,428.2	54.2	150.3	177.2	13.7
Sri Lanka	0.7	4.1	456.2	0.3	2.3	710.7	124.0	54.7	-55.9	0.6
St. Lucia	12.6	31.4	148.2	0.7	1.6	131.9				1.9
St. Vincent & the Grenadines	13.7	22.0	59.8	0.2	2.1	994.7				3.0
Sudan	0.3	1.2	396.0	0.0	0.1	600.0	155.4	82.3	-47.0	0.1
Suriname	10.0	17.4	73.2	0.4	9.5	2,207.3	172.7	192.5	11.5	2.7
Swaziland	1.8	3.2	82.3		3.3		802.3	830.1	3.5	0.3
Sweden	68.9	98.7	43.2	22.7	71.7	215.7	113.1	209.0	84.7	50.7
Switzerland	59.6	72.7	21.9	6.3	64.4	917.2	350.2	458.5	30.9	33.1
Syria	4.0	10.4	158.1		0.2		41.8	100.9	141.3	0.2
Tajikistan	4.7	3.6			0.0			29.4		0.0
Tanzania	0.3	0.5	69.0	0.0	0.5	5,000.0	36.7	74.6	103.5	0.3
Thailand	2.8	9.2	227.3	2.3	5.0	123.0	77.9	63.5	-18.5	2.0
Togo	0.3	0.9	217.2		1.1		661.0	238.5	-63.9	0.4
Trinidad & Tobago	14.7	23.1	57.4	0.5	10.3	1,917.6	206.9	244.1	18.0	3.6
Tunisia	4.0	9.0	123.6	0.0	0.6	1,350.0	174.7	164.6	-5.8	1.2
Turkey	14.2	28.0	96.9	0.7	24.6	3,408.6	24.2	39.8	64.7	3.1
Turkmenistan	6.3	8.2	29.1		0.2			43.1		0.1
Uganda	0.2	0.3	64.7	0.0	0.9	8,400.0	133.0	166.3	25.1	0.1
Ukraine	14.1	20.7	46.0	0.0	1.6	5,300.0		34.8		0.6
United Arab Emirates	22.1	39.1	77.1	5.5	54.8	892.8	0.6	1,101.9	183,194.8	28.2
United Kingdom	44.8	58.9	31.3	9.8	72.7	642.6	103.9	226.9	118.4	32.7
United States	55.2	67.3	22.0	12.8	39.8	209.9	64.5	179.9	179.2	52.2
Uruguay	14.5	27.8	92.0	1.3	13.2	955.2	62.0	90.4	45.8	11.1
Uzbekistan	7.0	6.7	-4.0	0.0	0.2	1,000.0		45.9		0.0
Vanuatu	2.0	3.4	66.8	0.1	0.2	171.4				1.6
Venezuela	8.1	10.8	33.4	1.9	21.8	1,063.1	58.2	72.1	24.0	4.0
Vietnam	0.2	3.2	1,495.0	0.0	1.0	3,200.0	58.4	18.5	-68.3	0.1
Yemen	1.1	1.9	71.8	0.1	0.2	240.0	168.0	103.8	-38.2	0.1
Yugoslavia	17.2	22.6	31.8	0.1	12.3	8,650.0	60.0	119.3	98.7	2.8
Zambia	0.9	0.8	-14.0	0.0	1.0	4,650.0	155.2	158.0	1.8	0.2
Zimbabwe	1.2	1.9	49.2		2.3		285.5	288.7	1.1	0.4

Region	Average no.main telephone lines per hundred population			Average no.cellular mobile telephone subscribers per hundred population			Average international outgoing telephone traffic minutes per mainline			Average estimated internet users as % population
	1991	2000	% change in avg.	1995	2000	% change in avg.	1991	2000	% change in avg.	2000
Low income	1.8	2.5	40.4	0.0	0.8	3,214.4	158.5	167.1	5.4	1.1
Middle income	8.5	16.0	88.3	0.7	9.3	1,257.2	153.7	144.6	-5.9	3.7
Low & middle income:										
East Asia & Pacific	4.2	8.2	95.2	7.8	54.6	602.9	135.2	154.0	13.9	3.4
Europe & Central Asia	13.6	21.2	55.3	0.3	10.7	3,022.1	70.1	84.8	21.0	4.9
Latin America & Caribbean	9.2	18.0	96.3	0.8	9.3	1,000.3	151.8	130.4	-14.1	3.2
Middle East & North Africa	6.4	10.6	66.4	0.4	5.3	1,173.3	201.4	221.7	10.1	1.7
South Asia	0.9	2.8	210.2	0.0	0.7	1,687.9	96.4	86.3	-10.4	0.6
Sub-Saharan Africa	1.3	2.7	111.9	0.1	2.6	3,178.6	256.0	232.1	-9.3	1.5
High income	41.6	53.9	29.6	7.0	46.1	555.9	139.1	245.2	76.3	19.8
World	16.6	24.0	44.7	2.5	18.3	619.0	210.5	234.5	11.4	6.1

*Data for Hong Kong and Macao are included in the aggregations but not listed individually in this table.

**Data for outgoing telephone traffic and internet use are for Israel only.

Where data for a particular year are not available, figures are taken from the year before or after as an estimate. These figures, and estimates based on them, are presented in italics.

Sources:International Telecommunications Union (ITU), Yearbook of Statistics; Telecommunications Services, 1991-2000 (Geneva: ITU, 2001); Internet Software Consortium, Internet Domain Survey, www.isc.org; RIPE (Reseaux IP Europeens), European Hostcount, www.ripe.net; NUA Publish (http://www.nua.com/surveys/how_many_online/index.html). NUA is the worlds leading resource for Internet trends and statistics

Record 8 Ratification of treaties

This table shows the major human rights, humanitarian, disarmament, and environmental treaties that countries have ratified, and in which years, up to 31 December 2001. The table also offers information on how many countries have ratified each particular treaty, and how many of the listed treaties each country has ratified. The graphs show a steady increase of ratifications, most pronounced in the 1980s, and how in the 1990s they are getting closer to an ideal global 'ceiling', where every country would have ratified every treaty. Global civil society is both dependent on the international rule of law and one of the main actors pushing for the adoption and enforcement of international law.

ICESCR – International Covenant on Economic, Social and Cultural Rights

ICCPR – International Covenant on Civil and Political Rights

ICCPR-OP1 – Optional Protocol to the International Covenant on Civil and Political Rights

ICCPR-OP2 – Second Optional Protocol to the International Covenant on Civil and Political Rights

CERD – International Convention on the Elimination of all forms of Racial Discrimination

CEDAW – Convention on the Elimination of All Forms of Discrimination Against Women

CAT – Convention against Torture and Other Cruel, Inhuman or Degrading Treatment or Punishment

Gen – Convention on the Prevention and Punishment of the Crime of the Genocide

ILO 87 – Freedom of Association and Protection of the Right to Organise Convention

CSR – Convention relating to the Status of Refugees

ICC – Rome Statute on the International Criminal Court

CWC – Chemical Weapons Convention

BWC – Biological Weapons Convention

LMC – Convention on the Prohibition of the Use, Stockpiling, Production and Transfer of Anti-Personnel Mines and on their Destruction

Geneva – Geneva Conventions

Prot 1 – First Additional to the Geneva Conventions

Prot 2 – Second Additional Protocol to the Geneva Conventions

BC – Basel Convention on the Control of Transboundary Movements of Hazardous Wastes and Their Disposal

CBD – Convention on Biological Diversity

UNFCCC – United Nations Framework Convention on Climate Change

KP – Kyoto Protocol to United Nations Framework Convention on Climate Change

VCPOL – Vienna Convention for the Protection of Ozone Layer

Country	Human Rights											Humanitarian Law						Environmental Law					Total
	ICESCR	ICCPR	CCPR-OP1	CCPR-OP2	CERD	CEDAW	CAT	Gen	ILO 87	CSR	ICC	CWC	BWC	LMC	Geneva	Prot 1	Prot2	BC	CBD	UNFCCC	KP	VCPOL	
Afghanistan	83	83			83		87	56					75		56								8
Albania	91	91			94	94	94	55		92		94	92	00	57	93	93	99	94	94		99	17
Algeria	89	89	89		72	96	89	63		63		95	01	01	62	89	89	98	95	93		92	19
Angola	92	92	92			86			01	81					84	84			98	00		00	9
Argentina	86	86	86		68	85	86	56	60	61	01	95	79	99	56	86	86	91	94	93	01	90	21
Armenia	93	93	93		93	93	93	93		93		94	94		93	93	93	99	93	94		99	17
Australia	75	80	91	90	75	83	89	49	73	54		94	77	99	58	91	91	92	93	92		87	20
Austria	78	78	87	93	72	82	87	58	50	54	00	95	73	98	53	82	82	93	94	94		87	21
Azerbaijan	92	92	01	99	96	95	96	96	92	93		00			93				01	00	95	00	96	17
Bahamas					75	93		75	01	93			86	98	75	80	80	92	93	94	99	93	15
Bahrain					90		98	90				97	88		71	86	86	92	96	94		90	12
Bangladesh	98	00			79	84	98	98	72			97	85	00	72	80	80	93	94	94	01	90	18
Barbados	73	73	73		72	80		80	67				73	99	68	90	90	95	93	94	00	92	17
Belarus	73	73	92		69	81	87	54	56			96	75		54	89	89	99	93	00		86	17
Belgium	83	83	94	98	75	85	99	51	51	53	00	97	79	98	52	86	86	93	96	96		88	21
Belize		96				01	90	86	98	83	90	00		86	98	84	84	84	97	93	94	97	17
Benin	92	92	92			92	92		60	62		98	75	98	61	86	86	97	94	94		93	17
Bhutan						81							78		91				95	95			5
Bolivia	82	82	82		70	90	99		65	82		98	75	98	76	83	83	96	94	94	99	94	19
Bosnia & Herzegovina	92	93	95	01	93	93	93	92	93	93		97	94	98	92	92	92	01		00		92	19

Country	Human Rights											Humanitarian Law						Environmental Law					Total
	ICESCR	ICCPR	CCPR-OP1	CCPR-OP2	CERD	CEDAW	CAT	Gen	ILO 87	CSR	ICC	CWC	BWC	LMC	Geneva	Prot 1	Prot2	BC	CBD	UNFCCC	KP	VCPOL	Total
Botswana		00			74	96	00		97	69	00	98	92	00	68	79	79	98	95	94		91	17
Brazil	92	92			68	84	89	52		60		96	73	99	57	92	92	92	94	94		90	17
Brunei												97	91		91	91	91					90	6
Bulgaria	70	70	92	99	66	82	86	50	59	93		94	72	98	54	89	89	96	96	95		90	20
Burkina Faso	99	99	99		74	87	99	65	60	80		97	91	98	61	87	87	99	93	93		89	19
Burundi	90	90			77	92	93	97	93	63		98			71	93	93	97	97	97	01	97	17
Cambodia	92	92			83	92	92	50	99	92			83	99	58	98	98	01	95	95		01	17
Cameroon	84	84	84		71	94	86		60	61		96			63	84	84	01	94	94		89	16
Canada	76	76	76		70	81	87	52	72	69	00	95	72	97	65	90	90	92	92	92		86	20
Cape Verde	93	93	00	00	79	80	92		99				77	01	84	95	95	99	95	95		01	17
Central African Republic	81	81	81		71	91			60	62					66	84	84		95	95		93	13
Chad	95	95	95		77	95	95		60	81				99	70	97	97		94	94		89	15
Chile	72	72	92		71	89	88	53	99	72		96	80	01	50	91	91	92	94	94		90	19
China & Tibet	01				81	80	88	83		82		97	84		56	83	83	91	93	93		89	15
Colombia	69	69	69	97	81	82	87	59	76	61		00	83	00	61	93	95	96	94	95	01	90	21
Comoros						94				78					85	85	85	94	94	94		94	9
Congo, Dem. Rep.	76	76	76		76	86	96	62	01	65			75		61	82		94	94	95		94	16
Congo, Rep.	83	83	83		88	82			60	62			78	01	67	83	83		96			94	14
Costa Rica	68	68	68	98	67	86	93	50	60	78	01	96	93	99	69	83	83	95	94	94		91	21
Côte d'Ivoire	92	92	97		73	95	95	95	60	61		95		00	61	89	89	94	94	94		93	18
Croatia	91	92	95	95	92	92	92	92	91	92	01	95	93	98	92	92	92	94	96	96		91	21
Cuba					72	80		53	52			97	76		54	82	99	94	94	94		92	14
Cyprus	69	69	92	99	67	85	91	82	66	63		98	73		62	79	96	92	96	97	99	92	20
Czech Republic	93	93	93		93	93	93	93	93	93		96	93	99	93	93	93	93	93	94	01	93	20
Denmark	72	72	72	94	71	83	87	51	51	52	01	95	73	98	51	82	82	94	93	93		88	21
Djibouti						98			78	77			98		78	91	91		94	95		99	11
Dominican Republic	78	78	78		83	82			56	78			73	00	58	94	94	00	96	98		93	16
Ecuador	69	69	69	93	66	81	88	49	67	55		95	75	99	54	79	79	93	93	93	00	90	21
Egypt	82	82			67	81	86	52	57	81					52	92	92	93	94	94		88	15
El Salvador	79	79	95		79	81	96	50		83		95	91	99	53	78	78	91	94	95	98	92	19
Equatorial Guinea	87	87	87			84			01	86		97	89	98	86	86	86		94	00	00	88	16
Eritrea	01				01	95		00					00		01	00			96	95			9
Estonia	91	91	91		91	91	91	91	94	97		99	93		93	93	93	92	94	94		96	18
Ethiopia	93	93			76	81	94	49	63	69		96	75		69	94	94	00	94	94		94	17
Fiji					73	95		73		72	99	93	73	98	71				93	93	98	89	13
Finland	75	75	75	91	70	86	89	59	50	68	00	95	74		55	80	80	91	94	94		86	20
France	80	80	84		71	83	86	50	51	54	00	95	84	98	51	01	84	91	94	94		87	20
Gabon	83	83			80	83	00	83	60	64	00	00		00	65	80	80		97	98		94	17
Gambia	78	79	88		78	93		78	00	66		98	91		66	89	89	97	94	94	01	90	18
Georgia	94	94	94	99	99	94	94	93	99	99		95	96		93	93	93	99	94	94	99	96	20
Germany	73	73	93	92	69	85	90	54	57	53	00	94	72	98	54	91	91	95	93	93		88	21
Ghana	00	00	00		66	86	00	58	65	63	99	97	75	00	58	78	78		94	95		89	19
Greece	85	97	97	97	70	83	88	54	62	60		94	75		56	89	93	94	94	94		88	19
Guatemala	88	92	00		83	82	90	50	52	83			73	99	52	87	87	95	95	95	99	87	19
Guinea	78	78	93		77	82	89	00	59	65		97		98	84	84	84	95	93	93	00	92	19
Guinea-Bissau	92					85				76			76	01	74	86	86		95	95			10

Country		Human Rights										Humanitarian Law						Environmental Law					
	ICESCR	ICCPR	CCPR-OP1	CCPR-OP2	CERD	CEDAW	CAT	Gen	ILO 87	CSR	ICC	CWC	BWC	LMC	Geneva	Prot 1	Prot2	BC	CBD	UNFCCC	KP	VCPOL	Total
Guyana	77	77	93		77	80	88		67			97			68	88	88	01	94	94		93	15
Haiti		91			72	81		50	79	84					57				96	96		00	10
Honduras	81	97				83	96	52	56	92			79	98	65	95	95	95	95	95	00	93	17
Hungary	74	74	88	94	67	80	87	52	57	89		96	72	98	54	89	89	90	94	94		88	20
Iceland	79	79	79	91	67	85	96	49	50	55	00	97	73	99	65	87	87	95	94	93		89	21
India	79	79			68	93		59				96	74		50			92	94	93		91	12
Indonesia					99	84	98		98			98	92		58			93	94	94		92	11
Iran	75	75			68			56		76		97	73		57			93	96	96		90	12
Iraq	71	71			70	86		59					91		56								7
Ireland	89	89	89	93	00	85		76	55	56		96	72	97	62	99	99	94	96	94		88	19
Israel & Occupied Territories	91	91			79	91	91	50	57	54					51			94	95	96		92	13
Italy	78	78	78	95	76	85	89	52	58	54	99	95	75	99	51	86	86	94	94	94		88	21
Jamaica	75	75			71	84		68	62	64		00	75	98	64	86	86		95	94	99	93	17
Japan	79	79			95	85	99		65	81		95	82	98	53			93	93	93		88	15
Jordan	75	75			74	92	91	50				97	75	98	51	79	79	89	93	93		89	16
Kazakhstan					98	98	98	98	00	99		00			92	92	92		94	95		98	13
Kenya	72	72			01	84	97			66		97	76	01	66	99	99	00	94	94		88	16
Kiribati														00	89					95	00		4
Korea, Dem. Rep.	81	81				01		89					87		57	88			94	94		95	10
Korea, Rep.	90	90	90		78	84	95	50		92		97	87		66	82	82	94	94	93		92	17
Kuwait	96	96			68	94	96	95	61			97	72		67	85	85	93		94		92	15
Kyrgyzstan	94	94	95		97	97	97	97	92	96					92	92	92	96	96	00		00	16
Laos					74	81		50				97	73		56	80	80		96	95		98	11
Latvia	92	92	94		92	92	92	92	92	97		96	97		91	91	91	92	95	95		95	18
Lebanon	72	72			71	97	00	53					75		51	97	97	94	94	94		93	14
Lesotho	92	92	00		71	95	01	74	66	81	00	94	77	98	68	94	94	00	95	95	00	94	21
Liberia					76	84		50	62	64				99	54	88	88	00				96	11
Libya	70	70	89		68	89	89	89	00				82		56	78	78	01	01	99		90	16
Lithuania	91	91	91		98	94	96	96	94	97		98	98		96	00	00	99	96	95		95	18
Luxembourg	83	83	83	92	78	89	87	81	58	53	00	97	76	99	53	89	89	94	94	94		88	21
Macedonia	94	94	94	95	94	94	94	94	91	94		97	96	98	93	93	93	97	97	98		94	20
Madagascar	71	71	71		69	89			60	67				99	63	92	92	99	96	99		96	15
Malawi	93	93	96		96	87	96		99	87		98		98	68	91	91	94	94	94	01	91	18
Malaysia						95		94				00	91	99	62			93	94	94		89	10
Maldives					84	93		84				94	93	00	91	91	91	92	92	92	98	88	14
Mali	74	74	01		74	85	99	74	60	73	00	97		98	65	89	89	00	95	94		94	19
Malta	90	90	90	94	71	91	90		65	71		97	75	01	68	89	89	00	00	94	01	88	20
Mauritius	73	73	73		72	84	92					93	72	97	70	82	82	92	92	92	01	92	17
Mexico	81	81			75	81	86	52	61	00		94	74	98	52	83		91	93	93	00	87	18
Moldova	93	93			93	94	95	93	96			96		00	93	93	93	98	95	95		96	16
Mongolia	74	74	91		69	81		67	69			95	72		58	95	95	97	93	93	99	96	17
Morocco & Western Sahara	79	79			70	93	93	58		56		95			56			95	95	95		95	13
Mozambique		93		93	83	97	99	83	96	83		00		98	83	83		97	95	95		94	16
Myanmar						97		56	55						92				94	94		93	7

Country	Human Rights											Humanitarian Law						Environmental Law					Total
	ICESCR	ICCPR	CCPR-OP1	CCPR-OP2	CERD	CEDAW	CAT	Gen	ILO 87	CSR	ICC	CWC	BWC	LMC	Geneva	Prot1	Prot2	BC	CBD	UNFCCC	KP	VCPOL	
Namibia	94	94	94	94	82	92	94	94	95	95		95		98	91	94	94	95	97	95		93	19
Nepal	91	91	91	98	71	91	91	69				97			64			96	93	94		94	14
Netherlands	78	78	78	91	71	91	88	66	50	56	01	95	81	99	54	87	87	93	94	93		88	21
New Zealand	78	78	89	90	72	85	89	78		60	00	96	72	99	59	88	88	94	93	93		87	20
Nicaragua	80	80	80		78	81		52	67	80		99	75	98	53	99	99	97	95	95	99	93	18
Niger	86	86	86		67	99	98		61	61		97	72	99	64	79	79	98	95	95		92	18
Nigeria	93	93			67	85	01		60	67		99	73	01	61	88	88	91	94	94		88	17
Norway	72	72	72	91	70	81	86	49	49	53	00	94	73	98	51	81	81	90	93	93		86	21
Oman												95	92		74	84	84	95	95	95		99	9
Pakistan					66	96			57	51		97	74		51			94	94	94		92	11
Panama	77	77	77	93	67	81	87	50	58	78		98	74	98	56	95	95	91	95	95	99	89	21
Papua New Guinea					82	95		82	00	86		94	80		76			95	93	93		92	12
Paraguay	92	92	95			87	90	01	62	70	01	96	76	98	61	90	90	95	94	94	99	92	20
Peru	78	78	80		71	82	88	60	60	64		95	85	98	56	89	89	93	93	93		89	19
Philippines	74	86	89		67	81	86	50	53	81		96	73	00	52		86	93	93	94		91	18
Poland	77	77	91		68	80	89	50	57	91		95	73		54	91	91	92	96	99		90	18
Portugal	78	78	83	90	82	80	89	99	77	60		96	75	99	61	92	92	94	93	93		88	20
Qatar					76		00					97	75	98	75	88		95	96	96		96	11
Romania	74	74	93	91	70	82	90	50	57	91		95	79	00	54	90	90	91	94	94	01	93	21
Russian Federation	73	73	91		69	81	87	54	56	93		97	75		54	89	89	95	95	94		86	18
Rwanda	75	75			75	81		75	88	80			75	00	64	84	84		96	98		01	15
Samoa						92				88				98	84	84	84		94	94	00	92	10
Sao Tome & Principe									92	78			79		76	96	96		99	99		01	9
Saudi Arabia					97	00	97	50				96	72		63	87		90		94		93	11
Senegal	78	78	78		72	85	86	83	60	63	99	98	75	98	63	85	85	92	94	94	01	93	21
Sierra Leone	96	96	96		67	88	01		61	81	00		76	01	65	86	86		94	95		01	17
Singapore						95		95				97	75		73			96	95	97		89	9
Slovakia	93	93	93	99	93	93	93	93	93	93		95	93	99	93	93	93	93	94	94		93	20
Slovenia	92	92	93	94	92	92	93	92	92	92		97	92	98	92	92	92	93	96	95		92	20
Solomon Islands	82				82					95			81	99	81	88	88	95	94			93	11
Somalia	90	90	90		75		90			78					62							01	8
South Africa		98			98	95	98	98	96	96	00	95	75	98	52	95	95	94	95	97		90	18
Spain	77	77	85	91	68	84	87	68	77	78	00	94	79	99	52	89	89	94	93	93		88	21
Sri Lanka	80	80	97		82	81	94	50	95			94	86		59			92	94	93		89	15
St. Lucia					90	82				80		97	86	99	81	82	82	93	93	93		93	13
St. Vincent & the Grenadines	81	81	81		81	81	01	81	01	93			99	01	81	83	83	96	96	96		96	18
Sudan	86	76			77					74		99			57				95	93		93	9
Suriname	76	76	76		84	93			76	78		97	93		76	85	85		96	97		97	15
Swaziland					69					78		96	91	98	73	95	95		94	96		92	11
Sweden	71	71	71	90	71	80	86	52	49	54	01	93	76	98	53	79	79	91	93	93		86	21
Switzerland	92	92		94	94	97	86	00	75	55		95	76	98	50	82	82	90	94	93		87	19
Syria	69	69			69			55	60						53	83		92	96	96		89	11
Tajikistan	99	99	99		95	93	95		93	93	00	95		99	93	93	93		97	98		96	17
Tanzania	76	76			72	85		84	00	64		98		00	62	83	83	93	96	96		93	16
Thailand	99	96				85							75	98	54			97		94		89	9

Country	ICESCR	ICCPR	CCPR-OP1	CCPR-OP2	CERD	CEDAW	CAT	Gen	ILO 87	CSR	ICC	CWC	BWC	LMC	Geneva	Prot 1	Prot2	BC	CBD	UNFCCC	KP	VCPOL	Total
	Human Rights											**Humanitarian Law**						**Environmental Law**					
Togo	84	84	88		72	83	87	84	60	62		97	76	00	62	84	84		95	95		91	18
Trinidad & Tobago	78	78			73	90			63	00	99	97		98	63	01	01	94	96	94	99	89	17
Tunisia	69	69			67	85	88	56	57	57		97	73	99	57	79	79	95	93	93		89	18
Turkey						85	88	50	93	62		97	74		54			94	97			91	11
Turkmenistan	97	97	97	00	94	97	99		97	98		94	96	98	92	92	92	96	96	95	00	93	20
Uganda	87	95	95		80	85	86	95		76		01	92	99	64	91	91	99	93	93		88	18
Ukraine	73	73	91		69	81	87	54	56			98	75		54	90	90	99	95	97		86	17
United Arab Emirates					74							00			72	83	83	92	00	95		89	9
United Kingdom	76	76		99	69	86	88	70	49	54		96	75	98	57	98	98	94	94	93		87	19
United States		92			94		94	88				97	75		55					92		86	9
Uruguay	70	70	70	93	68	81	86	67	54	70		94	81	01	69	85	85	91	93	94	01	89	21
Uzbekistan	95	95	95		95	95	95	99				96	96		93	93	93	96	95	93	99	93	17
Vanuatu						95							90		82	85	85		93	93	01	94	9
Venezuela	78	78	78	93	67	83	91	60	82		00	97	78	99	56	98	98	98	94	94		88	20
Vietnam	82	82			82	82		81				98	80		57	81		95	94	94		94	13
Yemen	87	87			72	84	91	87	76	80		00	79	98	70	90	90	96	96	96		96	18
Yugoslavia	01	01	01	01	01	82	01	01	00	01		00			01	01	01	00		97		92	17
Zambia	84	84	84		72	85	98		96	69		01		01	66	95	95	94	93	93		90	17
Zimbabwe	91	91			91	91		91		81		97	90	98	83	92	92		94	92		92	15
Total States Parties	139	141	98	43	153	159	124	128	134	128	32	134	137	112	176	149	141	137	169	169	39	170	

Sources: Office of the UN High Commissioner for Human Rights, http://www.unhchr.ch/html/intlinst.htm; United Nations, http://www.un.org/law/icc/statute/status.htm; Organisation for the Prohibition of Chemical Weapons, http://www.opcw.nl; Federation of American Scientists, http://www.fas.org/nuke/control/bwc/text/bwcsig.htm; Secretariat, Basel Convention on the Control of Transboundary Movements of Hazardous Wastes and Their Disposal, http://www.basel.int/ratif/ratif.html; Secretariat, United Nations Framework Convention on Climate Change, http://www.unfccc.de/resource/country/index.html; International Committee of the Red Cross, http://www.icrc.org/eng/party_gc and http://www.icrc.org/eng/party_cmines

Record 8b: Cumulative ratificaton of treaties (1949–2001)

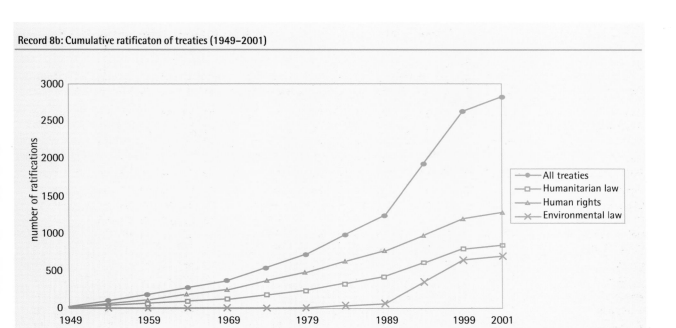

Record 8c: Cumulative ratificaton of treaties (1990–2001)

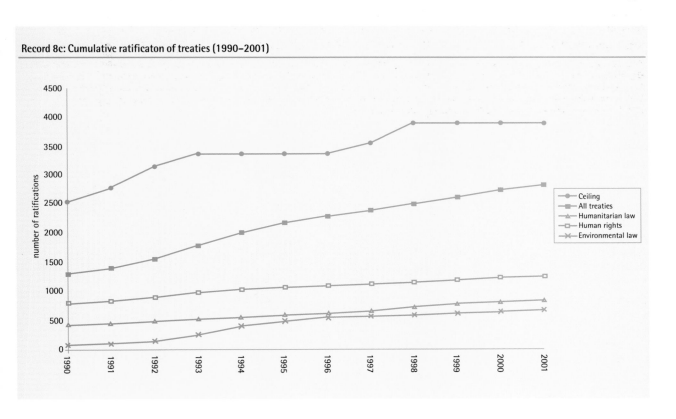

Record 9 Human rights violations

This table displays information on human rights abuses by country, covering extrajudicial executions and disappearances, arbitrary detentions, torture, freedom of expression, and the situation of minorities, using the latest information available from three different sources: Amnesty International, Human Rights Watch and the US State Department. The information offers an indication of whether certain basic human rights are violated, but it does not quantify the number of violations in each country. While Record 9 shows to what extent states have committed themselves to abide by international law, this table shows to what extent states actually respect international human rights law. Global civil society is instrumental in exposing human rights violations. At the same time, human rights violations form one of the main threats to the survival of local civil societies.

Country	Disappearances & extrajudicial executions			Arbitrary detentions			Torture			Discrimination against minorities			Freedom of expression & association		
	AI	HRW	SD	AI	HRW	SD	AI	HRW	SD	AI	HRW	SD	AI	HRW	SD
Afghanistan		yes	yes	yes	yes	yes	yes	yes	yes		yes	yes		no	no
Albania			yes			yes	yes	yes	yes		yes			no	
Algeria	yes	yes	yes	yes	yes	yes	yes	yes	yes		yes		no	no	no
Angola		yes	yes			yes			yes				no	no	no
Argentina	yes	yes	yes		yes	yes	yes	yes	yes					no	
Armenia						yes	yes	yes			yes	yes		no	
Australia				yes											
Austria		yes									yes			yes	
Azerbaijan		yes			yes	yes	yes	yes	yes		yes			no	no
Bahamas				yes		yes	yes								
Bahrain					yes		yes								no
Bangladesh		yes				yes	yes		yes		yes				no
Barbados															
Belarus	yes				yes	yes	yes				yes		no	no	no
Belgium		yes									yes				
Belize						yes	yes								
Benin	yes			yes							yes				no
Bhutan						yes	yes		yes		yes				no
Bolivia						yes	yes		yes		yes		no		
Bosnia & Herzegovina						yes					yes	yes	no	no	no
Botswana															
Brazil	yes	yes	yes			yes	yes	yes	yes		yes	yes		no	
Brunei								yes			yes				no
Bulgaria		yes	yes		yes		yes	yes	yes	yes	yes	yes	no	no	
Burkina Faso		yes	yes	yes	yes	yes			yes				no	no	no
Burundi	yes	yes	yes	yes	yes	yes	yes	yes	yes			yes		no	no
Cambodia	yes					yes	yes	yes	yes					no	no
Cameroon	yes	yes		yes		yes	yes		yes		yes		no		no
Canada															
Cape Verde															
Central African Republic		yes							yes		yes				no
Chad	yes	yes		yes		yes	yes		yes		yes				no
Chile							yes								
China & Tibet		yes		yes		yes	yes	yes	yes		yes		no	no	no
Colombia		yes				yes	yes		yes		yes				
Comoros						yes					yes				
Congo, Dem Rep.	yes	yes	yes	yes	yes	yes	yes	yes	yes		yes		no	no	no
Congo, Rep.		yes	yes	yes		yes					yes		no		

292

Record 9 continued	Disappearances & extrajudicial executions			Arbitrary detentions			Torture			Discrimination against minorities			Freedom of expression & association		
Country	AI	HRW	SD	AI	HRW	SD	AI	HRW	SD	AI	HRW	SD	AI	HRW	SD
Costa Rica															
Côte d'Ivoire	yes		yes			yes	yes								no
Croatia						yes					yes	yes			no
Cuba					yes							yes	no	no	no
Cyprus									yes						
Czech Republic				yes		yes			yes	yes	yes	yes			
Denmark															
Djibouti		yes				yes	yes		yes	yes		yes	no		no
Dominican Republic	yes		yes			yes	yes		yes			yes			
Ecuador	yes		yes			yes	yes		yes			yes			
Egypt		yes		yes	yes	yes	yes	yes	yes		yes	yes	no	no	no
El Salvador	yes					yes	yes					yes			
Equatorial Guinea						yes	yes		yes			yes	no		no
Eritrea				yes	yes				yes					no	no
Estonia						yes			yes			yes			
Ethiopia	yes		yes	yes	yes	yes		yes					no	no	no
Fiji	yes						yes						no		
Finland															
France		yes					yes		yes						
Gabon		yes							yes						no
Gambia		yes		yes		yes			yes				no		no
Georgia		yes			yes	yes	yes	yes	yes		yes	yes			no
Germany		yes							yes						
Ghana		yes		yes		yes							no		
Greece		yes							yes		yes	yes	no		no
Guatemala		yes	yes					yes	yes					no	no
Guinea						yes	yes		yes						no
Guinea-Bissau						yes									no
Guyana							yes		yes			yes			
Haiti		yes				yes	yes		yes					no	
Honduras		yes							yes	yes			no		no
Hungary									yes	yes	yes	yes			
Iceland															
India		yes				yes	yes		yes	yes	yes	yes		no	
Indonesia	yes	yes	yes	yes			yes	yes	yes						
Iran						yes	yes		yes		yes	yes	no	no	no
Iraq	yes	yes	yes			yes	yes	yes	yes	yes	yes	yes	no	no	no
Ireland									yes			yes			
Israel & Occupied Territories		yes			yes	yes	yes	yes	yes		yes	yes			
Italy						yes	yes		yes						
Jamaica	yes						yes		yes						
Japan							yes								
Jordan						yes	yes					yes			no
Kazakhstan		yes				yes	yes		yes		yes	yes		no	no
Kenya	yes	yes	yes			yes	yes		yes				no	no	no
Korea, Dem. Rep.			yes									yes			no

Record 9 continued	Disappearances & extrajudicial executions			Arbitrary detentions			Torture			Discrimination against minorities			Freedom of expression & association		
Country	AI	HRW	SD	AI	HRW	SD	AI	HRW	SD	AI	HRW	SD	AI	HRW	SD
Korea, Rep.						yes	yes		yes			yes			
Kuwait												yes	no		no
Kyrgyzstan						yes	yes		yes		yes	yes	no	no	no
Laos						yes	yes		yes				no		no
Latvia			yes			yes			yes						
Lebanon						yes	yes		yes			yes			no
Lesotho							yes								
Liberia	yes	yes	yes		yes	yes	yes	yes	yes		yes	yes	no	no	no
Libya				yes		yes	yes		yes			yes			no
Lithuania									yes						
Luxembourg															
Macedonia		yes	yes		yes		yes	yes	yes		yes	yes		no	
Madagascar						yes									no
Malawi			yes				yes								no
Malaysia			yes				yes		yes			yes	no	no	no
Maldives							yes								no
Mali						yes									
Malta															
Mauritania				yes		yes	yes					yes	no		no
Mauritius	yes						yes								
Mexico				yes	yes	yes	yes	yes	yes						
Moldova				yes		yes			yes			yes			no
Mongolia						yes									
Morocco & Western Sahara						yes	yes		yes			yes	no	no	no
Mozambique	yes	yes	yes			yes	yes	yes	yes						
Myanmar	yes		yes		yes	yes	yes	yes	yes			yes	no		no
Namibia	yes		yes				yes					yes	no		
Nepal	yes		yes	yes			yes		yes			yes			no
Netherlands															
New Zealand															
Nicaragua						yes									
Niger						yes	yes					yes	no		
Nigeria		yes	yes		yes	yes	yes		yes		yes				no
Norway						yes									
Oman												yes			no
Pakistan	yes		yes	yes		yes	yes		yes		yes	yes		no	no
Panama									yes			yes			
Papua New Guinea	yes						yes								no
Paraguay		yes				yes	yes		yes			yes			
Peru						yes	yes		yes			yes	no		
Philippines	yes		yes			yes	yes					yes			
Poland		yes		yes					yes			yes			
Portugal									yes			yes			
Qatar							yes					yes			no
Romania			yes				yes		yes		yes	yes			no
Russian Federation	yes	yes	yes	yes	yes	yes	yes	yes	yes			yes		no	no

Country	Disappearances & extrajudicial executions			Arbitrary detentions			Torture			Discrimination against minorities			Freedom of expression & association		
	AI	HRW	SD	AI	HRW	SD	AI	HRW	SD	AI	HRW	SD	AI	HRW	SD
Rwanda	yes	yes	yes	yes	yes	yes	yes	yes	yes	yes		yes		no	no
Samoa												yes			
Sao Tome & Principle															
Saudi Arabia				yes			yes	yes				yes	no	no	no
Senegal	yes		yes	yes		yes									no
Sierra Leone	yes			yes		yes	yes					yes			no
Singapore													no		no
Slovakia					yes			yes			yes	yes		no	
Slovenia															
Solomon Islands															
Somalia						yes			yes			yes	no		no
South Africa						yes	yes								
Spain							yes		yes			yes			
Sri Lanka	yes		yes	yes	yes		yes	yes	yes		yes	yes			no
St. Lucia							yes								
Sudan		yes	yes		yes	yes	yes	yes	yes		yes	yes	no	no	no
Suriname			yes												
Swaziland				yes			yes		yes			yes	no		no
Sweden															
Switzerland			yes						yes						
Syria				yes		yes	yes		yes			yes		no	no
Tanzania						yes			yes			yes	no		no
Tajikistan		yes				yes	yes	yes	yes			yes		no	no
Thailand							yes					yes			
Togo				yes		yes	yes					yes	no		no
Trinidad & Tobago													no		
Tunisia						yes	yes	yes	yes				no	no	no
Turkey	yes		yes			yes	yes	yes	yes		yes	yes	no	no	no
Turkmenistan			yes		yes	yes		yes	yes		yes	yes		no	no
Uganda	yes	yes	yes	yes		yes	yes	yes	yes				no		no
Ukraine	yes					yes	yes		yes						no
United Arab Emirates												yes	no		no
United Kingdom			yes			yes			yes			yes	no		
United States							yes	yes							
Uruguay							yes								
Uzbekistan			yes			yes	yes	yes	yes		yes	yes		no	no
Vanuatu															
Venezuela	yes	yes	yes			yes	yes		yes						
Vietnam			yes		yes	yes			yes		yes	yes	no	no	no
Yemen		yes		yes	yes	yes	yes	yes	yes			yes	no	no	no
Yugoslavia			yes		yes	yes	yes	yes	yes		yes	yes	no	no	no
Zambia		yes	yes			yes	yes	yes					no	no	no
Zimbabwe	yes		yes			yes	yes		yes			yes	no		no

In the first four categories 'yes' denotes a violation, whereas in the final category, 'no' denotes a violation. Absence of data indicates either no violations recorded or no data available.

Sources: Human Rights Watch World Report 2001; Amnesty International Report 2000; U.S. State Department Country Reports on Human Rights Practices for 2001

Record 10 Social justice

This table shows another measure of the spread of the international rule of law, namely, the level of realisation of social and economic rights, or social justice, for 1990 and 1999, unless otherwise indicated. It shows the Human Development Index (HDI), where higher numbers suggest higher levels of development. The HDI is a composite index of three separate indicators measuring GDP per capita, educational attainment, and life expectancy at birth. As further measures of social justice, we also show adult literacy, the extent of income inequality using the Gini coefficient, with higher numbers indicating greater inequality, and the percentage of women in secondary education (for 1995-97). The table thus shows indicators of poverty, inequality, and social exclusion. Growing inequality appears to be one of the characteristics of globalisation, as well as being one of the inhibitors of the emergence of global civil society.

Country	Human Development Index (HDI)			GDP per capita, PPP in current international $			Infant mortality rate (% live births)			Life expectancy at birth (years)			Adult illiteracy (% adult population)			Income inequality (Gini Index)*	Net enrolment in secondary education (% of women)
	value 1990	value 1999	% change 1990–1999	1990	1999	% change 1990–1999	1990	1999	% change 1990–1999	1990	1999	% change 1990–1999	1990	1999	% change 1990–1999	see note below	1995–1997
Albania	0.700	0.725	3.6	2,754	3,189	16	2.8	2.4	-14.1	72	72	-0.3	23	16	-30		
Algeria	0.641	0.693	8.1	4,545	5,063	11	4.6	3.4	-26.1	67	71	5.1	46	33	-27	35.3	54
Angola		0.422		1,594	3,179	99	13.0	12.7	-2.6	45	47	2.4					
Argentina	0.807	0.842	4.3	7,758	12,277	58	2.5	1.8	-27.0	72	74	2.7	4	3	-23		
Armenia		0.745		3,576	2,215	-38	1.9	1.4	-23.3	72	74	3.8	3	2	-34	44.4	
Australia	0.886	0.936	5.6	17,261	24,574	42	0.8	0.5	-38.7	77	79	2.3				35.2	89
Austria	0.889	0.921	3.6	19,006	25,089	32	0.8	0.4	-43.6	76	78	2.9				23.1	89
Azerbaijan		0.738		5,152	2,850	-45	2.3	1.6	-29.6	71	71	1.0				36	
Bahamas		0.820		14,458	15,258	6	2.8	1.8	-38.2	72	73	1.7	5	4	-19		
Bahrain		0.824		11,580	13,688	18	2.3	0.8	-66.2	71	73	2.2	18	13	-28		88
Bangladesh	0.414	0.470	13.5	1,004	1,483	48	9.1	6.1	-32.4	55	61	11.1	65	59	-9	33.6	
Barbados		0.864		11,298	14,353	27	1.2	1.4	23.4	75	76	1.0					
Belarus	0.808	0.782	-3.2	7,169	6,876	-4	1.2	1.1	-5.3	71	68	-3.4	1	1	-29	21.7	
Belgium	0.895	0.935	4.5	19,798	25,443	29	0.8	0.5	-32.0	76	78	2.7				25	87
Belize	0.751	0.776	3.3	3,864	4,959	28	3.4	2.8	-17.3	71	72	1.0	11	7	-36		
Benin	0.359	0.420	17.0	704	933	33	10.4	8.7	-16.2	52	53	2.4	72	61	-15		
Bhutan		0.477		887	1,341	51	0.0	5.9			61						
Bolivia	0.596	0.648	8.7	1,833	2,355	28	8.0	5.9	-26.5	58	62	6.4	22	15	-31	58.9	
Bosnia & Herzegovina							1.5	1.3	-15.0	71	73	2.3					
Botswana	0.654	0.577	-11.8	4,931	6,872	39	5.5	5.8	6.4	57	39	-30.6	32	24	-26		52
Brazil	0.710	0.750	5.6	5,568	7,037	26	4.8	3.2	-32.6	65	67	2.6	19	15	-21	59.1	
Brunei		0.857					0.9	0.9	-6.8	74	76	2.3	14	9	-37		
Bulgaria	0.783	0.772	-1.4	5,820	5,071	-13	1.5	1.4	-3.4	71	71	-0.4	3	2	-39	26.4	69
Burkina Faso	0.294	0.320	8.8	707	965	36	11.1	10.5	-5.6	45	45	-1.1	84	77	-8	48.2	
Burundi	0.344	0.309	-10.2	726	578	-20	11.9	10.5	-11.8	44	42	-3.4	62	53	-14	33.3	
Cambodia		0.541		985	1,361	38	12.2	10.0	-17.6	50	54	6.8	69	61	-12	40.4	16
Cameroon	0.511	0.506	-1.0	1,581	1,573	-1	8.1	7.7	-4.7	54	51	-6.1	37	25	-33		
Canada	0.925	0.936	1.2	20,203	26,251	30	0.7	0.5	-22.1	77	79	2.3				31.5	90
Cape Verde	0.624	0.708	13.5	2,941	4,490	53	6.4	3.9	-39.8	65	69	5.1	36	26	-27		48
Central African Rep.	0.370	0.372	0.5	1,060	1,166	10	10.2	9.6	-6.4	48	44	-7.4	67	55	-18		

Country	Human Development Index (HDI) value 1990	value 1999	% change 1990–1999	GDP per capita, PPP in current international $ 1990	1999	% change 1990–1999	Infant mortality rate (% live births) 1990	1999	% change 1990–1999	Life expectancy at birth (years) 1990	1999	% change 1990–1999	Adult illiteracy (% adult population) 1990	1999	% change 1990–1999	Income inequality (Gini Index)* see note below	Net enrolment in secondary education (% of women) 1995–1997
Chad	0.321	0.359	11.8	768	850	11	11.8	10.1	-14.6	46	49	5.1	72	59	-18		3
Chile	0.779	0.825	5.9	4,984	8,652	74	1.6	1.0	-37.7	74	76	2.5	6	4	-25	57.5	60
China & Tibet**	0.624	0.718	15.1	1,400	3,617	158	3.3	3.0	-8.5	69	70	1.7	23	17	-28	40.3	
Colombia	0.720	0.765	6.3	4,804	5,749	20	3.0	2.3	-25.1	69	70	2.2	11	9	-25	57.1	49
Comoros	0.498	0.510	2.4	1,658	1,429	-14	8.4	6.1	-27.6	56	61	8.2	46	41	-12		
Congo, Dem. Rep.		0.429		1,350	801	-41	9.6	8.5	-11.3	52	46	-11.2	52	40	-24		
Congo, Rep.	0.504	0.502	-0.4	752	727	-3	8.8	8.9	0.9	49	48	-2.6	33	21	-38		
Costa Rica	0.789	0.821	4.1	5,324	8,860	66	1.5	1.2	-16.4	75	77	1.9	6	5	-26	45.9	43
Côte D'Ivoire	0.414	0.426	2.9	1,553	1,654	6	9.5	11.1	17.1	50	46	-7.4	66	54	-18	36.7	
Croatia	0.794	0.803	1.1	7,104	7,387	4	1.1	0.8	-25.9	72	73	1.2	3	2	-42	29	80
Cuba							1.1	0.7	-35.7	75	76	1.7	5	3	-29		
Cyprus	0.843	0.877	4.0	12,839	19,006	48	1.1	0.7	-37.7	77	78	1.6	6	3	-46		
Czech Republic	0.833	0.844	1.3		13,018		1.1	0.5	-57.4	72	75	4.1				25.4	89
Denmark	0.889	0.921	3.6	19,592	25,869	32	0.8	0.5	-38.0	75	76	1.6				24.7	
Dominican Republic	0.675	0.722	7.0	3,386	5,507	63	5.1	3.9	-23.2	69	71	2.4	21	17	-18	47.4	33
Ecuador	0.700	0.726	3.7	2,792	2,994	7	4.5	2.8	-37.2	67	69	3.5	13	9	-29	43.7	
Egypt	0.573	0.635	10.8	2,517	3,420	36	6.9	4.7	-31.9	63	67	6.4	53	45	-14	28.9	64
El Salvador	0.642	0.701	9.2	2,978	4,344	46	4.6	3.0	-34.0	66	70	6.0	28	22	-21	50.8	23
Equatorial Guinea	0.507	0.610	20.3	1,056	4,676	343	12.1	10.4	-14.2	47	51	7.3	27	18	-33		
Eritrea		0.416			881		8.1	6.0	-25.8	49	50	3.1	57	47	-17		14
Estonia		0.812		8,092	8,355	3	1.2	1.0	-23.4	69	71	1.6				37.6	90
Ethiopia	0.294	0.321	9.2	489	628	29	12.4	10.4	-16.5	45	42	-5.8	72	63	-13	40	
Fiji	0.719	0.757	5.3	3,818	4,799	26	2.5	1.8	-26.5	71	73	2.5	11	7	-35		
Finland	0.894	0.925	3.5	17,868	23,096	29	0.6	0.4	-27.2	75	77	2.9				25.6	94
France	0.896	0.924	3.1	18,040	22,897	27	0.7	0.5	-34.2	77	79	2.2				32.7	95
French Polynesia				18,688	22,204	19	1.8	1.0	-42.4	70	73	4.3					
Gabon		0.617		5,207	6,024	16	9.6	8.4	-12.6	52	53	1.4					
Gambia	0.314	0.398	26.8	1,503	1,580	5	10.9	7.5	-31.1	49	53	8.0	74	64	-14	47.8	
Georgia		0.742			2,431		1.6	1.5	-4.9	72	73	0.8				37.1	74
Germany		0.921			23,742		0.7	0.5	-31.1	75	77	2.5				30	89
Ghana	0.505	0.542	7.3	1,409	1,881	33	6.6	5.7	-13.5	57	58	1.3	42	30	-29	39.6	
Greece	0.857	0.881	2.8	11,248	15,414	37	1.0	0.6	-37.9	77	78	1.2	5	3	-42	32.7	88
Guatemala	0.577	0.626	8.5	2,838	3,674	29	5.6	4.0	-28.5	61	65	5.6	39	32	-18	55.8	
Guinea		0.397		1,527	1,934	27	12.1	9.6	-20.4	44	46	6.1				40.3	
Guinea -Bissau	0.306	0.339	10.8	703	678	-4	14.5	12.7	-12.5	42	44	3.9	72	62	-13	56.2	

Country	Human Development Index (HDI)			GDP per capita, PPP in current international $			Infant mortality rate (% live births)			Life expectancy at birth (years)			Adult illiteracy (% adult population)			Income inequality (Gini Index)*	Net enrolment in secondary education (% of women)
	value 1990	value 1999	% change 1990–1999	1990	1999	% change 1990–1999	1990	1999	% change 1990–1999	1990	1999	% change 1990–1999	1990	1999	% change 1990–1999	see note below	1995–1997
Guyana	0.676	0.704	4.1	2,753	3,640	32	6.4	5.7	-11.0	63	64	1.6	3	2	-43	40.2	68
Haiti	0.449	0.467	4.0	1,746	1,464	-16	8.5	7.0	-18.1	53	53	0.6	60	51	-15		
Honduras	0.614	0.634	3.3	2,093	2,340	12	5.0	3.4	-31.2	67	70	4.6	32	26	-17	59	
Hungary	0.803	0.829	3.2	9,485	11,430	21	1.5	0.8	-43.2	69	71	1.9	1	1	-22	24.4	87
Iceland	0.910	0.932	2.4	21,267	27,835	31	0.6	0.3	-47.9	78	79	1.7					88
India	0.510	0.571	12.0	1,416	2,248	59	8.0	7.1	-11.4	60	63	5.6	51	44	-14	37.8	
Indonesia	0.622	0.677	8.8	1,960	2,857	46	6.0	4.2	-30.1	62	66	6.5	20	14	-33	31.7	
Iran	0.645	0.714	10.7	3,897	5,531	42	4.7	2.6	-45.7	66	71	7.4	36	24	-33		68
Iraq							10.2	10.1	-0.7	61	59	-3.3	55	45	-17		
Ireland	0.868	0.916	5.5	12,737	25,918	103	0.8	0.6	-32.9	75	76	2.1				35.9	88
Israel & Occupied Territories	0.859	0.893	4.0	13,504	18,440	37	1.0	0.6	-43.4	76	78	2.8	6	4	-31	35.5	
Italy	0.878	0.909	3.5	17,508	22,172	27	0.8	0.5	-33.8	77	78	1.5	2	2	-30	27.3	
Jamaica	0.722	0.738	2.2	3,473	3,561	3	2.5	2.0	-19.0	73	75	2.6	18	14	-24	36.4	
Japan	0.907	0.928	2.3	19,913	24,898	25	0.5	0.4	-21.7	79	81	2.3				24.9	
Jordan	0.677	0.714	5.5	3,380	3,955	17	3.0	2.6	-12.7	68	71	4.1	19	11	-42	36.4	
Kazakhstan		0.742		6,379	4,951	-22	2.6	2.2	-17.5	68	65	-5.1				35.4	
Kenya	0.531	0.514	-3.2	975	1,022	5	6.2	7.6	23.8	57	48	-16.5	29	19	-37	44.5	
Korea, Dem. Rep.							4.5	5.8	28.6	66	60	-8.1					
Korea, Rep.	0.814	0.875	7.5	8,923	15,712	76	1.2	0.8	-30.8	70	73	3.7	4	2	-41	31.6	97
Kuwait		0.818					1.4	1.1	-21.3	75	77	1.7	23	18	-20		58
Kyrgyzstan		0.707		3,687	2,573	-30	3.0	2.6	-14.7	68	67	-1.5				40.5	
Laos	0.402	0.476	18.4	904	1,471	63	10.8	9.3	-13.8	50	54	8.4	64	53	-17	37	21
Latvia	0.803	0.791	-1.5	8,519	6,264	-26	1.4	1.4	4.9	69	70	0.8	0	0	0	32.4	83
Lebanon		0.758		1,843	4,705	155	3.6	2.6	-27.6	68	70	3.4	20	14	-27		71
Lesotho	0.572	0.541	-5.4	1,073	1,854	73	10.2	9.2	-9.8	58	45	-22.6	22	17	-23	56	24
Liberia							16.8	11.3	-32.9	45	47	4.7	61	47	-23		
Libya		0.770					3.3	2.2	-31.9	68	71	3.3	32	21	-34		
Lithuania	0.814	0.803	-1.4	8,568	6,656	-22	1.0	0.9	-12.1	71	72	1.2	1	1	-29	32.4	85
Luxembourg	0.879	0.924	5.1	19,840	42,769	116	0.7	0.5	-36.2	75	77	2.2				26.9	70
Macedonia		0.766		4,644	4,651	0	3.2	1.6	-50.9	72	73	1.6					55
Madagascar	0.432	0.462	6.9	821	799	-3	10.3	9.0	-12.6	53	54	2.8	42	34	-18	46	
Malawi	0.363	0.397	9.4	475	586	23	13.5	13.2	-2.8	45	39	-11.5	48	41	-15		
Malaysia	0.720	0.774	7.5	4,763	8,209	72	1.6	0.8	-50.0	71	72	2.6	19	13	-32	49.2	
Maldives		0.739		2,845	4,423	55	6.0	2.9	-51.2	62	68	10.0	6	4	-38		
Mali	0.310	0.378	21.9	585	753	29	13.6	12.0	-11.8	45	43	-5.3	74	60	-19	50.5	
Malta		0.866		8,866	15,189	71	0.9	0.5	-42.6	75	77	2.6	12	8	-29		79
Mauritania	0.392	0.437	11.5	1,164	1,609	38	10.5	8.8	-15.8	51	54	6.5	64	58	-8	37.3	
Mauritius	0.721	0.765	6.1	5,639	9,107	61	2.0	1.9	-8.0	70	71	1.7	20	16	-21		61
Mexico	0.759	0.790	4.1	6,409	8,297	29	3.6	2.9	-19.2	70	72	2.5	12	9	-27	51.9	

R10 continued	Human Development Index (HDI)			GDP per capita, PPP in current international $			Infant mortality rate (% live births)			Life expectancy at birth (years)			Adult illiteracy (% adult population)			Income inequality (Gini Index)*	Net enrolment in secondary education (% of women)
Country	value 1990	value 1999	% change 1990-1999	1990	1999	% change 1990-1999	1990	1999	% change 1990-1999	1990	1999	% change 1990-1999	1990	1999	% change 1990-1999	see note below	1995-1997
Moldova	0.758	0.699	-7.8	5,237	2,037	-61	1.9	1.7	-8.4	68	67	-2.5	3	1	-50	40.6	
Mongolia	0.554	0.569	2.7	1,811	1,711	-6	7.3	5.8	-20.5	63	67	6.2	47	38	-20	33.2	61
Morocco & Western Sahara	0.539	0.596	10.6	2,900	3,419	18	6.4	4.8	-25.3	63	67	5.8	61	52	-15	39.5	
Mozambique	0.311	0.323	3.9	544	861	58	15.0	13.1	-12.8	43	43	-0.8	67	57	-15	39.6	5
Myanmar		0.551					9.4	7.7	-17.5	57	60	5.6	19	16	-19		
Namibia	0.551	0.601	9.1	4,332	5,468	26	6.4	6.3	-0.8	58	50	-13.1	25	19	-26		44
Nepal	0.415	0.480	15.7	892	1,237	39	10.1	7.5	-25.5	54	58	8.6	69	60	-14	36.7	
Netherlands	0.900	0.931	3.4	17,466	24,215	39	0.7	0.5	-28.2	77	78	1.0				32.6	91
New Zealand	0.873	0.913	4.6	14,247	19,104	34	0.8	0.5	-37.0	75	77	2.8					91
Nicaragua	0.596	0.635	6.5	1,782	2,279	28	5.1	3.4	-32.7	64	69	6.4	35	32	-9	60.3	35
Niger	0.254	0.274	7.9	742	753	1	15.0	11.6	-22.7	45	46	1.8	89	85	-4	50.5	4
Nigeria	0.423	0.455	7.6	767	853	11	8.6	8.3	-3.6	49	47	-3.2	51	37	-27	50.6	
Norway	0.899	0.939	4.4	19,606	28,433	45	0.7	0.4	-41.7	77	78	2.6				25.8	98
Oman		0.747					2.2	1.7	-21.0	69	73	6.3	45	30	-34		57
Pakistan	0.441	0.498	12.9	1,363	1,834	35	11.1	9.0	-19.1	59	63	5.8	64	55	-14	31.2	
Panama	0.746	0.784	5.1	3,904	5,875	50	2.6	2.0	-22.6	72	74	2.0	11	8	-25	48.5	
Papua New Guinea	0.481	0.534	11.0	1,618	2,367	46	8.3	5.8	-30.7	55	58	5.9	42	36	-15	50.9	
Paraguay	0.716	0.738	3.1	3,941	4,384	11	3.1	2.4	-24.2	68	70	2.7	10	7	-28	57.7	39
Peru	0.702	0.743	5.8	3,265	4,622	42	5.4	3.9	-27.4	66	69	4.5	14	10	-28	46.2	
Philippines	0.716	0.749	4.6	3,368	3,805	13	3.7	3.1	-14.9	65	69	5.4	8	5	-35	46.2	
Poland	0.790	0.828	4.8	5,922	8,450	43	1.9	0.9	-52.7	71	73	3.2	0	0	-25	31.6	
Portugal	0.818	0.874	6.8	11,238	16,064	43	1.1	0.6	-48.6	74	75	2.3	13	8	-36	35.6	
Qatar		0.801					2.1	1.6	-24.6	72	75	3.4	23	19	-17		70
Romania	0.775	0.772	-0.4	6,246	6,041	-3	2.7	2.0	-26.3	70	69	-0.4	3	2	-33	28.2	75
Russian Federation	0.823	0.775	-5.8	10,119	7,473	-26	1.7	1.6	-8.0	69	66	-4.5	1	1	-38	48.7	
Rwanda	0.344	0.395	14.8	957	885	-8	13.2	12.3	-7.0	40	40	-0.5	47	34	-27	28.9	
Samoa	0.661	0.701	6.1	3,151	4,047	28	2.7	2.3	-13.8	66	69	4.0	24	20	-17		
Sao Tome & Principe							0.0	0.0		62	65	4.1					
Saudi Arabia	0.706	0.754	6.8	9,448	10,815	14	3.2	1.9	-41.3	69	72	4.6	33	24	-27		41
Senegal	0.378	0.423	11.9	1,208	1,419	17	7.4	6.7	-9.1	50	52	5.7	72	64	-11	41.3	
Sierra Leone		0.258		894	448	-50	18.9	16.8	-11.1	35	37	6.3					
Singapore	0.816	0.876	7.4	12,843	20,767	62	0.7	0.3	-52.2	74	78	4.3	11	8	-29		
Slovakia	0.818	0.831	1.6	9,013	10,591	18	1.2	0.8	-30.6	71	73	2.5				19.5	
Slovenia	0.843	0.874	3.7		15,977		0.8	0.5	-41.4	73	75	2.5	0	0	0	28.4	90
Solomon Islands				1,816	1,975	9	2.9	2.1	-26.2	69	71	3.6					
Somalia							15.2	12.1	-20.5	42	48	14.9					

Country	Human Development Index (HDI)			GDP per capita, PPP in current international $			Infant mortality rate (% live births)			Life expectancy at birth (years)			Adult illiteracy (% adult population)			Income inequality (Gini Index)*	Net enrolment in secondary education (% of women)
	value 1990	value 1999	% change 1990–1999	1990	1999	% change 1990–1999	1990	1999	% change 1990–1999	1990	1999	% change 1990–1999	1990	1999	% change 1990–1999	see note below	1995–1997
South Africa	0.712	0.702	-1.4	8,324	8,908	7	5.5	6.2	11.9	62	48	-21.7	19	15	-19	59.3	67
Spain	0.875	0.908	3.8	12,914	18,079	40	0.8	0.5	-30.3	77	78	1.6	4	2	-35	32.5	
Sri Lanka	0.695	0.735	5.8	2,036	3,279	61	1.9	1.5	-16.6	71	73	2.9	11	9	-24	34.4	
St. Lucia				4,379	5,509	26	1.9	1.6	-16.4	71	72	0.8					
St. Vincent & the Grenadines				3,646	5,309	46	2.1	2.0	-6.2	70	73	4.0					
Sudan		0.439					8.5	6.7	-21.4	51	56	9.0	54	43	-20		
Suriname		0.758		2,596		-100	3.4	2.7	-19.9	69	70	2.2					
Swaziland	0.611	0.583	-4.6	3,704	3,987	8	7.9	6.4	-18.7	57	46	-18.3	28	21	-26	60.9	41
Sweden	0.892	0.936	4.9	18,247	22,636	24	0.6	0.4	-40.0	78	79	2.2				25	99
Switzerland	0.904	0.924	2.2	24,251	27,171	12	0.7	0.5	-32.9	77	80	2.9				33.1	
Syria	0.647	0.700	8.2	2,478	4,454	80	3.9	2.6	-33.0	66	69	4.6	35	26	-25		36
Tajikistan		0.660					4.1	2.0	-51.1	69	69	-0.9	2	1	-50		
Tanzania	0.422	0.436	3.3	455	501	10	11.5	9.5	-17.4	50	45	-10.1	36	25	-30	38.2	
Thailand	0.713	0.757	6.2	3,863	6,132	59	3.7	2.8	-23.6	69	69	0.2	8	5	-38	41.4	
Togo	0.466	0.489	4.9	1,395	1,410	1	8.1	7.7	-5.5	50	49	-2.7	54	44	-19		13
Trinidad & Tobago	0.778	0.798	2.6	6,065	8,176	35	1.8	1.6	-11.7	71	73	2.1	9	6	-25	40.3	
Tunisia	0.644	0.714	10.9	3,915	5,957	52	3.7	2.4	-35.6	68	73	6.5	41	30	-26	41.7	54
Turkey	0.684	0.735	7.5	4,846	6,380	32	5.8	3.6	-37.6	66	69	5.1	22	15	-30	41.5	43
Turkmenistan		0.730		5,920	3,347	-43	4.5	3.3	-27.8	66	66	-0.1				40.8	
Uganda	0.386	0.435	12.7	747	1,167	56	10.4	8.8	-15.4	47	42	-9.9	44	34	-23	37.4	
Ukraine	0.793	0.742	-6.4	6,759	3,458	-49	1.3	1.4	7.2	70	67	-4.0	1	0	-29	29	
United Arab Emirates		0.809		20,306	18,162	-11	2.0	0.8	-62.1	74	75	2.3	30	25	-16		71
United Kingdom	0.876	0.923	5.4	16,773	22,093	32	0.8	0.6	-27.8	76	77	2.1				36.1	93
United States	0.912	0.934	2.4	23,567	31,872	35	0.9	0.7	-26.6	75	77	2.2				40.8	90
Uruguay	0.800	0.828	3.5	6,202	8,879	43	2.1	1.5	-31.6	73	74	2.3	3	2	-32	42.3	
Uzbekistan	0.693	0.698	0.7		2,251		3.5	2.2	-35.5	69	70	0.5	17	12	-31	33.3	
Vanuatu				2,794	3,108	11	5.6	3.6	-35.6	61	65	6.7					
Venezuela	0.756	0.765	1.2	5,070	5,495	8	2.5	2.0	-17.9	71	73	2.7	11	8	-30	48.8	27
Vietnam	0.604	0.682	12.9		1,860		4.0	3.7	-8.2	67	69	3.0	10	7	-27	36.1	
Yemen	0.407	0.468	15.0	734	806	10	11.0	7.9	-27.9	52	56	7.3	67	55	-19	33.4	
Yugoslavia							2.3	1.2	-45.3	72	72	1.0					
Zambia	0.466	0.427	-8.4	840	756	-10	10.7	11.4	6.2	49	38	-21.7	32	23	-29	52.6	
Zimbabwe	0.598	0.554	-7.4	2,366	2,876	22	5.2	7.0	35.3	56	40	-28.0	19	12	-38	56.8	

Region	Human Development Index (HDI) value 1999	GDP per capita PPP in current international $ 1999	Infant mortality rate (percentage live births) 1999	Life expectancy at birth (years) 1999
Low income	0.549	1,910	8.0	59.4
Middle income	0.74	5,310	3.2	69.5
Low & middle income:				
East Asia & the Pacific	0.719	3,950	3.4	69.2
Europe & Central Asia	0.777	6,290	2.5	68.5
Latin America & Caribbean	0.76	6,880	3.2	69.6
Middle East & North Africa	0.648	4,550	4.4	66.4
South Asia	0.564	2,280	6.9	62.5
Sub-Saharan Africa	0.467	1,640	10.7	48.8
High income	0.926	25,860	0.6	78.0
World	0.716	6,980	5.6	66.7

*year is not listed as survey data for Gini index vary by country

**Data for China do not include Hong Kong

Where data for a particular year are not available, figures are taken from the year before or after as an estimate. These figures, and estimates based on them, are presented in italics.

Sources: World Bank, World Development Indicators 2001 (CD-Rom); United Nations Development Programme, Human Development Report 2001 Making New Technologies Work for Human Development (New York: Oxford University Press)

Record 11 Corruption

This table examines the state of the rule of law through the prism of corruption. It presents three different kinds of indicators of corruption: the corruption perception index by Transparency International, and the bribing and the transparency index by the Institute for Management Development. Since these are relatively new measures, we compare 1999 with 2001. Scores range between a score of 10, indicating high transparency and the absence of bribery and corruption, and 0, indicating lack of transparency and high levels of perceived corruption and bribery. Corruption does not only hinder economic development, it inhibits the formation of trust and social capital among people. It is therefore likely to be an obstacle to the growth of civil society more generally, as well as being a focus of civil society activism, locally as well as globally.

Country	Corruption Perception Index		Bribing and corruption		Transparency of government	
	1999	2001	1999	2001	1999	2001
Albania	2.3					
Argentina	3.0	3.5	1.4	1.5	5.4	3.4
Armenia	2.5					
Australia	8.7	8.5	7.9	8.2	6.8	6.8
Austria	7.6	7.8	5.9	6.9	6.1	6.2
Azerbaijan	1.7	2.0				
Bangladesh		0.4				
Belarus	3.4					
Belgium	5.3	6.6	4.2	5.2	5.4	5.6
Bolivia	2.5	2.0				
Botswana	6.1	6.0				
Brazil	4.1	4.0	2.7	2.6	5.2	5.0
Bulgaria	3.3	3.9				
Cameroon	1.5	2.0				
Canada	9.2	8.9	8.4	7.8	6.6	6.7
Chile	6.9	7.5	6.1	5.9	6.4	4.4
China & Tibet	3.4	3.5	1.9	2.3	6.4	6.1
Colombia	2.9	3.8	1.4	1.5	5.2	4.4
Costa Rica	5.1	4.5				
Cote d'Ivoire	2.6	2.4				
Croatia	2.7	3.9				
Czech Republic	4.6	3.9	2.0	2.3	3.8	3.7
Denmark	10.0	9.5	9.3	9.0	5.0	5.6
Dominican Rep.		3.1				
Ecuador	2.4	2.3				
Egypt	3.3	3.6				
El Salvador	3.9	3.6				
Estonia	5.7	5.6		4.3		5.4
Finland	9.8	9.9	9.3	9.5	7.4	7.3
France	6.6	6.7	5.2	4.2	5.7	4.9
Georgia	2.3					
Germany	8.0	7.4	6.1	6.9	4.6	5.7
Ghana	3.3	3.4				
Greece	4.9	4.2	2.9	3.0	5.3	4.7
Guatemala	3.2	2.9				
Honduras	1.8	2.7				
Hungary	5.2	5.3	2.8	2.5	6.2	4.7

Country	Corruption Perception Index		Bribing and corruption		Transparency of government	
	1999	2001	1999	2001	1999	2001
Iceland	9.2	9.2	8.7	9.0	6.7	6.7
India	2.9	2.7	1.8	1.3	3.8	4.5
Indonesia	1.7	1.9	0.9	1.6	2.7	2.7
Ireland	7.7	7.5	6.5	5.5	7.0	6.7
Israel & Occupied Territories	6.8	7.6	6.7	6.6	4.2	4.8
Italy	4.7	5.5	2.5	3.3	4.0	4.0
Jamaica	3.8					
Japan	6.0	7.1	4.6	4.3	3.3	2.5
Jordan	4.4	4.9				
Kazakhstan	2.3	2.7				
Kenya	2.0	2.0				
Korea, Rep.	3.8	4.2	2.2	3.5	3.5	4.1
Kyrgyztan	2.2					
Latvia	3.4	3.4				
Lithuania	3.8	4.8				
Luxembourg	8.8	8.7	6.8	7.4	7.5	7.1
Macedonia	3.3					
Malawi	4.1	3.2				
Malaysia	5.1	5.0	3.7	2.6	6.3	5.3
Mauritius	4.9	4.5				
Mexico	3.4	3.7	2.0	1.8	4.6	5.9
Moldova	2.6	3.1				
Mongolia	4.3					
Morocco & Western Sahara	4.1					
Mozambique	3.5					
Namibia	5.3	5.4				
Netherlands	9.0	8.8	7.6	8.0	7.0	6.9
New Zealand	9.4	9.4	9.0	8.8	5.7	5.9
Nicaragua	3.1	2.4				
Nigeria	1.6	1.0				
Norway	8.9	8.6	8.3	8.1	3.9	4.7
Pakistan	2.2	2.3				
Panama		3.7				
Paraguay	2.0					
Peru	4.5	4.1				
Philippines	3.6	2.9	1.6	1.3	5.3	3.9
Poland	4.2	4.1	1.8	1.4	3.6	3.2
Portugal	6.7	6.3	4.3	3.9	5.6	3.7
Romania	3.3	2.8				
Russian Federation	2.4	2.3	1.5	1.3	2.5	4.9
Senegal	3.4	2.9				
Singapore	9.1	9.2	8.5	8.0	8.5	8.0
Slovakia	3.7	3.7		1.8		5.4
Slovenia	6.0	5.2	2.6	2.8	2.1	3.6
South Africa	5.0	4.8	2.3	2.6	5.3	4.8
Spain	6.6	7.0	5.9	5.6	7.0	6.0

R11 continued	Corruption Perception Index		Bribing and corruption		Transparency of government	
Country	1999	2001	1999	2001	1999	2001
Sweden	9.4	9.0	8.1	8.6	4.1	4.6
Switzerland	8.9	8.4	7.2	7.2	6.2	6.6
Tanzania	1.9	2.2				
Thailand	3.2	3.2	2.4	2.1	5.4	4.6
Trinidad & Tobago		5.3				
Tunisia	5.0	5.3				
Turkey	3.6	3.6	2.5	1.6	4.4	3.7
Uganda	2.2	1.9				
Ukraine	2.6	2.1				
United Kingdom	8.6	8.3	6.9	6.8	6.1	5.3
United States	7.5	7.6	6.0	6.6	5.9	7.0
Uruguay	4.4	5.1				
Uzbekistan	1.8	2.7				
Venezuela	2.6	2.8	1.4	1.0	3.4	3.1
Vietnam	2.6	2.6				
Yugoslavia	2.0					
Zambia	3.5	2.6				
Zimbabwe	4.1	2.9				

Sources: Transparency International, 1999 Corruption Perceptions Index available at http://www.gwdg.de/~uwvw/; Transparency International, 2001 Corruption Perceptions Index available at http://www.globalcorruptionreport.org/download/data_and_research.pdf; Bribing and Corruption, and Transparency of Government, from International Institute for Management Development (1999), The World Competitiveness Yearbook 1999, Institute for Management Development, Lausanne, Switzerland; International Institute for Management Development (2001), The World Competitiveness Yearbook 2001, Institute for Management Development, Lausanne, Switzerland.

Record 12 Refugee populations and flows

This table presents data on refugee population, both in total and per 1,000 inhabitants for 1990 and 2000. In addition, the table provides information on the inflow and outflow of refugees for 2000, and includes estimates of internally displaced persons (IDPs). This table has two functions: if a country 'generates' many refugees or IDPs, it can be assumed that there is little respect for the rule of law in that country. On the other hand, countries that host a lot of refugees can be considered as extending international hospitality and bearing the associated financial burden.

| | Refugee populations | | | | | | Refugee flows | | |
| | Total of population | | | per thousand inhabitants | | | Inflow | Outflow | IDPs |
Country	1990	2000	% change	1990	2000	% change	2000	2000	2000
Afghanistan							2	447,777	758,600
Albania		523			0.2		231	917	
Algeria	169,110	169,656	0.3	5.4	5.6	3.7	92	1,012	
Angola	11,560	12,086	4.6	0.9	0.9	2.2	68	69,859	257,500
Argentina	11,740	2,396	-79.6	0.3	0.1	-80.0	93	67	
Armenia		280,591			74.1		5	1,670	
Australia	97,920	57,658	-41.1	5.2	3.0	-42.1	4,995		
Austria	34,940	17,092	-51.1	4.3	2.1	-50.7	2,569		
Azerbaijan		287					352	937	572,500
Bahamas		100			0.3				
Bahrain	1,780	1	-99.9	2.9			1		
Bangladesh	150	21,627	14,318.0		0.2		13	756	
Belarus		458					200	118	
Belgium	25,910	18,832	-27.3	2.5	1.8	-26.4	2,131		
Belize	30,660	1,250	-95.9	127.4	5.5	-95.7			
Benin	460	4,296	833.9	0.1	0.7	580.0	1,885		
Bolivia	200	351	75.5				4		
Bosnia & Herzegovina		38,152			9.6		2,203	2,643	518,300
Botswana	1,180	3,551	200.9	0.7	2.3	228.6	2,280		
Brazil	5,340	2,722	-49.0				316	21	
Bulgaria		1,474			0.2		688	179	
Burkina Faso	350	696	98.9		0.1		6		
Burundi	268,400	27,136	-89.9	40.1	4.3	-89.4	5,518	81,373	56,000
Cambodia		34					17	344	
Cameroon	49,880	43,680	-12.4	3.3	2.9	-10.9	70	530	
Canada	154,760	124,732	-19.4	5.0	4.1	-18.8	13,989		
Central African Republic	4,280	55,661	1,200.5	1.2	15.0	1,147.5	9,173		
Chad		17,692			2.2		148	186	
Chile		364					43	25	
China & Tibet	287,280	294,110	2.4	0.2	0.2	15.0	15	5,560	
Colombia	460	239	-48.0					4,706	525,000
Congo, Dem. Rep.		332,509			6.5		25,715	133,520	3,000
Congo, Rep.	2,990	123,190	4,020.1	1.0	40.8	3,981.0	85,803	7,162	
Costa Rica	276,210	5,519	-98.0	68.7	1.4	-98.0	534	29	
Côte d'Ivoire	272,280	120,691	-55.7	18.4	7.5	-59.0	180	120	
Croatia		22,437			4.8		4	255	34,100
Cuba	3,990	954	-76.1	0.4	0.1	-77.5	103	349	
Cyprus		76			0.1		39		
Czech Republic		1,186			0.1		134	97	

Country	Refugee populations Total of population 1990	2000	% change	per thousand inhabitants 1990	2000	% change	Refugee flows Inflow 2000	Outflow 2000	IDPs 2000
Denmark	32,910	71,035	115.8	6.2	13.4	115.3	3,868		
Djibouti	77,610	23,243	-70.1	121.7	36.8	-69.8	1,100	124	
Dominican Republic	1,970	510	-74.1	0.2	0.1	-70.0	15		
Ecuador	510	1,602	214.1		0.1		1,327	166	
Egypt	1,990	6,840	243.7		0.1		3,331	472	
El Salvador	20,300	59	-99.7	3.2				228	
Eritrea		1,984			0.5		382	98,960	1,100,000
Ethiopia	773,760	197,959	-74.4	12.4	3.2	-74.6	18,391	4,199	
Finland	2,350	13,276	464.9	0.5	2.6	414.0	507		
France	193,000	102,508	-46.9	3.3	1.7	-47.6	5,185		
Gabon	420	17,982	4,181.4	0.3	14.6	4,773.3	5,454		
Gambia		12,016			9.2		539	72	
Georgia		7,620			1.5		2,440	359	272,100
Germany	816,000	906,000	11.0	9.9	11.1	11.6	13,043		
Ghana	8,120	12,720	56.7	0.4	0.7	65.0	550	230	
Greece	8,490	6,653	-21.6	0.8	0.6	-21.3	383		
Guatemala	223,380	720	-99.7	19.6	0.1	-99.7	20	347	
Guinea	325,000	427,206	31.4	43.7	52.4	19.9	15,824	467	
Guinea-Bissau	3,000	7,587	152.9	2.5	6.3	153.2	525	60	
Haiti								1,011	
Honduras	237,100	12	-100.0	36.6			3	60	
Hungary	45,120	5,064	-88.8	4.5	0.5	-88.7	877	334	
Iceland		244			0.9		9		
India	212,740	170,941	-19.6	0.2	0.2	-15.0	2,011	1,464	
Indonesia & East Timor	3,280	122,618	3,638.4		0.6		423	1,045	
Iran	4,174,400	1,868,000	-55.3	61.7	26.6	-57.0	348,638	7,541	
Iraq	900	127,787	14,098.6		5.6		561	27,932	
Ireland		2,543			0.7		606		
Israel & Occupied Territories		4,075			0.7		6,010	1,133	
Italy	11,690	22,870	95.6	0.2	0.4		1,665		
Japan	6,820	3,752	-45.0	0.1			77		
Jordan	640	1,072	67.5	0.1	0.2	120.0	1,912	21	
Kazakhstan		20,574			1.3		5,620	129	
Kenya	14,250	206,106	1,346.4	0.5	6.7	1,244.0	9,256	910	
Korea, Rep.	230	6	-97.4				1	24	
Kuwait		2,776			1.5		270	98	
Kyrgyzstan		10,609			2.2		1,719	20	5,600
Laos								71	
Lebanon	2,550	2,672	4.8	0.8	0.8	-5.0	767	6,129	
Lesotho	210		-100.0	0.1					
Liberia		69,315			23.8		27	1,602	110,700
Libya		11,543			2.2		1,008	217	
Luxembourg	690	759	10.0	1.6	1.7	8.7	59		
Macedonia		9,050			4.5		76	50	
Malawi	926,730	3,900	-99.6	84.8	0.3	-99.6	1,957		

Country	Refugee populations Total of population			Refugee populations per thousand inhabitants			Refugee flows Inflow	Refugee flows Outflow	IDPs
	1990	2000	% change	1990	2000	% change	2000	2000	2000
Malaysia	14,860	50,487	239.8	0.7	2.3	224.3	132		
Mali	13,410	8,412	-37.3	1.2	0.7	-38.3	163		
Malta		190			0.5		29		
Mauritania	60,000	350	-99.4	22.5	0.1	-99.4	135	293	
Mexico	356,400	18,451	-94.8	3.6	0.2	-94.7	78	372	
Moldova		68					61	21	8,100
Morocco & Western Sahara	310	915	195.2				34	40	
Mozambique	420	207	-50.7				140		
Myanmar								1,359	
Namibia		27,263			15.5		9,651	1,609	
Nepal		129,237			5.6		42	21	
Netherlands	17,340	146,324	743.9	1.1	9.2	738.2	9,726		
New Zealand	4,670	4,923	5.4	1.2	1.3	8.3	324		
Nicaragua	16,000	332	-97.9	3.2	0.1	-97.8	2		
Niger	790	58	-92.7	0.1			10	66	
Nigeria	3,570	7,270	103.6		0.1		329	734	
Norway	19,580	47,693	143.6	4.4	10.7	142.5	3,310		
Pakistan	3,255,980	2,001,466	-38.5	20.8	14.2	-31.9	78,491	3,092	
Panama	1,350	1,313	-2.7	0.5	0.5	-8.0	124		
Papua New Guinea	7,100	5,864	-17.4	1.5	1.2	-18.7			
Peru	720	687	-4.6				1	414	
Philippines	19,860	176	-99.1	0.3			7		
Poland		1,020					78	150	
Portugal	870	410	-52.9	0.1					
Romania		1,685			0.1		171	246	
Russian Federation		26,265			0.2		277	10,246	490,700
Rwanda	23,600	28,398	20.3	3.1	3.7	20.3	455	17,692	
Saudi Arabia		5,309			0.3		31		
Senegal	58,110	20,766	-64.3	6.1	2.2	-63.9	35	389	
Sierra Leone	125,830	6,546	-94.8	25.9	1.5	-94.2	3	18,657	300,000
Singapore	150		-100.0				1		
Slovakia		457			0.1		10		
Slovenia		2,816			1.4		11		
Solomon Islands									
Somalia	460,000	558	-99.9	45.6	0.1	-99.9	6	29,775	18,000
South Africa		15,063			0.4		552		
Spain	8,300	6,696	-19.3	0.2	0.2	-15.0	350	761	
Sri Lanka		16					4	17,935	706,500
Sudan	1,031,050	414,928	-59.8	35.0	13.3	-61.9	95,065	39,544	
Swaziland	42,070	1,007	-97.6	41.7	1.1	-97.4	391		
Sweden	109,660	157,217	43.4	12.3	17.8	44.6	9,045		
Switzerland	40,940	57,653	40.8	5.5	8.0	46.2	25,205		
Syria	4,130	3,463	-16.2	0.3	0.2	-30.0	967	762	
Tajikistan		15,364			2.5		10,838	1,946	
Tanzania	265,180	680,862	156.8	7.9	19.4	145.4	99,525	157	
Thailand	99,820	104,965	5.2	1.6	1.7	4.4	704		

Country	\<Refugee populations — Total of population\> 1990	2000	% change	\<per thousand inhabitants\> 1990	2000	% change	\<Refugee flows\> Inflow 2000	Outflow 2000	IDPs 2000
Togo	3,480	12,223	251.2	0.8	2.7	237.5	141	496	
Tunisia		436			0.1			172	
Turkey	28,000	3,103	-88.9	0.4	0.1	-87.5	2,716	6,631	
Turkmenistan		14,188			3.0		633		
Uganda	145,720	236,622	62.4	6.7	10.2	51.6	18,913	565	
Ukraine		2,951			0.1		895	552	
United Arab Emirates		562			0.2		83		
United Kingdom	43,650	169,354	288.0	0.7	2.9	307.1	38,834		
United States	464,890	508,222	9.3	1.7	1.8	5.3	22,471		
Uruguay		79					3		
Uzbekistan		38,350			1.5		749	81	
Venezuela	1,750	132	-92.5	0.1			22	41	
Vietnam	21,150	15,945	-24.6	0.3	0.2	-33.3		221	
Yemen	2,940	60,545	1,959.4	0.2	3.3	1,550.0	8,125	69	
Yugoslavia	920	484,391	52,551.2	0.1	45.9	45,800.0	8	16,089	267,500
Zambia	138,050	250,940	81.8	15.1	24.1	59.5	50,069		
Zimbabwe	190,950	4,127	-97.8	16.4	0.3	-98.0	1,987	65	

Region	\<Refugee populations — Total\> 1990	2000	% change	Total inflow 2000	Total outflow 2000	Total IDPs 2000	Refugee populations per 1000 inhabitants 2000	Inflow per 1000 inhabitants 2000	Outflow per 1000 inhabitants 2000	IDPs per 1000 inhabitants 2000
East Asia & Pacific	563,140	660,538	17.3	6,696	8,624		1,998,197	0.003	0.004	
Europe & Central Asia	1,440,360	2,736,108	90.0	146,664	44,431	2,168,900	851,788	0.172	0.052	2.546
Latin America & Caribbean	1,188,080	37,792	-96.8	2,688	7,836	525,000	502,045	0.005	0.016	1.046
Middle East & North Africa	4,358,750	2,265,652	-48.0	371,830	45,598		310,823	1.196	0.147	
North America	619,650	632,954	2.1	36,460			313,987	0.116		
South Asia	3,468,870	2,323,287	-33.0	80,521	471,045	1,465,100	1,351,364	0.060	0.349	1.084
Sub-Saharan Africa	5,302,710	3,424,790	-35.4	462,421	509,416	1,845,200	630,906	0.733	0.807	2.925

Empty cells indicate that the value is below 100, zero or not available.

Inflows and Outflows based on primae facie arrivals and individually recognised refugees. IDPs refer to internally displaced persons of concern to/assisted by UNHCR at end of 1999.

Source: United Nations High Commissioner for Refugees, Refugees and Others of Concern to UNHCR - 1999 Statistical Overview, http://www.unhcr.org.

Record 13 Peacekeeping

This table reports the importance of peacekeeping forces relative to total military personnel for 1999, and the total number of forces per country committed to peace-keeping as per 31 January 2002. A country's preparedness to commit part of its armed forces to foreign conflicts can be seen as a commitment to the international rule of law.

Country	Total military personnel 1999	Peace-keeping forces as of 31 Jan 2002	Peacekeeping forces per thousand military personnel	Country	Total military personnel 1999	Peace-keeping forces as of 31 Jan 2002	Peacekeeping forces per thousand military personnel
Albania	52,000			Ecuador	58,000		
Algeria	124,000			Egypt	400,000	75	0.2
Angola	95,000			El Salvador	15,000		
Argentina	98,100	462	4.7	Equatorial Guinea	1,000		
Armenia	60,000			Eritrea	200,000		
Australia	65,000	1,427	22.0	Estonia	7,000	6	0.9
Austria	48,000	375	7.8	Ethiopia	300,000		
Azerbaijan	75,000			Fiji	4,000	789	197.3
Bahrain	9,000			Finland	35,000	5	0.1
Bangladesh	110,000	5,781	52.6	France	475,000	242	0.5
Belarus	65,000			Gabon	10,000		
Belgium	46,000	5	0.1	Gambia	1,000	2	2.0
Belize	1,000			Georgia	11,000		
Benin	8,000	3	0.4	Germany	335,000	14	0.0
Bhutan	8,000			Ghana	7,000	2,140	305.7
Bolivia	33,000	203	6.2	Greece	206,000	40	0.2
Bosnia & Herzegovina	40,000			Guatemala	30,000		
Botswana	8,000			Guinea	12,000	780	65.0
Brazil	204,700	72	0.4	Guinea-Bissau	7,000		
Brunei	5,000			Guyana	2,000		
Bulgaria	80,000	2	0.0	Honduras	11,244	12	1.1
Burkina Faso	9,000			Hungary	50,000	121	2.4
Burundi	35,000			India	1,140,000	2,216	1.9
Cambodia	60,000			Indonesia	281,000	7	0.0
Cameroon	13,000	1	0.1	Iran	575,000		
Canada	61,000	190	3.1	Iraq	400,000		
Cape Verde	1,000			Ireland	17,000	272	16.0
Central African Republic	5,000			Israel & Occupied Territories	173,000		
Chad	35,000			Italy	419,000	258	0.6
Chile	87,500	27	0.3	Jamaica	3,000		
China & Tibet	2,600,000	1	0.0	Japan	250,000	30	0.1
Colombia	260,086	1	0.0	Jordan	102,000	1,096	10.7
Congo, Rep.	10,000			Kazakhstan	34,000		
Costa Rica	10,000			Kenya	27,000	1,700	63.0
Côte d'Ivoire	15,000	1	0.1	Korea, Dem. Rep.	1,100,000		
Croatia	58,000	10	0.2	Korea, Rep.	670,000	459	0.7
Cuba	55,000			Kuwait	25,420		
Cyprus	10,000			Kyrgyzstan	14,000	6	0.4
Czech Republic	55,000	1	0.0	Laos	50,000		
Denmark	29,000	4	0.1	Latvia	5,000		
Djibouti	8,000			Lebanon	57,000		
Dominican Republic	22,000	15	0.7				

Country	Total military personnel 1999	Peace-keeping forces as of 31 Jan 2002	Peacekeeping forces per thousand military personnel
Lesotho	2,000		
Libya	70,000	3	0.0
Lithuania	12,000	9	0.8
Luxembourg	1,000		
Macedonia	15,000		
Madagascar	21,000		
Malawi	8,000	20	2.5
Malaysia	104,500	36	0.3
Mali	10,000	1	0.1
Malta	2,000		
Mauritania	11,000		
Mauritius	1,000		
Mexico	250,000		
Moldova	11,000		
Mongolia	20,000		
Morocco & Western Sahara	205,000	617	3.0
Mozambique	14,000	10	0.7
Myanmar	322,000		
Namibia	8,000	2	0.3
Nepal	35,000	969	27.7
Netherlands	57,000	3	0.0
New Zealand	10,000	645	64.5
Nicaragua	14,000		
Niger	5,000	1	0.2
Nigeria	76,000	3,321	4.4
Norway	33,000	6	0.2
Oman	38,000		
Pakistan	610,000	5,047	8.3
Panama	12,000		
Papua New Guinea	5,000		
Paraguay	16,000	1	0.1
Peru	122,000		
Philippines	107,000	58	0.5
Poland	230,000	836	3.6
Portugal	72,000	927	12.9
Qatar	11,000		
Romania	200,000		
Russian Federation	1,200,000	115	0.1
Rwanda	40,000		
Sao Tome & Principe	1,000		
Saudi Arabia	191,500		
Senegal	14,000	478	34.1
Sierra Leone	5,000		
Singapore	55,500	88	1.6
Slovakia	44,000	593	13.5
Slovenia	10,000		
South Africa	75,000	98	1.3

Country	Total military personnel 1999	Peace-keeping forces as of 31 Jan 2002	Peacekeeping forces per thousand military personnel
Spain	107,000	2	0.0
Sri Lanka	110,000		
Sudan	105,000		
Suriname	2,000		
Swaziland	3,000		
Sweden	60,000	1	0.0
Switzerland	39,000	1	0.0
Syria	320,000		
Tajikistan	10,000		
Tanzania	35,000	3	0.1
Thailand	290,000	735	2.5
Togo	12,000		
Trinidad & Tobago	2,000		
Tunisia	35,000	227	6.5
Turkey	716,600		
Turkmenistan	21,000		
Uganda	50,000		
Ukraine	310,000	1,278	4.1
United Arab Emirates	60,000		
United Kingdom	218,000	423	1.9
United States	1,530,000	1	0.0
Uruguay	25,000	793	31.7
Uzbekistan	65,000		
Venezuela	75,000		
Vietnam	650,000		
Yemen	69,000		
Yugoslavia	115,000		
Zambia	21,000	831	39.6
Zimbabwe	40,000		

Country of mission	Name of mission
Democratic Republic of Congo	MONUC
East Timor	UNTAET
India/Pakistan	UNMOGIP
Bosnia & Herzegovina	UNMIBIH
Cyprus	UNFICIP
Georgia	UNIMIG
Kosovo	UNMIK
Golan Heights	UNDOF
Iraq/Kuwait	UNOKOM
Lebanon	UNIFIL
Middle East	UNTSO

Data in italics are from 1998.

Sources: U.S. Department of State, Bureau of Arms Control, World Military Expenditures and Arms Transfers 1998; U.S. Department of State, Annual Report on Military Expenditures, 1999; United Nations, Department of Peacekeeping Operations, http://www.un.org/Depts/dpko/dpko/contributors/index.htm

Record 14 Emissions and environmental sustainability

This record shows to what extent countries protect or harm the global environment, using the latest data available. It is now generally agreed that carbon dioxide emissions are a major contributor to the problem of global warming: a large volume of emissions can therefore be considered as an infringement of the environmental element of the international rule of law. The Environmental Sustainability Index, shown here for 2002, aims to measure environmental sustainability in terms of performance on five dimensions (through 68 variables): the state of environmental systems such as air, water and soil; the reduction of environmental stresses such as pollution and exploitation; the reduction of human vulnerability, for example through exposure to environmental diseases; the social and institutional capacity to cope with environmental challenges; and the ability to act collectively in response to the demands of global stewardship. High values correspond to high levels of environmental sustainability.

| | Carbon dioxide emissions | | | | | | Environmental |
| | metric tons per capita | | % change | kg per PPP $ of GDP | | % change | Sustainability Index |
Country	1990	1997	1990–1997	1985	1997	1985–1997	2002
Afghanistan	0.2	0.0	-68.4				
Albania	2.3	0.5	-78.5		0.2		57.9
Algeria	3.3	3.4	1.7	0.8	0.7	-11.7	49.4
Angola	0.5	0.5	-12.0	0.4	0.2	-52.2	42.4
Argentina	3.4	3.9	14.9	0.5	0.3	-39.1	61.5
Armenia		0.8					54.8
Australia	15.8	17.2	9.2	1.1	0.8	-30.2	60.3
Austria	7.8	7.8	-0.1	0.6	0.3	-47.0	64.2
Azerbaijan		4.1			1.9		41.8
Bahamas	7.6	6.0	-21.0	0.6			
Bahrain	23.4	24.1	2.8	2.6			
Bangladesh	0.1	0.2	41.6	0.1	0.1	-32.3	46.9
Barbados	4.6	3.7	-18.6				
Belarus		6.1			0.1		52.8
Belgium	10.1	10.5	3.2	0.8	0.4	-49.5	39.1
Belize	1.6	1.7	2.9	0.5			
Benin	0.2	0.2	16.7	0.3	0.2	-34.7	45.7
Bhutan	0.2	0.6	199.6	0.2			56.3
Bolivia	0.9	1.4	64.9		0.6		59.4
Bosnia & Herzegovina		1.2			0.3		51.3
Botswana	1.7	2.2	28.8	0.4			61.8
Brazil	1.5	1.9	28.9	0.3	0.3	3.5	59.6
Brunei	22.6	17.7	-21.8				
Bulgaria	8.9	6.1	-32.0	2.6	1.2	-53.0	49.3
Burkina Faso	0.1	0.1	-17.1	0.1	0.1	-6.5	45.0
Burundi	0.0	0.0	-2.2	0.1	0.1	70.0	41.6
Cambodia	0.0	0.0	-7.4		0.0		45.6
Cameroon	0.2	0.2	22.3	0.4	0.1	-74.9	45.9
Canada	15.5	16.6	6.9	1.0	0.7	-33.0	70.6
Cape Verde	0.2	0.3	21.4				
Central African Republic	0.1	0.1	5.2	0.1	0.1	53.0	54.1
Chad	0.0	0.0	-37.6	0.1	0.0		45.7
Chile	2.8	4.1	48.0	0.6	0.5	-18.8	55.1
China & Tibet	2.2	2.9	32.3	2.4	0.9	-62.0	38.5
Colombia	1.7	1.8	6.5	0.4	0.3	-22.6	59.1
Comoros	0.2	0.1	-16.5	0.1			
Congo, Dem Rep.	0.1	0.1	-56.8	0.1	0.1	19.3	43.3

Carbon dioxide emissions

Country	metric tons per capita 1990	metric tons per capita 1997	% change 1990–1997	kg per PPP $ of GDP 1985	kg per PPP $ of GDP 1997	% change 1985–1997	Environmental Sustainability Index 2002
Congo, Rep.	0.9	0.1	-89.2	0.2	0.1	-57.4	54.3
Costa Rica	1.1	1.6	44.4	0.3	0.2	-23.4	63.2
Côte d'Ivoire	0.9	0.9	5.1	0.6	0.6	-5.2	43.4
Croatia		4.4			0.6		62.5
Cuba	3.1	2.3	-24.8				51.2
Cyprus	7.6	8.0	4.2	0.6			
Czech Republic		12.2			0.9		50.2
Denmark	10.0	10.9	8.8	0.9	0.4	-56.7	56.2
Djibouti	0.7	0.6	-13.7				
Dominican Republic	1.4	1.7	23.0	0.5	0.4	-15.8	48.4
Ecuador	1.7	1.8	5.3	1.0	0.6	-40.1	54.3
Egypt	1.6	2.0	24.5	0.9	0.6	-29.5	48.8
El Salvador	0.6	1.0	74.7	0.2	0.2	5.7	48.7
Equatorial Guinea	0.3	1.5	337.1				
Estonia		13.1			1.6		60.0
Ethiopia	0.1	0.1	2.6	0.1	0.1	-18.6	41.8
Fiji	1.2	1.0	-12.1	0.3			
Finland	10.8	11.0	2.1	0.8	0.5	-39.7	73.9
France	6.4	6.0	-6.8	0.6	0.3	-47.3	55.5
Gabon	7.0	3.0	-57.6	1.7	0.5	-70.5	54.9
Gambia	0.2	0.2	-11.6	0.2	0.1	-52.4	44.7
Georgia		0.8			0.3		
Germany		10.4			0.5		52.5
Ghana	0.3	0.3	1.9	0.2	0.1	-59.7	50.2
Greece	7.8	8.3	6.8	0.7	0.6	-19.5	50.9
Guam	16.9	27.9	64.8				
Guatemala	0.7	0.8	16.9	0.2	0.2	-5.7	49.6
Guinea	0.2	0.2	-10.2		0.1		45.3
Guinea-Bissau	0.2	0.2	-5.4	0.4	0.2	-44.4	38.8
Guyana	1.4	1.2	-14.8	1.0	0.1	-89.7	
Haiti	0.2	0.2	9.8	0.1	0.3	159.3	34.8
Honduras	0.6	0.8	29.4	0.3			53.1
Hungary	5.8	5.9	0.6	1.1	0.6	-46.6	62.7
Iceland	8.1	7.9	-3.4	0.5			63.9
India	0.8	1.1	34.4	0.7	0.5	-30.1	41.6
Indonesia & East Timor	1.0	1.3	30.0	0.7	0.4	-40.0	45.1
Iran	4.0	4.9	21.1	0.9	0.97	-1.4	44.5
Iraq	3.0	4.2	40.9				33.2
Ireland	8.7	10.2	16.5	1.0	0.5	-51.3	54.8
Israel & Occupied Territories	7.7	10.4	33.8	0.7	0.6	-13.7	50.4
Italy	7.4	7.4	-0.0	0.5	0.3	-44.7	47.2
Jamaica	3.4	4.3	26.9	1.1	1.2	12.9	40.1
Japan	9.0	9.6	6.0	0.6	0.4	-34.7	48.6
Jordan	3.5	3.5	0.4		0.9		51.7
Kazakhstan		8.0			1.7		46.5
Kenya	0.3	0.3	-8.2	0.3	0.2	-30.1	46.3
Korea, Dem Rep.	12.3	11.4	-7.8				32.3
Korea, Rep.	6.0	9.9	65.3	0.9	0.6	-35.4	54.1

Country	Carbon dioxide emissions metric tons per capita 1990	Carbon dioxide emissions metric tons per capita 1997	% change 1990-1997	kg per PPP $ of GDP 1985	kg per PPP $ of GDP 1997	% change 1985-1997	Environmental Sustainability Index 2002
Kuwait	20.1	28.2	40.5		1.8		23.9
Kyrgyzstan		1.4			0.6		51.3
Laos	0.1	0.1	28.3		0.1		56.2
Latvia		3.3			0.6		63.0
Lebanon	2.6	4.3	63.1		1.0		43.8
Lesotho							
Liberia	0.2	0.1	-41.6				37.7
Libya	8.9	8.4	-5.4				39.3
Lithuania		4.1			0.6		57.2
Luxembourg	26.7	19.6	-26.9	1.7			
Macedonia		5.5			1.2		47.2
Madagascar	0.1	0.1	3.8	0.2	0.1	-40.3	38.8
Malawi	0.1	0.1	1.2	0.2	0.1	-48.8	47.3
Malaysia	3.2	6.3	98.0	0.7	0.7	7.0	49.5
Mali	0.1	0.0	-5.3	0.1	0.1	-11.3	47.1
Malta	4.7	4.7	0.1	0.8			
Mauritania	1.3	1.2	-7.7	0.3	0.8	161.3	38.9
Mauritius	1.1	1.5	36.0	0.2	0.2	-10.0	
Mexico	3.7	4.0	9.7	0.7	0.5	-31.2	45.9
Moldova		2.4			1.1		54.5
Mongolia	4.8	3.3	-31.3	3.6	2.1	-42.2	54.2
Morocco & Western Sahara	1.1	1.3	23.5	0.4	0.4	-4.6	49.1
Mozambique	0.1	0.1	-0.6	0.3	0.1	-60.2	51.1
Myanmar	0.1	0.2	85.4				46.2
Namibia							57.4
Nepal	0.0	0.1	167.6	0.1	0.1	50.8	45.2
Netherlands	10.2	10.5	3.3	0.7	0.5	-33.2	55.4
New Zealand	7.0	8.4	20.3	0.6	0.5	-13.1	59.9
Nicaragua	0.8	0.7	-17.4	0.4	0.3	-16.0	51.8
Niger	0.1	0.1	-16.4	0.3	0.2	-22.2	39.4
Nigeria	0.9	0.7	-24.3	1.7	0.9	-46.8	36.7
Norway	11.4	15.6	36.3	1.6	0.6	-63.3	73.0
Oman	7.4	8.2	10.4				40.2
Pakistan	0.7	0.8	15.3	0.6	0.4	-31.7	42.1
Panama	1.4	2.9	114.1	0.4	0.5	38.1	60.0
Papua New Guinea	0.6	0.5	-13.9	0.4	0.2	-53.5	51.8
Paraguay	0.6	0.8	41.2	0.1	0.2	37.5	57.8
Peru	1.1	1.2	14.6	0.3	0.3	-13.2	56.5
Philippines	0.8	1.1	46.2	0.2	0.3	23.5	41.6
Poland	9.3	9.2	-0.5	3.0	1.2	-60.4	46.7
Portugal	4.6	5.4	16.5	0.5	0.4	-14.6	57.1
Qatar	28.4	72.9	156.4				
Romania	6.9	4.9	-28.3	1.5	0.8	-45.0	50.0
Russian Federation		9.8			1.4		49.1
Rwanda	0.1	0.1	-21.5		0.1		40.6
Samoa	0.8	0.8	1.5	0.3			
Sao Tome & Principe	0.6	0.6	-3.3				
Saudi Arabia	11.6	14.3	23.2	1.5	1.3	-13.6	34.2

Country	Carbon dioxide emissions metric tons per capita 1990	1997	% change 1990-1997	kg per PPP $ of GDP 1985	1997	% change 1985-1997	Environmental Sustainability Index 2002
Senegal	0.4	0.4	-7.4	0.4	0.3	-30.0	47.6
Sierra Leone	0.1	0.1	17.5	0.3	0.2	-31.9	36.5
Singapore	14.2	21.9	54.3	1.5	1.1	-27.1	
Slovakia		7.1			0.7		61.6
Slovenia		7.8			0.5		58.8
Solomon Islands	0.5	0.4	-20.5	0.5			
Somalia	0.0	0.0	-31.0				37.1
South Africa	8.4	7.9	-5.7	1.4	0.9	-34.6	48.7
Spain	5.8	6.6	12.7	0.6	0.4	-35.3	54.1
Sri Lanka	0.2	0.4	83.8	0.2	0.1	-43.1	51.3
St. Lucia	1.2	1.3	10.0	0.4			
St. Vincent & the Grenadines	0.8	1.2	55.8	0.3			
Sudan	0.1	0.1	-6.7	0.2			44.7
Suriname	4.6	5.2	13.8				
Swaziland	0.6	0.4	-24.6	0.3			
Sweden	5.8	5.5	-5.6	0.6	0.3	-47.1	72.6
Switzerland	6.7	6.0	-11.0	0.4	0.2	-45.7	66.5
Syria	3.1	3.3	7.9	1.2	1.0	-19.1	43.6
Tajikistan		0.9					42.4
Tanzania	0.1	0.1	-8.3		0.2		48.1
Thailand	1.9	3.8	102.7	0.5	0.6	27.0	51.6
Togo	0.3	0.2	-8.8	0.1	0.2	49.2	44.3
Trinidad & Tobago	14.1	17.4	23.7	3.3	2.4	-26.6	40.1
Tunisia	1.8	2.0	11.9	0.6	0.4	-28.3	50.8
Turkey	2.8	3.5	24.5	0.7	0.5	-30.7	50.8
Turkmenistan		6.7			2.5		37.3
Uganda	0.1	0.1	8.7	0.1	0.1	22.5	48.7
Ukraine		7.3			2.1		35.0
United Arab Emirates	33.9	32.0	-5.6	1.6	1.6	0.2	25.7
United Kingdom	9.9	8.9	-9.9	0.9	0.4	-54.7	46.1
United States	19.4	20.1	3.9	1.1	0.7	-38.7	53.2
Uruguay	1.3	1.8	31.1	0.3	0.2	-24.2	66.0
Uzbekistan		4.4			2.1		41.3
Vanuatu	0.4	0.3	-22.3	0.4			
Venezuela	6.0	8.4	40.9	1.5	1.4	-4.0	53.0
Vietnam	0.4	0.6	68.3		0.4		45.7
Yemen		1.0			1.3		
Yugoslavia		4.7					
Zambia	0.3	0.3	-19.3	0.7	0.4	-39.3	49.5
Zimbabwe	1.7	1.6	-6.1	0.7	0.6	-13.7	53.2

Sources: Environmental Sustainability Index © World Economic Forum, Yale Center for Environmental Law and Policy, Columbia University Center for International Earth Science Information Network (CIESIN: http://www.ciesin.columbia.edu/indicators/ESI/rank.html); World Bank, World Development Indicators 2001, CD-Rom; Carbon Dioxide Information Analysis Center, Environmental Sciences Division, Oak Ridge National Laboratory.

Man's Inhumanity to Man: Crime as a Measurement of Wrong

Shakespeare's phrase has been chosen as the title of this box because there is no agreed single term, at least in English, to encompass the aspect of life that is its subject. 'Crime' is the most obvious and most frequently used term, but it is potentially misleading. It is a legal term, and there are a lot more harms and evil deeds in life than appear in any crime statistics. Legal logic, which is two-value 'either/or' and categorises events as belonging to a dichotomous variable, and the logic of behavioural analysis which places events somewhere along a continuous variable, are different. Hence the difficulty of using legal outcomes to describe social situations.

Crime may be the best surrogate indicator we have, but it is a quite seriously flawed indicator, and official figures of recorded crime can be quite misleading. Many crimes, especially the less serious, are not reported, and some of those reported are not recorded. An increase in the recording of rape cases, for instance, need not reflect any actual increase at all. The numbers record the outcomes of decisions taken, first, by victims deciding to report the incident and, second, by public officials as to how to respond to those cases that do come to their notice.

Another source of possible misinterpretation is the aggregation of different but similar types of crime into one category for administrative purposes. Crime statistics are collected primarily for police administrative purposes, not primarily for research or science. For instance, when steering column locks and radios were introduced more or less simultaneously, fewer cars were stolen but more were broken into to obtain radios; but, unless the statistic were disaggregated into 'thefts *of*' and 'thefts *from*' motor vehicles, the figures for 'vehicle crime' continued the same trend as previously.

The United Nations secretariat has collected crime and criminal justice statistics for major crime types from countries willing to provide them covering the period 1975 to 2000, and is continuing to update that database. Most criminologists regard the rates of recorded crime more as indicators of the workload of the criminal justice system than as an accurate record of disorder in a country.

A source of much more reliable and valid data on the extent and nature of crime is the 'Victim Survey'. The methodology of such surveys has been improved over the last 30 years. Their drawback is cost and for that reason they have been conducted in relatively few countries. When data from victim surveys are available, however, they are usually more valid than official criminal justice statistics as a measure of the quality of life, and some use has been made of the two types in embryo triangulation exercises. The difference between the rates of officially recorded crime and rates as revealed by victim surveys is referred to in criminology as 'the dark figure', as it was unknown until victim surveys were developed.

A clear exposition of the limitations of the data in measuring the negative side of life is, however, necessary because, unless such warnings are given, conclusions are drawn and statements made about what is the case that the evidence does not justify.

Despite all these drawbacks, some reliable propositions are possible, particularly about the situation in developed countries, because the quantity and quality of data there are higher because resources are devoted to the matter. The following propositions apply to most countries for which adequate data exists:

- Officially recorded crime has risen in most countries; but the rate of increase in the number of cases of theft in richer countries is lower than the increase in the availability of desirable and movable things to steal (cars, cameras, mobile phones etc). In developed countries, the argument can be made that theft as a ratio of opportunity may actually have declined. Much of the increase of opportunistic theft seems to be associated with drug use. Crimes against the person have increased in most countries, at a lower rate than crimes against property, but in some developed countries serious crime, including homicide, has actually declined slightly in recent years

- If one type of crime can be considered a proxy indicator for the crime problem of a country, it should probably be robbery, which to the victim is a crime of violence or threat of violence, but to the offender is a crime of acquisition, against property. Robbery is also usually reported in most countries, so that the dark figure is relatively small.

- Some categories of crime such as paedophilia have become more widely reported, so that the incidence of these crime types appears to have increased greatly. but may in actuality may reflect increased reporting.

The moral state of the world, therefore, as inferred from official statistics on crime, is on the whole not improving; but neither, in most countries with stable governments, is it deteriorating by an order of magnitude, as the media sometimes suggest. In countries that do not enjoy stable government and in which the rule of law cannot be assumed, of course, the situation is very different. The evidence is scanty, it seems almost certain that much crime is not reported, interpersonal violence is more common, and theft is as likely to be function of the struggle for survival as much as of opportunity of obtaining 'luxury' goods.

There is one broad category of crime, however, that does seem to have increased significantly in the last decade or so, and that is organised crime, and especially its transnational aspect, often known in the criminological world as transnational organised crime (TOC). The word 'seem' is used because hard data on this are scarce, so evidence is largely anecdotal. The situation is also made less clear by the fact that some pressure groups and interest groups have portrayed organised and transnational crime as the fifth horseman of the apocalypse, being of such severity that only instant and comprehensive action will save the world. While it seems almost certain there is a serious and probably growing problem, institutionalised and relatively high-profile hysteria does not make it easier to establish the actual details.

Data exist in respect of drug trafficking and money laundering, and both shows a steady rise; but the problem of how much the change is due to increased criminal behaviour and how much to better recording remains unsolved.

Data are much scarcer on two other categories of TOC: trafficking in arms and smuggling of legitimate but highly taxed goods such as cigarettes. Obviously these are of a very different level of severity, but in both

the main data sources are individuals such as investigative journalists. While their work is important and valuable, 'extrapolated statistical estimates' from it should be treated very carefully.

All these types of TOC have been occurring, and reported up to a point, for many years. Types of crime which have occurred throughout history on a small scale, but which are now apparently becoming more frequent, such as trafficking in persons, have recently received more attention. The reasons suggested for this increase range from highly differentiated standards of living between countries to the increased ease of modern travel and transportation. Many of the victims of this trade are women and children being sold into what amounts to sexual slavery; others become more or less traditional domestic slaves. Concern over, study of, and action on such cases will become more widespread; but at the moment such study is embryonic.

Finally, modern information technology has made a great impact on some categories of crime that are nearly always organised, which can be roughly defined in this context as run on the lines of a commercial business, and usually transnational. The Internet and mobile phones are creating opportunities for new forms of perhaps old crimes, ranging from conspiracy to commit gross acts of terrorism to the exchange of sexually explicit pictures of children.

The situation regarding valid and reliable statistical data about TOC is even more beset by problems than that for 'ordinary' crime. All the same difficulties are encountered, and the non-reporting rate of most TOC offences is much higher, while there is no equivalent of victim surveys to throw light on the dark figure.

At the time of writing, officials responsible for the development of policy in respect to TOC and collaborating research criminologists tend to fall into two groups. The first maintains that the difficulties encountered in trying to measure TOC are so intrinsically intractable that it is impossible to develop accurate data. The second maintains that, without accurate data, the development of policies to counter TOC can only be a vague hit-and-miss activity. Regrettably, there is no reason why they cannot both be right.

Thus it is not surprising that our ability to describe the scope and nature of TOC currently is very limited. However, efforts are under way to investigate what can be done to establish the beginnings of a sound database.

One component of that effort currently being undertaken is a simple study of the way in which governments and intergovernmental organisations, in particular EUROPOL, INTERPOL, and the World Customs Organisation, set up and build up the statistical databases that they have. The philosophy of the study is that it is necessary to know how official agencies create their databases before it is possible to consider questions of best practice and any form of standardised reporting and recording. The feasibility of such standardisation must be regarded as an open question at the moment.

To sum up, enough is known about the nature of crime statistics, derived from official records or special surveys to provide a reasonably accurate account of crime within nations that enjoy the rule of law. Whether crime is to be regarded as an adequate indicator of social ills is a separate question. The possibility of developing a parallel knowledge of the different aspects of TOC is still in doubt; the problem is much harder. However, there are three factors that can give grounds for optimism. If the situation as regards TOC statistical data is regarded as parallel to the situation in respect of national, domestic crime in the early twentieth century, three things have changed markedly: officials are aware of the need for and use of statistical data; there is a good supply of criminologists who are comfortable with quantitative methods; and there is contemporary information technology. In a few years there may or may not be a good statistical data base on TOC, but it should be possible to answer both the question whether accurate data can be obtained and the question whether effective policies can be developed even in the absence of such data.

Bill Burnham has just retired as Professor of Applied Criminology at the University of Huddersfield. For twenty years he was a member of staff of the Crime Prevention and Criminal Justice Programme and of the International Drug Control Programme of the United Nations.

This table gives the total number of international organisation secretariats (headquarters) of international non-governmental organisations (INGOs) and internationally-oriented NGOs in a given country both for 1991 and 2001. It differs from the coverage of last year's Table R19 in two respects: that table combined coverage of INGOs and IGOs, but it did not cover internationally-oriented NGOs. The figures therefore cannot be compared. The table also indicates the number of secretariats per 1 million population for both years, and the expansion or contraction in the number of secretariats by country over the time period. In addition, Records 16b and 16c show in which cities the secretariats are primarily based.

Record 16a	1991		2001			
Country	Number of secretariats	Organisational density per million of population	Number of secretariats	Organisational density per million of population	Absolute growth % 1991–2001	Density growth % 1991–2001
Afghanistan						
Albania	1	0.3				
Algeria	13	0.5	10	0.3	-23.1	-36.6
Angola	1	0.1	3	0.2	200.0	119.2
Argentina	101	3.1	126	3.4	24.8	9.7
Armenia			1	0.3		
Australia	207	12.1	357	18.5	72.5	52.8
Austria	166	21.3	259	32.1	56.0	50.5
Azerbaijan			1	0.1		
Bahamas	1	3.8	5	16.2	400.0	323.7
Bahrain	5	9.9	5	7.7	0.0	-22.2
Bangladesh	14	0.1	17	0.1	21.4	-2.5
Barbados	24	93.0	23	85.8	-4.2	-7.7
Belarus			4	0.4		
Belgium	1,763	176.3	1,873	182.5	6.2	3.5
Belize	1	5.3	2	8.7	100.0	63.6
Benin	10	2.1	21	3.3	110.0	56.8
Bhutan	0	0.0	0	0.0		
Bolivia	2	0.3	14	1.6	600.0	453.2
Bosnia & Herzegovina	0	0.0	1	0.2		
Botswana	5	3.9	11	7.1	120.0	80.8
Brazil	65	0.4	96	0.6	47.7	28.7
Brunei	1	3.8	3	9.0	200.0	136.4
Bulgaria	25	2.9	29	3.7	16.0	27.7
Burkina Faso	12	1.3	20	1.7	66.7	30.1
Burundi	0	0.0	0	0.0		
Cambodia	0	0.0	6	0.4		
Cameroon	14	1.2	19	1.2	35.7	6.6
Canada	410	14.6	471	15.2	14.9	3.9
Cape Verde	0	0.0	0	0.0		
Central African Republic	3	1.0	0	0.0	-100.0	-100.0
Chad	0	0.0	0	0.0		
Chile	61	4.6	54	3.5	-11.5	-23.4
China & Tibet	36	0.0	36	0.0	0.0	-9.0
Colombia	43	1.2	48	1.1	11.6	-7.0
Comoros	0	0.0	0	0.0		
Congo, Dem. Rep.	18	0.5	4	0.1	-77.8	-83.7

Country	1991 Number of secretariats	1991 Organisational density per million of population	2001 Number of secretariats	2001 Organisational density per million of population	Absolute growth % 1991–2001	Density growth % 1991–2001
Congo, Rep.	14	6.1	2	0.6	-85.7	-89.4
Costa Rica	45	14.3	73	17.8	62.2	24.0
Côte d'Ivoire	36	2.8	33	2.0	-8.3	-27.3
Croatia	0	0.0	14	3.0		
Cuba	17	1.6	29	2.6	70.6	62.6
Cyprus	7	10.1	16	20.3	128.6	100.2
Czech Republic	46	4.5	45	4.4	-2.2	-1.7
Denmark	242	47.0	235	44.1	-2.9	-6.2
Djibouti	0	0.0	0	0.0	0.0	0.0
Dominican Republic	6	0.8	5	0.6	-16.7	-29.6
Ecuador	22	2.1	29	2.3	31.8	7.5
Egypt	57	1.0	75	1.1	31.6	9.4
El Salvador	8	1.5	10	1.6	25.0	1.7
Equatorial Guinea	0	0.0	0	0.0		
Eritrea	0	0.0	0	0.0		
Estonia	0	0.0	7	5.1		
Ethiopia	22	0.4	17	0.3	-22.7	-41.2
Fiji	18	24.7	30	36.5	66.7	47.8
Finland	126	25.2	144	27.8	14.3	10.6
France	1,674	29.4	1,460	24.6	-12.8	-16.3
Gabon	4	4.2	3	2.4	-25.0	-42.8
Gambia	3	3.1	3	2.2	0.0	-27.7
Georgia			2	0.4		
Germany	746	9.3	938	11.4	25.7	22.5
Ghana	29	1.9	37	1.9	27.6	0.6
Greece	37	3.6	96	9.0	159.5	149.5
Guatemala	12	1.3	18	1.5	50.0	15.2
Guinea	0	0.0	2	0.2		
Guinea-Bissau	1	1.0	0	0.0	-100.0	-100.0
Guyana	4	5.5	8	10.5	100.0	91.6
Haiti	2	0.3	0	0.0	-100.0	-100.0
Honduras	4	0.8	14	2.1	250.0	167.0
Hungary	40	3.9	59	5.9	47.5	53.7
Iceland	9	35.0	11	39.1	22.2	11.8
India	150	0.2	165	0.2	10.0	-7.6
Indonesia	34	0.2	34	0.2	0.0	-13.9
Iran	2	0.0	5	0.1	150.0	109.9
Iraq	44	2.5	11	0.5	-75.0	-81.2
Ireland	53	15.1	68	17.7	28.3	17.6
Israel & Occupied Territories	96	20.6	95	15.4	-1.0	-25.3
Italy	466	8.2	596	10.4	27.9	26.4
Jamaica	16	6.7	17	6.5	6.3	-2.4
Japan	247	2.0	286	2.2	15.8	12.7
Jordan	18	5.2	27	5.3	50.0	1.9
Kazakhstan			1	0.1		
Kenya	105	4.3	107	3.4	1.9	-20.7

Country	1991 Number of secretariats	1991 Organisational density per million of population	2001 Number of secretariats	2001 Organisational density per million of population	Absolute growth % 1991–2001	Density growth % 1991–2001
Korea, Dem. Rep.	0	0.0	0	0.0		
Korea, Rep.	53	1.2	54	1.1	1.9	-6.3
Kuwait	9	4.3	7	3.6	-22.2	-17.3
Kyrgyzstan			2	0.4		
Laos	0	0.0	1	0.2		
Latvia	0	0.0	11	4.6		
Lebanon	17	6.1	26	7.3	52.9	19.6
Lesotho	3	1.7	2	1.0	-33.3	-44.3
Liberia	1	0.5	9	2.9	800.0	507.8
Libya	15	3.4	2	0.4	-86.7	-89.1
Lithuania	0	0.0	9	2.4		
Luxembourg	58	149.9	46	104.1	-20.7	-30.6
Macedonia	0	0.0	1	0.5		
Madagascar	1	0.1	3	0.2	200.0	124.5
Malawi	3	0.3	3	0.3	0.0	-16.6
Malaysia	53	2.9	67	3.0	26.4	2.1
Maldives	0	0.0	0	0.0		
Mali	7	0.8	5	0.4	-28.6	-45.0
Malta	12	33.0	25	63.8	108.3	93.5
Mauritania	2	1.0	3	1.1	50.0	11.6
Mauritius	9	8.4	14	12.0	55.6	41.7
Mexico	89	1.0	118	1.2	32.6	12.0
Micronesia Fed. States	0	0.0	1	7.4		
Moldova			2	0.5		
Mongolia	2	0.9	5	2.0	150.0	121.4
Morocco & Western Sahara	15	0.6	19	0.6	26.7	3.7
Mozambique	2	0.1	0	0.0	-100.0	-100.0
Myanmar	0	0.0	0	0.0		
Namibia	1	0.7	2	1.1	100.0	59.2
Nepal	5	0.3	15	0.6	200.0	136.2
Netherlands	526	34.9	812	51.0	54.4	45.9
New Zealand	35	10.3	53	13.9	51.4	35.3
Nicaragua	11	2.8	13	2.5	18.2	-10.8
Niger	4	0.5	3	0.3	-25.0	-46.8
Nigeria	55	0.6	42	0.4	-23.6	-42.2
Norway	125	29.3	172	38.3	37.6	30.7
Oman	0	0.0	2	0.8		
Pakistan	31	0.3	27	0.2	-12.9	-32.4
Panama	15	6.1	18	6.2	20.0	1.2
Papua New Guinea	3	0.8	6	1.2	100.0	56.9
Paraguay	5	1.2	6	1.1	20.0	-7.6
Peru	55	2.5	48	1.8	-12.7	-26.5
Philippines	110	1.8	109	1.4	-0.9	-19.7
Poland	36	0.9	53	1.4	47.2	45.9
Portugal	34	3.4	62	6.2	82.4	79.7
Qatar	2	4.3	3	5.2	50.0	21.8

Country	1991 Number of secretariats	1991 Organisational density per million of population	2001 Number of secretariats	2001 Organisational density per million of population	Absolute growth % 1991–2001	Density growth % 1991–2001
Romania	8	0.3	16	0.7	100.0	106.9
Russian Federation*	45	0.3	77	0.5	71.1	75.9
Rwanda	2	0.3	0	0.0	-100.0	-100.0
Samoa	0	0.0	2	12.6		
Saudi Arabia	26	1.6	30	1.4	15.4	-13.3
Senegal	58	7.7	63	6.5	8.6	-15.5
Sierra Leone	6	1.5	4	0.9	-33.3	-40.5
Singapore	55	17.8	80	19.5	45.5	9.6
Slovakia	0	0.0	10	1.9		
Slovenia	0	0.0	20	10.1		
Solomon Islands	1	3.0	0	0.0	-100.0	-100.0
Somalia	0	0.0	0	0.0		
South Africa	41	1.1	143	3.3	248.8	195.5
Spain	165	4.2	300	7.5	81.8	79.5
Sri Lanka	18	1.0	20	1.0	11.1	0.3
St. Lucia	3	22.6	3	20.1	0.0	-10.7
St. Vincent & the Grenadines	1	9.3	3	25.9	200.0	176.7
Sudan	10	0.4	7	0.2	-30.0	-44.1
Suriname	1	2.5	0	0.0	-100.0	-100.0
Swaziland	3	3.8	2	2.1	-33.3	-44.1
Sweden	272	31.6	320	36.2	17.6	14.8
Switzerland	680	98.6	689	96.1	1.3	-2.5
Syria	23	1.8	12	0.7	-47.8	-59.9
Tajikistan			0	0.0		
Tanzania	12	0.4	18	0.5	50.0	12.5
Thailand	51	0.9	96	1.5	88.2	64.4
Togo	10	2.8	18	3.9	80.0	36.4
Trinidad & Tobago	18	14.7	34	26.2	88.9	77.8
Tunisia	34	4.1	30	3.1	-11.8	-23.2
Turkey	10	0.2	46	0.7	360.0	289.1
Turkmenistan			0	0.0		
Uganda	7	0.4	13	0.5	85.7	37.7
Ukraine			16	0.3		
United Arab Emirates	3	1.4	9	3.4	200.0	136.5
United Kingdom	1,460	25.3	1,884	31.6	29.0	25.2
United States	3,730	14.5	3,464	12.1	-7.1	-16.4
Uruguay	35	11.2	46	13.7	31.4	22.3
Uzbekistan			4	0.2		
Vanuatu	3	19.5	1	5.0	-66.7	-74.6
Venezuela	72	3.6	66	2.7	-8.3	-25.7
Vietnam	0	0.0	4	0.1		
Yemen	0	0.0	0	0.0		
Yugoslavia	36	3.5	11	1.0	-69.4	-70.3
Zambia	11	1.3	8	0.8	-27.3	-43.4
Zimbabwe	18	1.7	38	3.0	111.1	72.8

Record 16a continued	1991		2001			
Region	Number of secretariats	Organisational density per million of population	Number of secretariats	Organisational density per million of population	Absolute growth % 1991–2001	Density growth % 1991–2001
Low income	730	0.4	788	0.3	7.9	-8.1
Middle income	1,641	0.7	2,120	0.8	29.2	14.9
Low & middle income	2,371	0.5	2,908	0.6	22.6	7.0
East Asia & Pacific	364	0.2	517	0.3	42.0	26.3
Europe & Central Asia	237	0.5	422	0.9	78.1	74.9
Latin America & Caribbean	739	1.7	924	1.8	25.0	6.4
Middle East & North Africa	269	1.1	256	0.8	-4.8	-23.9
South Asia	218	0.2	224	0.2	2.8	-14.9
Sub-Saharan Africa	543	1.1	676	1.1	24.5	-6.1
High income	13,452	16.3	14,896	16.8	10.7	3.2
World	15,937	3.0	17,968	2.9	12.7	-1.7

*Russian Federation: 1991 data is for the entire USSR

Source: © Union of International Associations, Yearbook of International Organizations: Guide to Civil Society Networks, Brussels 1991 and 2001.

Record 16b

City	Country	Number of secretariats 2001
Amsterdam	Netherlands	162
Athens	Greece	64
Bangkok	Thailand	75
Barcelona	Spain	71
Berlin	Germany	101
Bonn	Germany	81
Brussels	Belgium	1,392
Buenos Aires	Argentina	110
Cairo	Egypt	62
Caracas	Venezuela	56
Copenhagen	Denmark	108
Dakar	Senegal	58
Frankfurt Main	Germany	51
Geneva	Switzerland	272
Helsinki	Finland	65
Jerusalem	Israel	50
Lausanne	Switzerland	67
Leiden	Netherlands	52
London	United Kingdom	807
Los Angeles	United States	50
Louvain	Belgium	50
Madrid	Spain	140
Mexico City	Mexico	87
Milan	Italy	82
Montreal	Canada	86
Moscow	Russia	61
Munich	Germany	61
Nairobi	Kenya	100
New Delhi	India	65
New York	United States	390

City	Country	Number of secretariats 2001
Oslo	Norway	95
Ottawa	Canada	68
Oxford	UK	52
Paris	France	729
Rome	Italy	228
San Francisco	United States	61
San Jose	Costa Rica	56
Singapore	Singapore	79
Stockholm	Sweden	133
Strasbourg	France	65
Tokyo	Japan	174
Toronto	Canada	70
Utrecht	Netherlands	80
Vienna	Austria	190
Washington DC	United States	487
Zurich	Switzerland	79

Only figures for those cities with more than 50 secretariats are listed here.

Source: © Union of International Associations, Yearbook of International Organizations: Guide to Civil Society Networks, Brussels 2001.

Record 16c: Share of NGOs: analysis of the top ten cities (2001)

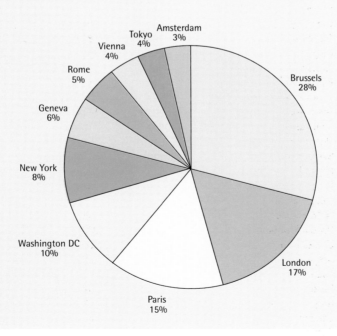

Record 17 Country participation in NGOs

This table indicates the extent to which organisations and individuals in each country are members of INGOs, for both 1991 and 2001. Data are for INGOs only; no information is available for internationally-oriented NGOs. Whether an INGO has a million members or a single member in a given country, this is counted as one membership. So a count of 100 for a country means that 100 INGOs each have at least one member or member organisation in that country. The table also offers data on membership density for each country, expressed as the number of memberships in INGOs per 1 million population, for the same years, and presents the percentage growth during the decade.

Country	Number of organisation memberships 1991	Membership density per million of population 1991	Number of organisation memberships 2001	Membership density per million of population 2001	Absolute growth % 1991–2001	Density growth % 1991–2001
Afghanistan	125	8.6	159	7.1	27.2	-17.9
Albania	95	28.8	767	243.9	707.4	746.6
Algeria	744	29.3	1,074	34.8	44.4	19.0
Angola	281	28.4	458	33.9	63.0	19.1
Argentina	1,922	58.3	2,900	77.4	50.9	32.7
Armenia			506	133.6		
Australia	2,393	139.7	3,879	200.6	62.1	43.6
Austria	2,788	357.9	4,548	563.2	63.1	57.4
Azerbaijan			378	46.7		
Bahamas	378	1,448.3	520	1,688.3	37.6	16.6
Bahrain	301	593.7	480	736.2	59.5	24.0
Bangladesh	694	6.2	1,153	8.2	66.1	33.4
Barbados	464	1,798.4	649	2,421.6	39.9	34.7
Belarus			766	75.5		
Belgium	3,726	372.6	5,732	558.5	53.8	49.9
Belize	253	1,338.6	402	1,740.3	58.9	30.0
Benin	420	87.3	720	111.7	71.4	28.0
Bhutan	73	42.3	137	64.0	87.7	51.3
Bolivia	803	119.3	1,205	141.5	50.1	18.6
Bosnia & Herzegovina			572	140.6		
Botswana	381	298.4	672	432.4	76.4	44.9
Brazil	2,119	14.1	3,220	18.7	52.0	32.4
Brunei	198	750.0	330	985.1	66.7	31.3
Bulgaria	1,011	116.7	2,123	269.9	110.0	131.2
Burkina Faso	418	45.2	713	60.1	70.6	33.2
Burundi	301	52.3	488	75.1	62.1	43.5
Cambodia	76	7.6	350	26.0	360.5	241.8
Cameroon	648	54.2	1,063	69.9	64.0	28.9
Canada	2,709	96.6	4,283	138.1	58.1	43.0
Cape Verde	110	316.1	245	560.6	122.7	77.4
Central African Republic	279	92.4	409	108.1	46.6	17.0
Chad	231	38.5	410	50.4	77.5	30.9
Chile	1,408	105.7	2,210	143.5	57.0	35.8
China & Tibet	1,106	0.9	2,240	1.7	102.5	84.4
Colombia	1,314	36.8	1,992	46.5	51.6	26.3
Comoros	112	206.6	168	231.1	50.0	11.8
Congo, Dem. Rep.	669	17.4	893	17.0	33.5	-2.2

Country	Number of organisation memberships 1991	Membership density per million of population 1991	Number of organisation memberships 2001	Membership density per million of population 2001	Absolute growth % 1991–2001	Density growth % 1991–2001
Congo Rep.	404	175.7	570	183.3	41.1	4.3
Costa Rica	947	301.2	1,416	344.4	49.5	14.3
Côte d'Ivoire	687	53.0	1,011	61.8	47.2	16.7
Croatia			1,894	406.9		
Cuba	600	56.0	1,049	93.4	74.8	66.7
Cyprus	715	1,033.2	1,316	1,665.8	84.1	61.2
Czech Republic	1,480	143.5	3,183	310.2	115.1	116.1
Denmark	3,309	642.2	4,842	907.9	46.3	41.4
Djibouti	152	292.9	226	350.9	48.7	19.8
Dominican Republic	672	93.5	932	109.6	38.7	17.1
Ecuador	911	86.8	1,334	103.6	46.4	19.4
Egypt	1,305	22.7	1,980	28.7	51.7	26.1
El Salvador	558	107.1	862	134.7	54.5	25.7
Equatorial Guinea	103	286.1	161	342.6	56.3	19.7
Eritrea			167	43.8		
Estonia			1,517	1,101.7		
Ethiopia	497	10.1	790	12.3	59.0	21.0
Fiji	427	584.9	660	801.9	54.6	37.1
Finland	2,748	548.6	4,515	872.0	64.3	58.9
France	4,204	73.7	6,562	110.4	56.1	49.7
Gabon	358	371.8	504	399.4	40.8	7.4
Gambia	336	347.8	492	368.0	46.4	5.8
Georgia			666	127.1		
Germany	4,116	51.5	6,436	78.5	56.4	52.4
Ghana	840	54.0	1,223	62.0	45.6	14.8
Greece	2,208	216.1	3,707	349.0	67.9	61.5
Guatemala	738	82.2	1,074	91.9	45.5	11.8
Guinea	277	43.5	488	59.0	76.2	35.4
Guinea-Bissau	135	139.0	248	202.1	83.7	45.4
Guyana	396	541.7	501	656.6	26.5	21.2
Haiti	442	62.8	618	74.7	39.8	19.1
Honduras	555	110.6	826	125.6	48.8	13.5
Hungary	1,674	162.0	3,495	352.4	108.8	117.5
Iceland	1,087	4,229.6	1,705	6,067.6	56.9	43.5
India	2,044	2.4	3,115	3.0	52.4	28.0
Indonesia & East Timor	1,171	6.3	1,911	8.9	63.2	41.0
Iran	637	10.6	955	13.4	49.9	25.9
Iraq	524	29.5	523	22.2	-0.2	-24.8
Ireland	2,180	619.1	3,628	944.5	66.4	52.6
Israel & Occupied Territories	1,831	393.3	2,951	478.1	61.2	21.6
Italy	3,807	67.0	5,906	102.7	55.1	53.3
Jamaica	710	297.6	909	349.9	28.0	17.6
Japan	2,361	19.0	3,721	29.2	57.6	53.4
Jordan	590	171.9	937	185.5	58.8	7.9

Country	Number of organisation memberships 1991	Membership density per million of population 1991	Number of organisation memberships 2001	Membership density per million of population 2001	Absolute growth % 1991–2001	Density growth % 1991–2001
Kazakhstan			491	30.5		
Kenya	1,057	43.4	1,611	51.5	52.4	18.6
Korea, Dem. Rep.	179	8.8	261	11.6	45.8	31.7
Korea, Rep.	1,234	28.5	2,193	46.6	77.7	63.4
Kuwait	560	267.2	784	397.8	40.0	48.9
Kyrgyzstan			257	51.5		
Laos	93	21.9	236	43.7	153.8	99.1
Latvia			1,286	534.5		
Lebanon	676	243.2	1,023	287.7	51.3	18.3
Lesotho	344	200.2	505	245.5	46.8	22.6
Liberia	421	200.6	447	143.8	6.2	-28.3
Libya	350	79.5	460	85.1	31.4	7.0
Lithuania			1,411	382.5		
Luxembourg	1,497	3,868.2	2,153	4,871.0	43.8	25.9
Macedonia			650	318.0		
Madagascar	507	41.2	710	43.2	40.0	4.8
Malawi	417	43.2	655	56.6	57.1	31.1
Malaysia	1,203	65.8	1,951	86.2	62.2	31.0
Maldives	81	364.9	154	513.3	90.1	40.7
Mali	394	43.8	631	54.0	60.2	23.4
Malta	616	1,692.3	1,162	2,964.3	88.6	75.2
Mauritania	277	135.6	435	158.4	57.0	16.8
Mauritius	562	526.7	807	689.2	43.6	30.8
Mexico	1,825	21.5	2,805	27.9	53.7	29.9
Micronesia Fed. States	34	354.2	104	770.4	205.9	117.5
Moldova			482	112.5		
Mongolia	126	55.6	412	161.0	227.0	189.5
Morocco & Western Sahara	954	37.7	1,384	44.7	45.1	18.7
Mozambique	310	22.1	637	34.2	105.5	54.6
Myanmar	265	6.4	401	8.3	51.3	29.1
Namibia	193	135.6	645	360.7	234.2	166.0
Nepal	415	22.3	820	34.8	97.6	55.6
Netherlands	3,736	248.2	5,826	365.7	55.9	47.4
New Zealand	1,636	480.9	2,606	684.3	59.3	42.3
Nicaragua	515	131.0	785	150.7	52.4	15.0
Niger	325	40.8	505	45.0	55.4	10.2
Nigeria	1,204	13.6	1,643	14.1	36.5	3.3
Norway	2,779	651.9	4,302	958.6	54.8	47.0
Oman	207	111.4	395	150.6	90.8	35.2
Pakistan	975	8.7	1,545	10.7	58.5	23.0
Panama	800	327.3	1,044	360.1	30.5	10.0
Papua New Guinea	495	128.3	717	145.7	44.8	13.6
Paraguay	636	146.5	963	170.9	51.4	16.6
Peru	1,230	56.0	1,784	68.4	45.0	22.1
Philippines	1,330	21.3	2,060	26.7	54.9	25.5
Poland	1,794	46.9	3,556	92.2	98.2	96.5

Country	Number of organisation memberships 1991	Membership density per million of population 1991	Number of organisation memberships 2001	Membership density per million of population 2001	Absolute growth % 1991–2001	Density growth % 1991–2001
Portugal	2,443	247.1	4,033	402.0	65.1	62.7
Qatar	202	432.5	358	622.6	77.2	43.9
Romania	939	40.5	2,358	105.3	151.1	159.8
Russian Federation*	1,376	9.3	3,068	21.2	123.0	129.1
Rwanda	335	51.8	527	270.4	57.3	422.5
Samoa	191	1,193.8	311	1,956.0	62.8	63.9
Sao Tome & Principe	68	591.3	125	757.6	83.8	28.1
Saudi Arabia	653	41.3	1,070	50.9	63.9	23.2
Senegal	814	108.3	1,118	115.7	37.3	6.9
Sierra Leone	484	118.3	632	137.8	30.6	16.5
Singapore	1,068	345.1	1,828	445.0	71.2	29.0
Slovakia			2,058	380.9		
Slovenia			1,972	993.5		
Solomon Islands	172	522.8	278	600.4	61.6	14.9
Somalia	241	33.5	226	24.7	-6.2	-26.3
South Africa	1,373	37.0	2,809	64.1	104.6	73.4
Spain	3,433	87.1	5,564	139.4	62.1	60.0
Sri Lanka	939	54.4	1,313	68.7	39.8	26.3
St. Lucia	240	1,804.5	347	2,328.9	44.6	29.1
St. Vincent & the Grenadines	184	1,719.6	278	2,396.6	51.1	39.4
Sudan	590	23.2	746	23.5	26.4	0.9
Suriname	269	665.8	354	844.9	31.6	26.9
Swaziland	312	396.9	476	507.5	52.6	27.8
Sweden	3,208	372.3	5,196	588.2	62.0	58.0
Switzerland	3,297	477.9	5,209	726.5	58.0	52.0
Syria	454	35.6	602	36.2	32.6	1.9
Tajikistan			189	30.8		
Tanzania	701	26.0	1,092	30.4	55.8	16.8
Thailand	1,170	21.1	1,893	29.8	61.8	41.3
Togo	468	132.6	678	145.6	44.9	9.8
Trinidad & Tobago	611	499.2	820	630.8	34.2	26.4
Tunisia	863	103.7	1,249	130.6	44.7	26.0
Turkey	1,270	22.2	2,345	34.7	84.6	56.2
Turkmenistan			156	32.3		
Uganda	575	32.3	999	41.6	73.7	28.8
Ukraine			1,569	31.9		
United Arab Emirates	360	172.1	740	278.8	105.6	62.0
United Kingdom	3,933	68.1	6,297	105.8	60.1	55.3
United States	3,073	11.9	5,031	17.6	63.7	47.4
Uruguay	1,065	340.6	1,546	460.0	45.2	35.1
Uzbekistan			362	14.3		
Vanuatu	156	1,013.0	275	1,361.4	76.3	34.4
Venezuela	1,365	68.3	1,900	77.1	39.2	12.9
Vietnam	283	4.2	851	10.7	200.7	156.3
Yemen	217	17.8	330	17.3	52.1	-3.3

Country	Number of organisation memberships 1991	Membership density per million of population 1991	Number of organisation memberships 2001	Membership density per million of population 2001	Absolute growth % 1991–2001	Density growth % 1991–2001
Yugoslavia	1,642	160.4	1,624	154.1	-1.1	-3.9
Zambia	675	81.5	945	88.7	40.0	8.9
Zimbabwe	855	81.3	1,330	103.5	55.6	27.3
Region						
Low income	25,474	12.4	44,279	17.9	73.8	44.2
Middle income	53,740	22.0	93,264	34.1	73.5	55.2
Low & middle income	79,214	17.6	137,543	26.4	73.6	50.1
East Asia & Pacific	9,869	6.0	17,264	9.4	74.9	57.3
Europe & Central Asia	11,295	24.7	37,729	81.9	234.0	231.2
Latin America & Caribbean	23,088	54.6	34,076	65.5	47.6	19.9
Middle East & North Africa	8,627	34.7	12,688	40.9	47.1	17.8
South Asia	5,346	4.7	8,396	6.1	57.1	29.8
Sub-Saharan Africa	20,989	40.8	31,709	48.1	51.1	17.7
High income	73,221	88.8	117,919	134.6	61.0	51.5
World	154,713	28.9	265,563	43.2	71.6	49.6

*Russian Federation: 1991 data is for the entire USSR

Source: © Union of International Associations, Yearbook of International Organizations: Guide to Civil Society Networks, Brussels 1991 and 2001.

Record 18 Links between international organisations

This table indicates different aspects of the inter-organisational network that links international and internationally-oriented NGOs to each other and to international governmental organisations (IGOs). It indicates the number of citations, or references, made by either NGOs or IGOs to any other international organisation (whether NGO or IGO). Examples of citations would be (1) ' ... founded under the auspices of "X"' ... , (2) '... financed by annual subventions from "X", "Y" and "Z" ... ', (3) '... consultative relations with "X"'. The number of links is shown for 1991 and 2001, in addition to a percentage growth figure.

Citations from NGO to IGO and NGO; Citations from IGO to IGO and NGO

Paragraph	1990	2000	% change	
Founded				
NGOs	2,710	5,051	86	The citing organisation cites another organisation as having had
IGOs	2,222	3,315	49	some role in its founding or establishment.
Total	4,932	7,511	52	
Aims				
NGOs	6	14	133	The citing organisation cites another organisation as having
IGOs	8	2	-75	something to do with its principle objectives.
Total	14	16	14	
Structure				
NGOs	747	1,555	108	The citing organisation has a structural link with another
IGOs	1,088	2,029	86	organisation, for instance as sister organisation or parent and
Total	1,835	3,584	95	subsidiary organisation.
Staff				
NGOs		3		The citing organisation shares key staff with, or is provided with
IGOs	72	120	67	key staff from, the other organisation it cites.
Total	72	123	71	
Finances				
NGOs	493	2,215	349	There is a financial link between the citing organisation and
IGOs	204	514	152	another organisation.
Total	697	2,718	290	
Activities				
NGOs	1,754	2,473	41	The citing organisation cites another organisation as having a
IGOs	1,845	4,011	117	role in its activities, for instance joint activities, or activities
Total	3,599	6,484	80	aimed at the cited organisation.
Publications				
NGOs	3	19	533	The citing organisation cites another organisation as having a
IGOs	20	25	25	role in its publications, for instance joint publications, or
Total	23	44	91	publications about the cited organisation.
Members				
NGOs	4,834	11,824	145	There is a membership link between the citing organisation and
IGOs	461	2,333	406	another organisation, for instance because one of them is a
Total	5,295	14,157	167	federation of organisations, or coordinating body of which the
				other is a member.

Citations from NGO to IGO and NGO; Citations from IGO to IGO and NGO

Paragraph	1990	2000	% change	
Consultative Status				The citing organisation has consultative status with another
NGOs	3,171	3,218	1	organisation. This mainly concerns NGOs having such a status
IGOs	3	357	11,800	with IGOs.
Total	**3,174**	**3,575**	**13**	
IGO Relations				
NGOs	7,883	23,240	195	
IGOs	9,901	14,472	46	The citing organisation has some other form of relation
Total	**17,784**	**26,875**	**51**	with an IGO.
NGO Relations				
NGOs	21,684	51,992	140	
IGOs	9,810	12,609	29	The citing organisation has some other form of relation
Total	**31,494**	**48,947**	**55**	with an NGO.
Total number of organisations cited				
NGOs	16,113	18,323	14	
IGOs	1,794	1,836	2	
Total	**17,907**	**20,159**	**13**	
Total number of citations				
NGOs	40,485	90,063	122	
IGOs	25,328	38,302	51	
Total	**65,813**	**112,112**	**70**	
Average number of citations				
NGOs	4.9	12.2	149	
IGOs	19.7	24.4	24	
Total	**6.7**	**14.1**	**110**	

Source: © Union of International Associations, Yearbook of International Organizations: Guide to Civil Society Networks, 1991 and 2001 (presenting data collected in 1990 and 2000, respectively). Data have been restructured from more comprehensive country and organisation coverage in the Yearbook of International Organizations.

Record 19 Meetings of NGOs

Meetings are an important vehicle for the constitution of global civil society. These tables present data on international meetings for the years 1999, 2000 and 2001 according to the country in which the event was held, and its purpose (largely following the International Classification of Nonprofit Organisations). These include meetings organised by INGOs, internationally-oriented NGOs and IGOs, and other significant international meetings recorded by the Union of International Associations. Most meetings are recorded as having several purposes. For each country, the number of meetings held in each country in a given year is shown as a percentage of all meetings held in that country for that year. The second table shows the number of meetings held for a particular purpose in each country in 2001, as a percentage of the total number of meetings for that purpose.

Record 19a

Meetings per country per year

	1999		2000		2001	
Country	no. of meetings	% of total meetings	no. of meetings	% of total meetings	no. of meetings	% of total meetings
Algeria	8	0.2	6	0.1	11	0.1
Argentina	94	0.8	178	1.1	85	0.9
Australia	332	2.8	441	3.4	296	2.4
Austria	277	2.9	267	3.0	274	3.0
Azerbaijan	5	0.1	4	0.0	6	0.1
Bahamas	2	0.0	7	0.1	6	0.1
Bahrain	13	0.1	16	0.3	9	0.1
Bangladesh	11	0.1	10	0.2	2	0.0
Barbados	9	0.1	8	0.1	6	0.1
Belarus	4	0.0	3	0.1	5	0.0
Belgium	383	3.8	384	4.2	321	3.2
Benin	10	0.1	9	0.2	8	0.1
Bolivia	7	0.1	7	0.1	10	0.2
Botswana	7	0.1	5	0.1	5	0.1
Brazil	107	1.4	145	1.6	90	0.8
Brunei	2	0.0	15	0.2	6	0.2
Bulgaria	28	0.3	22	0.3	29	0.5
Burkina Faso	15	0.2	10	0.2	7	0.1
Cambodia	5	0.1	6	0.1	8	0.3
Cameroon	8	0.1	7	0.1	13	0.2
Canada	283	2.6	329	3.0	246	2.3
Chile	42	0.5	42	0.4	29	0.4
China & Tibet*	90	1.0	134	1.6	87	1.0
Colombia	21	0.2	17	0.1	20	0.3
Costa Rica	19	0.4	13	0.2	19	0.3
Croatia	44	0.4	41	0.5	44	0.4
Cuba	201	1.3	88	0.9	54	0.6
Cyprus	22	0.2	12	0.2	15	0.2
Czech Republic	100	1.0	104	1.0	68	0.7
Denmark	177	1.6	151	1.3	158	1.4
Dominican Republic	15	0.1	14	0.2	11	0.1
Ecuador	11	0.1	14	0.2	13	0.2
Egypt	50	0.7	51	0.7	56	0.8
El Salvador	4	0.1	6	0.0	8	0.0
Estonia	11	0.1	11	0.1	13	0.1
Ethiopia	10	0.2	9	0.1	3	0.0

Meetings per country per year

Country	1999 no. of meetings	1999 % of total meetings	2000 no. of meetings	2000 % of total meetings	2001 no. of meetings	2001 % of total meetings
Fiji	9	0.2	8	0.2	4	0.0
Finland	272	2.9	185	1.5	217	2.0
France	857	9.4	963	10.6	723	7.9
Gabon	4	0.1	6	0.1	4	0.0
Gambia	6	0.1	1	0.0	1	0.0
Georgia	8	0.1	3	0.0	2	0.1
Germany	715	6.5	656	5.9	502	4.6
Ghana	22	0.2	10	0.1	11	0.1
Greece	137	1.3	103	1.1	98	1.0
Guatemala	6	0.1	8	0.1	10	0.1
Hungary	127	1.5	198	1.7	100	1.0
Iceland	16	0.1	26	0.3	10	0.1
India	119	1.5	120	1.4	89	1.0
Indonesia	26	0.3	28	0.4	32	0.8
Iran	16	0.2	13	0.2	5	0.1
Ireland	63	0.6	68	0.7	62	0.5
Israel & Occupied Territories	94	0.8	156	1.2	69	0.6
Italy	462	4.8	549	6.0	443	4.7
Jamaica	16	0.2	17	0.3	8	0.1
Japan	270	2.4	292	2.9	277	2.6
Jordan	15	0.2	20	0.3	12	0.2
Kazakhstan	7	0.2	3	0.1	6	0.1
Kenya	30	0.6	30	0.4	27	0.4
Korea, Rep.	97	0.9	116	1.1	154	1.4
Kuwait	8	0.1	4	0.0	4	0.1
Kyrgyzstan	1	0.0	1	0.0	6	0.1
Latvia	9	0.2	18	0.2	25	0.3
Lebanon	24	0.2	19	0.2	26	0.3
Lithuania	16	0.2	19	0.2	16	0.2
Luxembourg	27	0.4	19	0.3	22	0.3
Malaysia	64	0.7	58	0.7	54	0.8
Mali	3	0.0	8	0.2	5	0.1
Malta	22	0.3	23	0.2	1	0.1
Mauritius	7	0.1	8	0.1	3	0.0
Mexico	92	0.9	97	0.9	71	0.8
Morocco & Western Sahara	34	0.5	23	0.3		0.4
Mozambique	7	0.2	5	0.1	4	0.0
Namibia	4	0.0	8	0.2	4	0.0
Nepal	14	0.2	12	0.3	15	0.3
Netherlands	478	4.7	414	3.9	277	2.6
New Zealand	32	0.3	44	0.4	54	0.5
Nigeria	7	0.0	20	0.3	12	0.2
Norway	161	1.3	187	1.4	115	1.0
Pakistan	11	0.1	5	0.0	10	0.2
Panama	17	0.2	28	0.2	13	0.2
Peru	18	0.2	17	0.2	10	0.2
Philippines	46	0.5	39	0.5	34	0.5

Meetings per country per year

Country	1999 no. of meetings	1999 % of total meetings	2000 no. of meetings	2000 % of total meetings	2001 no. of meetings	2001 % of total meetings
Poland	117	1.2	119	1.3	110	1.0
Portugal	135	1.3	141	1.4	105	1.1
Qatar	6	0.1	2	0.0	2	0.0
Romania	38	0.4	15	0.2	28	0.3
Russian Federation	108	1.2	117	1.4	112	1.2
Saudi Arabia	3	0.0	4	0.0	13	0.2
Senegal	22	0.4	20	0.3	14	0.2
Singapore	157	1.1	151	1.2	138	1.1
Slovakia	33	0.4	27	0.3	18	0.2
Slovenia	45	0.5	55	0.6	37	0.4
South Africa	126	1.4	116	1.3	96	1.3
Spain	366	3.6	421	4.0	356	3.4
Sri Lanka	13	0.2	17	0.2	8	0.1
St. Lucia	7	0.1	7	0.1	3	0.0
Sweden	174	1.9	156	1.4	189	1.8
Switzerland	286	4.0	365	5.2	301	4.5
Syrian Arab Republic	9	0.2	7	0.1	11	0.1
Tanzania	9	0.2	7	0.1	16	0.2
Thailand	130	2.0	123	2.1	78	1.3
Togo	6	0.1	6	0.1	1	0.0
Trinidad & Tobago	15	0.3	13	0.2	9	0.2
Tunisia	25	0.3	27	0.4	13	0.2
Turkey	58	0.6	84	0.9	76	0.7
Uganda	13	0.2	5	0.1	10	0.1
Ukraine	31	0.2	22	0.3	28	0.4
United Arab Emirates	15	0.3	18	0.2	19	0.3
United Kingdom	754	6.3	765	6.7	510	4.1
United States	1376	13.3	1394	13.2	1146	11.5
Uruguay	11	0.1	24	0.2	14	0.1
Uzbekistan	4	0.1	6	0.1	3	0.0
Venezuela	19	0.2	17	0.2	13	0.2
Vietnam	15	0.2	8	0.1	21	0.4
Zambia	3	0.0	5	0.0	9	0.2
Zimbabwe	26	0.4	9	0.2	13	0.4
Total meetings in sample	11078		11514		9208	

*does not include Hong Kong or Macao

Source: © Union of International Associations,Yearbook of International Organizations:Guide to Civil Society Networks,Brussels 2001.

Record 19b: Purposes of meetings for selected countries*

2001 Country % of hits per purpose	Culture and recreation	Education	Research	Health	Social services
Argentina	1.4	0.7	0.8	1.4	1.0
Australia	3.1	3.0	2.7	3.8	2.4
Austria	2.8	3.3	3.0	2.6	3.0
Belgium	1.3	2.7	2.2	2.5	5.0
Brazil	0.7	0.8	1.0	0.8	0.9
Canada	2.3	2.6	2.7	2.7	2.0
China & Tibet***	1.1	1.1	1.1	0.7	0.6
Costa Rica		0.3	0.2	0.2	0.3
Croatia	1.7	0.1	0.3	0.3	0.3
Denmark	1.9	2.0	1.5	2.5	1.3
Egypt	0.4	0.8	0.6	0.7	0.8
Finland	3.2	3.0	2.0	2.5	2.5
France	12.9	6.8	7.4	8.5	8.9
Germany	3.8	5.8	5.0	5.4	4.4
Ghana	0.1	0.1	0.1		0.1
Greece	1.6	0.7	1.2	1.0	0.9
Hungary	1.0	1.2	1.0	1.2	0.9
India	0.5	1.4	0.9	0.9	1.2
Indonesia	0.6	0.7	0.6	0.1	0.4
Ireland	0.8	1.3	0.3	0.5	0.6
Israel & Occupied Territories	0.3	0.3	0.9	1.2	0.5
Italy	3.7	3.7	5.6	6.5	3.1
Japan	2.1	1.8	3.7	1.9	1.8
Korea, Rep.	1.4	1.6	1.6	0.9	1.3
Kyrgyzstan	0.1	0.1	0.1		0.0
Malaysia	0.7	0.9	0.7	0.3	0.8
Mexico	0.9	1.1	0.6	1.3	0.8
Namibia	0.1		0.0		
Netherlands	2.5	3.7	2.8	1.9	2.5
Norway	0.8	1.1	1.1	1.4	1.0
Philippines	0.3	0.5	0.4	1.0	0.8
Poland	0.8	0.9	1.3	0.7	0.6
Portugal	1.3	2.0	0.9	1.3	1.2
Russian Federation	1.1	0.7	1.4	0.3	1.5
Singapore	1.0	1.3	1.1	1.3	1.0
South Africa	1.3	1.8	1.1	1.2	1.1
Spain	3.6	3.3	3.3	3.7	3.1
Sweden	0.8	2.4	1.6	2.6	1.9
Switzerland	3.6	1.5	2.6	4.9	7.6
Thailand	1.3	1.8	1.0	0.8	1.3
Turkey	0.6	1.3	0.6	1.3	0.8
Ukraine	0.2	0.3	0.5	0.3	0.3
United Kingdom	4.2	3.9	4.7	5.7	3.4
United States	8.6	7.6	15.2	9.0	8.8
Zimbabwe		0.2	0.1	0.3	1.0

Covers only countries that had 1% of the meetings in at least one of the categories. Empty cells indicate that the share of meetings was below 0.05%

** One 'hit' is recorded for each meeting purpose: multi-purpose meetings may therefore generate several hits.*

Environment	Economic development, infrastructure	Law, policy and advocacy	Religion	Defence	Politics	Hits per country**	country % of all hits for year
0.8	0.9	0.7	0.3		0.5	362	0.9
2.3	2.3	1.6	3.1	1.6	1.3	991	2.4
2.1	2.6	3.2	1.9	2.8	4.6	1214	3.0
3.3	3.3	4.0	1.5	7.7	5.7	1329	3.2
0.7	0.7	0.8	1.0	0.4	0.7	338	0.8
2.3	2.1	2.0	0.5	1.2	2.6	957	2.3
1.6	1.3	0.6			0.8	408	1.0
1.1	0.3	0.3			0.4	113	0.3
0.2	0.3	0.2		0.8	0.2	148	0.4
1.4	1.2	1.1	0.3	0.4	1.1	579	1.4
0.7	1.0	0.7	0.9	0.4	1.2	310	0.8
2.4	1.8	1.3	0.2	0.8	1.4	817	2.0
6.4	6.3	9.9	6.0	6.9	9.6	3232	7.9
5.3	4.6	3.5	3.9	2.0	3.7	1873	4.6
	0.1	0.2	1.0		0.1	38	0.1
1.5	0.8	0.8	0.2	1.6	0.9	424	1.0
1.4	1.0	0.8	1.4	2.0	0.6	401	1.0
1.1	0.9	0.9	3.1	1.2	0.8	391	1.0
0.8	1.0	1.1	2.6		0.9	315	0.8
0.3	0.5	0.6		0.4	0.1	194	0.5
0.6	0.3	0.7	0.7		0.3	239	0.6
5.5	5.1	3.6	7.3	4.5	2.6	1910	4.7
3.0	2.5	1.2	0.5	1.2	1.9	1056	2.6
1.8	1.6	0.9	1.7	1.6	1.0	590	1.4
	0.0	0.2		2.0	0.0	28	0.1
1.2	1.1	0.8	1.5		0.7	336	0.8
1.2	0.6	1.1	0.2	0.8	0.5	307	0.8
	0.0		1.0		0.1	9	0.0
1.4	2.8	2.3	2.4	3.2	2.7	1077	2.6
1.4	1.0	0.4			0.7	403	1.0
1.7	0.4	0.4		0.4	0.1	197	0.5
0.5	1.3	0.5	0.9		0.6	402	1.0
0.9	1.1	1.3	0.2	0.8	0.8	448	1.1
0.7	1.0	1.9	0.2	2.0	1.4	504	1.2
0.9	1.4	0.6	0.2		1.0	461	1.1
1.5	1.4	1.7	0.3	1.6	1.6	543	1.3
3.3	3.9	3.4	1.7	4.0	2.1	1389	3.4
1.6	1.3	2.2	0.3	2.0	3.2	728	1.8
3.4	4.5	7.7	10.8	10.9	4.6	1831	4.5
1.2	1.7	1.9	2.2	0.4	1.2	551	1.3
0.8	0.6	0.9		0.4	0.8	305	0.7
0.2	0.4	0.4	0.3	1.2	0.5	159	0.4
3.7	4.2	2.8	11.4	5.3	3.6	1686	4.1
8.7	11.5	8.7	13.7	10.5	9.7	4698	11.5
0.2	0.3	1.0	0.3		0.2	144	0.4
						34,435	

*** Does not include Hong Kong or Macao

Source: © Union of International Associations, Yearbook of International Organizations: Guide to Civil Society Networks, Brussels 2001

Record 20 NGOs by purpose

Following the International Classification of Nonprofit Organisations, these tables present data on the purposes of activities by international and internationally-oriented NGOs by country, for 2000 and 2001. It expands the coverage of last year's Table R23, which only showed INGOs, and the figures therefore cannot be compared. The classification does not report actual activities or expenditures but only statements of intent. The summary table shows the overall growth rate by purpose over the last year.

Record 20a

Country	Culture & Recreation % total	Culture & Recreation % change 2000–2001	Education % total	Education % change 2000–2001	Research % total	Research % change 2000–2001	Health % total	Health % change 2000–2001	Social Services % total	Social Services % change 2000–2001
Argentina	5.0	0.8	6.0	1.0	23.3	-0.2	7.0	-0.9	14.0	0.2
Australia	8.3	-0.9	6.3	0.5	31.7	3.7	7.9	0.1	11.2	-0.9
Austria	8.6	-0.1	5.2	0.0	28.5	-0.0	3.3	0.2	10.5	0.0
Belgium	4.2	-0.3	4.6	-0.3	18.5	-0.4	4.9	0.1	11.4	-0.9
Brazil	6.8	-0.3	5.8	-0.5	30.5	0.4	8.4	-0.0	7.9	0.2
Canada	8.1	-0.3	6.7	-0.6	24.9	-1.2	6.4	1.2	11.1	0.6
Chile	2.8	-0.3	5.6	-0.4	25.4	2.8	3.5	0.2	16.2	-0.6
Colombia	3.5	-0.1	9.6	-0.8	21.7	-0.2	7.0	0.6	9.6	0.1
Costa Rica	1.4	0.2	9.4	1.1	20.1	0.3	2.2	0.1	17.3	-0.7
Côte d'Ivoire	14.2	-0.3	10.6	-0.5	17.7	-0.7	3.5	-0.9	7.1	-0.8
Czech Republic	3.0	0.3	4.4	-0.4	29.6	0.4	8.1	-0.3	15.6	-0.1
Denmark	7.0	-0.2	5.6	-1.2	28.1	-1.2	9.8	-0.3	10.9	0.5
Ecuador	0.8	0.8	5.9	0.4	16.1	0.9	1.7	-0.2	12.7	-0.6
Egypt	14.9	-0.3	2.7	-0.6	13.8	3.1	3.2	1.2	10.1	-1.2
Finland	5.6	-0.2	9.5	-0.0	28.1	0.4	10.9	-0.1	10.7	0.0
France	9.5	-0.0	5.1	0.2	23.6	0.3	4.6	0.2	11.4	-0.0
Germany	8.0	-0.1	4.4	-0.2	24.8	-1.1	7.1	-0.1	9.8	0.7
Ghana	4.6	1.5	10.1	0.6	10.1	0.8	2.8	-1.5	11.9	-0.5
Greece	12.1	-0.2	7.0	-1.8	26.6	0.5	9.0	-0.1	6.5	0.1
Hungary	16.1	0.1	5.0	-0.2	30.4	-1.4	1.2	0.3	5.6	0.5
India	2.5	-1.3	6.1	-1.7	24.5	-0.6	7.0	2.2	12.0	2.3
Ireland	5.4	-1.2	7.0	0.9	22.5	0.2	10.9	1.0	18.6	0.0
Israel	7.3	0.2	2.6	0.2	18.2	-0.0	2.1	0.4	6.3	-0.2
Italy	6.9	0.2	3.9	-0.3	29.3	-0.0	5.9	-0.8	9.1	-0.4
Japan	7.7	-0.0	4.1	-1.1	29.8	2.0	4.3	-0.6	10.6	1.2
Kenya	0.8	-0.3	6.2	0.7	28.3	-1.1	2.2	-0.4	13.5	0.9
Luxembourg	12.3	-0.4	1.6	0.1	11.5	3.6	4.1	-1.1	18.0	-1.5
Malaysia	4.1	-0.2	2.1	-0.3	24.9	0.7	7.3	-0.3	11.4	0.8
Mexico	6.5	-0.6	8.0	0.3	24.8	0.0	7.6	0.3	11.5	0.2
Netherlands	7.7	0.6	6.4	-0.2	24.0	-0.9	6.6	1.2	10.7	1.1
Nigeria	5.1	-0.1	5.8	-0.4	24.8	2.0	8.0	0.4	10.9	-1.0
Norway	6.9	-0.5	6.9	4.1	33.2	-0.3	5.0	0.4	7.9	-1.0
Peru	6.6	-0.2	5.0	-0.5	14.9	-1.5	5.8	-0.4	12.4	0.5
Philippines	2.0	-1.1	6.4	-0.4	15.3	-0.0	5.4	-0.5	12.9	0.4
Poland	13.0	2.3	5.0	0.3	38.0	-0.1	6.0	-0.2	8.0	1.0
Portugal	18.0	0.0	10.5	1.1	19.5	-1.5	4.5	-0.7	12.8	0.4

Environment		Economic development infrastructure		Law, policy and advocacy		Religion		Defence		Politics	
% total	% change 2000–2001	% total	% change 2000–2001	% total	% change 2000–2001	% total	% change 2000–2001	% total	% change 2000–2001	% total	% change 2000–2001
1.0	-0.0	23.3	0.4	14.0	-1.4	4.7	-0.2		0.0	2.0	0.2
2.6	0.2	17.6	-1.8	8.2	-0.7	4.0	-0.0		-0.1	2.2	-0.0
1.7	-0.1	23.3	-0.2	11.4	0.1	1.2	0.1	0.9	-0.0	5.4	-0.0
3.1	-0.1	36.9	2.9	9.9	-1.1	2.5	-0.2	0.5	0.0	3.4	0.4
2.6	-0.0	20.0	-0.2	10.5	0.4	3.7	0.3		-0.1	3.7	-0.1
3.5	1.0	21.5	-0.7	9.5	-0.2	4.8	-0.2	0.3	0.7	3.2	-0.2
4.9	-0.1	28.2	-0.0	9.2	-0.7	2.1	-0.7	0.7	0.0	1.4	-0.2
2.6	0.3	24.3	0.2	9.6	-0.7	11.3	0.0		0.0	0.9	0.5
5.0	0.1	24.5	-0.4	17.3	1.0		0.1		0.0	2.9	-1.7
4.4	-0.3	26.5	1.9	9.7	1.1	5.3	1.0		0.0	0.9	-0.5
3.0	-0.2	13.3	-0.1	12.6	0.3	5.9	0.6		-0.0	4.4	-0.4
3.4	-0.9	22.2	-2.1	7.5	6.7	2.5	-1.4	0.2	0.7	2.7	-0.5
4.2	-0.2	25.4	-0.7	16.9	-1.0	6.8	0.8	1.7	-0.0	7.6	-0.3
4.3	-0.6	21.8	-0.9	18.6	-0.4	5.3	0.0	0.5	0.0	4.8	-0.4
3.6	0.1	21.3	-0.3	6.2	0.0	1.8	0.2		-0.0	2.4	-0.0
2.7	0.0	25.9	-0.6	10.2	0.0	3.0	-0.1	0.6	-0.1	3.4	0.1
2.7	0.9	26.7	-0.4	8.6	-0.2	4.7	0.5	0.4	0.0	3.0	-0.1
2.8	-0.1	19.3	2.5	11.9	-2.3	21.1	-0.9		-0.3	5.5	0.4
4.0	-1.1	13.1	0.7	10.1	1.4	5.0	-0.3	2.0	-0.1	4.5	0.8
4.3	0.3	21.1	-0.5	6.2	1.1	3.1	-0.7	0.6	0.0	6.2	0.4
3.9	-0.4	17.0	-1.0	15.9	0.2	8.1	0.0		0.0	3.1	0.2
1.6	0.4	24.0	0.5	7.0	-0.0		-1.9		-0.1	3.1	0.2
1.6	0.1	14.1	-0.6	20.3	0.2	22.4	-0.2	1.0	-0.1	4.2	-0.1
2.3	0.1	19.9	0.6	9.9	-0.1	10.3	-0.1	0.7	0.2	1.7	0.6
2.5	0.3	24.2	-0.1	8.6	0.6	1.6	-1.8	1.1	0.0	5.6	-0.3
7.0	0.6	24.3	1.3	7.0	-1.6	10.0	-0.5		-0.1	0.8	0.6
3.3	-0.6	32.8	1.7	7.4	-0.9	4.9	-1.1	0.8	0.0	3.3	0.3
5.2	-0.2	30.1	-0.8	8.8	-0.7	4.7	0.3		0.0	1.6	0.6
6.1	0.0	21.8	-0.2	7.6	-0.0	1.5	0.1		-0.1	4.6	-0.1
3.6	-0.2	24.9	-0.7	9.5	-0.4	2.4	-0.3	0.9	-0.1	3.3	-0.1
5.1	-0.9	17.5	0.5	10.2	-0.0	8.0	-0.3	1.5	-0.1	2.9	-0.1
3.4	-0.5	22.2	0.7	9.5	-2.3	0.5	0.0	0.5	0.0	4.0	-0.6
5.8	-0.5	24.8	-0.6	17.4	0.9		1.3		0.0	7.4	1.1
6.4	0.0	27.5	-1.7	12.5	2.8	7.1	-0.1		-0.1	4.4	0.8
	0.7	20.0	-2.5	5.0	-0.3	1.0	-1.0	1.0	0.0	3.0	-0.1
1.5	0.9	19.5	-0.4	6.8	-0.3	3.8	0.1		0.1	3.0	0.1

Country	Culture & Recreation		Education		Research		Health		Social Services	
	% total	% change 2000–2001	% total	% change 2000–2001	% total	% change 2000–2001	% total	% change 2000–2001	% total	% change 2000–2001
Russian Federation	1.6	−0.3	9.6	1.1	26.4	−1.3	2.4	−0.0	12.8	0.1
Senegal	6.7	−1.8	4.2	4.2	17.0	−2.8	0.6	2.8	13.9	0.3
Singapore	7.4	−0.3	7.9	0.0	27.1	0.1	11.3	−0.6	8.9	−0.4
South Africa	6.9	1.0	3.6	0.7	24.5	−1.3	5.8	−0.7	8.8	0.6
Spain	8.0	−0.1	5.6	0.2	26.4	−1.5	5.6	0.4	9.9	−1.0
Sweden	7.2	0.5	4.3	−0.1	28.9	0.1	9.1	0.1	12.4	0.0
Switzerland	9.0	−0.1	3.9	0.2	16.7	−1.7	5.0	−0.8	13.5	−0.9
Thailand	0.8	−1.2	5.4	0.8	25.6	−3.4	5.4	−0.5	12.8	1.3
Turkey	1.0	0.1	3.0	0.3	31.0	0.2	6.0	0.1	11.0	−0.2
United Kingdom	6.2	−0.2	4.0	−0.1	23.6	0.2	5.4	−0.1	12.2	−0.1
United States	6.2	−0.3	4.0	−0.2	27.2	−0.2	5.9	−0.3	11.4	−0.0
Uruguay	4.4	−0.3	3.7	−0.2	28.7	0.4	5.1	−0.6	13.2	−0.3
Venezuela	5.4	−0.1	7.9	0.6	19.8	−0.3	2.5	0.7	17.8	1.2
Zimbabwe	3.9	0.0	6.2	0.0	13.2	0.0	3.1	0.0	15.5	0.0

Source: © Union of International Associations, Yearbook of International Organizations: Guide to Civil Society Networks, 1991 and 2001 (presenting data collected in 1990 and 2000, respectively). Data have been restructured from more comprehensive country and organisation coverage in the Yearbook of International Organizations.

Record 20b: Overall growth rate of number of NGOs by purpose

Purpose	2000	2001	% change 2000–2001
Culture and recreation	3,573	3,649	2.1
Education	2,812	2,982	6.0
Research	10,714	11,275	5.2
Health	2,559	2,653	3.7
Social services	5,735	5,985	4.4
Environment	1,567	1,637	4.5
Economic development, infrastructure	13,841	14,394	4.0
Law, policy and advocacy	6,054	6,374	5.3
Religion	2,761	2,866	3.8
Defence	382	384	0.5
Politics	2,703	2,887	6.8
Totals	**52,701**	**55,086**	**4.5**

Environment		Economic development infrastructure		Law, policy and advocacy		Religion		Defence		Politics	
% total	% change 2000–2001	% total	% change 2000–2001	% total	% change 2000–2001	% total	% change 2000–2001	% total	% change 2000–2001	% total	% change 2000–2001
5.6	0.5	12.8	0.5	16.8	-0.5	4.8	-0.0	2.4	0.0	4.8	-0.1
3.6	-0.1	37.6	-2.0	12.7	-0.5	1.2	-0.5		-0.1	2.4	0.5
0.5	-0.6	21.2	2.6	7.4	-0.2	7.4	-1.6	0.5	0.0	0.5	1.0
6.6	-0.3	23.0	0.2	6.2	-0.3	12.0	-0.1		-0.1	2.6	0.2
3.7	-0.1	25.8	3.1	9.5	-0.3	1.1	-0.3	0.7	-0.1	3.7	-0.1
2.7	0.0	23.1	-0.6	6.4	-0.3	2.0	0.1	1.2	-0.0	2.9	0.3
2.1	0.2	26.1	2.0	12.2	0.1	6.7	0.5	0.6	0.0	4.2	0.5
8.7	-0.2	19.0	1.0	16.1	2.5	3.3	-0.5		0.0	2.9	-0.1
2.0	-0.2	29.0	-0.1	9.0	-0.1	7.0	-0.0		0.0	1.0	-0.1
3.2	0.0	27.7	-0.1	9.7	-0.1	4.2	0.3	0.9	0.1	2.9	0.1
3.0	0.4	21.0	-0.4	10.8	0.6	6.3	0.6	0.6	0.0	3.6	-0.1
6.6	-0.6	18.4	-1.5	16.2	2.5	2.2	0.1		0.4	1.5	-0.0
1.5	2.3	23.8	-0.6	15.3	-4.3	1.5	0.6	0.5	0.0	4.0	-0.1
4.7	0.0	23.3	0.0	15.5	0.0	10.1	0.0		0.0	4.7	0.0

Record 21 Employment, volunteering and revenue of NGOs

For a selected number of countries that participated in the Johns Hopkins Comparative Nonprofit Sector Project, these tables offer employment and volunteering figures (21a), and revenue structure (21b), for non-profit organisations operating primarily at the international level. This includes prominently international humanitarian and relief organisations as well as INGOs active in supporting development, but also associations promoting international understanding, exchange, and friendship. The first part of the revenue table shows the percentages in terms of cash flow, while the second accounts for the financial value of volunteer input.

Record 21a: Employment and volunteering in NGOs

1995/1996	INGOs		Total non-profit sector		INGOs as % of total nonprofit sector	
Country	number of paid FTE workers	number of FTE volunteers	number of paid FTE workers	number of FTE volunteers	In % of paid employment	In % of paid employment and volunteers
Argentina	5,201	7	395,315	264,110	1.3	0.8
Australia	919	1,227	402,574	177,148	0.2	0.4
Austria	1,110		143,637	40,686	0.8	0.6
Belgium	594	1,018	357,802	99,099	0.2	0.4
Brazil	4,182		1,034,550	139,216	0.4	0.4
Colombia	181	22	286,861	90,756	0.1	0.1
Czech Republic	814	816	74,196	40,860	1.1	1.4
Finland	160	367	62,848	74,751	0.3	0.4
France	17,403	30,986	959,821	1,021,655	1.8	2.4
Germany	9,750	28,510	1,440,850	978,074	0.7	1.6
Hungary	342	226	44,938	9,878	0.8	1.0
Ireland	370	234	118,664	31,650	0.3	0.4
Israel	98		145,396	31,261	0.1	0.1
Italy	1,554	6,025	597,655	565,310	0.3	0.7
Japan	7,693	37,785	2,140,079	695,097	0.4	1.6
Netherlands	3,860	8,644	661,652	390,101	0.6	1.2
Norway	1,066	3,635	60,002	103,008	1.8	2.9
Peru	3		129,826	80,144	0.0	0.0
Poland	884	637	122,505	32,140	0.7	1.0
Romania	485	2,828	37,353	46,508	1.3	4.0
Slovakia	138	68	16,196	6,851	0.9	0.9
Spain	9,380	9,794	475,179	253,599	2.0	2.6
United Kingdom	53,726	7,298	1,415,743	1,120,283	3.8	2.4
United States		45,026	8,554,900	4,994,162		0.3

Percentages are in italics where information on numbers of INGO volunteers is not available for inclusion in this calculation.

Source: The Johns Hopkins Comparative Nonprofit Sector Project, 1999; Instituto Nazionale di Statistica, 1999

Record 21b: Revenue structure of INGOs

1995/1996/1997 Country	Cash revenue only			Cash and volunteer input		
	Public sector payments %	Private giving %	Private fees and charges %	Public sector payments %	Private giving %	Private fees and charges %
Argentina	100			100	0	
Australia	30	70		26	74	
Austria	40	55	5			
Belgium	33	58	9	28	64	8
Brazil			100			100
Colombia		99	1		99	1
Czech Republic	37	52	11	23	70	7
Finland	30	8	61	14	58	28
France	43	40	17	16	78	6
Germany	51	41	8	15	83	2
Hungary	66	14	20	64	17	19
Ireland	24	76		22	78	
Israel	23	51	26	23	51	26
Japan	19	27	54	5	82	14
Netherlands	45	35	20	35	50	15
Norway	35	24	41	25	46	29
Peru		3	97		3	97
Poland	19	36	45	19	38	44
Romania	47	31	22	8	88	4
Slovakia	22	21	57	22	24	55
Spain	56	36	8	32	63	5
United Kingdom	40	33	27	38	36	26

Source: The Johns Hopkins Comparative Nonprofit Sector Project, 1999.

Record 22 Networks

Global networks are part of the infrastructure of global civil society. They comprise NGOs and other civil society groups as well as individuals, and are becoming more and more prevalent. These maps offer a sample of the global reach and structure of five of the larger network structures.

Record 22a: Climate Action Network

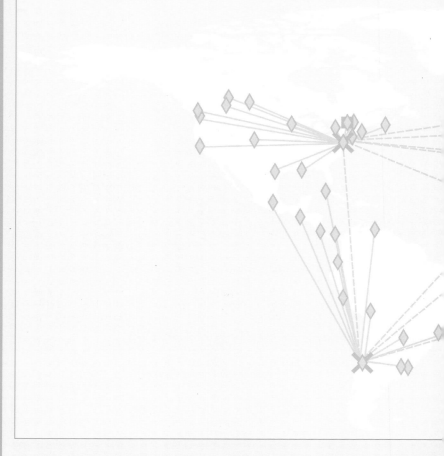

Affiliated Organisations

 Regional coordinator

 Focal Point

 Member

 Regional links

 Global links

Map elements by ESRI (Environmental Systems Research Institute, Inc. http://www.esri.com)
Mapping: Hagai Katz, UCLA

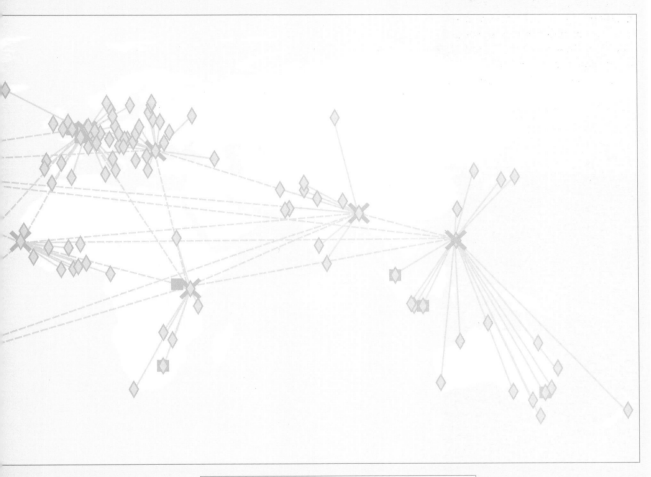

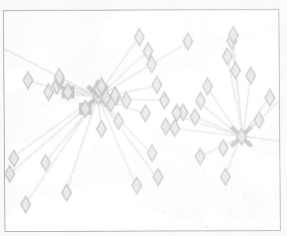

Affiliated Organisations

 Headquarters

 Network contact

Thematic working group

Steering committee member

Map elements by ESRI (Environmental Systems Research Institute, Inc. http://www.esri.co
Mapping: Hagai Katz, UCLA

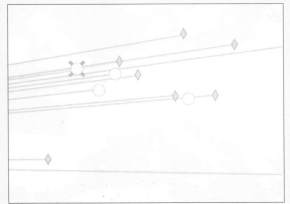

Record 22c: Coalition to stop the use of child soldiers

Affiliated Organisations

⚑ Headquarters

◇ National Coalition

✕ Regional representative

○ Steering committee member

▪ Observer

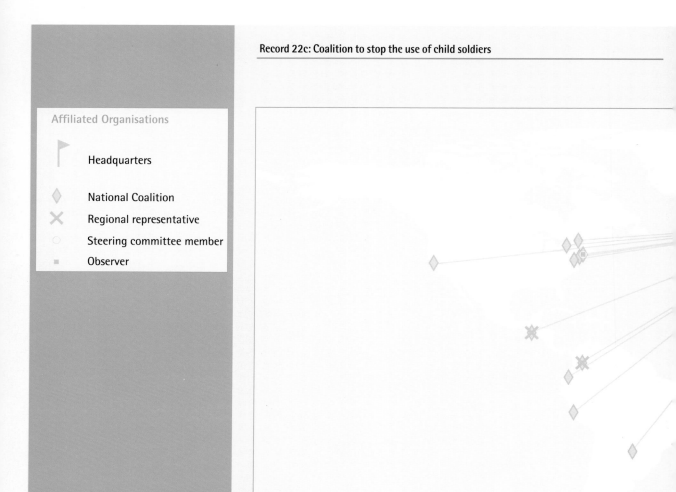

Map elements by ESRI (Environmental Systems Research Institute, Inc. http://www.esri.com)
Mapping: Hagai Katz, UCLA

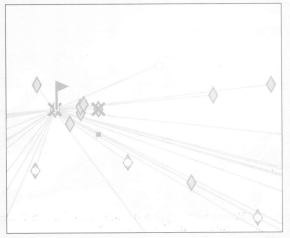

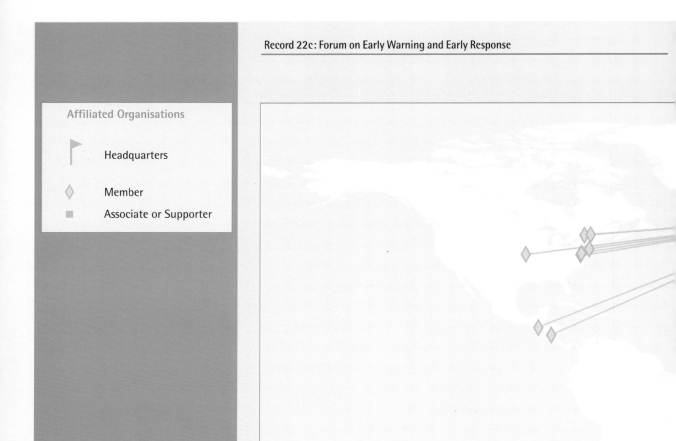

Affiliated Organisations

⚑ Headquarters

◇ Member

■ Associate or Supporter

Map elements by ESRI (Environmental Systems Research Institute, Inc. http://www.esri.com)
Mapping: Hagai Katz, UCLA

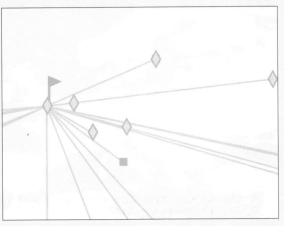

Affiliated Organisations

🚩 Headquarters

◇ Campaign contact

○ Coordinating Committee

Map elements by ESRI (Environmental Systems Research Institute, Inc. http://www.esri.com)
Mapping: Hagai Katz, UCLA

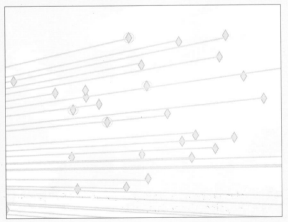

Record 23 Geographic identity

A more transnational or cosmopolitan sense of identity may be one of the features of participants in global civil society. Based on the latest population survey data available and provided by the European and World Values Surveys, this table offers the responses to the following question: 'Which of these geographical groups would you say you 'belong to' first of all?'

- Locality or town where you live
- Region of country where you live
- Your country as a whole
- Continent on which you live
- The world as a whole

Country	in % of all respondents per country	1990–1993 Locality or town	Region or county	Country	Continent	World	2000 Locality or town	Region	Country	Continent	World
Albania							62.0	15.2	21.3	1.4	0.1
Argentina		28.1	3.3	57.8	1.0	9.9	31.5	13.7	41.6	4.0	9.2
Armenia							33.1	10.0	45.5	1.5	10.0
Australia							32.7	12.8	43.8	0.8	10.0
Austria		34.5	31.5	27.3	3.5	3.2	35.0	33.9	24.0	4.2	2.9
Azerbaijan							20.6	16.2	45.1		18.0
Belarus							66.0	1.2	24.8	1.4	6.5
Belgium		49.0	14.0	20.1	7.8	9.1	32.1	20.3	27.9	9.3	10.4
Bosnia & Herzegovina							39.6	13.8	32.2	4.6	9.4
Brazil		36.9	11.2	30.6	1.8	19.6	30.9	11.6	28.5	2.2	26.8
Bulgaria		50.5	8.7	29.7	4.1	7.1	47.0	4.7	41.0	3.8	3.5
Canada		30.9	16.2	39.7	2.9	10.3					
Chile		32.5	14.5	39.6	5.1	8.3	32.4	13.9	39.7	6.1	7.9
China & Tibet		41.9	15.9	38.1	2.0	2.1	40.1	11.8	39.3	4.4	4.4
Colombia							34.5	8.8	25.1	5.4	20.7
Croatia							57.7	7.4	23.1	3.5	8.3
Czech Republic							42.9	13.7	35.5	2.7	5.3
Denmark		52.3	22.2	21.8	1.6	2.1	55.0	21.9	19.8	1.4	1.8
Dominican Republic							41.7	16.8	8.8	12.8	19.8
Estonia		31.2	55.7	8.4	1.4	3.3	61.4	12.2	21.4	1.4	3.6
Finland		32.5	11.9	41.3	5.4	8.8	48.9	12.3	31.2	3.2	4.4
France		40.5	13.8	27.9	7.9	9.9	43.7	12.1	28.5	4.3	11.4
Georgia							29.4	10.1	50.1	1.0	9.4
Germany*		38.0	33.2	15.7	5.9	7.3	55.7	28.8	11.3	2.2	2.0
Ghana							17.2	7.8	56.3	17.2	1.6
Greece							44.8	12.0	33.1	1.2	8.8
Hungary		58.0	5.8	27.4	5.9	2.8	67.3	6.3	20.1	2.0	4.3
Iceland		40.5	5.9	48.4	0.6	4.7	38.3	6.3	50.6	0.7	4.0
India		37.2	14.6	39.0	1.3	7.9	61.9	29.6	8.3	0.2	
Ireland		43.9	13.6	37.3	2.5	2.6	56.6	15.8	24.0	2.2	1.4
Italy		39.8	10.7	27.7	5.5	16.3	53.4	10.6	23.3	4.2	8.5
Japan		36.2	17.9	43.2	1.1	1.5	57.0	17.3	23.5	0.8	1.3
Korea, Rep.		18.1	23.7	58.3			41.5	21.2	33.7	0.5	3.2
Latvia		33.7	55.3	5.8	0.7	4.4	40.6	13.5	38.8	2.2	4.8

Country	in % of all respondents per country	1990–1993					2000				
		Locality or town	Region or county	Country	Continent	World	Locality or town	Region	Country	Continent	World
Lithuania		25.4	66.0	3.1	1.2	4.3	51.4	4.8	37.2	2.8	3.8
Luxembourg							43.1	11.0	24.4	13.4	8.0
Macedonia							*48.8*	*6.9*	*34.7*	*2.6*	*7.0*
Malta							44.1	24.8	25.3	3.9	1.9
Mexico		38.2	15.5	28.4	8.2	9.7	33.4	10.3	35.4	3.7	17.1
Moldova							34.8	9.6	31.4	1.8	22.4
Netherlands		44.1	7.3	35.1	4.4	9.2	39.1	7.7	41.2	4.8	7.2
New Zealand							*28.9*	*7.9*	*53.3*	*1.7*	*8.2*
Nigeria		39.7	10.4	29.7	11.6	8.6	41.7	16.4	30.7	8.9	2.2
Norway		69.2	13.1	14.1	1.2	2.3	*56.3*	*17.8*	*20.2*	*3.2*	*2.6*
Peru							*38.0*	*21.2*	*29.2*	*4.4*	*7.2*
Philippines							*46.6*	*24.8*	*19.9*	*1.5*	*7.2*
Poland		29.0	12.1	52.3	4.2	2.4	62.7	15.0	19.1	2.3	0.9
Portugal		39.8	23.0	23.6	4.0	9.6	36.3	16.0	41.6	1.6	4.5
Romania		48.0	15.0	31.8	2.0	3.2	45.2	19.5	30.4	1.6	3.3
Russian Federation		39.8	28.7	12.6	1.1	17.9	50.6	7.9	25.2	0.4	15.8
Slovakia		36.9	30.7	23.0	4.5	4.9	54.0	10.5	26.7	4.6	4.2
Slovenia		45.6	8.5	41.7	2.0	2.3	52.8	8.7	32.1	2.4	3.9
South Africa		35.6	16.4	38.1	4.6	5.2	*32.7*	*13.3*	*44.9*	*3.7*	*5.4*
Spain		43.6	17.5	30.4	1.4	7.2	45.6	16.5	26.8	1.7	9.4
Sweden		56.3	12.6	24.7	3.2	3.3	58.7	9.5	22.4	4.2	5.3
Switzerland		51.2	20.2	16.6	3.6	8.4	*28.7*	*22.8*	*26.5*	*7.2*	*14.7*
Turkey		33.6	11.7	45.5	1.2	8.0	*25.0*	*7.2*	*51.3*	*0.6*	*15.9*
Ukraine							49.5	7.7	26.1	1.8	14.9
United Kingdom		41.9	19.5	28.2	2.3	8.1	56.1	12.4	24.8	1.9	4.7
United States		38.1	12.1	30.2	3.7	15.9	32.6	10.9	34.4	2.6	19.5
Uruguay							23.0	7.7	52.0	6.9	10.4
Venezuela							26.4	18.8	42.1	3.8	9.0
Yugoslavia							55.1	11.3	25.8	2.6	5.3
Average		40.1	19.0	30.6	3.5	7.2	43.4	13.6	31.6	3.5	8.0

Values in italics indicate that 1995-1997 data have been used.

*1990-1993 data West Germany only

Sources: © European Values Survey, WORC, Tilburg University, Netherlands, 1999-2000, by permission; © World Values Survey, Institute for Social Research, University of Michigan, by permission; Inglehart, R., Basañez, M., and Moreno, A., Human Values and Beliefs: A Cross-Cultural Sourcebook: Political, Religious, Sexual, and Economic Norms in 43 Societies: Findings from the 1990-1993 World Values Survey, The University of Michigan Press, Ann Arbor, 1998.

Record 24 Tolerance

Using two different questions from the latest available European and World Values Surveys, these tables present the idea of tolerance as part of a general value system and as an attitudinal measure of discrimination against 'outsiders'. The first (24a) shows percentages of respondents who mention 'tolerance' in answer to the following question: 'Here is a list of qualities which children can be encouraged to learn at home. Which, if any, do you consider to be especially important?' (Multiple responses possible.)

- Tolerance and respect for other people
- Independence
- Responsibility
- Obedience
- Unselfishness

The second table (24b) shows responses to the following question: 'On this list are various groups of people. Could you please tell me any that you would not, generally speaking, like to have as your neighbours?'

- People of different races
- Immigrants/foreign workers

Record 24a

in % all respondents per country Country	Mentioned 1990-1993	Mentioned 2000	% change 1990-2000
Albania		85.5	
Argentina	77.6	70.2	-9.5
Armenia		48.5	
Australia		80.9	
Austria	65.7	71.4	8.7
Azerbaijan		59.1	
Bangladesh		69.2	
Belarus	79.8	71.8	-10.0
Belgium	67.2	83.5	24.3
Bosnia & Herzegovina		61.3	
Brazil	65.7	59.4	-9.6
Bulgaria	51.5	58.9	14.4
Canada	80.2	81.6	1.7
Chile	79.0	76.0	-3.8
China & Tibet		43.0	
Colombia		68.5	
Croatia		64.6	
Czech Republic	66.1	62.9	-4.8
Denmark	80.5	87.0	8.1
Dominican Republic		67.9	
El Salvador		58.8	
Estonia	70.2	70.9	1.0
Finland	78.9	82.6	4.7
France	78.0	84.4	8.2
Georgia		57.0	
Germany	75.8	71.7	-5.4
Greece		55.9	
Hungary	61.6	64.7	5.0
Iceland	93.0	84.1	-9.6

in % all respondents per country Country	Mentioned 1990-1993	Mentioned 2000	% change 1990-2000
India	59.2	63.2	6.8
Ireland	76.4	75.0	-1.9
Israel		84.1	
Italy	66.9	74.7	11.7
Japan	59.5	71.2	19.7
Korea, Rep.	55.4	46.9	-15.3
Latvia	69.7	69.5	-0.3
Lithuania	56.7	56.5	-0.4
Luxembourg		78.0	
Macedonia		*70.6*	
Malta		61.0	
Mexico	64.3	71.8	11.7
Moldova		*63.4*	
Netherlands	87.1	90.4	3.8
Nigeria	75.0	59.1	-21.2
Norway	63.7	*65.9*	*3.5*
Pakistan		53.8	
Peru		*63.0*	
Philippines		60.2	
Poland		79.6	
Portugal	67.1	65.3	-2.7
Puerto Rico		*74.4*	
Romania	56.0	55.6	-0.7
Russian Federation*	70.2	66.9	-4.7
Slovakia	55.0	57.0	3.6
Slovenia	74.5	70.1	-5.9
South Africa	58.6	73.6	25.6
South Korea	55.4	64.7	16.8
Spain	73.3	82.1	12.0
Sweden	90.8	92.5	1.9
Switzerland	77.4	*78.6*	*1.6*
Tanzania		83.4	
Turkey	69.1	64.0	-7.4
Uganda		56.6	
Ukraine		65.0	
United Kingdom	79.6	78.8	-1.0
United States	72.4	79.8	10.2
Uruguay		*71.1*	
Venezuela		79.6	
Vietnam		67.9	
Yugoslavia		61.0	
Zimbabwe		76.7	
Average:	70.1	69.4	-1.1

Values in italics indicate that 1995-1997 data has been used

* Russian Federation figures for 1990 are for USSR

Sources: © European Values Survey, WORC, Tilburg University, Netherlands, 1999-2000, by permission; © World Values Survey, Institute for Social Research, University of Michigan, by permission; Inglehart, R., Basañez, M., and Moreno, A., Human Values and Beliefs: A Cross-Cultural Sourcebook: Political, Religious, Sexual, and Economic Norms in 43 Societies: Findings from the 1990–1993 World Values Survey, The University of Michigan Press, Ann Arbor, 1998.

Record 24b: Unwillingness to have people of a different race, immigrants or foreign workers as a neighbour

| in % all respondents per country | 2000 | | | |
| | Immigrants & foreign workers | | Different race | |
Country	Not mentioned	Mentioned	Not mentioned	Mentioned
Albania	89.4	10.6	91.2	8.8
Albania	89.4	10.6	91.2	8.8
Argentina	94.3	5.7	95.4	4.6
Armenia	78.3	21.7	80.8	19.2
Australia	95.4	4.6	95.2	4.8
Austria	87.8	12.2	93.3	6.7
Azerbaijan	80.1	19.9	87.7	12.3
Bangladesh	70.5	29.5	82.7	17.3
Belarus	82.9	17.1	83.5	16.5
Belgium	83.9	16.1	85.7	14.3
Bosnia & Herzegovina	80.0	20.0	75.5	24.5
Brazil	96.5	3.5	97.2	2.8
Bulgaria	75.4	24.6	71.9	28.1
Chile	88.3	11.7	88.0	12.0
China & Tibet	78.7	21.3	76.1	23.9
Colombia	93.1	6.9	97.9	2.1
Croatia	80.7	19.3	82.7	17.3
Czech Republic	80.6	19.4	90.1	9.9
Denmark	89.4	10.6	92.6	7.4
Dominican Republic	82.4	17.6	81.5	18.5
Estonia	79.1	20.9	84.9	15.1
Finland	87.0	13.0	87.7	12.3
France	88.0	12.0	91.1	8.9
Georgia	89.2	10.8	90.7	9.3
Germany	89.5	10.5	94.5	5.5
Ghana	86.4	13.6	88.6	11.4
Greece	80.6	19.4	75.6	24.4
Hungary	38.0	62.0	48.0	52.0
Iceland	97.0	3.0	96.9	3.1
India	66.9	33.1	62.7	37.3
Ireland	87.7	12.3	87.9	12.1
Italy	83.5	16.5	84.5	15.6
Korea, Rep.	60.5	39.5	0.0	0.0
Latvia	90.2	9.8	95.2	4.8
Lithuania	76.4	23.6	90.3	9.7
Luxembourg	91.6	8.4	93.7	6.3
Macedonia	76.3	23.7	73.6	26.4
Malta	84.3	15.7	81.0	19.0
Mexico	72.9	27.1	73.3	26.7
Moldova	86.8	13.2	92.2	7.8
Netherlands	94.7	5.3	94.5	5.5
Nigeria	72.6	27.4	75.5	24.5
Norway	88.8	11.2	90.8	9.2
Peru	89.7	10.3	88.4	11.6
Philippines	80.1	19.9	75.8	24.2

Record 24b continued

| in % all respondents per country | 2000 Immigrants & foreign workers | | Different race | |
Country	Not mentioned	Mentioned	Not mentioned	Mentioned
Poland	76.4	23.6	82.7	17.3
Portugal			92.4	7.6
Romania	78.9	21.1	75.8	24.2
Russian Federation	89.0	11.0	91.9	8.1
Slovakia	77.1	22.9	83.0	17.0
Slovenia	84.0	16.0	88.0	12.0
South Africa	*78.7*	*21.3*	*88.8*	*11.2*
Spain	90.7	9.3	89.7	10.3
Sweden	97.2	2.8	97.5	2.5
Switzerland	*90.0*	*10.0*	*91.3*	*8.7*
Turkey	*63.6*	*36.4*	*67.8*	*32.2*
Ukraine	85.1	14.9	89.5	10.5
United Kingdom	83.2	16.8	90.1	9.9
United States	89.9	10.1	91.8	8.2
Uruguay	*92.9*	*7.1*	*93.2*	*6.8*
Venezuela	*78.1*	*21.9*	*80.0*	*20.0*
Yugoslavia	*72.4*	*27.6*	*15.8*	*84.2*
Average	82.9	17.1	83.2	15.2

Values in italics indicate that 1995-1997 data have been used

Sources: © European Values Survey, WORC, Tilburg University, Netherlands, 1999-2000, by permission; © World Values Survey, Institute for Social Research, University of Michigan, by permission.

Record 25 Value attached to democracy

This table shows to what extent people in different countries believe in democracy, using the latest available data from the European and World Values Surveys. The surveys ask respondents whether they agree or disagree more or less with the following statements about democracy:

- Democracy may have problems but it's better than any other form of government
- In a democracy, the economic system runs badly
- Democracies are indecisive and have too much squabbling
- Democracies aren't good at maintaining order

The average level of agreement is given for each country, on a 1–10 scale, where 1 indicates strong disagreement with the item and 10 indicates strong agreement.

| Country | in average agreement score per country | 2000 | | | |
		Best despite problems	Bad for economy	Indecisive/ squabbling	Not good at order
Albania		8.9	4.6	5.5	4.9
Argentina		8.1	5.0	6.0	4.4
Armenia		6.5	5.4	6.0	5.6
Australia		7.6	4.8	5.5	4.8
Austria		8.7	3.6	4.9	3.2
Azerbaijan		7.5	4.3	4.1	4.1
Bangladesh		9.1	3.8	4.6	4.1
Belarus		7.5	4.7	5.0	5.1
Belgium		8.5	4.6	6.2	4.8
Bosnia & Herzegovina		8.0	4.0	4.7	4.0
Brazil		7.8	6.8	8.0	5.8
Bulgaria		7.7	5.1	5.2	4.8
Chile		7.3	4.5	5.5	4.9
Croatia		8.2	4.5	4.3	3.8
Czech Republic		8.0	5.0	5.6	5.7
Denmark		9.1	3.8	5.0	3.8
Dominican Republic		8.5	4.4	5.0	4.8
Estonia		7.3	4.9	5.4	4.8
Finland		7.8	4.4	5.4	4.2
France		8.6	5.5	6.8	5.8
Georgia		7.4	4.7	5.4	5.3
Germany		8.4	3.6	4.6	3.7
Greece		8.7	5.9	5.7	5.5
Hungary		7.1	5.0	6.1	5.0
Iceland		8.5	3.8	3.9	3.5
India		8.0	6.1	6.2	5.2
Ireland		7.9	4.3	5.0	4.4
Italy		8.1	4.9	5.7	4.2
Japan		7.3	4.3	5.1	4.3
Korea, Rep.		7.7	4.3	4.9	4.3
Latvia		7.3	5.5	6.3	5.3
Lithuania		7.3	5.2	6.2	5.6

Country	in average agreement score per country	Best despite problems	Bad for economy	Indecisive/ squabbling	Not good at order
			2000		
Luxembourg		8.7	3.8	5.4	3.7
Macedonia		*6.9*	*5.3*	*5.7*	*5.3*
Malta		8.2	4.0	4.3	3.9
Mexico		*6.9*	*5.5*	*5.7*	*5.3*
Moldova		*6.7*	*5.7*	*6.0*	*5.6*
Netherlands		8.3	3.7	5.2	4.5
New Zealand		*7.5*	*4.5*	*5.3*	*4.5*
Nigeria		*8.3*	*4.3*	*4.9*	*4.7*
Norway		*9.0*	*4.2*	*5.7*	*4.3*
Peru		*7.4*	*5.0*	*5.7*	*5.3*
Philippines		*6.7*	*5.3*	*5.5*	*5.5*
Poland		7.4	5.5	7.0	6.5
Portugal		8.0	5.1	6.0	5.3
Romania		7.2	5.8	6.8	5.5
Russian Federation		6.1	5.8	6.7	6.4
Slovakia		7.4	5.5	5.9	5.1
Slovenia		7.4	5.5	6.5	5.4
South Africa		*7.7*	*4.8*	*5.4*	*5.0*
Spain		8.0	4.7	5.1	3.9
Sweden		8.3	3.7	5.4	3.8
Switzerland		*8.0*	*4.4*	*6.5*	*4.5*
Turkey		7.8	4.6	5.7	4.6
Ukraine		7.1	5.1	5.8	5.6
United Kingdom		7.7	4.1	4.8	4.4
United States		7.8	4.4	5.1	4.4
Uruguay		*8.2*	*4.4*	*5.2*	*4.4*
Venezuela		*7.9*	*7.6*	*7.3*	*6.2*
Yugoslavia		*7.9*	*4.5*	*5.3*	*4.7*
Average		**7.8**	**4.8**	**5.6**	**4.8**

Information restructured from original 1-4 scale to facilitate comparisons. Values in italics indicate that 1995-1997 data has been used.

Sources: © European Values Survey, WORC, Tilburg University, Netherlands, 1999-2000, by permission; © World Values Survey, Institute for Social Research, University of Michigan, by permission; Inglehart, R., Basañez, M., and Moreno, A., Human Values and Beliefs: A Cross-Cultural Sourcebook: Political, Religious, Sexual, and Economic Norms in 43 Societies: Findings from the 1990–1993 World Values Survey, The University of Michigan Press, Ann Arbor, 1998.

Record 26 Confidence in institutions

This table shows the latest available data from the European and World Values Surveys to show to what extent people in different countries have confidence in civil society institutions such as the church, trade unions, and the press, as well as state institutions such as parliament and government, and how their confidence in these institutions has evolved over the years. For 2000, it also illustrates faith in the main global governance institution, the United Nations. The higher the number, the greatest the average degree of confidence in the institution in question.

Country	in average agreement score per country	1990–1993						2000						
		Church	Press	Trade unions	Companies	Parliament	Government	Church	Press	Trade unions	Companies	Parliament	Government	United Nations
Albania								5.8	4.0	3.5	4.1	5.8	5.2	7.9
Argentina		5.5	4.3	2.6	3.9	3.4		5.8	4.7	2.8	4.3	3.3	4.0	4.7
Armenia								6.5	4.5	3.5	5.2	3.8	4.7	6.3
Australia								5.3	3.9	4.2	5.8	4.6	4.2	5.5
Austria		5.6	4.0	4.7	5.1	5.1		5.0	4.7	4.5	5.1	5.2		5.0
Azerbaijan								6.5	4.2	4.4	4.8	6.8	7.9	4.1
Bangladesh								9.5	6.5	5.3	6.2	7.5	7.3	7.2
Belarus		5.9	4.5	4.1	4.9	4.5	4.0	6.5	4.9	4.3	5.8	4.6		5.4
Belgium		5.4	5.0	4.7	5.4	5.0		4.9	4.7	4.6		4.7		5.1
Bosnia & Herzegovina								6.8	5.5	5.9	6.0	5.8	6.6	6.1
Brazil		7.2	5.6	5.2	5.8	3.4		6.9	5.8	5.3	6.2	3.8	4.8	6.4
Bulgaria		4.1	4.8	4.5	4.7	5.4	4.3	4.6	4.3	3.4		4.2		4.9
Canada		6.4	5.3	4.7	5.5	5.0	4.9							
Chile		7.7	5.5	5.7	6.0	6.5	5.7	7.6	5.3	5.1	5.8	4.6	5.5	6.1
Colombia								7.8	5.1	4.4	5.8	3.7	4.5	
Croatia								6.2	3.8	4.3	4.1	4.0		4.9
Czech Republic		4.7	5.2	4.2	4.2	5.3	5.3	3.6	5.0	3.9	4.2	3.5		5.4
Denmark		5.4	4.6	5.2	5.0	5.1		5.8	4.7	5.4		5.4		6.0
Dominican Republic								7.5	4.9	4.0	5.5	3.5	3.4	5.3
Estonia		5.7	6.1	4.3	3.6	6.4	3.1	5.1	5.0	4.5		4.3		5.0
Finland		4.6	5.0	4.7	5.0	4.7		5.9	4.9	5.6	5.1	5.2		5.2
France		5.1	4.6	4.2	6.0	5.1		4.8	4.4	4.4	5.1	4.6		5.4
Georgia								7.3	5.7	3.8	5.4	4.6	5.1	5.7
Germany		5.1	4.5	4.6	5.0	5.3		4.4	4.7	4.9	4.9	4.7		5.3
Ghana								8.9	7.2	7.6	7.9	8.3		8.7
Greece								6.4	4.4	3.4	3.4	4.1		3.1
Hungary		5.8	4.8	4.2	4.5	4.8		5.2	4.3	3.7		4.5		5.7
Iceland		6.5	4.1	5.6	4.9	5.6		6.2	5.0	5.5	5.0	6.5		6.5
India		8.2	6.4	5.5	6.0	6.3	5.6	6.9	6.1	5.6	6.0	6.0	5.7	5.7
Ireland		7.2	4.8	5.2	5.6	5.6		5.9	4.9	5.4		4.6		6.1
Italy		6.2	4.8	4.5	5.9	4.4		6.6	4.8	4.3	5.3	4.7		6.4
Japan		3.3	5.7	4.5	4.6	4.6		3.1	6.3	5.3	4.8	4.3	4.6	5.9
Korea, Rep.		5.9	6.2	6.1	4.5	4.6		5.2	6.1	5.7	4.7	4.5	5.2	7.0
Latvia		6.1	6.1	4.0	3.0	6.9	3.2	6.4	5.2	4.3		4.1		5.1
Lithuania		6.6	6.1	4.4	3.7	6.1	3.3	6.6	6.4	5.1	3.9	3.5		5.1
Luxembourg								5.3	5.2	5.5	4.8	5.9		6.2
Macedonia								4.6	4.0	3.4	4.2	3.3	3.5	5.3

Country	in average agreement score per country	1990–1993						2000						
		Church	Press	Trade unions	Companies	Parliament	Government	Church	Press	Trade unions	Companies	Parliament	Government	United Nations
Malta								7.9	4.6	5.3		5.4		5.9
Mexico		7.4	5.3	4.6	5.1	4.4	3.9	7.4	5.5	4.5	5.4	4.8	4.7	5.2
Moldova								7.2	4.7	4.5	5.2	4.7	4.9	6.8
Netherlands		4.4	4.7	5.3	5.2	5.5		4.5	5.7	5.7		5.7		5.7
New Zealand								5.1	4.7	3.9	5.1	3.7	3.7	5.7
Nigeria		8.8	7.2	7.0	7.6	5.9	4.9	8.4	6.3	5.8	6.6	4.8	3.9	7.1
Norway		5.3	5.3	5.8	5.6	5.9		5.7	4.8	6.0	5.8	6.2	6.1	6.5
Peru								7.4	4.8	3.7	4.6	3.6	5.2	5.7
Philippines								8.8	6.8	5.9	6.3	6.0	6.0	7.0
Poland		8.0	5.5	3.7	6.8	7.1	2.2	6.9	5.4	4.6		4.6		5.9
Portugal		6.4	4.9	4.5	5.3	4.7		7.3	6.1	5.2	5.4	5.2		6.3
Romania		7.2	4.3	4.4	4.7	3.7		7.8	5.0	4.4		3.5		5.0
Russian Federation*		6.3	5.2	5.1	5.1	5.2	5.1	6.0	4.2	4.1	3.3	3.4		3.7
Slovakia		5.4	4.8	4.0	4.4	4.6	4.6	6.6	5.3	4.9		4.8		5.2
Slovenia		4.9	5.5	4.2	4.7	4.8		4.6	6.1	4.5		4.3		5.4
South Africa		7.8	5.6	5.3	6.9	6.4	6.0	8.1	5.7	4.7	6.8	6.2	6.3	5.6
Spain		5.5	5.4	4.9	5.2	4.7	3.9	5.0	5.0	4.3	4.6	5.3		4.9
Sweden		4.7	4.6	4.9	5.6	5.3		5.3	5.3	5.1		5.5		6.5
Switzerland								4.9	4.2	4.7	5.1	5.1	5.4	5.0
Turkey		6.8	5.2	5.0	4.4	6.0	5.3	6.0	5.4	5.4	5.8	5.0	4.9	4.9
Ukraine								6.4	5.2	4.6	3.6	3.9		5.5
United Kingdom		5.9	3.7	4.3	5.4	5.3		5.7	3.6	4.5	4.9	4.8		5.6
United States		7.3	5.6	4.8	5.6	5.2	5.8	7.5	4.5	4.9	5.6	4.6	4.6	5.4
Uruguay								5.9	5.8	4.5	4.9	4.7	4.7	5.6
Venezuela								7.5	6.2	3.8	5.7	3.5	3.8	4.9
Yugoslavia								4.7	4.1	4.1	4.6	4.5	4.7	3.8
Average		6.1	5.1	4.8	5.1	5.2	4.5	6.2	5.1	4.7	5.2	4.8	5.0	5.6

Information restructured from original 1-4 scale to facilitate comparisons. Values in italics indicate that 1995-1997 data has been used.

*Russian Federation figures for 1990 are for USSR

Sources: © European Values Survey, WORC, Tilburg University, Netherlands, 1999-2000, by permission; © World Values Survey, Institute for Social Research, University of Michigan, by permission; Inglehart, R., Basañez, M., and Moreno, A., Human Values and Beliefs: A Cross-Cultural Sourcebook: Political, Religious, Sexual, and Economic Norms in 43 Societies: Findings from the 1990–1993 World Values Survey, The University of Michigan Press, Ann Arbor, 1998.

Record 27 Willingness to help immigrants

This table is a measure of the extent to which people are willing to translate cosmopolitan values into concrete action. Using the European Values Survey for 2000, it shows responses to the question 'Would you be prepared to actually do something to improve the conditions of immigrants in your country'? Unfortunately, these data are available only for European/developed countries.

| Country | in % of all respondents per country | | 2000 | | |
	Absolutely Yes	Yes	Maybe	No	Absolutely No
Austria	2.8	17.1	47.6	24.8	7.7
Belarus	0.0	1.3	7.9	41.6	49.2
Belgium	8.6	22.3	36.5	19.1	13.6
Bulgaria	1.9	13.9	41.5	32.6	10.1
Croatia	5.7	27.2	47.5	15.6	4.0
Czech Republic	0.9	13.9	53.1	27.5	4.5
Denmark	5.6	24.5	36.0	24.1	9.9
Estonia	1.3	7.7	40.0	40.1	10.9
Finland	2.6	20.2	45.8	23.4	7.9
France	6.6	18.7	37.4	18.8	18.5
Germany	3.9	19.4	53.1	17.0	6.6
Greece	2.1	19.6	52.7	22.6	2.9
Hungary	1.5	6.1	29.2	35.7	27.4
Iceland	3.6	31.0	49.8	13.1	2.5
Ireland	7.4	27.2	48.7	15.6	1.1
Italy	6.0	40.2	41.7	10.8	1.3
Latvia	0.9	11.2	27.8	45.6	14.5
Lithuania	0.9	3.3	24.8	54.3	16.7
Luxembourg	11.7	29.4	35.6	18.1	5.2
Malta	3.1	23.4	53.7	17.4	2.3
Netherlands	2.8	33.2	46.3	15.7	2.0
Poland	2.6	13.4	44.6	32.1	7.4
Portugal	7.6	12.8	53.3	21.1	5.2
Romania	9.1	12.7	33.9	20.2	24.0
Russia	0.8	10.5	30.6	38.4	19.6
Slovakia	2.6	18.0	42.2	24.5	12.7
Slovenia	4.9	23.3	48.9	18.8	4.1
Spain	5.5	29.5	54.4	9.3	1.3
Sweden	10.7	56.8	25.5	6.2	0.8
Ukraine	1.7	6.8	19.5	37.7	34.2
United Kingdom	3.4	28.7	42.1	29.7	9.4
Average	4.2	20.1	40.4	24.9	10.9

Source: © European Values Survey, WORC, Tilburg University, Netherlands, 1999-2000, by permission.

This table, using the latest available data from the European and World Values Surveys, shows the extent to which respondents are members of community action groups, organisations concerned with the environment, those concerned with development and human rights, and peace organisations. The table also offers data showing what proportion of respondents volunteers for these types of associations. The following question was asked: 'Look carefully at the following list of voluntary organisations and activities and say...

a) Which, if any, do you belong to?
b) Which, if any, are you currently doing unpaid work for?

- community action on issues like poverty, employment, housing, racial equality
- Third world development and human rights
- Environment, conservation, ecology
- Peace movement'

in % of respondents per country who are members of or volunteers in organisations, by type — Country	1990–1993 Membership				1990–1993 Volunteering (unpaid)				2000 Membership				2000 Volunteering (unpaid)			
	Community action	Third world/human rights	Environment	Peace	Community action	Third world/human rights	Environment	Peace	Community action	Third world/human rights	Environment	Peace	Community action	Third world/human rights	Environment	Peace
Argentina	1.3	0.4	0.2	0.2	1.1	0.2	0.1	0.1	3.2	0.5	2.2		2.6	0.3	1.4	0.7
Austria	2.2	1.6	2.9	0.8	1.4	0.7	1.4	0.3	3.0	3.2	9.6	1.2	1.3	0.8	2.3	2.7
Bangladesh									25.9	10.9	20.3	23.0	27.0	12.0	21.6	30.0
Belarus									0.1	0.5	0.9	0.1	0.9	0.7	2.2	0.5
Belgium	4.6	6.5	7.7	2.2	2.9	3.3	2.6	1	5.0	9.9	10.5	2.4	2.7	5.0	3.3	2.9
Bulgaria	2	1.5	3.8	1.1	1.7	1.4	3.4	0.9	1.1	0.4	1.5	0.7	0.8	0.3	1.5	0.8
Canada	5.1	4.6	7.5	2	4	2.7	3.5	1.6	7.3	4.5	8.1	1.8	4.6	2.4	3.9	5.4
Chile	4.1	1.3	1.6	0.8	3.3	0.9	0.9	0.5	4.9	2.0	3.1	1.7	3.8	1.7	2.2	4.8
China	0.5	0.2	0.8	0.3	3.9	0.1	1.5	0.5	1.5	0.4	1.2	0.9	14.2	4.6	27.9	15.1
Croatia									1.3	0.5	3.0	1.0	0.7	0.4	2.1	1.4
Czech Republic									3.2	0.8	6.6	1.4	1.9	0.4	3.0	1.1
Denmark	5.2	2.8	12.5	2.1	1.9	0.9	0.9	0.2	6.2	4.1	13.2	0.8	3.1	1.2	2.3	0.8
Estonia	4.5	0.6	2.7	1.3	4	0.9	2	0.9	1.8	0.1	1.7	0.2	1.8	0.3	1.2	1.4
Finland	3.2	5.9	5.5	1.7	2.9	2.9	4.3	1.2	2.6	5.9	4.8	1.3	1.5	3.3	2.1	1.8
France	3.3	2.6	2.3	0.5	2.9	1.4	1.5	0.5	2.5	1.2	2.1	0.4	1.7	0.6	0.9	0.1
Germany*	1.7	2.1	4.5	2	1	0.8	1.4	1	0.7	0.4	2.2	0.2	0.3	0.1	0.9	1.8
Greece									4.3	5.0	11.0	4.1	6.7	5.7	9.5	3.0
Hungary	1.4	0.2	1.4	0.5	1.5	0.3	1.3	0.2	1.2	0.4	1.9	0.3	1.1	0.2	1.9	0.2
Iceland	2	3.4	4.8	1.4	0.6	0.4	2	0.3	2.5	7.5	4.6	1.1	0.7	1.3	1.3	2.3
India									6.0	2.8	7.0	4.8	5.3	2.2	5.3	5.5
Ireland	3.3	1.6	2.2	0.6	2.8	1.3	0.6	0.2	5.8	3.0	3.2	1.5	3.4	2.0	1.3	2.8
Italy	2.5	1.1	2.9	1.1	2	0.7	1.4	0.6	2.4	2.9	3.8	1.4	1.8	1.9	1.8	0.4
Japan	0.2	0.2	1.1	0.6	0.5	0.2	1.2	0.8	1.2	1.7	3.2	2.0	0.4	0.3	1.2	1.2
Korea, Rep.	12.5	2.4	2	2	3.4	1.8	2.4	2.1	6.9	2.3	6.2	1.8	6.9	1.3	4.5	3.9
Latvia	5.4	1.3	4.3	1.2	8.4	4	4.9	0.9	0.7	0.6	0.7	0.2	1.7	0.3	0.5	0.3

in % of respondents per country who are members of or volunteers in organisations, by type	1990–1993 Membership				1990–1993 Volunteering (unpaid)				2000 Membership				2000 Volunteering (unpaid)			
Country	Community action	Third world/human rights	Environment	Peace	Community action	Third world/human rights	Environment	Peace	Community action	Third world/human rights	Environment	Peace	Community action	Third world/human rights	Environment	Peace
Lithuania	2.1	1	2.1	0.6	1.5	0.9	1.8	0.8	0.7	0.4	0.8	0.2	0.7	0.3	0.6	0.3
Luxembourg									5.1	9.7	9.7	2.2	2.8	5.0	4.1	2.3
Malta									2.8	0.3	2.0	0.2	3.9	1.6	1.9	1.7
Mexico	4.3	0.9	2.8	1.4	2.7	0.6	2.4	0.7	5.0	2.5	4.7	2.8	4.2	1.4	3.4	3.3
Netherlands	5	14.1	23.3	2.9	2.5	3	2.9	1.3	6.9	24.4	45.1	2.8	4.0	4.1	2.4	0.5
Philippines									7.2	5.0	8.2	11.8	6.5	5.7	9.0	8.8
Poland		0.1	1.5	0.2		0.5	1.6	0.1	1.9	0.3	1.4	0.4	1.3	0.2	0.7	0.5
Portugal	1.7	0.6	1.5	0.5	0.8	0.6	0.7	0.2	1.5	1.0	0.9	0.9	1.1	0.8	0.6	0.1
Romania	1.1	0.2	1	0.2	0.6	0.1	0.9	0.1	0.9	0.6	1.0	0.1	0.6	0.4	0.6	0.3
Russian Federation**	2.5	0.3	1.6	1.1	1.7	0.3	1.3	0.8	0.9	0.1	0.7	0.1	0.6	0.0	0.4	0.3
Slovakia		0.4	5.8	1.6		0.2	3	0.1	8.3	0.2	2.6	0.3	6.8	0.2	2.0	4.7
Slovenia	5.8	0.1	1.7	0.1	2.7	0.5	1.4	0.3	9.2	0.8	3.3	0.8	5.8	0.4	2.9	1.3
South Africa									6.6	2.2	3.8	4.1	4.5	1.3	1.8	6.1
Spain	1.2	1	1.4	0.7	0.4	0.8	1	0.5	2.1	2.7	2.0	1.1	1.7	1.4	1.1	0.8
Sweden	2.2	9.3	10.6	3.1	1	3.2	2.5	1.5	9.4	15.0	35.3	1.5	5.5	4.5	3.8	0.4
Uganda									10.5	4.9	9.7	10.3	6.2	2.9	6.9	12.3
Ukraine									1.9	0.6	0.6	0.1	1.0	0.2	0.3	0.4
United Kingdom***	3.5	2.3	5.9	1.3	1	1.1	1.8	0.6	3.2	2.5	1.4	1.2	1.4	2.9	8.2	1.1
United States	4.6	1.7	8.5	2	3	0.9	3.5	0.7	12.9	5.5	15.9	4.3	7.3	2.9	8.8	9.3
Venezuela									10.3	8.9	11.9	5.8				
Vietnam									26.2	1.5	7.6	9.2	25.8	1.3	7.9	26.9
Yugoslavia									0.6	0.8	2.5	0.4	0.3	0.3	1.3	0.8
Zimbabwe									4.8	1.6	2.6	2.9	2.1	0.5	1.4	6.0
Average	3.3	2.3	4.3	1.2	2.3	1.2	1.9	0.7	5.0	3.4	6.4	2.5	4.1	1.9	3.7	3.8

Data in italics are for 1995-1997.

*1990-1993 data West-Germany only

** Russian Federation figures for 1990 are for USSR

***UK excluding Northern Ireland for 1990-1993 data

Sources: © European Values Survey, WORC, Tilburg University, Netherlands, 1999-2000, by permission; © World Values Survey, Institute for Social Research, University of Michigan, by permission; Inglehart, R., Basañez, M., and Moreno, A., Human Values and Beliefs: A Cross-Cultural Sourcebook: Political, Religious, Sexual, and Economic Norms in 43 Societies: Findings from the 1990–1993 World Values Survey, The University of Michigan Press, Ann Arbor, 1998.

Record 29 Participation in political action

The extent to which people are prepared to take political action for or against a particular cause can be considered as a general measure of political mobilisation. This table, based on the latest European and World Values Surveys, shows responses to the question to what extent people have taken such action. The responses on 'lawful demonstrations' for the former Eastern bloc countries, which are high, may be skewed by past participation in the quasi-obligatory manifestations of the old regime.

Country	in % of all respondents per country	1990–1993 Sign petition	Join boycott	Attend lawful demonstration	Join unofficial strike	Occupy building	2000 Sign petition	Join boycott	Attend lawful demonstration	Join unofficial strike	Occupy building
Argentina		22.4	3.4	15.0	7.3	2.7	30.4	1.4	16.7	5.9	3.1
Armenia		0.0	0.0	0.0	0.0	0.0	17.8	12.1	28.2	15.0	1.2
Australia		0.0	0.0	0.0	0.0	0.0	78.4	21.5	17.8	8.1	2.0
Austria		47.7	5.2	10.4	1.1	0.7	56.7	9.8	16.7	2.2	0.7
Azerbaijan		0.0	0.0	0.0	0.0	0.0	10.1	2.6	20.5	9.0	0.2
Belarus		27.0	4.6	18.1	2.3	0.8	8.8	4.1	16.3	1.1	0.6
Belgium		50.2	10.2	25.4	7.2	4.3	71.4	12.0	39.6	8.9	6.0
Bosnia & Herzegovina		0.0	0.0	0.0	0.0	0.0	22.0	8.8	9.0	5.8	0.7
Brazil		50.8	10.5	17.9	7.9	1.9	47.1	6.4	24.8	6.5	2.7
Bulgaria		21.6	3.4	14.5	3.2	1.5	11.2	3.6	14.8	4.9	3.1
Canada		76.8	22.3	20.8	7.0	3.0	0.0	0.0	0.0	0.0	0.0
Chile		22.9	4.0	30.1	8.2	4.2	16.6	2.4	14.6	5.3	2.2
Colombia		0.0	0.0	0.0	0.0	0.0	18.9	7.7	11.5	4.9	1.3
Croatia		0.0	0.0	0.0	0.0	0.0	37.4	8.0	7.7	3.2	1.2
Czech Republic		0.0	0.0	0.0	0.0	0.0	58.7	9.2	27.8	10.2	1.0
Denmark		51.0	10.7	27.6	17.4	2.0	56.8	24.9	29.3	22.2	2.8
Dominican Republic		0.0	0.0	0.0	0.0	0.0	14.9	5.6	26.5	8.4	4.6
Estonia		39.0	3.3	25.9	4.2	0.8	20.7	2.9	11.1	1.3	0.1
Finland		40.7	13.5	14.2	8.1	1.6	49.5	19.9	19.8	9.6	6.8
France		53.7	12.5	32.7	10.1	7.9	68.3	13.2	39.7	12.6	9.0
Georgia		0.0	0.0	0.0	0.0	0.0	14.0	5.8	19.3	9.8	0.8
Germany*		56.5	10.0	20.5	2.3	1.1	54.5	8.5	34.1	1.8	0.8
Ghana		0.0	0.0	0.0	0.0	0.0	11.9	5.1	11.3	1.6	5.6
Greece		0.0	0.0	0.0	0.0	0.0	33.7	3.8	38.7	6.8	18.8
Hungary		18.0	2.2	4.4	2.9	0.1	14.7	2.8	4.5	0.8	0.5
Iceland		47.3	21.4	23.7	5.0	1.3	53.0	17.8	20.7	3.4	0.7
Ireland		42.1	7.4	16.4	3.5	1.7	59.5	9.0	20.9	6.3	2.3
Italy		48.1	10.9	36.0	6.1	7.6	54.6	10.3	34.8	5.4	8.0
Japan		61.5	3.8	13.2	3.0	0.4	56.1	8.1	11.1	2.9	0.0
Korea, Rep.		42.0	11.3	19.8	0.0	10.7	39.8	16.0	14.5	3.9	2.3
Latvia		64.6	4.1	35.6	6.1	1.1	19.1	4.0	25.1	1.1	0.3
Lithuania		58.3	7.3	34.0	2.6	0.2	27.3	4.6	11.5	2.2	1.4
Luxembourg		0.0	0.0	0.0	0.0	0.0	53.2	8.9	28.3	6.5	1.6
Macedonia		0.0	0.0	0.0	0.0	0.0	15.4	8.0	10.8	2.5	0.5
Malta							33.1	10.6	25.5	4.6	1.2

Country	in % of all respondents per country	1990–1993					2000				
		Sign petition	Join boycott	Attend lawful demonstration	Join unofficial strike	Occupy building	Sign petition	Join boycott	Attend lawful demonstration	Join unofficial strike	Occupy building
Mexico		34.7	6.9	22.0	7.4	5.2	30.4	9.5	11.5	6.2	4.6
Moldova		0.0	0.0	0.0	0.0	0.0	10.4	1.0	8.3	1.9	0.3
Netherlands		50.8	7.8	25.3	1.9	3.0	61.3	23.4	34.1	4.6	5.5
New Zealand		0.0	0.0	0.0	0.0	0.0	90.6	19.1	21.4	5.2	1.2
Nigeria		7.2	13.1	20.2	5.5	2.3	6.7	10.2	16.9	5.2	5.5
Norway		61.1	12.0	19.5	24.4	1.0	0.0	0.0	0.0	5.1	1.8
Peru		0.0	0.0	0.0	0.0	0.0	20.6	2.8	12.2	4.1	2.9
Philippines		0.0	0.0	0.0	0.0	0.0	12.0	6.0	8.0	3.1	1.6
Poland		14.0	5.8	11.7	6.2	3.8	22.6	4.2	10.0	4.7	2.9
Portugal		29.1	4.7	24.8	3.6	1.4	22.6	4.6	14.9	3.0	1.2
Romania							10.7	1.9	14.8	1.2	0.5
Russian Federation**		27.1	4.2	34.5	2.4	0.7	11.6	2.6	23.3	1.6	0.7
Slovakia		0.0	0.0	20.2	0.0	0.0	59.3	4.3	14.3	2.3	0.9
Slovenia		27.6	8.0	10.1	1.5	0.8	32.4	8.2	9.8	3.6	1.6
South Africa		24.2	21.5	18.8	8.5	2.5	0.0	0.0	10.4	3.7	2.4
Spain		20.4	5.6	23.5	6.9	2.9	28.6	5.6	26.9	8.7	3.1
Sweden		71.7	16.5	22.6	3.1	0.2	87.4	33.0	35.2	4.6	2.6
Switzerland		62.9	0.0	15.4	2.1	0.0	63.6	12.2	16.9	1.9	1.1
Turkey		13.6	5.6	5.7	1.5	1.2	13.8	6.6	6.3	2.0	0.5
Ukraine		0.0	0.0	0.0	0.0	0.0	14.2	5.0	18.9	2.7	0.9
United Kingdom***		75.4	14.7	13.6	8.5	2.3	69.9	15.2	17.6	9.6	2.3
United States		70.9	17.9	15.5	4.4	2.0	81.1	24.7	20.0	5.4	3.8
Uruguay		0.0	0.0	0.0	0.0	0.0	35.5	4.0	5.0	10.2	7.6
Venezuela		0.0	0.0	0.0	0.0	0.0	22.7	2.4	9.7	2.4	2.6
Yugoslavia		0.0	0.0	0.0	0.0	0.0	19.4	6.7	7.5	4.6	1.2
Average:		26.4	5.6	13.1	3.5	1.5	34.4	8.5	18.0	5.2	2.6

Values in italics indicate that 1995-1997 data have been used.

*West-Germany only for 1990

**Russian Federation figures for 1990 are for USSR

***UK excluding Northern Ireland for 1990

Sources: © European Values Survey, WORC, Tilburg University, Netherlands, 1999-2000, by permission; © World Values Survey, Institute for Social Research, University of Michigan, by permission; Inglehart, R., Basañez, M., and Moreno, A., *Human Values and Beliefs: A Cross-Cultural Sourcebook: Political, Religious, Sexual, and Economic Norms in 43 Societies: Findings from the 1990–1993 World Values Survey*, The University of Michigan Press, Ann Arbor, 1998.

Glossary of Terms in Table Programme

Arbitrary detention. Deprivation of liberty imposed arbitrarily, that is, where no final decision has been taken by domestic courts in conformity with domestic law and with the relevant international standards set forth in the Universal Declaration of Human Rights and with the relevant international instruments accepted by the states concerned.

Corruption Perceptions Index (CPI). Measures corruption in the public sector and defines corruption as the abuse of public office for private gain. The CPI makes no effort to reflect private sector fraud. The index is based on surveys compiled by Transparency International from other organisations which tend to ask questions about the misuse of public power for private benefits, with a focus, for example, on bribing of public officials, taking kickbacks in public procurement, or embezzling public funds, etc. Surveys consulted:

- Economist Intelligence Unit (Country Risk Service and Country Forecasts);
- Gallup International (50th Anniversary Survey);
- Institute for Management Development (World Competitiveness Yearbook);
- Political & Economic Risk Consultancy (Asian Intelligence Issue);
- Political Risk Services (International Country Risk Guide);
- World Development Report (private sector survey by the World Bank); and
- World Economic Forum & Harvard Institute for International Development (Global Competitiveness Survey).

Crime. Crimes recorded in criminal (police) statistics, including attempts to commit crimes.

Daily newspapers. The number of newspapers published at least four times a week.

Discrimination. Any distinction, exclusion, restriction, or preference based on any ground such as race, colour, sex, language, religion, political or other opinion, national or social origin, property, birth, or other status which has the purpose or effect of nullifying or impairing the recognition, enjoyment, or exercise, on an equal footing, of human rights and fundamental freedoms in the political, economic, social, cultural, or any other field of public life.

Emissions. Emissions refer to the release of greenhouse gases and/or their precursors and aerosols into the atmosphere over a specified area and period of time.

Enforced disappearances. Enforced disappearances occur when persons are arrested, detained, or abducted against their will or otherwise deprived of their liberty by officials of different branches or levels of government, or by organized groups or private individuals acting on behalf of, or with the support, direct or indirect, consent, or acquiescence of the government, followed by a refusal to disclose the fate or whereabouts of the persons concerned or a refusal to acknowledge the deprivation of their liberty, which places such persons outside the protection of the law.

Environmental Sustainability Index (ESI). The ESI is based on 68 variables which together make 20 core indicators of environmental sustainability. It aims to measure environmental sustainability on five dimensions: the state of environmental systems (air, water, soil, ecosystems), the reduction of environmental stresses such as pollution and exploitation, the reduction of human vulnerability (e.g. loss of food resources or exposure to environmental diseases), the social and institutional capacity to cope with environmental challenges, and the ability to act collectively in response to the demands of global stewardship. High values correspond to high levels of environmental sustainability.

Extrajudicial executions. Full expression 'extrajudicial, summary, or arbitrary executions': all acts and omissions of state representatives that constitute a violation of the general recognition of the right to life embodied in the Universal Declaration of Human Rights and the International Covenant on Civil and Political Rights.

Foreign direct investment (FDI). Investment to acquire a lasting management interest (10 per cent or more of voting stock) in an enterprise operating in an economy other than that of the investor. It is the sum of equity capital, reinvestment of earnings, other long-term capital, and short-term capital as shown in the balance of payments. FDI stock is the value of the share of capital and reserves (including retained profits) attributable to enterprises based outside the domestic economy, plus the net indebtedness of domestic affiliates to the parent enterprise. UNCTAD FDI stock data are frequently estimated by accumulating FDI flows over a period of time or adding flows to an FDI stock that has been obtained for a particular year.

Freedom of association. The right to establish and, subject only to the rules of the organisation concerned, to join organisations of one's own choosing without prior authorisation.

Freedom of expression. Freedom to hold opinions without interference and to seek, receive, and impart information and ideas through any media and regardless of frontiers.

Full-time equivalent employment. Indicates total employment in terms of full-time jobs. Part-time employment is converted into full-time jobs and added to the number of full-time jobs, based on country-specific conventions.

Gross domestic product (GDP). Total domestic expenditure of a country, minus imports, plus exports of goods and services.

GDP per capita, PPP. GDP per capita based on purchasing power parity (PPP). GDP PPP is gross domestic product converted to international dollars using purchasing power parity rates. An international dollar has the same purchasing power over GDP as the US dollar in the United States. Data are in current international dollars.

Gini index. Measures the extent to which the distribution of income (or, in some cases, consumption expenditures) among individuals or households within an economy deviates from a perfectly equal distribution. A Lorenz curve plots the cumulative percentages of total income received against the cumulative number of recipients, starting with the poorest individual or household. The Gini index measures the area between the Lorenz curve and a hypothetical line of absolute equality, expressed as a percentage of the maximum area under the line. Thus, a Gini index of zero represents perfect equality, while an index of 100 implies perfect inequality.

Gross national income (GNI). Formerly known as gross national product or GNP. The sum of value added by all resident producers plus any product taxes (less subsidies) not included in the valuation of output plus net receipts of primary income (compensation of employees and property income) from abroad.

Human Development Index (HDI). A composite index based on three indicators: longevity, as measured by life expectancy at birth; educational attainment, as measured by a combination of adult literacy (two-thirds weight) and the combined gross primary, secondary, and tertiary enrolment ratio (one-third weight); and standard of living, as measured by GDP per capita (PPP US$).

Illiteracy rate. Calculated as 100 minus the adult literacy rate, which refers to the people aged 15 and above who can, with understanding, both read and write a short, simple statement on their everyday lives.

Imputed value for volunteers. Calculated by converting the total volunteer hours into full-time equivalent employment, multiplied by the average wage for the group, industry, or the economy as a whole.

Infant mortality rate. The probability of dying between birth and exactly one year of age times 1,000.

Internally displaced persons (IDPs). Individuals or groups of people who have been forced to flee their homes to escape armed conflict, generalised violence, human rights abuses, or natural or man-made disasters, and have remained within the borders of their home country.

International NGOs. These are currently active, autonomous non-profit making organisations with operations or activities in at least three countries, or members with voting rights in at least three countries, a formal structure with election of governing officers from several member countries and some continuity of activities. Notably excluded are obviously national or bilateral organisations, informal social movements and ad hoc bodies, and international business enterprises, investment houses or cartels and other obvious profit making bodies. Irrelevant are size, importance, degree of activity, financial strength, political or ideological position, field of interest or activity, location of headquarters and language.

Internationally-oriented NGOs. These are national currently active, autonomous non-profit making organ-

isations with various forms of international activity or concern such as research, peace, development or relief. They may also include national bodies which have relations with international organisations and which are listed by them in conjunction with truly international bodies or which appear from their titles to be international themselves. This criterion includes organisations having consultative status with United Nations and other intergovernmental organisations.

Meetings. These are meetings organised or sponsored by 'international organisations'(INGOs, internationally-oriented NGOs and IGOs) that appear in the Union of International Associations' Yearbook of International Organizations, and other meetings of significant international character. Excluded are purely national meetings, as well as those of an essentially religious, didactic, political, commercial or sporting nature and meetings with strictly limited participation, such as those of subsidiary (internal) statutory bodies, committees, groups of experts etc., and corporate and incentive meetings.

Merchandise trade. Includes all trade in goods. Trade in services is excluded.

Network. Interpersonal or inter-organisational ties that report structural or legal relations, information flows and other exchanges. Network analysis seeks to identify patterns in complex networks.

Official development aid (ODA). Official development assistance and net official aid record the actual international transfer by the donor of financial resources or of goods or services valued at the cost to the donor, minus any repayments of loan principal during the same period. ODA data consist of disbursements of loans made on concessional terms (net of repayments of principal) and grants by official agencies of the members of the Development Assistance Committee (DAC) of the OECD, by multilateral institutions, and by certain Arab countries to promote economic development and welfare in recipient economies listed as 'developing' by DAC. Loans with a grant element of at least 25 per cent are included in ODA, as are technical cooperation and assistance.

Passengers carried. Air passengers carried include both domestic and international aircraft passengers.

Peacekeeping forces. Military personnel and civilian police serving in United Nations peacekeeping missions.

Public sector or government. All branches of the government, including the executive, judicial, and administrative and regulatory activities of federal, State, local, or regional political entities; the terms 'government' and 'public sector' are used synonymously.

Public sector payments. Include grants and contracts, i.e. direct contributions by the government to the organisation in support of specific activities and programmes; statutory transfers, i.e. contributions by the government, as mandated by law, to provide general support to an organisation in carrying out its public programmes, and third-party payments, i.e. indirect government payments reimbursing an organisation for services rendered to individuals (e.g. health insurance, 'vouchers', or payments for day care).

Private giving. Includes foundation giving, including grants from grant-making foundations, operating foundations, and community foundations; business or corporate donations, which includes giving directly by businesses or giving by business or corporate foundations; and individual giving, i.e. direct contributions by individuals and contributions through 'federated fund-raising' campaigns.

Private fees and charges (or 'programme fees'). Essentially include four types of business or commercial income: fees for service, i.e. charges that clients of an agency pay for the services that the agency provides (e.g. fees for day care or health care); dues, i.e. charges levied on the members of an organisation as a condition of membership. They are not normally considered charges for particular services; proceeds from sales of products, which includes income from the sale of products or services and income from for-profit subsidiaries; and investment income, i.e. the income a non-profit earns on its capital or its investments.

Refugee. As defined by the UN High Commissioner for Refugees, a person is a refugee if she/he qualifies under the Arrangements of 12 May 1926 and 30 June 1928 or under the Conventions of 28 October 1933 and 10 February 1938, the Protocol of 14 September 1939 or the Constitution of the International Refugee Organisation. See http://www.unhcr.ch for further information.

Revenues. Inflows of spendable resources received by the organisation during the year.

Telephone mainlines. Telephone lines connecting a customer's equipment to the public switched telephone network.

Transnationality Index (TNI). The average of three ratios: a corporation's foreign assets to total assets, foreign sales to total sales, and foreign employment to total employment.

Transparency of government. Indicates the extent to which a government communicates its policy intentions clearly and publicly. Included in the International Institute for Management Development's World Competitiveness Yearbook as part of its corruption measurements.

Torture. Any act by which severe pain or suffering, whether physical or mental, is intentionally inflicted on a person for such purposes as obtaining from him or a third person information or a confession, punishing him for an act he or a third person has committed or is suspected of having committed, or intimidating or coercing him or a third person, or for any reason based on discrimination of any kind, when such pain or suffering is inflicted by or at the instigation of or with the consent or acquiescence of a public official or other person acting in an official capacity. It does not include pain or suffering arising only from, inherent in, or incidental to lawful sanctions.

Total military personnel. Active duty military personnel, including paramilitary forces if those forces resemble regular units in their organisation, equipment, training, or mission.

Total trade. The sum of the market value of imports and exports of goods and services.

Tourists. Visitors who travel to a country other than that where they have their usual residence for a period not exceeding 12 months and whose main purpose in visiting is other than an activity remunerated from within the country visited.

PARALLEL SUMMITS OF GLOBAL CIVIL SOCIETY: AN UPDATE

Mario Pianta

Introduction

In 2001 and in the first half of 2002 the international events organised by global civil society have multiplied at an unprecedented rate. Besides *parallel summits* which have long shadowed the meetings of states and supranational institutions—from the G8 to the IMF, from UN conferences to regional summits—a growing number of independent gatherings of global social movements has taken place, such as the second World Social Forum held in Porto Alegre, Brazil, in January-February 2002. Following up on the chapter on Parallel Summits of Global Civil Society (Pianta 2001a) published in *Global Civil Society 2001*, this section provides an update showing the evolution of these events, based on wider work on these issues (Pianta 2001b; 2002).

A survey was undertaken in order to investigate the nature of parallel summits, the events that occurred, their forms of organisation, and their impact. A questionnaire was circulated to hundreds of civil society organisations; and dozens of newspapers, journals, NGO publications, and web sites were monitored in order to gather systematic information. From the findings, 89 cases of parallel summits have been selected, which are considered representative of the range of events, topics, and locations, covering the period 1988-June 2002. The focus here is on the 35 main events of 2001 and the first half of 2002. They will be compared with the evolution over the past 20 years presented in Pianta (2001a).

With all the limitations that such data may have, they leave little doubt that global civil society is coming of age. Global movements are active in all continents on a great variety of issues. Moving from protest against official summits, they have developed their own agenda, where the critique of neo-liberal globalisation is joined by the proposal of alternatives and the exploration of new forms of political action. They have shown a great organisational capacity in preparing global events and a growing autonomy in charting their own course, independently of the pressure of the policy agenda of international institutions, and of the short-term considerations of national politics. Even the surge of terrorism with the attacks of 11 September 2001 against the United States, and the ensuing war in Afghanistan, did not slow down global activism of civil society; rather, this led to greater attention to the issues of peace, war, and violence. The millions of people around the world mobilised in the last year and a half show that global civil society has now reached a role and relevance which should not be ignored either by national politics or by supranational institutions.

Record 30 Growth of parallel summits

How many parallel summits take place? In 2000 the same number of parallel summits are recorded as in the four previous years, while in 2001 close to a quarter of all events are concentrated, and the first semester of 2002 alone accounts for 15% of all gatherings of global civil society. This exponential growth is the most effective indicator of the booming relevance of global civil society events.

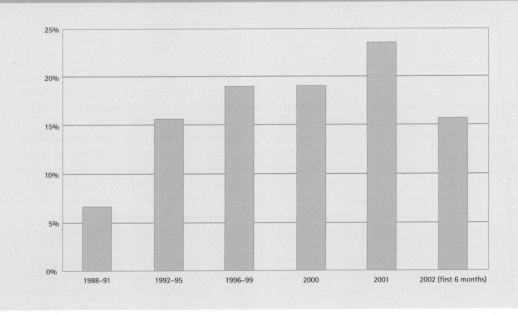

Record 31 Location of parallel summits

Where do parallel summits occur? In the last year and a half, close to a third of parallel summits have taken place in Europe, a quarter in Latin America, a sixth each in North America and Africa, and the rest in Asia and Oceania, as shown in Record 31: a large shift to the South from the 1988 to June 2001 figures, where Europe and North America had much higher shares (53 and 23%).

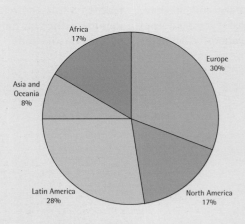

Record 32 Types of parallel summits

What type of summits does civil society set out to challenge? Record 32 shows that since 2001, 40% of events are meetings of global movements organised independently of official summits, while this was only about 10% in the past 13 years. Close to 30% of parallel summits deals with regional conferences (European Union, American or Asian government meetings), and fewer than one third shadow UN, G8, IMF or WTO meetings. In the past this group accounted for two-thirds of all parallel summits.

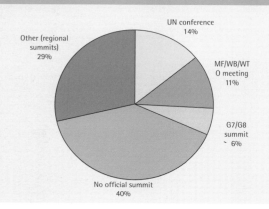

Record 33 Fields of activity of the organisations involved

Who are the organisers of parallel summits? Nothing has changed in the key actors of the organisation of parallel summits; they generally are civil society groups of the hosting country, in 80% of cases involving also international networks and NGOs. In a third of cases local groups are also active, with a lesser involvement by trade unions and local authorities. Record 33 shows that two-thirds of events—in recent months as well as in the whole period—have resulted from the work of civil society organisations active in development and economic issues (trade, finance, debt, and so on). Groups involved on democracy issues are active now in half of global events, as opposed to a quarter in the past. Human rights and peace organisations are stable in 25-30% of parallel summits, while environmental groups lose importance and are found only in one fifth of events (about half as much as in the past); a similar fall is found for the presence of trade unions. Groups active on gender, youth and other issues also appear to be less relevant than in the past. Multiple responses were possible and totals therefore do not add up to 100%.

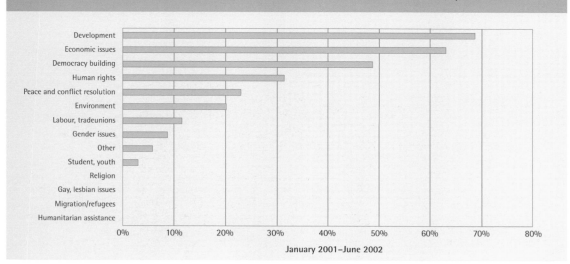

PARALLEL SUMMITS OF GLOBAL CIVIL SOCIETY: AN UPDATE   Mario Pianta

Record 34 Types of events

What type of event is a parallel summit? Record 34 shows that it is always a conference, associated with street demonstrations in 80% of the cases (in contrast to one half of past parallel summits). In recent months media events and grass-roots meetings have lost importance, while a broader range of fringe actions and initiatives is carried out.

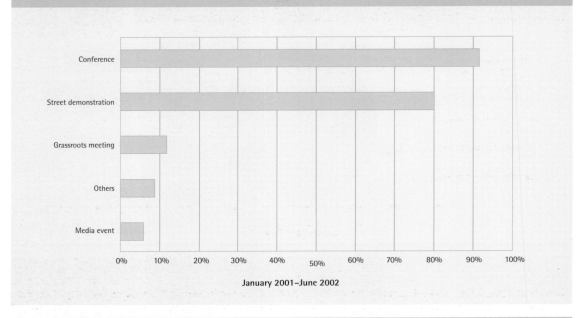

January 2001–June 2002

Record 35 Number of participants

How many people attend? Since January 2001, one-third of global civil society events has had more than 10,000 participants—in seven parallel summits the people involved are above 80,000. Record 35 shows that one-fifth of cases involve between 1,000 and 10,000 people, and one quarter between 200 and 500, suggesting that global meetings with a more focused participation are also on the rise. Relative to past trends, there is an increase of large demonstrations and of small events, while the smallest ones basically disappear.

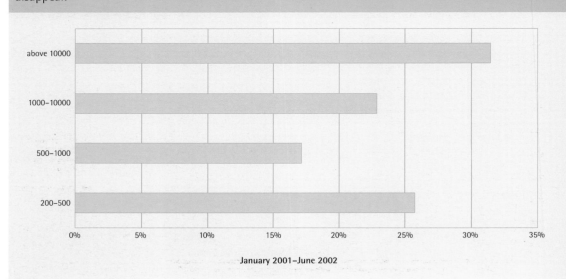

January 2001–June 2002

What are the objectives of the gatherings of global movements? Record 36 shows that, since 2001, in three quarters of the cases parallel summits have had three parallel aims: networking among civil society organisations, disseminating public information, and proposing alternative policies. The latter objective maintains the same relevance as in the past, while the other two aims have rapidly grown in importance. The development of stable networks of civil society organisations has emerged as a major recent priority for their action, while the attempt to inform public opinion has also broadened.

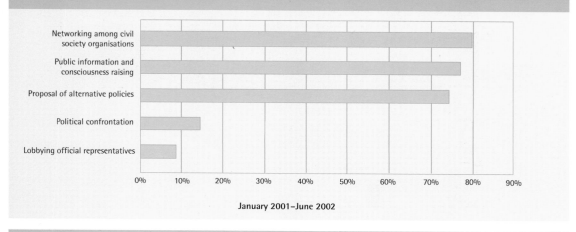

January 2001–June 2002

How much impact do parallel summits have? The evaluation shown in Record 37 is based on the judgement of organisers or participants or from media reports, and clearly these results have to be treated with great caution. From the evidence available, the strongest impact of parallel summits appears to be on global civil society itself, where three-quarters of events judged to have a medium or strong effect; this is no different from the past. In half of the cases there is a similarly medium or strong impact on public opinion, followed by the effect on international media. While the impact of parallel summits on specific national and international policies has remained very weak, official summits have begun to feel the pressure of civil society. In the last year and a half, more than 60% of parallel summits have had a medium or strong impact on official conferences—interrupting their activities, influencing their location or agenda - an impact that is twice as great that estimated in the past.

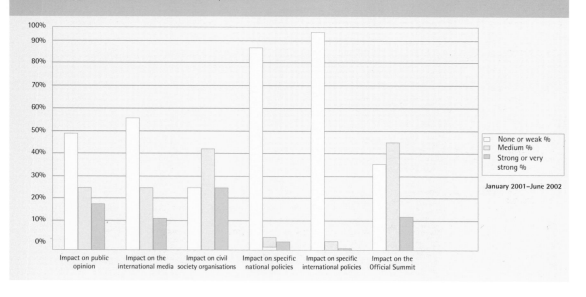

January 2001–June 2002

PARALLEL SUMMITS OF GLOBAL CIVIL SOCIETY: AN UPDATE   Mario Pianta

Record 38 Factors of success

What are the strengths of parallel summits? These did not change much after 2001. Record 38 shows that in 60% of cases the wide international network of organisations is the main factor of success, followed by the strong political alliance among them; this underlines again the importance of the 'internal' development of global movements. Mass participation is considered as a success in one-third of parallel summits, while radical protest emerges as less important.

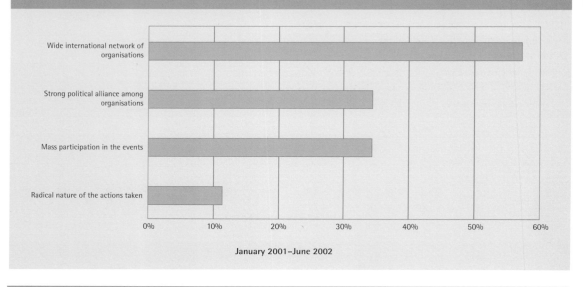

January 2001–June 2002

Record 39: Factors of weakness

What are the weaknesses of parallel summits? These are mainly due to the lack of attention of policy-makers (or the failure to make them listen to civil society) and the lack of 'external' visibility (or the failure to make media and public opinion listen to the message of parallel summits), both relevant in more than 50% of cases. A much lower number of cases point to 'internal' weaknesses, such as divisions among organisers (small, but on the increase), or poor participation.

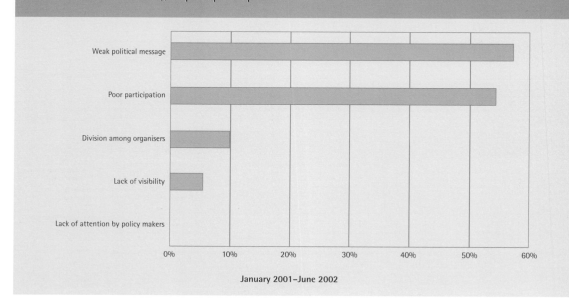

January 2001–June 2002

References

Pianta, M. (2001a). 'Parallel Summits of Global Civil
    Society', in Helmut Anheier, Marlies Glasius, and Mary
    Kaldor (eds), *Global Civil Society 2001*. Oxford: Oxford
    University Press.
—(2001b). Globalizzazione dal basso. Economia mondiale e
    movimenti sociali. Rome: Manifestolibri.
(2002) 'I controvertici e gli eventi della società civile
    globale'. in Lunaria (ed.) *Capire i movimenti globali. Da
    Porto Alegre al Forum Sociale Europeo.* Trieste: Asterios.

CHRONOLOGY OF GLOBAL CIVIL SOCIETY EVENTS

Compiled by Jill Timms, with contributions from Mustapha Kamel Al-Sayyid, Leonardo Avritzer, Reine Borja, Joabe Cavalcanti, Hyo Je Cho, Bernard Dreano, Marlies Glasius, Nihad Gohar, Anil Gupta, Svitlana Kuts, Natalia Leshchenko, Alejandro Martinez, Nuria Molina, Alejandro Natal, Ebenezer Obadare, Mario Pianta, Jasmin San Juan, Jirina Siklova, Thomas Ruddy, Guy Taylor, Yulia Tykhomyrova, Sebastien Ziegler, Csengeri Zsolt

Note on the Chronology

In this section of the Yearbook we provide accounts of global civil society events which occurred during 2001. Whereas chronologies of the year usually focus on events and personalities from the North/West and depend on media coverage which tends to be biased against civil society activities, our aim here is to offer a different type of chronology. We include the activities of diverse types of groups and organisations which belong to a broad understanding of what global civil society is and which can help us to understand the process of globalisation from below. Some of these types of events do not necessarily get included in statistics on the growth of civil society activities and organisations, and our chronology enables us to capture civil society actvities in the South/East.

This chronology builds on the chronologies provided in *Global Civil Society 2001*, which detailed events of 2000 and of the decade 1989–1999. The chronologies are thus being built up as a reference tool, part of the records section of each Yearbook. They also provide information about the variety of events that take place in different parts of the world, and so can contribute to the development of a type of global collective memory. These objectives can be fulfilled only with the help of a global team of correspondents, and we would like to invite you to become part of this team (please see the details in the following section).

When is something important enough to be a 'global civil society event'? For the first Yearbook we developed the criterion that, in our entirely subjective opinion, a global civil society event was one that involved or had implications for civil society and that resonated, or had implications, beyond national boundaries. The range of activities included as events is diverse, as is the size and scale of actions. Government actions are occasionally included when they had significant impact on, or were a reaction to, global civil society. Events involving violence have been included where the perpetrators may be seen by some as broadly part of civil society or where the action can have significant implications for civil society. On the whole natural disasters have not been included unless they act as a catalyst for civil society action. In a similar way election-related events have also been included only when civil society mobilisation has had a direct bearing on the event. We expect that our criteria will continue to be refined and adapted as each chronology is compiled and as our team of correspondents expands. The chronology presented here should therefore not be seen as a definitive list of all that has happened in global civil society, but as an indication of the variety, growth, and diversity of events we have learnt about.

Become a global correspondent for the Global Civil Society Yearbook

The success of this initiative is dependent on the contributions made by our team of global correspondents. We are very grateful to this team (whose names appear at the top of this section) for their efforts. We aim to include entries from every part of the world and to focus on events that may not otherwise be known or be included in dominant understandings of global civil society. Therefore, we are continually looking to enlist new contributors. Are you interested in global civil society and in contributing to this project?

We are looking for people who take an active interest in the activities of global civil society in their part of the world. We would like to have a mix of journalists, students and academics, and activists/practitioners, with men and women, young people and older people from all regions of the world represented. Correspondents would submit events to be included in the next chronology, so would need to be looking out for suitable activities to report on. Preferably, they would know about or be involved in activism on more than one type of issue (for instance peace, human rights, the environment, consumer activism), possibly in more than one country.

If you are interested in becoming a correspondent, know someone who might be, would like to know more, or have comments to make on this year's chronology, then please do contact us. Further details can be found at http://www.lse.ac.uk/Depts/global//Yearbook/yearbook.htm. As well as becoming part of the Yearbook team, all correspondents are acknowledged and receive complimentary copies of the Yearbook.

Global Civil Society Events of 2001

January

15–16 January Appeal proceedings are heard in Montpellier, France, of the 12 peasant activist members of the Confederation Paysanne prosecuted for the dismantling of a McDonald's restaurant in Millau in 1999. The dismantling was a protest against US and World Trade Organisation (WTO) policy imposing hormone beef on the European market. The first trial was held in August 2000, with 100,000 people demonstrating in support of the activists. In this appeal, several thousand come together to protest against the appeal and against the larger consequences of globalisation.

17–20 January In the Philippines, thousands of civilians march in the streets of Manila to protest against corruption and demand that the government of President Joseph Estrada leave office. This is a reaction to news of his acquittal from an impeachment trial. Over several days, labour union power unites with other civil society activists in a move to finally bring Estrada down from power. 30,000 workers and urban poor are mobilised by militant groups to rally at the People Power Monument, with the protest being described as 'People Power II' as reminiscent of a previous action against dictator Marcos. The military then withdraws its support from the Estrada government, and Gloria Arroyo is being sworn in.

22 January A teenage girl, Bariya Ibrahim Magazu, is sentenced to 100 lashes for engaging in pre-marital sex in Zamfara state, Nigeria. Her earlier conviction by a Sharia court has attracted widespread international condemnation coordinated mainly by the government and civil society groups in Canada.

25–30 January The first World Social Forum is held in Porto Alegre, Brazil, as an alternative to the World Economic Forum being held in Davos, Switzerland. 11,000 activists gather to protest against neo-liberalism and discuss alternatives to capitalist globalisation under the banner of 'another world is possible'. The event is organised by a number of civil society organisations, including many progressive Brazilian ones such as the Landless Movement and trade union groups, with ATTAC-France also being prominent. It is decided during the forum that the event should be held annually.

26 January The earthquake that hits Gujarat in India on this date, causing the deaths of an estimated 20,000 people, is followed by a tremendous outpouring of civil society support for emergency relief and rehabilitation. By the end of the year, almost half the houses are already reconstructed or on the way to being constructed.

29 January–3 February The World Economic Forum is held in Davos, Switzerland, and, despite police efforts to seal off the event, anti-capitalist protesters still attempt to demonstrate but are held back with water cannons. Pressure groups invited by the Davos organisers to encourage dialogue respond to the police actions by threatening to boycott future participation in the forums if demonstrations are to be banned.

February

3 February The Mexican government hands over the Argentine ex-captain Ricardo Miguel Cavallo to Spanish courts to be tried for crimes against humanity during the 'Dirty War' which occurred at the time of the military dictatorship in Argentina between 1976 and 1983. The actions of the Mexican government are largely a consequence of the pressure exerted by civil society organisations in Argentina, Spain, and Mexico.

10 February After a week of protests against rising domestic violence, more than 1,000 Ethiopian women march to the centre of Addis Ababa in the first public action of this kind in the country. Organised by the Ethiopian Women's Lawyers Association, the demonstrators call for tougher laws to protect women and especially young girls from the rising number of sexual offences.

12 February In the Philippines more than 20,000 wage-earners and friends of the slain labour leader Felimon 'Popoy' Lagman of Buklurang Manggagawa ng Pilipinas (BMP) wear red shirts as a sign of their protest. They march in protest against his death and call for justice carrying placards and banners bearing the symbol of labour and his name.

17 February Police disperse pro-democracy protesters in Osogbo, capital of western Osun state in Nigeria. The self-styled '2 million man march' is led by the National Conscience Party.

20 February The Syrian government undertakes a series of measures to restrict the freedom of the civil forums, which have flourished since President Bashar al Assad assumed power in July 2000.

22–27 February Anti-capitalists initiate a series of activities to parallel the regional World Economic Forum (WEF) held in Cancun, Mexico. These include an important encounter between anti-globalists and globalisers as the leaders of the WEF and Mexican authorities meet with 25 civil society organisations, 15 of which are Mexican. Jose Maria Figuerez, director of the Agenda of the World Economic Forum, declares that the encounter is a success for there has been a series of shared arguments around globalisation, such as the demand for inclusion of marginal groups and access to the economy, education, and health for everyone. Representatives of various organisations, unions, peasants, and NGOs take the opportunity to urge President Vicente Fox to conduct a 'real' dialogue and to encourage accountability to civil society for the economic policies of the country. Outside the forum many activist groups come together to protest, and there is a heavy police presence throughout the city as well as in the bay, where Greenpeace moors its Rainbow Warrior ship. More radical activists protest fiercely in the area surrounding the hotels of the WEF participants.

25 February–5 March The Zapatistas leave their refuges in the highlands of Chiapas to initiate a march to Mexico City called the 'Zapatour'. Passing through several major cities, the Zapatistas raise large numbers of people in protest against the historical oppression of indigenous peoples. The caravan is supported permanently by civil society organisations from Mexico, and participants from all over the world, especially from Italy, take part. They create an enclosure for the leaders, the so-called 'enclosure of peace'.

26 February Protesting Nigerian youths from Oben, Ikobi, Obozogbenugu, and Igueleba, all in Orhionmwon Local Government Area of Edo state, invade oil and gas stations belonging to Shell.

March

9–11 March Zapatistas enter Mexico City after the 'Zapatour'. This event is particularly symbolic for its resemblance to the entry of Emiliano Zapata to the city, during the aftermath of the Mexican Revolution at the beginning of the twentieth century. 150,000 people join a rally in support of the campaign, where sub-commandante Marcos demands publicly the right of the indigenous leaders to address the National Congress.

15 March The Sudanese government is accused by Christian Aid of systematically depopulating oil-rich areas for the benefit of foreign companies.

17 March A Global Forum is held in Naples, Italy on governance and the impact of the Internet on government. Parallel initiatives are organised by an estimated 20,000 anti-capitalist protesters, and violent street clashes also take place between demonstrators and the police.

19 March Meetings are held at the WTO's headquarters in Geneva to negotiate a liberalising of world trade in services, such as in telecoms, financial services, and tourism. Outside, protesters and anti-capitalist groups gather to voice their opposition, dressed up as business people waving butterfly nets at other protesters dressed up as mobile phones and first-aid kits.

20 March In the Middle East a loose coalition of civil society organisations, including religious leaders, politicians, and intellectuals, demonstrate against a visit scheduled for 20–24 March by a delegation from the US Commission on International Religious Freedom (USCIRF). This is the first leg of a regional tour, which includes Saudi Arabia, Israel, and the Occupied Territories.

23 March In an unprecedented event in Mexico, indigenous leaders are given the opportunity to address the national Congress. To a large extent this is due to the enormous pressure that civil society organisations and the Zapatista demonstrations put on the government to find legal solutions to allow them to speak in the Tribune, the area designated for members of the Congress only. Four indigenous leaders speak in their native languages to the Congress and the country, as the event is broadcast by all national TV channels.

30 March An umbrella group called the National Coalition for Press Reform is formed to campaign for the independent press in Korea. The coalition demands an end to the government practice of granting special tax exemption to media companies.

April

14 April On Easter Saturday the Campaign for Nuclear Disarmament organises a demonstration in London which marches to Downing Street to oppose and call a halt to any UK/US collaboration on nuclear missile defence plans. About 400 demonstrators complete the march, carrying a giant Darth Vader puppet and are then addressed by a number of speakers.

19 April The court case initiated by pharmaceutical companies against the South African government over the production of generic copies of AIDS/HIV drug treatments is unconditionally dropped. Activists see this as a landmark victory in their attempts to secure medication for the millions of sufferers of the disease in Africa.

19–21 April The first International Citizens Meeting is held in Barcelona, organised by UBUNTU, the world forum of networks whose president is Federico Mayor Zaragoza. This meeting has the aim of offering a forum for NGOs to analyse and discuss world affairs and to concentrate on issues such as human rights, international disarmament, human development and social justice, ecology, globalisation, peace, and conflict prevention.

21 April Tens of thousands of protesters from diverse groups demonstrate against the Free Trade Area of the Americas (FTAA) project at the Summit of the Americas held in Quebec, Canada.

23 April The opening session of a symposium 'Towards an Arab Developmental and Cultural Project' is held in the Moroccan city of Fez. More than a 100 Arab intellectuals, activists, and academics participate in an attempt to analyse the Arab world within the framework of an Arab developmental and cultural project that encompasses concepts such as independent development, democracy, social justice, national independence, and cultural renewal.

26 April The Belarussian democratic opposition organises a demonstration with other civil society groups to commemorate the catastrophe at the Chernobyl nuclear power station in 1986. The Chernobyl radioactive fallout affected one-fifth of the Belarussian population and contaminated one-third of the country's territory.

May

1 May Protesters, trade unionists, and anti-capitalist demonstrators take to the streets throughout the world in global May Day protests. Protests are held in many Australian cities, with activists in Brisbane attempting to raid the stock exchange. Throughout France, hundreds of thousands of trade unionists march to defend workers' rights. In a number of German cities, police are deployed to disperse demonstrators, and clashes become violent with many arrests. In Iran, protesters call for stricter action against illegal foreign workers and in Italy trade unionists organise a huge rock concert. In Japan, nearly half a million people join a workers' march in Tokyo, and Japanese trade unionists are joined by delegates from Burma. In London, 10,000 police are deployed to control demonstrators. Police use a strategy of trapping protesters in the central Oxford Circus, surrounding them with riot police for up to 8 hours. As this is done without arrest; legal battles continue against the action. In Norway protesters show their dissatisfaction by throwing a cream pie at Foreign Minister Thorbjoern Jagland. In Pakistan, thousands of security forces are deployed in Karachi to block a May Day rally against military rule, and hundreds are arrested. In South Korea thousands march through Seoul to protest against economic reforms, and in Turkey protests focus on the plight of left-wing prisoners on hunger strike. Riot police are used in Zimbabwe to break up confrontations between trade unionists and government-backed 'war veterans' during the traditional May Day rally. Other demonstrations are held at sites including Russia, Ukraine, Austria, Greece, Spain, and Indonesia where workers march to demand more rights.

25 May A network of environmental NGOs organises an international campaign to halt plans for further reclamation in Saemankum tidal wetlands, South Korea, and hold an inauguration meeting for the campaign. The government's decision, announced on 17 June, to go ahead with the reclamation project later raises further international concerns. Ricardo Navarro, president of Friends of the Earth International, visits South Korea just after the government announcement to show international solidarity for local NGOs, and urges the government to reconsider the plan.

31 May The 'second popular conference for the resistance of normalisation with the Zionist state' is opened in Kuwait. It stresses the importance of popular mobilisation in the Arab and Islamic world to exert pressures on the Arab governments to sever all kinds of relations with Israel.

June

Early June Ten Ukrainian NGOs start the 'your vote' initiative to ensure fair parliamentary elections, to take place in Ukraine in the end of March 2002. The 'your vote' initiative's goal is to ensure conscious choice, make fraud and ballot-box stuffing impossible, and crush the attempts to abuse or garble information.

2 June An Arab Women's Forum is held in Tunisia under the headline 'women and politics', calling upon Arab states to promote the political participation of women through literacy campaigns for girls, and the preparation of women to activate their role in political parties.

8 June Ijaw youth protesters of the Sangana Local Government Area of Bayelsa state in Nigeria take over oil production platforms of multinational corporation Texaco Overseas Petroleum Company Limited (TOPCON), and hold some staff on duty hostage.

9 June Protests are coordinated against European fiscal paradises, with demonstrations being held in Jersey, Andorra, and Monaco. These are organised by ATTAC-France in conjunction with other organisations.

14 June The Council of the Arab Organization for Human Rights holds its closing session in Cairo after discussing a number of field reports reflecting the state of human rights in Arab nations. Issues discussed include Palestine, Iraq, the Algerian and Sudanese crisis, and also the pressures exerted by some Arab states on human rights organisations. The session calls for more freedom of action for these organisations.

14–16 June In Gothenburg, European leaders meet to discuss the future direction and expansion plans of the EU. During the meeting Gothenburg is overtaken by protests, and violent clashes take place with the Swedish police. Protests focus on privatisation and economic plans of the EU leaders. Demonstrators also march against US President George Bush and his stance on climate change.

19 June A World Bank meeting planned to take place in Barcelona is cancelled due to fears that anti-capitalist protests would disrupt the event. The conference is instead held partially on the Internet; however, 20,000 demonstrators still gather to protest in Barcelona's Central Square.

22 June A case is filed in Washington by the human rights group, International Labour Rights Fund (ILRF), against ExxonMobile Oil Company. This is done on behalf of 11 Acehnese villages in Indonesia, accusing Exxon of complicity in the torture, murder, and sexual abuse of the local population by the Indonesian military.

25 June The United States drops its legal case against Brazil, allowing generic Aids-treatment drugs to be produced within South America. This follows intense pressure from a range of civil society organisations in Brazil, the US, and elsewhere.

26 June Protests are held by students and other activist groups in Papua New Guinea against the World Bank and the government's privatisation policies in Papua New Guinea. Demonstrations in Port Moresby, the capital, leave three protesters dead and more injured.

28 June As a result of South Korean NGOs joining forces with international organisations such as Transparency International, the National Assembly of South Korea passes an anti-corruption law. This is a direct result of NGO campaigns that have called for legislation for more transparent practices in politics as well as in business.

July

6–7 July In Geneva, a symposium is held with the World Trade Organization and 450 representatives of NGOs on issues confronting the world trading system. The meeting is part of the preparations for the 2001 Ministerial Meeting in Doha, Qatar and is seen as a progressive step towards civil society involvement.

16–20 July An initial planning meeting is held for the World Civil Society Forum (WCSF), aiming to bring together large numbers of different kinds of civil society organisations in Geneva. The actual forum will be held in Geneva in July 2002.

16–27 July The UN conference on climate control held in Bonn, Germany, reach agreement about the Kyoto Protocol. Discussions are hampered by US resistance, and pressure is kept up by a diverse mix of demonstrators, including anti-capitalist and environmentalist civil society groups.

18–21 July The G8 Summit is held in Genoa, Italy, and is marked by large-scale protests, marches, and demonstrations as a contingent of 250,000 protesters from 700 groups descend on the city. The majority march in peaceful protests, and many alternative conferences, meetings, and events are organised. However, the police are prepared for violence and use many tactics which an Italian police chief later admits involved excessive force. This includes the raiding of demonstrators' accommodation during the night, unnecessary use of tear-gas, and mistreatment of those arrested. One protester is killed by the police and approximately 200 others are injured. Legal battles continue against the actions of the police.

19–20 July A general strike brings most of Argentina to a standstill as trade unionists join with dissatisfied citizens to protest against the government's handling of the economy and the dramatic social spending cuts.

August

8 August NGOs hand over a collection of signatures to the Japanese embassy in Seoul to protest against the Japanese government's decision earlier in the year to grant permission for the use of right-wing history textbooks in state schools. This decision provokes public outrage and eventually leads more than 100,000 people to sign a petition to cancel the policy. Protesters claim the books gloss over episodes of Japanese aggression, such as the violence of the Japanese Empire during the first half of the last century. Both the South Korean and the Chinese governments have insisted on amendments to the textbooks written by a group of right-wing scholars. The signature gathering and public denouncement campaigns have drawn support from Japan as well as South Korea.

9 August A 'living chain of concerned people' is formed by several hundred people along the main street in the Belarussian capital Minsk, holding portraits of prominent political leaders who have disappeared during the years of President Lukashenka's rule. The disappeared include the former parliamentary deputy chairman, the head of the electoral commission Hanchar, former minister of interior Zakharanka, and a cameraman of the Russian TV company Zavadsky. These disappearances have been linked to the activity of an alleged death squad under the president's personal command. 'Living chains' are held in other cities and towns throughout the year.

15 August More than 500 citizens and activists gather in Seoul to protest against Japanese Prime Minister Koizumi's visit to Yaskuni war shrine. The gathering is a part of a bigger pan-Asian network including China, Taiwan, and the Philippines, which seeks to prevent the Japanese military from reviving itself in the region.

15–21 August A group of South Korean delegates of NGOs and labour movements visit North Korea to attend the ceremony for the 56th anniversary of the national liberation from Japanese colonial rule. It is the first time that South Korean activists are allowed to visit North Korea in an official capacity. The 337 delegates from South Korea reached agreements with the North to build solidarity for peaceful reunification and peace-keeping.

17 August Guy Verhofstadt, Prime Minister of Belgium and President of the European Union, writes an open letter to the anti-globalisation movement. Newspapers around the world publish this letter and the responses are collected for publication.

28 August A global delegation, spearheaded by groups and networks such as the Kakammpi, Platform of Filipino Migrant Organizations in Europe (Platform), Global Coalition for the Political Empowerment of Filipinos (Empower), and eLaAGDA (Connecting Filipinos through Technology) lobby for the passage of a bill on absentee voting in the Philippines. The consolidated version of the bill extends absentee voting rights to overseas Filipinos who can prove their Filipino citizenship by showing either their passport or any other relevant document. It also proposes to include undocumented Filipino workers overseas, temporary workers, and permanent residents.

28 August–1 September An NGO Forum Against Racism is held in Durban, South Africa, in preparation for and parallel to the World Conference Against Racism, Racial Discrimination, Xenophobia and Related Intolerance. NGOs from around the world attend meetings and stage marches and protests. However, the event is marred by many disagreements and incidents, as is the main conference, mostly centring around the issues of Zionism, anti-Semitism, and slavery.

30 August Members of Greenpeace Southeast Asia and representatives of the Crusade for Sustainable Environment (a local NGO) plant 200 white crosses in the ash field to protest the toxic wastes produced by the National Power Corporation (Napocor) plant in Calaca, Philippines. The wooden crosses signify potential graves for the communities surrounding the plant.

September

Early September Two world summits due to be held in Italy this month are cancelled due to fears of protests such as were seen in Genoa in July. The UN Food and Agricultural Organisation's World Food Summit and a planned NATO conference are the two events affected.

7 September Under the banner of 'the cry of the excluded', protests take place in cities throughout Brazil, on this annual day of demonstration which coincides with Brazil's Independence Day. The event brings together a diverse range of religious movements with other organisations including trade unions and neighbourhood associations. This year's protest also focuses on the external debt, the creation of the Free Trade Area of the America's (FTAA), and neo-liberal globalisation.

11 September Four aircraft are hijacked in the USA. Two of the planes are flown into the World Trade Centre Twin Towers, causing both towers to collapse with an estimated death toll of 4,000, including 250 firefighters and police who attended the scene. The third plane is crashed into the Pentagon in Washington, the centre of America's military operations, and the fourth crashes 80 miles south-east of Pittsburgh.

13 September The Australian government cites the terrorist attacks on the US to justify its hard stance on asylum seekers entering the country. It is claimed that Australia is becoming a target for refugees from a number of countries due to its geographical accessibility, and that a strong line is necessary to discourage the increasing number of refugee boats heading for the country. This and future action is met with fierce resistance by a variety of civil society groups, including Amnesty International, resulting in protests inside and outside many of Australia's detention centres for asylum seekers.

16–22 September Environmental activists from South Korea join together to visit the headquarters of a German multinational corporation, BASF, in Ludwigshafen, Germany, to protest against its expansion plans in South Korea. The company is accused of having used heavily toxic materials. The activists meet the company's CEO and visit the German Bundestag in Berlin. German local environmental groups join the Korean activists in generating publicity.

19 September Activists from 20 Islamabad-based NGOs hold a protest at Aabpara to express solidarity with the families of the victims of the September 11 terrorist attacks on World Trade Centre and the Pentagon. The demonstration is organised by the Citizen Peace Committee.

22 September The government of the Philippines and the leftist Rebolusyonaryong Partido ng Manggawa (RPM-P) renew their commitment to the peace treaty they signed in December 2000. Representatives of the church and student groups, local government officials, and the business sector participate in the dialogue.

26 September–3 October The Asian Network for Free and Fair Elections (ANFREL) takes part in election monitoring in Bangladesh. This is a Bangkok-based network consisting of six countries in Asia, and aims to help prevent election irregularities and ensure a free and fair election. It later also contributes to election monitoring activity in Sri Lanka. The experience of South Korean NGOs in the democratisation struggle during the 1970s and 1980s is contributing to this by helping to establish democracy in other parts of the developing world, particularly Asia.

27 September An anti-war demonstration is held in Naples, Italy to protest against the possibility of using military action in response to the September 11 attacks on the US. 10,000 people attend the event to demonstrate against war and NATO.

29 September In Washington DC, civil society groups come together for a march to 'stop war and racism'. This is attended by 25,000 anti-war protesters.

October

7 October Air strikes are launched on Afghanistan by the US in the 'war on terror'. Training camps and military installations of the Al Qaeda network are targeted with the objective of capturing those involved in the organisation of the terrorist attacks of September 11, including the leading figure of Osama Bin Laden. Anti-war protesters around the world voice their opposition and step up campaigns to stop the military action.

8 October In Santiago, Chile, an anti-war protest is held to demonstrate against the military action of the US, with activists claiming that the Americans are now committing terrorism themselves through their bombing of Afghanistan.

9 October Environmentalist groups and anti-war protesters come together in South Korea to demonstrate against the war.

12 October Thousands of Muslims in the Kenyan capital, Nairobi, defy a police ban and come out to protest against the American-led attacks on Afghanistan.

12 October Clashes between Christians and Muslims in response to the World Trade Centre and Pentagon attacks leave an undetermined number dead in Kano state, Nigeria.

13 October In London a march and rally for peace and justice is attended by more than 20,000 from a wide range of communities.

13 October An anti-war demonstration in Berlin is attended by 30,000 people, calling for peace, solidarity, and social justice.

13 October In Italy, 250,000 anti-war demonstrators participate in a 23-mile peace walk between Assissi and Perugia, making it one of the biggest peace demonstrations so far in the protest against the US-led strikes on Afghanistan.

14 October Activists in India take part in an anti-war march and rally in Calcutta with 70,000 people involved in the demonstration.

15 October A protest to denounce the US-led air strikes on Afghanistan is held in Ankara, Turkey.

17 October In Paris commemorations take place for the massacre perpetrated by the French police against unarmed Algerian demonstrators on 17 October 1961. Thousands of people demonstrate in the street, supported by anti-racist and human rights movements, left-wing political parties and trade unions.

18 October The activist for human rights Digna Ochoa is murdered in her house in Mexico City. This unchains a series of declarations and mobilisations of groups within Mexico and abroad to urge President Vincente Fox to issue a statement marking a new position for Mexico vis-à-vis human rights. The new government is also pressed by civil society organisations to free the indigenous peasants jailed for protecting the environment.

18 October After a two-year legal struggle that has been supported by Brazilian organisations and international NGOs such as Greenpeace, the Denie Indians of Manaus in the Amazon win the right to protect their land from illegal logging and industrial practices.

26 October Student demonstrations in Sao Paulo, Brazil, result in police captain Francisco Roher having a cream pie thrown at him as he is presented with his degree from PUC University. The captain is the commander of police who had violently repressed protesters from different organisations at a previous demonstration against the Free Trade Area of the Americas (FTAA), resulting in 69 arrests and 100 injured.

31 October With the upcoming legal registration period for a right to vote which lasts three months every year, a renewed campaign is launched by Egyptian women's NGOs to increase the percentage of Egyptian women's participation in the elections and to fill a gap in the Egyptian law which registers males automatically while making female registration optional.

November

6 November In Delhi, 15,000 people gather to protest against the World Trade Organisation ahead of its planned meeting in Doha, the capital of Qatar. The protesters include farm labourers, slum-dwellers, and low-caste Hindus, who condemn the Indian government's failure to protect its own interests.

9–15 November A World Trade Organisation meeting is held in Doha, Qatar. Tight security and the geography of the location prevent protesters from attending in great numbers. Some of the main issues discussed include workers' rights and access to cheap pharmaceuticals. A small contingent of 100 NGOs is invited to attend, with their activities limited to lobbying and quiet protest. Many complaints are made by protesters at the lack of opportunity to voice opinions, and fuel their criticisms of the WTO's undemocratic nature.

18 November Another anti-war demonstration is held in London with up to 100,000 marching to the capital's Trafalgar Square for a rally.

18 November A revision of the Earth Charter announced at the Earth Summit in Rio in 1992 takes place in Amman, where a number of Arab thinkers who have an interest in civil society, representing Egypt, Syria, Tunisia, Lebanon, Palestine, and Bahrain, meet to formulate a collective viewpoint on the Charter and the necessary amendments reflecting an Arab point of view.

21 November A court of appeal in the Moroccan capital of Rabat acquit 36 human rights activists, who had been sentenced earlier to 3 months' incarceration for participating in the organisation of an unauthorized demonstration in the previous December. A number of groups have been campaigning on their behalf.

26 November More than 100 Arab scientists, activists, academics, and politicians meet at the Arab League Headquarters in Cairo to discuss the 'dialogue between civilisations'.

30 November An international solidarity network is founded in Los Angeles to exchange information about, and to launch a campaign against, the imperial Japanese atrocities during the Second World War. The network comprises more than 50 groups in 13 countries including North and South Korea, Japan, China, Indonesia, the Philippines, Taiwan, US, and the Netherlands. The network is to launch a lawsuit in a US court for a former victim of forced labour during the war.

December

2–6 December In Lille, France, the World Citizens' Assembly of the Alliance for a Responsible, Plural and United World meet. This brings together 400 civic activists and personalities from all over the world, representing youth movements, peasants and fishermen unions, women movements, NGOs, municipalities, and journalists. The participants work towards a new concept of governance and sustainable development.

5 December This is International Volunteer Day, and the global closing of what has been the UN-sponsored International Year of the Volunteer. This draws together a year of diverse events held worldwide, such as parades, volunteer fairs, workshops, conferences, and work camps, some of which are aimed directly at young people.

7–9 December A seminar is held in Istanbul, Turkey, on the 'clash of civilisations' organised by Euro-Arab Dialogue, the Dutch Interchurch Peace Council (IKV), and the Helsinki Citizens' Assembly. The participants attend from European, Mediterranean, and Middle Eastern countries. At this event the project of a Middle East Citizens' Assembly (MECA) is launched.

9 December National Blanket day is celebrated in India, promoted by different student groups. The idea behind this initiative is to encourage people to donate a blanket to homeless people all around the world.

11 December The biggest general strike for more than 40 years paralyses Venezuela, as people throughout the country take part in a 12-hour stoppage. Fedecamaras, the country's largest business association, claims that 95 per cent of businesses have taken part. Business leaders have called the strike to protest that they were not consulted in the development of new labour laws. However, other protesters gather in Caracas in support of President Hugo Chavez. The president addresses them to claim this was a strike of the rich and he will not abandon the poor of Venezuela.

13 December A 24-hour general strike is held by public workers in Argentina, bringing the country to a virtual standstill. This is in protest against government restrictions, such as curbs on bank withdrawals, implemented in response to the deepening economic crisis the country faces. With a national debt of $132 billion the government's plans are thrown into turmoil when the International Monetary Fund refuses a payment of $1.3 billion, which was part of a larger loan package; however Argentina has repeatedly failed to meet economic targets. The mood of the country becomes increasingly discontented.

13–14 December The European summit is held in Brussels, with European leaders launching a review of the future direction and shape of the EU with the aim of increasing efficiency. This takes place, however, amidst mass protests. A march organised by trade unions is attended by up to 80,000 people. There are later clashes between some protesters and police.

20 December Mass public protests by Argentinian citizens lead to the resignation of President Fernando de la Rua, a culmination of prolonged protests at the government's handling of the economy. At least 25 people are killed during the riots. Some neighbourhood councils are set up to try to restore order in the communities.

24–25 December After the September 11 attacks more than 600 NGOs in South Korea organise a peace network to campaign for the end of the Afghanistan war. They also hold a big concert on Christmas day to raise funds for the refugees in the region. In particular, NGOs express concern over the Korean and Japanese decision to send troops to Afghanistan.

CHAPTER UPDATES

Note on Chapter Updates

This section refers to the themes discussed as part of the first Yearbook, *Global Civil Society 2001*. The pieces included here are written by some of the authors from the first Yearbook, with the aim of updating readers about further developments in the chapter areas since the time of writing. Chapters have been selected for update where recent events, developments, and changes in approach have occurred and have an impact on the discussion in the original chapter. This feature of the Yearbook is designed to facilitate continued debate about the major themes and issues that are important for understanding the development of global civil society.

Chapter 3:
The New Anti-Capitalist Movement:
Money and Global Civil Society

2002 Update: A Roller-Coaster Ride for the Anti-Capitalists

Meghnad Desai and Yahia Said

This update addresses critical events over the past year which affected global finance and provides an update on the new anti-capitalist movement in the light of the September 11 events.

The anti-capitalist movement experienced a roller-coaster ride over the past year. Throughout 2001 and especially after the massive Genoa demonstrations in July, where an estimated 250,000 demonstrators took to the streets, mainstream attitudes gradually shifted from ridicule and condemnation to understanding and support. Mainstream media expanded their coverage beyond violent demonstrators and began to engage the movements on the issues. Politicians and officials from various quarters were expressing understanding, sympathy, and even support. German and French political leaders went as far as to come out in support one of the movement's main projects, the 'Tobin tax'.

All this came to an abrupt halt on September 11. The movement's anti-Americanism, even if it was reserved for acts by the US administration in the service of multinational corporations, seemed improper in the light of the atrocities in New York and Washington. Some argue that the terrorist attacks represented a logical extension of the anti-capitalist argument, the implication being that capitalism with its emphasis on individualism, responsibility, and opportunity is the only answer to the murderous nihilism and tribal fanaticism of the terrorists. The civilised world, according to this line of thinking, needs to stand united against the terrorist threat, setting aside differences over detail, such as the side effects of global capitalism.

Anti-capitalists counter that unbridled capitalism, far from being the only answer to terrorism, is actually part of the problem. One of the main by-products of global capitalism, they argue, is exclusion, which breeds frustration and violence including terrorism. They point at collapsing states and economies in the aftermath of state mismanagement and structural adjustment which are merging into large swaths of 'bad lands'. Criminal economic networks spread from these areas providing the blood-line for global terrorist and fundamentalist networks. Anti-capitalists also argue that public spending cuts, privatisation, and deregulation weaken public services including policing and health care, and create an opening for terrorists even in the world's most advanced countries.

Notwithstanding these arguments, there was serious doubt whether the movement could survive the aftermath of September 11, 2001. The IMF/World Bank meeting scheduled originally for September was postponed. Attempts by activists to turn the event into a protest against the war in Afghanistan

Above: The opening march of the World Social Forum II. Porto Allegre, Brazil © Joabe Cavalcanti.

swept by angry demonstrations, banging of pots and pans, and looting and storming of banks after devaluation left thousands unable to meet their dollar-denominated mortgage payments. At least 25 people were killed in clashes with the police. The crisis led to the collapse of the Argentinian government and constitutional crisis.

As for Turkey, the new US administration, which vowed to abandon its predecessor's policy of international bail-outs, had to reverse course and assemble a rescue package for Turkey out of fear of losing one of its few remaining Muslim allies. The conservative conditions attached to the package, however, sent thousands of protesters to the streets in Istanbul and other Turkish cities. Further action against IMF and World Bank policies over the last year included protest marches in Ecuador, a doctors' strike in El Salvador, student action in Ghana, strikes in India, riots over fuel prices in Indonesia, teacher and student demonstrations in Malawi, railway strikes in Mozambique, student protests in Papua New Guinea, anti-privatisation protests in South Africa, and massive trade union demonstrations in South Korea (http://www.wdm.org.uk/cambriefs/Debt/Unrest2.pdf).

The fortunes of the anti-capitalist movement in the developed world, too, have since improved with tens of thousands turning out for the EU summit in Brussels in December 2001 and the World Social Forum in Brazil and concurrent demonstrations in New York targeted at the annual meeting of the World Economic Forum in February 2002. Over 700 NGOs participated in parallel events at the Monterey conference of March 2002, largely protesting against the anaemic outcome of the conference.

The best sign, however, of the enduring vitality and relevance of the anti-capitalist movement came in spring 2002, when hundreds of thousands turned out for demonstrations around the EU Council Meeting in Barcelona, in March, and subsequently across the Atlantic, at the World Bank/IMF meeting in Washington, DC in April. The familiar cacophony of slogans characteristic of these demonstrations was expanded to include new grievances with the ever-expanding 'war on terrorism' and the onslaught on civil liberties associated with it.

fell flat. Activities around the WTO ministerial meeting in Doha in November were weak, even if one takes into account the difficulty in accessing the actual meeting venue. At the same time the meeting presented a rare occasion where Third World participants succeeded in pushing through some of their demands in relation to the new round of trade negotiations.

Over the past year, Turkey and Argentina encountered severe financial crises. This was largely expected since both economies had been showing signs of distress for some time. In both countries, the IMF stepped in with the customary policy prescriptions, which further exacerbated social discontent. Public frustration was compounded by the Fund's failure to assist the government in averting the crises despite ample forewarning.

Argentina was for a long time the poster boy of the currency board mechanism, the most conservative approach to economic policy. This rigid exchange-rate mechanism, which severely restricts a government's ability to influence demand, was largely credited with defeating hyperinflation and was considered the most viable fixed exchange-rate mechanism in the aftermath of the Asian crises. After a year of protests and strikes, in December the country was

Chapter 4:
Dig It Up: Global Civil Society's Responses to Plant Biotechnology

2002 Update: Terminal Leaky Genes?

Diane Osgood

In 2001, the world estimate for genetically modified (GM) crops measured over 52 million hectares, a 19 per cent leap from 2000. The crops are still concentrated in the USA, Canada, Argentina, and now China. GM crops were also grown in Australia, South Africa, Mexico, Bulgaria, Uruguay, Romania, Spain, Germany, and Indonesia. Herbicide tolerance remains the dominant trait with insect resistance second. Much of the increase took place without making headline news.

Global civil society was a bit quieter towards the end of 2001 than in 1999–2000. There were fewer demonstrations and no violent farmers' riots. Civil society groups, both reformers and supporters of plant biotechnology, participated in intergovernmental and national meetings, mainly with the aim of bolstering governments' ability to regulate and monitor change.

As this update goes to press, two battles are being waged by both rejectionists and reformers. The first is an 'old' theme: Terminator technology. 'Terminator' is a genetically engineered plant in which certain genes are 'switched' on or off so that it produces sterile seeds in the field. There are many other 'gene switch' technologies—not all of which are Terminator. For example, if sterility is used in the production of hybrid seeds but does not impact plant fertility in the farmers' fields, it is not considered 'Terminator'.

Terminator technology brings out an emotional response from just about everyone. It's the lowest common denominator issue uniting many diverse civil society organisations dealing with development, religion, food security, farmers' rights, and the environment. The message is: this technology is repugnant and we want to stop it. Scientists respond by saying: it brings many possible benefits, including stopping gene drift, 'you don't understand'. If the past is a valid indicator, civil society will win this media battle.

Taking advantage of the global meetings in 2002—World Food Summit, Conference of the Parties for the Convention on Biodiversity (COP-CBD), and the World Summit on Sustainable Development—a large international campaign to get governments to ban 'Terminator' technology was launched in early 2002 by a wide range of NGOs.

Has the campaign started to work? India has passed legislation to prohibit the importation of 'Terminator' technology seeds, and other countries are reportedly planning similar legislation. The issue is on most agendas for preparatory committees for the above international meetings.

The second issue is 'gene drift', which occurs when genes from the GM plant are found in the offspring of the pollen of the GM plant and a nearby 'native'. To have an impact, the 'leaky genes' needs to 'introgress': that is, to be passed on to future generations of plants. If the genes are present for only one generation, the environmental impact is limited to that generation. If the genes do introgress, the hazard is that this new crossbreed may push out the locals, in the most extreme cases causing extinction, displacement, or ecosystem disruption.

Gene drift is most serious in the world's centres of crop genetic diversity. Rejectionists, reformers, and most agricultural scientists all argue that this kind of biodiversity feeds the planet's people. We are risking a globally valuable resource if we lose the original varieties and landraces of maize, wheat, rice, potato, and other staple crops.

Using GM Terminator to halt GM seed contamination is like...

...using DDT to kill the ants on your sandwich.

Right: US public opinion campaign against Terminator. © Reymond Page.

Global civil society is responding to these issues by calling for intergovernmental policy as well as national regulation to ban imports of GM seeds into the centres of crop diversity to avoid gene leak.

But have genes already leaked in critical places? Global civil society is rapidly engaging in this rather scientific, if emotional, debate. A huge controversy erupted in early 2002 over evidence in Oaxaca, Mexico, that maize plants in farmers' fields were contaminated by GM maize material. This has provoked an international outcry, as there are genuine concerns about threats to genetic diversity, especially in areas of the Meso-American centre of genetic diversity for maize.

An article by Drs Quist and Chapela in *Nature* reported the initial evidence. The ink had not dried on the presses at *Nature* before scientists were claiming the study was deeply flawed. Many picked 'easy' holes in the methodology and others published scorching criticisms (Chapela and Quist 2002). Later, the magazine revoked the article, publishing both letters of criticism and responses from the authors. Almost simultaneously, rejectionists and reformist global civil society players raised an outcry about perceived corruption and intimidatory tactics to silence potentially dissident scientists. A global civil society Joint Statement (2002)was launched in February, with the aim of having the issue added to the agendas of the World Food Summit (June 2002) and Conference of the Parties of the Convention on Biodiversity (April 2002), as well as at the World Summit on Sustainable Development (September 2002).

After an initial lull, 2002 promises much global civil society action on biotechnology issues. With these issues to hand, the organisations involved will have to engage with science rather than play on emotions, and to work with intergovernmental bodies as much as with national governments.

References

Chapela, I. and D. Quist (2002). 'Transgenetic DNA Introgressed into Traditional Maize Landraces in Oaxaca, Mexico'. *Nature*, 20/2: 106–7.

Joint Statement on the Mexican GM Maize Scandal (2002). The ETC Group Press Release, 19 February. http://www.etcgroup.org.

Chapter 8: Funding Global Civil Society Organisations

2002 Update: Developments in Funding

Frances Pinter

The main argument of last year's chapter was that the bulk of funding for global civil society organisations (CSOs) comes from development initiatives of one form or another. The history of development aid has steered development agencies and civil society organisations into a mutually interdependent relationship. By 2000 about $7 billion originating from the multilateral agencies and bilateral government programmes could be identified as flowing through NGOs, and, whilst not necessarily earmarked specifically for civil society-building directly, these projects and programmes are, in one way or another, thought to foster the development of civil society links across borders precisely because of their cross-border nature. The aims and objectives of this kind of funding are more limited than the wide array of activities carried out by local civil society entities.

Hampering international funding are legal restrictions on cross-border financial flows. The lack of incentives such as tax concessions plays a role in determining funding levels, as do the natural instincts of people to care more about local issues than those further afield. Nonetheless, matters concerning globalisation and the increasing interconnectedness of issues has generated an increased awareness of the functions of civil society around the world. Activist and advocacy groups, often considered as a specific sector of the wide array of civil society organisations, rely more on individual contributions and support from independent foundations.

The second largest source of global civil society funding, of just over $2 billion in 2000, comes from Western (primarily US) foundations for international projects. In addition, there is funding from individuals, small organisations (often re-packing large grants into smaller donations and funding even smaller NGOs) and diaspora bodies. The growing availability of digital communication technologies continues to play an increasingly important role in facilitating fund flows between funders and funded around the world.

What has changed?

In 2001 the following factors impacted on the levels of funding: (1) the global economy, particularly the recession in the US; (2) the events of September 11; and (3) an increased linking of development to both the economic and security well-being of the whole world.

According to the Foundation Center in New York, foundation grant-making in 2001 in the United States increased by 5.1 per cent to just over $29 billion. While higher than anticipated, this growth is largely due to the 8.4 per cent increase in foundation assets in 2000. Although increases are still likely for 2002, the rate of growth will probably be lower, because of the downturn in the economy in 2001. A substantial number of foundations have their assets invested in the stock market, and fluctuations there impact on sums available for distribution. Corporate giving in 2001 experienced its lowest growth since 1994. International programmes (16 per cent of US giving), which increased by 86.4 per cent in 2000, are unlikely to grow substantially as 50 per cent of this increase was due to a one-off grant of $210 million from the Gates Foundation for international research scholarships at the University of Cambridge, UK.

The Foundation Center estimated that $1.5 billion was raised in philanthropic funds to deal with the aftermath of September 11, much of it aimed at providing for the families of the victims of the attacks on the World Trade Centre and the Pentagon. Over a third came from corporations, employing 6 per cent of the overall corporate giving total. There has been some concern that this concentration of funding may be to the detriment of international programmes.

Paradoxically, official aid to developing countries appears to have declined by 5 per cent in 2001 according to the World Bank. However, intended involvement of civil society in World Bank projects increased slightly in 2001 but is still down from an all-time high in 1999. Much of the heightened political rhetoric from world leaders linking development to security came after September 11, so any possible increases in funding are unlikely to be evident for another couple of years.

For details of relevant URLs, please see the references in Chapter 8 of *Global Civil Society 2001*.

INDEX